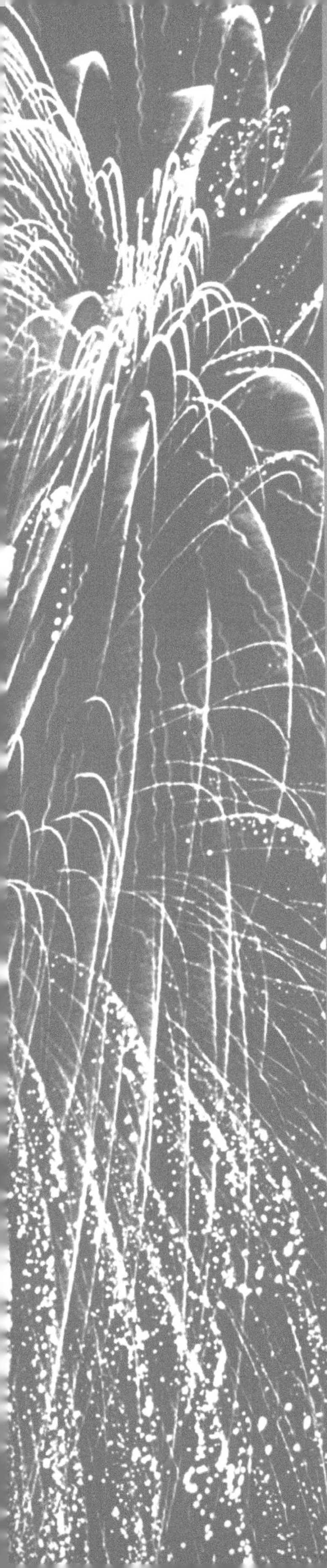

Advanced Photoshop Elements 7 For Digital Photographers

Philip Andrews

Routledge
Taylor & Francis Group
NEW YORK AND LONDON

First edition published 2009 by Elsevier

Published 2021 by Routledge
605 Third Avenue, New York, NY 10017
2 Park Square, Milton Park, Abingdon, Oxon OX14 4RN

First issued in hardback 2021

Routledge is an imprint of the Taylor & Francis Group, an informa business

Publisher's Note
The publisher has gone to great lengths to ensure the quality of this reprint but points out that some imperfections in the original copies may be apparent.

British Library Cataloguing in Publication Data
A catalogue record for this book is available from the British Library

Library of Congress Cataloging-in-Publication Data
A catalog record for this book is available from the Library of Congress

Layout and design by Karen and Philip Andrews in Adobe InDesign CS3

Acknowledgements

Karen for your support, love and patience always and Adrian and Ellena for keeping me balanced. And as always, my thanks goes to the great team at Focal Press, especially Ben Denne, David Albion, Melissa Read and Lisa Jones – you always make me look good. Cheers to Richard Coencas and Don Day for their technical comments and direction and to the supportive staff at Adobe in the UK, Australia and USA offices. Much appreciation to Mike Leavy, Adobe Engineering Manager for Elements products and Nigel Atherton, editor of *What Digital Camera* magazine for your kind words of introduction to this text.

Picture credits

ISBN 13: 978-1-138-40116-7 (hbk)
ISBN 13: 978-0-240-52158-9 (pbk)

DOI: 10.4324/9780080951218

Contents

Foreword vi
Introduction viii

1 The Next Level 1

The comprehensive Photoshop Elements workflow 4
Elements basics 6
Basic Elements workflow 10

2 Scanner and Camera Techniques 13

The basics – resolution 14
2.01 How many pixels do I need? 16
The basics – color depth 18
2.02 More colors equal better quality 20
Digital shooting technique 22
2.03 Exposure compensation 24
Frame-by-frame control 25
2.04 Contrast 26
2.05 Color saturation 27
2.06 Image sharpness 28
2.07 White balance control 29
2.08 Applying fine-tuning automatically 33
2.09 Customizing your white balance 34
2.10 Shooting Raw for ultimate control 35
So what is in a Raw file? 37
The Raw advantage 39
2.11 Shooting workflows 40
2.12 Scanning resolution – 'Know where you are going before you start the journey' 42
2.13 Color depth 43
2.14 Multi-sample 44
2.15 Highlight and shadow capture 45
2.16 Color cast correction 46
2.17 Dust and scratches 47
2.18 Noise Reduction technologies 48
2.19 Color regeneration features 49
2.20 Scanning workflow 50
Fixing common shooting problems 51
Fixing common scanning problems 53

3 Processing Raw files 55

The Photoshop Elements approach to Raw processing 56
3.01 Enabling your Raw camera 57
3.02 Modifying your capture workflow for Raw 59
3.03 Using the Adobe Photo Downloader 61
3.04 The Adobe Camera Raw interface 64
3.05 The new Camera Calibration tab 83
3.06 The raw conversion process 87
3.07 Keeping ACR up to date 92
3.08 Other Raw plug-ins 92

4 Photo Organization and Management

Organizing your photos with Photoshop Elements 94
4.01 Add picture details in-camera 94
4.02 Organize photos while downloading 94
4.03 Captioning 96
4.04 Naming and renaming 96
4.05 Tagging your photos 99
4.06 Auto Face Tagging 100
4.07 Albums and how to group photos 101
4.08 Using Smart Albums 103
4.09 Synchronizing and Backing Up Albums 106
4.10 Changing your view 108
4.11 Locating files 110
Protecting your assets 112
4.12 Creating a backup 113
4.13 Versioning your edits 115
4.14 Creating Image Stacks 117

5 Pathways to Editing in Elements 119

Automatic editing 120
5.01 Auto Smart Fix 121
5.02 Auto Red Eye Fix 121
5.03 Other auto options 121
Automating editing of several pictures at once 123
5.04 Processing multiple files 123
5.05 Multi-selection editing 124
5.06 Bulk Red eye fixing 124
Semi-automatic editing 125
5.07 Using the Quick Fix Editor 125
Semi-auto editing summary: 125
5.08 Adjust Smart Fix 126
Manual editing 127
5.09 The Full Edit workspace 127
Three Editing Modes in Elements plus one Online 129
5.10 Guided Edits 129
5.11 Enhancing via Photoshop.com 130
Non Destructive editing, the professional's choice 132
5.12 Adjustment Layers 133
5.13 Select and adjust in one stroke 134
5.14 'All Layers' tool options 136
5.15 Blend Modes 137
5.16 Layer Masking 138
5.17 Duplicate layers 139
Giving Elements a helping hand 141
5.18 Borrowing Photoshop features 141
5.19 Advanced layer masks 143

6 Image Changes – Beyond the Basics 145

Advanced selection techniques 146
6.01 Adding to and subtracting from selections 146
6.02 Using the Selection Brush 146
6.03 The Quick Selection Tool 148
6.04 Advanced refining of selection edges 149
6.05 Saving and loading selections 151
6.06 Modifying selections 152
6.07 Transforming a selection 153
6.08 Precise control of selection size 155
Understanding layers 156

Masking techniques 161
6.09 Painting masks with the Selection Brush 161
6.10 Fill and adjustment layer masks 162
6.11 Using selections with layer masks 163
6.12 'Group with Previous' masks 163
6.13 Changing the mode to grayscale 164
6.14 Desaturate the color file 165
6.15 A more sophisticated approach 167
6.16 The Convert to Black and White feature 168
6.17 Custom entries in Convert to Black and White 170
6.18 The Gradient Map conversions 171
6.19 Borrowing Photoshop's Black and White 172
Advanced dodging and burning-in 173
6.20 Using selections to change tone 173
6.21 Erase back through tonal layers 175
6.22 Paint on dodging and burning-in 177
6.23 Blend mode Dodge and Burn 178
Enhance your poorly exposed pictures 179
6.24 Screening image layers to enhance tones 179
6.25 Adding detail to highlights and shadows 182
Tinted monochromes 183
6.26 Using Hue and Saturation to tone your pictures 184
6.27 Tinting borrowed from Photoshop 186
Split toning 187
6.28 Select and tone 187
6.29 Two-layer erase 189
6.30 Color Variations based split toning 190
6.31 Photoshop's Color Balance split toning in Elements 190
Black and white and color 192
6.32 Layer mask and gradient map 192
Border techniques 193
6.33 Simple borders 193
6.34 Sophisticated edges using grayscale masks 194
6.35 Creating frames with Frame layers 195
Adding texture 197
6.36 Add Noise filter 197
6.37 Grain filter 198
6.38 Non-destructive textures 199
Advanced sharpening secrets 200
6.39 Unsharp Masking to the rescue 201
6.40 Adjust Sharpness for the ultimate control 203
6.41 Another approach 204

7 Darkroom Techniques on the Desktop 205
7.01 Diffusion printing 206
7.02 Instant film transfer effect 208
7.03 Using the Unsharp Mask filter to add contrast 212
7.04 Lith printing technique 214
7.05 Correcting perspective problems 216
7.06 Add emphasis with saturation 218
7.08 Cross-processing effects 220
7.09 Digital hand coloring 222
7.10 Realistic depth of field effects 225
7.11 Beyond the humble drop shadow 229
7.12 Ring flash shadow 233
7.13 Elements' Curves features 234
7.14 Using Photoshop's Curves in Elements 237
7.15 Combining images seamlessly 238
7.16 Believable montages – a step further 240
7.17 Producing high-key pictures 243
7.18 Correcting lens problems 245
7.19 Change to old 247
7.20 Painterly photos 249

8 Professional Retouching 253
Visual surgery without a hint of anything plastic 255
8.01 Adding a dreamy effect 256
8.02 Softening freckles 257
8.03 Eliminating blemishes 258
Clone Stamp tool 258
Healing Brush tool 258
Spot Healing Brush 259
Clone Stamp tool step-by-step 260
Healing Brush tool step-by-step 261
Spot Healing Brush tool step-by-step 261
8.04 Removing the Red 262
8.05 Brighten Eyes 264
8.06 Tone down skin highlights and shadows 265
8.07 Retouching non-destructively 266

9 Photo Restoration 267
9.01 Restoration basics 270
9.02 Dust and scratches be gone 272
9.03 Uncovering the faded 274
9.04 Levels based color restoration 276
9.05 Working with a scanned print 278
9.06 Extra correction help 280
9.07 Adjusting shadow tones 281
9.08 Recreating missing content 282
9.09 Removing stains 283

10 Making Better Panoramas 285
Advanced shooting techniques 293
10.01 Positioning the camera 293
10.02 Camera support 294
Other capture methods 297
10.03 Exposure 298
10.04 Focus and zoom 299
10.05 Depth of field 299
10.06 White balance 301
10.07 Timing 302
10.08 Ensuring consistent overlap 303
10.09 Dealing with the moving subject 304
10.10 Advanced panorama editing in Photoshop Elements 7/6 306
10.11 Fixing misaligned picture parts 309
10.12 Coping with extremes of brightness 309
10.13 Creating artificially increased DOF 312

10.14 Correcting exposure differences 313
10.15 Adjusting for changes in color balance 314
10.16 Vertical panoramas 316
10.17 High-resolution mosaics 317
10.18 Panoramic printing 318
10.19 Spinning panorama movies 320
10.20 Panorama workflow 324

11 Extending Your Web Abilities 325

Building websites – the basics 327
11.01 Elements' Online Album websites 329
Creating individual web assets using Photoshop Elements 334
11.02 Optimizing photos for the web 335
11.03 Making seamless backgrounds 337
11.04 Using background matting 338

12 Free Form Photo Collages 339

Before you start – edit then layout 341
12.01 Basic steps for layout creation 342
12.02 The new super Project Bin 344
12.03 Editing existing Photo Collages 346
12.04 Adding, removing and replacing photos 348
12.05 Adding, moving and deleting pages 350
12.06 Using the Content and Effects panes 352
12.07 Align, arrange and distribute your frames 356
12.08 Printing your Photo Collages and Photo Books 358
Order a Kodak Photo Book or Kodak Prints 359

13 Finely Crafted Output 361

Printing basics 362
The inkjet printer 364
Laser 366
Dye Sublimation 366
Other printing processes 367
Image resolution vs printer resolution 368
13.01 Basic steps 369
13.02 Creating contact sheets 372
13.03 Multiple prints on a page 373
Ensuring color consistency between devices 374
13.04 Setting up a color-managed workflow 377
13.05 Calibrating your screen – ColorVision Spyder 382
Getting intimate with your printer 384
13.06 Calibrating your printer – resolution, color, tone and sharpness tests 384
13.07 Calibrating your printer – ColorVision PrintFIX 388
13.08 Making great black and white prints 390
13.09 What about permanence? 393
13.10 Preparing your images for professional outsourcing 397
13.11 Shoot small print big 399
13.12 Printing workflow 402

14 Extending the Power of Elements 403

Photoshop Elements and Photoshop Lightroom 404
Why Lightroom plus Elements 405
Enough talk, let's get to it! 406
The workspace 407
The Lightroom workflow modules 408
Using Elements to edit Lightroom managed images 416
Edit Photo dialog 418

Appendices 419

Blend modes 420
Faster Elements at no extra cost 422
Plug-ins 424
Jargon buster 426
Keyboard shortcuts 431
Elements/Photoshop feature equivalents 434

Index 435

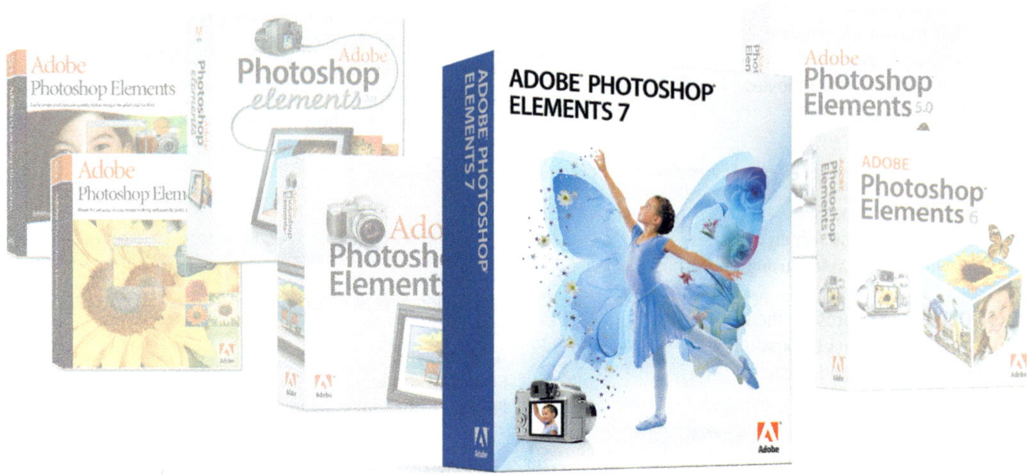

Foreword

Nearly without exception, human beings the world over are fascinated by the photograph. A photograph is a timeless, compelling, emotive and honest representation of our world; of the places we've been, the events we've witnessed, the people we've met and loved. The photograph is a reflection of our world and ourselves; our mind's eye projected onto cotton vellum or computer screen. The persistence of vision *ex machina*. Indeed, the photographic image is the true iconography of the modern world.

For the photography enthusiast, these are very exciting times. In the span of less than 10 years, we have witnessed the evolution of photography from a mostly silver halide film-based process to a completely digital process. The individual photographer now has the capability to shoot, 'develop', and create prints using an entirely digital workflow, and completely within the comfortable confines of his or her own study.

This new-found freedom from film and the complicated processing thereof is largely due (of course) to the ready availability of affordable digital cameras and photo-quality printers; but it is due also, in no small part, to the efforts of the people at Adobe Systems. Adobe is committed to empowering the digital photographer by providing the most powerful and excellent tools available for rendering, manipulating and printing digital images. Among the most popular and successful of these tools is Adobe Photoshop Elements.

Although one of the original design intents behind Photoshop Elements was to make many of the most common image enhancement tools more readily available and noticeable to the novice user, there is still much depth behind this initial surface. Fortunately for both Adobe and its customers, talented writers such as Philip Andrews have resolved to explore this depth and, in easy-to-understand language and step-by-step guidance, provide access to you, the reader.

Advanced Photoshop Elements 7 for Digital Photographers is a beautifully rendered and compellingly written exploration of the advanced features and techniques that can be accomplished with Photoshop Elements. Through the use of many sample photographs, screen shots and clearly illustrated examples, Mr Andrews provides us with the tools to turn our images into exciting and compelling works of art.

From careful and thoughtful descriptions of the basics of tonal adjustments and camera and scanner settings to detailed explanations for creating traditional photographic effects such as lith print style reproductions, *Advanced Photoshop Elements 7 for Digital Photographers* will provide you with an entire arsenal of tools for adding emphasis, detail, and clarity to your images and for exposing and enhancing their inherent beauty.

If you love photography as much as I do, you are in luck with this book.

Enjoy.

Mike Leavy
Engineering Manager for Elements products
Adobe Systems, Inc.

Introduction

When Photoshop Elements came out it was assumed by many that, because it was so inexpensive, it would be the sort of program that you could master in a couple of hours – it certainly wouldn't require a huge learning curve and probably, let's face it, a chunky manual to get to grips with it, as its professional sibling, Photoshop, does. But how wrong we were. Budget certainly doesn't mean basic in this case, and Adobe has packed so much into Photoshop's little brother that you really do need an expert guide to get the best out of it, to lead you through all those nooks and crannies and show you all the cool tricks that are not obvious to the casual user.

But who to choose to be that guide? Well for me there's only one person, and luckily for you it's the one whose name is on the cover of this book. Philip Andrews is an enigma. As editor of the UK's leading digital photography magazine I require two main qualities from my contributors: they have to be real experts who possess a truly in-depth knowledge of their subject, and they have to be able to communicate that knowledge in simple layman's terms that anyone can understand. (They also have to be reliable and hand their copy in on time, but that's another story!) Well there are plenty of experts and plenty of communicators, but you'd be amazed at how rare it is to find someone who is both, as Philip is.

Philip Andrews knows Elements better than anyone else I know. He also writes in a friendly, entertaining and non-academic style – despite the fact that he is a senior lecturer in photography. He has a great understanding of the needs of the end user and his knowledge and enthusiasm for digital imaging (and photography in general) shine from every sentence. He's an accomplished photographer too, so he not only talks the talk but walks the walk, and uses many of his own excellent images to illustrate his points.

Having already covered the fundamentals of Elements in his last book Philip now moves on to more complex themes and ideas, things which you might (wrongly) have considered a bit ambitious for Elements. As before he puts the software into the wider context of digital imaging in general and explains the why as well as the how. Once again there's a great linked website that allows you to download some of the images used in the book and try the techniques out for yourself.

With Philip as your guide you'll be using Elements like a pro and making great images in no time.

Good luck.

Nigel Atherton
Editor of *What Digital Camera* magazine, UK

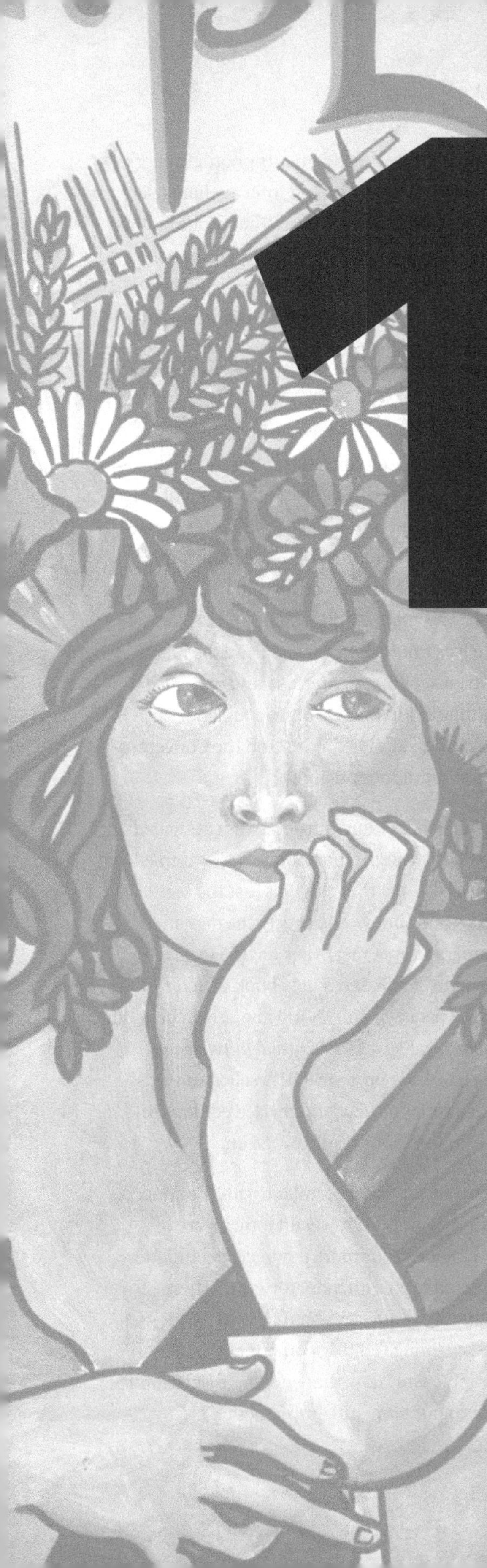

1

The Next Level

There is no doubt that when Adobe decided to release Photoshop Elements photographers the world over rejoiced. Not content with their offerings for entry and intermediate users in the past and ever conscious of the growing digital camera user base, the Adobe boffins created the new package with you, the digital photographer, firmly in their mind. Despite the rumors spread by the 'Photoshop Snobs' that the product was just a cut down version of Adobe's professional package and that any serious editing will need to be completed in Photoshop, users the world over are realizing just how well Photoshop Elements fits their needs.

A true photographer's tool

Adobe had finally heard the cries of the mortals and produced an image manipulation package that has the strength of Photoshop with the price tag more equal to most budgets. Elements gives desktop image-makers top quality image editing and management tools that can be easily used for preparing pictures for printing or sharing via the web or CD. Features like the panoramic stitching option, called Photomerge, and the Photo Browser are firm favorites and were featured in this package before they ever appeared in Photoshop. The color management and vector text and shape tools are the same robust technology that drives Photoshop itself, but Adobe has cleverly simplified the learning process by providing an easier-to-use interface and options like step-by-step interactive recipes for common image manipulation tasks. These, coupled with features like the Smart Brush and Quick Selection tools, Adjust Color Curves and the Convert to Black and White features, make the package a digital photographer's delight.

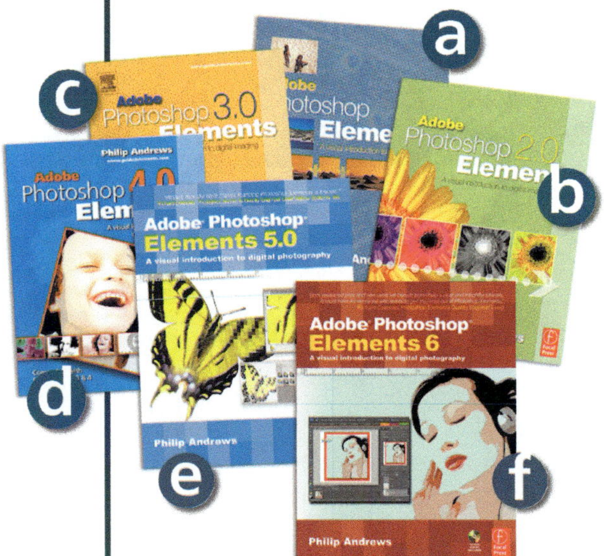

Beyond the companion introduction title >> *This book is the result of many requests to provide a 'next step' that will take Elements users beyond the basic concepts and skills outlined in the introductory text,* Adobe Photoshop Elements – A visual introduction to digital imaging. *(a) Edition 1. (b) Edition 2. (c) Edition 3. (d) Edition 4. (e) Edition 5. (f) Edition 6.*

As a photographer, teacher and author I was captivated by the simplicity and strength that Adobe has crammed into the package and knew that this was just the sort of image editing program that would satisfy the demands of the digital camera users I met every day. So to accompany Elements, I released a new book which was an introduction to the package and digital imaging in general. Titled *Adobe Photoshop Elements – A visual introduction to digital imaging* it quickly became a best-seller and was followed up with a series of new and revised editions to accompany ongoing versions of the program.

As Elements users became more familiar with the concepts and tools used in the program it wasn't long before I started to receive requests for more advanced techniques than those presented in this introductory text. These were quickly followed by queries about how to position Elements as the key 'image editing component' in a high quality photographic workflow that encompassed capture, management, manipulation and output activities.

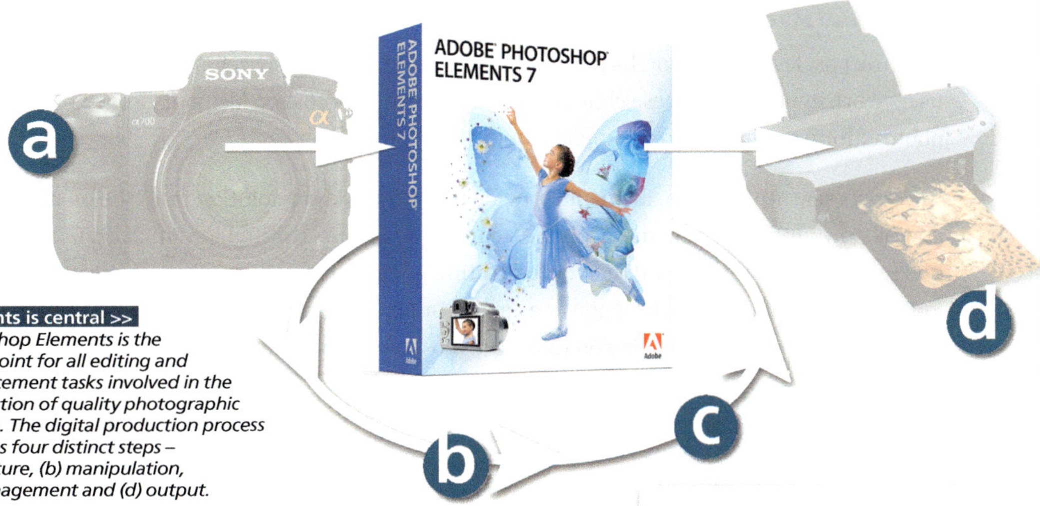

Elements is central >> *Photoshop Elements is the pivot point for all editing and enhancement tasks involved in the production of quality photographic images. The digital production process involves four distinct steps – (a) capture, (b) manipulation, (c) management and (d) output.*

This book is my answer to these requests. With well over 150 new techniques it provides professional tips aimed at advancing your Elements skills beyond the basics. It is presented in a series of highly illustrated step-by-step color tutorials that show you what can be achieved. The techniques are discussed in the greater context of professional quality workflows that cover camera and scanner capture, raw processing, picture management, panorama production and quality print and web production. There is even a new section that looks at how to use Elements as a linked editor for Lightroom providing an even more comprehensive and professional workflow for experienced Elements users.

Each technique is cross-referenced with related skills and ideas in the book and there are on-line resources and video tutorials at the book's website –

www.photoshopelements.net

Here you can download and practise with many of the example images, video tutorials and resources used in the production of the book. Key settings for important dialog boxes are presented along with the illustrated steps needed for you to complete each technique. By working side by side with this text, your favorite image editing program and the associated web resources, you will quickly build both your Elements skills and your general understanding of the processes involved in creating quality photographic images.

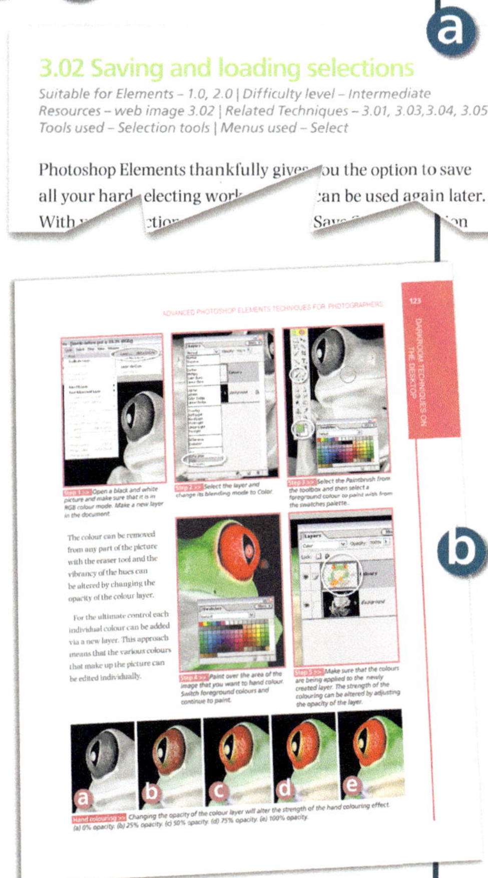

Step-by-step >> *The techniques in the book are presented in a highly illustrated step-by-step fashion that will progressively build your Elements skills. (a) Cross-referenced techniques. (b) Step-by-step illustrations.*

The comprehensive Photoshop Elements workflow

Over the past few versions of the program Adobe has made massive changes to the way that users work in Elements. These changes have converted Photoshop Elements from simply being a photo editing program into a complete digital photography system.

Now in its seventh revision, Elements provides a total workflow solution from the moment you download your files from camera, phone, scanner or the net, through organization, archiving and manipulation phases and then onto printing or outputting the pictures electronically (online albums, email attachments) or as print. Understanding how the various components in the system fit together will help you make the most of the software and its powerful features.

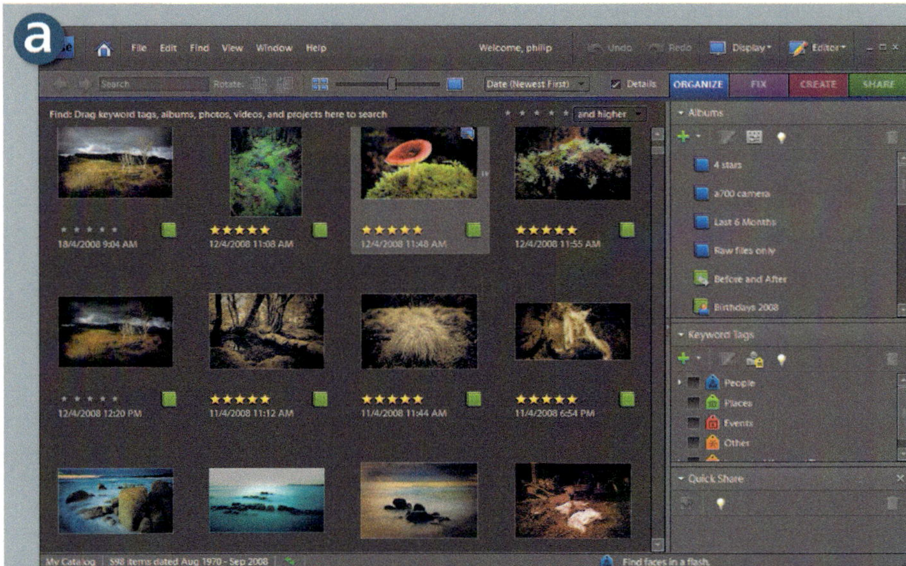

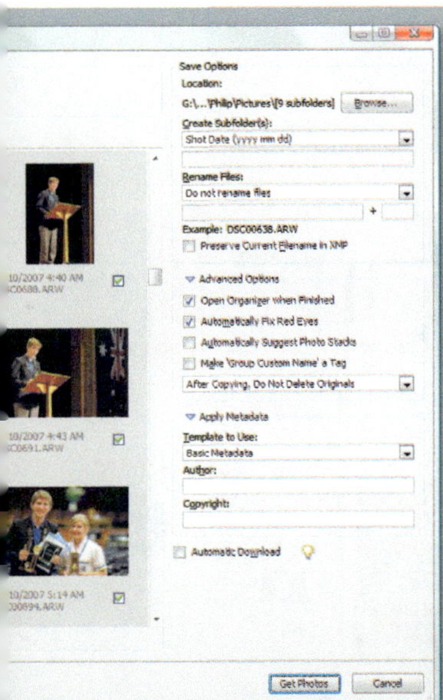

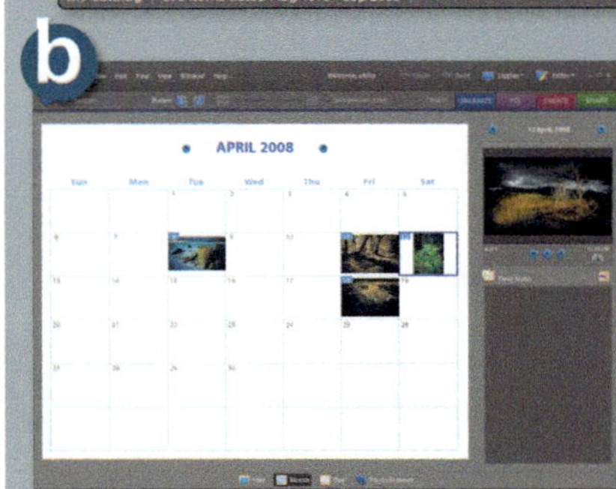

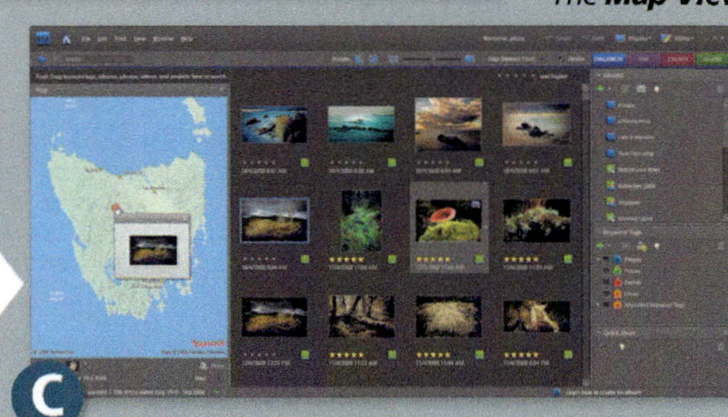

The Adobe Photo Downloader feature and **Get Photos** command allow you to preview, select and download files from a variety of different sources.

*The **Organizer** component (a) of Elements works like a 'super' file browser allowing you to import and organize pictures straight from your camera, scanner, the net or your hard drive. You can view the photographs via the **Photo Browser** or **Date View** options. Pictures can be grouped into Albums (previously called Collections) and you can find specific images via the unique 'keyword tags' that you attach to the files. In **Date View** (b) images are grouped and displayed based on the date they were taken. The **Map View** (c) displays photos according to their location on a map with options to share the referenced map with others.*

IMPORT

ORGANIZE

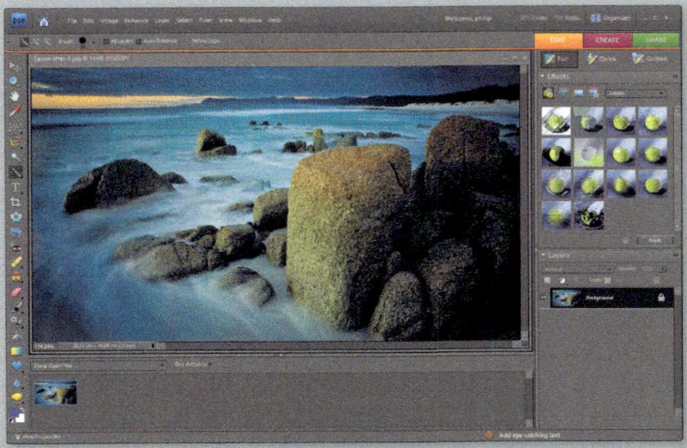

The **Full** Edit workspace contains all the familiar editing and enhancement tools that Elements users have come to expect. It is here that you can take full control over the manipulation and fine-tuning of your pictures. You can also add text, play with layers, create multi-picture composites and combine all manner of special effects with your original photo.

EDIT & ENHANCE

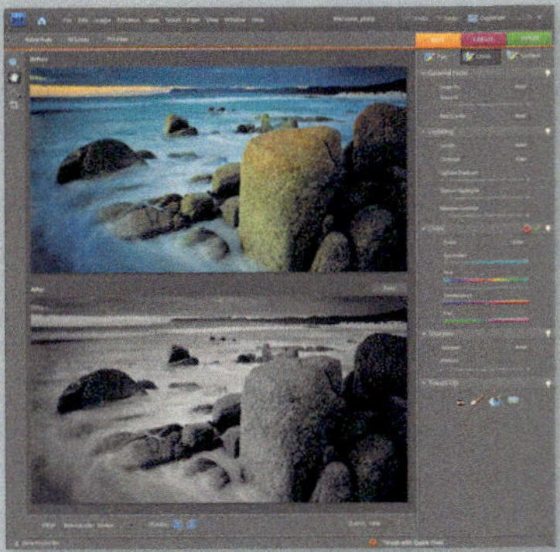

QUICK EDITS

The **Quick Fix** editor provides a series of one-click or semi-automatic fixes for common problems with lighting, contrast, color and sharpness. All the controls are contained in the one screen for speed and you can configure the display to show before and after versions of the photo.

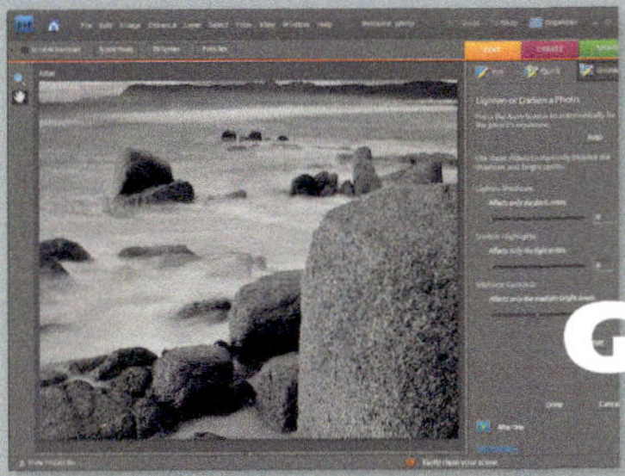

GUIDED EDITS

The **Guided Edit** mode combines step-by-step instructions with controls and tools embedded into the instructions. This is a good place to learn new techniques or get up to speed on how to use new tools and features.

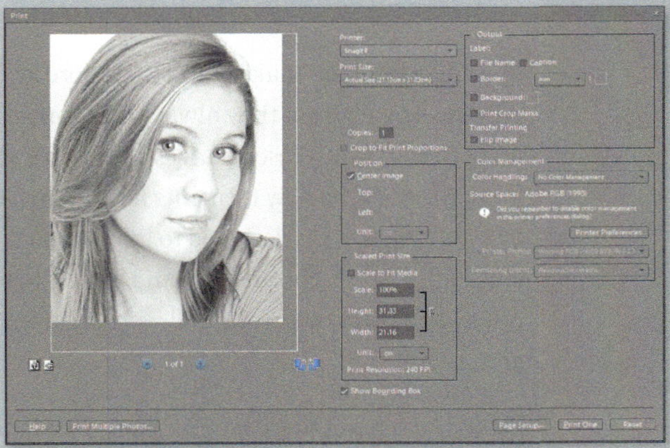

The **Print** options in Elements 6.0 and 7.0 are a little different from earlier versions of the program. You can choose to print individual photos or multiple pictures on a single sheet of paper. You can also preview and print individual pages of the multi-page .PSE document. As an added bonus, when printing from the Organizer workspace, decorative frames can be added to the images right from the Print Multiple Photos dialog box.

PRINT

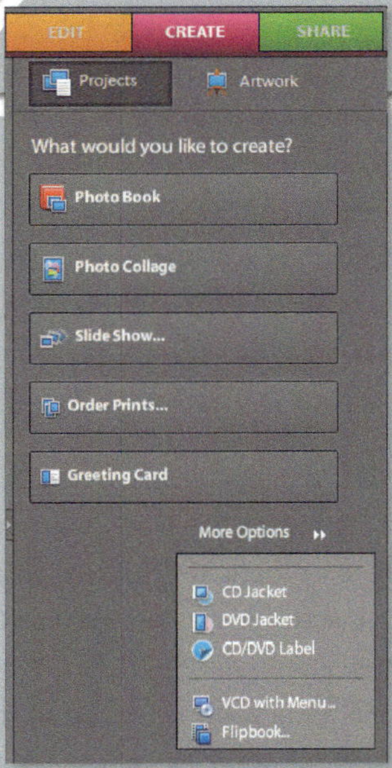

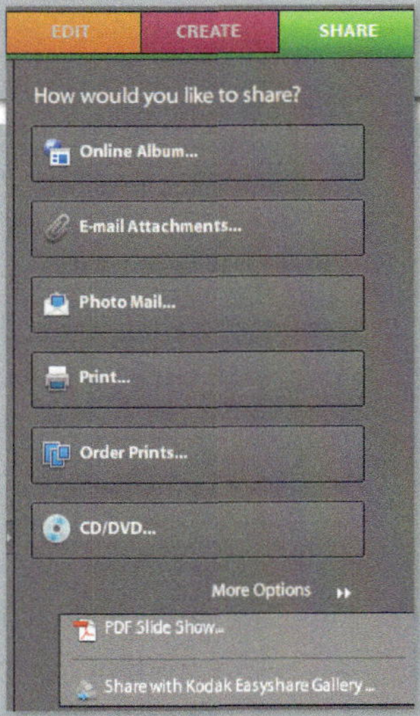

CREATE & SHARE

In versions 6 and 7, the photo projects options are split into two different categories. You can select the various project options from either the Create or Share panels on the right of the Organizer or Editor workspaces. Entries found here use a step-by-step approach to create such projects as slide shows, VCD presentations, photo album pages and greetings cards and photo galleries.

Elements basics

Most digital image-makers find that there are several enhancing steps that they always perform on a newly acquired picture. These changes are often among the first skills that the new Elements user learns. Despite the fact that this book is designed to build upon such basic techniques I thought that it would be best to revisit them briefly to ensure that we are all working from the same game plan.

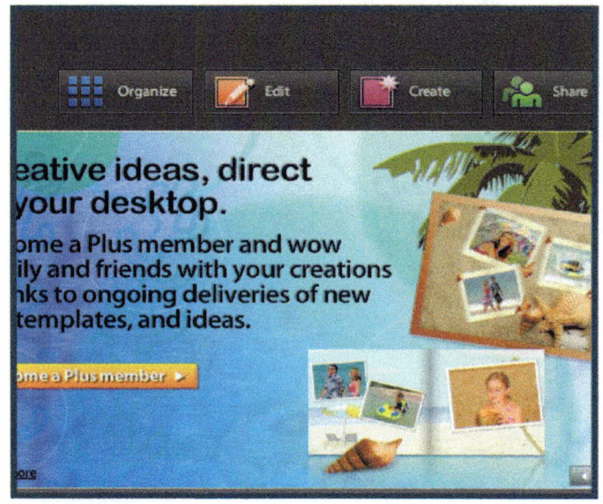

Step 1 >> *The Welcome screen provides simple and easy access to different parts of the Photoshop Elements system.*

For the most part these changes follow a predictable sequence:
Import, Organize, Orientate or Straighten, Crop, Adjust Tones, Alter Color, Apply Sharpness and Save.

These basic alterations take an image captured by a camera or scanner and tweak the pixels so that the resultant picture is cast-free, sharp and displays a good spread of tones.

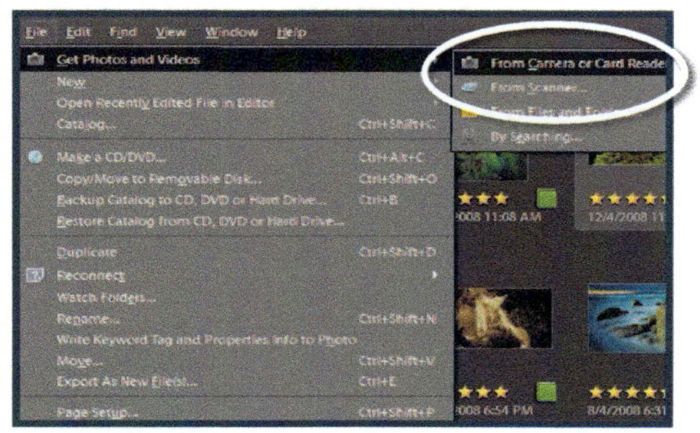

Step 2 >> *Choose the location of the files to import from the list in the File > Get Photos and Videos menu or shortcut.*

Importing photos

When opening Elements the user is confronted with the Welcome screen containing a variety of options. From this screen you can choose to organize, edit, get creative or share your pictures. The first step for most Elements users is to import their photos from a digital camera or scanner. This task is generally handled by the Adobe Photo Downloader which will automatically start when a camera or card reader is attached to the computer. The files are downloaded and cataloged in Elements with the utility.

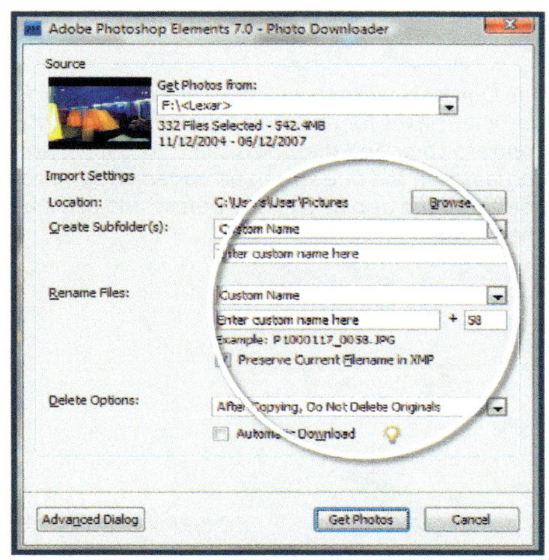

Step 3 >> *Add naming, destination folder and deletion details for the transferred files in the Downloader dialog.*

Alternatively you can import files from other sources or activate the downloader manually from inside the Organizer workspace, which is accessed via the View and Organize selection in the Welcome screen. See Step 1. This feature provides a visual index of your pictures and can be customized to display the images in Browser, Date or Folder mode and thumbnails can be sorted by keyword tags, title, media, metadata or collection.

To start your first catalog simply select the Organizer: File > Get Photos and Videos menu option. Choose one of the listed sources of pictures provided and follow the steps and prompts in the dialogs that follow. See Step 2.

Basic organization

When using the Photo Downloader you can add naming, destination folder and deletion details and in the Advanced dialog you can also apply metadata, auto stack, fix red eye and add group tags to photos automatically. See Step 3. After downloading, or importing, the files are previewed as thumbnails in the Organizer workspace. At this time it is a good idea to make use of some of Elements' brilliant organizational features to help manage the files before jumping into editing and enhancement activities. Add keyword tags to your photos by click-dragging existing entries from the Keyword Tags pane onto your photos. See Step 4. Alternatively, add your own Keyword Tag entries using the new option (+ button) at the top of the pane. See Step 5. Adding Keyword Tags to your photos means that you can search for and locate individual files based on this association.

Along with Keyword Tags you can also group your images into Albums (previously called Collections) and Smart Albums that automatically update each time you add pictures to Elements. In version 7.0 you also have the option to synchronize Albums online.

Changing a picture's orientation

Turning your camera to shoot images in Portrait mode will generally produce pictures that need to be rotated to be viewed correctly. Elements provides a series of dedicated rotate options that are available from inside the Photo Browser workspace. Simply right-click the thumbnail and select an option from the pop-up list. See Step 6. While organizational tasks and some simple automatic enhancement changes are handled in the new Fix pane of the Photo Browser workspace, more controllable edits are applied in either the Quick, Guided or Full Edit workspaces. So for the next set of changes the picture is passed to the Editing workspace. Do this by selecting the Go to Full Edit option from the right-click thumbnail menu. See Step 7.

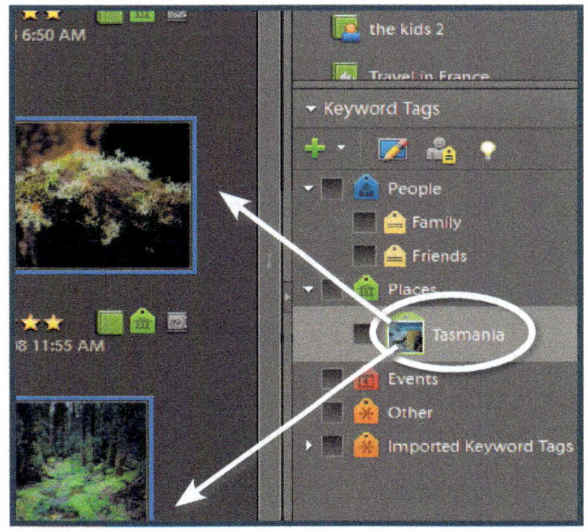

Step 4 >> *Add Tags to the thumbnails by click-dragging the entry from the Tags pane onto the photo.*

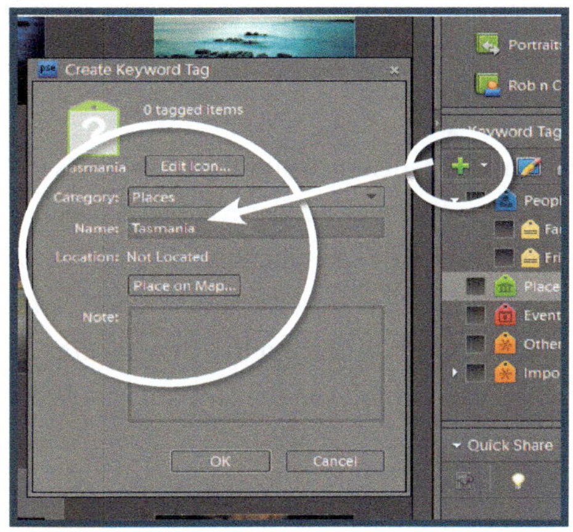

Step 5 >> *Add a different Tag entry by clicking the New button and adding details in the Create Keyword Tag dialog.*

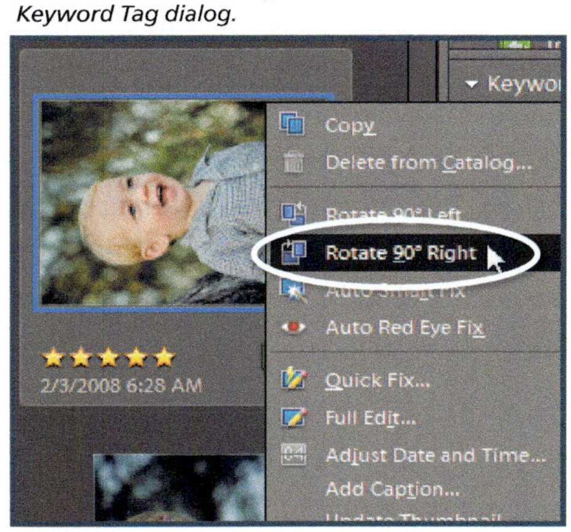

Step 6 >> *Orientate the photo using one of the options in the right-click menu of the Photo Browser workspace.*

Cropping and straightening

Most editing programs provide tools that enable the user to crop the size and shape of their images. Elements provides two such methods. The first is to select the Rectangular Marquee tool and draw a selection on the image the size and shape of the required crop. Next choose Image > Crop from the menu bar. The area outside of the marquee is removed and the area inside becomes the new image. The second method uses the dedicated Crop tool that is located just below the Magic Selection Brush in the tool box. Just as with the Marquee tool, a rectangle is drawn around the section of the image that you want to retain. The selection area can be resized at any time by click-dragging any of the handles positioned in the corners of the box. To crop the image click the Tick button at the bottom of the crop marquee or double-click inside the selected area. See Step 8.

An added benefit to using the Crop tool is to not only pre-visualize the crop but also rotate the selection by click-dragging the mouse when it is positioned outside the box. To complete the crop click the Tick button at the bottom of the crop marquee, but this time the image is also straightened based on the amount that the selection area was rotated.

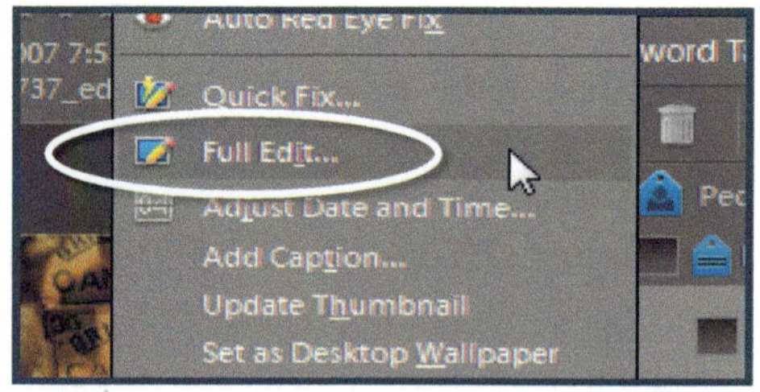

Step 7 >> *Pass the photo to one of the editing spaces by selecting the option from the right-click menu.*

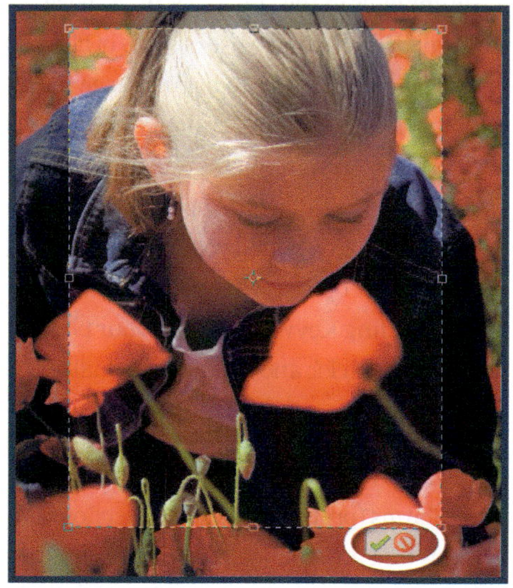

Step 8 >> *The Crop tool gives the user the ability to crop and straighten selected areas of the image.*

Spreading your image tones

When photographers produce their own monochrome prints they aim to spread the image tones between maximum black and white. So too should the digital image-maker ensure that their pixels are spread across the whole of the possible tonal range. In a 24-bit image (8 bits per color channel – red, green and blue), this means from a value of 0 (black) to 255 (white). Elements provides both manual and automatic techniques for adjusting tones.

The Auto Contrast and Auto Levels options are both positioned under the Enhance menu. Both features will spread the tones of your image automatically, the difference being that the Auto Levels function adjusts the tones of each of the color channels individually whereas the Auto Contrast command ignores differences between

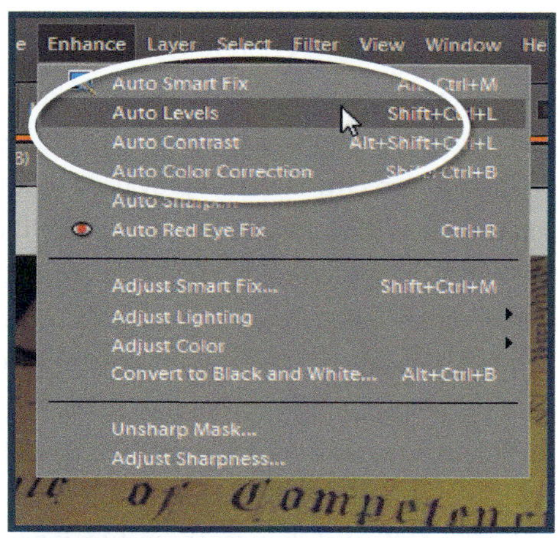

Step 9 >> *The Auto Levels and Auto Contrast functions spread the tones of your image automatically.*

the spread of the red, green and blue components. If your image has a dominant cast then using Auto Levels can sometimes neutralize this problem. The results can be unpredictable though, so if after using the feature the colors in your image are still a little wayward, undo the changes and use the Auto Contrast feature instead. See Step 9.

If you want a little more control over the placement of your pixel tones then Adobe has also included the slider-based Contrast/Brightness and Levels features used in Photoshop in their entry-level software. Both these features, plus the new Adjust Color Curves feature, take back the control for the adjustment from the program and place it squarely in the hands of the user. See Step 10. Jump to the end of the chapter for more details on manual control of tones.

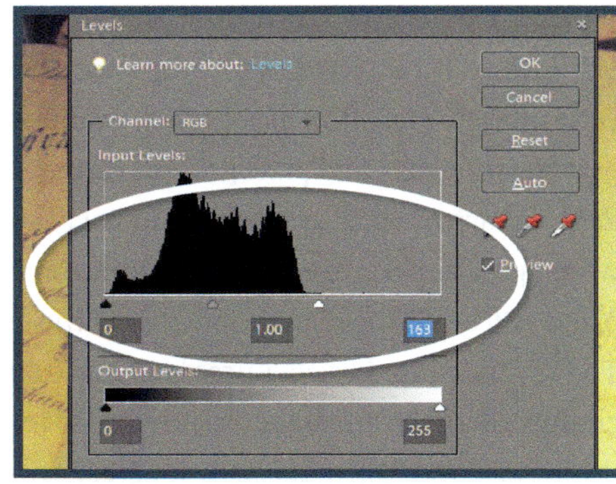

Step 10 >> *The Levels feature provides manual control of the position of white, mid and black tones in your image.*

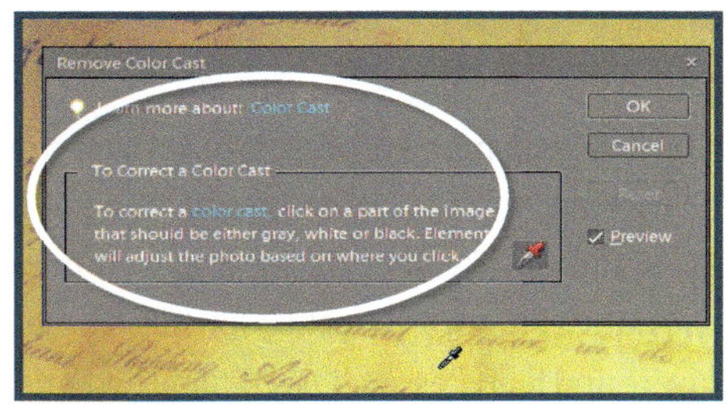

Step 11 >> *The Color Cast tool uses an Eyedropper feature to neutralize color casts in your images.*

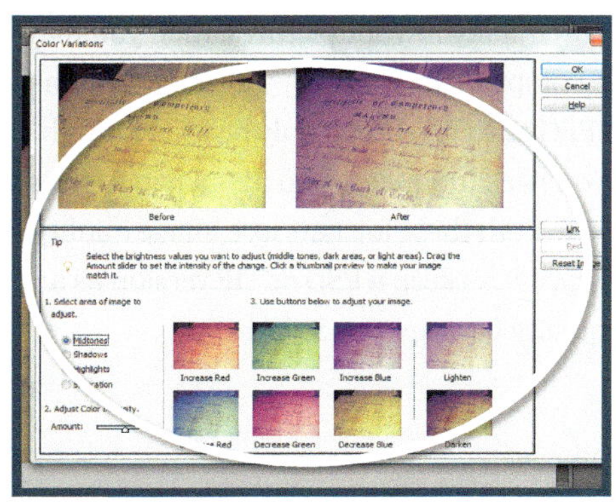

Step 12 >> *The Variations control provides a 'ring around' approach to cast removal.*

Ridding your pictures of unwanted color casts

Despite the quality of modern digital cameras' White Balance systems, images shot under mixed lighting conditions often contain strange color casts. The regularity of this problem led Adobe to include the specialized Color Cast tool (Enhance > Adjust Color > Remove Color Cast) in Elements. Simply click the eyedropper on a section of your image that is meant to be gray (an area that contains equal amounts of red, green and blue) and the program will adjust all the colors accordingly. See Step 11. This process is very easy and accurate, if you have a gray section in your picture. For those images without the convenience of this reference, the Variations feature (Enhance > Adjust Color > Variations) provides a visual 'ring around' guide to cast removal. See Step 12.

Applying some sharpening

The nature of the capture or scan process means that most digital images can profit from a little careful sharpening. I say careful, because the overuse of this tool can cause image errors, or artifacts, that are very difficult to remove. Elements provides several sharpening choices, most automatic, and one with a degree of manual control.

The Auto Sharpen feature found in the Enhance menu provides automatic techniques for improving the clarity of your images. The effect is achieved by altering the contrast of adjacent pixels and pixel groups. Elements also includes the Unsharp Mask filter and the Adjust Sharpness feature, which provides the user with manual control over which pixels will be changed and how strong the effect will be. The key to using these features is to make sure that the changes made by the filter are previewed in both the thumbnail and full image at 100 percent magnification. This will help to ensure that your pictures will not be noticeably over-sharpened. See Step 13.

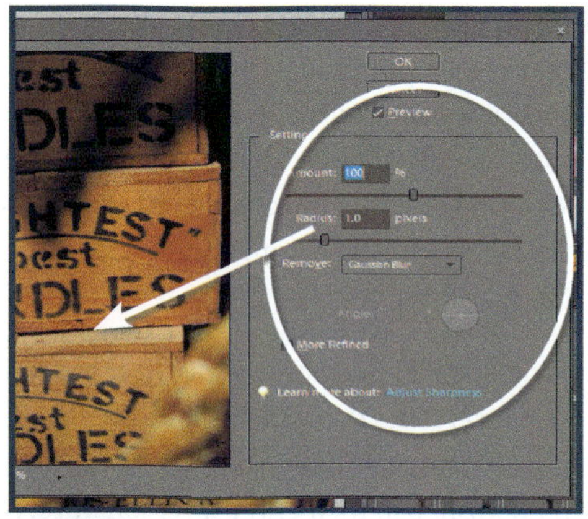

Step 13 >> *Adjust Sharpness improves the overall appearance of sharpness in the image by increasing the contrast of adjacent pixels.*

Saving your images

The final step in the process is to save all your hard work. The format you choose determines a lot of the functionality of the file. If you are unsure of your needs always use the native PSD or Photoshop format. These files maintain layers and features such as editable text and saved selections, and do not lose any picture details due to compression. If space is a premium, and you want to maintain the best quality in your pictures, then you may decide to use a compressed version of TIF or Tagged Image File Format. JPEG and GIF should only be used for web work or when you need to squeeze you files down to the smallest possible size. Both these formats lose image quality in the reduction process, so keep a PSD or TIF version as a quality backup. See Step 14.

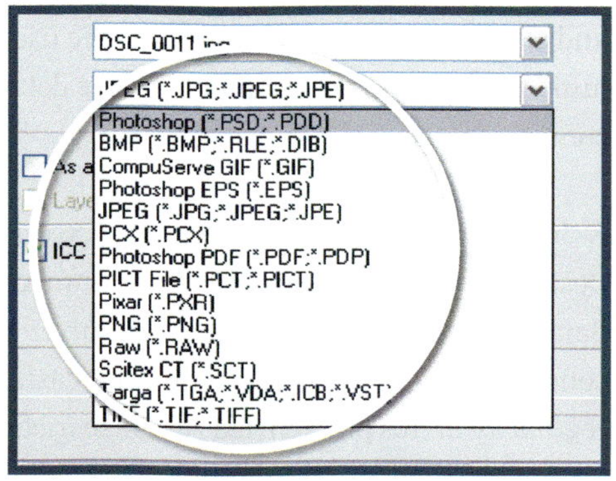

Step 14 >> *Elements provides a range of file formats that can be used to save your images.*

Basic Elements workflow

These steps should be the first changes and enhancements you make to new digital photographs. It is upon these basics that the rest of the book will build. So make sure that the sequence and skills included here are second nature before moving on to extending your Elements knowledge.

Basic Elements Adjustments Workflow		
Download image from camera	Import picture from scanner	Open image via Photo Browser
Tag photos (Right-click > Attach Tag)		
Rotate picture (Image > Rotate menu)		
Straighten picture (Crop or Straighten tool or Image > Rotate menu)		
Crop picture (Crop tool or Marquee then Image > Crop)		
Adjust brightness (Enhance > Adjust Brightness/Contrast menu)		
Alter contrast (Enhance > Adjust Lighting menu)		
Remove color casts (Enhance > Adjust Lighting menu)		
Apply sharpening (Enhance menu)		
Save file (File > Save As)		

Take manual control of your tones >>

One of the most basic, yet critical, tasks for any digital photographer involves adjusting the contrast and brightness of their images. This action is often one of the first undertaken by novices and professionals alike when enhancing newly shot pictures. Well-executed contrast and brightness adjustments can take an 'okay' image and turn it into a dramatic picture.

Though at first glance making these changes seems like a simple task, don't be too eager to play with the Brightness/Contrast sliders. These controls though upgraded in version 6 are often too coarse for quality work. Careful manipulation of the pixels is the key to making quality images and these features don't allow the subtlety of adjustment that is necessary to achieve good results. Instead, employ the aid of either the Levels feature (Enhance > Adjust Lighting > Levels) or the new Adjust Color Curves feature (Enhance > Adjust Color > Adjust Color Curves) when making these changes. Professional digital photographers prefer to use tools like these as they not only provide sliders to alter brightness and contrast but also show a visual representation of the spread of the pixels or preview of the image changes.

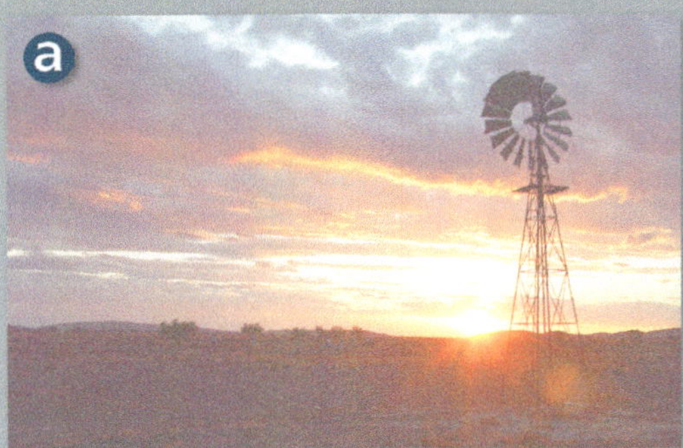

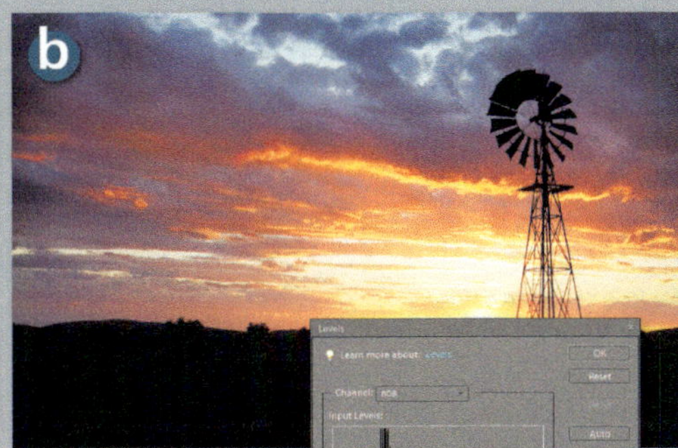

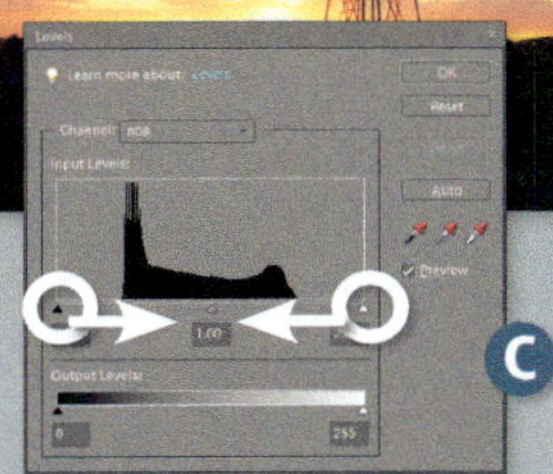

Levels adjustments >> *The Levels and Adjust Color Curves features provide fine manual control over the contrast and brightness of your pictures. (a) Before. (b) After. (c) The Levels adjustment used to correct contrast and brightness.*

Advanced tonal control

The first step in taking charge of your pixels is to become aware of where they are situated in your image and how they are distributed between black and white points. The Histogram palette (Window > Histogram) displays the same graph of your picture's pixels as the Levels feature. Viewing the histogram can be one of the quickest ways to diagnose the source of brightness and contrast problems in your pictures.

The left-hand side represents the black values, the right the white end of the spectrum and the center area the midtones (see Levels feature illustrations on page 12). As you may be already aware, in a 24-bit image (8 bits per color channel) there are a total of 256 levels of tone possible from black to white – each of these values are represented on the graph. The number of pixels in the image with a particular brightness or tone value is displayed on the graph by height. Where the graph is high there are many pixels of this tone present in the image. In contrast, low areas of the graph mean that few pixels of this tone can be found in the picture.

Knowing your images

After a little while of viewing the histograms of your images you will begin to see a pattern in the way that certain styles of photographs are represented. Overexposed pictures will display a large grouping of pixels to the right end of the graph, whereas underexposure will be represented by most pixels bunched to the left. Flat images or those taken on an overcast day will show all pixels grouped around the middle tones and contrasty pictures will display many pixels at the pure white and black ends of the spectrum.

These tonal problems can be fixed automatically by applying one of the standard correction features, such as Auto Contrast or Auto Levels, found in Elements. Both these commands re-map the pixels so that they sit more evenly across the whole of the tonal range of the picture. Viewing the histogram of a corrected picture will show you how the pixels have been redistributed. If you want to take more control of the process than is possible with the auto solutions, open the Levels dialog.

Using the Levels control

Looking very similar to the histogram this feature allows you to interact directly with the pixels in your image. As well as a graph, the dialog contains two slider bars. The one directly beneath the graph has three triangle controls for black, midtones and white and represents the input values of the picture. The slider at the bottom of the box shows output settings and contains black and white controls only.

To adjust the tones, drag the input shadow and highlight controls until they meet the first set of pixels at either end of the graph. When you click OK the pixels in the original image are redistributed using the new white and black points. Be careful though as moving the black point slider beyond the first pixels in the graph will convert these tones to straight black, losing any shadow detail that was present. Similarly, dragging the white point too far towards the middle will change delicate highlight details to pure white. Moving the midtone slider will change the brightness of the middle values of the image without changing the black and white points in the image. Altering the output black and white points will flatten, or decrease, the picture's contrast.

Pro's Tip: Hold down the Alt key whilst moving the black or white input slider and you will see a reversed version of the image showing the pixels that are being converted to black or white by the action.

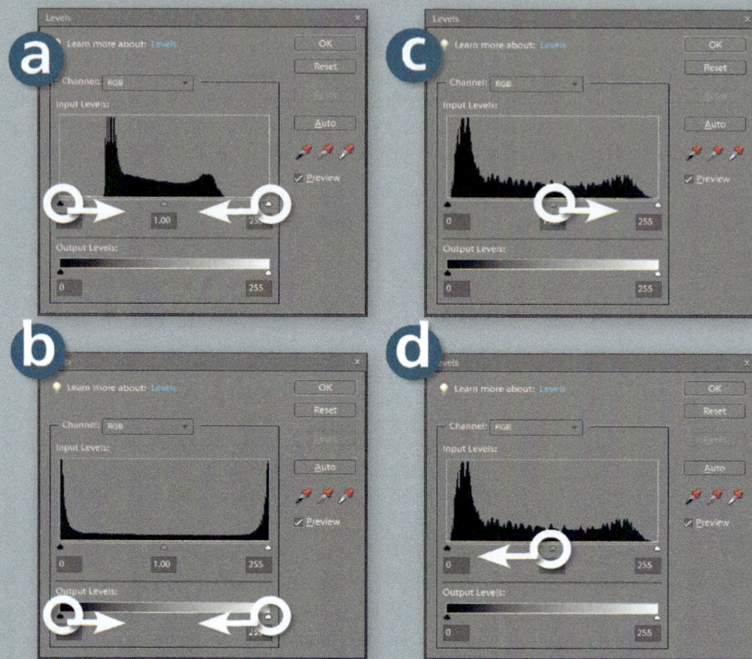

Basic changes >>
(a) To add contrast drag white and black input sliders inwards.
(b) To reduce contrast drag white and black output sliders inwards.
(c) To darken midtones drag mid input slider to the right.
(d) To lighten midtones drag mid input slider to the left.

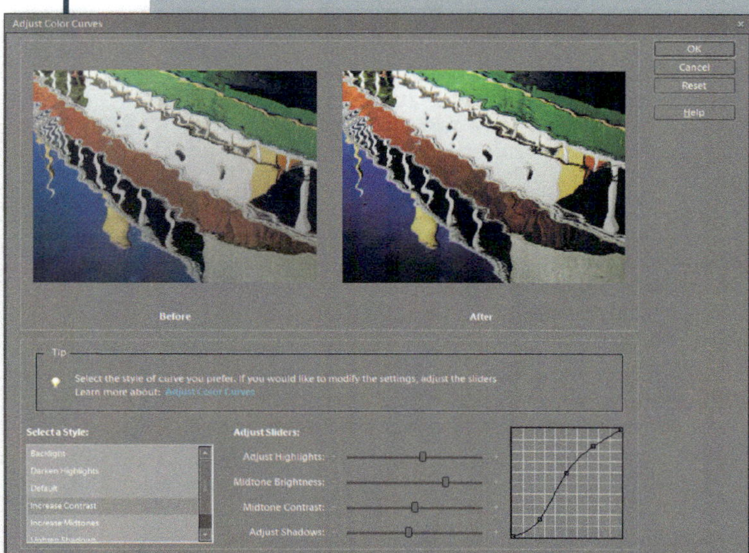

***Protip for Adjust Curves usage:** Holding Shift while moving the Shadows or Highlights slider lets you move on the horizontal axis instead of the vertical.*

The Adjust Color Curves control

The Adjust Color Curves option provides another way that you can alter brightness and contrast in your photo. Unlike the very basic Brightness/Contrast control, Adjust Color Curves provides separate controls for altering the brightness of highlights, shadows and midtones as well as a single slide for changing midtone contrast.

The feature is divided into two different sections – Style and Adjust Sliders. The Styles section contains several preset adjustments. Selecting one of these entries will apply the adjustment to your photo. The After image shows the enhancement changes.

The Adjust Sliders section contains four controls plus a curves graph that plots the tonal relationships in the picture. Whereas the Styles presets provide a one-click image adjustment, the controls contained here allow multiple, additive, fine-tuning changes. The best approach is to select a Styles preset that matches the change that you are requiring first, e.g. Lighten Shadows, and then fine-tune the results with the Adjust Sliders controls. Pressing the Reset button restores the dialog's control to the default 'Increase Midtones' values.

2

Scanner and Camera Techniques

There is no way to get around the fact that the quality of your final digital pictures is dependent on how well they were captured initially. Poorly photographed or badly scanned images take their problems with them throughout the whole production process and end up as poor quality prints. One of the best ways to increase the level of your work is to ensure that you have the skills and knowledge necessary to create the best digital file possible at the time of capture. This is true for the majority of you who now shoot with a digital camera as well as those who are converting existing photographic images to digital with a scanner.

To help gain this level of control let's go back to the basics and see how factors like resolution and numbers of colors affect the quality of image capture.

The basics – resolution

Most of us, no matter how new to digital photography, are aware that resolution has a direct link with picture quality. It is true that this factor, along with the numbers of colors (bit depth) saved in the file, or captured by the camera, helps determine the overall quality of the image.

The rule of thumb that most new users adhere to goes something like this – the higher the resolution and the greater the bit depth the better the image will be – and to a large extent this is true. High-resolution images with lots of colors are generally better quality than those with a limited color range and fewer pixels, but to understand how integral resolution is to making great digital images we must look a little deeper.

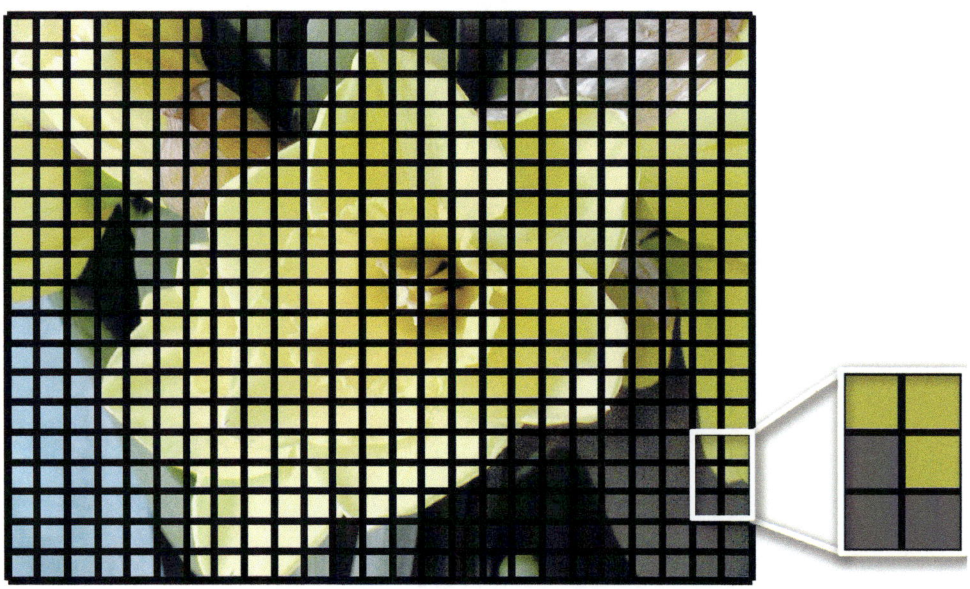

Digital photography basics >> *All digital photographs are constructed of a grid of colored pixels which when seen at a distance combine to form the appearance of a continuous color and tone picture.*

Image capture – input resolution

Computers can only work with digital files. The world as we view it, and as we capture it in silver-based photographs, is not in a digital format. Tones and colors merge gradually from one extreme to another. For the computer to be able to work with such images they must be changed from this 'analog' or continuous tone format to a digital one. Scanners and digital cameras make this change as part of the capturing process.

The scene or print is tested, or sampled, at regular intervals and a specific color and brightness allocated for each sample area. The testing continues in a grid pattern all over the scene, gradually building a pattern of the image which is made up of discrete areas of specific color/ brightness. Each of these areas, or samples, becomes a pixel in the resultant digital file.

Resolution at this capturing stage refers to the frequency that samples are made of the image. Generally this measurement is represented as the number of samples taken in a one inch space; for this reason it is sometimes called Samples Per Inch or spi. Unfortunately most scanner software does not use this terminology but prefers to refer to this setting as Dots per inch (dpi). This is a hangover from language used in the printing industry and does more to confuse than clarify the situation.

If you are using a digital camera to capture your image then the resolution will be determined by the sensor, which has a specific number of CCDs set into a grid that is used to digitize the image. Scanner users, on the other hand, are able to control the sampling rate by changing the settings 'in the scanner's dialog box'.

A high sampling rate will result in a higher quality image with a much greater file size. A low SPI will provide a smaller file of less quality. These facts lead a lot of new users to a situation where all images are scanned at the highest resolution possible. Do this and your hard drive will soon be completely used up. High-resolution scans require huge amounts of storage space.

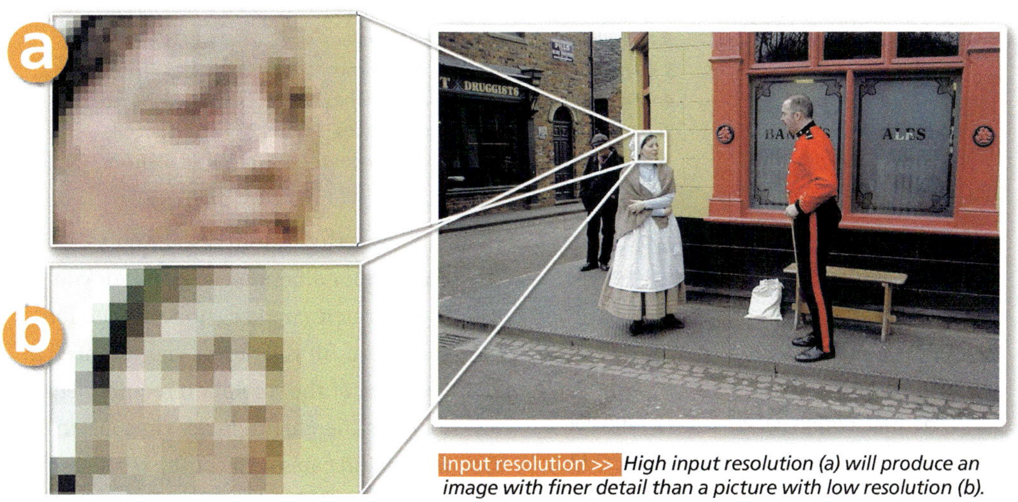

Input resolution >> *High input resolution (a) will produce an image with finer detail than a picture with low resolution (b).*

Input resolutions should be decided on the basis of what the image's final use will be. If the image is to be printed the size of a postage stamp then there is no point scanning at a resolution that will result in a file large enough to print an A2 poster. Remember the end usage determines the scanning resolution, or to put it in a way more easily remembered, 'Know where you are going before you start the journey'.

2.01 How many pixels do I need?

Suitable for Elements – 7.0, 6.0, 5.0, 4.0, 3.0, 2.0, 1.0 | Difficulty level – Intermediate
Related techniques – 2.02, 2.12, 2.13, 13.07

The trick to knowing how many pixels you require is to think carefully about the end product you want to create. As an example, if you want to produce a 10 x 8 inch photographic quality print and you know that the lab you will use to output the image suggests a resolution of 250 dpi, then you have all the information to determine the number of pixels you will need to capture. Essentially the lab is saying that to produce photographic quality they need 250 pixels for every inch of the print. For the photograph to be 10 inches high then your file must contain a minimum of 2500 pixels for this dimension and to ensure the 8 inch width, you will need 2000 pixels. With this knowledge you can adjust the settings on your scanner so that you will end up with a picture file that contains the minimum pixel dimensions of 2500 x 2000.

For digital camera shooters, understanding this concept will not only give you an indication of the maximum print size available from your camera's sensor, but will also allow you to accurately select the correct resolution, or more precisely the correct pixel dimension, setting on your camera for specific tasks. The table below will give you a good starting point.

Chip pixel dimensions:	Chip resolution: (1 million = 1 megapixel)	Print size at 200 dpi: (e.g. photo print)	Image size at 72 dpi: (e.g. web use)
640 x 480 pixels	0.30 million	3.2 x 2.4 inches	8.8 x 6.6 inches
1440 x 960 pixels	1.38 million	7.4 x 4.8 inches	20.0 x 13.2 inches
1600 x 1200 pixels	1.90 million	8.0 x 6.0 inches	22.0 x 16.0 inches
2048 x 1536 pixels	3.15 million	10.2 x .7.6 inches	28.4 x 21.3 inches
2304 x 1536 pixels	3.40 million	11.5 x 7.5 inches	32.0 x 21.3 inches
2560 x 1920 pixels	4.92 million	12.8 x 9.6 inches	35.5 x 26.6 inches
2000 x 3000 pixels	6.0 million	10 x 15 inches	27.7 x 41.6 inches
2336 x 3504 pixels	8.2 million	11.6 x 17.5 inches	32.4 x 48.6 inches
2592 x 3888 pixels	10.2 million	12.9 x 19.44 inches	36 x 54 inches

Proposed use	Suggested image resolution
Screen or web use	72 dpi
Draft quality inkjet	150 dpi
Photo-quality inkjet	200-300 dpi
Photo lab output (min)	250 dpi
Photo lab output (max)	400 dpi
Offset printing (good quality)	300 dpi

The suggested output resolution changes for different end uses. For you to accurately capture enough pixels for the end result you desire, you will need to be aware of the resolution requirements for different end products. The table to the left indicates some of the resolution requirements for different uses.

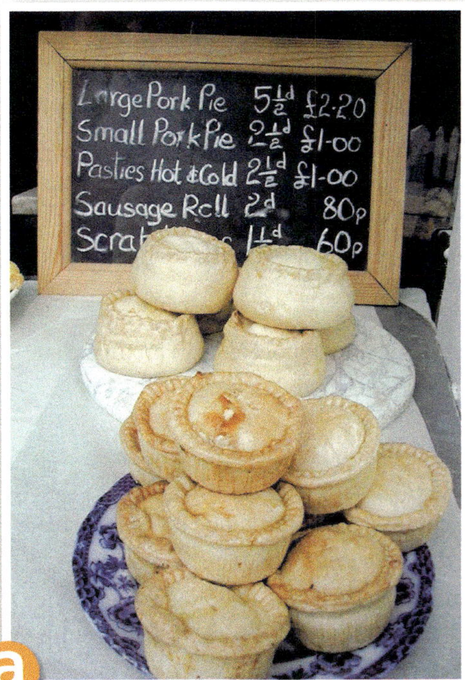

a

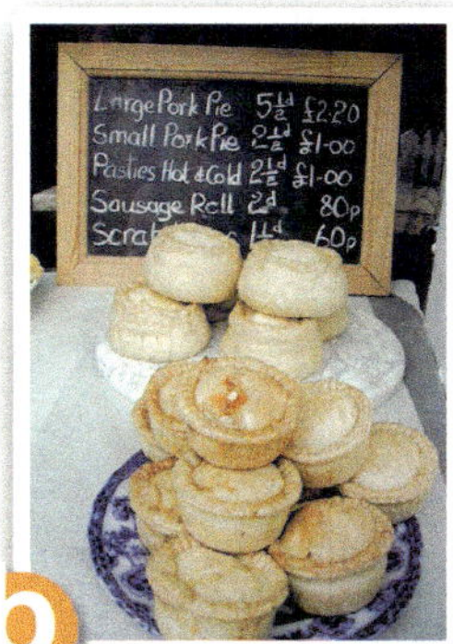

b

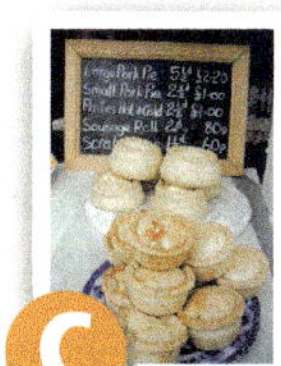

c

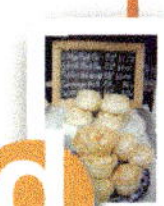

d

Spreading the pixels >> In the example, the digital file has dimensions of 800 x 1200 pixels. Though the number of pixels remains the same, each of the prints ranges in size because of the numbers of pixels used to print each inch.
(a) 16 x 24 inch printed at 50 pixels per inch (ppi).
(b) 8 x 12 inch printed at 100 ppi.
(c) 4 x 6 inch printed at 200 ppi.
(d) 2 x 3 inch printed at 400 ppi.

Pro's Tip

Pro's Tips:

• **Know where you are going before you start the journey** – your scanner resolution should be based on the end use of the digital file. A poster will need a higher resolution initial scan, and a bigger file, than a postcard.

• **Balance print quality with practical file sizes** – test your printer to see at what image resolution increases in print quality cease to be perceived. Make this your base image resolution and scan your files according to this setting.

Once you know the image resolution needed for the printer, the final size of the print and the size of your original you can easily calculate the scanning resolution and the total pixel dimensions you need for your digital file. Use the formula in the table below to give yourself an indication of the number of pixels you need for any size print job.

	Pro's Scanning Resolution Formulae				
1.	*Final image dimensions (pixels)*	=	*Original image dimensions (inches)*	x	*Scanning resolution (samples per inch)*
	3000 x 2400 pixels	=	*10 x 8 inch print*	x	*300 samples per inch*
	6000 x 4000 pixels	=	*1.5 x 1 inch (135 mm film)*	x	*4000 samples per inch*
2.	*Print size (inches)*	=	*Image dimensions (pixels)*	/	*Image resolution (pixels per inch)*
	15 x 12 inches	=	*3000 x 2400 pixels*	/	*200 pixels per inch*
	20 x 13.33 inches	=	*6000 x 4000 pixels*	/	*300 pixels per inch*

The basics – color depth

This growing understanding of how important resolution is to high quality imaging underpins the continual push by digital consumers for higher pixel output from their cameras. In the last couple of years sensor sizes have pole-vaulted from the diminutive 1.5 megapixels to the more commonplace 8.0 and even 10.0 megapixel models that now fill the shelves of many photographic suppliers. The power to create truly photographic quality output up to A3 size is well within our grasp.

But high resolution is only half the 'image quality' story. The number of colors in an image is also a factor that contributes to the overall quality of the photograph.

Discrete colors (or levels)

Photographs in either print or negative (or slide) form contain a range of subtle tones and colors that blend smoothly into each other. These are referred to as 'continuous tone images'. For instance, in a traditional black and white print it is difficult to see where one shade of gray starts and another one finishes. The effect is a smooth transition from the deepest shadows through to the most delicate highlights.

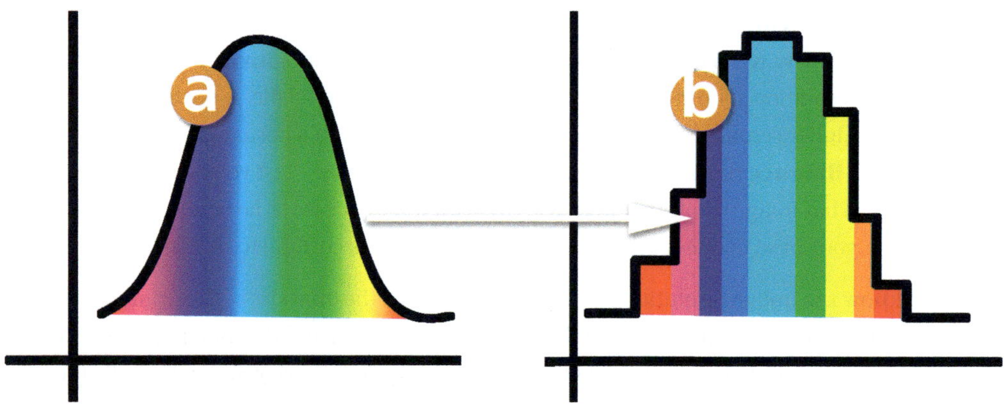

Analog to digital >> *In the capture process, via digital camera or scanner, a continuous tone original or scene is converted into discrete colors that can be represented by a series of numbers. (a) Analog original containing continuous tones. (b) Digital version containing discrete colors.*

In contrast, a digital image is made up of discrete tones and colors. When a scene or a print is captured by a device such as a camera or scanner the continuous original is converted into a digital file. The file describes the image as a series of numbers representing these discrete colors and tones. When we scan a negative or slide, or photograph a scene, we make this conversion by sampling the picture at regular intervals. At each sample point, a specific color is chosen to represent the hue found in the original. In this way, a grid of colors is put together to form a digital version of the continuous tone original.

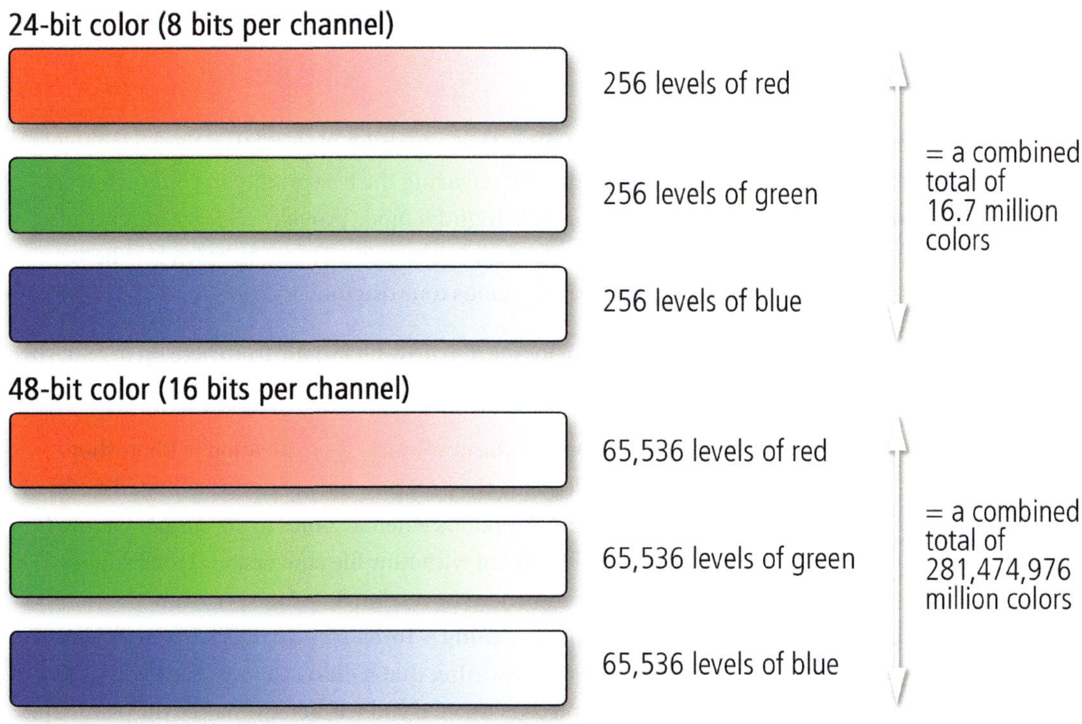

8-bit versus 16-bit >> *Digital photographs captured in 16-bit per channel mode contain a greater number of colors than those captured with 8 bits.*

Comparing bits

Each digital file you create (capture or scan) is capable of representing a specific number of colors. This capability, usually referred to as the 'mode' or 'color depth' of the picture, is expressed in terms of the number of 'bits'. Most images these days are created in 24-bit mode. This means that each of the three color channels (red, green and blue) is capable of displaying 256 levels of color (or 8 bits) each. When the three channels are combined, a 24-bit image (8 + 8 + 8) can contain a staggering 16.7 million discrete tones/hues.

This is a vast amount of colors and would be seemingly more than we could ever need, see, or print, but many modern cameras and scanners are now capable of capturing 16 bits per channel or 'high-bit' capture. This means that each of the three colors can have 65,536 different levels and the image itself a whopping 281,474,976 million colors (last time I counted!). But why would we need to capture so many colors?

12-bit capture

Many cameras capture 12 rather than 16 bits per channel. These files contain 4096 tones per channel, as opposed to the 65,536 possible with 16-bit capture. Generally these 12-bit files are captured as raw files and when converted with the Adobe Camera Raw feature, you can choose between producing a 16- or 8-bit converted file.

2.02 More colors equal better quality

Suitable for Elements – 7.0, 6.0, 5.0, 4.0, 3.0, 2.0, 1.0 | Difficulty level – Intermediate
Related techniques – 2.13

Most readers would already have a vague feeling that a high-bit file is 'better' than a low-bit alternative, but understanding why is critical for ensuring the best quality in your own work. The main advantage is that capturing images in high-bit mode provides a larger number of colors for your camera or scanner to construct your image with. This in turn leads to better color and tone in the digital version of the continuous tone original or scene.

'Fantastic!' you say, 'No more 8-bit capture for me, I'm a 16-bit fanatic from here on in'. But there is a catch (you knew there had to be).

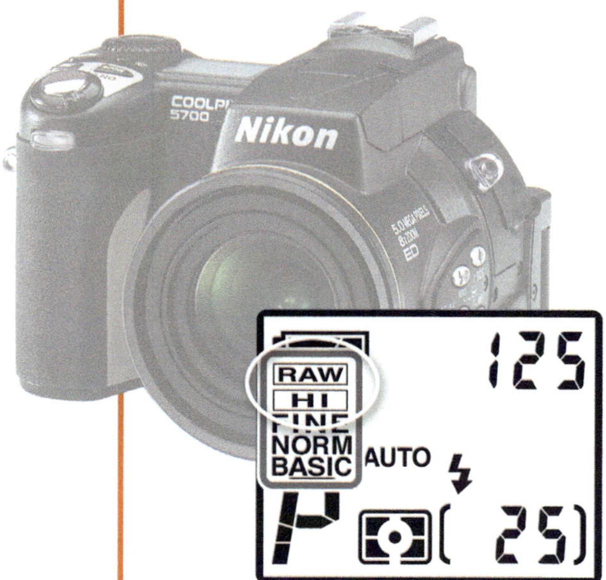

Capture commandment >> *If you want the best quality pictures always make sure that your scanner or camera captures in 16-bit per channel or 48-bit mode.*

On most cameras this is referred to as the 'Tiff' or 'Raw' setting. See technique 2.10 for more details on Raw files.

Despite the power and sophistication of Photoshop Elements the program only contains a limited range of editing options when it comes to 16-bits per channel files. Along with Raw file conversion, 16-bit support commenced in version 3.0 of the program. Previously when opening a 16-bit picture the program displayed a dialog warning that it didn't support the high-bit mode and then asked if you wanted to change the picture to an 8-bit form.

In these recent versions of the program the Rectangular and Elliptical Marquee and Lasso, Eyedropper, Move and Zoom tools all function in 16-bit mode. In addition, you can rotate, resize, apply auto levels, auto contrast or auto color correct, or use more manual controls such as Levels, Shadow/Highlights and Brightness/Contrast features. The Sharpen, Noise, Blur and Adjustment filter groups also work here as well.

Does this mean that making enhancement changes in 16-bit mode is unworkable? No, you just need to use a different approach. Read on.

Global versus local enhancement

Because of the limitations when working with a 16-bits per channel file in Elements some digital photographers break their enhancement tasks into two different sections – global and local.

Global, or those changes that are applied at the beginning of the process to the whole picture. These include general brightness and contrast changes, some color correction and the application of a little sharpening.

Local changes are those that are more specific and are sometimes only applied to certain sections of the picture. They may include dodging and burning-in, removal of unwanted dust and scratches, the addition of some text and the application of special effects filters.

This separation of enhancement tasks fits neatly with the way that the 16-bit support works in Photoshop Elements. Global changes can be applied to the photograph whilst it is still in 16-bit mode; the file can then be converted to 8 bits per channel (Image > Mode > 8 Bits/channel) and the local alterations applied. This is the process that the professionals have been using for years and now Elements gives you the power to follow suit.

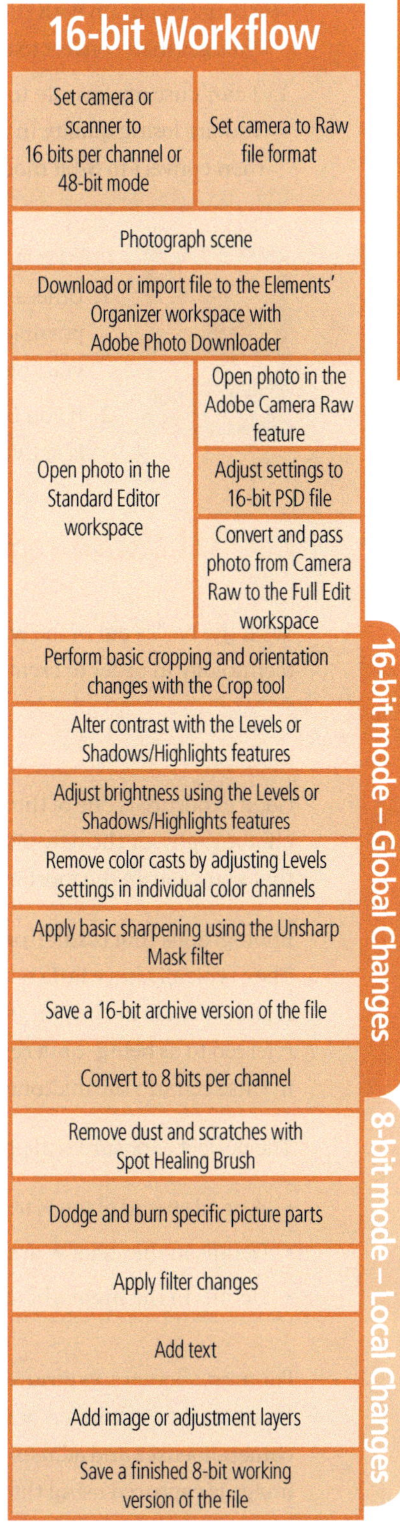

The advantages of 16-bit or high-bit capture

Here are the main advantages in a nutshell:

1. Capturing images in high-bit mode provides a larger number of colors for your camera or scanner to construct your image with. This in turn leads to better color and tone in the digital version of the continuous tone original or scene.
2. Global editing and enhancement changes made to a high-bit file will always yield a better quality result than when the same changes are applied to a low-bit image.
3. Major enhancement of the shadow and highlight areas in a high-bit image is less likely to produce posterized tones than if the same actions were applied to a low-bit version.
4. More gradual changes and subtle variations are possible when adjusting the tones of a high-bit photograph using tools like Levels than is possible with low-bit images.

Common high-bit misconceptions

1. Elements can't handle high-bit images. Not true. Previous versions of the program couldn't handle high-bit pictures, but since Elements 3.0 the program has contained a reduced feature set that can be used with 16-bits per channel images. And even with this limitation there are enough tools available to ensure quality enhancement of your images.
2. High-bit images are too big for me to handle and store. Yes, high-bit images are twice the file size of 8-bit images and this does slow down machines with limited resources, but if this is

a concern put up with the inconvenience of a slow machine whilst you make tonal and color changes then convert to a speedier 8-bit file for local changes.

3. I can't use my favorite tools and features in high-bit mode so I don't use high-bit images at all. You are losing quality in your images needlessly. Perform your global edits in 16-bit mode and then convert to 8-bit mode for the application of your favorite low-bit techniques.

Pro's Tip

Ensure quality capture and enhancement with 16-bit and Raw files

1. Unless space is an issue capture all images in the highest color depth possible. This will help to ensure the best possible detail, tone and color in your pictures.
2. If you have a camera that can capture Raw files then ensure that this feature is activated as well, as it provides the best quality files to work with.

Digital shooting technique

With the basics out of the way let's now look at how to manipulate some of your camera's technology in order to create the best digital files possible.

Exposure

Good exposure is one of the cornerstones of great imaging. Whether it be traditional silver-based photography, or the new pixel-centered picture making, getting your exposure right will ensure that you capture the most information possible.

Photographs that result from the sensor receiving too much light are said to be 'overexposed'. They typically have little or no details in the highlight portions of the image and the midtone regions are far too bright. In contrast, pictures that have been captured with too little light are referred to as being 'underexposed'. In these images it is the shadow areas that lose details and in this scenario the midtones are too dark.

The perfect exposure will produce a picture that contains:

- A good spread of tones from light to dark,
- Details in the shadow areas, and
- Details in the highlight areas.

For most shooters, exposure is something that the camera does automatically. You frame the image in the viewfinder, or via the preview screen, push the button down halfway and the camera focuses and adjusts the exposure for the scene. Push the button down fully and the image is captured using the exposure settings selected by the camera.

Generally speaking, letting the camera do the work produces great results, but in some circumstances where the lighting is a little tricky, the 'auto' exposure route can result in images that are either 'under' or 'over' exposed. It's here that the photographer needs to 'step in' and make some adjustments to the exposure settings. Modern cameras have a range of features designed to override the camera's auto exposure settings.

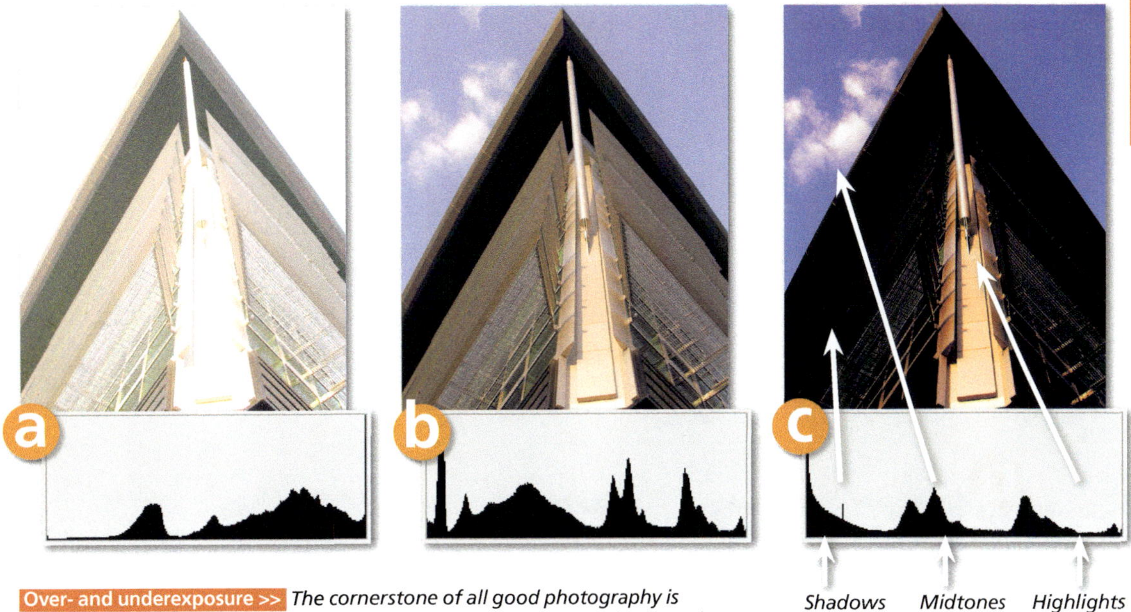

Over- and underexposure >> *The cornerstone of all good photography is accurate exposure. (a) Overexposed images are too light and lose details in the highlights and mid tone areas. (b) Well-exposed pictures have a good distribution of tones over a range from dark to light. (c) Underexposed images have little or no shadow detail as these areas are converted to pure black.*

Exposure control

Two devices – the **shutter** and the **aperture** – control the amount of light that hits your camera's sensor.

The shutter is either an electrical or mechanical device that controls the length of time that the light falls upon the sensor. The longer the shutter is 'open' the more exposure the sensor will receive and, conversely, the shorter the shutter speed the less exposure is received. Shutter speeds have traditionally been measured in fractions of a second and are represented by a number sequence of halves and doubles. With some cameras, one step either way in the sequence is referred to as a change of a 'full stop', other modes step in 1/2 or 1/3 stops, and so multiple steps will be needed to make a full stop change in exposure.

The aperture works in a similar way to the iris in your eyes. The amount of light hitting the sensor, or entering your eye, is controlled by the size of the aperture, or iris, hole. Using a large hole will transmit more light than when a small aperture is in place. Again a series of numbers represent a doubling or halving of the amount of light entering through a given aperture.

This sequence is called F-stops and causes some confusion with new camera users as the scale equates the biggest aperture hole with the smallest F-stop number.

By varying the combination of aperture and shutter speed the camera, or photographer, can adjust the amount of light entering the camera to suit the sensitivity of the sensor. In bright conditions it is normal to use a fast shutter speed coupled with a large aperture number (small hole). Conversely, in low light situations a slow shutter speed and small aperture number (large hole) would be selected.

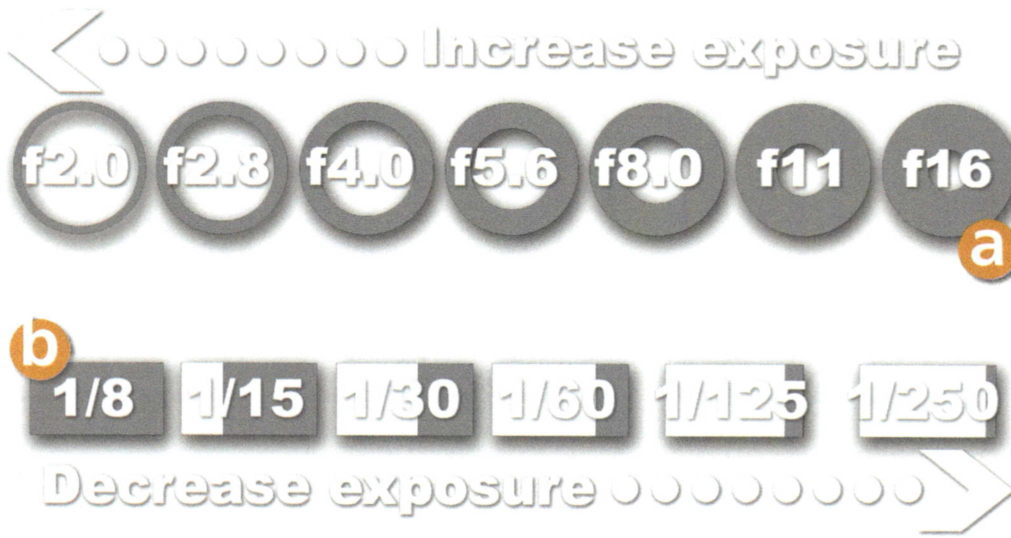

Mechanics of exposure >> *Aperture and shutter in combination control the amount of light that hits the sensor. (a) The aperture opens to allow more light into the camera and closes to reduce exposure. (b) The length of time the shutter is opened is displayed in fractions of a second. In addition to these mechanisms controlling exposure they also change the way that the photo looks. The aperture also controls the depth of field or zone of focus in the photo and the shutter manipulates how motion or movement is recorded.*

2.03 Exposure compensation

Suitable for Elements – 7.0, 6.0, 5.0, 4.0, 3.0, 2.0, 1.0 | Difficulty level – Intermediate
Related techniques – 2.02

One of the real advantages of photographing digitally is the ability to review your efforts immediately after shooting via the built-in screen on the back of the camera. With this tool it is easy to determine the times when the auto exposure system is producing images that are not quite the perfect exposure. When this occurs you can increase or decrease the amount of light reaching the sensor by using the Exposure Compensation feature.

This control effectively changes the shutter speed or aperture selected in steps of a third of an F-stop (sometimes also called EV – exposure value). Most cameras allow changes of up to plus, or minus, 3 stops. In tricky lighting scenarios I generally shoot a test image, review the results, adjust my exposure compensation settings and shoot again. I continue this process of shooting and reviewing until I am satisfied with the exposure.

A more precise way to determine over- or underexposure is to consult the histogram display of your camera. The histogram can be accessed from your camera's playback menu and it visually graphs the spread of the pixels in the image. This feature takes the guesswork out of determining whether your image has exposure problems.

A bunching of pixels to the left-hand end of the graph usually indicates underexposure and the need for more light, whereas a grouping to the right signals overexposure and requires a reduction in either the aperture or shutter speed setting.

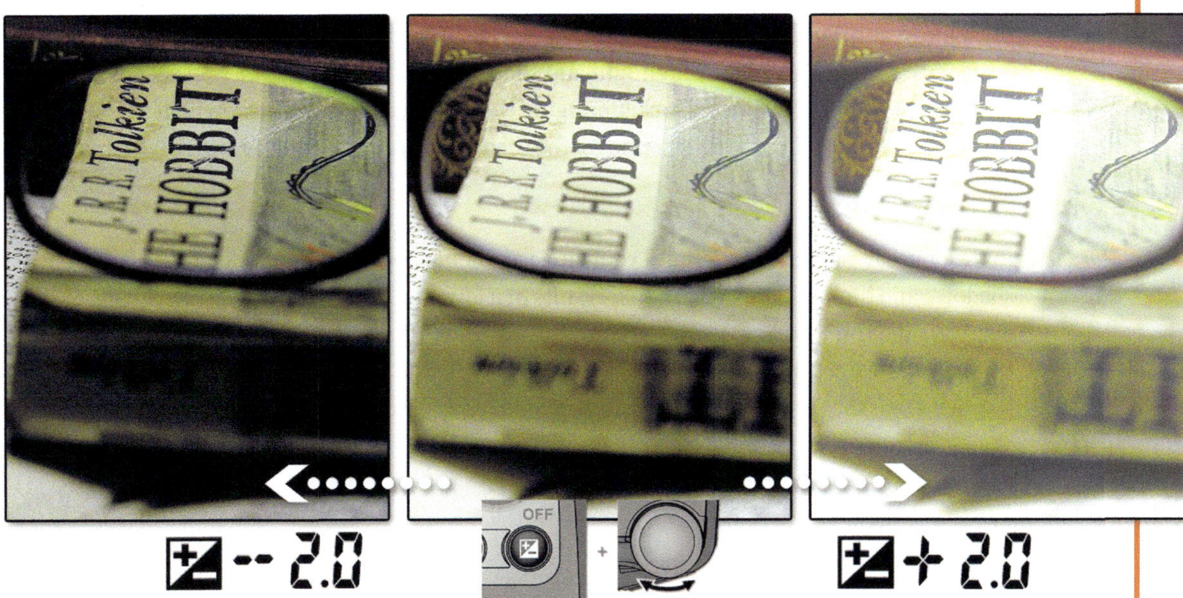

Exposure compensation >> *Many digital cameras contain a special feature that can be used to modify your exposure settings without altering the aperture or shutter speed values directly. This Exposure Compensation control allows you to increase or decrease the overall exposure of the picture.*

Frame-by-frame control

Apart from the absence of film, the typical digital camera has many familiar features. Experienced shooters on the whole have no difficulty understanding technology such as the shutter, aperture, or ISO sensitivity as these options have their traditional counterparts, but most new digital cameras contain several often overlooked functions that are designed to help you produce the 'ultimate images – shot by shot'.

Some of these features include:

- Contrast control,
- Saturation adjustment, and
- In-built Sharpness control.

These controls are now found on all but the most basic entry-level models and provide a level of flexibility that was never possible in the days when 'film was king'.

2.04 Contrast

Suitable for Elements – 7.0, 6.0, 5.0, 4.0, 3.0, 2.0, 1.0 | Difficulty level – Basic

The contrast control is one of the most useful features for the digital camera owner. When you are faced with shooting a beach, or snow scene, on a sunny day the range of brightness between the lightest and darkest areas can be extremely wide. Set to normal your camera's sensor will probably lose detail in both the highlight and shadow areas of the scene. Delicate tones will either be converted to white or black. Changing the setting to 'less contrast' will increase your camera's ability to capture the extremes of the scene and preserve otherwise lost light and dark details.

In the opposite scenario, sometimes your subject will not contain enough difference between shadows and highlights. This situation results in a low contrast or 'flat' image. Typically, pictures made on an overcast winter's day will fall into this category. Altering the camera's setting to 'more contrast' will spread the tonal values of the scene over the whole range of the sensor so that the resultant picture will contain acceptable contrast.

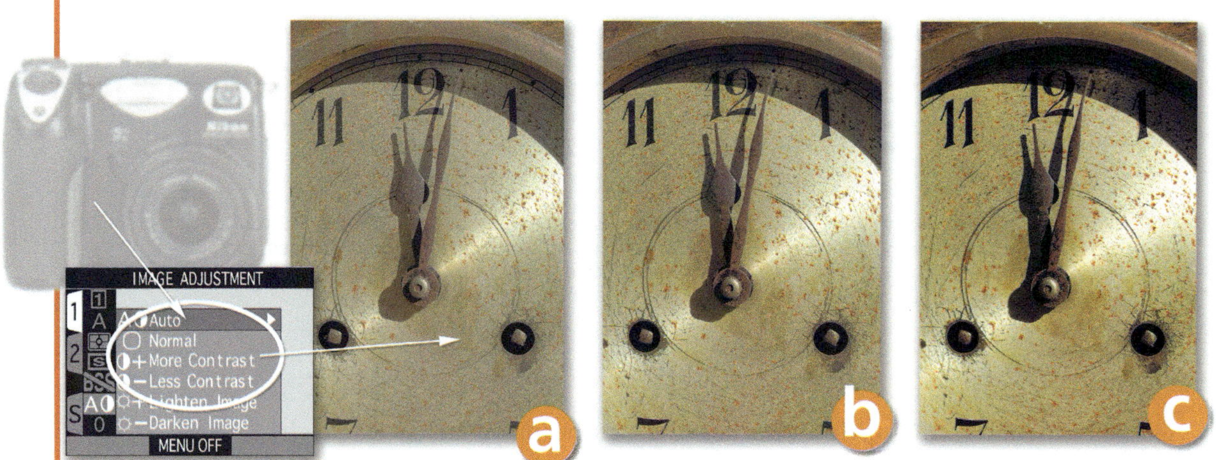

In-camera contrast adjustment >> *Altering the way that your camera records the contrast or the extremes of brightness in a scene can help to ensure that you capture important highlight and shadow details.*
(a) Less contrast setting.
(b) Normal contrast setting.
(c) More contrast setting.

'How do I know if my scene has either too much or too little contrast?' The beauty of shooting digitally is that we can preview our image immediately. In particular check the shadow and highlight areas using the camera's histogram feature. If the display contains pixels bunched at either end of the graph then the picture is too contrasty and will warrant a contrast change and a re-shoot. Pixels concentrated in a group in the center of the graph indicate an image that is too flat and needs to be re-shot using a higher contrast setting.

Pro's Tip: Contrast correction that is applied via your favorite image editing software package is possible and often used, but it is always preferable to capture the image with the best contrast at the time of shooting. This will guarantee you are making images of the best quality.

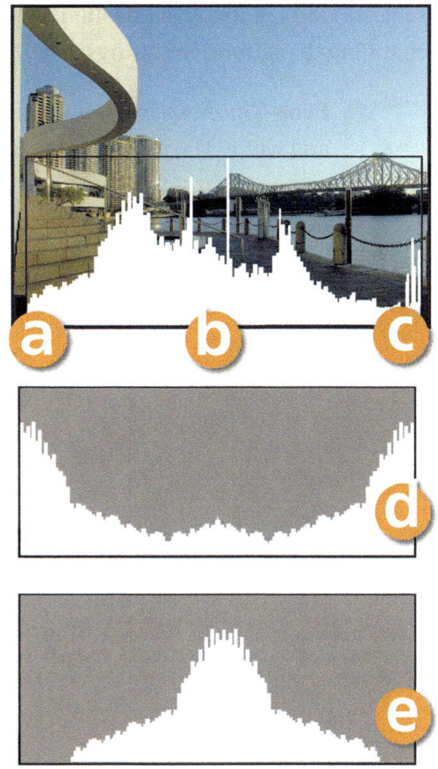

Histograms >> *Mid to high range cameras usually contain a Histogram function which displays the spread of the tones in the image. This feature is very useful for determining if a picture is exposed correctly or contains too much or too little contrast. (a) Shadow tones. (b) Middle tones. (c) Highlight tones. (d) High contrast picture. (e) Low contrast picture.*

2.05 Color saturation

Suitable for Elements – 7.0, 6.0, 5.0, 4.0, 3.0, 2.0, 1.0
Difficulty level – Basic

The saturation, or vividness, of color within your images can either make or break them. Sometimes color is the cornerstone of a picture, providing both the focal point and the design for the whole photograph. In these circumstances, desaturated or pastel hues will only serve to weaken the strength of the picture. In contrast, strong color elements can distract from important subject matter, causing the viewer to concentrate on the color rather than the subject of the picture.

Digital shooters can take more control of the color content of their images by selecting just how dominant or vivid the hues will be in their pictures. For shots that rely on their color the vividness can be increased; for those that work more effectively with subdued hues, the color strength can be reduced by way of the camera's saturation control.

Again, the effectiveness or suitability of each setting should be previewed and if necessary, several images with different color settings can be captured and the final choice made later. Though not as critical for retention of details as the contrast settings, it is important to capture as much color information as possible when shooting. This does not mean that you shoot all subjects with maximum saturation; it is just a reminder that if color is important, consider changing the saturation settings to suit your needs and your picture.

Pro's Tip

Pro's Tip: Always shoot in Color mode even if the photograph is to be used as a black and white. The picture can easily be converted to black and white in your image editing program at any time and you have the advantage of a color version if ever you need it.

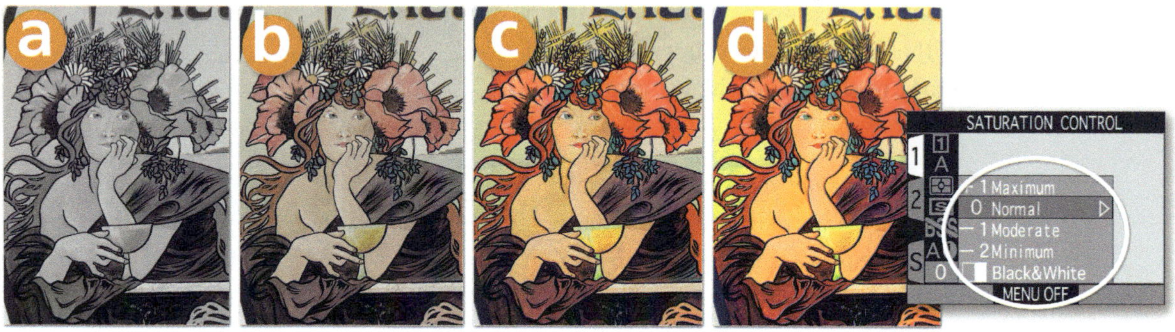

In-camera saturation adjustment >> *Using the saturation control in your camera you can alter the strength of the colors in your pictures. (a) Black and white. (b) Minimum saturation setting. (c) Normal saturation setting. (d) Maximum saturation setting.*

2.06 Image sharpness

Suitable for Elements – 7.0, 6.0, 5.0, 4.0, 3.0, 2.0, 1.0 | Difficulty level – Basic

The digital equivalent of film is a grid of sensors situated behind the lens in your camera. Each of these sensors records the light and color of the image that is focused upon it. In doing so a digital version of the scene is constructed. Despite the high resolution of modern sensors and specially developed lenses, the final image contains a degree of softness that is the direct result of this capturing process.

To help create crisper images the camera manufacturers include in-camera sharpening as one of their auto enhancement tools. Designed to improve the appearance of sharpness across the picture these features enhance the edge of objects by increasing the difference in tones between adjacent pixels. Sound confusing? Just remember that the act of sharpening changes the pixels in your image and just like the other image enhancement tools, too much sharpening can destroy your picture.

How do I know what settings to use? There are two schools of thought for deciding when and where to apply sharpening to your images. Some shooters apply a little sharpening in-camera, using either the minimum or auto setting. Others prefer to leave their images untouched and will use the sharpening tools built into their favorite image editing program to enhance their pictures. I lean towards the second option, as it offers me the greatest control over the sharpening effects and where they occur in my photographs.

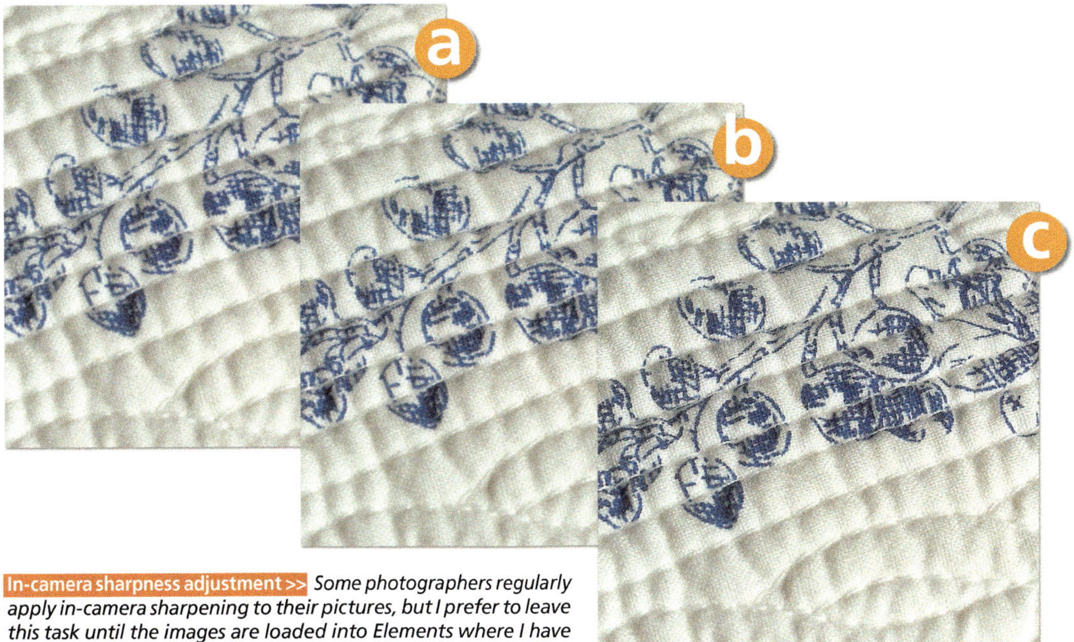

In-camera sharpness adjustment >> *Some photographers regularly apply in-camera sharpening to their pictures, but I prefer to leave this task until the images are loaded into Elements where I have more control. (a) No sharpening applied. (b) Normal sharpening setting. (c) Maximum sharpening setting.*

Pro's Tip

Pro's Tip: When sharpening in your editing program always view the image to be sharpened at 100% so that you can see the effects of the filter at the magnification that the picture will be used at.

2.07 White balance control

Suitable for Elements – 7.0, 6.0, 5.0, 4.0, 3.0, 2.0, 1.0 | Difficulty level – Basic

Our eyes are extremely complex and sophisticated imaging devices. Without us even being aware they adjust automatically to changes in light color and level. For instance, when we view a piece of white paper outside on a cloudy day, indoors under a household bulb or at work with fluorescent lights, the paper appears white. Without realizing it our eyes have adapted to each different light source.

Unfortunately digital sensors, including those in our cameras, are not as clever. If I photographed the piece of paper under the same lighting conditions, the pictures would all display a different color cast. Under fluorescent lights the paper would appear green, lit by the household bulb (incandescent) it would look yellow and when photographed outside it would be a little blue. This situation occurs because camera sensors are designed to record images without casts in daylight only. As the color balance of the light for our three examples is different to daylight, that is, some parts of the spectrum are stronger and more dominant than others, the pictures record with a cast. The color of the light source illuminating the subject in your picture determines the cast that will result.

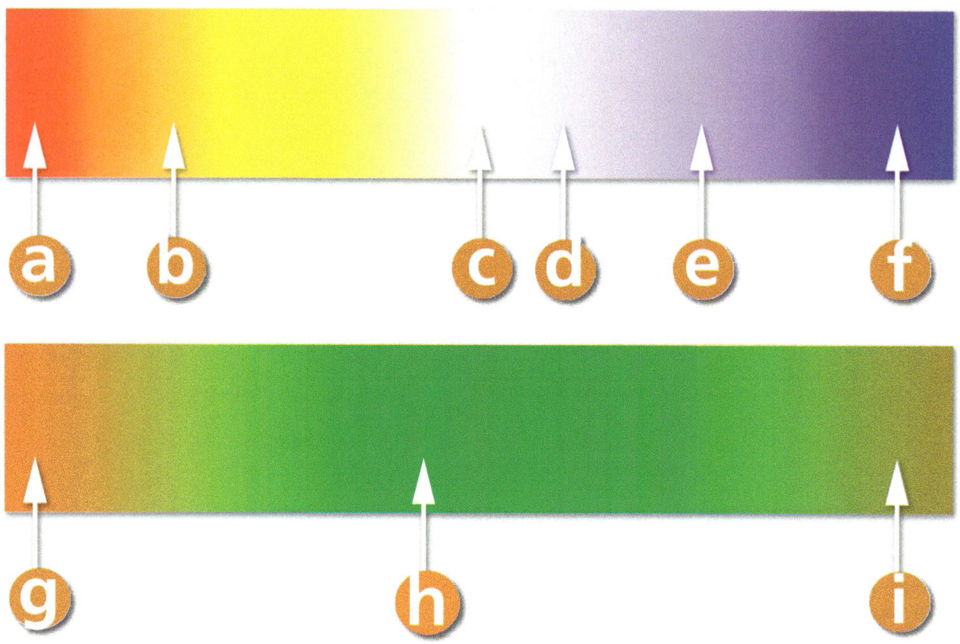

When is white light not white? >> *The color of white light varies from source to source. Our eyes adjust to these changes but the camera will record the differences as a color cast in your pictures. The White Balance feature is designed to rid your images of these casts. (a) Candle. (b) Household bulb. (c) Daylight. (d) Flash. (e) Cloud. (f) Skylight (no sun). (g) White fluorescent. (h) 'Daylight White' fluorescent. (i) 'Daylight' fluorescent.*

Traditional shooters have been aware of this problem for years and because of the limitations of film, most photographers carried a range of color conversion filters to help change the light source to suit the film. Digital camera producers, on the other hand, are addressing the problem by including White Balance functions in their designs. These features adjust the captured image to suit the lighting conditions it was photographed under. The most basic models usually provide automatic white balancing, but it is when you start using some of the more sophisticated models that the choices for white balance correction can become a little confusing.

Most modern digital cameras provide a vast array of options that should have you shooting 'cast-free' in any lighting conditions. The selections include:

- Auto,
- Fine or Daylight,
- Incandescent,
- Fluorescent,
- Cloudy,
- Speed light or Flash, and
- White Balance Preset.

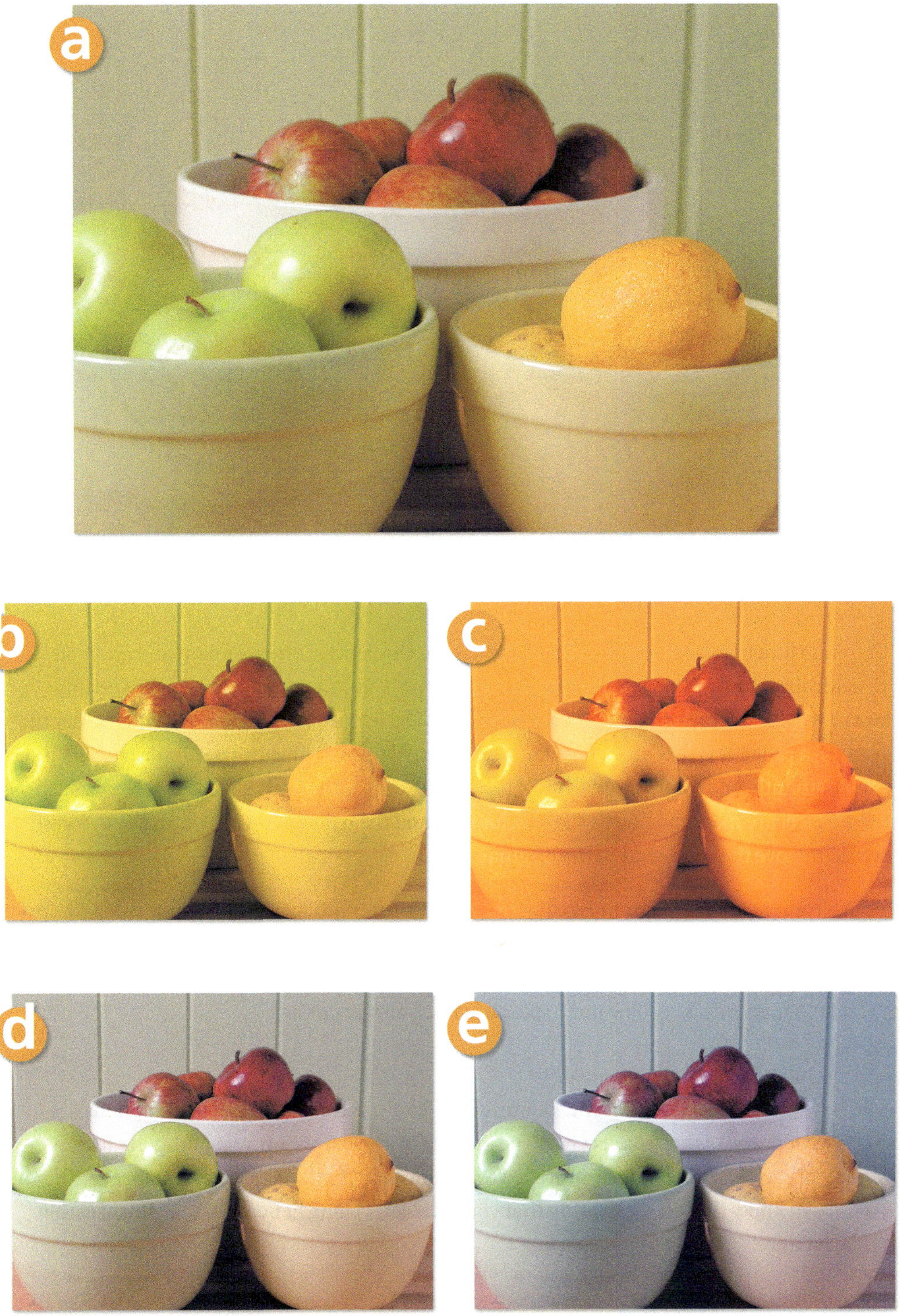

Color casts from different light sources >> *Camera sensors are balanced for daylight. Shooting pictures under non-daylight light sources will result in the color casts we see above. (a) Daylight. (b) Fluorescent. (c) Household bulb or incandescent. (d) Flash. (e) Cloudy day.*

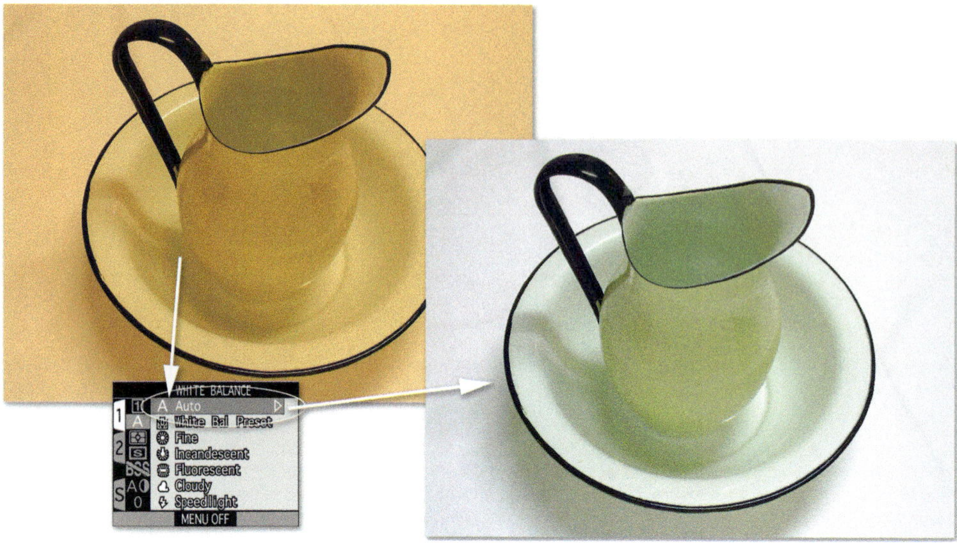

Auto white balance >> *The modern digital camera has a highly developed auto white balance system. It performs well under most lighting scenarios and should be your first choice when shooting under difficult conditions.*

Auto white balance

The Auto function assesses the color of the light in the general environment and attempts to neutralize the mid tones of the image. As with most 'auto' camera features, this setting works well for the majority of 'normal' scenarios. The feature does a great job with scenes that contain a range of colors and tones, but you may strike some difficulty with subjects that are predominantly one color, or are lit from behind. Also keep in mind that some subjects, such as cream lace, are meant to have a slight color shift and the use of the Auto feature in this case would remove the subtle hue of the original.

Apart from these exceptions most cameras' Auto features produce great results that require little or no post-shooting color correction work. So it's my suggestion that if in doubt try the Auto setting first. Check the results on the preview screen of the camera and if there is a color cast still present then move on to some more specific white balance options.

Light source white balance settings

The Daylight (Fine), Incandescent, Fluorescent, Cloudy and Flash (Speed light) options are designed for each of these light types. The manufacturers have examined the color from a variety of each of these sources, averaged the results and produced a white balance setting to suit. If you know the type of lighting that your subject is being lit by, then selecting a specific white balance setting is a good move.

Again, for the majority of circumstances these options provide great results, but for those times when the source you are using differs from the 'norm', companies like Nikon have included a fine-tuning adjustment. With the light source set, the command dial is turned to adjust the color settings.

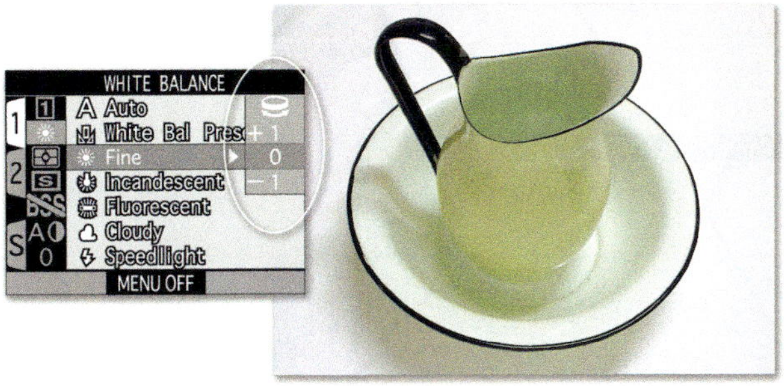

Fine-tuning white balance >> *With some models white balance settings can be fine-tuned to suit specific lighting scenarios. With this camera plus values add blue to the picture and negative values add red.*

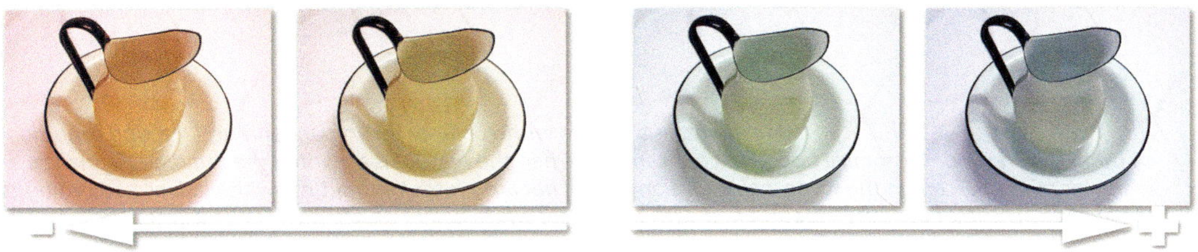

For Daylight, Incandescent, Cloudy and Flash options selecting positive values will increase the amount of blue in the image. Alternatively, negative numbers will increase the red content.

If you have selected Fluorescent as your light source then the Fine-tuning feature will allow you to select one of three different white balance settings. FL1 is suitable for tubes marked 'White', FL2 should be used with 'Daylight White' fluorescents and FL3 is for those labelled 'Daylight'.

2.08 Applying fine-tuning automatically

Suitable for Elements – 7.0, 6.0, 5.0, 4.0, 3.0, 2.0, 1.0 | Difficulty level – Intermediate
Related techniques – 2.07

If you are like me and find manually fine-tuning hampers the flow of your photography – shoot, stop, switch to menu, fine-tune white balance, shoot again, stop, switch to menu … you get the idea – then check to see if you camera has an Auto White Balance Bracketing option. This feature automatically shoots a series of three images starting with the standard white balance settings and then adding a little blue and finally a little red.

I find white balance bracketing particularly useful when shooting difficult subjects like the hand-blown colored glass in the example. As three separate images are saved I can make decisions about the most appropriate color by previewing them on my workstation's large color calibrated monitor later rather than the small preview screen on the back of my camera in the field.

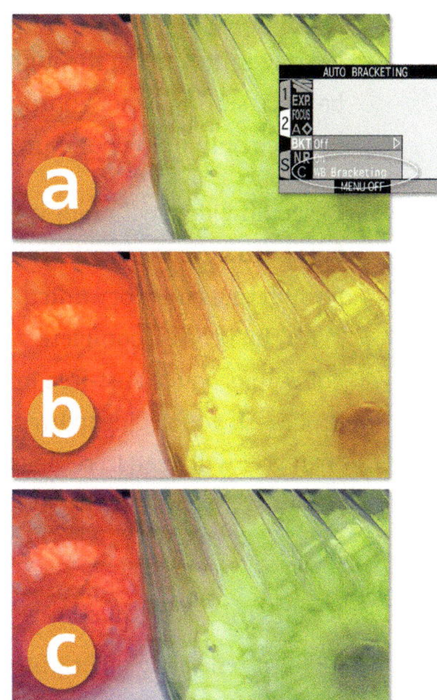

Auto fine-tuning >> *The White Balance Bracketing option automatically captures several pictures with slightly different color settings. (a) Standard setting. (b) + Red. (c) + Blue.*

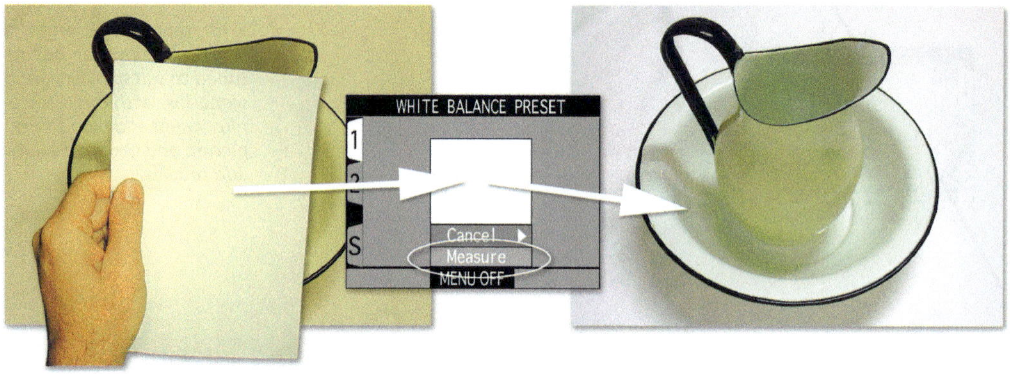

Preset white balance options >> *You can obtain a precise white balance setting under mixed lighting conditions by using the Preset or Customize option in your camera. When the feature is activated the camera will analyze a white (or mid gray) card in the scene, neutralize any casts that are present and set the white balance according to the analysis. The images now photographed with this preset white balance setting will be cast-free.*

2.09 Customizing your white balance

Suitable for Elements – 7.0, 6.0, 5.0, 4.0, 3.0, 2.0, 1.0 | Difficulty level – Intermediate
Related techniques – 2.07, 2.08

In a perfect world the scene you want to shoot will always be lit by a single source. In reality most scenarios are illuminated by a variety of different colored lights. For instance, what seems like a simple portrait taken in your lounge could have the subject partially lit by the incandescent lampstand in the corner, the fluorescent tube on the dining room ceiling and the daylight coming through the windows. Because of the mixed light sources a specific white balance setting is not appropriate. Instead, you should use the customize, or preset, white balance option on your camera.

Based on video technology, this feature works by measuring the light's combined color as it falls onto a piece of white paper. The camera then compares this reading with a reference white swatch in its memory and designs a white balance setting specifically for your shooting scenario. With the process complete you are now set to shoot your portrait secure in the knowledge that you will produce cast-free images. Always remember though, because this is a customized process, if you decide to turn a light off, or move your subject to another position in the room, then you will need to remeasure and reset your white balance. This way of working is by far the most accurate way to correct the color casts resulting from mixed lighting sources in your pictures.

It takes into account changes in color that result from:

- Light reflecting off brightly painted walls,
- Bulbs getting older,
- Mixed light sources,
- Light streaming through colored glass, and
- Shooting through colored filters.

2.10 Shooting Raw for ultimate control

Suitable for Elements – 7.0, 6.0, 5.0, 4.0, 3.0, 2.0, 1.0 | Difficulty level – Intermediate | Related techniques – 2.02

More and more medium to high end cameras are being released with the added feature of being able to shoot and save your pictures in Raw format. For most users this option on the camera's file menu has no real significance, but there are a growing number of photographers who having tried the new file type vow never to go back to using any other format. They boast of the extra quality and control that is achievable when using Raw for their image making and probably most impressive of all often refer to images in this format as being the closest thing to a digital 'negative' that we have yet seen. But why all this talk about Raw? What does the term actually mean and how can it help me take better pictures?

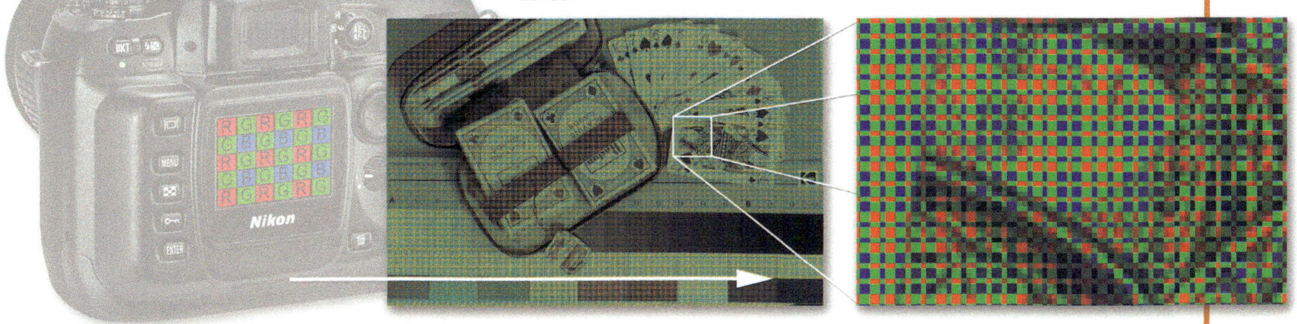

Raw files >> *Unlike TIFF and JPEG formats, Raw files contain the unprocessed image and shooting data. In many cameras the visual information is laid in the Bayer pattern of the original sensor.*

Back to the beginning

To start to understand the importance of Raw formats we need to go back to the beginning of the capture process. All single shot digital cameras (except those using the Foveon chip) contain a sensor that is made up of a grid of light-sensitive sites. Each site responds to the amount of light that hits its surface. By recording and analyzing each of these responses a tone is attributed to each sensor site in the grid. In this way a digital picture can be created from the range of scene brightnesses that are focused through the lens onto the sensor's surface. Fantastic though this is, this process only results in a monochrome (black, white and gray) picture as the CCD or CMOS sensors by themselves cannot record the color of the light, only the amount.

To produce a digital color photograph a small filter is added to each of the sensors. In most cameras these filters are a mixture of the three primary colors red, green and blue, and are laid out in a special design called a Bayer pattern. It contains 25% red filters, 25% blue and 50% green with the high percentage of green present in order to simulate the human eye's sensitivity to this part of the visible spectrum. In their raw, or unprocessed, format the output from these sensors is made up of a grid of red, green and blue patches (pixels) of varying tones. And yes this does mean that in any individual picture only 25% of the sensor sites are actually capturing information about the red or blue objects in the scene.

Interpolated color

I hear you saying 'But the images that I download from my camera are not split into discrete RGB colors'. This is true. What emerges from the camera is a full color picture which contains 100% red, 100% blue and 100% green pixels. This occurs because as an integral part of the capture process the raw RGB data that comes from the sensor is interpolated to create a full color image. Using special algorithms, the extra detail for a non-red site, for instance, is created using the information from the surrounding red, green and blue sites. This process is called interpolation and though it seems like a lot of 'smoke and mirrors' it works extremely well on most cameras.

When you opt to save your images in JPEG or TIFF formats this capture and interpolation process happens internally in the camera each time you push the shutter button. In addition your camera will also reduce the number of colors and tones from the 16-bit color depth that was captured to the 8 bits that are stored in the file. Selecting a Raw format stops the camera from processing the color-separated (primary) data from the sensor and reducing the image's bit depth, and saves the picture in this unprocessed format. This means that the full description of what the camera 'saw' is saved in the image file and is available to you for use in the production of quality images.

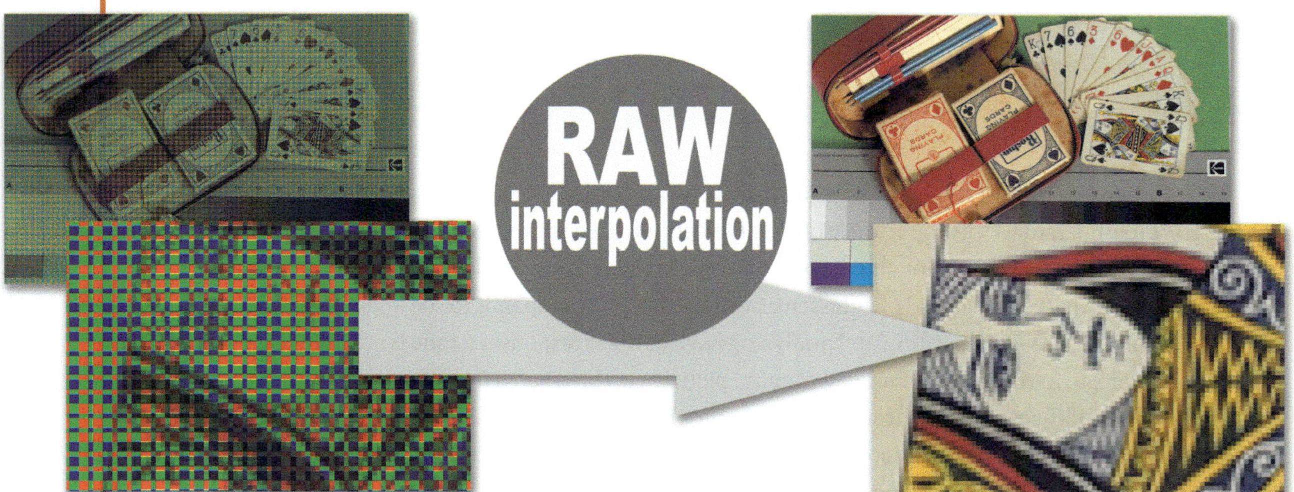

Raw images >> *The image stored in a Raw file is based upon the base data that comes directly from the sensor and needs to be interpolated to create the full color digital file we normally associate with camera output.*

DIY Raw processing

Sounds great, doesn't it? All the quality of an information-rich image file to play with, but what is the catch? Well, Raw files have to be processed before they can be used in a standard image editing application. To access the full power of these digital negatives you will need to employ a special dedicated Raw editor. Photoshop Elements 3.0 was the first version of the program to have such an editor built into the program. Called Adobe Camera Raw this feature is designed specifically to allow you to take the unprocessed Raw data directly from your camera's sensor and convert it into a usable image file format. Chapter 3 is dedicated to the processing of raw files using Photoshop Elements.

Adobe Camera Raw also provides access to several image characteristics that would otherwise be locked into the file format. Variables such as color depth, White Balance mode, image sharpness and tonal compensation (contrast and brightness) can all be accessed, edited and enhanced as a part of the conversion process. Performing this type of editing on the Raw data provides a better and higher quality result than attempting these changes after the file has been processed and saved in a non-Raw format such as TIFF or JPEG.

So what is in a Raw file?

To help consolidate these ideas in your mind try thinking of a Raw file as having three distinct parts:

Camera Data, usually called the EXIF or metadata, includes things such as camera model, shutter speed and aperture details, most of which cannot be changed.

Image Data which, though recorded by the camera, can be changed in the Elements Raw editor and the settings chosen here directly affect how the picture will be processed. Changeable options include color depth, white balance, saturation, distribution of image tones and application of sharpness.

The **Image** itself. This is the data drawn directly from the sensor in your camera in a non-interpolated form. For most Raw-enabled cameras, this data is supplied with a 12-, 14- or 16-bits per channel color depth providing substantially more colors and tones to play with when editing and enhancing than found in a standard 8-bits per channel camera file.

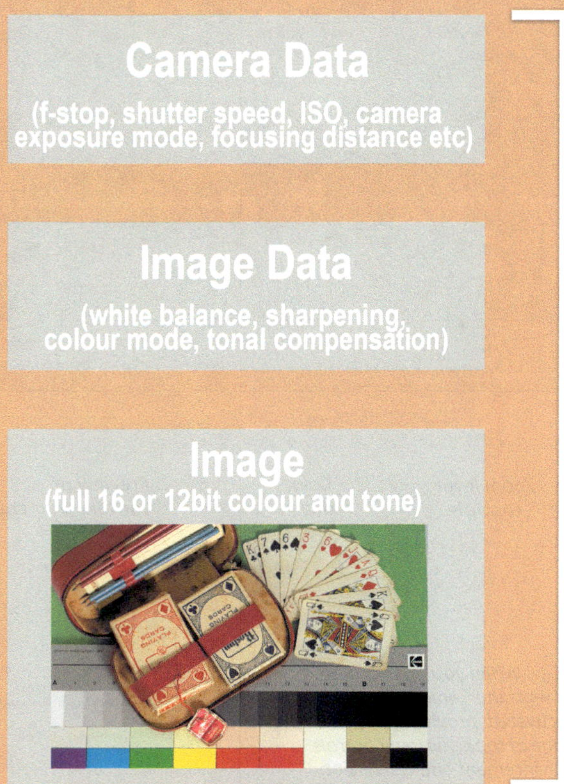

Raw files make-up >> *The Raw file is composed of three separate sections: Camera Data, Image Data and the Image itself. By keeping these components separate it is possible to edit variables like white balance and color mode which are usually a fixed part of the file format.*

Raw processing in action

When you open a Raw file in Elements you are presented with the Adobe Camera Raw dialog containing a full color interpolated preview of the sensor data. Using a variety of menu options, dialogs and image tools you will be able to interactively adjust image data factors such as tonal

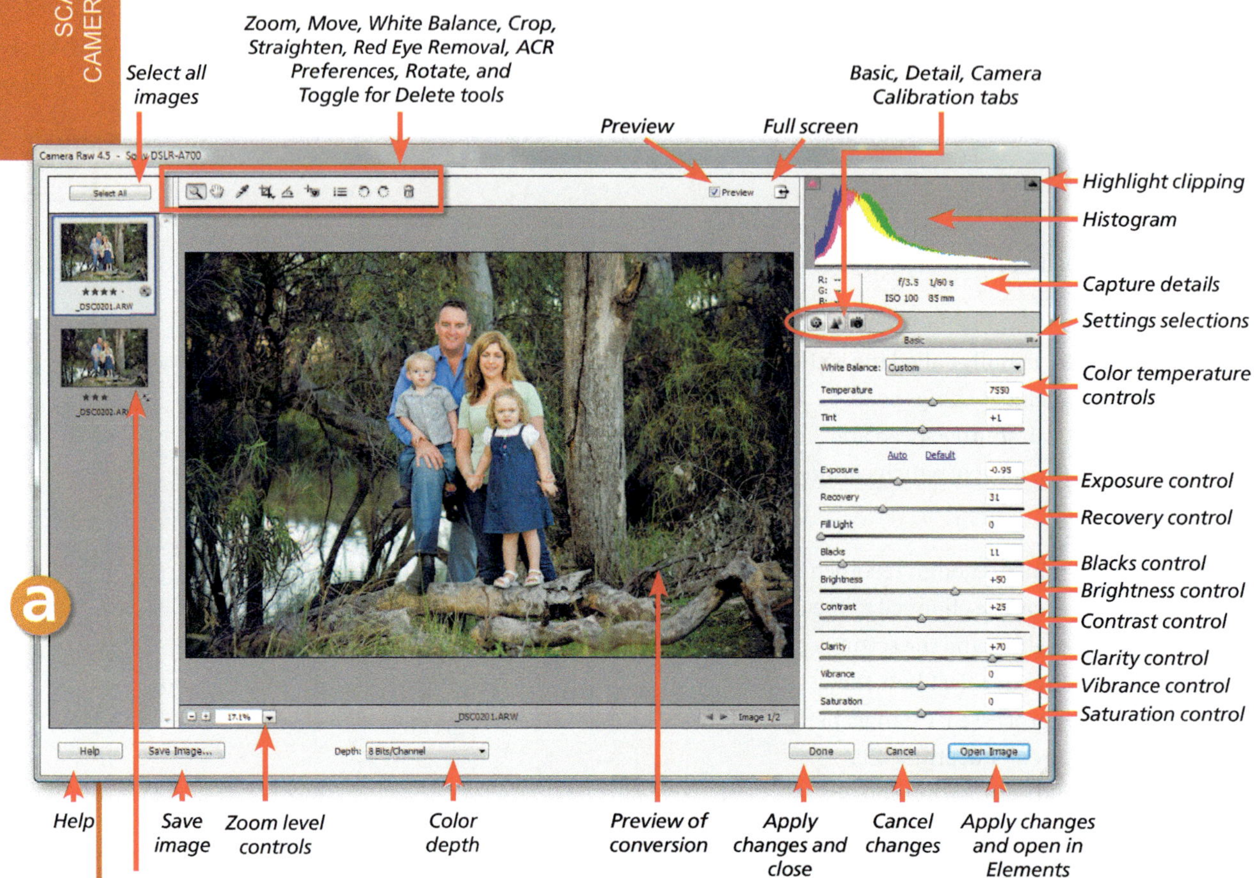

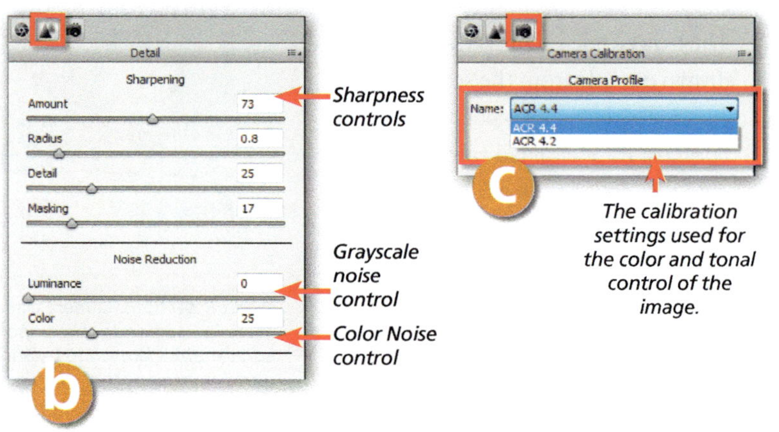

Raw files >> *When you open a raw file in Elements the Camera Raw editor is activated, providing you with a range of sophisticated controls for the enhancement and conversion of your raw files.*
After making your changes, click Open – the plug-in closes and the converted file is placed into the Elements workspace.
(a) Adjust tab options.
(b) Detail tab options.
(c) Camera Calibration options.

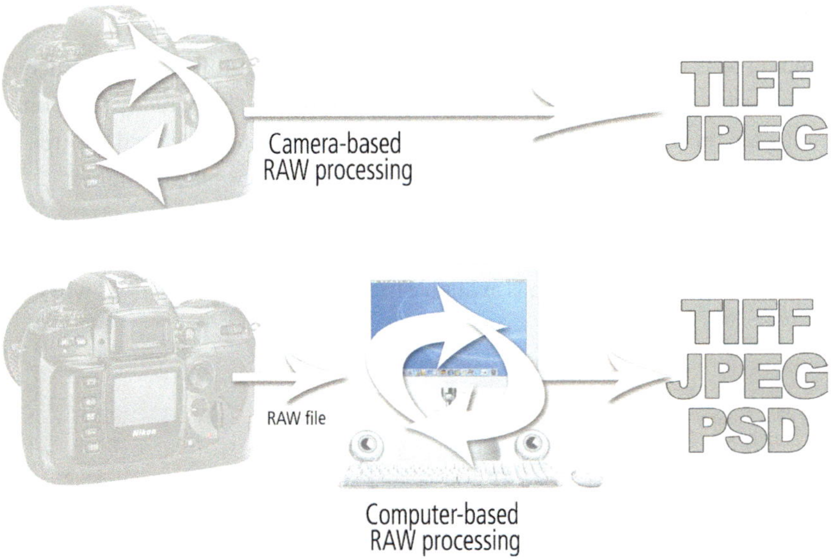

Capture workflow >> *Selecting JPEG or TIFF as your picture's file format means that the image processing is handled by the camera. In contrast choosing the Raw format removes this task from the camera and places it firmly with you and your computer. Working this way means that you have a say in decisions about white balance, contrast, brightness, sharpness and color mode.*

distribution and color saturation. Many of these changes can be made with familiar slider controlled editing tools normally found in features like Levels and the Shadows/Highlights control. The results of your editing can be reviewed immediately via the live preview image and associated histogram graph.

After these general image editing steps have taken place you can apply some enhancement changes such as filtering for sharpness, removing color noise and applying some smoothing. The final phase of the process involves selecting the color depth and image orientation. Clicking the Open button sets the program into action applying your changes to the Raw file, whilst at the same time interpolating the Bayer data to create a full color image and then opening the processed file into the Elements Full Edit workspace.

The Raw advantage

The real advantages of editing and enhancing at the Raw stage are that these changes are made to the file at the same time as the primary image data is being converted (interpolated) to the full color picture. Editing after the file is processed (saved by the camera in 8-bits per channel versions of the JPEG and TIFF format) means that you will be applying the changes to a picture with fewer tones and colors. A second bonus for the dedicated Raw shooter is that actions like switching from the white balance option selected when shooting, to another choice when processing are performed without any image loss. This is not the case once the file has been processed with the incorrect white balance setting, as anyone who has inadvertently left the tungsten setting switched on whilst shooting in daylight can tell you.

For a more in-depth look at raw processing steps in Photoshop Elements go to Chapter 3.

2.11 Shooting workflows

Having an understanding of all these camera techniques is one thing but putting them together when you are out shooting is another. To capture the most detail and in the best quality that your camera offers is a multi-step process. The following table summarizes the steps involved in three different approaches to capturing images using the techniques discussed above. The highest quality is obtained by shooting with a Raw file which is then enhanced using a dedicated editor. If your camera doesn't contain Raw capabilities then the next best option is to shoot TIFF and make your adjustments in Elements. If neither option is available then using 'best quality' JPEG will give good results.

<table>
<tr><th colspan="4">Recommended Digital Camera Workflow</th></tr>
<tr><td rowspan="8">Before Shooting</td><td colspan="3">Select highest resolution</td></tr>
<tr><td colspan="3">Pick best color depth
(16 bits per channel or 48-bit overall)</td></tr>
<tr><td>Select file format – JPEG</td><td>Select file format – TIFF</td><td>Select file format – Raw</td></tr>
<tr><td>Choose finest quality
(least compression)</td><td>No compression</td><td>No compression</td></tr>
<tr><td colspan="3">Set Color mode
(sRGB for web work, AdobeRGB for print work)</td></tr>
<tr><td colspan="3">Set Saturation</td></tr>
<tr><td colspan="3">Set White balance
(Either for the dominant light source or using the Customize option)</td></tr>
<tr style="display:none"><td colspan="3"></td></tr>
<tr><td rowspan="3">During Shooting</td><td colspan="3">Arrange composition</td></tr>
<tr><td colspan="3">Adjust focus
(Check Depth of Field)</td></tr>
<tr><td colspan="3">Set exposure
(Check Histogram)</td></tr>
<tr><td rowspan="5">After Shooting</td><td colspan="2">Adjust Highlight and Shadow
(Elements)</td><td>Adjust Highlight and Shadow
(Adobe Camera Raw plug-in)</td></tr>
<tr><td colspan="2">Alter contrast
(Elements)</td><td>Alter contrast
(Adobe Camera Raw plug-in)</td></tr>
<tr><td colspan="2">Remove color casts
(Elements)</td><td>Remove color casts
(Adobe Camera Raw plug-in)</td></tr>
<tr><td colspan="2">Apply some sharpening
(Elements)</td><td>Apply some sharpening
(Adobe Camera Raw plug-in)</td></tr>
<tr><td colspan="2">Save processed file
(Elements)</td><td>Save processed file
(Elements)</td></tr>
<tr><td>Image Quality</td><td>Good</td><td>Better</td><td>Best</td></tr>
</table>

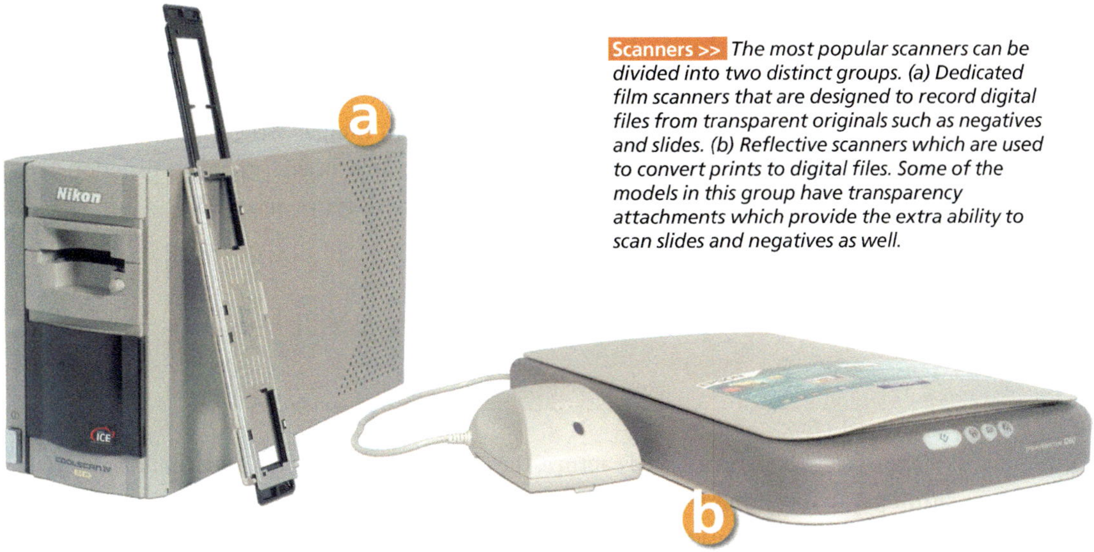

Scanners >> *The most popular scanners can be divided into two distinct groups. (a) Dedicated film scanners that are designed to record digital files from transparent originals such as negatives and slides. (b) Reflective scanners which are used to convert prints to digital files. Some of the models in this group have transparency attachments which provide the extra ability to scan slides and negatives as well.*

Film and print scanners

It was not too long ago that an activity like scanning was the sole responsibility of the repro house. The photographer's job was finished the moment that the images were placed on the art director's desk. But as we all know, the digital revolution has changed things forever, and scanning is one place where things will never be the same.

Desktop scanners that are capable of high-resolution color output are now so cheap that some companies will throw them in as 'freebies' when you purchase a complete computer system. The proliferation of these devices has led to a large proportion of the photographic community now having the means to change their prints, negatives or slides into digital files. But as all photographers know, having the equipment is only the first step to making good images.

For the most part, scanners can be divided into three distinct varieties – film, print and the more recent hybrid or combination scanner.

Dedicated film – This device is set up specifically for negative or slide capture and is usually restricted to a single format (135 mm x 120 mm/5 x 4 inch). The hardware is not capable of reflective scanning. If your business involves the repeated capture of images of the one film type, a dedicated scanner is a good investment.

Dedicated print – The scanners in this category are the most affordable and easily obtainable of the three types. If you can't afford a digital camera of the quality that you desire and you have loads of prints in boxes lying around the house then spending a couple of hundred dollars here will have you enhancing high quality digital versions of your pictures in no time.

Hybrid – These scanners are capable of both reflective and transmission scanning. This means that the one device can capture both film and print images. Starting life as flatbeds with added transparency adapters, these scanners have developed into multi-function devices that are capable of producing quality files from both types of originals.

2.12 Scanning resolution – 'Know where you are going before you start the journey'

Suitable for Elements – 7.0, 6.0, 5.0, 4.0, 3.0, 2.0, 1.0 | Difficulty level – Intermediate
Related techniques – 2.01

Just as is the case with camera-based capture, the quality of the digital picture that results from our scanning activities is based primarily on resolution and color depth. It is critical that these two factors are carefully considered before any scanning capture takes place.

Scanning resolution, as opposed to image or printing resolution, is determined by the number of times per inch that the scanner will sample your image. The number of pixels generated by a digital camera has an upper limit that is fixed by the number of sensors in the camera. This is not the case for scanner capture. By altering the number of samples taken for each inch of the original print or negative you can change the total number of pixels created in the digital file. This figure will affect both the 'enlargement' potential of the final scan and its file size. The general rule is the higher the resolution the bigger the file and the bigger the printed size possible (before seeing pixel blocks or digital grain).

Scanning resolution (samples per inch)	Image size to be scanned	Output size (pixels)	Output size (inches for print @ 200 dpi)	File size (Mb)
4000	35 mm film frame (24 mm x 36 mm)	4000 x 6000	20 x 30	72.00
2900	35 mm	2900 x 4350	14.5 x 21.75	37.80
1200	35 mm	1200 x 1800	6 x 9	6.40
600	35 mm	600 x 900	3 x 4.5	1.62
400	5 x 4 inch print	2000 x 1600	10 x 8	9.60
1000	5 x 4 inch print	5000 x 4000	25 x 20	60.00
400	10 x 8 inch print	4000 x 3200	20 x 16	38.40

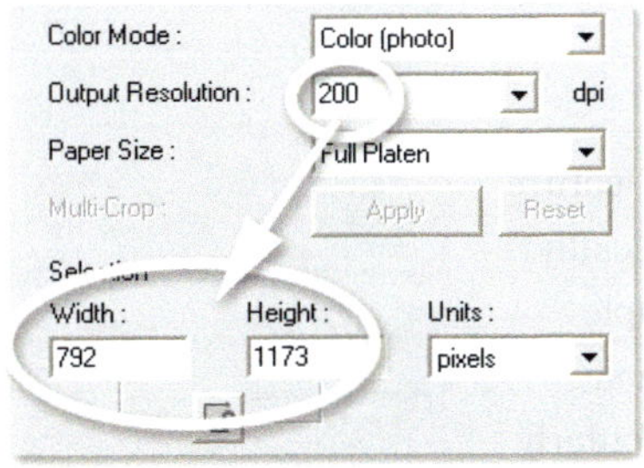

Scanning resolution >> *Adjusting the resolution that you scan at will directly affect the pixel dimensions of your final file. High scanning resolution will create more pixels in the files which translates into bigger prints.*

Does this mean that we always scan at the highest resolution possible? The intelligent answer is NO! The best approach is to balance your scanning settings with your printing needs. If you are working on a design for a postage stamp you will need less pixels to play with than if you want your masterpiece in poster format. For this reason it is important to consciously set your scanning resolution keeping in mind your required output size. See section 2.01 for more details about resolution.

Some scanning software will give you an indication of resolution, file size and print size as part of the dialog panel but for those of you without this facility use the table on page 42 as a rough guide.

2.13 Color depth

Suitable for Elements – 7.0, 6.0, 5.0, 4.0, 3.0, 2.0, 1.0 | Difficulty level – Basic | Related techniques – 2.02

As we have seen already color depth refers to the number of possible colors that make up the digital file upon the completion of scanning. If you have the choice always select 16-bit scanning mode (sometimes called 48-bit – 16 bits for red + 16 bits for green + 16 bits for blue) instead of 8-bit as this provides you with the opportunity to capture as much information from your photographic original as possible. Remember this is true even if you intend to convert these files to 8-bit immediately upon opening. The more accurately the image is scanned in the first place the better quality the down sampled file will be after the conversion has been made.

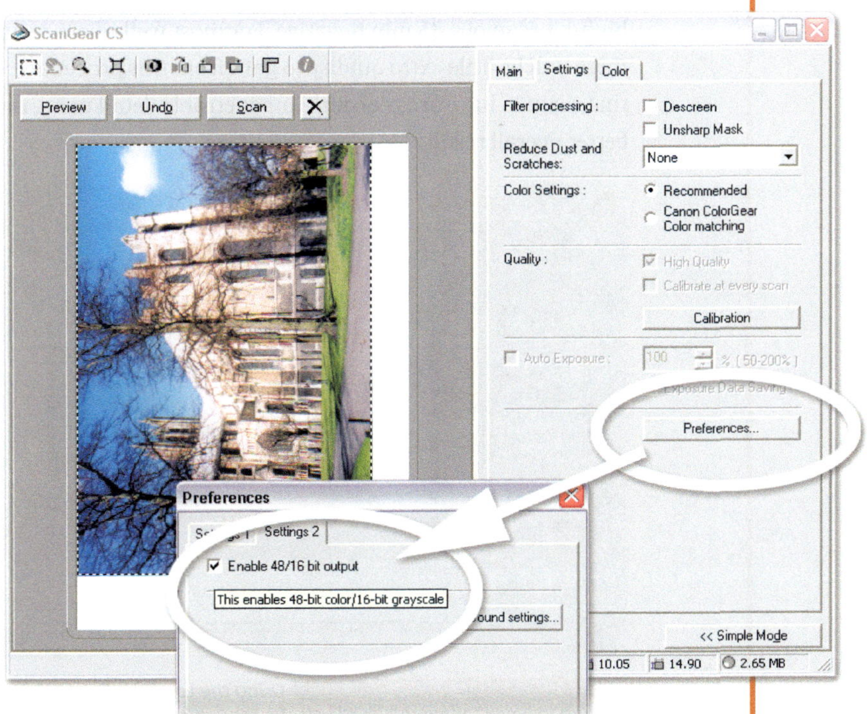

Scan in 16-bit mode >> *To capture the best detail, colour and tone always scan in 16-bit mode.*

2.14 Multi-sample

Suitable for Elements – 7.0, 6.0, 5.0, 4.0, 3.0, 2.0, 1.0
Difficulty level – Intermediate

Scanners in the mid to high end range often contain another feature that is designed to increase the quality of digital capture, especially in the darkest parts of the negative or print. Called Multi-Sample Scanning, it is a process where the image is sampled or scanned several times and the results averaged. This approach is particularly helpful when the scanner is trying to penetrate the shadow areas of a print or the highlight parts of a negative. It is in these parts of the picture that a single pass scan will most likely provide a 'noisy' result.

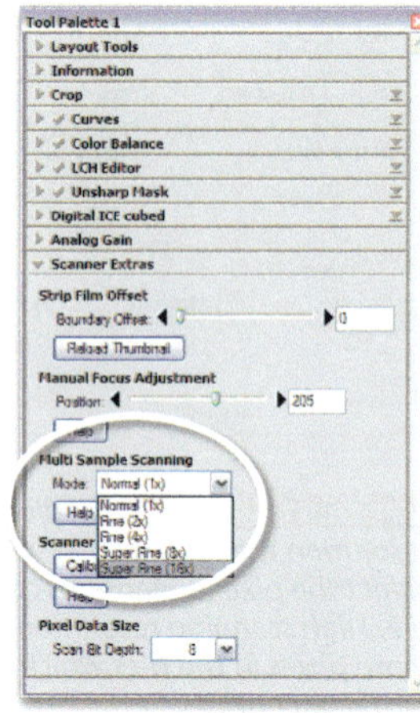

Multi-sample scan >> *Some scanners offer the option of 'multi-scanning' your film original. Select this setting for the best overall capture of difficult negatives or slides, but be warned – using this feature dramatically increases your scanning time.*

You can reduce this noise by making several scans of the same area and then averaging the result. The theory is that the level of noise reduction is directly proportional to the number of samples to be averaged. Therefore machines that offer a multi-sample rate of '16x' will produce better results than those that only contain a '4x' version. The down side to the technology is that all this extra scanning and averaging does take time. For instance the Minolta Dimage Dual III set to 8x Multi-Sample can take up to 14 times longer to make a high-resolution, high-bit scan of a 35 mm negative. For most well-exposed and processed negatives or prints there will be little extra quality to gain from this procedure, but for those troublesome images that seem to have areas of dark impenetrable detail using multi-sample will definitely produce a better overall result.

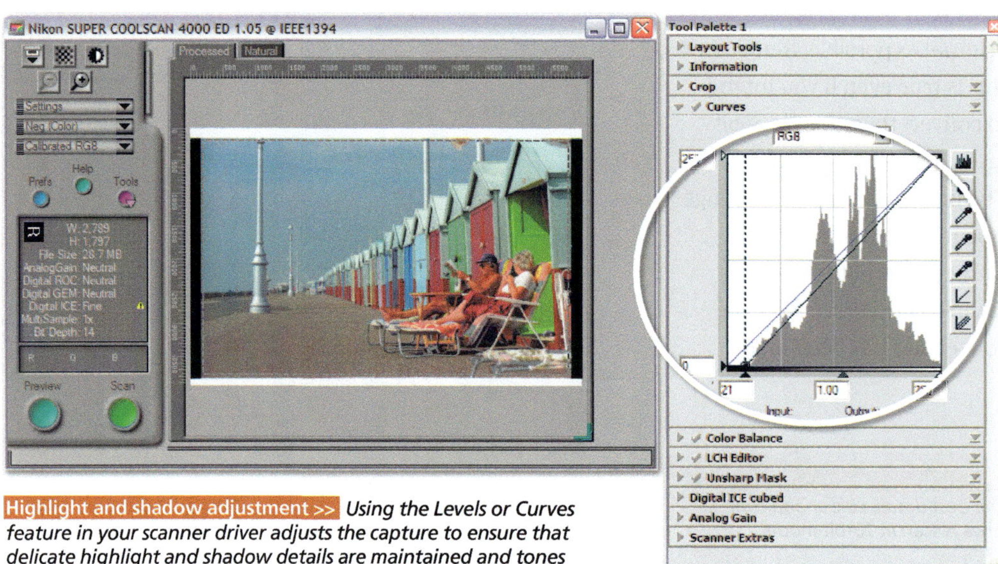

Highlight and shadow adjustment >> *Using the Levels or Curves feature in your scanner driver adjusts the capture to ensure that delicate highlight and shadow details are maintained and tones are well spread.*

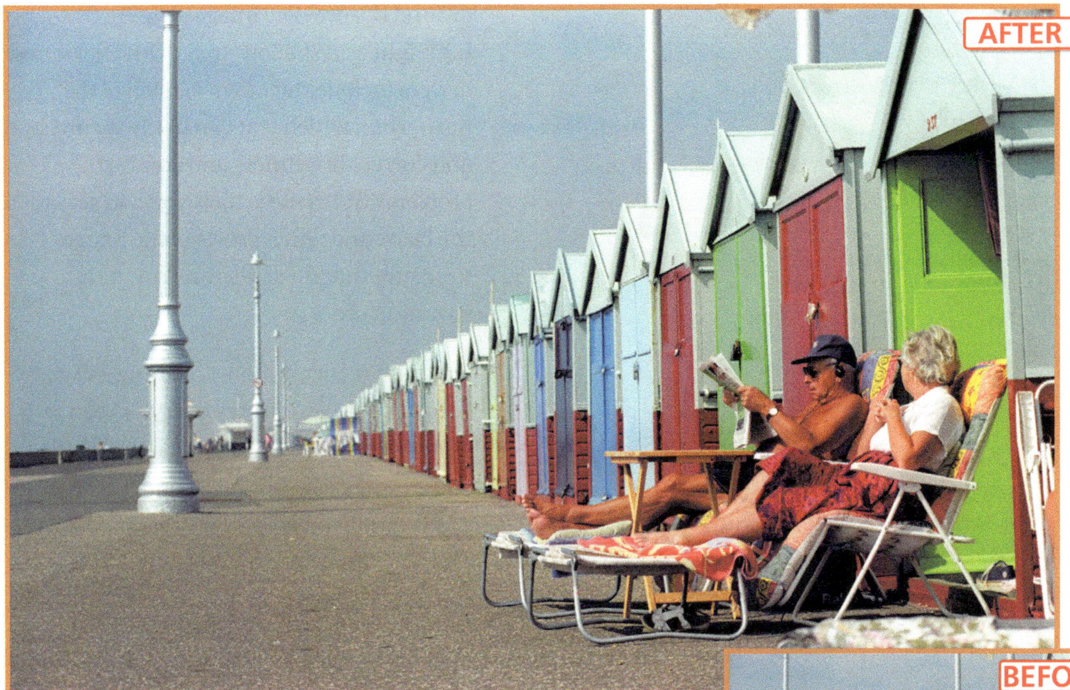

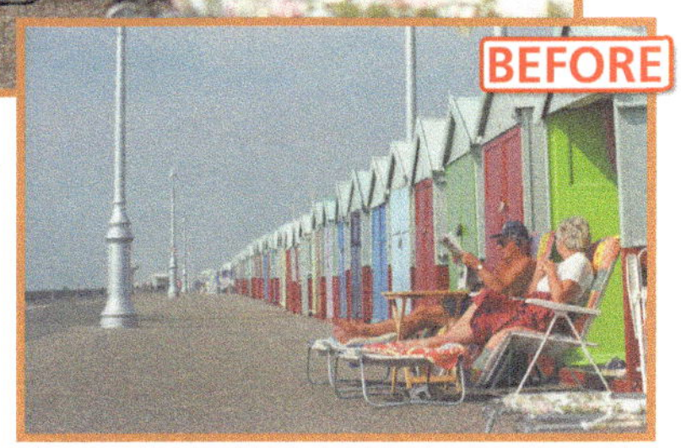

Contrast changes >> *Flat pictures can be corrected at scanning time by adjusting black and white using the Brightness or Contrast tools in the scanner driver.*

2.15 Highlight and shadow capture

Suitable for Elements – 7.0, 6.0, 5.0, 4.0, 3.0, 2.0, 1.0 | Difficulty level – Basic

With resolution and color depth set we can now scan the image – well almost! Just as exposure is critical to making a good photograph, careful exposure is extremely important for achieving a good scan.

All but the most basic scanners allow some adjustment in this respect. Preview images are supplied to help judge exposure and contrast, but be wary of making all your decisions based on a visual assessment of these often small and pixelated images. If you inadvertently make an image too contrasty then you will lose shadow and highlight detail as a result. Similarly, a scan that proves to be too light or dark will also have failed to capture important information from your print or film original.

It is much better to adjust the contrast, sometimes called gamma, and exposure settings of your scan based on more objective information. For this reason a lot of desktop scanner companies provide a method of assessing what is the darkest, and lightest, part of the image to be scanned. Often looking like the Info palette in Elements these features give you the opportunity to move

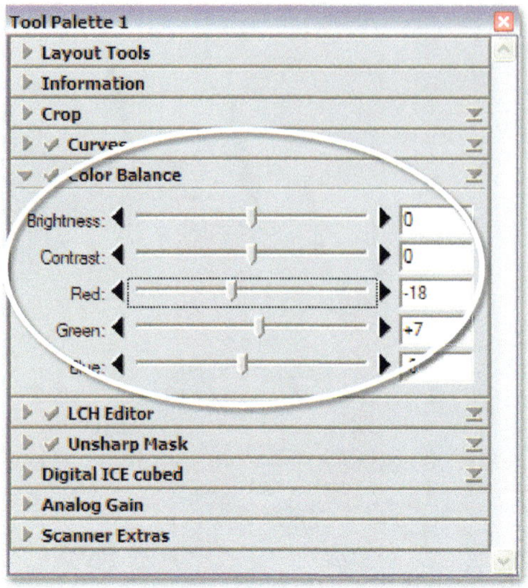

Color cast correction >> *Color casts can be removed from scanned originals using the slider controls found in the scanner driver.*

around the preview image pegging the highlight and shadow areas. Other scanner drivers include their own version of the histogram, which you can use to diagnose and correct brightness and contrast problems. With these tools you can set the black and white points of the image to ensure that no details are lost in the scanning process.

For those readers whose scanning software doesn't contain this option, try to keep in mind that it is better to make a slightly flat scan than risk losing detail by adjusting the settings so that the results are too contrasty. The contrast can be altered later when you edit the picture in Elements.

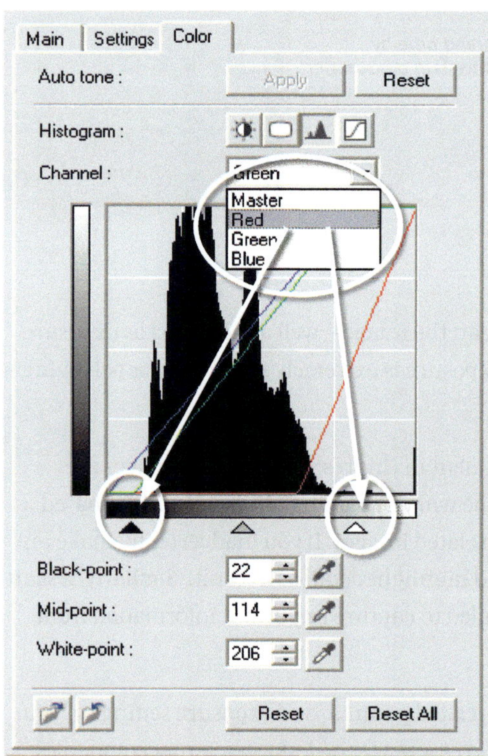

Removing casts with histograms >> *In the absence of dedicated cast removal sliders careful adjustment of the histogram for each channel can achieve the same results.*

2.16 Color cast correction

Suitable for Elements – 7.0, 6.0, 5.0, 4.0, 3.0, 2.0, 1.0 | Difficulty level – Intermediate

Despite our best abilities some photographs are captured with a dominant color cast that pervades the whole picture. Using the scanner driver's own color adjustment feature you can neutralize this tint at the time of capture. Frequently the scanner software provides a before and after thumbnail of your color adjustments so that you can preview your changes before committing the final settings. Now when the picture is scanned the color balance is adjusted and the color cast removed.

It is true that this process can be handled by Elements using the Color Cast or Color Variations features but, as we have already seen with the camera techniques above, the best quality images are generated when adjustments such as these are made at the capture stage.

2.17 Dust and scratches

Suitable for Elements – 7.0, 6.0, 5.0, 4.0, 3.0, 2.0, 1.0 | Difficulty level – Basic

One of the hidden enemies of quality scans is dust. Though the presence of dust won't reduce the ability of the scanner to record highlight and shadow detail accurately it does decrease the overall quality of the file because the affected area must be retouched later in Elements. No matter how proficent the retouching is, the 'rebuilt' section of the picture that is created to cover the dust mark will never be the same as the detail that existed in the original negative, slide or print. More important, especially for the photographer with hundreds of scans to complete, is the massive amount of time needed to retouch these dusty areas.

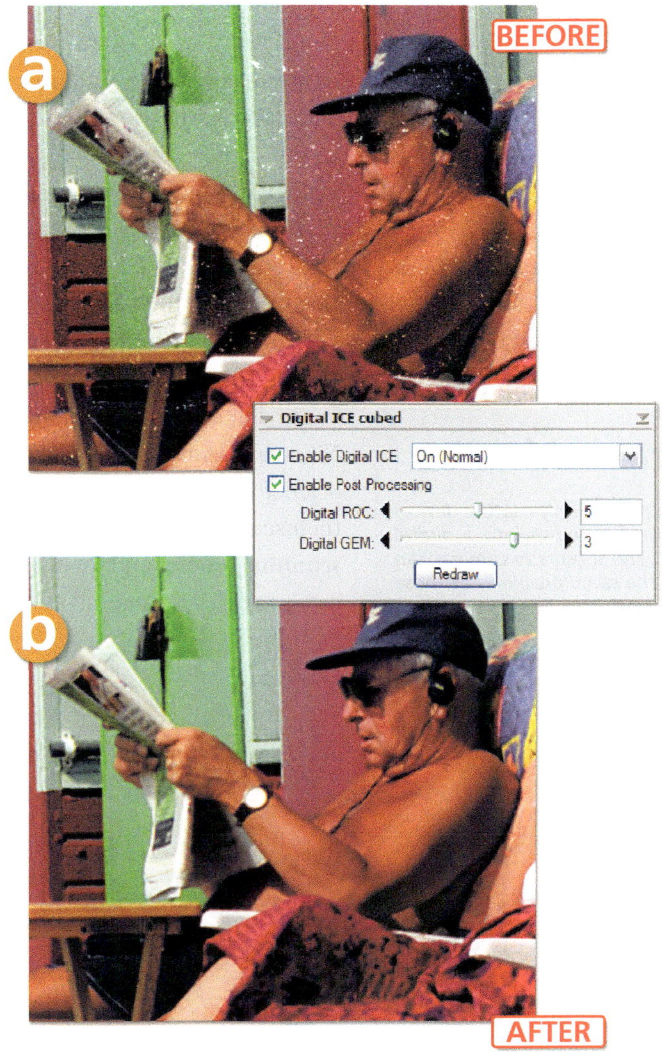

Auto dust removal >> *Features like ASF's Digital ICE can remove dust and scratch marks automatically at the time of scanning. (a) Before Digital ICE. (b) After Digital ICE.*

Some scanner models will include features designed to remove dust (and scratches) automatically from the picture during the scanning process. This technology when applied carefully can produce truly amazing results. One example is the Digital ICE technology produced by Applied Science Fiction (www.asf.com). Unlike post-capture processing where the dust mark is covered over using samples of other picture detail that surrounds the area, ICE isolates the marks during the scanning process and then proceeds to erase the defects from the picture. As the process is directly linked to the scanning hardware the Digital ICE technology cannot be applied to a dust affected image after it has been captured.

If you are considering buying a scanner then it is worth considering a make and model that incorporates the ASF Digital ICE feature. It's true that the defect detecting and erasing processes do add to the overall scanning time, but the retouching time saved more than makes up for it.

2.18 Noise Reduction technologies

Suitable for Elements – 7.0, 6.0, 5.0, 4.0, 3.0, 2.0, 1.0 | Difficulty level – Basic

As part of the process of scanning an image, visual errors are introduced into the file that were not part of the original. This is true to varying degrees for both entry level and high end scanners. The most noticeable of these errors is called noise and usually shows up in shadow or highlight areas of the picture as brightly colored random pixels or speckles. Image noise can be caused by a variety of factors including high speed film grain (high ISO), under- or overexposed negatives or slides, lighting conditions with brightness extremes, and image enlargement, as well as the CCD sensor itself. At worst, high levels of noise within a picture cause the image to appear unsharp and less detailed and have the potential to distract a viewer's attention away from the content of the image. To help correct or, more accurately minimize, the impact of noise in our digital photographs, scanner manufacturers like Kodak, Minolta, Nikon and Umax have banded together with software producer Applied Science Fiction (www.asf.com) to include ASF's Digital GEM product in their scanning software. GEM reduces image noise and grain during the scanning process and should be used when standard scanner settings produce noisy results.

Cameras and noise

Scanners are not the only capture devices that can introduce noise into a digital photograph. The sensors in cameras can suffer from the same problems as those found in scanners.

Generally, noise is at its worst in photographs taken with high ISO (equivalent) settings or when the shutter speed is longer than one second.

To help remove the noise in camera-captured pictures ASF also produces a plug-in version of their GEM software that can be activated via the Filter menu in Elements. This version of the software provides a little more control than that provided as part of the scanner driver as it allows separate adjustments for highlight and shadow noise as well as a slider control to alter the sharpness of the picture.

Alternatively, Elements versions 6 contains the Reduce Noise filter (Editor: Filter > Noise > Reduce Noise). As with the GEM plug-in the filter contains several sliders that help balance noise removal and overall sharpness of the processed picture.

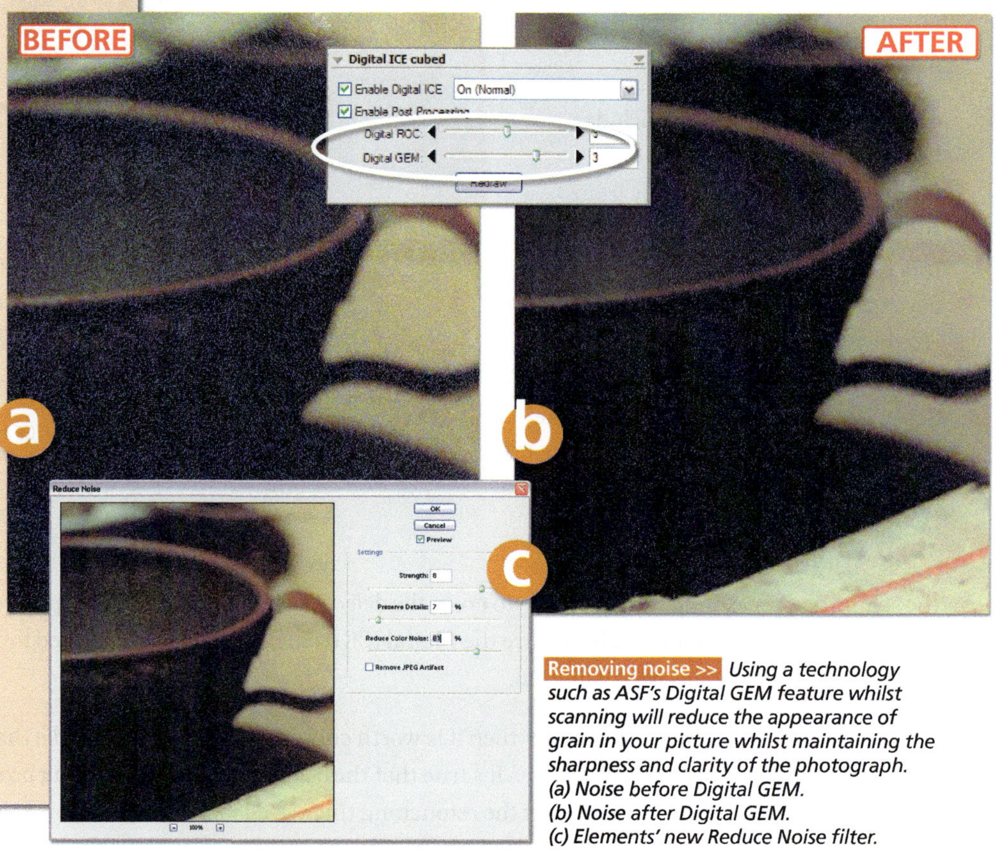

Removing noise >> *Using a technology such as ASF's Digital GEM feature whilst scanning will reduce the appearance of grain in your picture whilst maintaining the sharpness and clarity of the photograph.*
(a) Noise before Digital GEM.
(b) Noise after Digital GEM.
(c) Elements' new Reduce Noise filter.

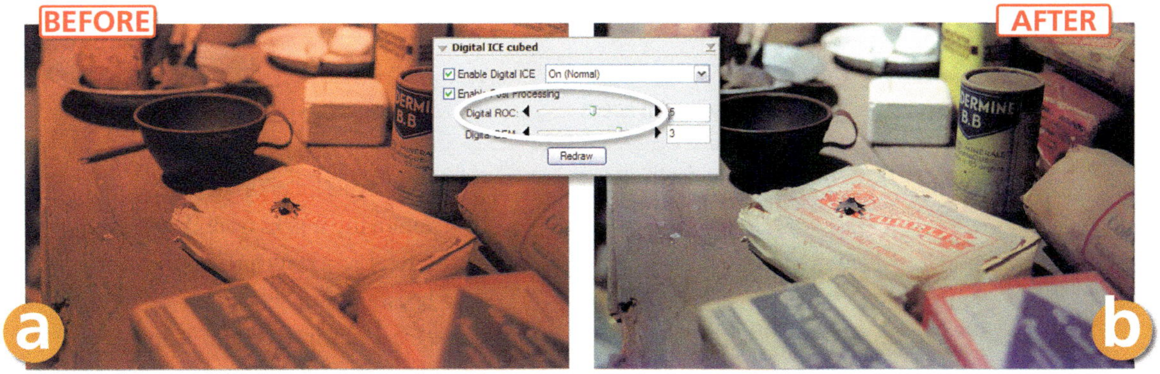

Re-creation of color >> *ASF's Digital ROC feature re-creates the color lost in original pictures due to fading or incorrect color balance at the time of shooting. (a) Before and (b) after color regeneration.*

2.19 Color regeneration features

Suitable for Elements – 7.0, 6.0, 5.0, 4.0, 3.0, 2.0, 1.0
Difficulty level – Basic

The last feature in the Applied Science Fiction trinity of scanning products is Digital ROC. Starting life as a feature designed specifically for use in the restoration of faded negatives or prints, many scanner operators now regularly leave the ROC option turned on for their non-restoration jobs as well. It provides a fast and effective way to automatically adjust the scanned image to account for over- and underexposure, color casts and, of course, fading. The feature analyses the data from the blue, green and red layers, identifying areas of loss and carefully recreating density and detail. ROC can also be used to restore density to faded black and white prints or negatives if the original is scanned in RGB mode initially.

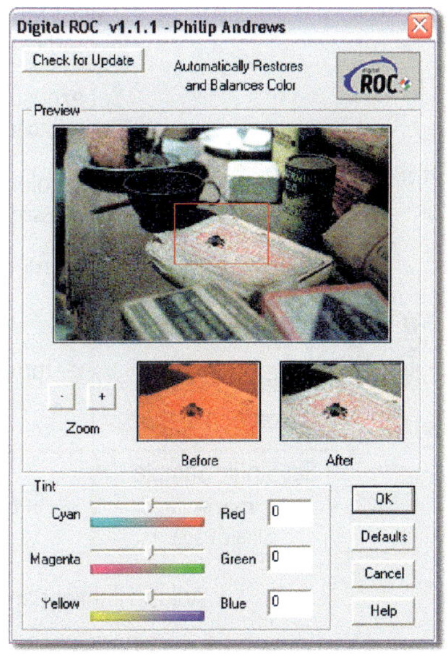

Digital ROC for cameras >> *The ROC and GEM components of the Digital ICE suite are also available as plug-ins for Photoshop Elements, providing grain reduction and color balancing options for camera-based images.*

The product is available as a plug-in for Elements or as part of your scanner software. Most scanners that included ICE and GEM also contain the ROC feature as well. The plug-in offers more control over the color regeneration process by providing slider adjustments for the red–cyan, green–magenta and blue–yellow tints.

Recommended Scanning Workflow

Before Scanning	Select resolution to suit print needs (samples per inch)	
	Pick best color depth (16-bit per channel or 48-bit overall)	
	Set Color mode (sRGB for web work, AdobeRGB for print work)	
	Set media type (reflection – print or transmission – negative, slide)	
	Set original type (negative, slide, print)	
After Preview Scan	Flip or rotate (if necessary)	
	Crop out unwanted detail (if necessary)	
	Adjust focus (Manual or Auto)	
	Set exposure (Check Histogram)	
	Remove color cast (if necessary)	
	Turn off Dust and Scratch Removal feature	Turn on Dust and Scratch Removal feature (if necessary)
	Turn off Color Restoration feature	Turn on Color Restoration feature (if necessary)
	Set Single Sample mode (Single Pass)	Set Multi-Sample mode
After Scanning in Elements	Adjust Highlight and Shadow	
	Alter contrast	
	Remove color casts	
	Apply some sharpening	
	Save processed file	
Image Quality	Good	Best

2.20 Scanning workflow

Making sure that your negatives/prints are clean before scanning can save a lot of time spent removing marks from the picture later. Use a soft cloth or a blower brush to remove surface particles before placing the film strip into the holder or the print on the platen. Don't forget to clean the glass of the scanner as well.

Check with your scanner manual to see which way the film should be placed in the holder. Inserting the film the wrong way round will mean that any writing in the picture will be back to front. Place the film in the holder ensuring the strip aligns with holder edges. Insert the film holder into the scanner. For flatbed scanners, place the photograph face down on the glass surface making sure that the edges are parallel with the scanner's edge.

Start the scanner software. You can do this from inside Elements. Simply select the scanner name from the Import (Editor: File > Import) menu. This will open the software that controls the scanner. Some scanners are supplied with a stand-alone version of this software that you can access from your program's menu without having to open an editing package first.

Fixing common shooting problems

Use the guide below to help diagnose and solve shooting problems.

1. Focus not on main subject

Problem: The main subject in the image is not sharply focused.

Cause: This is usually caused by not having the auto focus area on the main subject at the time of shooting.

Solution: If your subject is off to one side of the frame make sure that you lock focus (pressing the shutter button down halfway) on this point before re-composing and releasing the shutter button.

2. Picture too light

Problem: The photograph appears washed out or too light with no detail in the light areas of the print.

Cause: This is caused by too much light entering the camera causing the overexposure.

Solution: You can resolve this problem by adjusting the camera's exposure compensation control so that it automatically reduces the overall exposure by one stop. Shoot again and check exposure. If still overexposed, change the compensation to two stops. Continue this process until the exposure is acceptable.

3. Picture too dark

Problem: The photograph appears muddy or too dark with no detail in the shadow areas of the print.

Cause: Again this is a problem of exposure. This time not enough light has entered the camera.

Solution: Adjust the exposure compensation control to add more light or alternatively use a flash to help light your subject.

4. Subject too blurry

Problem: The main subject, or the whole picture, appears blurry and unsharp.

Cause: When images appear blurry it is usually the result of the subject, or the photographer, moving during a long exposure.

Solution: Use a tripod to reduce the risk of camera shake and try photographing the subject at a point in the activity when there is less movement.

5. Flash off glass

Problem: This problem results from the flash bouncing straight back from the glass into the lens of the camera.

Cause: The flash travels directly from your camera hitting the glass and bouncing directly back into the lens.

Solution: Using available light rather than the flash is one solution. Another is to move a little to one side so that the flash angles off the glass surface away from the camera.

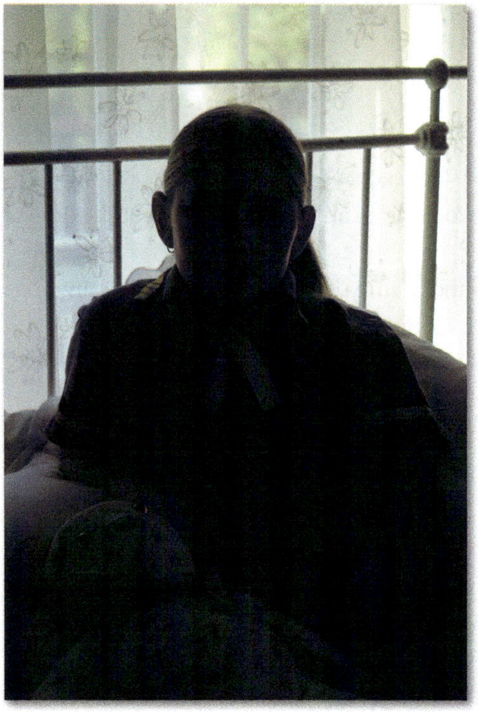

Adjusting for backlighting >> *The camera's exposure system can be easily fooled when there is a source of bright light in the photo and the subject is in shadows. Here the portrait sitter is a silhouette because the camera is basing the exposure on the light coming from the window. To correct this situation:*
1) Move the subject so that they are no longer framed by the window, or
2) Use fill flash to illuminate the subject in the foreground, or
3) Fill the frame with the subject and then take your exposure reading.

6. Portrait too dark

Problem: Instead of a clear picture of your subject framed by the window you end up with a silhouette effect, where the subject is too dark but the window is well exposed. See above.
Cause: When your subject is sitting against an open window the meter is likely to adjust exposure settings for the light around your subject.
Solution 1: Move the subject so that the light from the window falls onto them from the front or side rather than behind.
Solution 2: Use the camera's flash system, set to 'fill flash mode', to add some more light to the subject.
Solution 3: Move closer to the subject until it fills the frame. Take an exposure reading here (by holding the shutter button down halfway) and then reposition yourself to make the exposure using the saved settings.

7. Portrait too light

Problem: The main subject is 'blown out' or too light (overexposed).
Cause: This problem is the reverse of what was happening in the example above. Here the meter is seeing the large dark areas within the frame and overcompensating for it, causing the main subject to be too bright.
Solution 1: Manually compensate for the overexposure by adjusting the camera's exposure compensation mechanism so that the sensor is receiving one, two or three stops less light.
Solution 2: Move close to the subject until it fills the frame. Take an exposure reading here and then reposition yourself to take the picture using the saved settings.

Fixing common scanning problems

Use the guide below to help diagnose and solve scanning problems.

1. Marks on the picture

Problem: The photograph contains marks on the surface after scanning.
Cause: This usually occurs because of dust or scratches on the glass plate on the top of the scanner or on the photograph or negative.
Solution: Clean the glass plate and photograph carefully before placing and scanning your picture. If you still have marks use a retouching tool to remove them (see the Eliminating blemishes technique in Chapter 8 for more details).

2. Color picture appears black and white

Problem: After scanning a color picture it appears black and white on screen.
Cause: The 'original' or 'media' option in the scanner software is set to black and white and not color.
Solution: Re-scan the picture making sure that the software is set to color original or color photograph.

3. Picture is too bright

Problem: The picture looks too bright overall. Light areas of the photograph appear to be completely white with no details.
Cause: The picture has been scanned with the wrong 'exposure' or 'brightness' setting.
Solution: Re-scan the picture, but this time move the brightness or exposure slider towards the dark end of the scale before scanning.

4. Picture is too dark

Problem: The picture looks too dark overall. There is no detail in the shadow parts of the photograph.
Cause: The picture has been scanned with the wrong 'exposure' or 'brightness' setting.
Solution: Re-scan the picture, but this time slide the Brightness or Exposure slider towards the light end of the scale before scanning.

5. Picture looks washed out

Problem: The picture has no vibrant colors and looks washed out.
Cause: The contrast control in the scanner software is set too low.
Solution: Re-scan the photograph altering the scanner's contrast setting to a higher value.

6. Writing is back to front

Problem: The message on a billboard in the picture is back to front.
Cause: The negative or slide was placed into the scanner back to front.
Solution: Turn the film or slide over and scan again.

7. The picture has too much contrast

Problem: The delicate light areas and shadow details of the picture can't be seen and have been converted to completely white and completely black.

Cause: The contrast control in the scanner software is set too high.

Solution: Re-scan the photograph altering the scanner's contrast setting to a lower value.

8. When I print my scanned picture it is fuzzy

Problem: The print of a scanned image is fuzzy, not very clear or is made up of rectangular blocks of color.

Cause: To get the best quality prints from your scanned pictures you must make sure that you match the scan quality (resolution) with the output requirements. A fuzzy or unclear print is usually the result of using a scan quality setting that is too low.

Solution: Re-scan the picture using a higher scan quality setting (resolution).

3 Processing Raw Files

Raw is the new buzz word in photographic circles the world over. Professionals and serious amateurs alike are switching their cameras from the standard JPEG and TIFF capture options to the Raw format. This is despite the fact that doing so will mean that they add another processing step to their digital photography workflow. It seems that the extra level of control possible when processing your own Raw files (rather than letting the camera do the work) is worth the effort. So how do Photoshop Elements users become part of the Raw Revolution? Well this chapter will outline both the workflow and conversion techniques that you can employ to make Raw capture and processing a regular part of your photographic routine.

The Photoshop Elements approach to Raw processing

As we saw in Chapter 2 Raw files contain both the image and metadata along with the actual picture information in a format which cannot be directly opened into Photoshop Elements. Instead the Raw photo is opened first into a conversion utility where global image characteristics such as white balance, brightness, contrast, saturation, noise reduction and sharpness are adjusted before the converted file is opened into the Full Edit workspace. Alternatively the converted file can be saved as an Adobe Digital Negative or DNG file. Once the converted file is opened in the Elements Editor workspace it is no longer a Raw file and can be edited and enhanced just like any other photo.

This approach to Raw processing is often called Convert then Edit as the original Raw file must be converted before any pixel-based or local editing can take place. In contrast other Raw processing solutions such as Adobe Lightroom provide a full Raw workflow which includes editing functions and output to print and web without ever converting the Raw file.

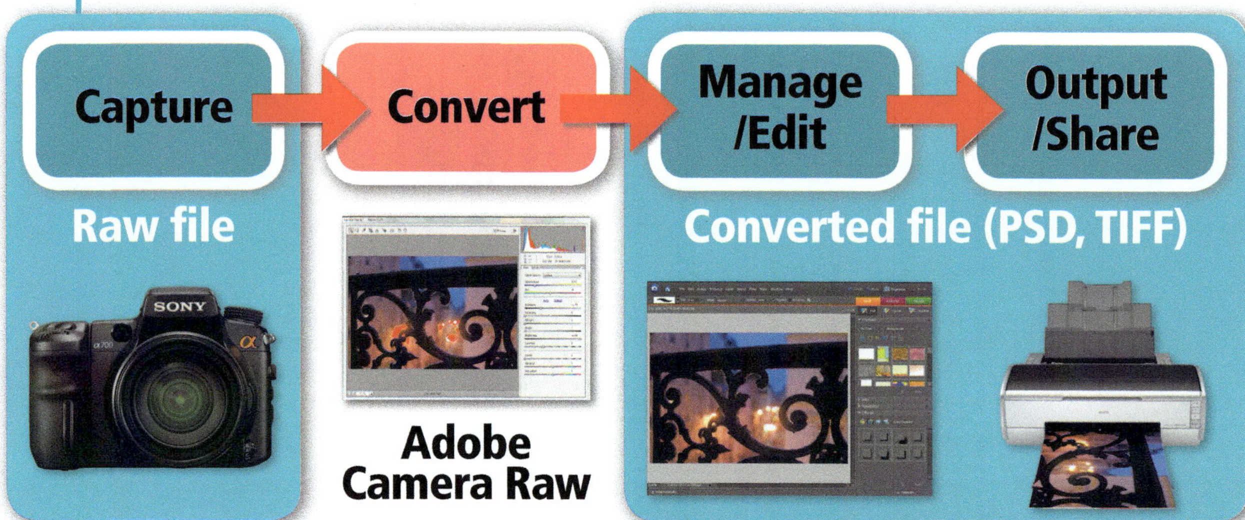

Raw Processing >> *The **Convert then Edit** approach is the most popular workflow currently used by Raw shooting photographers. The Raw file is downloaded from the camera and the first task in the process is to convert the file to a type that is more readily supported by photo editing programs such as TIFF or PSD.*

3.01 Enabling your Raw camera

Suitable for Elements – 7.0, 6.0, 5.0, 4.0, 3.0, 2.0, 1.0
Difficulty level – Basic

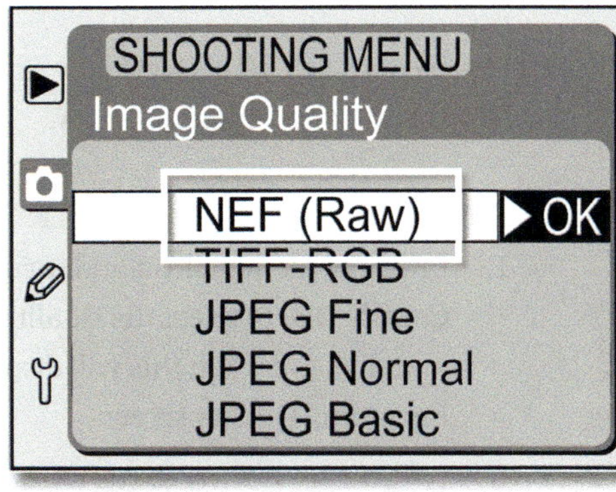

With most Raw-enabled cameras, switching from one capture format to another is a simple matter of entering the camera Set up menu and selecting the Raw entry from the Image Quality or File Format options. With some models you can also make this change via a Quality toggle or switch elsewhere on the camera.

Occasionally there is also a choice between saving compressed and non-compressed versions of the Raw file. Unlike the algorithms used for compressing JPEG files, the method used when compressing Raw files is 'lossless', meaning that all the detail that was captured is retained in the compressed file. Compressing will mean that pictures will take up less space on the memory card, but the process of compression does result in longer saving times. For most shooters this isn't an issue but if you like to photograph sports or action, then the extra time taken to compress the file will reduce the frames per second rate of your camera. In practice most Raw shooters opt for non-compressed files and just buy more memory cards to accommodate the larger file sizes that need to be saved.

CAPTURE FILE SIZE COMPARISONS	JPEG file size (Fine setting)	JPEG file size (Normal setting)	JPEG file size (Basic setting)	TIFF file size	Raw file size	Raw file size (compressed)
Example file 1	2997 Kb	1555 Kb	782 Kb	17708 Kb	9777 Kb	5093 Kb
Example file 2	2466 Kb	1575 Kb	748 Kb	17712 Kb	9776 Kb	4275 Kb

Capture format versus file size >> *The capture format you select directly affects not only the way the file is saved and its visual quality but also the size of the final file. JPEG produces the smallest files but uses a 'lossy' compression system to do so. In the JPEG format you can adjust the level of compression used when saving the photo. In this table the Fine setting uses the least compression and the Basic option the most. Both TIFF and Raw formats preserve all the image detail and any compression used with these formats is 'lossless'.*

There are several cameras on the market that also have the ability to save both Raw and JPEG versions of the same file at the time of capture. This option can be a real time saver if you need to access your pictures quickly, but the feature is less of an advantage if you regularly perform many enhancement steps to your files, as in the end the captured JPEG will not resemble the processed Raw file.

At the big end of town most of the high-resolution camera backs, which are destined for use with medium format camera bodies, only capture in Raw formats. Many make use of dedicated software to control the camera, capture the photo and then process the Raw file. Other manufacturers, such as Hasselblad, Samsung, Ricoh and Leica even use Adobe's DNG format as the capture format, making the transition to Elements a simple one.

In practice – enabling your camera

For the purposes of this workflow example I have included step-by-step instructions for both Nikon and Canon cameras below.

Canon workflow

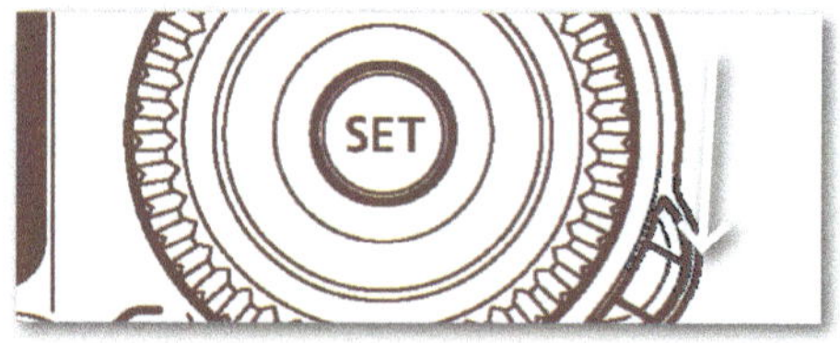

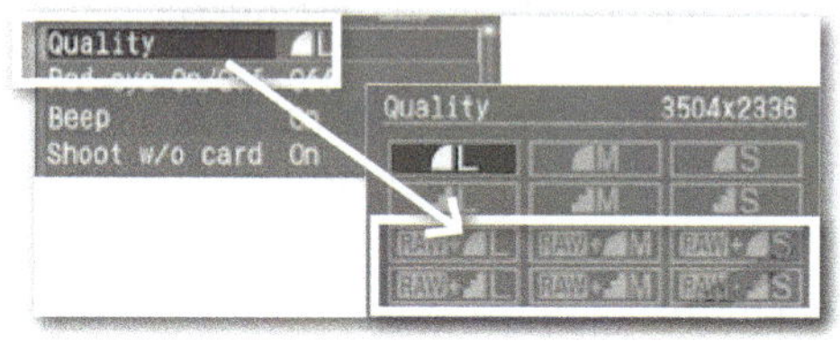

1. Press the Menu button and turn the Quick Control Dial to select the Quality heading and then press Set; this will display the Recording Quality screen.

2. Next, use the Quick Control Dial again to choose one of the Raw options from those listed. Depending on the camera model your choices may include Raw and Raw + JPEG. Press Set to set the selected capture mode.

Note: Canon cameras divide the controls into two levels: Basic and Creative (advanced). They name these control subsets different 'Zones'. If your camera is currently in the Basic Zone you won't be able to choose any Raw caption options. To do this, you will need to switch to the Creative Zone first, and then alter the Recording Quality. Canon's menu system also varies from consumer to pro models so check with the manual if you are unsure.

Nikon workflow

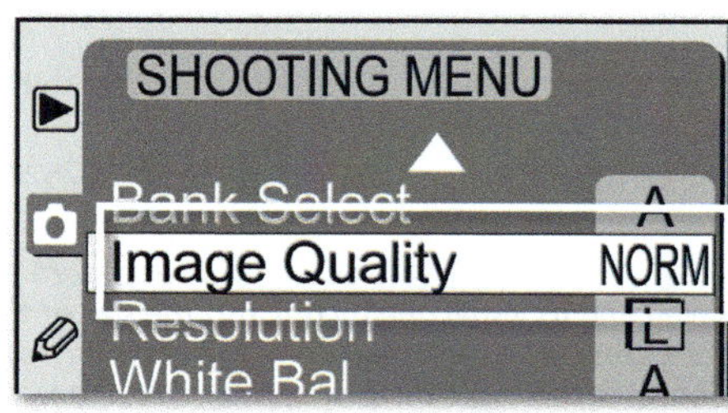

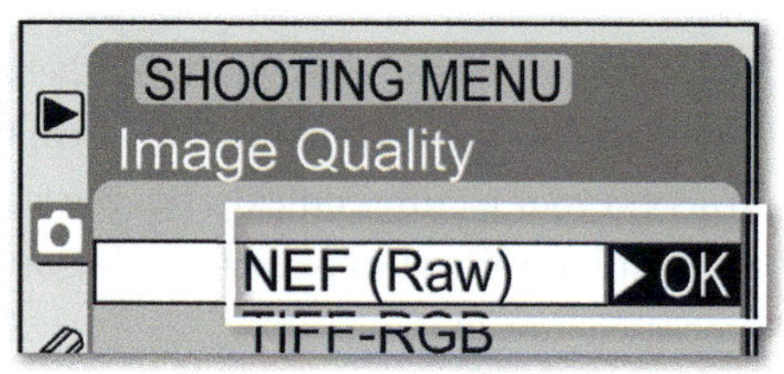

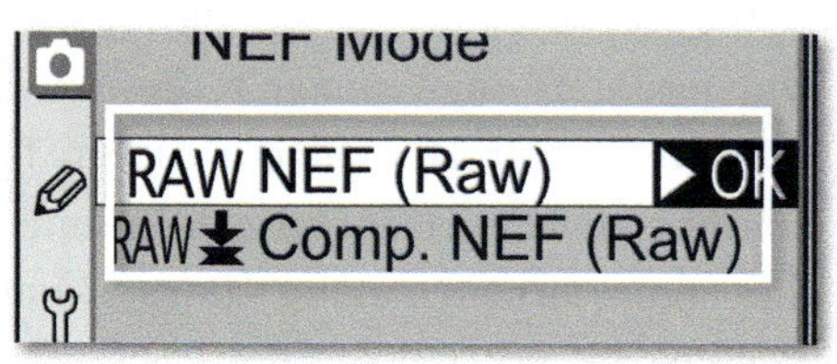

1. To switch the default capture format to Raw, activate the menu on the back of the camera and then use the Multi-selector control to navigate to the Shooting Menu (second option on the left side of the screen). Use the right arrow on the Multi-selector control to pick menu options.

2. From the first page of the menu list, select the Image Quality entry. This will display another screen containing a list of quality options – three JPEG, one TIFF and one NEF (Nikon's version of Raw). At this screen choose the NEF (Raw) heading.

3. Selecting NEF will display a final screen with a choice of two different Raw capture modes – 'Comp. NEF (Raw)' compressed and 'NEF (Raw)' uncompressed. Select one of these options and then exit the menu.

3.02 Modifying your capture workflow for Raw

Suitable for Elements – 7.0, 6.0, 5.0, 4.0, 3.0, 2.0, 1.0 | Difficulty level – Basic

In the previous chapter we looked at the controls that are available to digital camera users that enable them to capture great images. These include such digital-only options as Saturation, Sharpness, White Balance and Contrast Control. Using such features it is possible for the digital photographer to customize their image capture more than was ever possible when film was king. But switching capture formats to Raw impacts directly on the role that these controls play in your digital capture. As we already know factors such as white balance, contrast, saturation and sharpness settings are not fixed in Raw files. These controls are only applied to the file at the time of conversion or after the image exits the Adobe Camera Raw utility and is opened in the Editor workspace. So rather than these factors being applied in-camera, as is the case with JPEG and TIFF capture, they are applied via the ACR utility. In fact any of the adjustments you make to these settings on the camera can be reversed or tweaked in ACR. Remember the white balance illustration? You forget to change from tungsten to daylight and shoot outside. No problem, just make the switch back to the daylight setting in the ACR dialog and the photo is corrected without loss of image quality.

So if these factors are controllable at conversion then should the Raw shooting photographer bother with them at time of capture? This is a good question to which you will receive many answers. Unfortunately many shooters believe that capturing in Raw is a 'fix all' for poor camera technique. Haven't selected the right white balance? No problem, fix it in Raw. Haven't judged the light quite right? Again, not a big deal just fix it in Raw. Nor adjusted your lighting for good contrast? Again, not an issue, there is contrast control in Raw. But to my mind although many factors can be altered in Raw this approach has four main drawbacks:

1. Correctly captured pictures need less correction when converting, saving valuable time.
2. The white balance settings determined at time of capture provide a good starting point for further fine-tuning during the conversion process.
3. If a Raw + JPEG capture mode is being used then the color in the accompanying JPEG photo will better match the processed Raw file as it was more accurate at the time of capture.
4. Correct exposure provides better quality edited images as ideally no shadow or highlight details are clipped when the picture is taken.

Raw capture will fix it!

Raw capture implications on workflow

So what changes to standard capture workflow should the Raw shooter make? Let's examine the impact of Raw capture on some of the standard camera controls.

Resolution – When working with Raw as the capture format, most cameras will not provide the ability to alter the dimensions of your photo. The largest photo possible (one sensor site to one pixel) is generally recorded in the Raw file.

Color Depth – Raw photographers automatically get access to the increased levels of tone afforded by high-bit capture because nominating Raw as the capture format negates the camera's bit depth settings and automatically provides the full depth capable by the sensor. At time of conversion in ACR you can elect the bit depth of the converted file.

Saturation – As the vibrancy or saturation of the converted image can be controlled on a picture-by-picture basis in ACR it is a good idea to leave this camera setting on the default or normal value. This will display your photo with standard saturation in ACR and then give you the option to boost or reduce vibrancy according to the requirements of the photo.

White Balance – Despite the fact that white balance can be losslessly adjusted in ACR it is good practice to match white balance settings with the dominant light source in your scene. This helps to maintain the photographer's own capture skill as well as ensuring speedier color cast removal in ACR, as the camera settings are loaded as default when opening the image. The more accurate these capture settings are the less fiddling the photographer will need to do to ensure a great result.

Contrast – Most cameras have the choice to increase or reduce contrast. The feature is invaluable when shooting in difficult lighting scenarios and saving the results back to TIFF or JPEG files. Raw shooters have the luxury of being able to make these types of contrast adjustments much more accurately and on an image-by-image basis back at the desktop.

Sharpening – Professionals now employ a workflow that applies sharpening at three different times during the enhancement process – at time of capture, during enhancement and then when preparing for output. For Raw shooters adopting this approach means adding a little global sharpening in-camera or at the time of conversion. Both approaches are fine as long as the sharpening is kept to a minimum with the idea that it will be fine-tuned later to account for subject matter and output destination.

Noise Reduction – Reducing noise on the desktop, either during Raw conversion or afterwards inside Photoshop Elements, provides better control over the process and therefore better results than the auto approach adopted by in-camera systems.

ISO – Shooting in Raw doesn't directly affect the selection of ISO setting used for capture. These settings will be based on the available light in the scene or the shutter speed required to freeze or blur motion.

Camera Exposure – Shooting in Raw doesn't change the fact that exposure is key to the creation of high quality images. It is true that the slider controls in ACR provide a great deal of flexibility when it comes to processing the tones in a photo and that this means that slight problems with exposure (under- or overexposure) can be corrected more easily than with other capture formats. What is important to remember though is that this doesn't provide photographers with a license for poor exposure control. The best conversions are made with images that are well exposed.

3.03 Using the Adobe Photo Downloader

Suitable for Elements – 7.0, 6.0, 5.0, 4.0, 3.0, 2.0, 1.0 | Difficulty level – Basic

Over the history of the development of Photoshop Elements one of the most significant additions to the program has been the Organizer workspace. This feature provides a visual index of your pictures and can be customized to display the images in Photo Browser Mode, date mode or sorted by keyword tags or album (collection). Unlike the standard file browsers of previous editions which created the thumbnails of your pictures the first time that the folder is browsed, the Organizer creates the thumbnail during the process of adding your photographs to a collection.

To commence downloading your Raw files and, in the process, create your first collection, simply select the View and Organize option from the Welcome screen and then proceed to the Organizer: File > Get Photos and Videos menu option. Select one of the listed sources of pictures (camera or folders) provided and move through the steps and prompts in the dialogs that follow. If you are sourcing your files from a camera or card reader then the Adobe Photo Downloader (APD) automatically starts when you attach these devices, removing the need for you to go to the Get Photos menu to start the downloading process.

Option 1: Getting your Raw files from camera or card reader

To demonstrate the process let's start by downloading some photographs from a memory card or camera. This will probably be the most frequently used route for your Raw images to enter the Elements program. Connect the camera, being sure that you have first installed the drivers for the unit. Alternatively you may wish to eject the memory card from the camera and insert it into a card reader that is already attached to the computer. The Adobe Photo Downloader utility should automatically start; if it doesn't then manually select the From Camera or Card Reader option from the File > Get Photos and Videos menu.

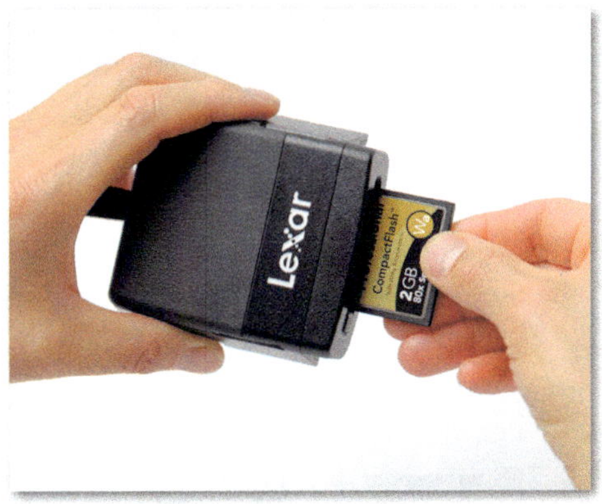

Downloading files >> *Raw files can be imported directly from the camera or by inserting the memory card into an attached reader.*

After attaching the camera, or inserting a memory card into the reader, you will see the Adobe Photo Downloader dialog. This is a utility designed specifically for managing the download process and has both a Basic and Advanced dialog mode. The **Basic Dialog** is displayed by default. The first step is to select the location of the pictures (the card reader or memory card in the camera) from the Source drop-down menu in the top right of the dialog. The first photo in the group is shown as a thumbnail on the left of the window. Below this area is the Import

Settings section where you can choose the folder location for the pictures that are downloaded as well as options to create new subfolders, rename photos and delete successfully downloaded files. There is also a checkbox for activating the new Automatic Download feature which imports photos directly from card reader or camera, bypassing the Adobe Photo Downloader dialog and instead using the import options saved in the Camera or Card Reader preferences (Edit > Preferences > Camera or Card Reader).

Clicking the **Advanced Dialog** button at the bottom left switches the window to a more sophisticated version of the feature. Here all the photos on the card/camera are previewed and you have the additional options of fixing red eyes, creating photo stacks and adding group tags

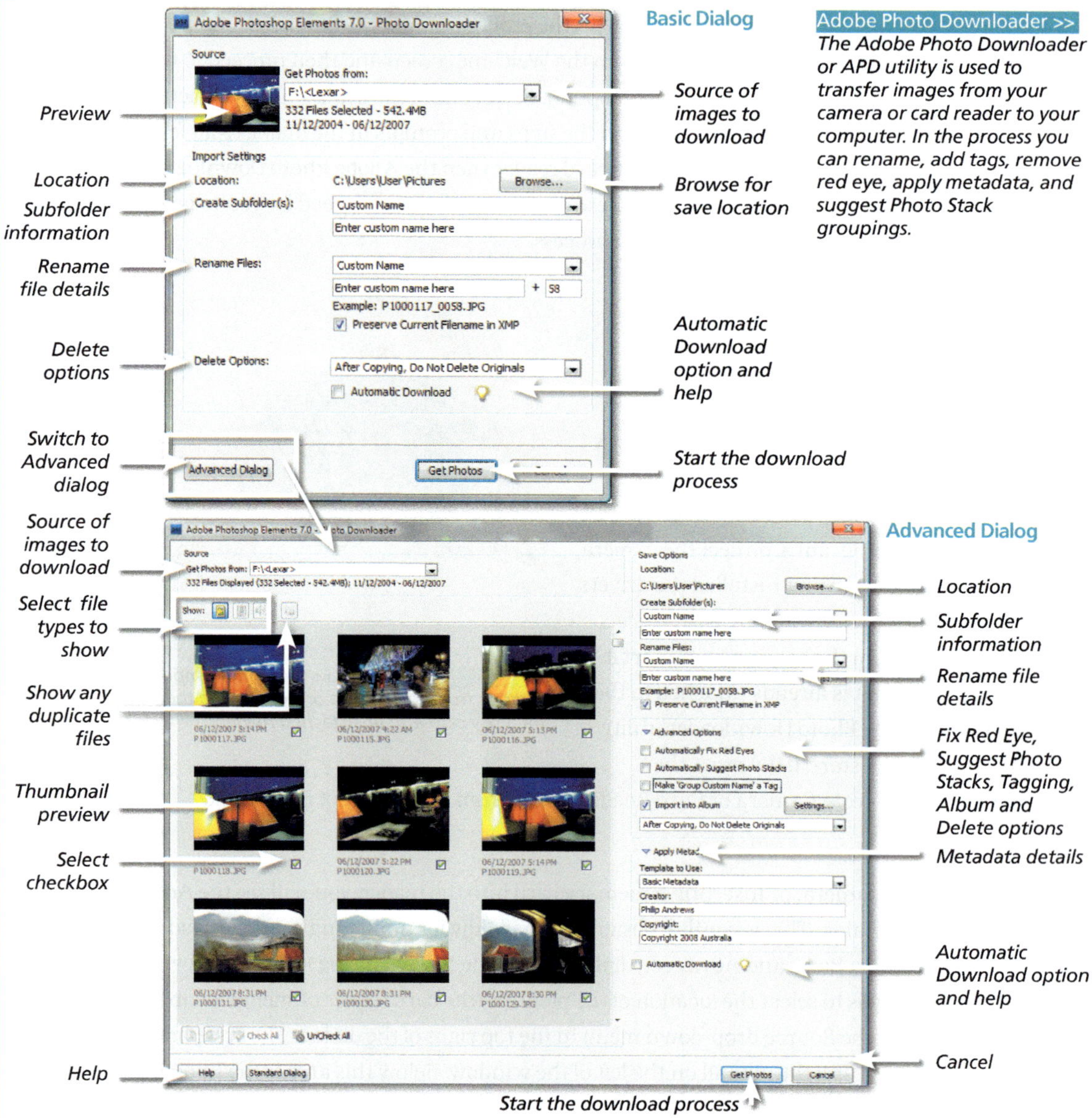

Adobe Photo Downloader >>

The Adobe Photo Downloader or APD utility is used to transfer images from your camera or card reader to your computer. In the process you can rename, add tags, remove red eye, apply metadata, and suggest Photo Stack groupings.

and metadata information automatically as files are downloaded. By default all pictures on the card will be selected ready for downloading and cataloging. If for some reason you do not want to download all the images then you can deselect them by unchecking the tick box at the bottom right-hand of the thumbnail.

After selecting the options in either the Basic or Advanced dialog click the Get Photos button to transfer the pictures. After the process is complete Elements will tell you that the files have been successfully imported.

Option 2: Loading Raw files from an existing archive, disk or drive

Acting much like the File > Open option common to most programs the Get Photos and Videos > From Files and Folders selection provides you with the familiar operating system browse window that allows you to search for and open pictures that you have already saved to your computer. You generally have the option to view your files in a variety of ways including Thumbnails, Tiles, Icons, List and Detail Views using the drop-down menu from the top of the window.

However, for Windows XP users, the Thumbnail option will only display small previews of your Raw files if the Microsoft Raw Image Thumbnailer and Viewer utility is installed. This is available free from http://www.microsoft.com/windowsxp/using/digitalphotography/prophoto/Raw.mspx. Vista users will only be able to preview their raw files in Windows Browsers after installing a Raw file CODEC available from the camera manufacturer's website.

Users can also elect to automatically fix red eyes or suggest photo stacks here as well. After selecting the image, or images, you wish to import into Elements, select the Get Photos button.

How to multi-select the files to import

To select several images or files at once hold down the Ctrl key whilst clicking on the pictures of your choice. To select a complete list of files without having to pick each file in turn click on the first picture and then, whilst holding down the Shift key, click on the last file in the group.

Activating and deactivating APD

Disable the Adobe Photo Downloader

1. Select Organizer: Edit > Preferences > Camera Or Card Reader.
2. Deselect 'Auto Launch Adobe Photo Downloader on Device Connect'.

Enable the Adobe Photo Downloader

1. For Elements 6.0/7.0 users select Organizer: Edit > Preferences > Camera Or Card Reader.
2. Select 'Auto Launch Adobe Photo Downloader on Device Connect'.

Enabling the Automatic Download option in Adobe Photo Downloader (APD)

1. Choose the Automatic Download option from the APD Basic or Advanced dialogs. The downloader will commence automatically the next time a card/camera is connected.
2. Select Organizer: Edit > Preferences > Camera Or Card Reader and set the preferences for the download in the Files and Download sections of the dialog.

3.04 The Adobe Camera Raw interface

Suitable for Elements – 7.0, 6.0, 5.0, 4.0, 3.0, 2.0, 1.0 | Difficulty level – Basic

Before commencing to process our first raw file, let's take a close look at the Adobe Camera Raw feature as it appears in Photoshop Elements 7.0. The ACR dialog, the user interface between you and what goes on inside the Camera Raw plug-in, provides tools to adjust, process, convert and save raw files. After opening a raw photo from inside either the Organizer or Editor workspaces, this dialog will be displayed.

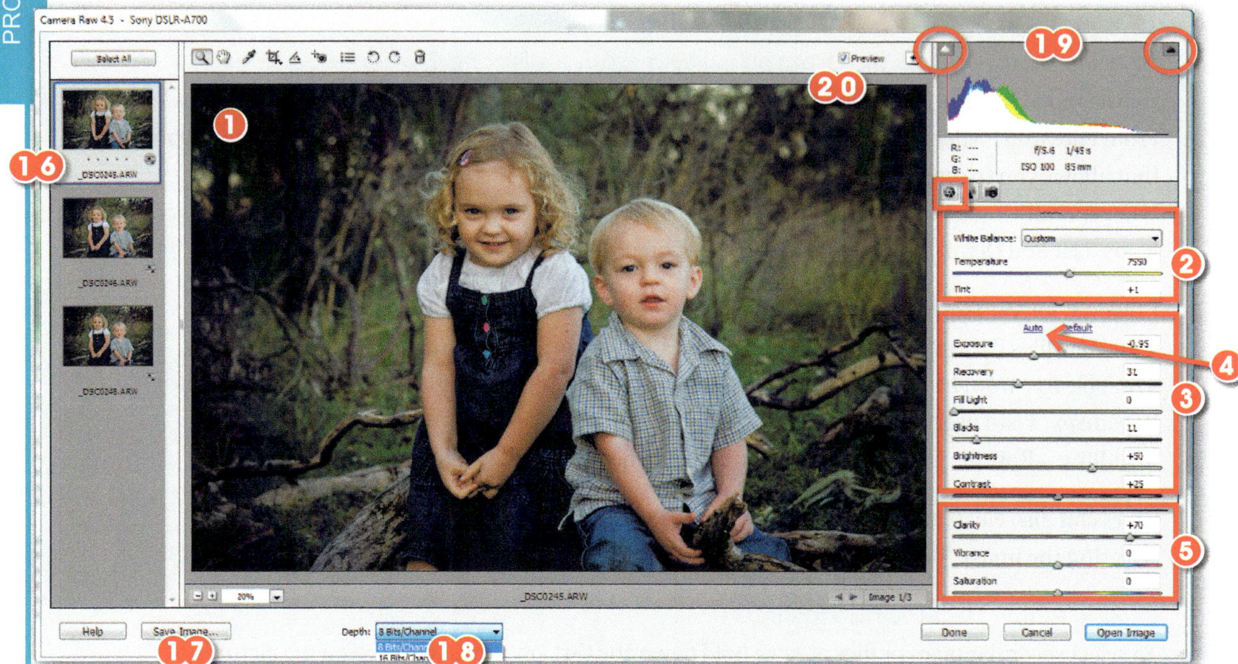

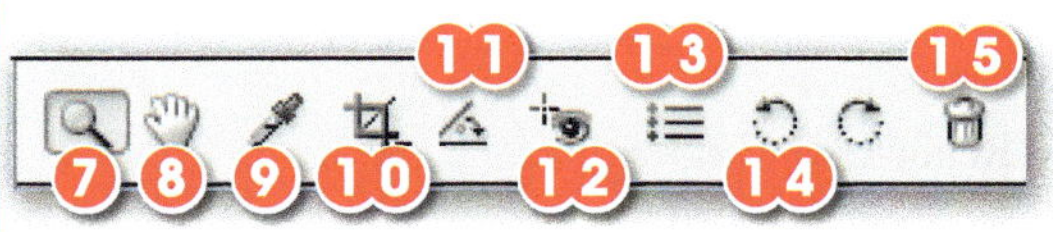

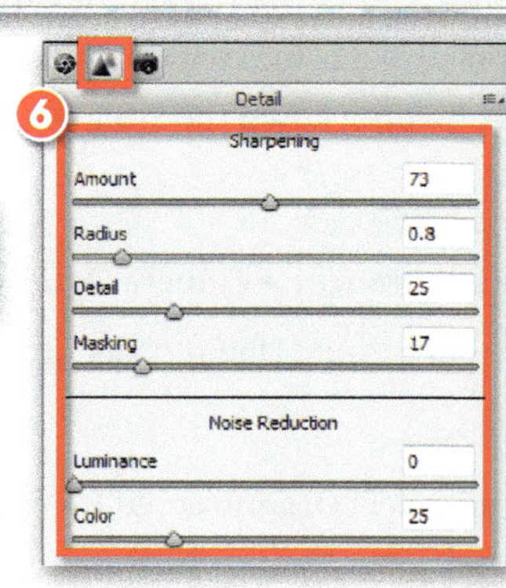

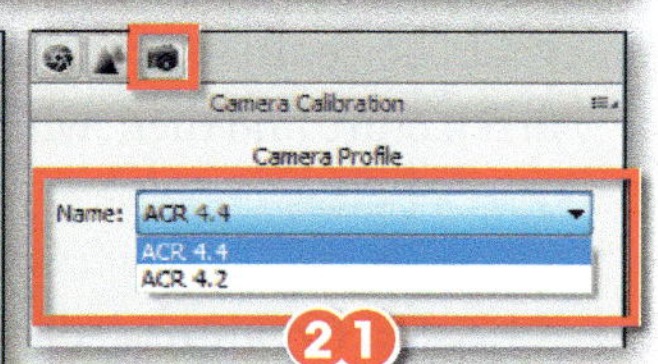

Adobe Camera Raw interface >> *Features of the Adobe Camera Raw dialog box in Photoshop Elements 7.0.*

1. *Preview area.*
2. *White balance settings.*
3. *Tonal controls.*
4. *Auto option for tonal control settings.*
5. *Color controls.*
6. *Detail tab containing the sharpness and noise options.*
7. *Zoom tool.*
8. *Hand tool.*
9. *White balance tool.*
10. *Crop tool.*
11. *Straighten tool.*
12. *Red eye removal tool.*
13. *ACR preferences.*
14. *Rotate buttons.*
15. *Mark for deletion button.*
16. *Queued raw files.*
17. *Save button.*
18. *Bit depth options.*
19. *Shadow and highlights clipping warnings.*
20. *Preview checkbox.*
21. *Camera Calibration tab containing the Camera Profile menu.*

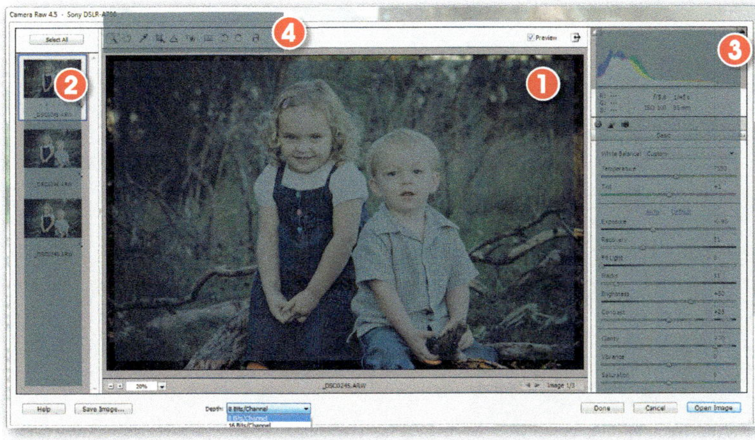

ACR dialog work areas >>
The ACR dialog can be broken into four separate areas: 1. Preview. 2. Image adjustment controls. 3. Raw file queue. 4. Toolbar.

The feature's window is broken into four distinct areas:

1. A preview of the file is displayed in the center of the dialog. Any editing or development changes made to the file will be reflected automatically in this preview.

2. A queuing area for raw files awaiting processing. This area of the dialog is only present when multiple raw files are selected for opening and is new for Photoshop Elements 7.0.

3. Controls or settings area. This part of the dialog contains all the processing and development controls for altering the look of the color, tone, sharpening and noise in the photo. The settings are grouped under two tabs – Basic and Detail. A new third tab called Camera Control lists Camera Profiles that are available for the current image. A histogram graph is also displayed here.

4. The toolbar sits at the top of the dialog and houses options such as the Zoom, Hand, Crop and Straighten tools.

The Help and Save buttons are located at the bottom left of the window. In the center is the bit depth menu and on the right, are the Done, Cancel and Open Images buttons. To ensure that you have the best selection of tools to use on your raw files, make sure that your ACR plug-in is always up to date. See section 3.05 for more details on how to obtain and install the latest version of the plug-in. By way of introduction let's look at each of these work areas in turn.

The preview space

The preview displays the changes you make to your image via the develop or enhancement settings. Any adjustment of controls are reflected immediately in the preview image, providing a visual reference to the effect of the alterations. The preview can be enlarged or reduced in size to suit the screen area available. When making some changes, such as Sharpening or Noise

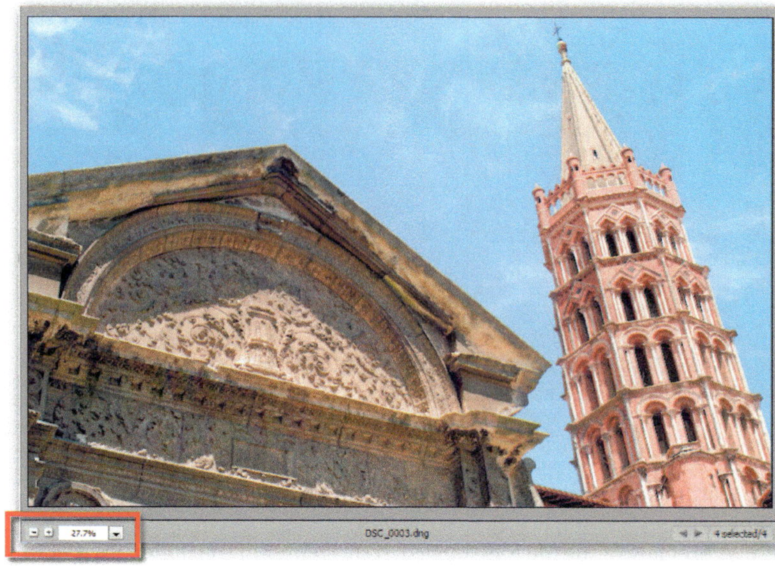

The preview >>
The preview image in ACR's dialog is capable of being magnified to a range of levels. The current magnification value is shown in the bottom left corner of the window.

Reduction, the preview should be magnified to at least 100%. At this zoom setting, you will be able to preview the results of the adjustments of these controls.

There are three ways for you to change the magnification level of the preview to 100%:

1. Double-click the Zoom tool,
2. Select the 100% entry from the zoom menu at the bottom left of the dialog, or
3. Use the Ctrl+ to magnify or Ctrl - to reduce the size of the preview to the zoom value in the window at the bottom left of the dialog.

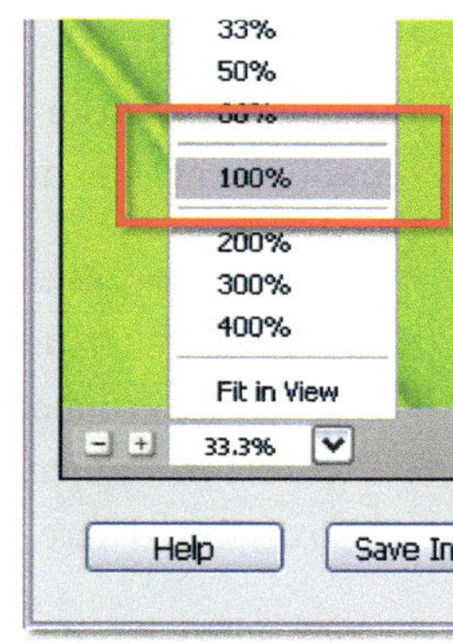

Zoom to 100% >>
The zoom menu at the bottom left of the dialog provides a variety of zoom levels for quick access.

Image adjustment controls

The right-hand side of the ACR dialog is reserved for the core adjustment features.

Histogram

A full color histogram is located under the RGB values. The feature graphs the distribution of the pixels within your photo. The graph updates after changes are made to the color, contrast and brightness of the picture. By paying close attention to the shape of the graph you can pre-empt many image problems. The aim with most enhancement activities is to obtain a good spread of pixels from shadow through midtones to highlights without clipping (converting delicate details to pure black or white) either end of the tonal range.

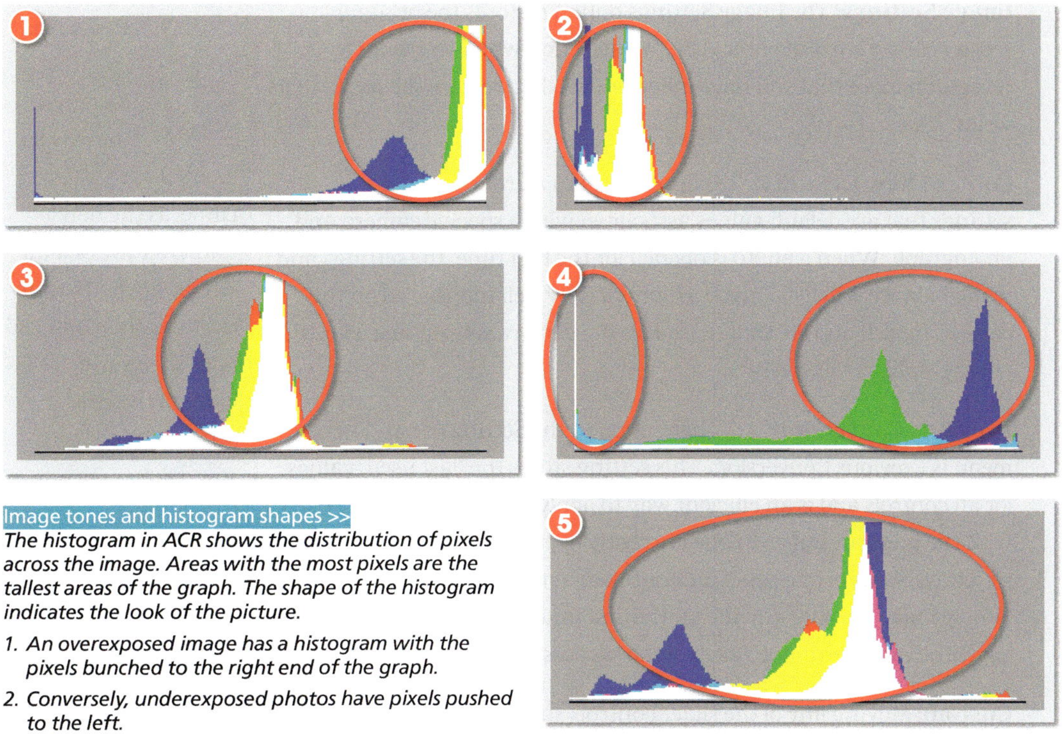

Image tones and histogram shapes >>
The histogram in ACR shows the distribution of pixels across the image. Areas with the most pixels are the tallest areas of the graph. The shape of the histogram indicates the look of the picture.

1. *An overexposed image has a histogram with the pixels bunched to the right end of the graph.*
2. *Conversely, underexposed photos have pixels pushed to the left.*
3. *Flat or low-contrast pictures typically have all their pixels grouped in the middle.*
4. *High-contrast photos or those that have 'clipped' highlights and shadow areas usually have many pixels at the extreme ends of the graph.*
5. *For the best results, with most images, you should always aim to spread the pixels between the maximum black and white points without clipping any of the image pixels.*

This is not the case for all photos though. Take, for instance, the case of a black cat in a darkened room, the correct histogram for this photo will show a bunching of the pixels towards the left side of central, whereas a shot of the ski slopes, also correctly exposed, will display most pixels to the right of the histogram graph.

The Basic tab

Below the histogram is a tab area containing two options – Basic and Detail. The Basic tab contains all the tone and color controls. On the other hand, the Sharpening and Noise Reduction features are grouped under the Detail tab. Here we will concentrate on the controls under the Basic tab.

Image Settings menu

The Settings drop-down menu is displayed by clicking the Settings button on the right side of the Tabs. The menu contains the Image Settings, Camera Raw Defaults, Previous Conversion, Custom, Clear Imported Settings, Save New Camera Raw Defaults, and Reset Camera Raw Defaults entries. Here are some more details on each entry:

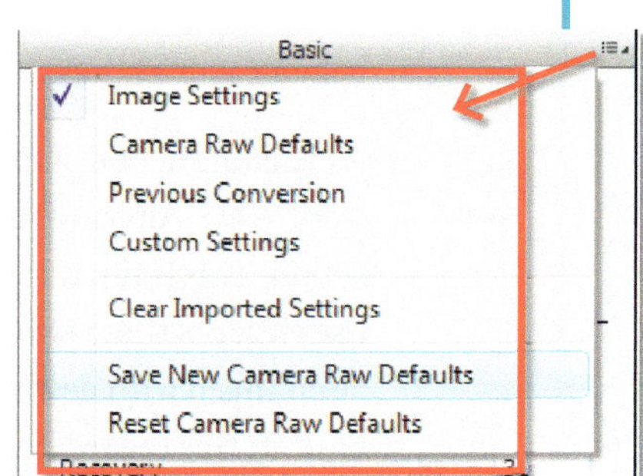

The Settings menu >>
The Settings menu contains options for saving or recalling image settings associated with specific cameras.

Image Settings: The Image Settings option restores the original settings of the current photo. Use this selection when you want to reverse changes that you have made and wish to restore the photo to its virgin state.

Camera Raw Defaults: This option applies a group of slider settings that are default values associated with a specific camera and photograph. When a photo is opened for the first time, the settings and white balance will be altered to Camera Raw Defaults (based on the camera model) and As Shot (based on the camera settings used for the photograph), respectively.

Previous Conversion: Another option in the Settings drop-down menu is Previous Conversion. This setting stores the 'last used' values for all controls and is an efficient way to apply the enhancements used with the previous image to one currently open in the dialog. Using this option will help speed up the conversions of a series of photos taken at the same time under the same lighting conditions. Simply make the adjustments for the first image and then use the Previous Conversion option to apply the same settings to each of the successive photos from the series in turn.

Pro's tip: As ACR recognizes the raw file created with different cameras the new Camera Raw Default will be applied to only those photos captured with the specific camera that the settings have been saved for.

Custom: Moving any of the slider controls such as Temperature or Tint sliders under the White Balance menu automatically changes the settings entry to Custom. Once the settings have been customized for a particular photograph the values can be saved as a new Camera Raw Default entry using the save option in the pop-up menu accessed via the sideways arrow next to the Settings menu.

White balance correction

White balance is used to correctly balance the color of the scene to the lighting conditions at the time the shot was taken. Leaving white balance set at As Shot means you elect to keep the white balance values that were used when taking the picture.

As you know, one of the advantages shooting raw is that this setting is not a fixed part of the picture file. Altering the specific white balance setting at the time of raw conversion is a 'lossless' action. This is not the case if you have used an incorrect setting and have shot in JPEG or TIFF. Use either of these two formats and the white balance setting will be fixed in the file and can only be changed with destructive adjustments using features like Color Variations or Remove Color Cast. In this regard raw shooters have much more flexibility.

White Balance drop-down menu: For instance, if you selected a Daylight setting in-camera and think that Shade or another white balance preset may be closer to the actual lighting conditions you may select one of the options from the list of presets under the White Balance drop-down menu. Moving either the Temperature or Tint sliders switches the setting to

PROCESSING RAW FILES

Custom. These controls are used for matching the image color temperature with that of the scene.

Temperature slider: The Temperature slider is a fine-tuning device that allows you to select a precise color temperature in units of degrees Kelvin. When an image is too yellow, meaning it has a lower color temperature than you prefer, move the Temperature slider to the left to make the colors bluer and compensate for the lower color temperature. When an image is too blue, or higher in temperature than you prefer, move the slider to the right to make the image warmer, adding more yellow compensation. So, left is to make image colors cooler and right is to make image colors warmer.

Tint slider: The Tint slider fine-tunes the white balance to compensate for a green or magenta tint. Moving the Tint slider to the left adds green and to the right adds magenta. This control is often used to neutralize a color cast caused by lighting from fluorescent tube or strip sources.

White Balance tool: The quickest and perhaps easiest way to adjust white balance is to select the White Balance tool and then click in an area that should be neutral gray or even amounts of red, green and blue. For best results, use a dark to midtone as the reference and be careful not to click on an area with pure white or specular highlights. These will produce unreliable results so keep away from the bright highlight areas of highly reflective or chrome surfaces. One suggestion for working with neutral gray is to:

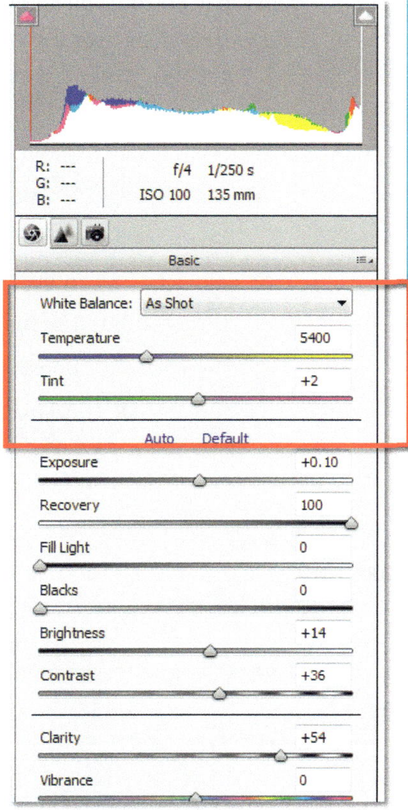

White Balance control >>
When an original file is opened for the first time in the dialog, the settings and white balance values will be set to Camera Raw Defaults (based on camera model and make) and As Shot (determined by the camera settings at the time of capture), respectively.

WB tool workflow

1. Click on the White Balance tool.
2. Move the White Balance tool cursor over a midtone area which should be neutral gray (e.g. textured white area) but contains a color cast in the preview.
3. Click on the image location to neutralize the cast not just in the selected area but in the whole photo.

Making tonal adjustments

Below the white balance controls are the Exposure, Recovery, Fill Light, Blacks, Brightness, Contrast, Clarity, Vibrance and Saturation sliders which are also available for making adjustments to raw files. Adobe has positioned these controls in the dialog so that when working from top to bottom you follow a specific enhancement workflow. For this reason you should follow these steps in order:

Tonal changes workflow

1. Set the white clipping points using the **Exposure** slider.
2. Set the black clipping points using the **Shadows** slider.
3. Use **Recovery/Fill Light** controls (if needed).
4. Adjust the overall brightness using the **Brightness** slider.
5. Adjust contrast using the **Contrast** slider.
6. Use the **Clarity** slider to adjust local contrast.
7. Boost specific desaturated colors with the **Vibrance** slider.
8. Adjust saturation, if needed, using the **Saturation** slider.

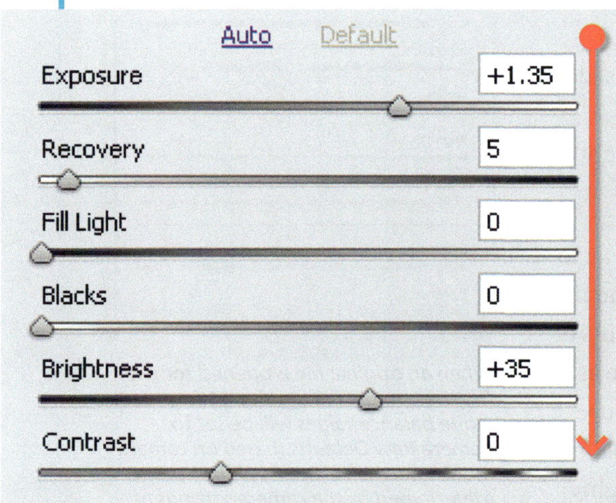

Tonal adjustment sequence >>
Adobe has positioned the slider controls that adjust the tones within the image in the order (top to bottom) that they should be applied within the ACR dialog.
The Exposure and Blacks sliders should be used first to set the white and black points in the photo. Use the Alt/Option keys in conjunction with these sliders to preview the pixels being clipped and to accurately peg the white/black points. Or alternatively switch on the Shadows/Highlights Clipping Warnings which perform the same function whilst leaving the full color preview visible.
Next lighten or darken the photo using the Brightness slider. Unlike the Exposure control this slider doesn't affect the white and black points of the image but rather adjusts the appearance of the photo by compressing or extending the altered tones.
Recovery and Fill Light sliders are new for this release of Elements' ACR. Use the Recovery control to rebuild highlight areas where one channel has been clipped. The Fill Light slider brightens mid to dark shadow areas.

Exposure

The Exposure slider adjusts the brightness or darkness of an image using value increments equivalent to f-stops or EV (exposure values) on a camera. An image is underexposed when it is not light enough or too dark and it is overexposed when it is too light. Simply move the slider to the left to darken the image and to the right to lighten (brighten) the image.

What do the f-stop or EV equivalents indicate? An adjustment of -1.50 is just like narrowing the aperture by 1.5 (one and a half) f-stops. Moving the slider 1.33 places to the left will dramatically darken an image and to the right the same amount will result in a bright image. If you have to move more than two full stops in either direction this probably indicates your settings at capture were inaccurate. Making adjustments beyond two stops starts to deteriorate image quality as invariably shadow or highlight detail is lost (clipped) in the process.

For those of you who are interested, the Exposure slider sets the white clipping points in the image. Clipping shows as values creeping up the left (shadow) and right (highlight) walls of your histogram (and red and blue areas in the image if shadow and highlight previews are turned on), and occurs when the pixel values shift to the highest highlight value or the lowest shadow value. Clipped areas are completely black or white and contain no detail. As you want to maintain as much detail in the shadows and highlights as possible your aim should always be to spread the picture tones but not to clip delicate highlight or shadow areas.

Blacks (Shadows)

Moving the Blacks or Shadows slider adjusts the position of the black point within the image. Just as was the case with the Exposure slider you should only make shadows adjustments when the clipping warning is active. This will ensure that you don't unintentionally convert shadow detail to black pixels. Remember movements of the slider to the left decrease shadow clipping. Moving it to the right increases or produces clipping.

Brightness and Contrast

The Brightness slider is different to the Exposure slider although both affect the brightness of an image. Brightness compresses the highlights and expands the shadows when you move the slider to the right. When adjusting your photos your aim is to set the black and white points first and then adjust the brightness of the midtones to suit your image.

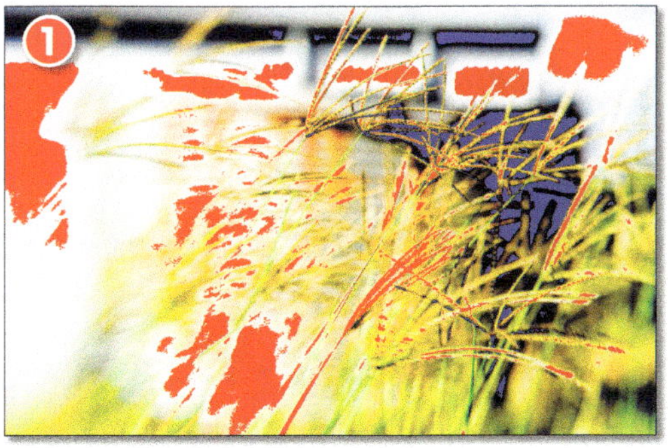

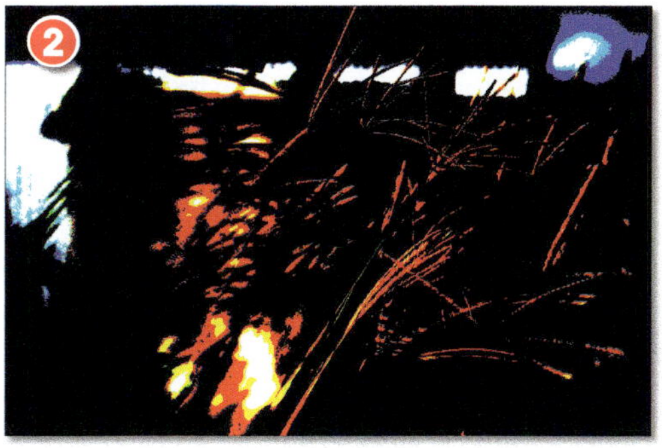

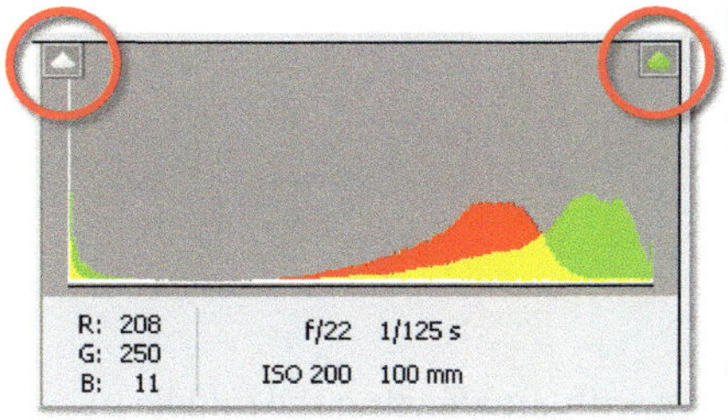

Highlight and Shadow clipping warnings >>
To ensure that you don't accidently convert shadow or highlight detail to pure black or white pixels ACR contains two different types of 'Clipping' warnings.

1. *When the Shadows and Highlights Clipping Warning features are selected at the top of the Histogram graph, areas of highlight clipping are displayed in the preview as red and shadows as blue.*
2. *Holding down the Alt key whilst moving either the Exposure or Shadows sliders will convert the preview to black (for Exposure) or white (for Shadows). Any pixels being clipped will then be shown as a contrasting color against these backgrounds.*

Contrast adjusts the spread of the midtones in the image. A move of the Contrast slider to the right spreads the pixels across the histogram, actually increasing the midtone contrast. Conversely movements to the left bunch the pixels in the middle of the graph. It is important to adjust the contrast of midtones after working on exposure, shadows and brightness.

Recovery

When a photograph is overexposed one of the consequences can be that the lighter tones in the image lose detail and are converted to pure white. This process is called clipping. Digital images are created with details from three color channels (red, green, blue). In situations of slight overexposure, when only one channel is clipped, it is possible to recreate the lost detail with the highlight information from the other two (non-clipped) channels. The Recovery slider attempts to recreate lost highlight details in such cases. Moving the slider to the right progressively increases the degree of highlight recovery.

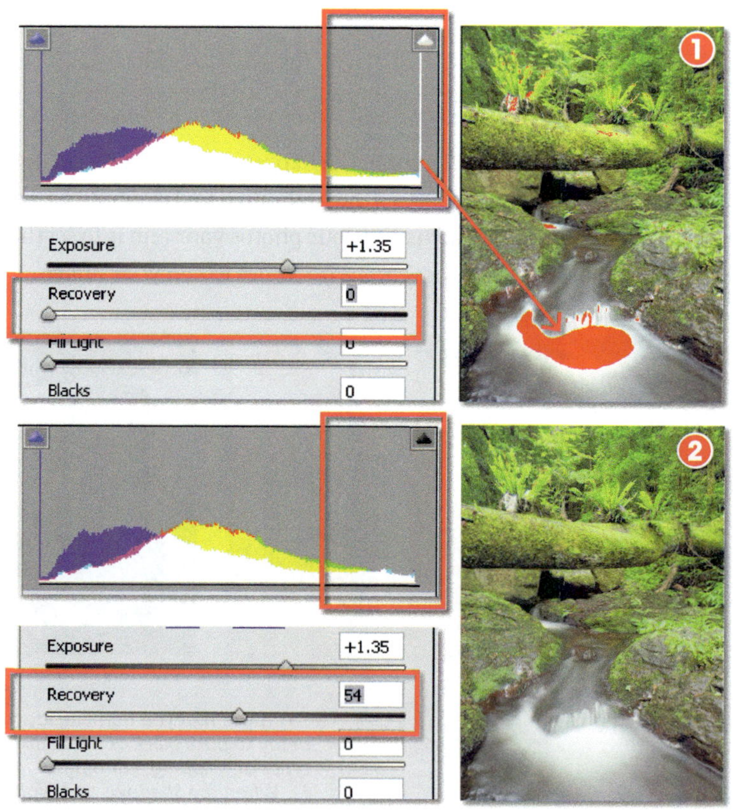

Recovering highlights >>
The Recovery slider is used for correcting clipped highlights. With the clipping warning activated it is easy to see problem highlights (1). When moving the slider to the right, ACR will attempt to reconstruct clipped details from the information stored in the non-clipped channels (2).

Fill Light

The Fill Light slider is used to lighten the darker tones in a picture without affecting the middle to highlight values. Use this control to brighten backlit subjects or boost shadow details. The beauty of this control is that the changes it makes do not generally impact on mid to highlight values.

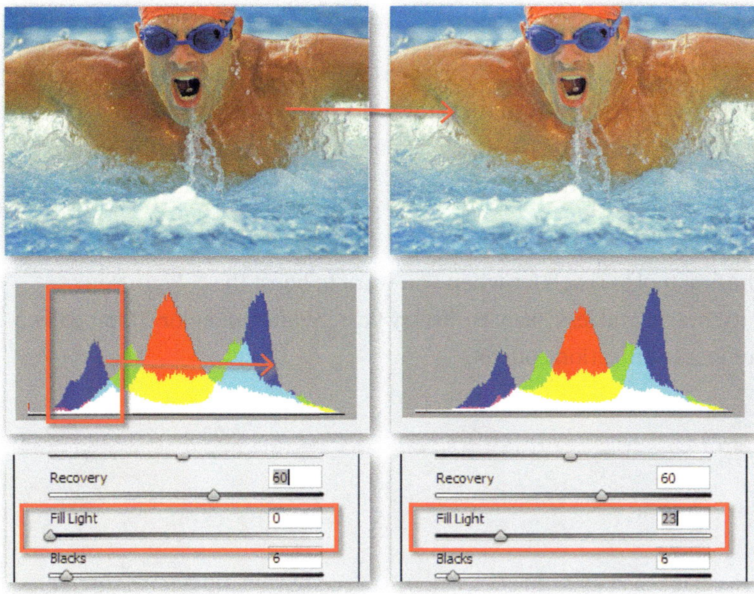

Pro's tip: In some instances you may need to readjust Exposure and Blacks sliders after Brightness, Recovery, Fill Light and Contrast to fine-tune your enhancements.

Boosting shadows >> *The Fill Light slider manipulates the mid to dark tones in the photo. Moving the slider to the right pushes these tones towards the highlight end of the histogram, lightening them.*

Clarity

Located along with Vibrance and Saturation controls at the bottom of the Basic panel, this new slider produces localized contrast changes to otherwise flat images.

Rather than adding contrast to the whole image by stretching the tones between black and white points, Clarity works on changing contrast on the detail in your photos. There are many sophisticated, multi-step, sharpening techniques that produce similar effects but thankfully Adobe has managed to squeeze much of their contrast-increasing abilities into a single control. Moving the slider to the right increases the effect.

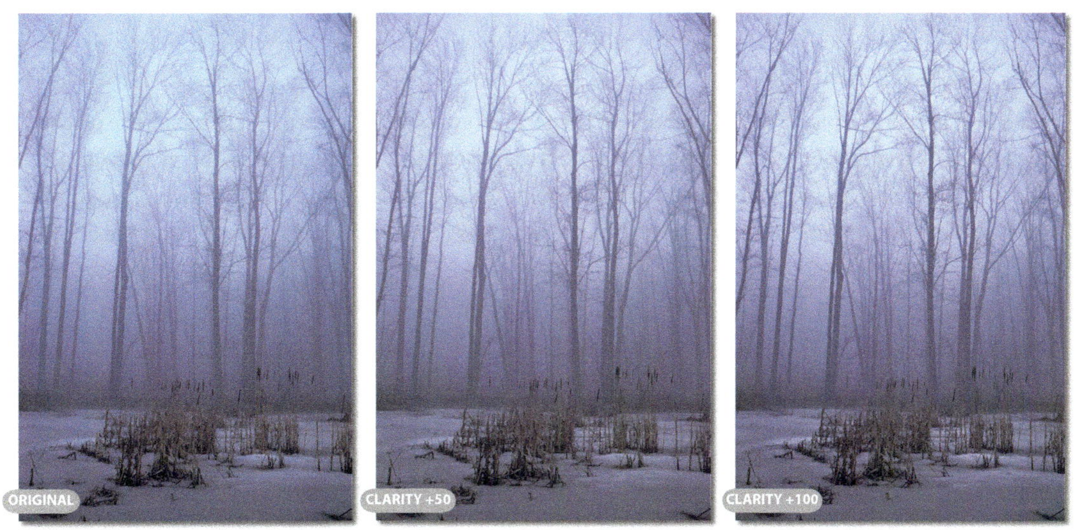

Adding contrast using the Clarity slider >> *The Clarity slider gradually increases the contrast of details in the photo.*

Vibrance

The Vibrance slider is a new addition to the Basic panel of Adobe Camera Raw. Like the Saturation control, Vibrance controls the strength of the color in the photo. Movements to the right boost the color and movements to the left make the vividness of the hue more subtle. But unlike the Saturation slider, Vibrance manages these changes selectively, targeting the least saturated colors and protecting (to some extent) skin tones.

This makes the new control the first tool to reach for when you want to boost the color in your photos. The results are easier to control and less likely to display posterization or color clipping from over-application than the traditional Saturation control.

Saturation control >>
The Saturation slider controls the strength of the color within your raw photos.
(1) Dragging the slider all the way to left (-100) will remove all color from the photo, creating a monochrome picture.
(2) A value of 0 is the default setting where the saturation is neither boosted nor reduced.
(3) Moving the slider all the way to the right to a setting of +100 produces twice the saturation of the normal or default setting.

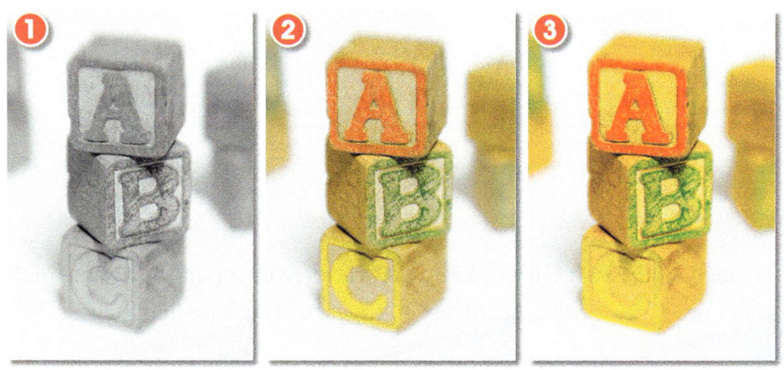

Saturation

If desired, the Saturation slider may be used to adjust the strength of the color within the photo. A setting of -100 is a completely desaturated monochrome image and a value of +100 doubles the saturation. Watch changes in the histogram when you move the Saturation slider in either direction.

Auto tonal control

When first opening a picture ACR will adjust the tonal controls to an average setting for the picture type and camera make/model. When the Auto setting is selected, ACR examines the picture and adjusts the controls according to the images' content. When these settings are in place, moving the associated slider will remove the selection but these values can be reinstated by selecting the check box again.

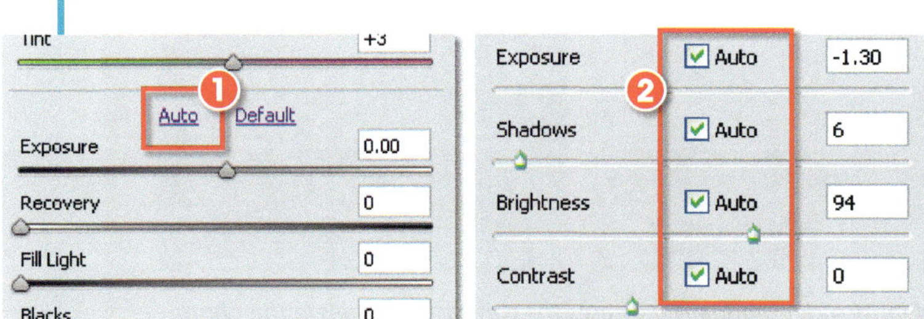

ACR auto options >>
(1) A single Auto button is provided with the version of ACR that ships with Photoshop Elements 7.0.
(2) There are individual Auto options for Exposure, Shadows, Brightness and Contrast controls inside earlier versions of the ACR dialog.

Sharpening, Luminance Smoothing and Color Noise Reduction

Sharpening (Amount, Radius, Detail, Masking), Luminance Smoothing and Color Noise Reduction are all controls that can be accessed under the Detail tab.

Sharpening

Sharpening is an enhancement technique that is easily overdone and this is true even when applying the changes at the time of raw conversion. The best approach is to remember that sharpening should be applied to photos as the very last step in the editing/enhancement process and that the settings used need to match the type of output the photo is destined for. In practice this means images that are not going to be edited after raw conversion should be sharpened within ACR, but those pictures that are going to be enhanced further should have a small amount of subtle sharpening applied in ACR and specific output sharpening applied later using the specialist filters in Photoshop Elements.

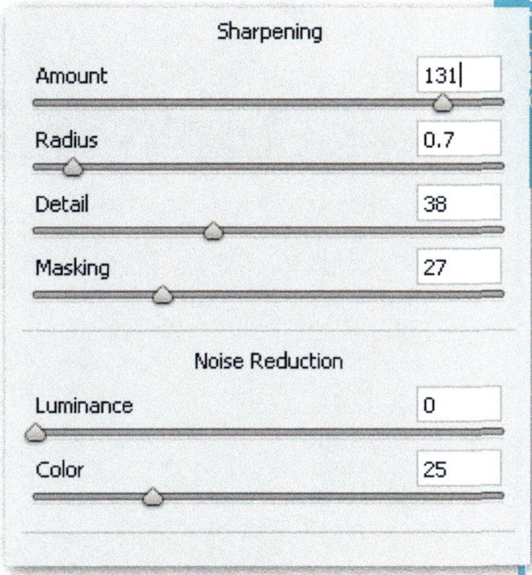

Detail Tab controls >>
The Detail tab contains both Sharpening and Noise Reduction options.

When a picture is first opened into the ACR the program sets the sharpening and noise values based on the camera type and model used to capture the image. For many photographers making further adjustments here is an exception rather than a rule as they prefer to address sharpening in the Editor after cropping, straightening, enhancing, resizing and going to print.

The inclusion of two new controls in the Detail section of the Camera Raw dialog contributes substantially to the user's ability to fine-tune the sharpening in their images. Added to the existing Amount (strength of the effect) and Radius (number of pixels from an edge that will be changed in the sharpening process) sliders is the Detail and Masking controls. Both sliders are designed to control which parts of the image the sharpening effect is applied to. As with all sharpening techniques ensure that the preview is set to 100% before playing with the new controls. In fact, this magnification level is essential if you are to see the masking previews mentioned below.

Moving the Detail slider to the right increases the local contrast surrounding edge areas and therefore enhances the appearance of details. Moving the slider to the left decreases the effect and also reduces the appearance of halos.

The Masking control interactively applies an edge locating mask to the sharpening process. Sharpening through an edge mask is nothing new but encapsulating the process in a single slider control is. A setting of 0 applies no mask and therefore all detail in the photo is sharpened. Moving the slider to the right gradually isolates the edges within the photo until, at a setting of 100, sharpening is only being applied to the most contrasty or dominant edges in the picture. Holding

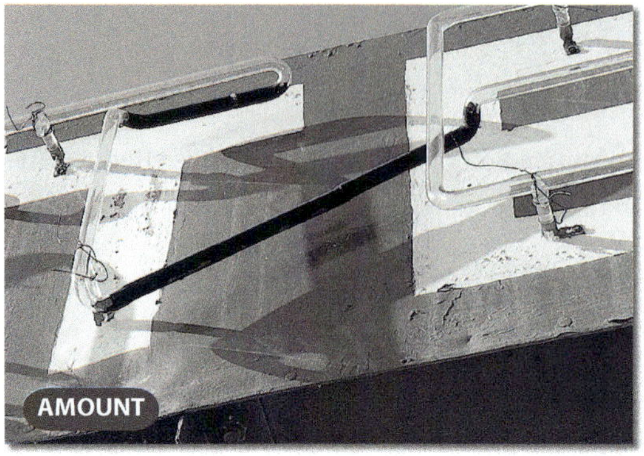

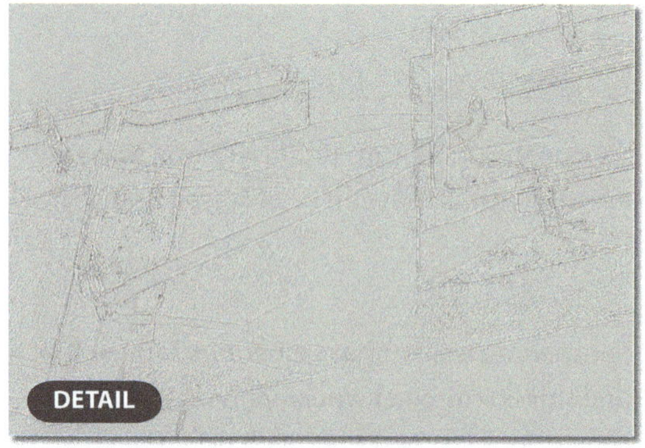

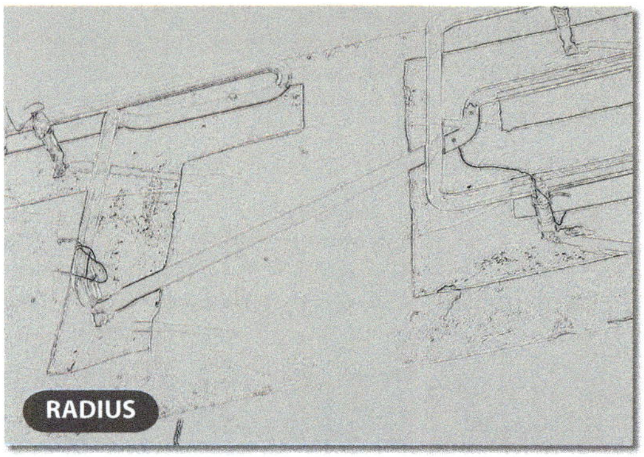

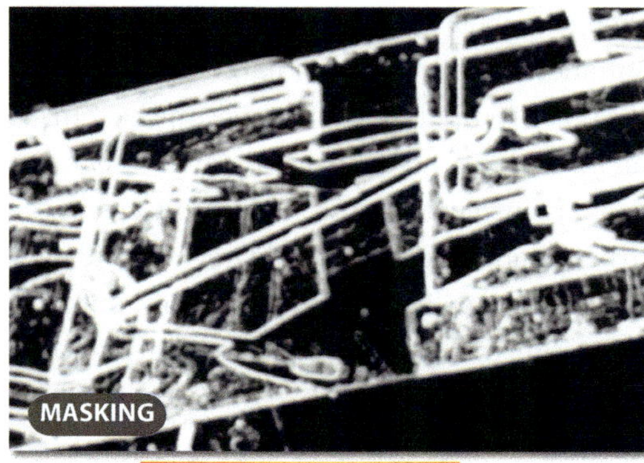

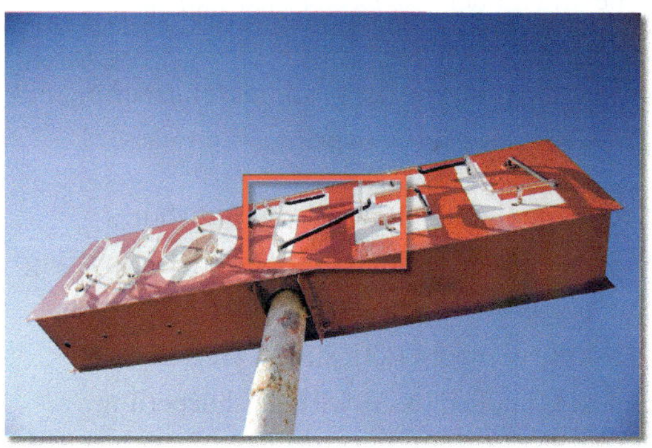

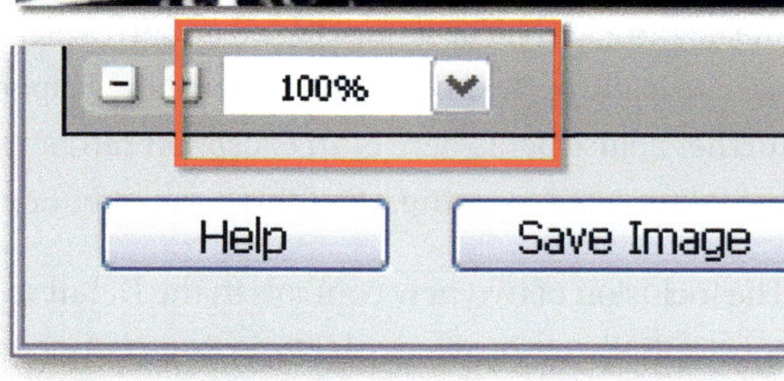

Sharpening preview options >>
After magnifying the preview to 100% there are four different preview options available when holding down the Alt keys and sliding one of the Sharpening sliders.

down the Alt key (at 100% magnification) as you move the slider previews the masked areas, allowing you to fine-tune exactly where the sharpening is being applied. Remember no sharpening is occurring in the black parts of the mask, in the areas masked by gray tones only partial sharpening is being applied and in white mask sections the full effect is revealed.

As well as including a mask display option, in the latest version of ACR you can also preview the settings for the other sharpening sliders. Holding down the Alt keys while moving the Amount slider displays a 'luminosity only' version of the image so that you can gauge the sharpening effect without the distraction of color. This preview also reminds us that in the latest version of ACR sharpening is applied to detail only and not the color information in the photo. When the Alt/Opt keys are used with the Radius slider the preview highlights the 'edges' in the image that will be sharpened and the width of the sharpening effect.

Noise Reduction

ACR contains two different noise reduction controls. The Luminance Smoothing slider and the Color Noise Reduction control. The Luminance Smoothing slider is designed to reduce the appearance of grayscale noise in a photo. This is particularly useful for improving the look of images that appear grainy. The second type of noise is the random colored pixels that typically appear in photos taken with a high ISO setting or a long shutter speed. This is generally referred to as chroma noise and the effect is reduced using the Color Noise Reduction slider in ACR. The noise reduction effect of both features is increased as the sliders are moved to the right.

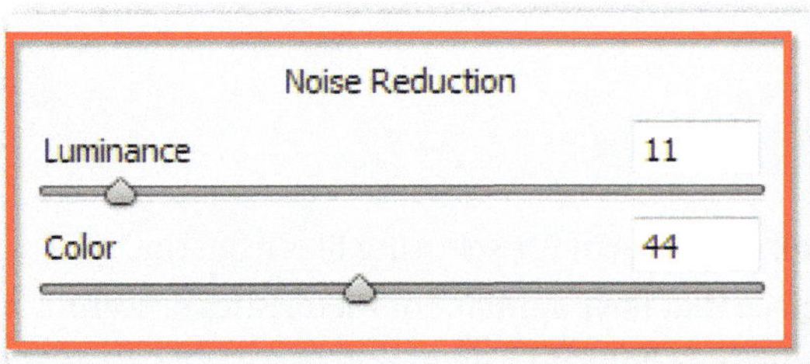

ACR noise reduction controls >>
Along with the masking options for Sharpening, the ACR design team also took the opportunity to tweak the noise reduction algorithms in the latest release of the product. Though the effects are not as dramatic as those possible via other methods, the changes are definitely an improvement.

Raw file queue

The third section of the Photoshop Elements version of the ACR dialog only appears when you select multiple raw files inside the Organizer workspace and then choose the Full Edit option from the right-click menu. The selected files are opened into the ACR dialog and listed on the left-hand side of the main workspace. This function, though available in the Photoshop version of ACR, was only introduced to the edition that ships with Photoshop Elements in version 6.0.

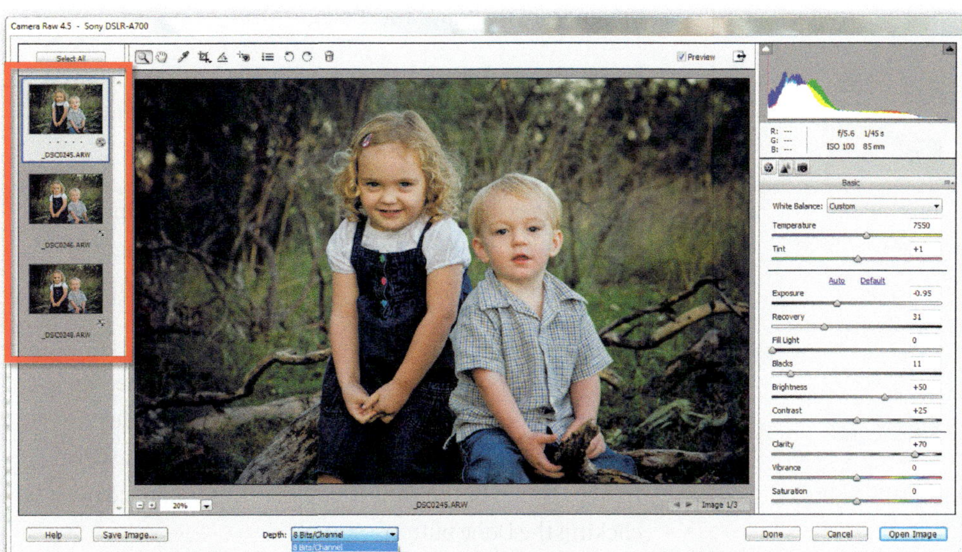

Queued Raw files >>
When selecting multiple raw files to open in Photoshop Elements the pictures are listed on the left side of the Adobe Camera Raw dialog.

In general, only one image can be selected from the grouping, and displayed in the preview area, at a time. All changes made to the image settings are applied to the selected photo only. Users can move from image to image making the necessary enhancements before clicking the Done key to apply the changes without transferring the files, or Open to display the converted pictures in the Full Edit workspace. But this is not the only way to work with the files.

Synchronizing enhancements across multiple files

The Select All button at the top of the queued files can be employed for a more efficient workflow. With this feature enhancement changes made to a single photo can be applied across the whole range of images queued in the dialog.

Step-by-step

Applying changes across multiple raw files

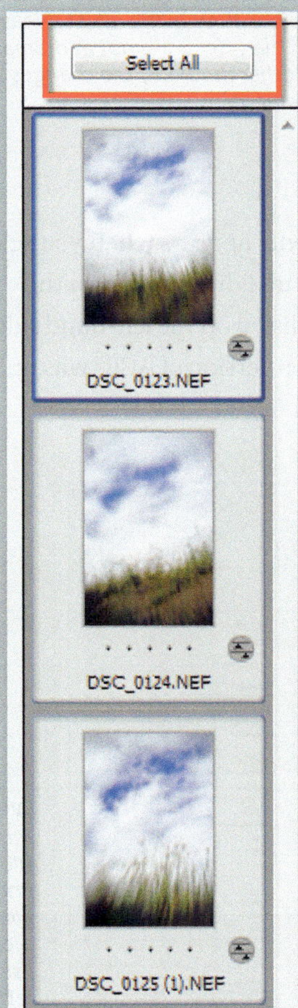

1. For best results, start by multi-selecting files from the Organizer space that have similar characteristics or were shot under the same lighting conditions.

2. Next, open the pictures in ACR by selecting the Full Edit option from the right-click menu. The ACR dialog opens with the selected files listed as thumbnails on the left.

3. Now select a single photo from the queue that is indicative in tone and color of the whole group. With this photo displayed in the preview area, choose the Select All option from the top of the dialog.

4. Proceed to make enhancement changes to the previewed files as you would normally. Notice that these changes are also applied to the other photos in the queue.

5. The changes made to all the photos can then be fine-tuned to suit the characteristics of individual images (if needed) by selecting each picture in turn and adjusting the controls.

6. If no changes for individual files are necessary, then the selected photos can be saved, using the Save Images button, transferred to the Edit workspace with the Open Images option or the enhancement settings applied by clicking the Done button.

Applying changes across rated raw files

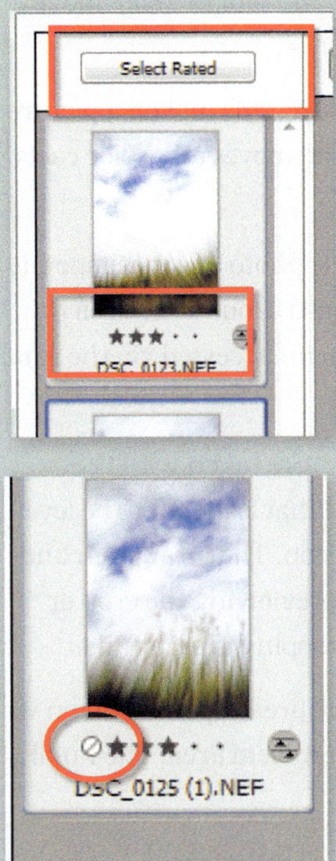

1. In addition to being able to apply image changes across all the queued files by choosing the Select All button, it is also possible to adjust a subset of the files listed. Start by reviewing each of the queued files in turn by clicking onto the thumbnail on the left of the dialog.

2. During the review process rate those files that you want to adjust as a group. Do this by clicking the star rating section located under each thumbnail.

3. Once the review process is completed and all files to be enhanced as a group are rated, hold down the Alt key and choose the Select Rated button at the top of the queued list. Notice that this action selects only those files with a star rating attached.

4. Now you can set about applying the changes to those selected as before.

5. If you want to remove an image from the Rated grouping simply click on the no rating option under the thumbnail.

Step-by-step

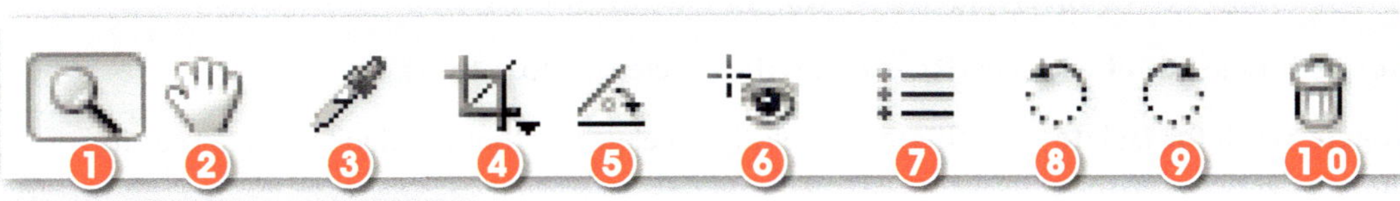

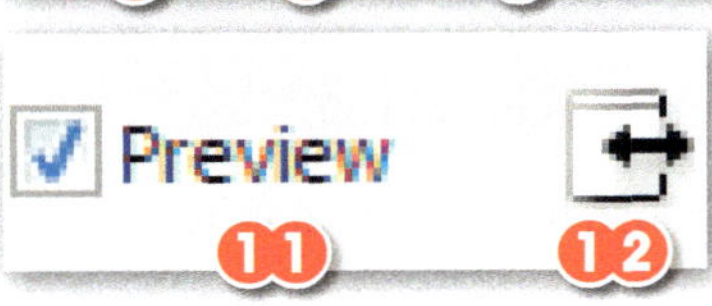

The ACR toolbar >>
Photoshop Elements users have access to a range of tools via the toolbar at the top of the ACR dialog.
1. *Zoom tool*
2. *Hand tool*
3. *White Balance tool*
4. *Crop tool*
5. *Straighten tool*
6. *Red Eye Removal*
7. *Preferences dialog*
8. *Rotate image 90°CC*
9. *Rotate image 90°C*
10. *Toggle Mark for Delete*
11. *Preview*
12. *Toggle Full Screen*

Toolbar

Like the image adjustment tabs on the right of the ACR dialog, the contents of the program's toolbar are different depending on if you are working on files inside Photoshop Elements or Photoshop/ Bridge. Elements users have the following tools at their disposal (left to right):

Zoom tool (shortcut key = Z) – The Zoom tool is useful for looking closely at the image for problems with focus and execution – slow shutter speed, lack of stabilization, incorrect aperture setting. At 25% an image may appear to be quite impressive, yet when examining it at 100% often a bit of movement and/or lack of focus appear.

Hand tool (H) – When the preview image is enlarged you can use the Hand tool to easily move around the screen.

White Balance tool (I) – The White Balance tool is very powerful. Clicking this tool on a picture portion that is meant to be neutral (even amounts of red, green and blue) removes any color casts and adjusts the hue of the entire image in one fell swoop.

Crop tool (C) – Use the Crop tool to remove unwanted areas around your photo or to reshape the format of the image to fit a specific paper type. The tool can be click-dragged around the area to keep or a specific cropping format can be selected from the drop-down menu accessed via the small downward-facing arrow in the bottom right of the tool button.

Straighten tool (A) – The Straighten tool can automatically rotate a picture taken with the horizon slightly crooked. Simply drag the tool along the line in the image that is meant to be level and ACR will automatically rotate and crop the photo to realign the horizon. The Straighten and Crop tools don't actually remove parts of the Raw image, in fact it is just previewing the crop or horizon line that is going to be opened in the Editor, but is not actually cropping the Raw file.

Red Eye Removal (E) – Use the Red Eye Removal tool to recolor the pupil area of photos taken with flash. Either click onto the red pupil or click-drag a marquee around the problem area. The Pupil Size and Darken sliders can be used to adjust the quality of the results.

Open Preference dialog (Ctrl + K) – Displays the Camera Raw Preferences dialog.

Rotate image 90° counter-clockwise (L) – Rotates the selected photo to the left.

Rotate image 90° clockwise (R) – Rotates the selected photo to the right.

Toggle Mark for Delete – Use this tool carefully to delete files that you don't want to keep in the catalog.

Preview (P) – Switches the preview of current image adjustments settings on and off.

Toggle Full Screen (F) – Switches the display mode of the dialog from a floating window to full screen.

Output options

Now to the business end of the conversion task – outputting the file. At this stage in the process ACR provides several options that will govern how the file is handled from this point onwards. In previous versions of the dialog the lower right-hand corner house all the output options, now they are spread along the bottom of the window. The options include Save Image, Cancel, Open Image, Done and Help, and a further three: Save Image (without the options dialog), Reset and Open Copy, when the Alt button is pushed.

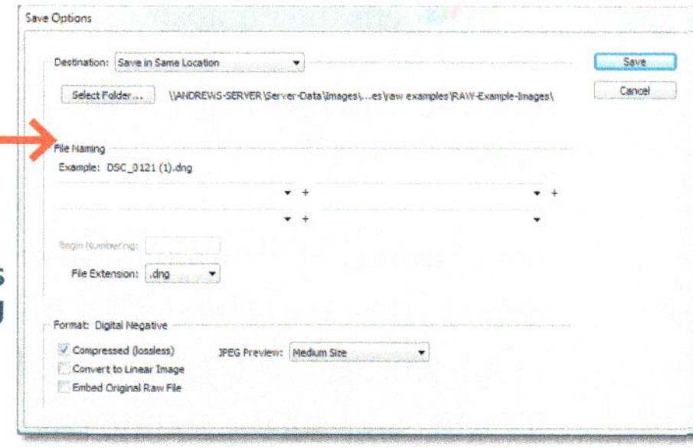

Save Options dialog

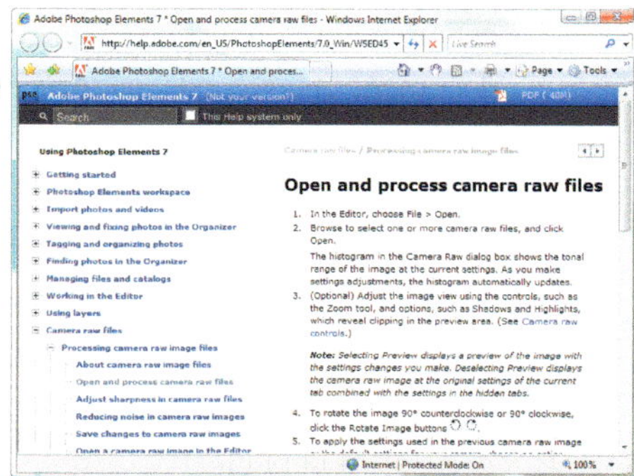

Help

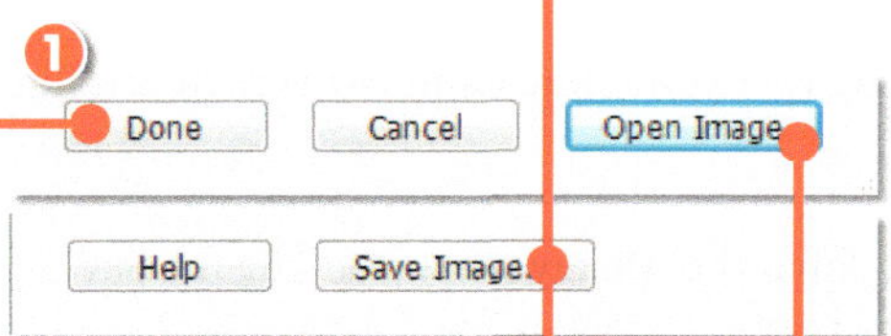

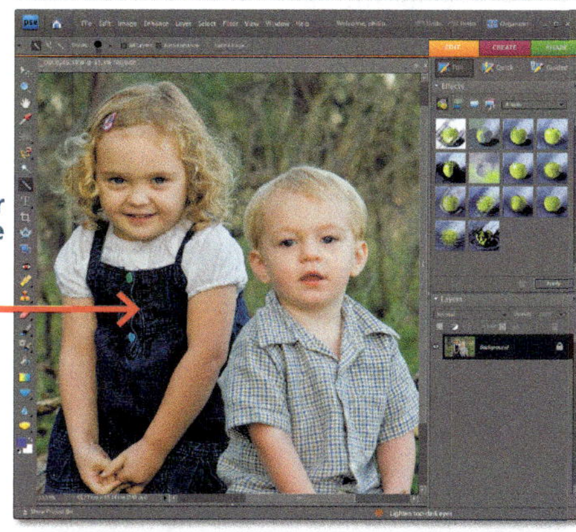

The Editor workspace

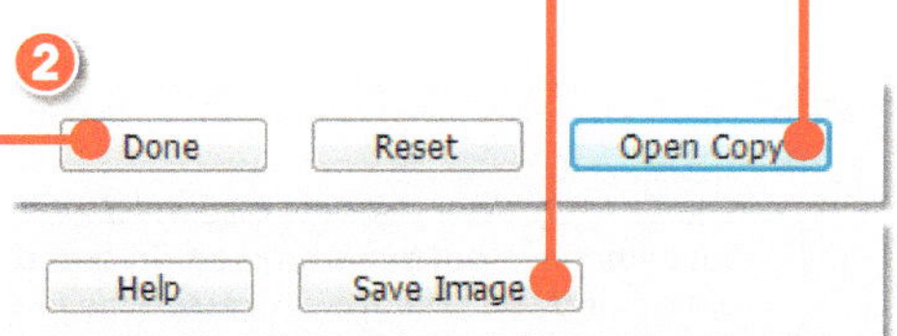

Alternative ACR button layout displayed when Alt key is pressed

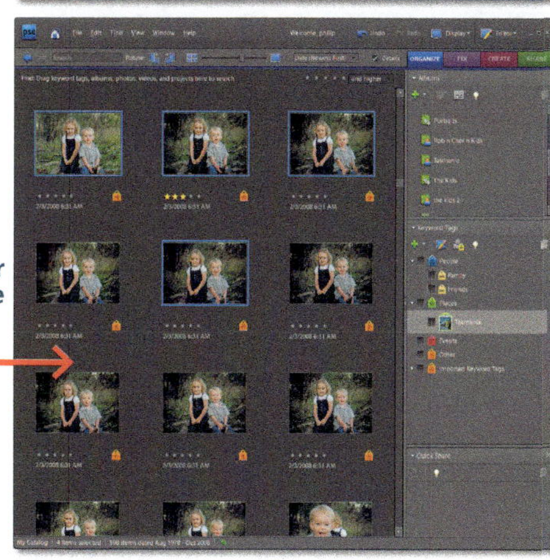

The Organizer workspace

Outputting the file >>

Once all controls for the raw conversion have been set ACR provides a range of options for the next step in the process. Save, Help, Cancel, Done and Open are available by default (1). Holding down the Alt key switches the button set to Save (without a dialog), Help, Reset, Open Copy and Done (2).

Help: Opens the Photoshop Elements help system with raw processing topics already displayed.

Cancel: This option closes the ACR dialog not saving any of the settings to the file that was open.

Save Image: The normal Save Image button, which includes several dots (...) after the label, displays the Save Options dialog. Here you can save the raw file, with your settings applied, in Adobe's own DNG format. The dialog includes options for inputting the location where the file will be saved, the ability to add in a new name as well as DNG file-specific settings such as compression, conversion to linear image and/or embed the original raw file in the new DNG document. It is a good idea to Select Save in Different Location in the Destination drop-down at the top to separate processed files from archive originals. Clearly the benefits of a compressed DNG file are going to help out in the storage issue arena and compression is a big advantage with DNG. Embedding the original raw file in the saved DNG file begs the questions of how much room you have in the designated storage device and whether you really want to have the original raw file here.

Save Image (without save options): Holding down the Alt key when clicking the Save button skips the Save Options dialog and saves the file in DNG format using the default save settings.

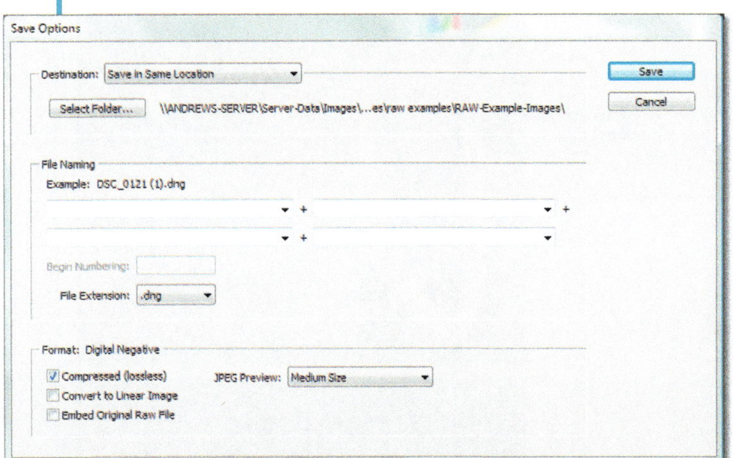

Options for saving >>
The Save Options dialog is displayed when the Save Image ... button is pressed. To skip this dialog and still save the processed file in DNG format hold down the Alt/Option key whilst clicking the Save Image button.

Open Image: If you click on the Open button Elements applies the conversion options that you set in ACR and opens the file inside the Editor workspace. At this point, the file is no longer in a raw format so when it comes to saving the photo from the Editor workspace Elements automatically selects the Photoshop PSD format for saving.

Open Copy: The Open Copy option differs from Open Image in that it applies the development settings to a duplicate of the file which is then opened into the Elements Editor workspace.

Reset: The Reset option resets the ACR dialog's settings back to their defaults. This feature is useful if you want to ensure that all settings and enhancement changes made in the current

PROCESSING RAW FILES

session have been removed. To access the Reset button click the Cancel button while holding down the Alt key.

Done or Update: The Done button applies the current settings to the photo and the dialog is then closed. The thumbnail preview in the PhotoBrowser workspace will also be updated to reflect the changes. In previous versions of the dialog clicking the Open button in conjunction with the Alt/Option key (the Update button) will update the raw conversion settings for the open image in the same way.

Pro's Tip **Pro's tip:** If the thumbnail doesn't update automatically, select the picture and then choose Edit > Update Thumbnail in the PhotoBrowser workspace.

Skip: In previous versions of Adobe Camera Raw holding down the Shift key whilst clicking the Open button will not apply the currently selected changes and just close the dialog. In this way it is similar to the Cancel button.

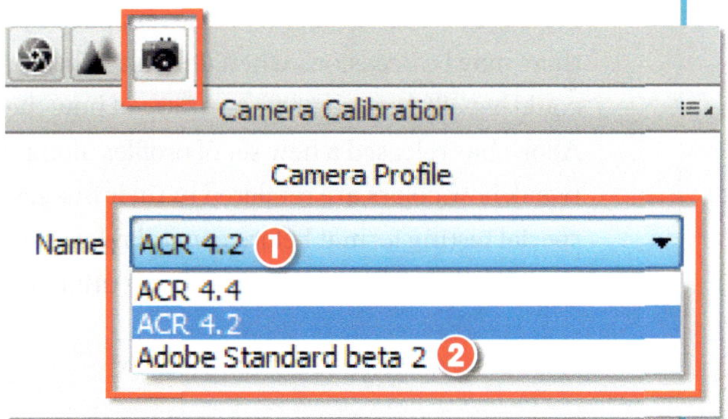

Camera Calibration >>
The Camera Calibration tab is new for the version of Adobe Camera Raw that ships with Photoshop Elements. The section contains a single drop down menu where you can select the camera profile that is used to interpret the colors, tones and white balance of your raw images. For many camera models there will be several options available with the highest numbered ACR entry representing the most recent profile (1). Adobe has also released a very new set of profiles titled Adobe Standard (2) which don't ship with Elements but can be downloaded and installed.

3.05 The new Camera Calibration tab

Suitable for Elements – 7.0 | Difficulty level – Advanced

The Camera Calibration pane contains a drop down menu of the camera profiles that ship with Adobe Camera Raw. These profiles tell ACR how to interpret the colors in an image. They are specific to individual manufacturers and camera models and the default selection will suit most users' needs straight out of the box. Depending on the camera you are using there may be several profiles available for use with your images. The default profile displayed will either be the most recent version available for your camera for new pictures, or for images you have already enhanced in ACR it will be the profile that was used for making these changes.

It is easy to switch from one profile to another by selecting and alternative entry from the drop-down menu. Because each profile renders colors differently, switching profiles will change the way that the colors appear in you photo which may in turn require a little tweaking of tones and colors in order to account for the different rendering. Keep in mind that the highest numbered entry will be the most recent profile available for your camera.

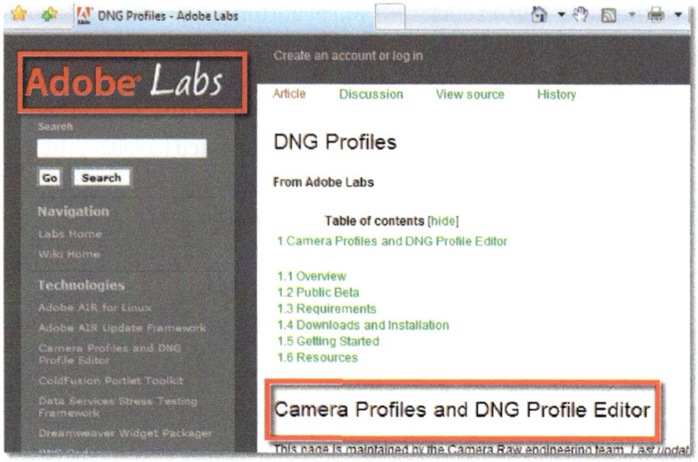

New Camera Profiles >>
At the time of writing the new camera profiles as well as the DNG Profile Editor utility are available in beta format from the labs.adobe.com website.

New Camera Profiles

For most users the general profiles supplied by Adobe are more than sufficient for their needs, but there may be occasions when difficult lighting, or the wayward characteristics of a specific camera, could benefit from some fine-tuning of how the raw data is interpreted by ACR. For this reason Adobe has released a new set of profiles along with a special editor utility designed to allow users to tweak how colors are rendered in their images. At the time of writing these are both in beta form (a special testing format before general release) and are available as a free download from labs.adobe.com. The formal name for the editing utility is the DNG Profile Editor.

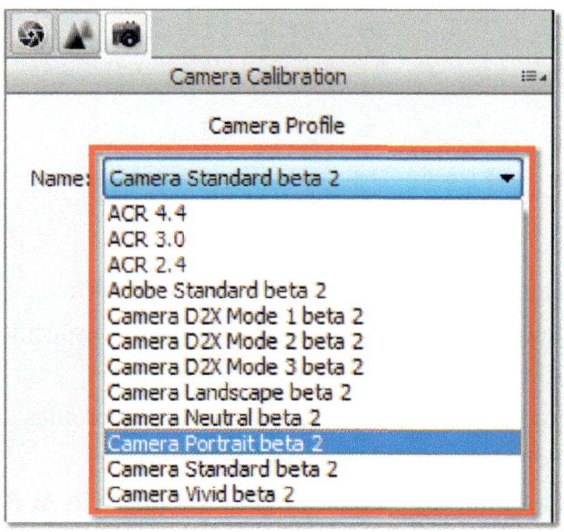

Multiple Profiles >>
As the DNG Profile Editor provides the ability to quickly and easily create new profiles for a camera, installing the new camera profiles will display a variety of entries in the drop down menu. In this example the user has the option of selecting a way of rendering the colors, tones and white balance in a image from a list of 12.

Adding Adobe's new camera profiles

The new camera profiles can be downloaded from the beta website and when installed will automatically be available for use in the Camera Calibration tab of Adobe Camera Raw the next time you open it. You will find at least one new general profile available for all cameras supported by ACR. This is titled the Adobe Standard Beta. For some manufacturers and camera models there will also be a variety of other profiles available. These include profiles customized for different looks and styles. There are some suitable for landscape imagery, others that work well with portraits, as well as options for creating more vivid colors or a more subtle rendition of hues. Once installed you can quickly flip through each of the camera profiles to see which works best with your particular image.

Note: If you only see the Adobe Standard profile entry then there are currently no extra custom profiles available for you camera. For this reason it is a good idea to check adobe.com regularly to see which new camera profiles are available for download.

DNG Profile Editor >>
The DNG Profile Editor provides a set of controls for creating custom Camera Profiles.

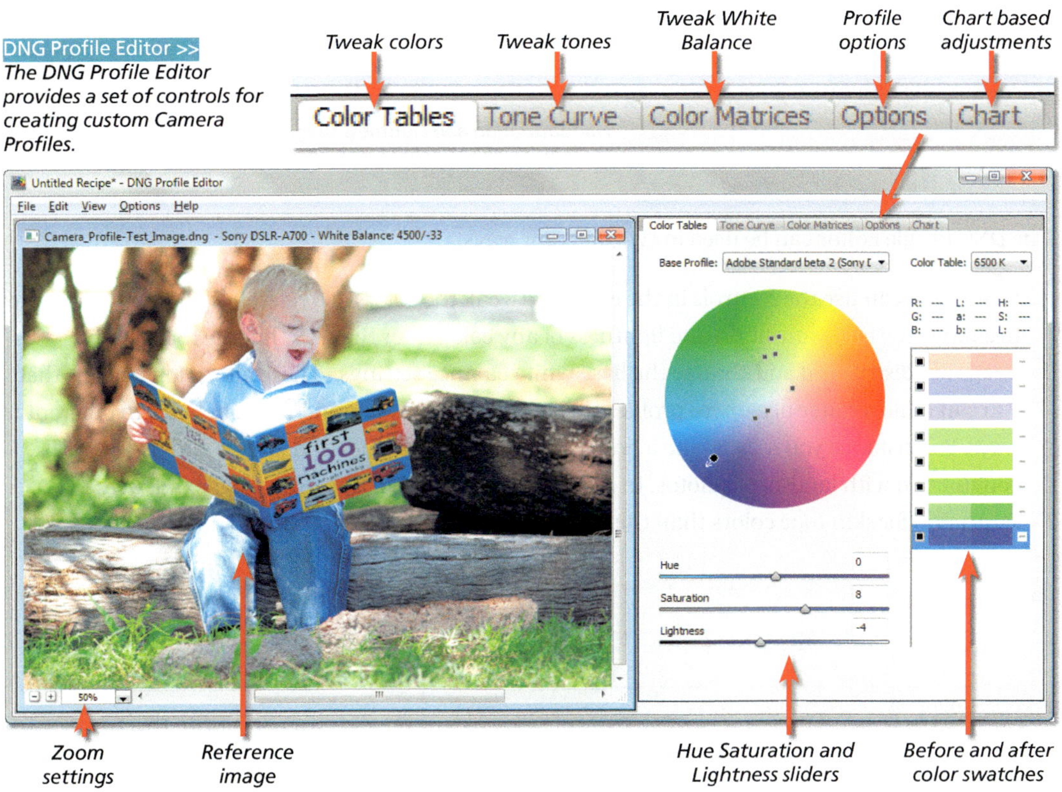

Creating your own custom camera profiles

Now for those of you who really like to 'tinker under the hood', Adobe also provides an editor utility that can be used to create your own camera profiles. Called the DNG Profile Editor, at the time of writing the program is available from labs.adobe.com as a free beta download.

With this tool it is possible to fundamentally change how the hues that are recorded by the camera are translated into colors in the photo; for this reason, I must provide a cautionary note here. This an advanced technique and accompanying this level of color rendering power, comes the ability to really screw up how your photos appear. Thankfully creating and using a crazy profile with your photo won't permanently change your picture. To revert the image back to its original settings all you need to do is select one of the Adobe created profiles from the Camera Profile menu.

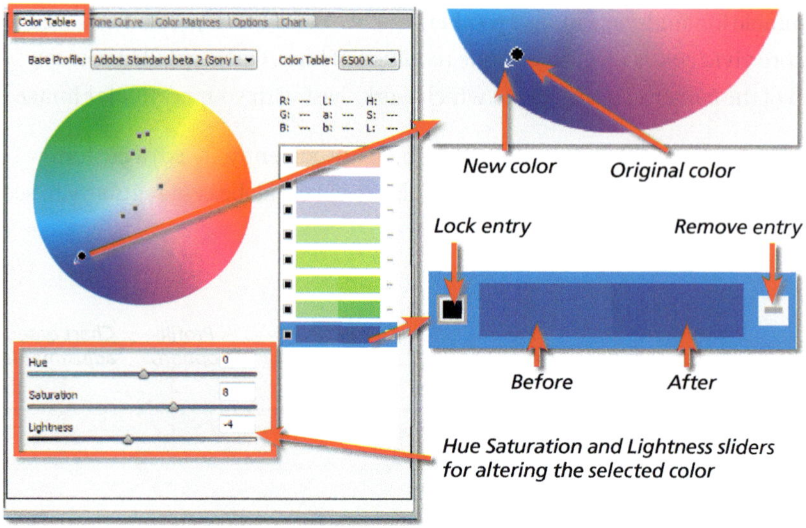

Customizing profiles >>
The Color Tables (pictured), Tone Curve, and Color Matrices sections in the DNG Profile Editor contain tools for adjusting the colors, tones and white balance.

The DNG Profile Editor can be used in two different ways.

1. Firstly, you can use the controls in the editor to tweak the colors of a reference photo. It is possible to change the hue, saturation and lightness of any color, alter the way that the tones in the image are distributed and change the base white balance settings. These alterations means that you can build a range of camera profiles that render colors, tones and white balance in different ways. For instance you may create a profile that emphasizes blues and greens and use this in conjunction with landscape photos. In contrast you may build a portrait profile that uses less saturation for skin tone colors than the other hues in the scene.

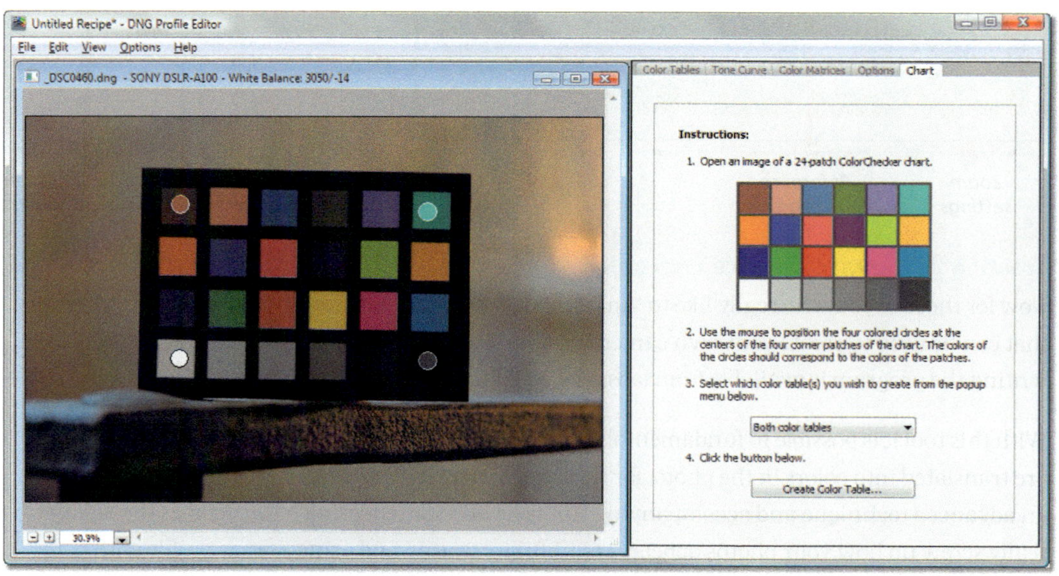

Creating camera profiles for specific lighting >>
The Chart section of the DNG Profile Editor is specifically designed to be used with the X-Rite ColorChecker to create accurate color rendition under difficult lighting or mixed light sources.

2. Secondly, the DNG Profile Editor can be used together with a color calibration target calibrate your camera's response to color under different light sources. The utility is designed to use the ColorChecker that is available from X-Rite (previously Gretagmacbeth). The process involves shooting the color checker using representative lighting for the scene. This image is then opened in the DNG Profile Editor and processed via the tools in the Chart section of the utility. The editor compares the colors of each swatch in the photo with the known values of these hues and then creates a 'recipe' of adjustments to correct any casts present in the photo. The recipe settings can then be exported as a new camera profile and used in Adobe Camera Raw. This is not a task that you would undertake for all images; instead, it is a calibration activity that you perform when encountering a difficult shooting scenario such as capturing under mixed lighting.

Note: In order to open photos in the DNG Profile Editor they must first be saved in or converted to Adobe's DNG or digital negative format. The easiest way for Elements users to do this is to open the raw file in Adobe Camera Raw and then use the Save Image .... (yes the one with the dots) with DNG selected as the file format.

3.06 The raw conversion process

Suitable for Elements – 7.0, 6.0, 5.0, 4.0, 3.0, 2.0, 1.0 | Difficulty level – Basic

Okay, now that we have a good understanding of the features and controls within the Adobe Camera Raw dialog let's move on and look at a typical conversion workflow.

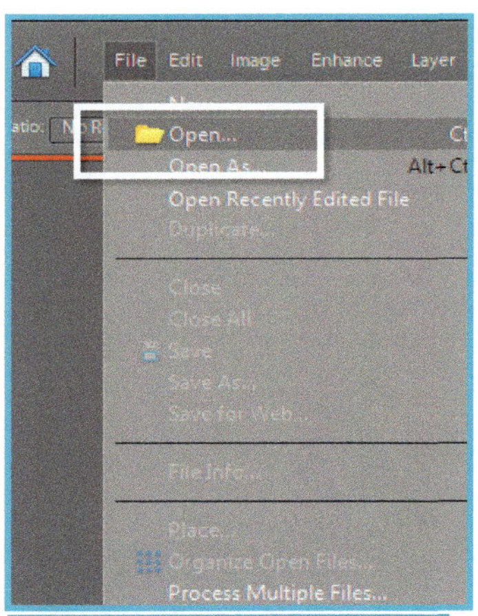

1. Opening the raw file in the Editor workspace *Once you have downloaded your raw files from camera to computer you can start the task of processing. Keep in mind that in its present state the raw file is not in the full color RGB format that we are used to, so the first part of all processing is to open the picture into Adobe Camera Raw. Selecting File > Open from inside Elements will automatically display the photo in this.*

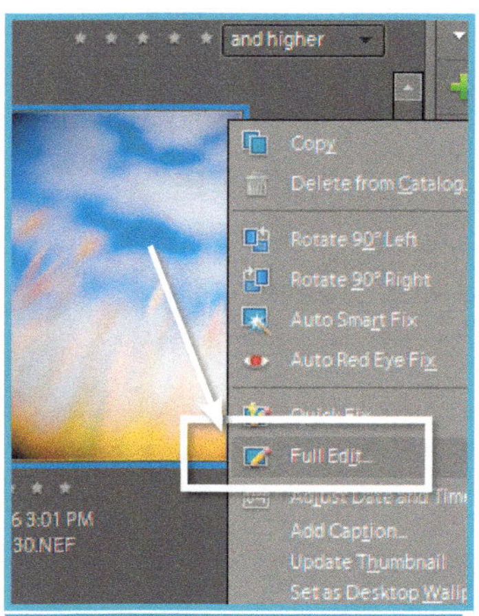

2. Starting with the PhotoBrowser *Starting in the PhotoBrowser or Organizer workspace simply right-click on the thumbnail of the raw file and select Full Edit or Go to Standard Edit from the pop-up menu to transfer the file to the Elements version of ACR in the Editor workspace.*

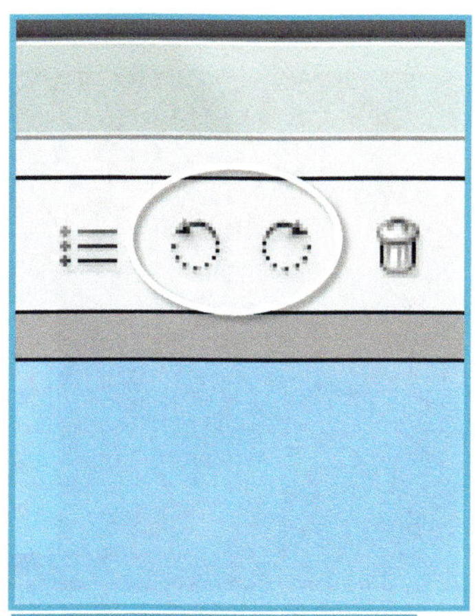

3. Rotate right (90 CW) or left (90 CCW) *Once the raw photo is open in ACR you can rotate the image using either of the two Rotate buttons at the top of the dialog. If you are the lucky owner of a recent camera model then chances are the picture will automatically rotate to its correct orientation. This is thanks to a small piece of metadata supplied by the camera and stored in the picture file that indicates which way is up.*

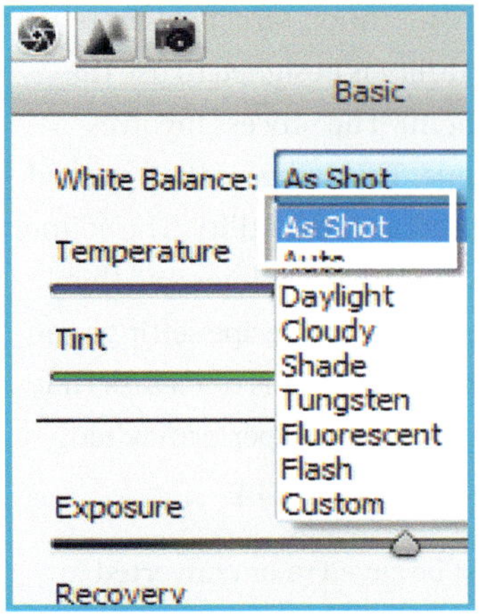

4. Preset changes *As we have seen you can opt to stay with the settings used at the time of shooting ('As Shot') or select from a range of light-source-specific settings in the White Balance drop-down menu of ACR. For best results, try to match the setting used with the type of lighting that was present in the scene at the time of capture. Or choose the Auto option from the drop-down White Balance menu to get ACR to determine a setting based on the individual image currently displayed.*

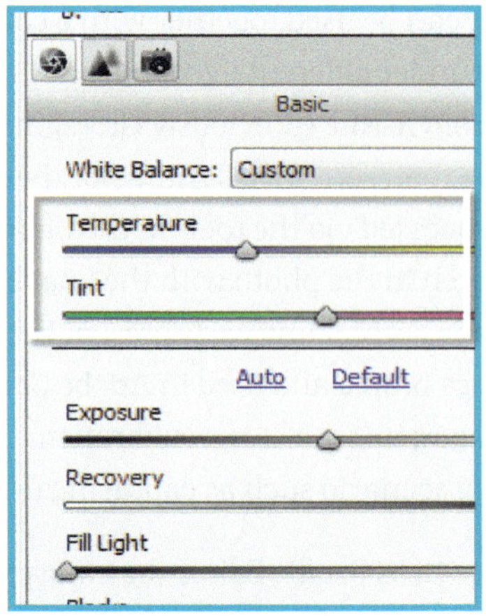

5. Manual adjustments *If none of the preset white balance options perfectly matches the lighting in your photo then you will need to fine-tune your results with the Temperature and Tint sliders (located just below the Presets drop-down menu). The Temperature slider settings equate to the color of light in degrees Kelvin – so daylight will be 5500 and tungsten light 2800. It is a blue to yellow scale, so moving the slider to the left will make the image cooler (more blue) and to the right warmer (more yellow). In contrast the Tint slider is a green to magenta scale. Moving the slider left will add more green to the image and to the right more magenta.*

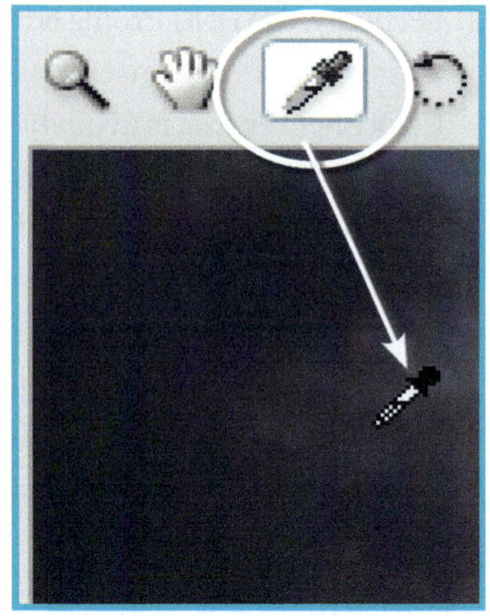

6. The White Balance tool *Another quick way to balance the light in your picture is to choose the White Balance tool and then click on a part of the picture that is meant to be neutral gray. ACR will automatically set the Temperature and Tint sliders so that this picture part becomes a neutral gray and in the process the rest of the image will be balanced. For best results when selecting lighter tones with the tool ensure that the area contains detail and is not a blown or specular highlight.*

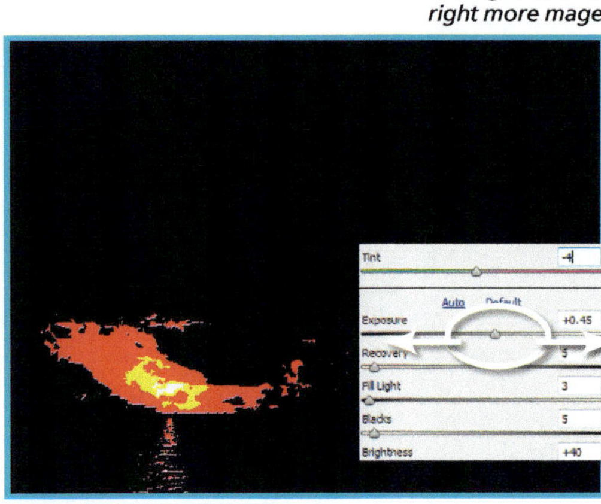

7. Setting the white areas *To start, adjust the brightness with the Exposure slider. Moving the slider to the right lightens the photo and to the left darkens it. The settings for the slider are in f-stop increments, with a +1.00 setting being equivalent to increasing exposure by 1 f-stop. Use this slider to peg or set the white tones. Your aim is to lighten the highlights in the photo without clipping (converting the pixels to pure white) them. To do this, hold down Alt/Option whilst moving the slider. This action previews the photo with the pixels being clipped against a black background. Move the slider back and forth until no clipped pixels appear but the highlights are as white as possible.*

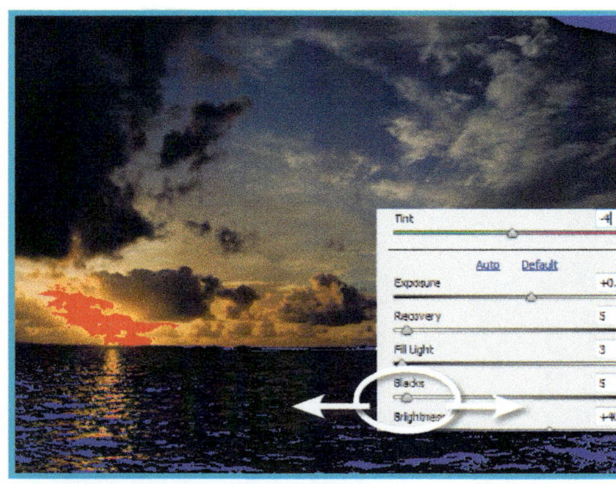

8. Adjusting the shadows (blacks) *The Blacks or Shadows slider performs a similar function with the shadow areas of the image. Again the aim is to darken these tones but not to convert (or clip) delicate details to pure black. Just as with the Exposure slider, the Alt/Option key can be pressed whilst making Shadows adjustments to preview the pixels being clipped. Alternatively the Shadow and Highlights Clipping Warning features (top left and right corners of the histogram) can be used to provide instant clipping feedback on the preview image. Shadow pixels that are being clipped are displayed in blue and clipped highlight tones in red.*

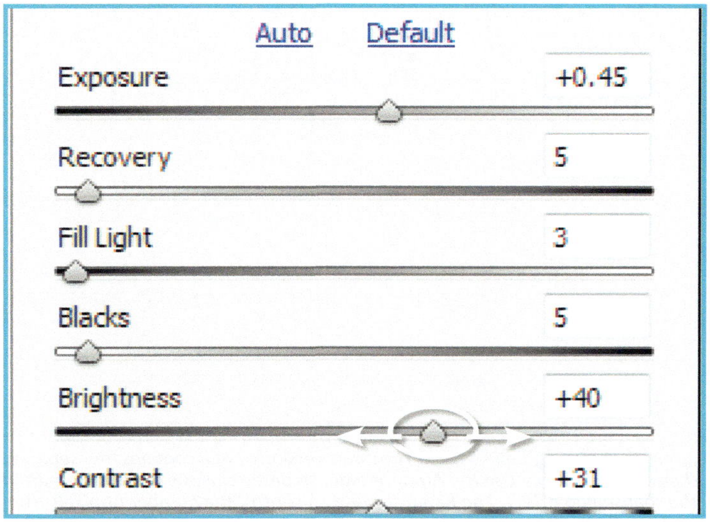

9. Brightness changes *The next control, moving from top to bottom of the ACR dialog, is the Brightness slider. At first the changes you make with this feature may appear to be very similar to those produced with the Exposure slider but there is an important difference. Yes, it is true that moving the slider to the right lightens the whole image, but rather than adjusting all pixels the same amount the feature makes major changes in the midtone areas and smaller jumps in the highlights. In so doing the Brightness slider is less likely to clip the highlights (or shadows) as the feature compresses the highlights as it lightens the photo. This is why it is important to set white and black points first with the Exposure and Shadows sliders before fine-tuning the image with the Brightness control.*

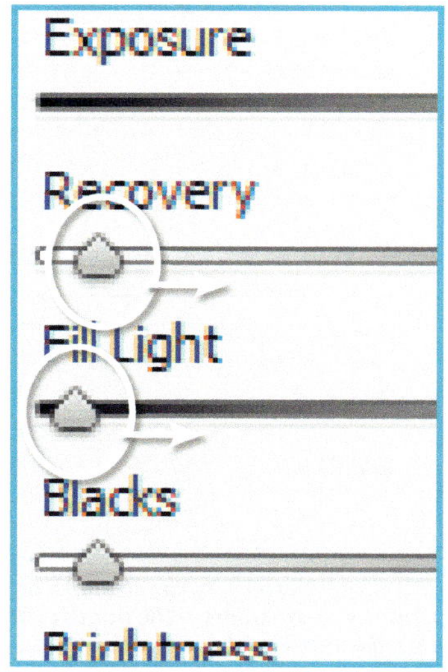

10. Recovering highlights and shadow detail *If the highlights are still being clipped then use the Recovery slider to recreate detail in the problem area. Likewise if the shadow areas are too dark then drag the Fill Light slider to the right to lighten these tones in the photo. Be careful with over-application of either of these controls as it can make the image look low in contrast.*

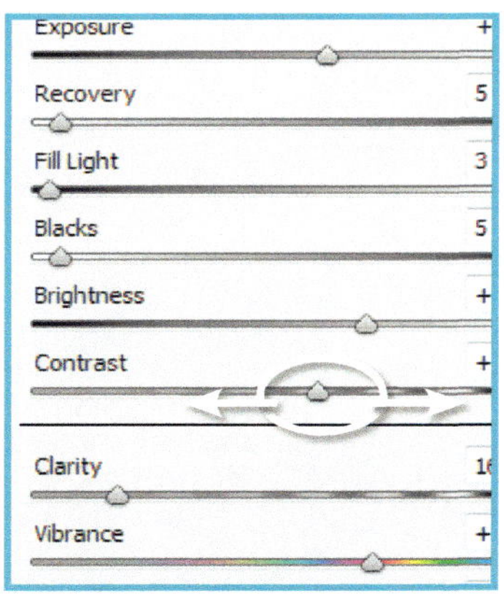

11. Increasing/decreasing contrast *The last tonal control in the dialog, and the last to be applied to the photo, is the Contrast slider. The feature concentrates on the midtones in the photo with movements of the slider to the right increasing the midtone contrast and to the left producing a lower contrast image. Like the Brightness slider, Contrast changes are best applied after setting the white and black points of the image with the Exposure and Blacks sliders.*

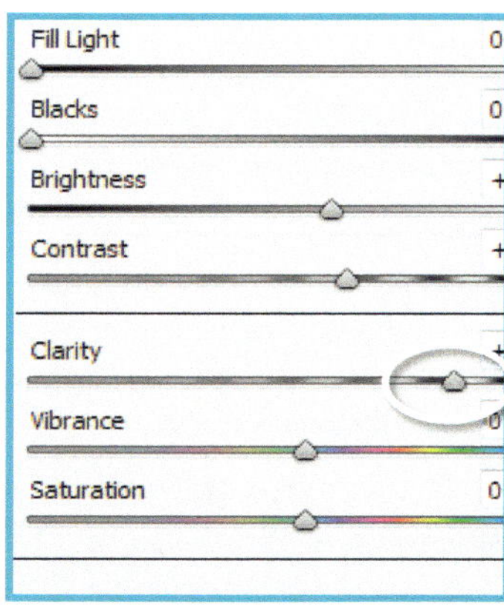

12. Local contrast control *The Clarity slider is used to alter the local contrast or the contrast of details within the photo. It works well with photos that have been photographed with diffused light or on a cloudy day. Use Clarity and Contrast sliders together. You can now also apply negative Clarity values to soften details or provide a diffused look to your images.*

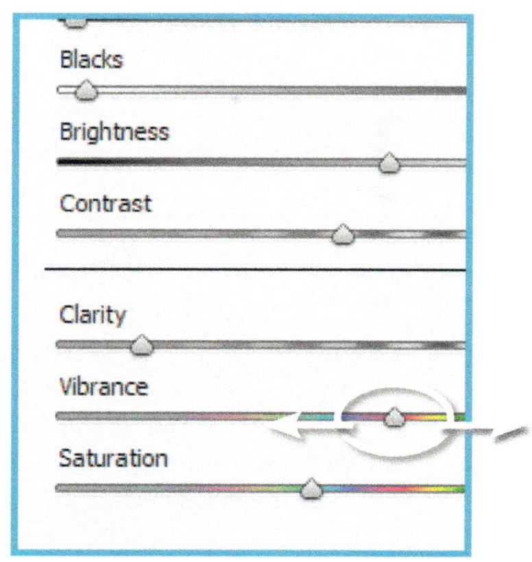

13. Vibrance adjustment *Unlike the Saturation slider, which increases the strength of all colors in the photo irrespective of their strength in the first place, Vibrance targets its changes to just those colors that are desaturated. Use this control to boost the strength of colors in the photo with less risk of posterized results.*

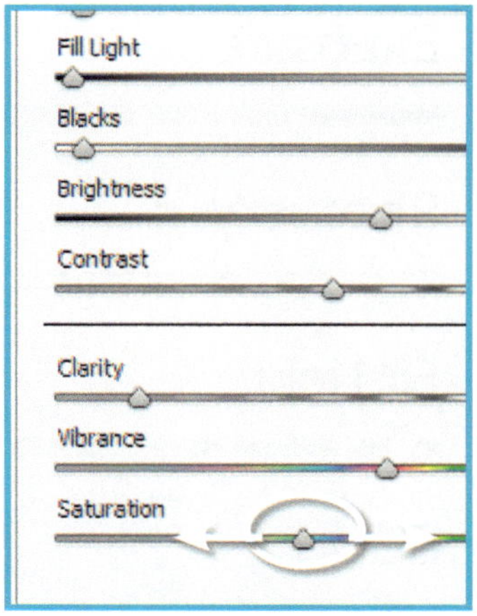

14. Saturation control *The strength or vibrancy of the colors in the photo can be adjusted using the Saturation slider. Moving the slider to the right increases saturation, with a value of +100 being a doubling of the color strength found at a setting of 0. Saturation can be reduced by moving the slider to the left, with a value of -100 producing a monochrome image. Some photographers use this option as a quick way to convert their photos to black and white but most prefer to make this change in Photoshop Elements proper, where more control can be gained over the conversion process with features such as the Convert to Black & White.*

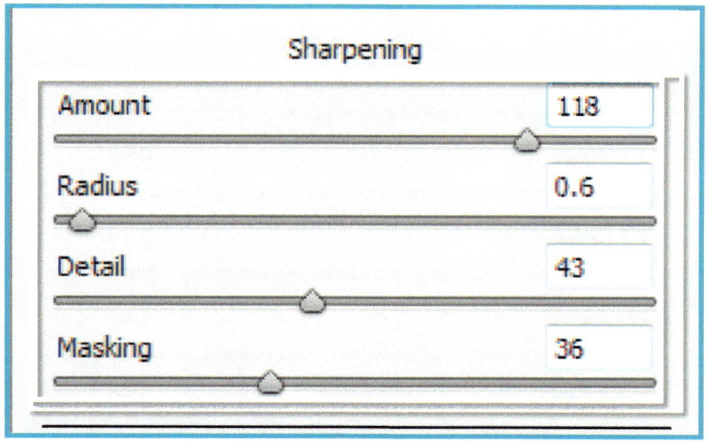

15. To sharpen or not to sharpen *The latest version of ACR contains four separate sharpening controls. Use the Amount slider to determine the overall strength of the sharpening effect. The Radius is used to control the number of pixels from an edge that will be changed in the sharpening process.*

The Detail and Masking sliders are both designed to help target the sharpening at the parts of the image that most need it (edges) and restrict the sharpening effects from being applied to areas that don't (skin tone and smooth graded areas). Moving the Detail slider to the right increases the local contrast surrounding edge areas and therefore enhances the appearance of details. Moving the slider to the left decreases the effect and also reduces the appearance of halos.

The Masking control interactively applies an edge locating mask to the sharpening process. A setting of 0 applies no mask and therefore all detail in the photo is sharpened. Moving the slider to the right gradually isolates the edges within the photo until, at a setting of 100, sharpening is only being applied to the most contrasty or dominant edges in the picture.

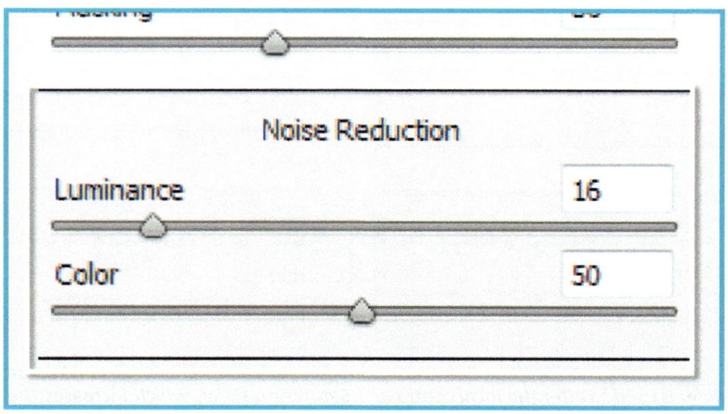

16. Reducing noise *ACR contains two different Noise Reduction controls. The Luminance Smoothing slider is designed to reduce the appearance of grayscale noise in a photo. This is particularly useful for improving the look of images that appear grainy.*

The second type of noise is the random colored pixels that typically appear in photos taken with a high ISO setting or a long shutter speed. This is generally referred to as chroma noise and is reduced using the Color Noise Reduction slider in ACR.

The noise reduction effect of both features is increased as the sliders are moved to the right.

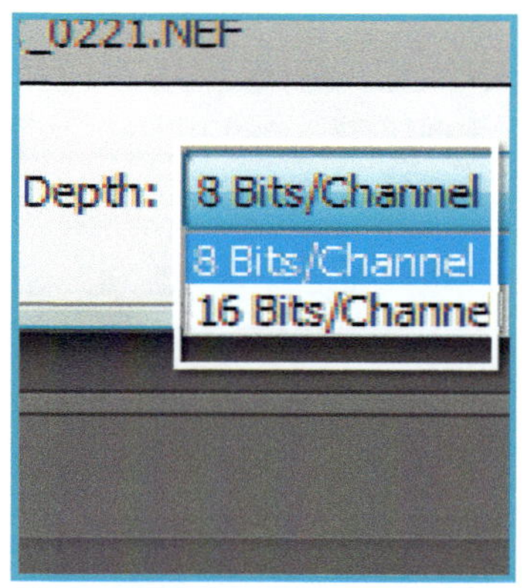

17. Color depth *The section below the main preview window in ACR contains the output options settings. Here you can adjust the color depth (8 or 16 bits per channel) of the processed file. Earlier versions of Photoshop Elements were unable to handle 16 bits per channel images but the last two releases have contained the ability to read, open, save and make a few changes to these high color files.*

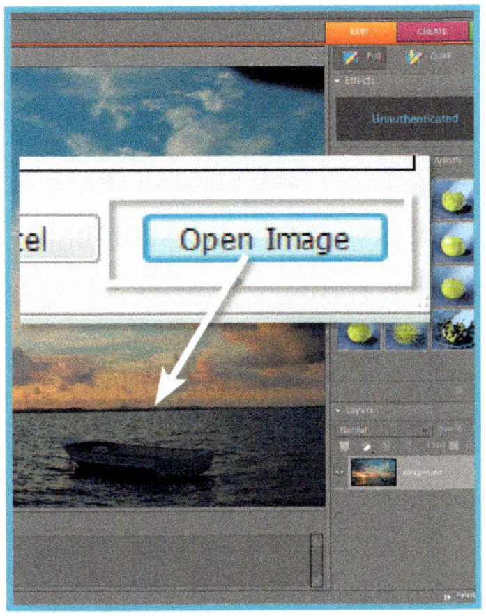

18. Opening the processed file in Photoshop Elements *The most basic option is to process the raw file according to the settings selected in the ACR dialog and then open the picture into the Editor workspace of Photoshop Elements. To do this simply select the Open Image button. Select this route if you intend to edit or enhance the image beyond the changes made during the conversion.*

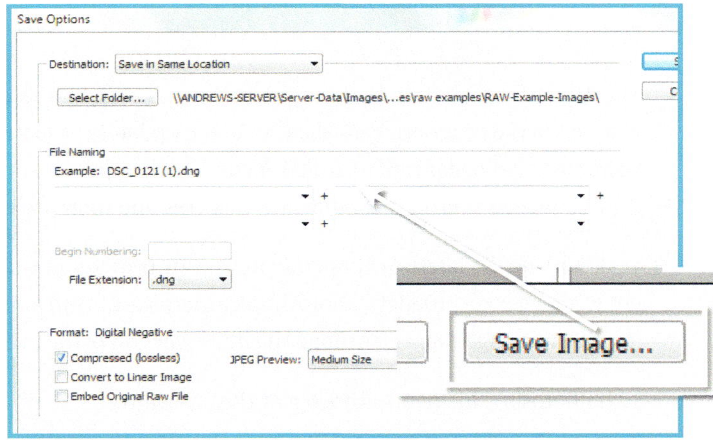

19. Saving the processed raw file *Users also have the ability to save converted raw files from inside the ACR dialog via the Save Image button. This action opens the Save Options dialog which contains settings for inputting the file name as well as file type-specific characteristics such as compression. Use the Save option over the Open command if you want to process photos quickly without bringing them into the editing space.*

Pro's Tip

Pro's tip: *Holding down the Alt key whilst clicking the Save button allows you to store the file (with the raw processing settings applied) without actually going through the Save Options dialog*

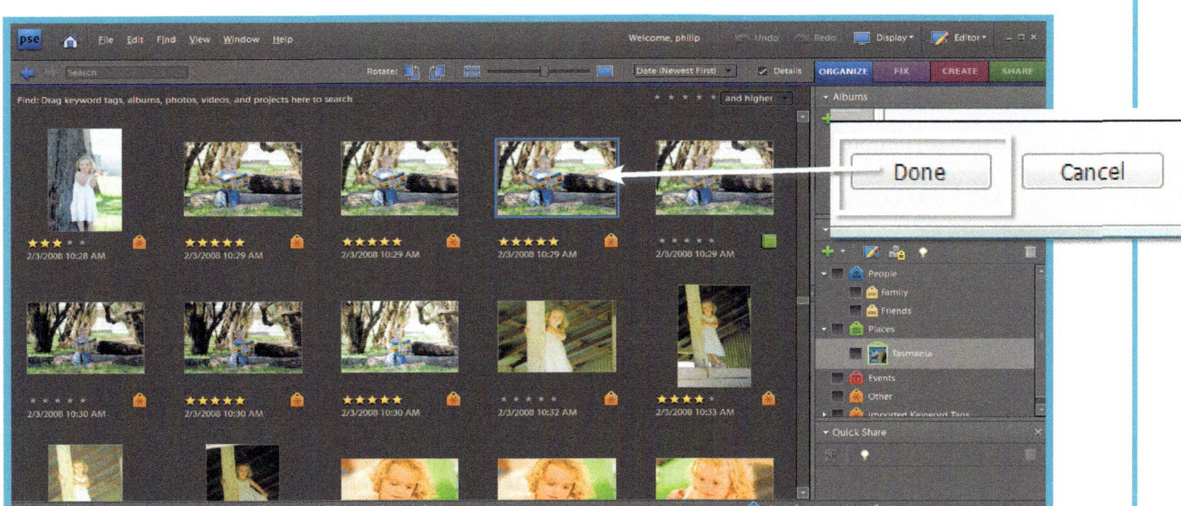

20. Applying the raw conversion settings *There is also an option for applying the current settings to the raw photo without opening the picture. By Clicking the Done button (or Alt-clicking the OK button – holding down Alt key changes the button to the Update button in previous versions of the dialog), you can apply the changes to the original file and close the ACR dialog in one step.*

The great thing about working this way is that the settings are applied to the file losslessly. No changes are made to the underlying pixels, only to the instructions that are used to process the raw file.

When next the file is opened, the applied settings will show up in the ACR dialog ready for fine-tuning, or even changing completely.

3.07 Keeping ACR up to date

Suitable for Elements – 7.0, 6.0, 5.0, 4.0, 3.0, 2.0, 1.0 | Difficulty level – Basic

The Adobe Camera Raw feature is installed as a plug-in inside Photoshop Elements when you first install the program. Periodically Adobe updates the feature releasing a new version that can be freely downloaded and installed. Typically the updates contain support for the latest digital camera models and occasionally new features and tools are included as well.

To download the latest ACR update point your browser to **www.adobe.com** (specifically http://www.adobe.com/products/photoshop/cameraRaw.html) and then look for the Adobe Camera Raw update page. Next download the latest version of the utility and install using these steps:

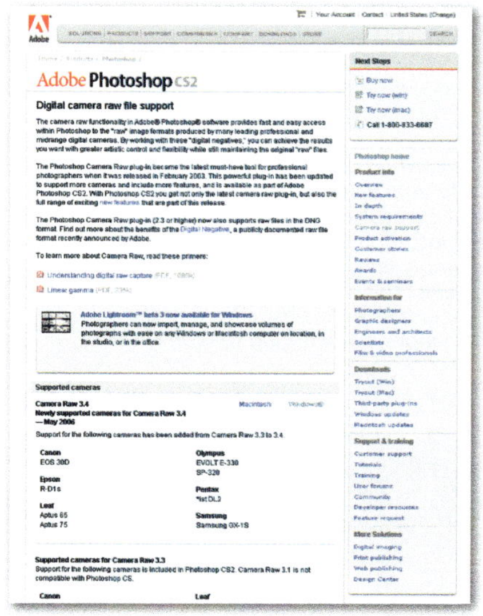

1. If Photoshop Elements is open exit the program.
2. Open the system drive (usually C:).
3. Locate the following directory:
   Program Files\Adobe\Photoshop Elements 7\Plug-Ins\File Formats
4. Find the Adobe Camera Raw.8bi file in this folder.
5. Move the plug-in to another folder and note down its new location just in case you want to restore the original settings.
6. Drag the new version of the Adobe Camera Raw plug-in, the Adobe Camera Raw.8bi file (that you downloaded), to the same directory as in Step 3.
7. Restart Photoshop Elements.

3.08 Other Raw plug-ins

Suitable for Elements – 7.0, 6.0, 5.0, 4.0, 3.0, 2.0, 1.0 | Difficulty level – Basic

Often when installing the support software that was supplied with your digital camera an extra Raw utility is installed on your computer. This can mean that after installing the camera drivers you find that you no longer have access to Adobe Camera Raw and that instead the camera-based plug-in keeps appearing when you are attempting to open Raw files. If this occurs and you want to restore ACR as the default Raw utility then you will need to remove the camera-based plug-in from the plug-ins\Adobe Photoshop Elements 7\File Formats folder in Elements and add in the Adobe Camera Raw.8bi instead.

This is a problem that is often seen with Nikon users as the NEF.8bi plug-in designed to display and adjust Nikon Raw or NEF files takes precedence over the ACR utility.

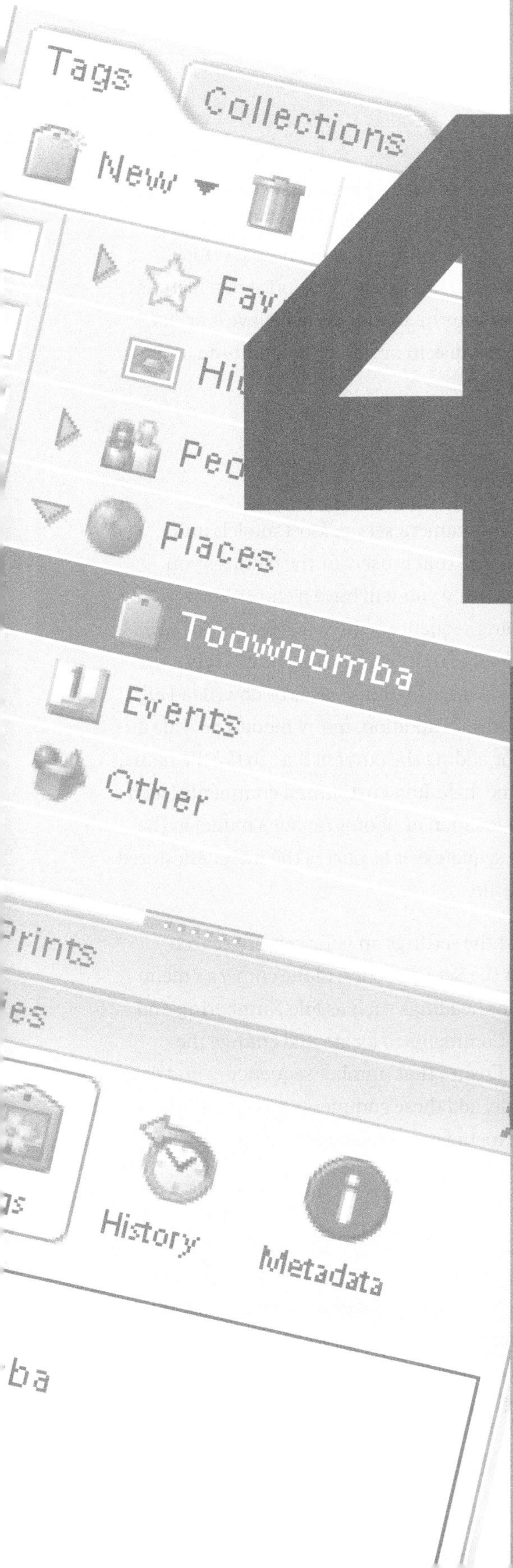

4

Photo Organization and Management

Organizing your photos with Photoshop Elements

With no film or processing costs to think about each time we take a picture, it seems that many of us are pressing the shutter more frequently than we did when film was king. The results of such collective shooting frenzies are hard drives all over the country full of photos. Which is great for photography but what happens when you want to track down that once in a lifetime shot that just happens to be one of thousands stored on your machine? Well, believe it or not, being able to locate your files quickly and easily is more a task in organization, naming and camera set up than browsing through loads of thumbnails.

4.01 Add picture details in-camera

Suitable for Elements – 7.0, 6.0, 5.0, 4.0, 3.0, 2.0, 1.0 | Difficulty level – Basic
Related techniques – 4.02, 4.03, 4.04, 4.05

Getting those pesky picture files in order starts with your camera set up. Most models and makes have options for adjusting the numbering sequence that is used for the pictures you take. Generally you will have a choice between an ongoing sequence, where no two photos will have the same number, and one that resets each time you change memory cards or download all the pictures. In addition, many models provide an option for adding the current date to the file name, with some including customized comments (such as shoot location or photographer's name) in the naming sequence or as part of the metadata stored with the file.

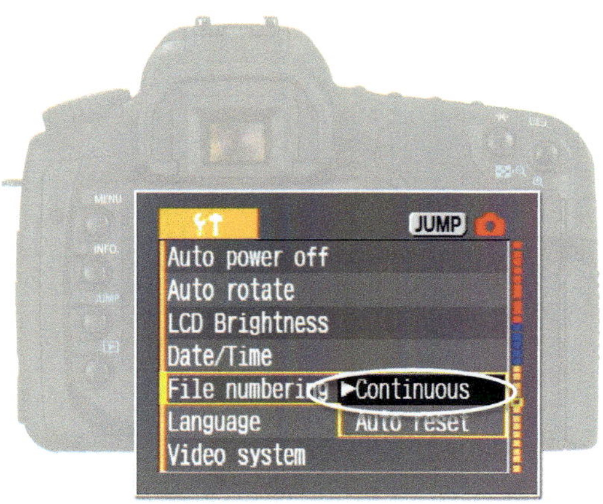

In-camera labelling >> *Most cameras provide options for selecting the way in which files are numbered. The continuous option ensures that a new number is used for each picture even if memory cards are changed in the middle of a shoot.*

To adjust the settings on your camera search through the Set Up section of the camera's menu system for headings such as File Numbering and Custom Comments to locate and change the options. Ensure that number sequencing and date inclusion options are switched on and, where available, add these comments along with the photographer's name and copyright statement to the metadata stored within the picture file.

4.02 Organize photos while downloading

Suitable for Elements – 7.0, 6.0, 5.0, 4.0, 3.0 | Difficulty level – Basic | Related techniques – 4.01, 4.03, 4.04, 4.05

As we saw in the last chapter Photoshop Elements includes the Adobe Photo Downloader utility that moves pictures from your camera or memory card to the computer. As part of the download process, the user gets to select the location of the files and the way that the files are to be named and numbered, and automatically stack, tag and apply metadata to the photos.

It is at this point in the process that you need to be careful about the type of folder or directory structure that you use. Most photographers group their images by date, subject, location or client, but the approach that you employ is up to you. Once you have selected a folder structure though, try to stick with it. Consistency is the byword of photo organization.

If your camera doesn't provide enough Automatic Naming and metadata options to satisfy your needs then use the Elements Photo Downloader feature to enhance your ability to distinguish the current images with those that already exist on your hard drive by setting the location and filename of the picture files as you transfer them.

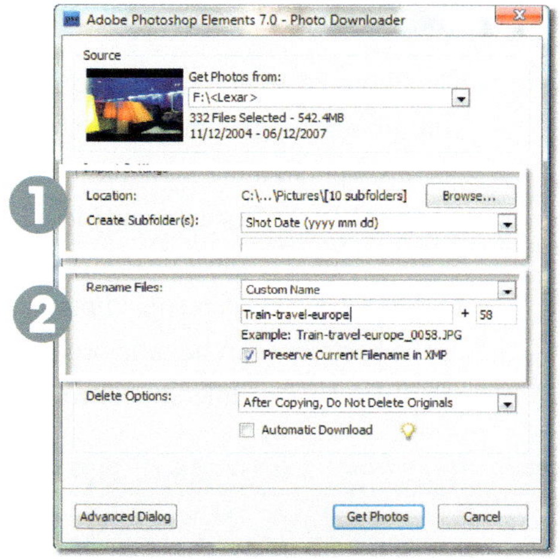

Naming via the downloader >> *Use the options in the Photo Downloader to thoughtfully locate (1) and name (2), your digital photos.*

Pro's Tip Nominate and create a new directory for each session of downloaded photos. Add extra metadata captions, keywords, photographer and copyright details using the tagging options in Elements.

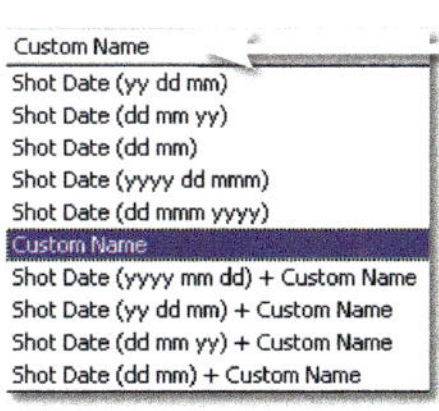

You can select from a range of different naming schemes in the Rename drop-down menu.

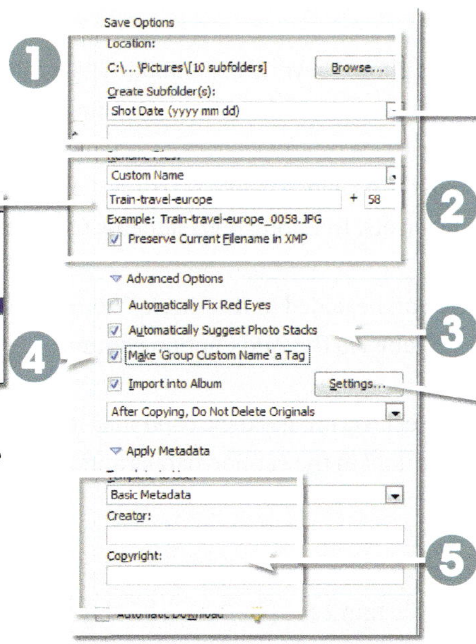

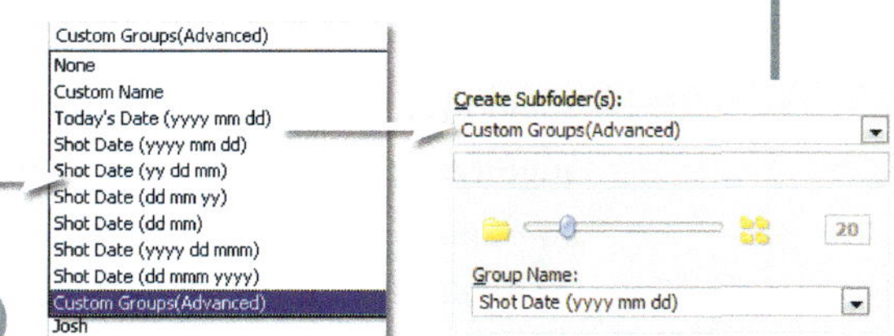

A variety of names for any subfolders that are created for the downloaded photos can also be selected. Choosing the Custom Groups (Advanced) option redisplays the thumbnails in groups based on setting of the Slider control.

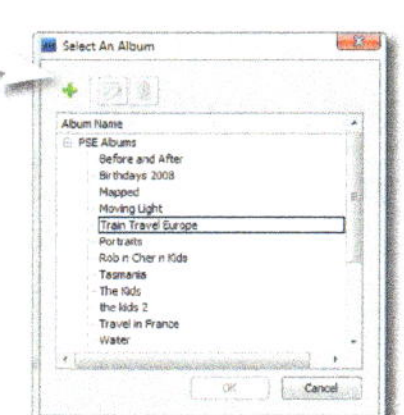

Automatically add files to a Photoshop Elements Album using the new Import to Album option.

Organize as you download >> *The Adobe Photo Downloader allows the user to automatically apply naming changes, metadata, group tags, suggest photo stacks and determine the location where transferred files will be saved. The downloader features provide five different ways to organize your pictures: (1) Locating existing, or creating new, folders for downloading. (2) Renaming pictures with meaningful titles. (3) Suggesting Photo Stack groupings. (4) Applying Group Custom Name as a Tag. (5) Adding custom metadata to the picture file which can be used as search criteria inside the Organizer workspace. New for Photoshop Elements 7.0 is the ability to add photos to an Album as they are being downloaded.*

Organizing using Photo Browser

The Photo Browser mode in the Organizer workspace not only provides thumbnail previews of your photos but the images can be categorized with different Keyword Tags, Notes and Caption entries, split in different Albums (previously Collections) and then searched based on the Keyword Tags, shot date and Metadata associated with each photo. Unlike a traditional browser system, which is folder based (i.e. it displays thumbnails of the images that are physically stored in the folder), the Elements Photo Browser creates a catalog version of the pictures and uses these as the basis for searches and organization. With this approach it is possible for one picture to be a member of many different collections and to contain a variety of different keywords.

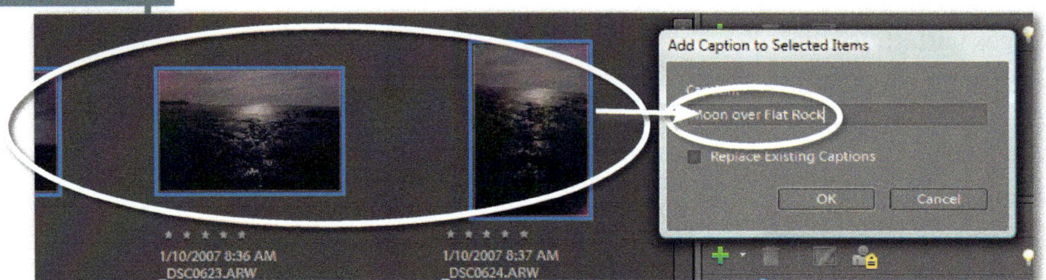

Adding captions to several photos >>
After multi-selecting pictures in the Photo Browser workspace press the Change Caption option located in the Properties palette and then add the new caption in the dialog that is displayed. These captions can be added to or used to replace existing captions.

4.03 Captioning

Suitable for Elements – 6, 5.0, 4.0, 3.0 | Difficulty level – Basic | Related techniques – 4.01, 4.02, 4.04, 4.05

Captions are another way to 'title' your photos beyond the standard file name. Adding a meaningful caption provides yet another avenue for searching for individual photos as the Find > Find by Caption or Note feature targets the entries you make here. Captions can also be used, printed or displayed in Photo Projects (but need to be added before starting the creation process) and Online Galleries as well as on contact sheets. In Photoshop Elements 6.0 captions can be added and used in a range of different ways.

Adding a single caption – Captions can be added in the Single Photo View of the Photo Browser, the Properties pane (General tab), via the Add Caption command or in the Caption field in the Date View.

Adding multiple captions – Multi-select the images to be captioned and press the Change Caption button in the Properties palette, add in the caption details and click OK.

4.04 Naming and renaming

Suitable for Elements – 6, 5.0, 4.0, 3.0 | Difficulty level – Basic | Related techniques – 4.02, 4.03, 4.04, 4.05

Along with captioning, adding logical file names to photos is probably the most popular way that photographers organize their pictures. If the downloading utility that you use doesn't provide the opportunity to rename on-the-fly, the file titles can be changed either individually, via the Name section of the Properties palette, or as a group, using the Editor: File > Rename feature or as a group in the Editor using the File Renaming section of Process Multiple Files (File > Process Multiple Files). Be sure to use a unique name for your photos and preferably one that will help you locate them later.

Changing names >> *Rename a file by selecting its thumbnail in the Photo Browser workspace and then clicking on the General tab in the Properties palette. Type in the new title for the file in the Name section of the dialog that is displayed.*

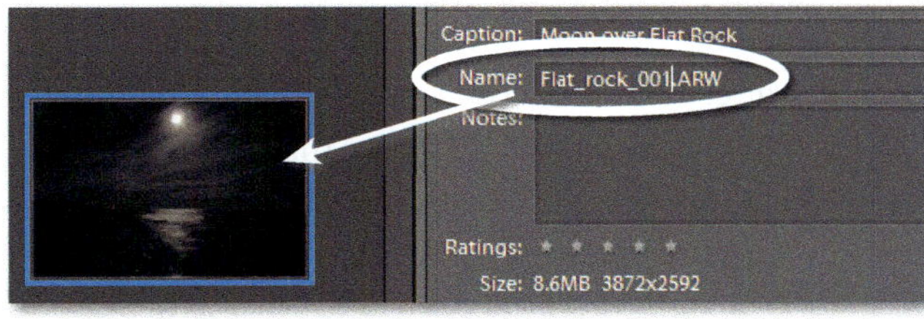

Pro's Tip: Renaming as you download

As we saw in the previous section Elements ships with a specialised transfer utility called the Adobe Photo Downloader. Designed to make the process of transferring photos from your camera, or memory card reader, more efficient, this utility also contains options for renaming of files as they are being downloaded. Here we will take a closer look at the renaming feature and, in particular, the different naming schemes that are possible.

The download contains the option of two dialogs – Standard and Advanced dialog. Both contain a drop down Rename Files menu. The renaming options revolve around three key pieces of data – the current date, the shot date, a custom name and a sub-folder name. Each menu entry uses a different combination or sequence of these details. Elements users have the choice of 21 different naming schema. Unfortunately APD doesn't include the option to create your own customized naming schema, or Template, as is available in Lightroom's own transfer utility.

It is good to see that when dates are part of the renaming process that Adobe has thought to include both US and UK based date formats. It is also very handy to have the option to include the original filename stored in the XMP data associated with the photo. XMP data is search-able via the new Search option in the Organizer's shortcuts bar.

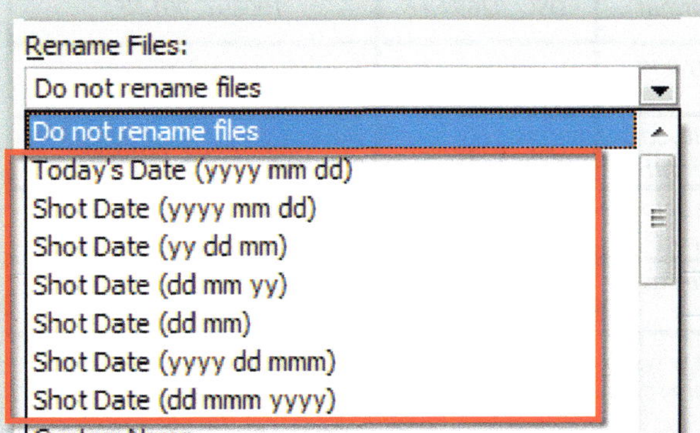

Renaming via the downloader >> *Elements users can retitle photos as they are downloading them via the Rename Files setting in the Adobe Photo Downloader utility.*

Step-by-step APD renaming:

Using a the Subfolder name

1. To create some consistency across your naming scheme some photographers will use the same title for both the download folder and the images contained within it. To do this start by selecting the Custom Name option in the Create Subfolder drop down menu.

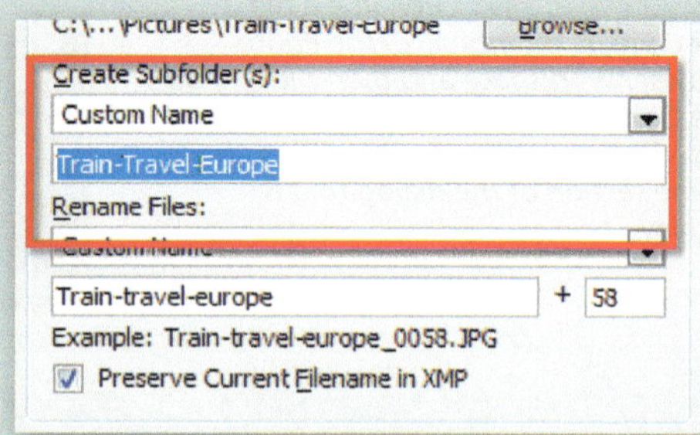

2. Next input the title you wish to use in the text box directly below the Custom Name entry. This action sets the name of the folder that will be created on your hard drive and used to store the transferred photos.

3. Now select the Same as Subfolder Name entry from the options in the Rename Files drop down menu. APD will automatically insert the Subfolder custom name in the Rename Files text box. You still have the option to choose a different starting value for the sequential number by inputting this number in the box to the right of the text.

4. Finally, double check that the naming scheme provides the results that you expect by looking at the Example entry at the bottom of the Rename Files area. This text should display the subfolder custom name, the sequential number and the file extension.

Renaming Option	Action	Original Name	After Renaming
Do not rename files	Keeps the name allocated by the camera set up	DSC_0269.NEF	DSC_0269.NEF
Today's Date (yyyymmdd)	Substitutes the computer's date	DSC_0269.NEF	20070812_001.NEF
Shot Date (yyyymmdd)	Substitutes the shot date as determined by the camera	DSC_0269.NEF	20070810_001.NEF
Shot Date (yyddmm)	Substitutes shot date with the year noted in two digits	DSC_0269.NEF	070810_001.NEF
Shot Date (ddmmyy)	Substitutes shot date in UK date format	DSC_0269.NEF	100807_001.NEF
Shot Date (ddmm)	Substitutes shot date with only day and month recorded	DSC_0269.NEF	1008_001.NEF
Shot Date (yyyyddmmm)	Substitutes shot date with four digit year, two digit date and a three letter month	DSC_0269.NEF	200710Aug_001.NEF
Shot Date (ddmmmyyyy)	Substitutes shot date with the same details above but using the UK Date format	DSC_0269.NEF	10Aug2007_001.NEF
Custom Name	Changes the file name to one that the user has entered	DSC_0269.NEF	Jills_Birthday_001.NEF

Example renaming settings >> *With 21 different ways to change the names of your photos when downloading it can be hard to know where to start. Here are some examples of the type of changes possible.*

Using a Custom name

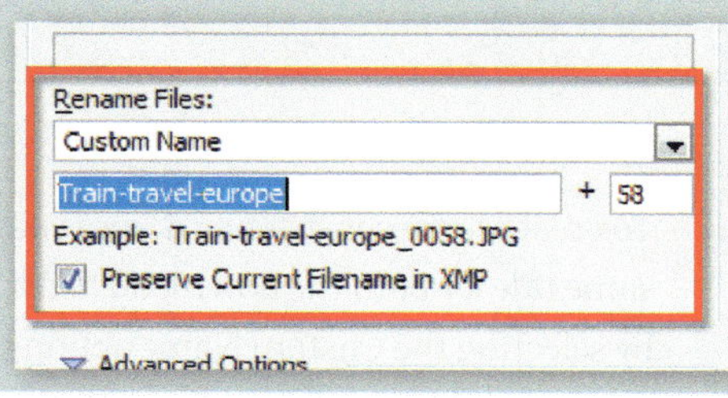

1. To substitute a custom name for the one allocated by the camera choose the Custom Name option from the Rename Files drop down menu.

2. Next input the title you wish to use in the text box directly below the Custom Name entry. At

this point you can also add a starting number for the numbering sequence that will be used if more than one image is to be renamed. Here the value is set to 58.

3. Double check that the naming scheme provides the results that you expect by looking at the Example entry at the bottom of the Rename Files area. This text should display the custom name, the sequential number and the file extension.

4.05 Tagging your photos

Suitable for Elements – 7.0, 6.0, 5.0, 4.0, 3.0 | Difficulty level – Basic | Related techniques – 4.01, 4.02, 4.03, 4.05

In Elements descriptive words can be added to your photos in the form of Keyword Tags. The Keyword Tags panel stores the entries, provides an easy drag and drop approach to adding tags to selected photos and sits on the right of the Photo Browser workspace. The panel is grouped together with the Albums (previously Collections), Quick Share and Properties panels in the new Organize pane. Tags are applied to a picture by selecting and dragging them from the pane onto the thumbnail or alternatively the thumbnail can be dragged directly onto the Tags pane. Multiple Tags can be attached to a single picture by multi-selecting the Tags first and then dragging them to the appropriate thumbnail.

FEATURE SUMMARY

1. To add a Tag to a single image click-drag the tag entry from the Keyword Tags panel to the thumbnail image in the browser (Organizer) workspace.
2. To add a single Tag to multiple thumbnails, multi-select the thumbnails in the workspace and then drag the Tag entry from the pane onto one of the selected thumbnails.

Creating new Keyword Tags

New Keyword Tags are created and added to the pane by selecting the New Keyword Tag option from the menu displayed after pressing the New button (+ icon) at the top left of the pane. Next, fill out the details of the new entry in the Create Keyword Tag dialog, select a suitable icon for the Keyword Tag label and click OK. The first picture that you drag to the new tag determines the thumbnail you see on the Tag. This is the quickest way to add an image to the Tag icon.

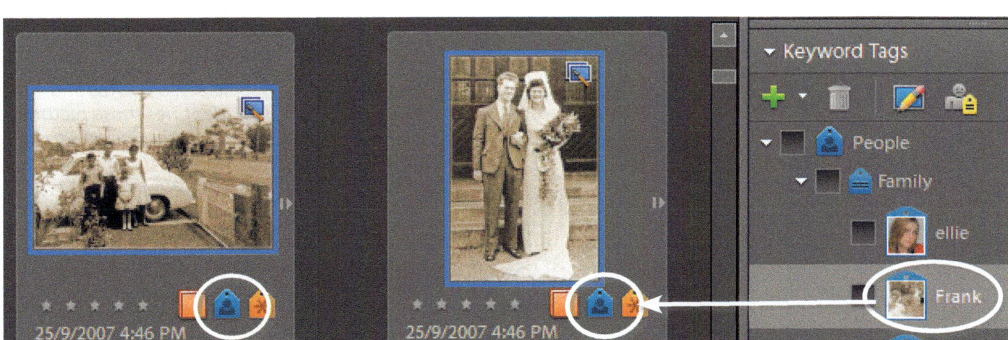

Keyword Tags and Albums >> *Keyword Tags and Albums (Collections) are used to organize the pictures in the Organizer workspace. One photo can belong to many different Albums and contain multiple Keyword Tags.*

FEATURE SUMMARY

1. To create a new Keyword Tag, select the New Tag option from the New Button (+ icon) menu at the top of the Tags pane.
2. In the Create Keyword Tag dialog that is displayed, select a category for the Tag, add in a name and include any explanatory notes.
3. Next press the Edit Icon button and import for a picture to include the Tag label before sizing and cropping the photo in the Edit Tag Icon dialog.
4. Click OK to close both dialogs and add the new entry to the Keyword Tag list.

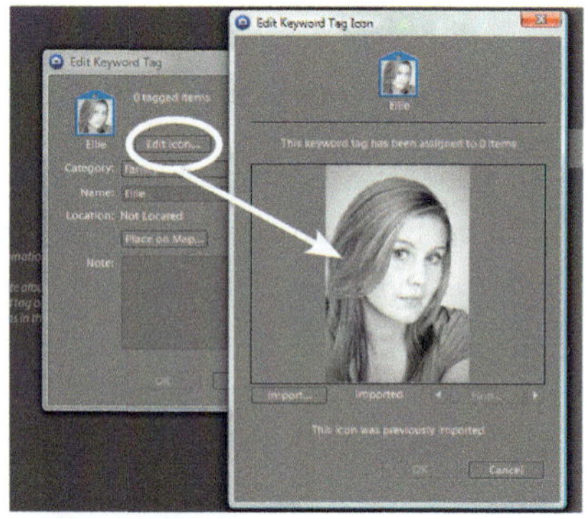

Make a new Tag >> *You can add to the existing set of Tags using the New Tag option. There is even an option to add your own pictures as the Tag icon.*

4.06 Auto Face Tagging

Suitable for Elements – 7.0, 6.0, 5.0, 4.0, 3.0 | Difficulty level – Basic | Related techniques – 4.05

First introduced in version 5.0 was the ability to search through a group of photos and automatically select those that contain faces. Using this feature makes it much easier to locate and tag photos of family and friends in the batches of pictures that you import. Start by selecting a group of photos from inside the Organizer workspace. Next, click the Find Faces for Tagging button in the Tags pane. The faces identified will be displayed in a new dialog box which also includes the Tags pane. From here your Keyword Tags can be quickly dragged onto individual or groups of selected face photos.

FEATURE SUMMARY

1. Multi-select a group of images from inside the Organizer workspace.
2. Either choose Find > Find Faces for Tagging or press the Find Faces for Tagging button at the top of the Keyword Tags pane.
3. Drag Tags onto the pictures that are displayed in the Face Tagging dialog. Click Done to return to the Photo Browser workspace.

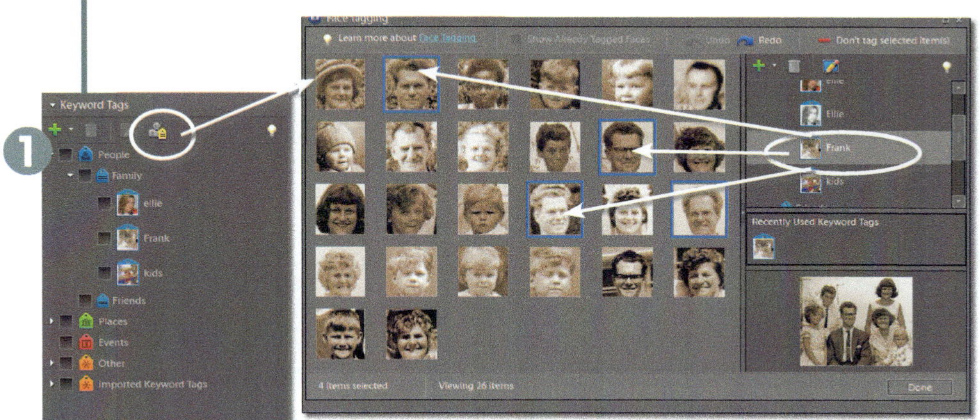

Tagging by faces >> *The Face Tagging option in Elements 6 quickly scans a group of selected photos and identifies those pictures that contain faces then displays these in a separate dialog ready for tagging.*
(1) Organizer pane.

4.07 Albums and how to group photos

Suitable for Elements – 7.0, 6.0, 5.0, 4.0, 3.0 | Difficulty level – Basic | Related techniques – 4.11, 4.12

Apart from tagging, Photoshop Elements also uses Albums (previously called Collections) as a way to organize your photos. Albums allow you to group images of a similar theme together in the one place making it easier to locate these images at a later date. After creating an Album in the Albums pane, photos can be dragged from the Photo Browser workspace to the Album heading to be added to the group, or alternatively the Album entry can be dragged to the photo to produce the same result. The Albums feature allows you to allocate the same image to several different groups. Unlike in the old days, this doesn't mean that the same file is duplicated and stored multiple times in different folders. Instead the picture is only stored or saved once and a series of Album associations is used to indicate its membership in different groups.

When you want to display the contents of an Album just click the entry in the pane and the program searches through its database of collection keywords and only shows those images that meet your search criteria. The Albums pane is the pivot point for all your grouping activities. Here you can view, create, rename and delete Albums. Albums are part of the Organize pane, which you can show by choosing Window > Show Task Pane then clicking the blue Organize tab. Alternatively, the Task Pane can be hidden or shown by clicking on the vertical resize bar on the left edge of the pane.

In Elements 7.0 Albums can be synchronized/backed up online via an active Photoshop.com account.

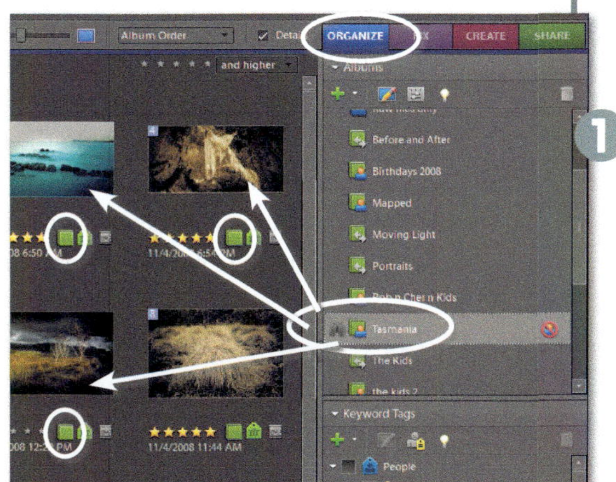

Grouping with Albums >> *Sort your pictures into groups of the same subject or theme using the Elements' Albums feature. (1) Album Pane.*

Adding photos to an Album

To start using Albums make a new Album entry first and then add your photos to it.

FEATURE SUMMARY

1. Start making a new Album by clicking on the New button (+ icon) in the Albums pane and select the New Album menu item. In the Create Album dialog choose the group that the new album will belong to, add the name and include any explanation details for the group. Click OK.
2. Select the photos to be included in the album in the Photo Browser and drag them to the Album heading in the Albums pane.
3. To view all the pictures contained in an album double-click on the Album heading or click near the album's thumbnail. A Binoculars icon will appear.
4. Single photos or even groups of pictures can be added to more than one album at a time by multi-selecting the album names first (use Ctrl–click to multi-select Albums without displaying their contents) before dragging the images to the pane.

Using Album groups

Different albums (and the photos they contain) can also be organized into groups that have a common interest or theme. For instance, albums that contain pictures of the kids, family vacations, birthday parties and mother- and father's-days events can all be collated under a single 'Family' Album Group heading.

Create an Album group by selecting the New Album Group option from the New menu (+ icon) in the Album Pane. Next, click-drag existing album entries listed in the pane to the Album Group heading. Alternatively, create the Album Group entry first and then create new albums selecting the new Album Group in the Create Album dialog. This will automatically add the new Album under the group heading in the Album pane.

The Album Advantage

The advantage of using an album over just viewing tagged files in the Photo Browser is that files in an album can be reordered by dragging them. Each member image of the Album is displayed with a small sequence number in the upper left of the thumbnail indicating the position in the Album order. The image sequence arranged in an Album is respected when the photos are used in the production of Elements' creation projects such as Photo Books, Online Albums and Slide Shows. Files in the Photo Browser window cannot be reordered in this way.

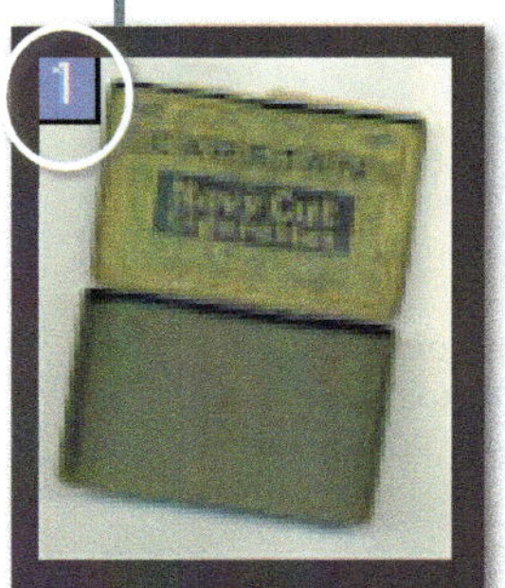

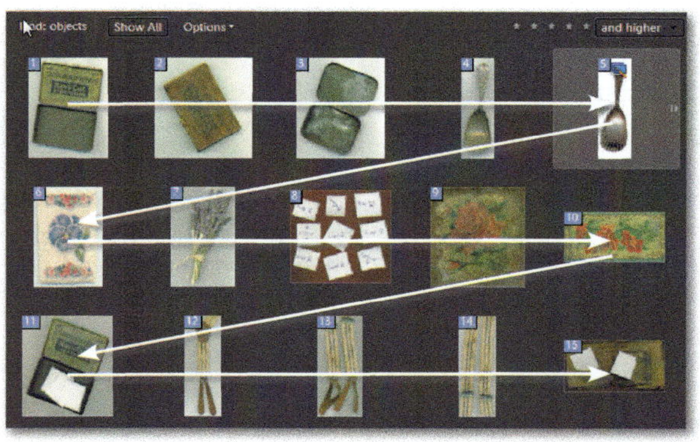

Sequencing with Albums >>
Placing images in an Album has the advantage that the photos can be arranged in a set sequence. The power of this ability is that the order is respected when the photos are incorporated into Elements projects.

Pro's Tip: Add photos to Albums as you download

Many photographers see the task of organizing their photos with features such as keywords and albums as tasks that just detract from the real work of editing and enhancing the images. It's true that that image management is not nearly as exciting as creating, editing and printing photos but you will quickly find that a little time spent arranging your photos will reap rewards later when you are trying to locate the best of your images.

For this reason, I always rejoice when Adobe adds an auto option to Elements that makes my management tasks less painful. New for Photoshop Elements is the ability to add photos to Albums as they are transferred from camera card to computer. This is terrific as, used

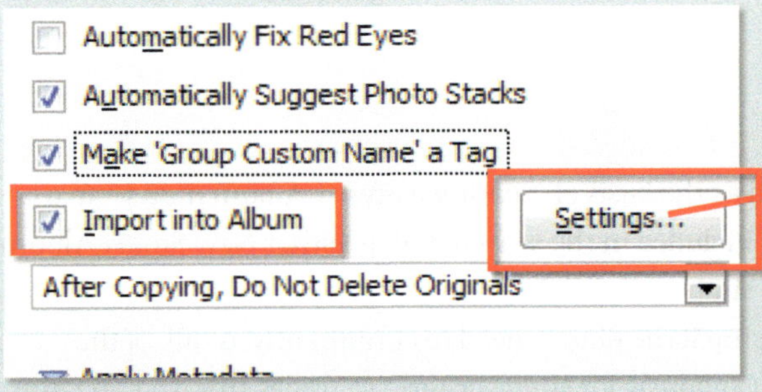

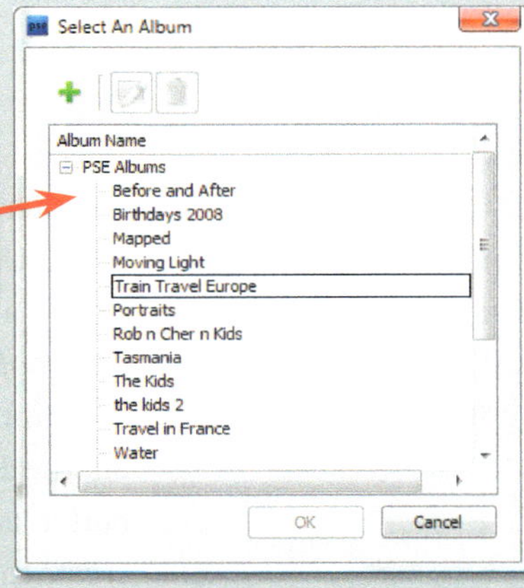

Auto Album addition >> *Use the new Import into Album option available in the Advanced dialog of the Adobe Photo Downloader to add the files you transfer to specific Elements Albums.*

correctly, this new feature can save you loads of time that you would use to manually add images to albums. The new Import to Album feature is located in the Advanced dialog of the Adobe Photo Downloader and is used in the following way:

1. After selecting the Import Into Album option in the Advanced dialog of the Adobe Photo Downloader, press the Settings button to display the Select an Album window.

2. Here you can choose which Album to add the photos to. The window also contains buttons to add new tags, edit the name of tags and delete tags. The edit and delete options are only available when selecting empty Albums that have been added in the window.

3. After setting up a new Album for the download, clicking OK will close the Settings window and Get Photos will download the pictures and add them to the new Album.

4. If you only want a selection of all the images stored in the camera, or located on the memory card, to be added to a specific album, then use the checkbox at the bottom right of each thumbnail to include or exclude the photo from both download and being added to the album.

4.08 Using Smart Albums

Suitable for Elements – 7.0, 6.0, 5.0, 4.0, 3.0 | Difficulty level – Basic | Related techniques – 4.06, 4.07

Adobe introduced a new album type in Photoshop Elements 6.0 called Smart Albums. Images are included in a Smart Album based on one or more search criteria established at the time that the album is created. Each time the Smart Album entry is selected Elements automatically adds any new photos that meet the criteria to the group. Smart Albums are a great way to keep important collections of images up to date without the need to manually find and add images to the album.

You can create Smart Albums either via the New Smart Album entry in the new album pop-up menu (click the '+' button at the top of the panel to display), or by executing a search using the Find > By Details (Metadata) feature. Both avenues provide the user with the chance to choose the search criteria used for the basis of the Smart Album. With the Find > By Details option, it is necessary to select the Save this Search Criteria as Smart Album setting at the bottom of the dialog before starting the search.

Establishing search criteria

The idea of setting up specific search criteria as the basis of creating a Smart Album may seem a little daunting, but the range of possibilities included in the search dialog, either New Smart Album, or the Find by Details, makes the process as simple as selecting options from several drop-down menus. With the dialog open, start by choosing if the photos need to contain any, or all, of the search criteria to be included in the album. Obviously for single criteria searches this isn't an issue, but the dialog allows the user to add several criteria (click the '+' button at the right end of the criteria entry) for searching. Next, create the basis for the search by selecting the criteria.

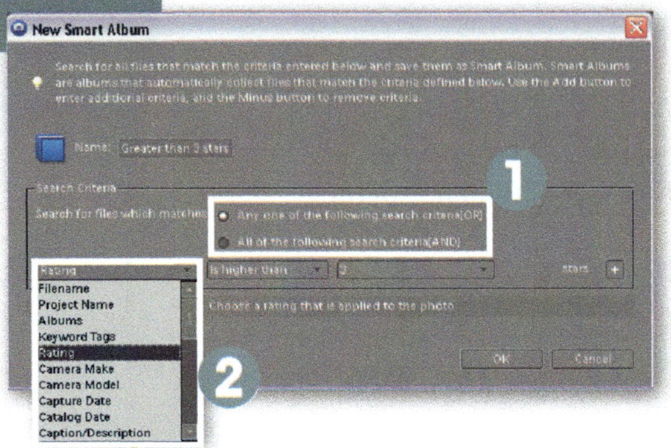

Smart Album creation >> *To set up the search criteria used for a Smart Album pick the matching option first (1) and then the criteria from the drop-down menus (2).*

There are no less than 30 different criteria that can be used for the search. These include most camera settings (sometimes called EXIF data) such as lens, ISO, F-stop and Shutter Speed, individual photo details including file size, pixel dimensions and filename as well as Elements-specific criteria like keyword tags, project name, version set, project type or even map location. Once you are comfortable with creating search criteria the whole Smart Album system provides a very powerful and efficient way to locate and manage groups of images in your catalog.

Creating a new Smart Album

There are three ways to create Smart Albums in Elements. The first is via the options in the Album panel.

FEATURE SUMMARY

1. Start by selecting the New Smart Album entry from the menu displayed by clicking on the '+' button in the Albums panel.
2. Next, add in a name for the album in the text box at the top of the New Smart Album dialog.
3. Choose how the files will match the criteria. You can select between matching **any** of the criteria or **all** of the criteria.
4. Now start with the drop-down menu on the left of the dialog and select the criteria group to use for the search, i.e. Filename, Project Name, Keyword Tags, Camera Model, etc.
5. Depending which entry you choose in the first menu the number of menus (and their content) on the right will change accordingly. The entries in these menus are designed to refine the search. For instance, if you choose the Project Type as your main search criteria then you will have a second menu containing Gallery, Photo Book and Slideshow.
6. With one criteria established you can add other criteria by clicking the '+' button on the right of the Search entry. This displays a new search criteria menu set.

Using Find to make Smart Albums

The second way to create Smart Albums in Elements is to use the search abilities in the Find > By Details (Metadata).

FEATURE SUMMARY

1. Select the By Metadata entry from the Find menu to display the Find by Details dialog. Input the match option and search criteria in the same way as outlined in steps 3–6 above.
2. Next, select the Save this Search Criteria as Smart Album option at the bottom of the dialog. This makes the Name text box active. Add a title for the New Smart Album here.

Naming, Album and Tagging strategies

The best way that you choose to make use of the Keyword Tagging and Album features in Elements will depend a great deal on the way that you work, the pictures you take and the type of content that they include, but here a few different proven methods that you can use as a starting point.

Subject:

Photos are broken down into subject groups using headings such as family, friends, holidays, work, summer, night shots, trip to Paris, etc. This is the most popular and most applicable approach for most readers and should be the method to try first.

Time line:

Images are sorted and stored based on their capture date (when the picture was photographed), the day they were downloaded or the date that they were imported into the organizational package. This way of working links well with the auto file naming functions available with most digital cameras but can be problematic if you can't remember the approximate dates that important events occurred. Try using the date approach as a sub-category for subjects headings, e.g. Bill's Birthday > 2005.

File type:

Image groups are divided into different file type groups. Although this approach may not seem that applicable at first glance it is a good way to work if you are in the habit of shooting RAW files which are then processed into PSD files before use.

Project:

This organizational method works well for the photographer who likes to shoot to a theme over an extended period of time. All the project images, despite their age and file type, are collated in the one spot making for ease of access.

Client or Job:

Many working pros prefer to base their filing system around the way that their business works, keeping separate groups for each client and each job undertaken for each client.

Smart Albums via the new Search feature

The Adobe guys decided to include a new Search feature in the shortcuts bar at the top of the Organizer workspace. Like other such features typically found in computer operating systems this dedicated search box provides a speedy way to locate images based on a text entries associated with an image. This information may be stored in the filename, as a keyword or as part of the EXIF data for the photo.

Elements refines the results of the search as you type. Locating pictures in this way has the added bonus that the search term that you employed can be used to create a new Smart Album.

1 Start by typing the search term into the new text box located on the left of the Shortcuts bar. You may need to try a range of different search terms.

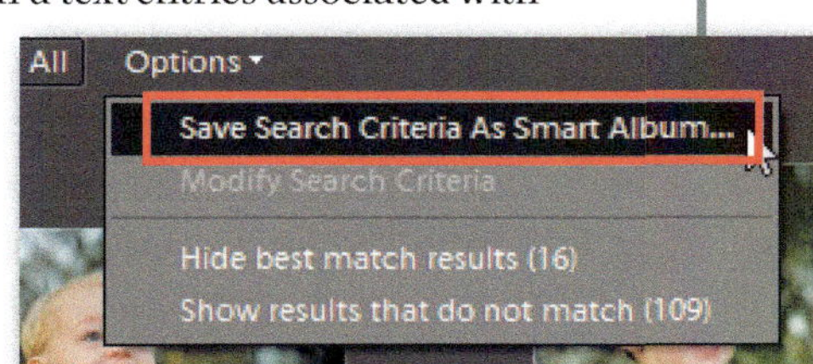

Search results become Albums >> Use the criteria for the new search feature as the basis of a new Smart Album.

2 Once the correct photos are displayed in the Organizer workspace choose the Save Search Criteria As Smart Album entry from the Options menu.

Converting Keyword Tags to Smart Albums

The last way to create Smart Albums is to use existing Keyword Tags as the basis for creating a new Smart Album.

FEATURE SUMMARY

1 After clicking the Keyword Tag entry to display the images containing the tag, choose the Save Search Criteria As Smart Album entry from the Options menu at the top left of the workspace.

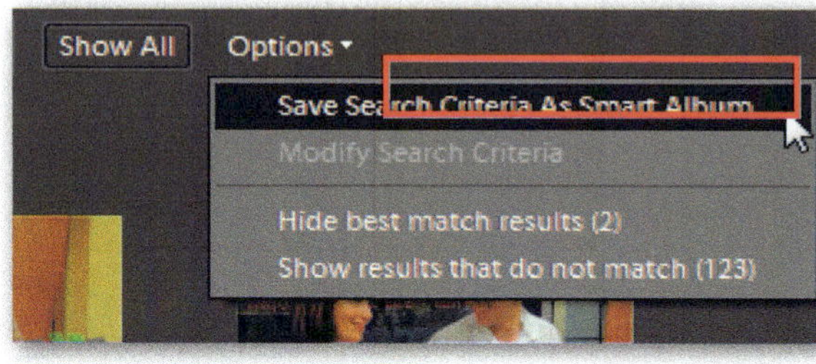

Keywords become Albums >> Click onto the Keyword Tag entry to display the pictures with the associated keyword then choose the Save Search Criteria As Smart Album entry from the Options menu.

4.09 Synchronizing and Backing Up Albums

Suitable for Elements – 7.0 | Difficulty level – Medium | Related techniques – 4.07, 4.08

In Photoshop Elements 7.0, Adobe introduces a new option for synchronizing the albums you create in the Organizer workspace with copies stored at Photoshop.com. This feature means that not only can you share your Elements pictures via the web using the Online Albums, but you also have a secure backup of your photos as well. Now before we start, it is important to realize a couple of facts about working with synchronized albums:

- You need to have an active Photoshop.com account before being able to backup/synchronize your photos,
- Smart Albums cannot be synchronized,
- The Web Galleries feature found in previous versions of Elements has been replaced by 'Online Albums' which is part of the new synchronized album feature, and
- You need a good internet connect if you are wanting to sync more than just a few pictures.

Signing up for a Photoshop.com account is an easy process and can be initiated from either the Photoshop Elements 7.0 Welcome Screen or by visiting Photoshop.com. There are two levels of membership, Standard, which provides the user with webspace, a dedicated web address (URL), tutorials and access to the features of the website and online links from inside Photoshop Elements, and Plus, which gives the user more storage space for photos and albums and extra tutorials, artwork and themes for use with Elements' projects. Once you have signed up, you can log in at the home screen each time you start Elements, which in turn will give you access to all the features of the Photoshop.com website.

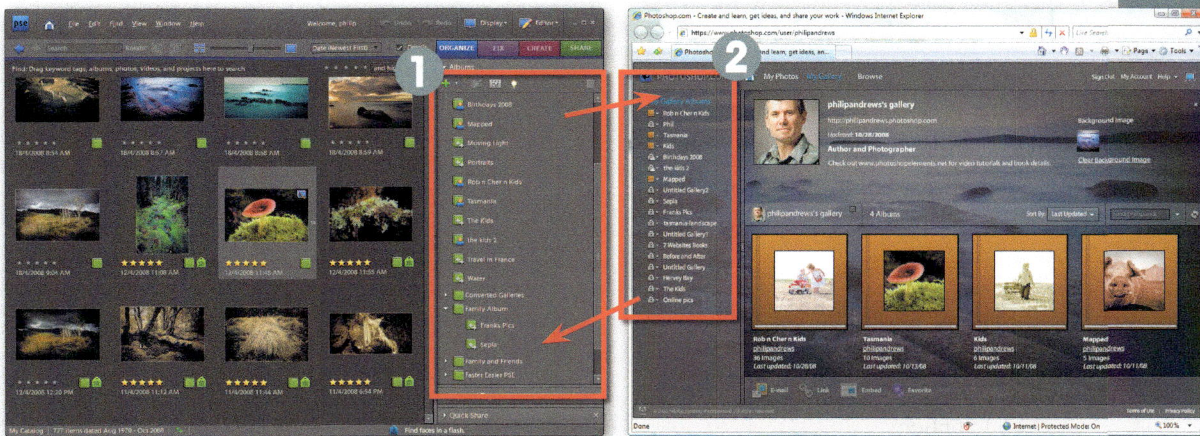

Synchronizing Photoshop.com and Photoshop Elements >> *New for version 7.0 is the ability to synchronize/backup Elements' albums to Photoshop.com. In the screenshots above you can see the Album list from Elements (1) duplicated in the Photoshop.com account (2). Synchronized Albums can be created in Elements or online.*

Rather than synchronizing your whole Photoshop Elements Catalog, the new synchronization system uses Albums which are common to both Photoshop.com and the Organizer. The Welcome screen in version 7.0 contains a series of new online options that are available to registered Elements users. One of these options is titled Backup Settings. Clicking this entry will display the Backup/Synchronization section of the Elements' Preferences dialog. This window can also be displayed by selecting the Preferences entry from the Edit screen in the Organizer workspace or by clicking the Backup/Synchronization preferences button at the top of the Albums pane.

The settings contained here allow you to turn the synchronization feature on and off, choose for all new albums to synchronized online by default, options for resolving synchronization conflicts and scenarios when you delete photos online as well as maximum size files included in the synchronization process. The dialog also provides a visual summary of the albums that are currently stored in both locations and whether they are synchronized, a space usage meter and the option to upgrade your membership to access more backup space and exclusive Elements tips and techniques.

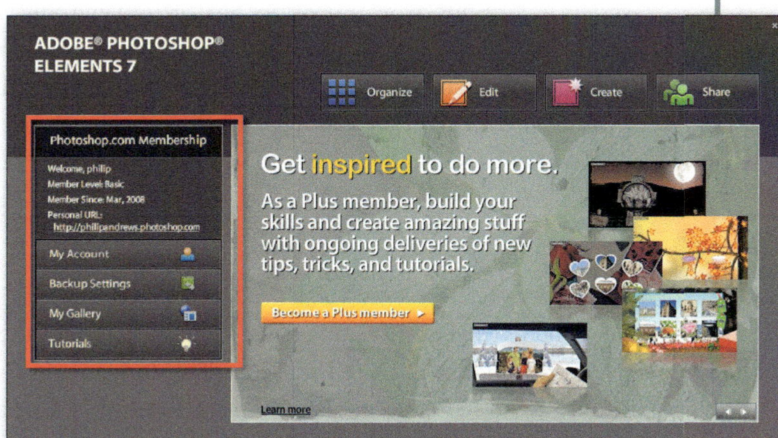

Sign In at the Home Screen >> *You can sign up and sign in to use the new online options available in version 7.0 of Photoshop Elements at the Home screen that is displayed when first starting the program. Here you have options for adjusting you account and backup (synchronization) settings as well as quick links to any web galleries you are hosting at Photoshop.com. The last option available at the Home screen is a link to the new Inspirational Browser where authors like myself post video and step by step tutorials about how to get the most out of Elements.*

Creating a Synchronized Album

FEATURE SUMMARY

1. Start by selecting the New Album entry from the menu displayed by clicking on the '+' button in the Albums panel.
2. Next, add in a name for the album in the text box at the top of the New Album dialog.
3. Select the Backup/Synchronize option.
4. Complete the rest of the dialog settings, drag images from the Photo Browser workspace to the Items area and click the Done button to finish.
5. Alternatively, click the Share button to create a styled web gallery from the images in the new album.

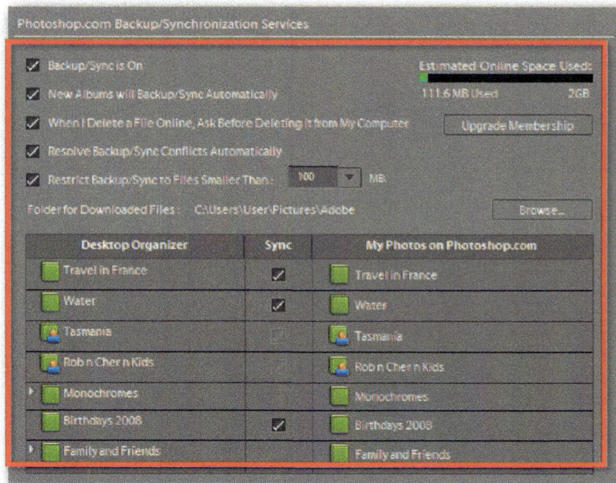

Synchronization settings >> *The options for the new backup feature are grouped together in the Backup/Synchronization Services section of the Photoshop Elements Preferences.*

When the backup/synchronization feature is active on your computer a new icon is added to your system tray. Called the Sync Monitor, right-clicking on the icon will display several options which indicate the current status of the feature. If the Pause or Stop entries are shown, then the sync system is currently active. Choosing the Backup/Sync only when Idle option restricts update activity (which occurs via an active internet connection) to times when the connection is not being used by other programs such as a web browser or email program. There is also another version of the Sync Monitor located in the bottom left of the Organizer workspace. Here there are options for viewing backup, not backed files as well as those that are waiting ('pending') to be backup.

4.10 Changing your view

Suitable for Elements – 7.0, 6.0, 5.0, 4.0, 3.0 | Difficulty level – Basic
Related techniques – 4.11

Your photos can be viewed in a range of different ways in the Organizer or Photo Browser workspace. The standard view (**Photo Browser View**) displays the pictures as a series of thumbnails in a 'rows and columns' format. You can sort the sequence of the photos according to date and import batch or folder location using the drop-down menu at the bottom left of the workspace. It is also possible to display only those images with a specific associated Tag or belonging to a particular collection by double-clicking on the entry in Keyword Tags or Albums or clicking on the column on the left of the palette.

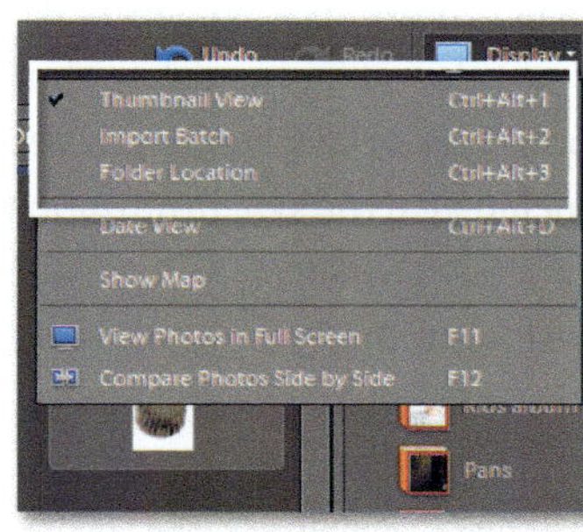

Selecting the View >> *Choosing one of the options from the drop-down Display menu at the end of the Photo Browser options bar, determines how the pictures are presented in the workspace.*

Another option is to view the photos in **Date View** mode. Here the images are also grouped and displayed based on the date they were taken, but they are shown in a calendar format. You can choose a year-, month- or day-based calendar with each view containing a slide show feature that will automatically flick through all the photos taken on a specific date. Pictures displayed in Date View can be edited, printed, shared and included in Photo Creation projects by clicking one of the shortcut buttons at the top of the screen.

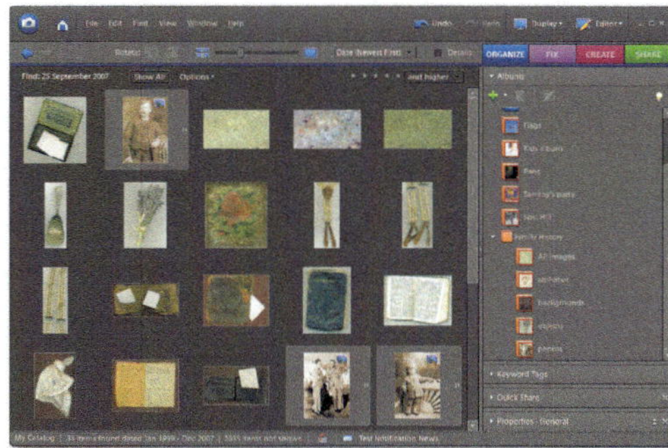

Photo Browser View >>

The **View Photos in Full Screen** option provides an instant slide show of the files that you have currently displayed in the Photo Browser. Seeing the photos full size on your machine is a good way to edit the shots you want to keep from those that should be placed in the 'I will remember not to do that next time' bin. With the provided menu you can play, pause, or advance to next or last photos, using the VCR-like controls. You can enlarge or reduce the size that the picture appears on screen with the Magnification slider (Zoom Level control). For quick magnification changes there are also 'Fit to Window' and 'Actual Pixels' buttons. But the real bonus of the feature is the list of actions that you can perform to pictures you review. You can automatically enhance, add and remove tags, mark the file for printing and add the file to a chosen collection using the choices listed under the Action menu. Specific picture properties such as Tag, History, and Metadata are available by hitting the Alt + Enter keys to display the properties window. As well as showing all the photos currently in the browser you can also multi-select the images to include in the review session before starting the feature, or even limit those pictures displayed to a particular collection. The Full Screen View options can be set when the feature is first opened or accessed via the last item on the Action menu.

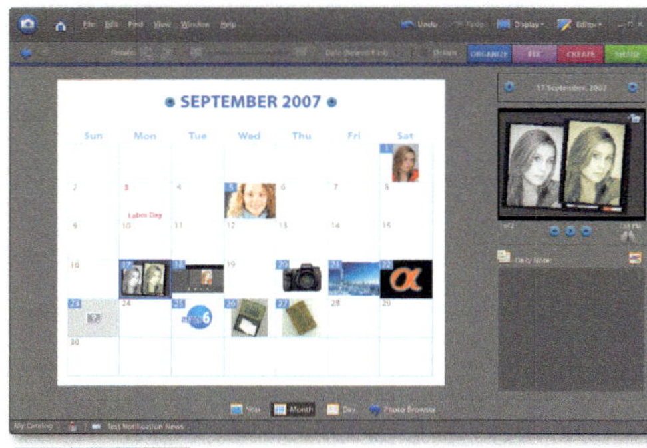

Date View >>

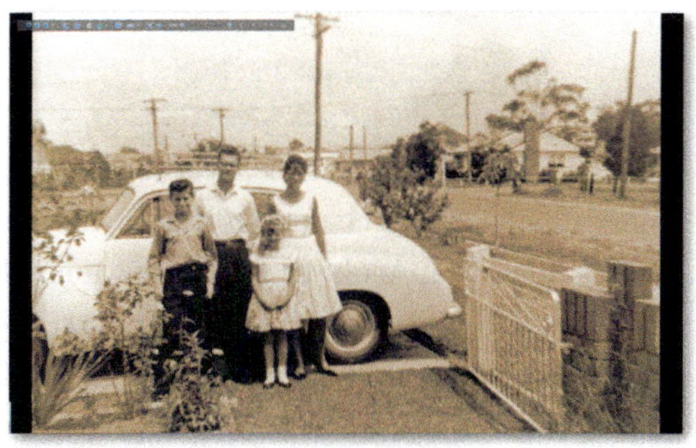

View Photos in Full Screen mode >>

Closely linked to the View Photos in Full Screen feature detailed above is the **Compare Photos Side by Side** option which allows users to display two similar pictures side by side. This is a great way to choose

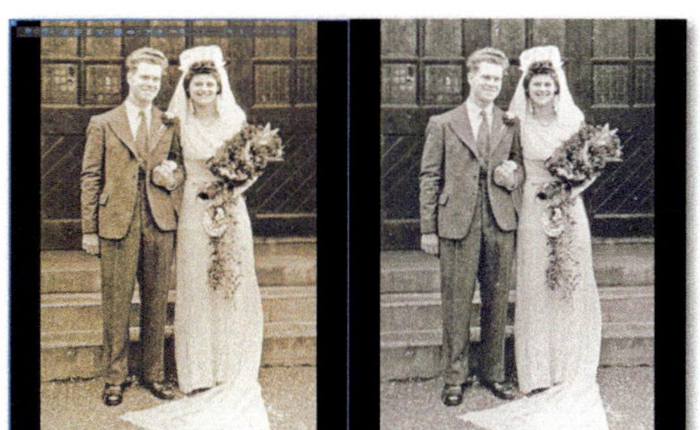

Compare Photos Side by Side mode >>

between several images taken at the same time to ensure that the best one is used for printing or passed on to the Editor for enhancement. To select the images to display click onto one of the compare workspaces and then click on a thumbnail. Now select the other workspace and click the comparison image thumbnail. Pressing the X key switches the photos in the display so that you can always keep the best images on the left of the screen as you flip through other photos on the right. All the same Full Screen adjustment and organizational controls are available in the Compare Photos feature, including the Zoom Control which provides the ability to examine candidate files more closely.

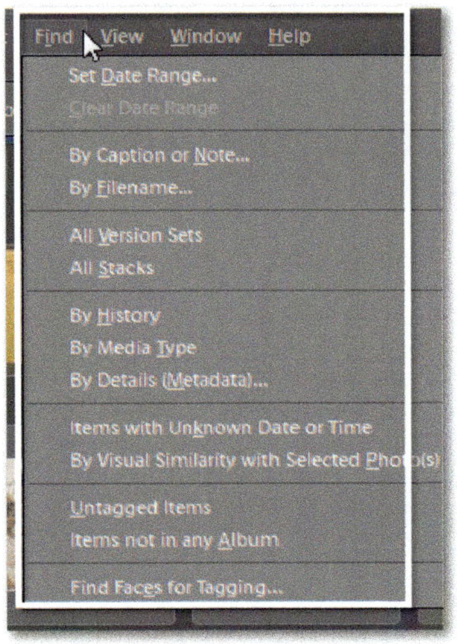

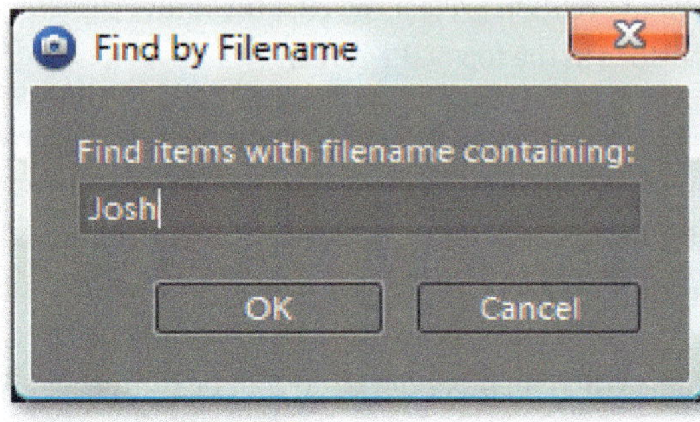

Locate by filename >> *When choosing the Date Range, Caption or Note, Filename (see above), History, and Details find options Elements displays a new dialog into which your search criteria can be entered.*

Find options >> *The Find menu in the Photo Browser workspace lists the many different ways to locate images within Elements.*

4.11 Locating files

Suitable for Elements – 7.0, 6.0, 5.0, 4.0, 3.0 | Difficulty level – Basic | Related techniques – 4.08

One of the great benefits of organizing your pictures in the Photo Browser workspace is the huge range of search options that then become available to you. In fact there are so many search options that Adobe created a new menu heading 'Find' specifically to hold all the choices. Here you will be able to search for your photos based on a selected date range, filename, caption, media type (video, photo, audio or creation), history (when an item was emailed, printed, received, imported, used in a creation project or even shared on-line) and even by the predominant color in the photo. After selecting one of the Find menu options Elements either displays files that meet the search criteria in a new view of the same window (Find by Version Sets, Media Type, Untagged Items) or opens a new dialog where the user must enter specific details (dates, filenames, details, captions) which will be used to base the search.

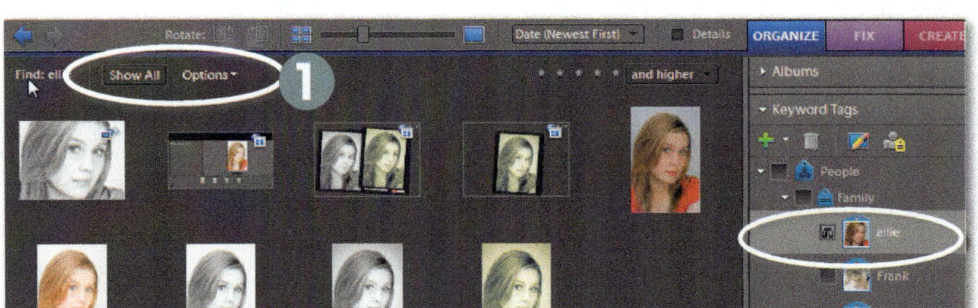

Locate tagged photos >> *To display all images tagged with a specific entry, click the Tag name in the Tags pane. Return the view to the whole collection by clicking the Show All photos button (1).*

Finding tagged photos or those contained in an Album

As well as the search options located in the Organizer: Find menu, you can make use of the Keyword Tags and Albums features to quickly locate and display sets of photos from your catalog.

To find tagged photos: Click the Keyword Tag entry in the Keyword Tags pane.

To display all the images in a collection: Click on the Album entry in the Albums pane or click on the column on the left of the pane. This will display the Binoculars icon.

To return the browser back to the original catalog of thumbnails: Click on the Show All Photos button at the top of the thumbnail group.

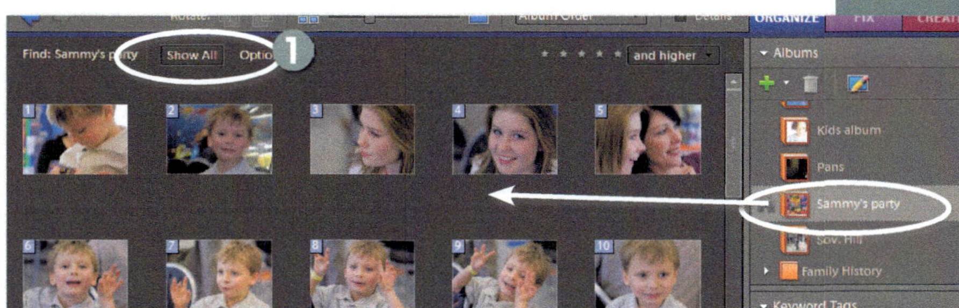

Finding Albums >> *To show all the photos in an album click the Album name in the Album Pane. Again, press the Show All Photos button to return to the catalog (1).*

Find by details or metadata

Version 6.0 of Elements also contains a Find option that is designed to allow users to search the details or metadata that is attached to their picture files. Most digital cameras automatically store shooting details from the time of capture within the photo document itself. Called metadata, you can view this information by clicking the Metadata button inside the Properties palette.

The Find > By Details (Metadata) option displays a sophisticated Search dialog that allows you to nominate specific criteria to use when looking within the metadata portion of the picture file. The dialog provides a section to input the text to search for as well as two drop-down menus where you can set where to look (Filename, Camera Make, Camera Model, Capture Date, etc.) and how to match the search text (Starts with, Ends with, Contains, etc.).

Beyond camera-based metadata you can also use this dialog to search for any Captions, Notes, Keyword Tags or Albums that you have applied to your pictures.

FEATURE SUMMARY

1. Select Find > By Details (Metadata) from the Photo Browser workspace.
2. Choose the type of details that you are looking for – Filename, Camera Make, Camera Model, etc. from the drop-down list in the Find by Details dialog.
3. Enter the text you want to search for (if needed).
4. Enter how the search text should appear in the located files (contained, not contained, etc.)

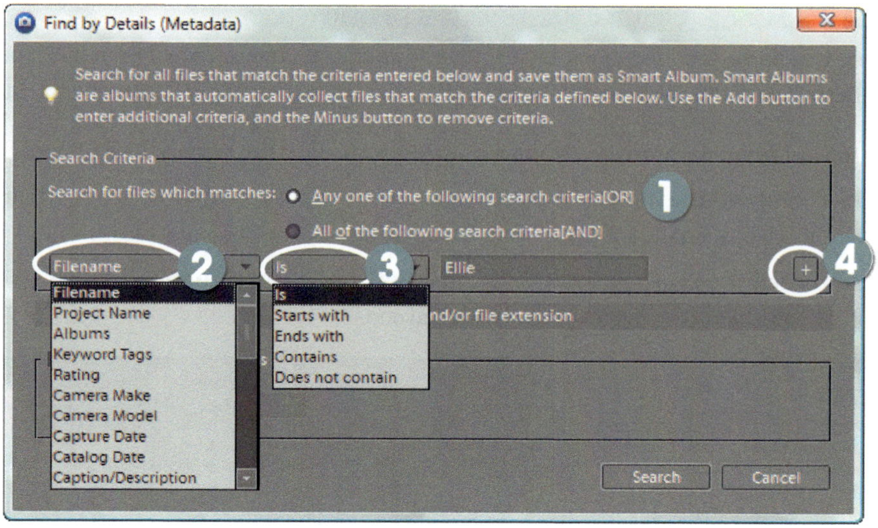

Find using details >> *The Find by Details feature allows you to customize the search options used via settings within the dialog. Choosing the type of detail to look for from the drop-down list (1) determines the contents of the rest of the dialog. In this instance selecting 'Filename' displays a second list (2) describing how to match the text you input (3). Extra search criteria can be added or removed by pressing the Plus or Minus buttons to the right of the dialog (4).*

Protecting your assets

Ensuring that you keep up-to-date duplicates of all your important pictures is one of the smartest work habits that the digital photographer can learn. Ask yourself 'What images can't I afford to lose – either emotionally or financially?' The photos you include in your answer are those that are in the most need of backing up. If you are like most image-makers then every picture you have ever taken (good and bad) has special meaning and therefore is worthy of inclusion. So let's assume that you want to secure all the photos you have accumulated.

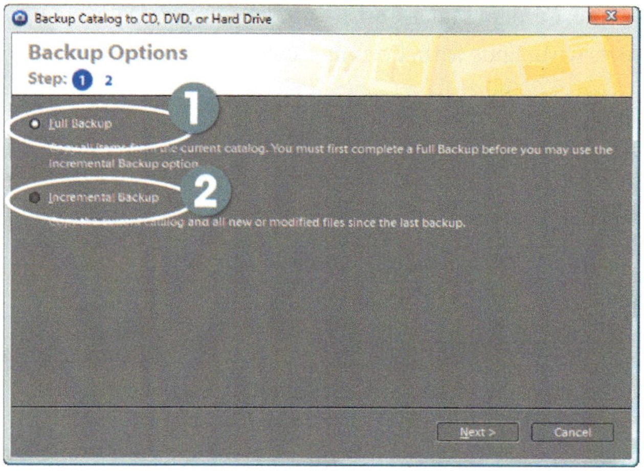

Backup files >> *The first screen of the Elements' Backup feature contains the choice of two different actions:*

(1) Full Backup – This option is for first time use. It will create an archive for the full catalog.

(2) Incremental Backup – Once you have created a full backup then it is only necessary to copy changed or new files to the backup in order to keep the archive current. The incremental option is designed specifically for this purpose.

4.12 Creating a backup

Suitable for Elements – 7.0, 6.0, 5.0, 4.0, 3.0 | Difficulty level – Basic | Related techniques – 4.09

Gone are the days when creating a backup of your work involved costly tape hardware and complex server software. Now you can archive your pictures from inside the very software that you use to enhance them – Photoshop Elements.

The Backup feature (Organizer: File > Backup Catalog to CD, DVD or Hard Drive) is designed for copying your pictures (and catalog files) onto DVD, CD or an external hard drive for archiving purposes. To secure your work simply follow the steps in the wizard. The feature includes the option to backup all the photos you currently have cataloged in the Photo Browser and then just copy changed files for successive backups.

FEATURE SUMMARY

1. To start the backup process select File > Backup Catalog to CD, DVD or Hard Drive from the Photo Browser workspace.
2. At the next screen choose **Full Backup** for first time archiving or **Incremental Backup** for all backups after the first one. Click Next.
3. And finally select the place where you want the backup to be stored. This may be on a series of CDs or DVDs, an internal or external drive. Then click Done to backup your files.

Backup glossary

Multi-disk archive – A process, often called spanning, by which chunks of data that are larger than one disk can be split up and saved to multiple CD-ROMs or DVDs using spanning software. The files can be recompiled later using utility software supplied by the same company that wrote the disks.

Full backup – Duplicates all files even if they haven't changed since the last time an archive was produced.

Incremental – Backs up only those files that have changed since the last archive was produced. This makes for faster backups but means that it takes longer to restore files as the program must look for the latest version of files before restoring them.

Restore – Reinstates files from a backup archive to their original state on your hard drive.

Backup hardware

CD-ROM or DVD writer – This option is very economical when coupled with writing software that is capable of writing large numbers of files over multiple disks. The sets of archive disks can easily be stored off site insuring you against theft and fire problems but the backup and restore process of this approach can be long and tedious.

Internal hard drive – Adding an extra hard drive inside your computer that can be used for backing up provides a fast and efficient way to archive your files but won't secure them against theft, fire or even some electrical breakdowns such as power surges.

External hard drive – Connect via USB or Firewire, these external self-contained units are both fast and efficient and can also be stored off site providing good all-round protection. Some, like the Maxtor One Touch models, are shipped with their own backup software. Keep in mind that these devices are still mechanical drives and that care should be taken when transporting them.

Backup regularly

There is no point having duplicate versions of your data if they are out of date. Base the interval between backups on the amount of work you do. In heavy periods when you are downloading, editing and enhancing many images at a time backup more often; in the quieter moments you won't need to duplicate files as frequently. Most professionals backup on a daily basis or at the conclusion of a work session.

Store the duplicates securely

In ensuring the security of your images you will not only need to protect you photos from the possibility of a hard drive crash but also from such dramatic events as burglary and fire. Do this by storing one copy of your files securely at home and an extra copy of your archive disks or external backup drives somewhere other than your home or office. I know that this may sound a little extreme but swapping archive disks with a friend who is just as passionate about protecting their images will prove to be less painful than losing all your hard work.

Multi-disk and multi-session backups

From version 5.0 the Backup Catalog feature was enhanced so that it was possible to archive your catalog over a series of CD or DVD disks. In previous versions, the Backup feature only allowed writing to a single disk and even with the growing use of DVD-ROMs for archive scenarios, many digital photographers have a catalog of photos that far exceeds the space available on a single disk. The feature can estimate the space required for creating the backup copy of the catalog and, after selecting the drive that will be used for archiving, the feature also determines the number of disks required to complete the action. During the writing process the feature displays instruction windows at the end of writing each disk and when you need to insert a new disk. All disks need to be written for the backup to be complete. To restore a catalog from a set of backup disks use the File > Restore Catalog from CD, DVD or Hard Drive option in the Organizer workspace.

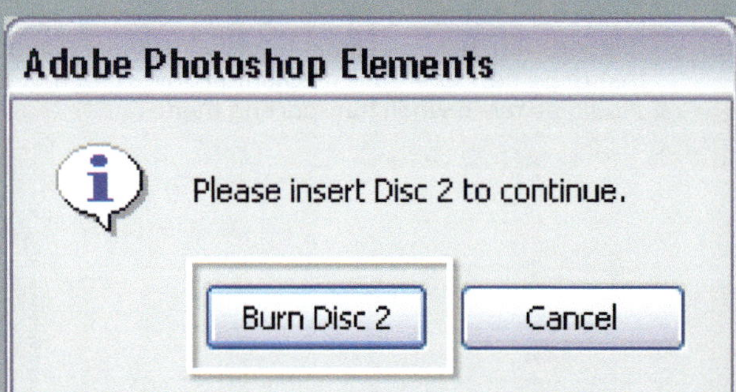

The backup feature also allows multi-session recording of archives. Multi-session DVD or CD-ROM recording means that you can add extra backup files to disks that you have already recorded to. Most Elements users will find this useful when performing incremental backups.

The online archive option that was included with version 5.0, called Online Backup; is no longer available. In its place is the much more sophisticated Synchronized/Backup Albums features found in Photoshop Elements 7.0.

4.13 Versioning your edits

Suitable for Elements – 7.0, 6.0, 5.0, 4.0, 3.0 | Difficulty level – Basic | Related techniques – 4.07, 4.12

Creating a good archival system goes a long way to making sure that the images you create are well protected, but what about the situation where the original photo is accidentally overwritten as part of the editing process? Embarrassing as it is, even I have to admit that sometimes I can get so involved in a series of complex edits that I inadvertently save the edited version of my picture over the top of the original. For most tasks this is not a drama as the edits I make are generally non-destructive (applied with adjustment layers and the like) and so I can extract the original file from inside the enhanced document but sometimes, because of the changes I have made, there is no way of going back. The end result of saving over the original untouched digital photo is equivalent to destroying the negative back in the days when film was king. Yep, photographic sacrilege!

So you can imagine my relief to find that in the last few versions of Photoshop Elements Adobe have included a technology that protects the original file and tracks the changes made to the picture in a series of successively saved photos. The technology is called Versioning as the software allows you to store different versions of the picture as your editing progresses. What's more, the feature provides options for viewing and using any of the versions that you have previously saved. Let's see how this file protection technology works in practice.

Versions and Photoshop Elements

Versioning extends the idea of Elements image stacks by storing the edited version of pictures together with the original photo in a special Version Set. All photos enhanced in the Photo Browser space using a tool like Auto Smart Fix are automatically included in a Version Set. Those images saved in the Quick, Guided and Full Edit workspaces with the Save As command can also be added to a Version Set by making sure that the Save in Version Set with Original option is ticked before pressing the Save button in the dialog.

Saving in this way means that edited files are not saved over the top of the original; instead a new version of the image is saved in a Version Set with the original. It is appended with a file name that has the suffix '_edited' attached to the original name. This way you will always be able to identify the original and edited files. The two files are 'stacked' together in the Photo Browser with the most recent file displayed on top.

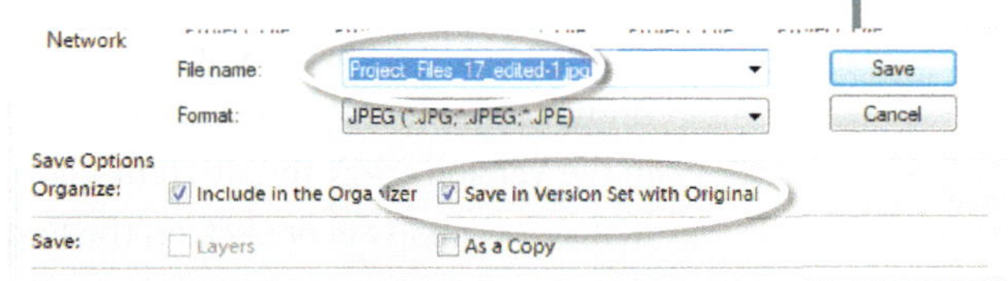

Save a version from Editor >> *To create a Version Set when saving an edited file from inside the Quick Fix or Full Edit workspace make sure that the 'Save a Version Set with Original' option is selected.*

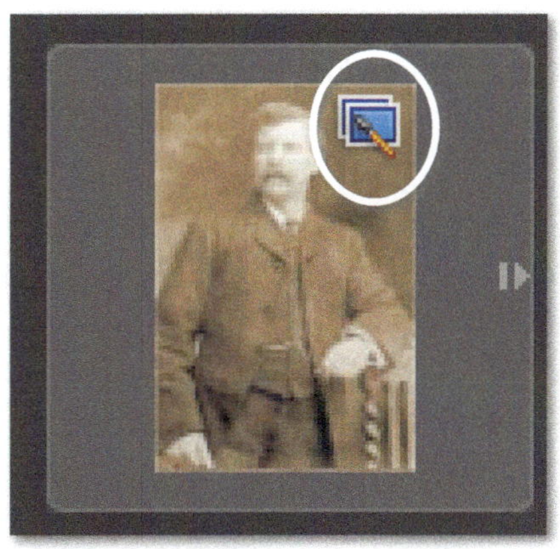

Version Set icon >> *The Bundled photos icon at the top right of the thumbnail shows that the photo is part of a version set.*

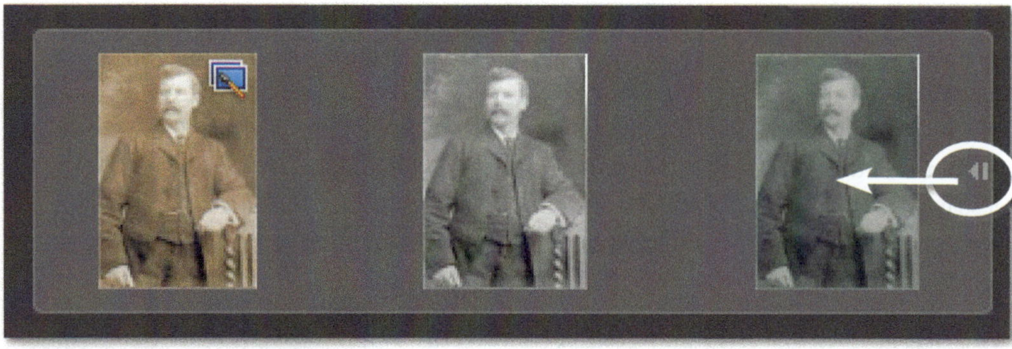

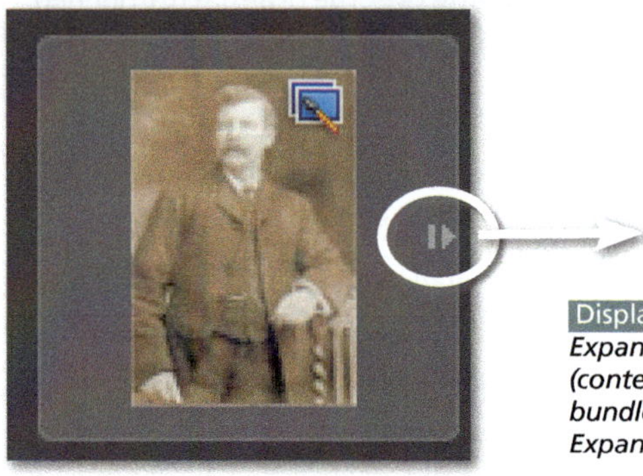

Displaying Version Set photos >> *Selecting the Version Set > Expand Items in Version Set option from the right-click menu (context menu) displays the various pictures that have been bundled together in the set. Alternatively you can click the Expand/Collapse arrow on the right of the version set.*

When a photo is part of a Version Set, there is a small icon displayed in the top right of the Photo Browser thumbnail. The icon shows a pile of photos and a paint brush. To see the other images in the Version Stack simply right-click the thumbnail image and select Version Set > Expand Items in Version Set or click on the Expand/Collapse arrow button on the right of the version set thumbnail.

Using the other options available in the right-click pop-up menu the sets can be expanded or collapsed, the current version reverted back to its original form or all versions flattened into one picture. Version Set options are also available via the Photo Browser Edit menu. Unlike Stacks, you cannot add other images to a Version Set as the set only contains edits of the same image.

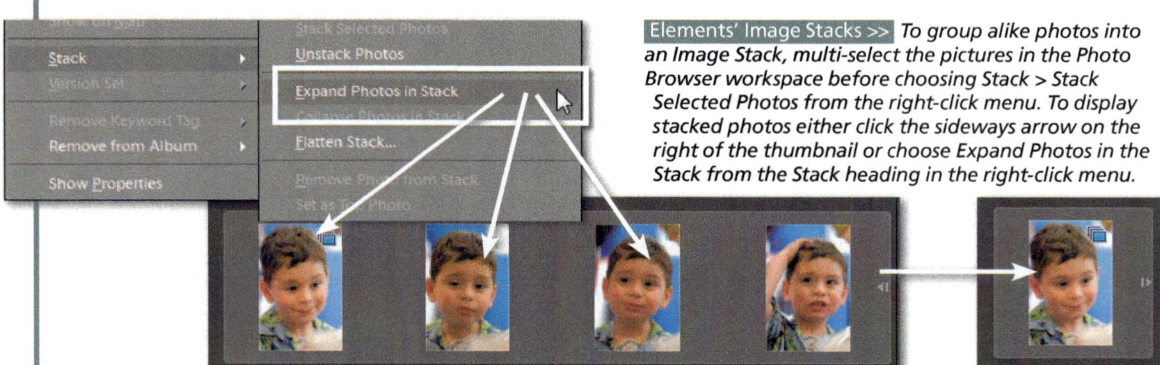

Elements' Image Stacks >> *To group alike photos into an Image Stack, multi-select the pictures in the Photo Browser workspace before choosing Stack > Stack Selected Photos from the right-click menu. To display stacked photos either click the sideways arrow on the right of the thumbnail or choose Expand Photos in the Stack from the Stack heading in the right-click menu.*

4.14 Creating Image Stacks

Suitable for Elements – 7.0, 6.0, 5.0, 4.0, 3.0 | Difficulty level – Basic | Related techniques – 4.07, 4.11

An Image Stack is slightly different from a Version Set as it is a set of pictures that have been grouped together into a single place in the Organizer workspace. Most often Stacks are used to group pictures that have a common subject or theme and the feature is one way that Elements users can sort and manage their pictures. To create a Version Stack, multi-select a series of thumbnails in the workspace then right-click on one of the selected images to show the menu and from here select the Stack > Stack Selected Photos option. The thumbnail you right-click on will be the top photo in the stack. You can identify stacked image groups by the small icon in the top right of the thumbnail.

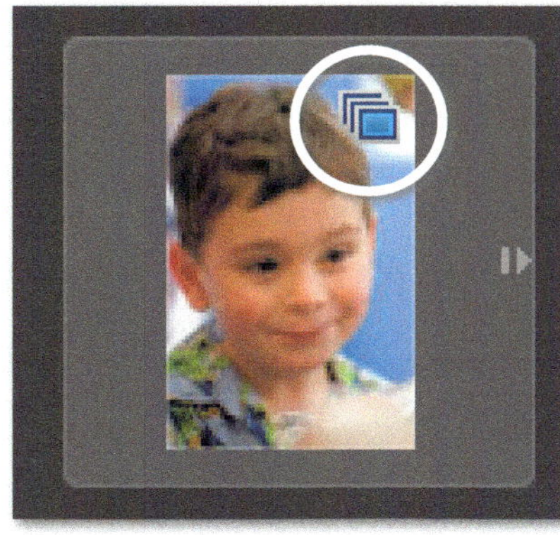

Image Stacks icon >> *Image Stacks use a Layered Photos icon in the top right of the thumbnail to indicate that the picture is one of several images that have been grouped.*

Auto photo stacking

The idea of grouping together like photos in a single stack was introduced in version 3.0 of the program. Version 5.0 introduced the ability to auto stack images as they are downloaded from camera, imported into Elements from folders or even when displayed in the Organizer workspace. The feature searches for similar images, either visually similar, or multiple photos taken within a short period of time, and then assembles these in groups in the 'automatically suggest photo stacks' window. From here you can choose to remove selected photos from a group or even remove a group all together from the window. Once you have fine-tuned which photos to include, clicking the Stack All Groups button will create Photo Stacks from all the groups in the window.

To auto stack pictures that are already in your catalog select a group of thumbnails first and then choose Automatically Suggest Photo Stacks from either the Edit > Stack or the right-click pop-up menus. Alternatively, to stack when importing pictures from a folder, camera or card reader choose the Automatically Suggest Photo Stacks option in the Get Photos or Adobe Photo Downloader dialog.

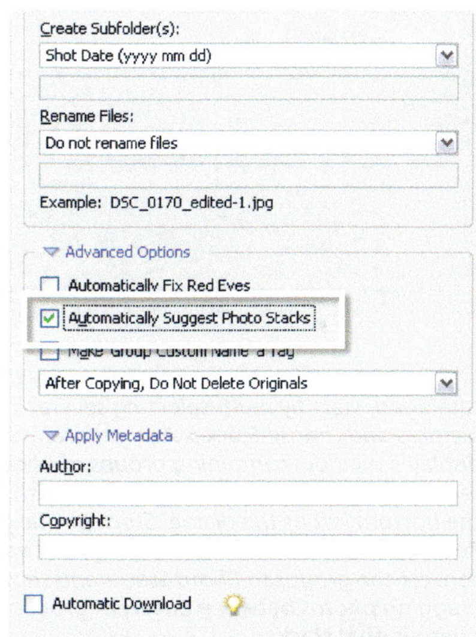

Auto stack whilst downloading >> *The Advanced dialog of the Adobe Photo Downloader contains the Automatically Suggest Photo Stacks option so you can group alike images as you transfer your files from camera to computer.*

Either of these two options will then display a new window with alike pictures pre-grouped. Choosing the Stack All Groups button converts the groups to stacks. The Remove Group or Remove Selected Photos buttons prevent individual images or group of pictures being made into a stack.

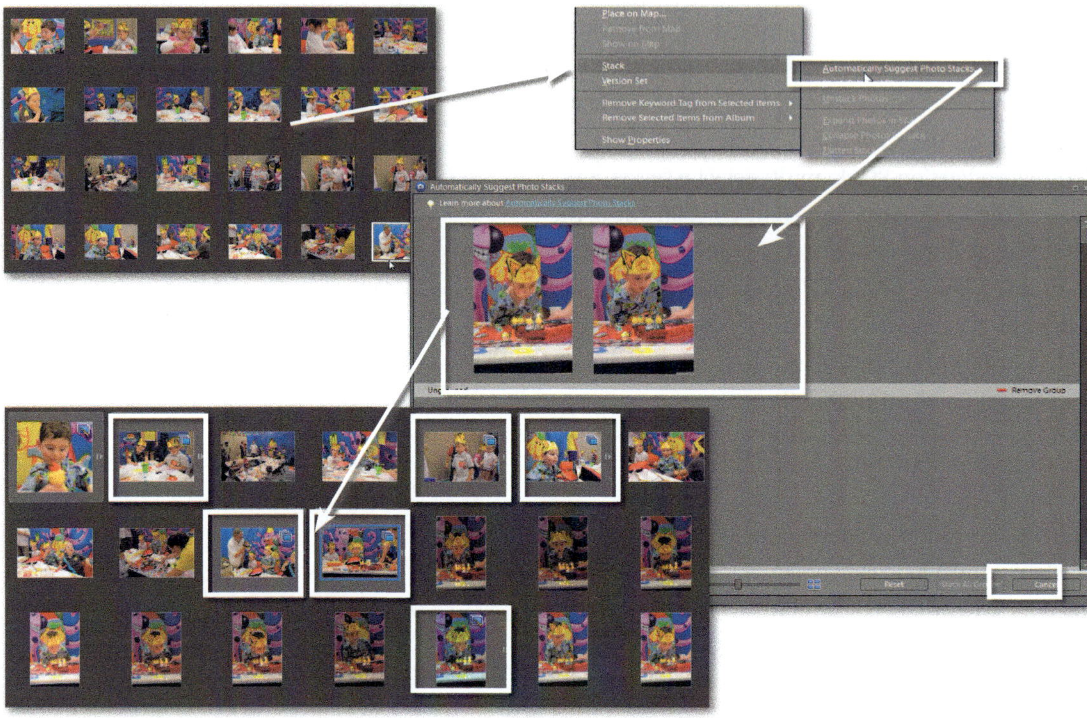

Stacking cataloged photos >> *To employ the Auto Stacking feature with photos that you have already cataloged, start by multi-selecting several images in the Photo Browser workspace. Next right-click one of the pictures and choose Stack > Automatically Suggest Photo Stacks from the pop-up menu. Elements will then display a window containing groups of photos that are suitable for converting into Photo Stacks. You can remove images from groups by selecting the photo and then pressing the Remove Selected Photos button at the bottom left of the dialog. Stop specific groups from being converted to a Photo Stack by clicking on the Remove Group button at the top right of each group section. Finally, press the Stack All Groups button to convert the groups to Photo Stacks and show these in the Photo Browser. You can edit the groups by click-dragging photos between different groups or within the same group. The left-most thumbnail will be the top photo in that stack.*

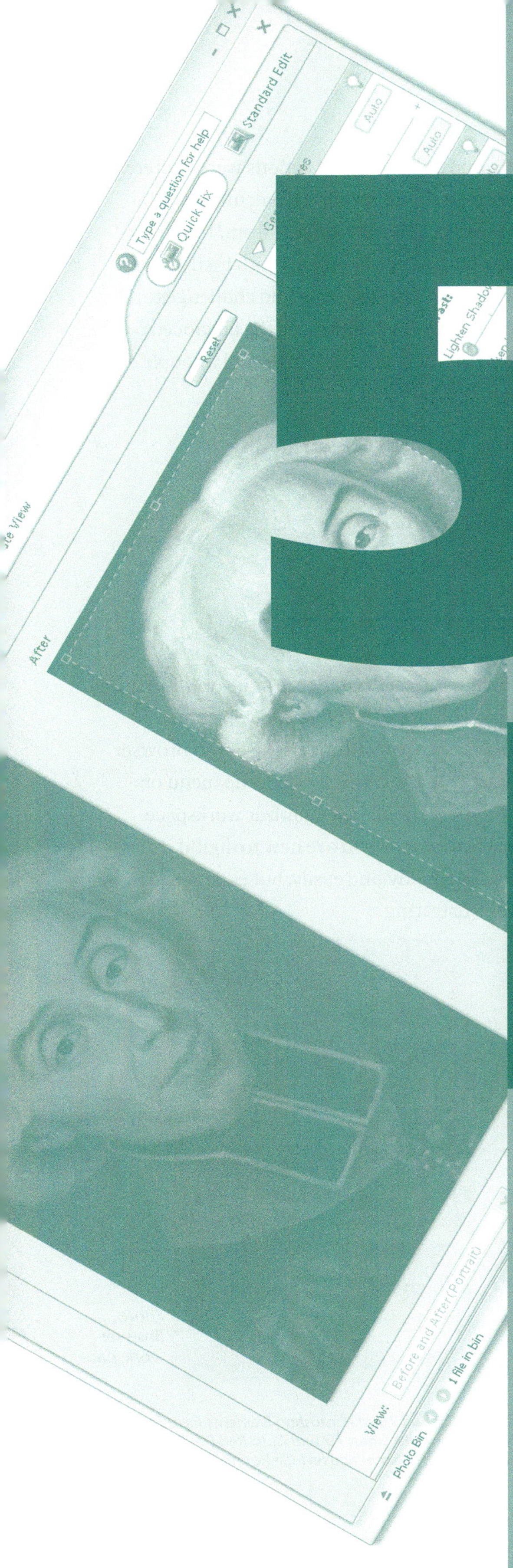

5

Pathways to Editing in Elements

In earlier editions of Photoshop Elements all editing and enhancement actions were centered around the tools and features in the Full Edit workspace. More recently Elements has provided the photographer with several different levels of editing to choose from. In the last edition we were introduced to a new option, the Guided Edit, which combines both instructions and tools in a single panel. All editing approaches have their own strengths and challenges and in this chapter I will overview each option in turn. In addition I will introduce the advanced concept of 'non-destructive editing' using some of Elements most powerful tools and a couple of features that we sneakily borrow from Photoshop. So let's get started!

Editing Options

The options can be grouped around five different approaches to the task:

- Automatic,
- Semi-automatic,
- Manual,
- Guided edits,
- Non-destructive and
- Photoshop assisted.

Auto editing summary

- Simple control using Auto Smart Fix, Auto Color, Auto Levels, Auto Contrast, Auto Sharpen and Auto Red Eye Fix
- Rotate left or right options
- Manual cropping
- Changes applied automatically
- New users start here for good, quick results
- Automatic control of: contrast, color, shadow and highlight detail and sharpness.

Automatic editing

The simplest tools are almost always fully automatic with the user having little control over the final results. These are the types of color, contrast, brightness and sharpness controls that are available in the Photo Browser either via option in the Edit menu, from the right-click pop-up menu or displayed in the new Fix panel on the right of the Organizer workspace. These options provide a great place to start if you are new to digital photography and want good results quickly and easily, but experienced users will find the lack of control frustrating.

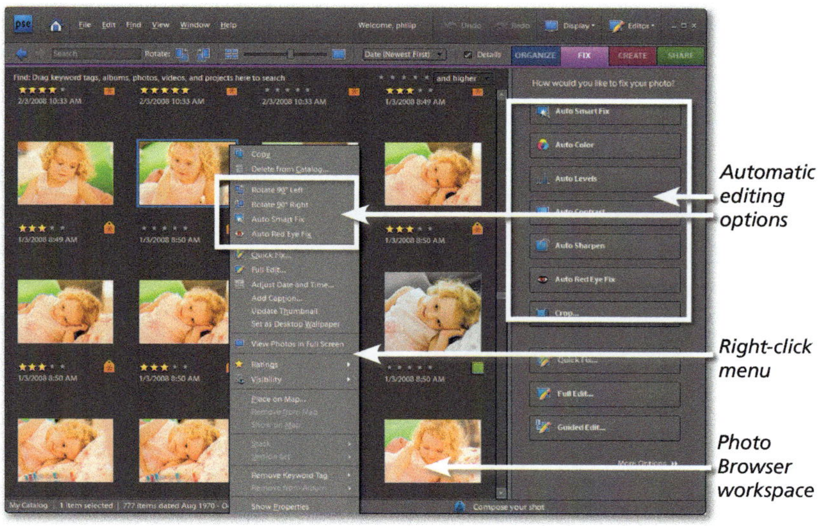

Auto-editing options >> *The range of auto enhance options in versions 6.0 and 7.0 of Photoshop Elements includes Auto Color, Auto Levels, Auto Contrast and Auto Sharpen options as well as Auto Smart Fix and Auto Red Eye Fix features found in the previous version. The features are grouped in the new Fix panel and include Rotate buttons and a new Crop option.*

5.01 Auto Smart Fix

Suitable for Elements – 7.0, 6.0, 5.0, 4.0, 3.0 | Difficulty level – Basic
Related techniques – 5.02, 5.03

The Auto Smart Fix feature enhances both the lighting and color in your picture automatically. The command is used to balance the picture hues and improve the overall shadow and highlight detail. Most images are changed drastically using this tool. In some cases the changes can be too extreme. If this occurs, the effect should be reversed using the Edit > Undo command and the more controllable version of the tool – Adjust Smart Fix – used instead. Adjust Smart Fix is located in the Editor workspace.

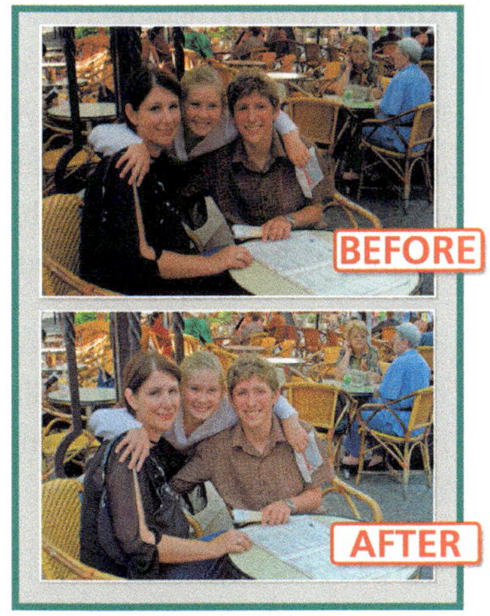

Auto Smart Fix >> *The Auto Smart Fix feature enhances color, brightness, shadow and highlight detail automatically.*

5.02 Auto Red Eye Fix

Suitable for Elements – 7.0, 6.0, 5.0, 4.0 | Difficulty level – Basic
Related techniques – 5.01, 5.03

One of the possible side effects of using the inbuilt flash on your compact digital camera is the appearance of red eyes in the subject. Elements has always had great options for correcting this problem and the current release is no different containing a specific Red Eye Removal tool. First introduced in Elements 5.0 was the ability to automatically detect the presence of red eye in a photo and then correct the problem. The feature cleverly checks out the metadata attached to the photo to see if flash was used to record the image before searching for the problem eyes and automatically correcting the red hue. This feature can also be applied when transferring images from camera to computer by selecting the Automatically Fix Red Eyes option in the Photo Downloader.

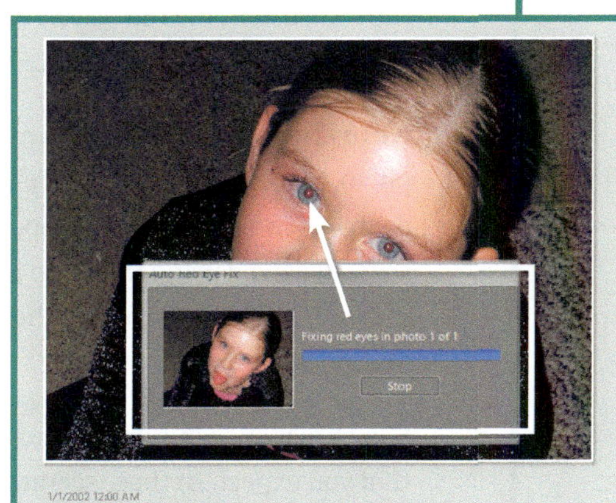

Auto Red Eye Fix >> *The Auto Red Eye Fix feature searches for and corrects the red eyes caused by on-camera flash.*

5.03 Other auto options

Suitable for Elements – 7.0, 6.0
Difficulty level – Basic | Related techniques – 5.01, 5.02

In Photoshop Elements 6.0 and 7.0 four auto enhance options that were previously only available in the Enhance menu of the Edit workspace, have been added to the new Fix pane in the Organizer. Unlike the Auto Smart Fix option which enhances several different image characteristics in the one action, features like Auto Levels, Auto Contrast, Auto Sharpen, and Auto Color Correction generally concentrate on adjusting just one aspect of the photo, providing more specific and controllable changes to your photo.

Quick guide to the Fix panel's auto enhance features

Correction needed	Feature to use
Low contrast problem	Auto Contrast
High contrast problem	Auto Contrast
Color cast problem	Auto Color Correction or Auto Levels
Color cast and contrast problem	Auto Levels
Sharpness or clarity problem	Auto Sharpen

Auto Contrast is designed to correct images that are either too contrasty (black and white) or too flat (dull and lifeless). Unlike the Auto Levels feature, Auto Contrast ensures that the brightest and darkest pixels in the picture (irrespective of their colors) are converted to pure white and black. In doing so all the tones in between are expanded or contracted to fit.

Auto Color concentrates on correcting the color in the midtones of the picture and adjusting the contrast by reassigning the brightest and darkest pixels to white and black.

Auto Levels is similar to Auto Contrast in that it maps the brightest and darkest parts of the image to white and black but differs in that each individual color channel is treated separately. In the process of mapping the tones (adjusting the contrast) in the red, green and blue channels, dominant color casts can be neutralized.

Auto Sharpen applies a set amount of sharpening to the photo. Most photographers prefer to be able to adjust the degree of sharpening that is applied to their images and so would avoid using this auto feature in favor of a more manual approach involving the Editor: Enhance > Adjust Sharpness filter.

Sometimes such automatic fixes do not produce the results that you expect. In these scenarios use the Undo (Edit > Undo) command to reverse the changes and try one of the manual correction tools detailed in the next section.

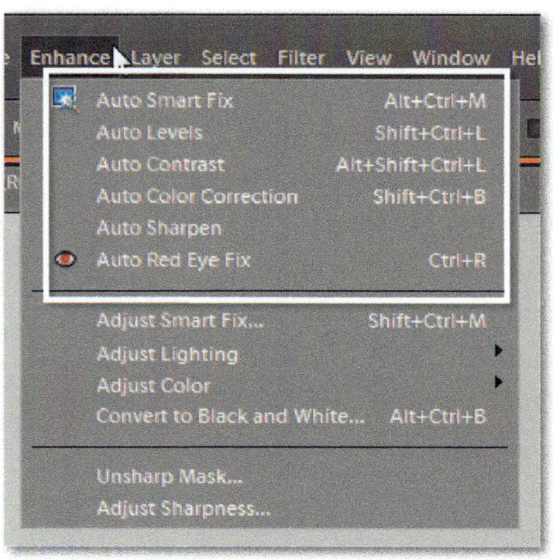

Auto options also found in Edit >> *The Fix panel's auto features can also be found in the Enhance menu of the Full Edit or Quick Fix workspaces.*

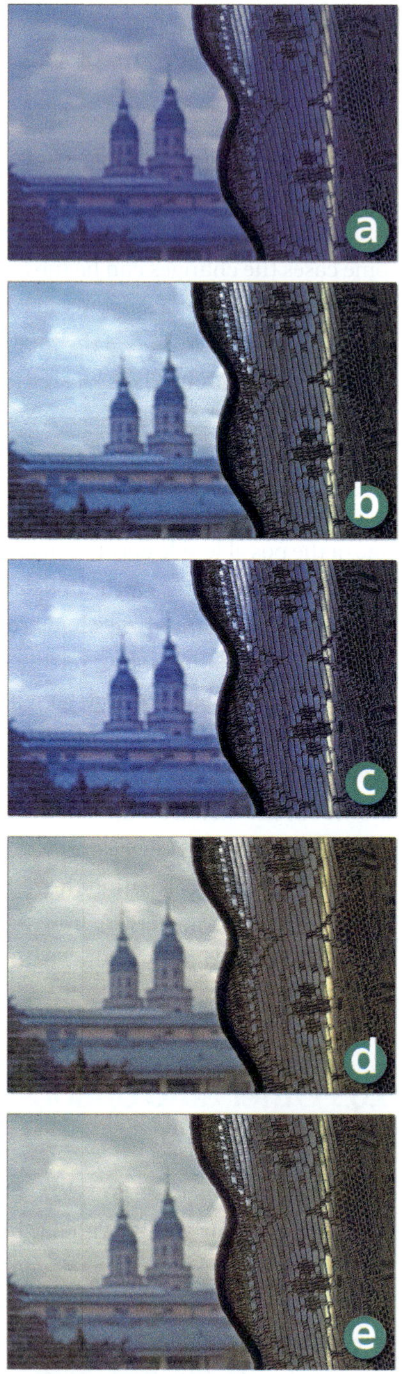

Auto options examples >>
(a) Original uncorrected image.
(b) After applying Auto Levels.
(c) After applying Auto Contrast.
(d) After applying Auto Color Correction.
(e) After Auto Color and Auto Sharpen

Automating editing of several pictures at once

It's true that shooting digital has meant that many photographers have saved the time that they used to spend in the darkroom processing their images. The flip side to this coin is that now we while away the hours in on-screen production instead. Surely with all the power of the modern computer and flexibility of Elements there must be quicker ways to process files. Well yes there is!

5.04 Processing multiple files

Suitable for Elements – 7.0, 6.0, 5.0, 4.0, 3.0 | Difficulty level – Basic
Related techniques – 5.05, 5.06

Photoshop Elements users are able to automate a variety of editing functions with the Process Multiple Files feature located in the File menu of the Full Edit workspace. The feature is like a dedicated batch processing tool that can name, size, enhance, label and save in a specific file format a group of photos stored in a folder or selected via the file browser or Open Files.

The dialog's options include:

Source – Files to be processed can be stored in a single folder, the files currently open in the workspace, pictures in the Project Bin or images multi-selected in the file browser.

Destination – Sets the location where processed files will be saved.

File naming – Options for naming or renaming of selected files including a range of preset naming styles.

Image Size – Specify size and resolution changes after choosing the unit of measure to work with from the drop-down menu. Proportions can be constrained.

File type – Select the file format that processed files will be saved or converted to.

Quick Fix enhancement – Use the options here to apply automatic enhancement of the files being processed.

Add Labels – Add caption or file name labels to each of the processed files. Also contains an option for watermarking the pictures.

After setting the options for each of the sections in the dialog press the OK button to process the pictures.

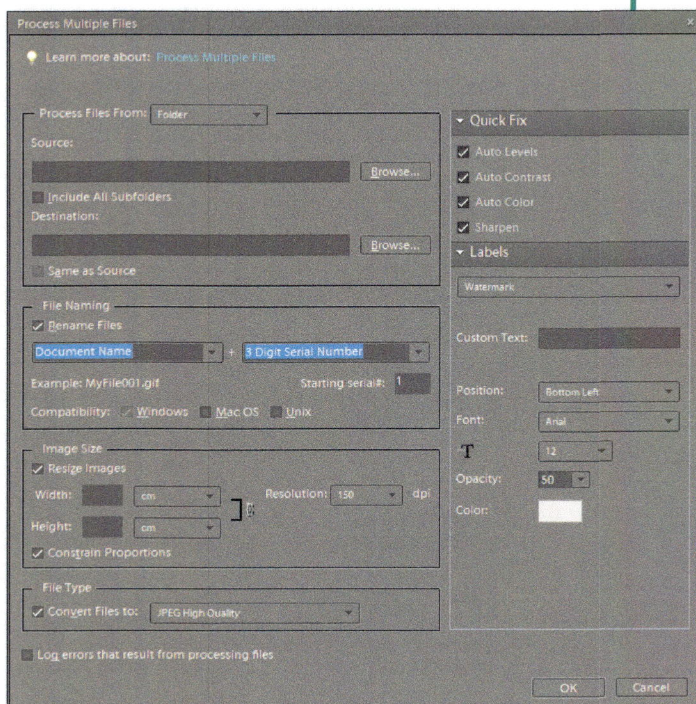

Batch processing of files >> *Elements users can automate the application of basic enhancement and editing features to a group of files using the Process Multiple Files feature located in the Full Edit workspace.*

5.05 Multi-selection editing

Suitable for Elements – 7.0, 6.0, 5.0, 4.0, 3.0 | Difficulty level – Basic | Related techniques – 5.04, 5.06

Another method of applying automatic changes to several photos at once is to multi-select photos in the Photo Browser workspace then choose an editing option from the right-click pop-up menu or the new Fix panel. There are a multitude of options available using this approach, all of which provide quick editing changes to the selected photos. For best results always apply critical edits and enhancements manually, but multi-select edits are particularly useful if you want to process a bunch of files quickly. The added bonus is that the edited versions of the pictures are not saved over the original file, but rather they are kept in a Version Set, so that it is always possible to extract the original file, or reverse the enhancement changes, if need be.

Keystrokes for fast edits of multi-selected photos

Rotate Photos 90° Left – Ctrl + Left

Rotate Photos 90° Right – Ctrl + Right

Auto Smart Fix – Ctrl + Alt + M

Auto Red Eye Fix – Ctrl + R

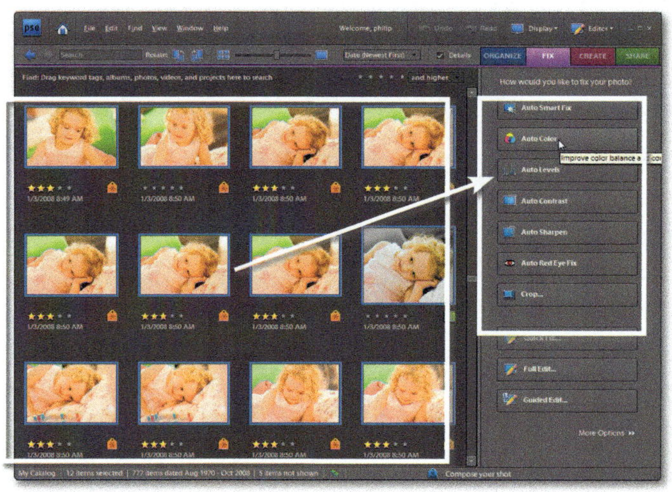

Auto enhance several files >> *The editing and enhancement options located on the right-click menu or the new Fix panel in the Photo Browser workspace can be just as easily applied to several photos that have been multi-selected as to a single picture.*

This method is a quick and easy means of making automatic changes to a group of photos.

5.06 Bulk Red Eye fixing

Suitable for Elements – 6, 5.0, 4.0 | Difficulty level – Basic
Related techniques – 5.04, 5.05

As well as being able to apply the Auto Red Eye Fix feature to individual photos this correction option is also available in the Adobe Photo Downloader dialog. So now it is possible to download pictures from your camera, or import them from a folder, and at the same time be searching the images for red eye and correcting it when it is present. This is a great time saver if you regularly photograph with on-camera flash but as always for the absolute best results apply the Red Eye Fix yourself manually.

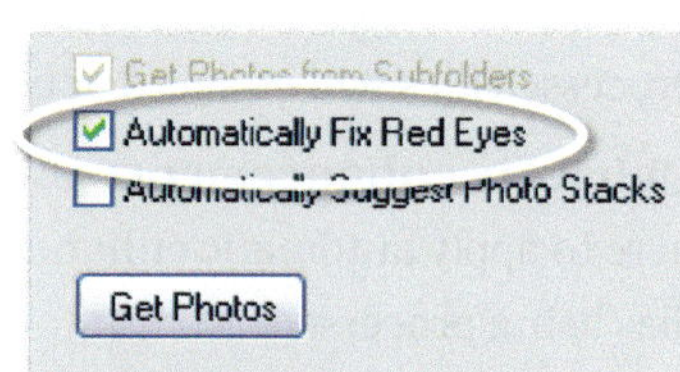

Auto Red Eye Fix >> *The Auto Red Eye fix option is also available in dialogs that are used to import or download pictures onto your computer. Selecting this option instructs Elements to search and correct any occurrence of red eye in the photos you are loading into the Organizer workspace.*

Semi-automatic editing

The second level of features sits in the middle ground between total user control and total program control over the editing results. The tools in this group are primarily available in the Quick Fix editor but also encompass some of the more automatic or easy-to-use controls available in the Full Edit workspace. Move to these tools once you feel more confident with the digital photography process as a whole (downloading, making some changes, saving and then printing) and find yourself wanting to do more with your pictures. Again, for the advanced user the tools listed here will provide a degree of frustration as the amount of control over the results is still limited.

5.07 Using the Quick Fix Editor

Suitable for Elements – 7.0, 6.0, 5.0, 4.0, 3.0 | Difficulty level – Basic
Related techniques – 5.08, 5.09

The Quick Fix Editor contains a reduced tool and feature set designed to facilitate the fast application of the most frequent of all enhancement activities undertaken by the digital photographer.

The Zoom, Hand, Crop tools and the Quick Selection Tool and Selection Brush are located in a small toolbar to the left of the screen and are available for standard image editing changes; the fixed Palette Bin, to the right, contains the necessary features to alter and correct the lighting, color and sharpness of your pictures. Rotate buttons are located at the bottom of the dialog. Three new retouch tools have been added to the red eye removal brush and positioned at the bottom of the pane on the right side of the workspace.

You can choose to apply each image change automatically, via the Auto button, or manually using the supplied sliders. This approach provides both convenience and speed when needed, with the option of a manual override for those difficult editing tasks.

The adjustment features are arranged in a fashion that provides a model enhancement workflow to follow – simply move from the top to the bottom of the tools starting with smart fixing, working through lighting and color alterations, applying sharpening and, lastly, paint on retouching to specific areas of the photo.

There is no doubt that for making speedy adjustments of your favorite images with the option of some override control, the Quick Fix editor is a great place to start. And the best thing of all is you can see the before and after results of your changes on screen via the zoomable preview windows.

Semi-auto editing summary

- Middle-level control using the features in the Quick Fix and Full Edit workspaces
- Some changes applied automatically, others via a user controlled slider
- New users progress here with experience and understanding
- Control of: cropping, rotation, contrast, color, saturation, hue, temperature, tint, shadow and highlight detail, red eye, midtone contrast and sharpening.

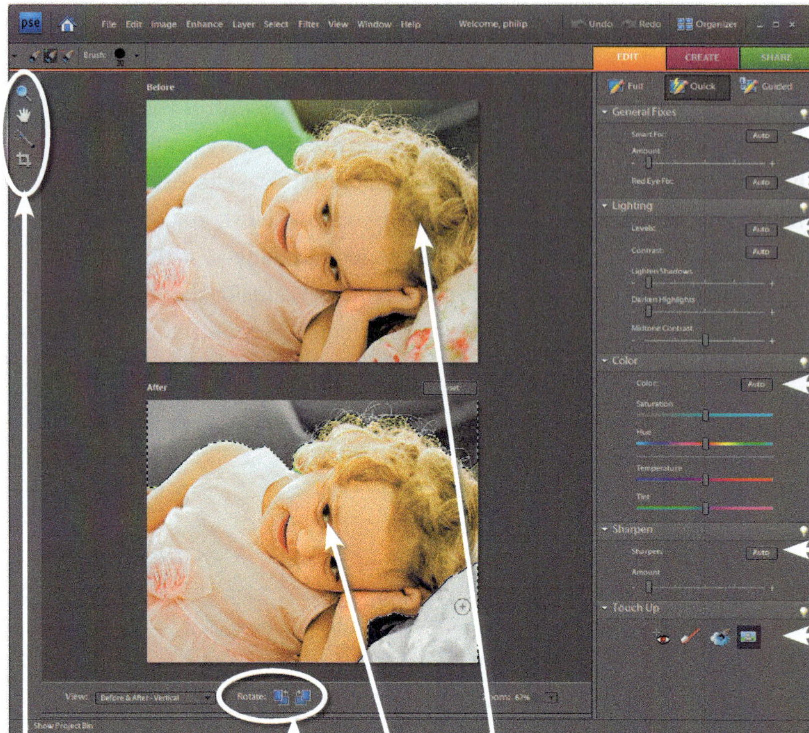

Smart Fix control

Red Eye Fix

Lighting control for changes to levels, contrast, shadows and highlights

Color control for changes to saturation, hue, color temperature and tint

Sharpening control

Retouch Tools

Zoom, Move, Crop, Quick Selection Brush and Selection Brush tools

Rotate image buttons

After preview

Before preview

The Quick Fix Editor >> *The Quick Fix editor combines the major automatic enhancing tools with manual override slider controls, great before and after preview pictures and now three new retouch tools in addition to the red eye removal tool.*

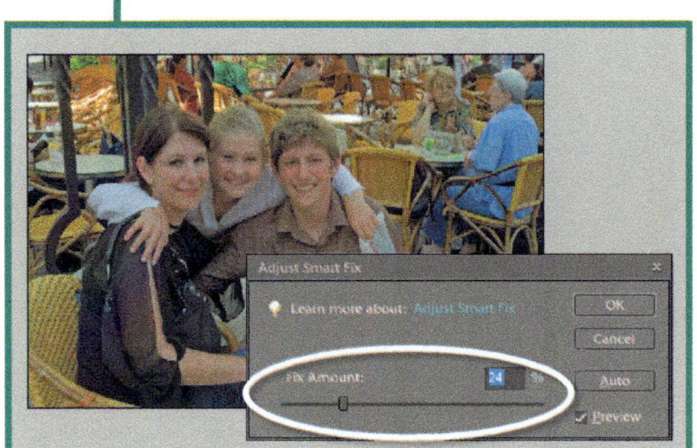

Adjust Smart Fix >> *The Adjust Smart Fix option provides a slider control for the auto enhancement effects applied by the feature.*

5.08 Adjust Smart Fix

Suitable for Elements – 7.0, 6.0, 5.0, 4.0, 3.0 | Difficulty level – Basic
Related techniques – 5.01, 5.03

The Adjust Smart Fix (Editor: Enhance > Adjust Smart Fix) version of the Auto Smart Fix feature provides the same control over color, shadow and highlight detail but with the addition of a slider control that determines the strength of the enhancement changes. Moving the slider from left to right will gradually increase the amount of correction applied to your picture. This approach provides much more control over the enhancement process and is a preferable way to work with all but the most general photos.

The Auto button, also located in the dialog, automatically applies a fix amount of 100% and provides a similar result to selecting Enhance > Auto Smart Fix.

Manual editing

The next approach to editing includes tools and features designed to give the user professional control over their editing and enhancement tasks. Many of the features detailed here are very similar to, and in some cases exactly the same as, those found in the Photoshop itself. These tools provide the best quality changes available with Elements, but they do require a greater level of understanding and knowledge to use effectively.

The extra editing and enhancement power of these tools comes at a cost of the user bearing all responsibility for the end results. Whereas the automatic nature of many of the features found in the other two groups means that bad results are rare, misusing or over-applying the tools found here can actually make your picture worse. This shouldn't stop you from venturing into these waters, but it does mean that it is a good idea to apply these tools cautiously rather than with a heavy hand. In fact once most users develop a good level of understanding and skill with the manual tools and features in the Full Edit workspace they seldom return to using automatic enhancement options, preferring to remain in complete control over the pixels in their pictures.

5.09 The Full Edit workspace

Suitable for Elements – 7.0, 6.0, 5.0, 4.0, 3.0, 2.0, 1.0 | Difficulty level – Basic
Related techniques – 5.07

The Full Edit contains the features and tools used for the most sophisticated of the three different editing pathways provided in Elements. The groups of tools included in this workspace are designed to give the user professional control over all their editing and enhancement tasks.

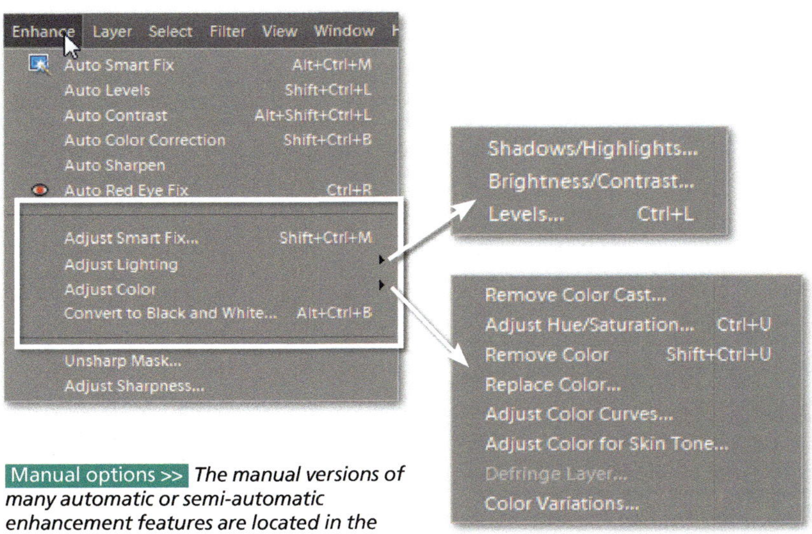

Manual options >> *The manual versions of many automatic or semi-automatic enhancement features are located in the lower part of the Enhance menu.*

Manual editing summary

- Sophisticated control using the features in the Full Edit workspace
- Most editing changes applied manually via settings input by the user
- Great for complex editing and enhancement tasks performed by more experienced users
- The most control of all the major editing and enhancing of your digital photographs.

As well as providing manual versions of all the automatic enhancement options that we have looked at so far, the Full Edit workspace also includes tools that enable the user to isolate where and how the editing changes are applied to photos. For this reason most advanced techniques detailed in the ensuing chapters of this book make use of the extensive tool and feature set provided in this Editor workspace.

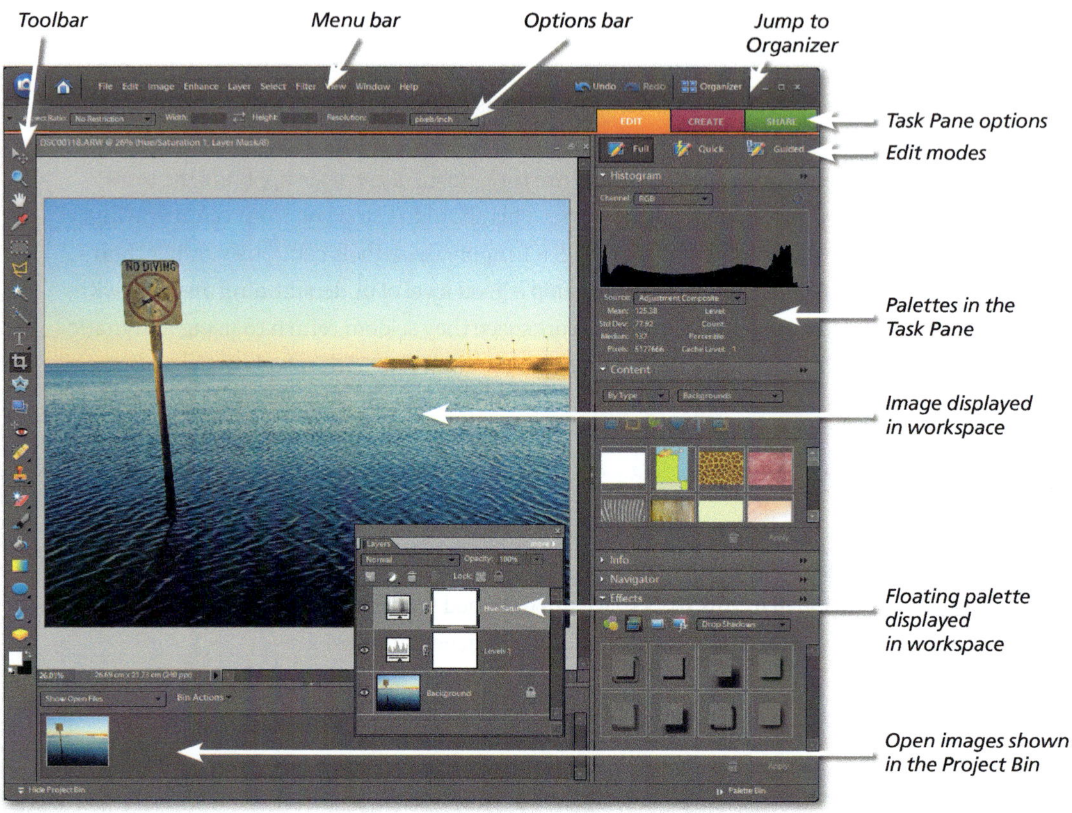

The Full Edit >> *Advanced editing and enhancement techniques are generally applied in the Full Edit workspace.*

Auto/manual feature equivalents

Automatic feature	Manual equivalent
Auto Levels	Levels or Shadows/Highlights or Brightness/Contrast or Adjust Color Curves
Auto Color Correction	Remove Color Cast or Color Variations or Adjust Color For Skin Tones
Auto Contrast	Levels or Shadows/Highlights or Brightness/Contrast or Adjust Color Curves
Auto Red Eye Fix	Red Eye Removal Tool
Auto Smart Fix	Levels or Shadows/Highlights or Brightness/Contrast or Adjust Color Curves together with Remove Color Cast or Color Variations or Adjust Color For Skin Tones
Auto Sharpen	Unsharp Mask or Adjust Sharpness

Manual pathway choices >> *Photoshop Elements provides manual alternatives for all its automatic and semi-automatic editing options. This table summarizes the specific manual features that can be used as alternatives.*

Three Editing Modes in Elements plus one Online

The Guided Edit workspace was introduced into Elements in version 6. This mode combines the step-by-step instructions that used to be found in the How To feature with the direct enhancement control of the Quick Fix edit space. As part of the interface changes that also occured in Photoshop Elements 6, the guys at Adobe grouped features, tools and options into several task headings. The Task Pane and the associated headings are displayed on the right of the Element's workspaces with different options available in each. In the Edit workspace these include Edit, Create and Share, where as in the Organizer the choices include Organize, Fix, Create and Share. With all the management, editing, enhancement, and production options now available in Elements the inclusion of these task based headings helps the user navigate through the various phases of photographic workflow.

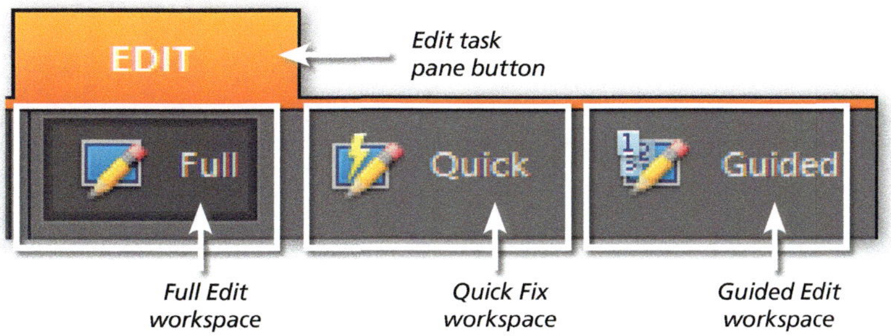

Three edit options >> *In version 6.0 the Guided edit mode was added to help users with their enhancement activities.*

In the Edit workspace, Elements users have the luxury of three different ways of conducting their enhancement activities. Once you have selected the Edit heading you can then choose between Full Edit, Quick Fix and Guided Edit workspaces. New for Photoshop Elements 7.0 is the ability to perform simple editing tasks online via the tools and function available at Photoshop.com. Though these 'web' tools do not provide the level of manual control available in the Full edit workspace, they do provide a very usable alternative to many of the enhancement options available in Quick and Guided edit modes. When linked with Online Albums any changes made in the webspace are reflected in the duplicated photos stored in the Organizer..

We have already looked at the Full Edit and Quick Fix workspaces so let's now turn our attention to the newly created Guided Edit option.

5.10 Guided Edits

Suitable for Elements – 7.0, 6.0 | Difficulty level – Basic

Selecting the Guided tab from the Edit task pane displays a list of the tutorials that ship with Elements. Clicking a tutorial heading will reveal subheadings for specific topics. Selecting a heading topic will display a set of instructions together with associated buttons and controls. For instance, in the example on the next page, two Rotate buttons (rotate left and rotate right) are displayed in the panel. Clicking either of these buttons will perform the same action as selecting the same options from the Image > Rotate menu.

Guided edit is best used for learning how to use new tools and techniques or, as is the case with the new Photomerge Faces and Group Shot options, as a way to step through complex techniques.

The Guided Activities > Guide for Editing a Photo entry contains a collection of guided edits that are useful when correcting images. These include crop, lighten, darken, touch up and sharpen.

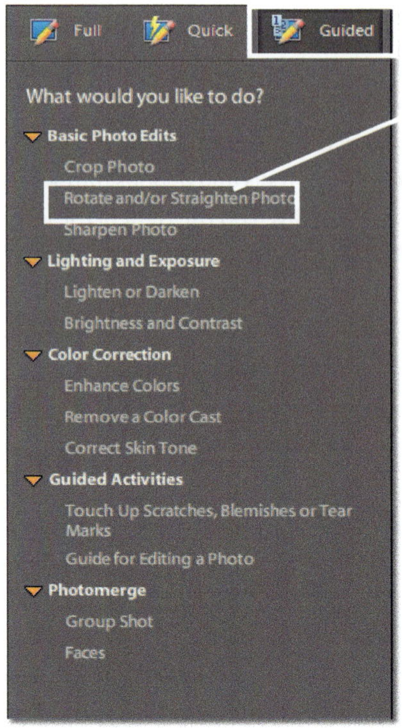

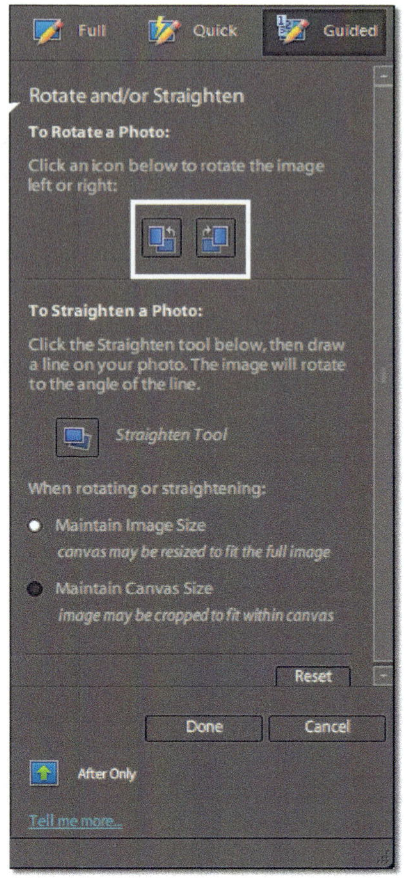

Guided Edits >> *The Guided edit workspace combines step-by-step instruction with embedded enhancement or edit controls.*

5.11 Enhancing via Photoshop.com

Suitable for Elements – 7.0 | Difficulty level – Basic

The partnership between Photoshop Elements and Photoshop.com goes way beyond merely providing a space on the web to view the pictures that you process in Elements. Because Photoshop.com grew out of Photoshop Express the site also contains simple editing features such as the ability to crop, resize, auto correct, alter white balance, adjust highlights, boost color, tint and distort photos.

To adjust an image online, click onto the My Photos heading first and then navigate to the photo. You can look for the photos visually by selecting an Album entry or Library heading on the left of the screen and then scrolling through the thumbnails in the main workspace. Alternatively, you can locate the photo by typing a search term into the Search box at the top right of the workspace and then hitting the Enter key. Photoshop.com tries to match the search term with album and file names, tags associated with the photos and picture captions.

Once you have located the photo, clicking on the picture's thumbnail switches the workspace to the edit mode and displays the photo as large as possible within the window. All the adjustments that can be applied to the photo, are grouped under three headings Basics, Tuning and Effects on the left.

For most options, when an adjustment is selected from the list, a series of thumbnails displaying varying degrees of application for the adjustment are displayed above the image. Clicking a thumbnail will preview a change to the photo. With some adjustments a slider control is also provided below the thumbnails for finer control. One thumbnail of the group will be displayed with a curved yellow arrow. Click this entry to reset the photo to the way it was before selecting the current adjustment. Click the green tick (top right) to save the current adjustment changes and click the red cross to cancel the alterations.

Despite the preview being updated to reflect the changes that you have made, the adjustments are not actually applied to the image until they are saved upon exiting the Editing mode. This way of working allows you to revert the photo to its original state by clicking the Reset All button at the bottom of the window. Also contained at the bottom of the editing window is the View Original image which allows you to see how the photo looked before your adjustments. Hold down the button to see the before image, let go of the button to return the picture to its current state.

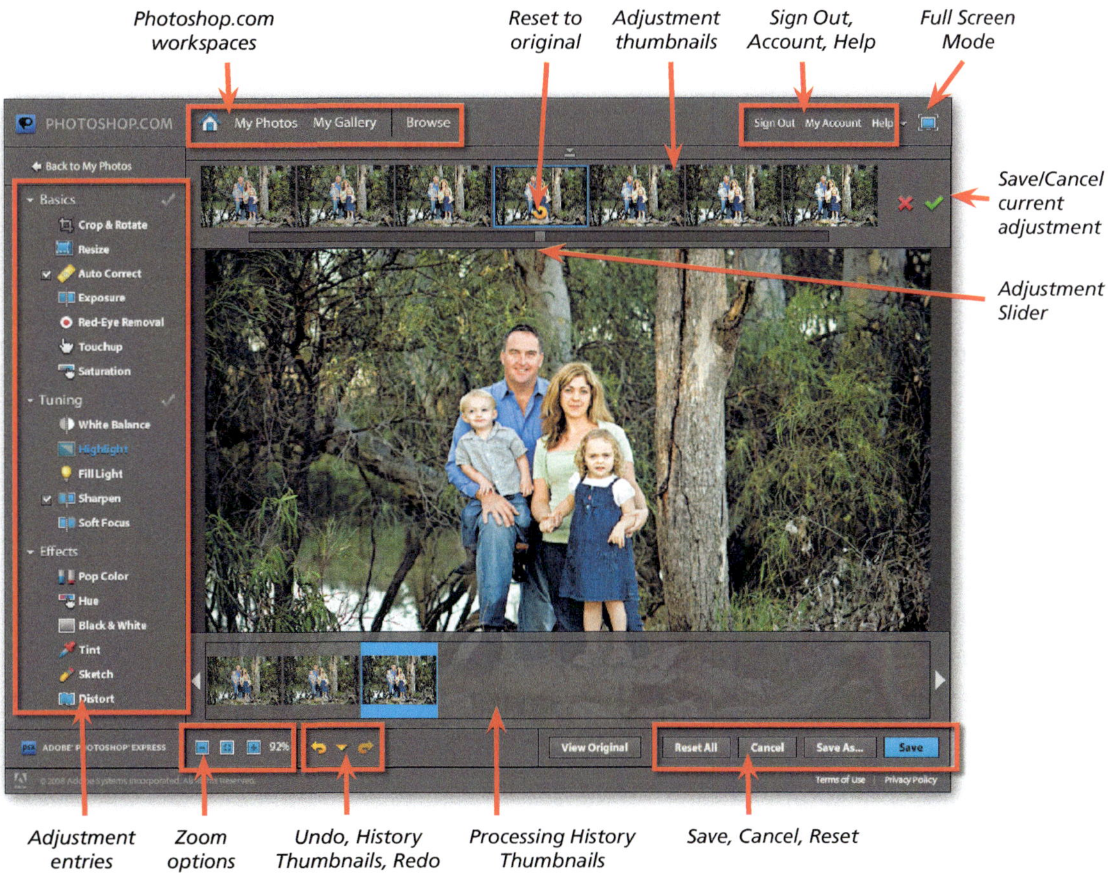

Enhancing at Photoshop.com >> All image adjustments performed in Photoshop.com are undertaken in the Editing mode pictured to the left.

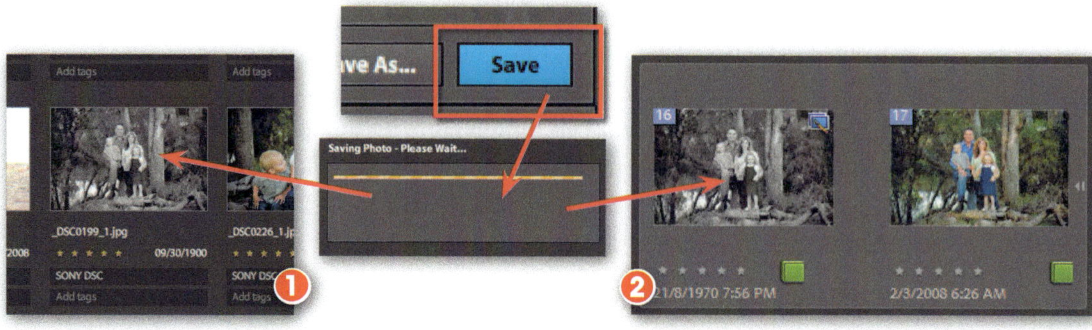

Synchronized Updating >> *For photos that you have edited, and are part of a synchronized album, clicking the Save button updates the image at Photoshop.com (1) and in your Photoshop Elements catalog (2).*

Some enhancement options, such as Red-Eye Removal and Touchup, require the user to interact directly with the image. With these tools you will need to click on or paint over the parts of the photo that you want to change. The Touchup tool in particular is very useful as it provides a way to remove small dust marks and spots from your photo. Once selected, you simply click and drag a circle around the dust mark and then let the mouse button go. Automatically the dust spot is removed. If the result didn't work as you expected, just click the circular orange arrow icon at the top right of the window. This is the Reset button and pressing it will remove all your retouching changes, allowing you to start again.

Once you are satisfied with your changes, you can saved the altered photo by clicking the blue Save button at the bottom of the editing window. This action will update the photo in the Photoshop.com library and will also update the picture in your Photoshop Elements Catalog if the picture belongs to an Album that is set for Backup/Synchronization.

Non-destructive editing, the professional's choice

Though not strictly an editing mode in itself, the idea of making changes to your images in a non-destructive fashion is key to all professional workflows. For this reason I feel that it is appropriate to introduce the idea here. When digital photography was in its infancy, all changes made to the photo were applied directly to the original pixels captured by the camera or scanner. At the time, the abilities of the software and hardware allowed frustratingly few alternatives to this destructive way of working.

For me, as a photographer who trained when film was king, I found the idea of changing my captured image rather distressing, as I would never have altered, cut, or intentionally marked my negatives, so why should I have to work this way when opting for a digital workflow. This would lead me to make countless copies of my original images to ensure that I had at least one copy of the primary capture file to refer to at all times.

Thankfully times have changed and digital photography is now well out of 'short trousers' and software and hardware has developed to a stage where many of the editing activities we regularly carry out in Photoshop Elements can be executed non-destructively, that is, without altering the pixels of the captured file.

Throughout the rest of the text I will use non-destructive editing and enhancement techniques wherever possible, but to get you up to speed, here I introduce a selection of tools, techniques and features that can be employed to enhance your images non-destructively.

5.12 Adjustment Layers

Suitable for Elements – 7.0, 6.0, 5.0, 4.0, 3.0, 2.0, 1.0 | Difficulty level – Basic

These special layers alter the look of the layers that are arranged below them in the layers stack. They act as a filter through which the lower layers are viewed. You can use adjustment layers to perform many of the enhancement tasks that you would normally apply directly to an image layer without changing the image itself. When you choose to use an Adjustment Layer rather than applying the enhancement change directly to the image you are choosing to work non-destructively.

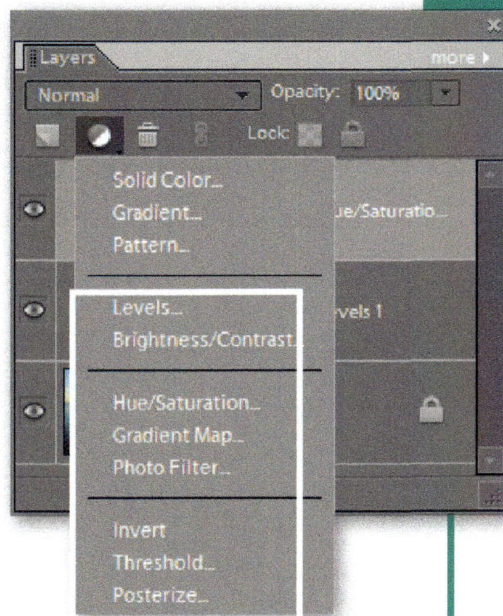

Adjustment Layers >> *Photoshop Elements contains eight different adjustment layers.*

Creating an adjustment layer adds a new entry to the layers palette just above the active layer. The adjustment layer entry contains two thumbnails – the Layer Thumbnail on the left and the Layer Mask thumbnail on the right. Double clicking the Layer Thumbnail will display the adjustment layer's dialog. For instance, in the case of a Levels adjustment layer, double clicking the thumbnail will display the Levels dialog. This provides the user with the ability to make adjustments to existing settings, or even rest the dialog, at any time. The Layer Mask is used to customize where and how the adjustment layer's changes are applied. See Technique 5.15 for more details.

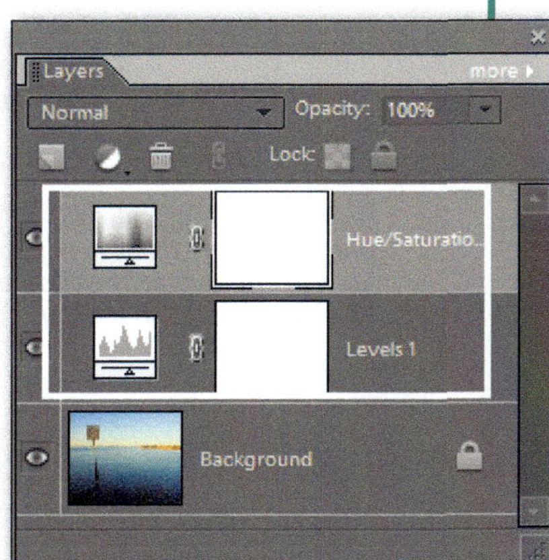

Adjustments applied downwards >> *Adjustment layers alter the look of the image layers that are positioned below them in the layers palette.*

Elements contains eight different types of adjustment layers which are grouped together with the fill layers under the Create Adjustment Layer button in the Layers palette. The same options can also be found in the Layer > New Adjustment Layer menu. They are:

Levels – Adjusts the tones in the picture.

Brightness/Contrast – Lightens, darkens and controls contrast.

Hue/Saturation – Changes the color and strength of color in photos.

Gradient Map – Changes the photo so that all the tones are mapped to the values of a selected gradient.

Photo Filter – Reproduces the color changes of traditional photo filters.

Invert – Reverses all the tones in a picture, producing a negative effect.

Threshold – Converts the picture to pure black and white with no grays present at all.

Posterize – Reduces the total number of colors in a picture and creates a flat paint (or poster)-like effect.

Placing an adjustment layer at the top of a stack of layers will ensure that the editing changes will be applied to the content of all the layers beneath. If instead of changing all the lower layers you want to restrict the effects of the adjustment layer to a single layer then after selecting the adjustment layer, pick the Group with Previous option from the Layer menu. This will indent the adjustment layer in the palette and, more importantly, 'group' the adjustment with the layer immediately below it. This technique is an important one as it changes the way that adjustment layers work and allows their non-destructive editing powers to be applied to individual image layers only.

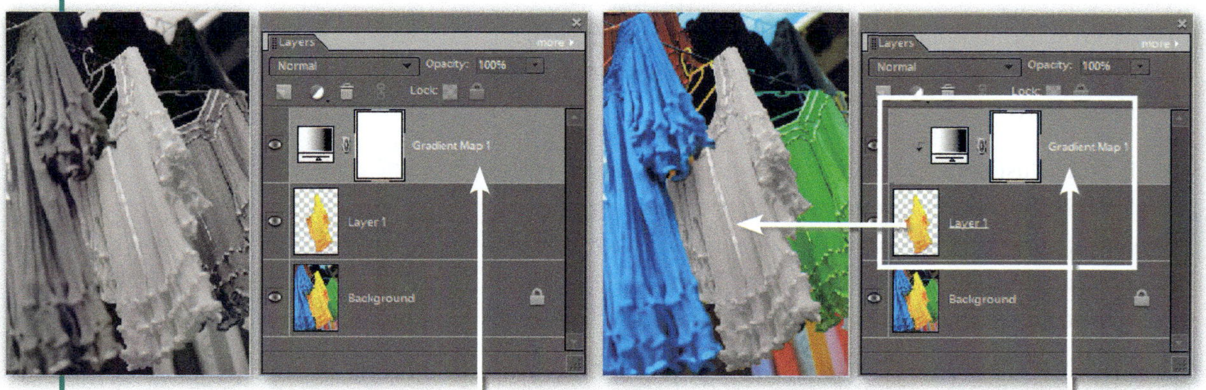

Gradient Map adjustment layer being applied to both image layers

Gradient Map adjustment layer grouped with Layer 1 so that the convert to gray change only occurs in one layer only

Restricting adjustments to a single layer >> *To link the changes made via an adjustment layer to a single layer only, make sure that the adjustment layer is directly above the image layer to be changed and then with the adjustment layer active, choose Layer > Group with Previous, or Ctrl + G.*
Pro Tip: *Alt-click on the border between a layer and the one below it to Group With Previous.*

5.13 Select and adjust in one stroke

Suitable for Elements – 7.0 | Difficulty level – Basic

One of the major changes introduced in Photoshop Elements 7.0 is the ability to select and make changes with the one tool. The new Smart Brush tool brings a whole new level of ease to the process of changing specific areas of your photo. By combining the selecting abilities of the Quick Selection tool and the enhancement options available via adjustment layers, the Adobe engineers have created a new way to change the look of your photos.

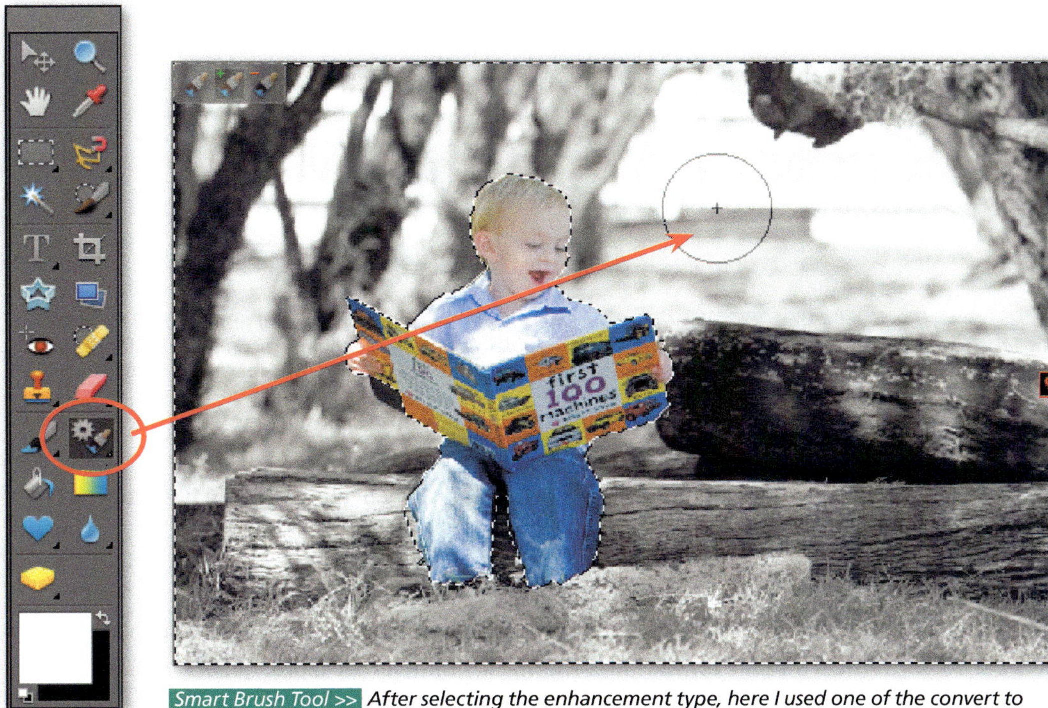

Smart Brush Tool >> *After selecting the enhancement type, here I used one of the convert to black and white options, all you need to do is paint over the parts of the photo that you want to change. If the tool selects too much of the photo, switch to the Subtract from Selection mode (hold down the Alt key) and paint over the unwanted change to remove it.*

Unlike the traditional way of applying adjustments where the user must first make a selection and then apply the adjustment, the Smart Brush Tool creates the selection and applies the adjustment as the user paints over the image. You can select the type of adjustment that will be applied with the tool from a list of over 65 that ships with Elements. These presets are grouped under general headings in the Preset Chooser located in the options bar. Here you will find options for altering image characteristics such as color, tone and saturation as well as subject based enhancements such as brightening teeth or making a dull sky bluer and, of course, a bunch of special effects changes. Preset entries can be displayed in a list or thumbnail form by selecting one of the options displayed when pressing the double sideways arrows in the top left of the Presets window.

The Smart Brush Tool is only available in Full editor workspace.

FEATURE SUMMARY

1 With the Smart Brush tool active, go to the Options Bar and select the type of enhancement from the Preset Chooser pop-up menu.

2 Now paint over the areas that you wish to select and enhance.

3 After the first selection area is drawn, the tool's mode automatically changes to Add to Selection so that you can include extra areas in the selection.

4 Subtract from the selection by painting over new areas after switching to the Subtract from Selection mode using the buttons in the Options Bar or the floating palette at the top right of the photo.

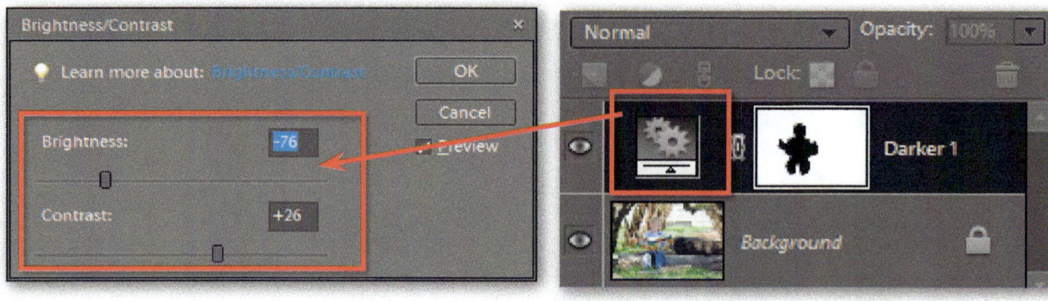

Fine-tuning Smart Brush Tool effects >> *With some Smart Brush Tool entries the actual settings used for making the image adjustments can be edited. In this example, double-clicking on the thumbnail on the left of the entry displays the Brightness/Contrast dialog. In the dialog you can change the settings used for the adjustment.*

When you paint on a photo with the Smart Brush Tool, Elements creates a new Adjustment Layer and adds it to the layer stack with a mask based on the painted selection. Cool! We get the power of masked adjustment layers without any of the pain of creating them manually, but how do we alter Smart Brush Tool effects once they are added?

To alter the strength of a Smart Brush Effect: Changing the strength of the effect is a simple matter of selecting the Smart Brush Tool entry in the layers palette and then adjusting the Opacity slider at the top right of the palette. The lower the opacity number the more subtle the effect.

To change how the effect combines with the picture: Photoshop Elements controls how the contents of two layers are mixed together via the Blend Mode setting. Elements uses this setting to adjust how the Smart Brush Tool layer interacts with the background or image layer. To change Blend Modes just select a new entry from the drop down list at the top left of the layers palette.

To change the settings of the effect itself: As all Smart Brush Tool effects are based on masked adjustment layers, to change the style of the effects, it should be possible to double-click on the layer thumbnail and simply change the settings in the dialog that appears. For most Smart Brush Tool adjustments this is true (check out the Lighting options) as they are built upon Elements Adjustment Layers, but this is not always the case as some effects are based on features that are only available in Photoshop itself. If you try to adjust these you will get a warning notice saying that it is not possible to tweak the settings.

5.14 'All Layers' tool options

Suitable for Elements – 7.0, 6.0, 5.0, 4.0, 3.0, 2.0, 1.0 | Difficulty level – Basic

Removing dust and scratches is a regular correction activity for digital photographers, irrespective of if they are working on scanned historical photos, or recently captured portraits, where the client wants slight skin blemishes disguised. These changes are often performed with Elements' features such as the Clone Stamp tool, Spot Healing and Healing Brushes on the main or background layer. Working this way changes the original pixels forever. A non-destructive work around that provides the same results, makes use of the 'All Layers' options of these tools to keep the changes in a separate retouching layer that sits above the background.

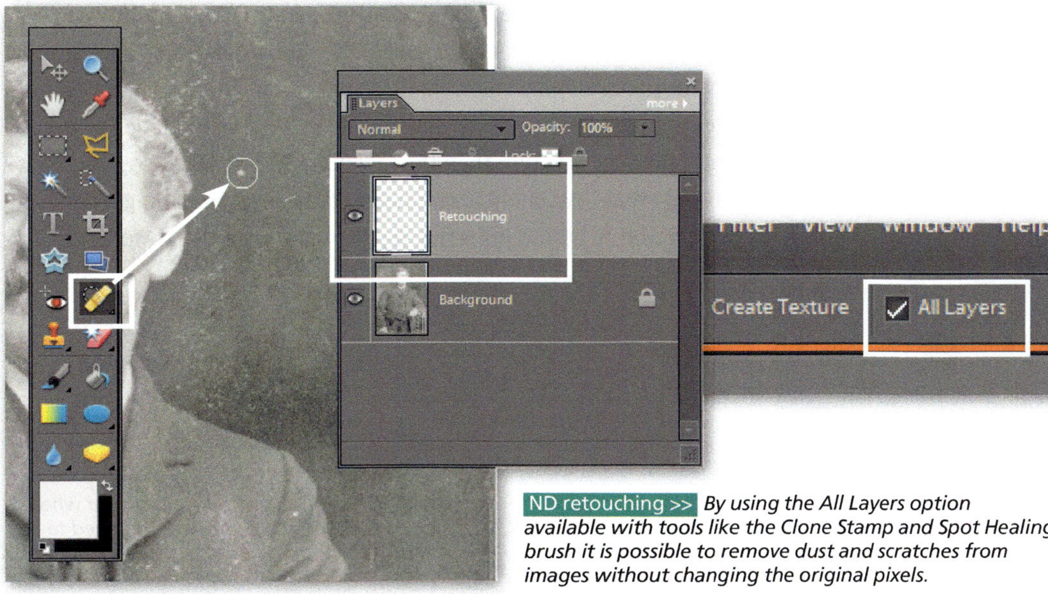

ND retouching >> *By using the All Layers option available with tools like the Clone Stamp and Spot Healing brush it is possible to remove dust and scratches from images without changing the original pixels.*

To use this technique start by creating a new layer above the background layer. Rename this layer Retouching. Next select the layer to make sure that it is active and choose the desired tool from the Elements' toolbar. Before commencing the repair work, select the All Layers option in the tool's options bar. Now proceed to use the tool normally. The retouching changes though stored in a separate layer are seamlessly blended with the background. For specific restoration and retouching techniques turn to Chapters 8 and 9.

5.15 Blend Modes

Suitable for Elements – 7.0, 6.0, 5.0, 4.0, 3.0, 2.0, 1.0 | Difficulty level – Basic

As we have seen with the Smart Brush Tool the way that individual layers interact with other layers in the stack is determined by the blending mode setting. By default the layer's mode is set to Normal, which causes the picture content on the upper layer to obscure the picture parts beneath, but Photoshop Elements has many other ways (modes) to control how these pixels interact.

Called 'blend modes', the different options provide a variety of ways to control the mixing, blending and general interaction of the layer content. The modes are grouped into several different categories based on the type of changes that they make. The layer blend modes are located in the drop-down menu at the top left of the Layers palette. Blend modes can also be applied to the painting and drawing tools via a drop-down menu in the tool's options bar. For a complete list of the Blend Modes available in Photoshop Elements go to the Appendix at the end of this book.

So how can blend modes help us when it comes to altering out images non-destructively? By providing us with a range of ways to mix the image content from two layers, Blend Modes increase our ability to edit and enhance without changing original pixels. Let's take the example of coloring a grayscale image to simulate the look of a hand colored photo of old. You may first think that the task is a simple one, select the color, choose the Brush tool and then paint over the grayscale background layer. Do this and you will get a paint stroke of solid color, that obscures all the detail of the original image. Not the look that we are wanting! However, if you change the Brush's Blend Mode (using the drop-down menu in the tool's option bar) to Color then the tool magically applies color in direct proportion as tone of the background image. All detail is retained in the underlying image, but this detail is colored the hue of the foreground swatch. This is the magic of the Color Blend Mode.

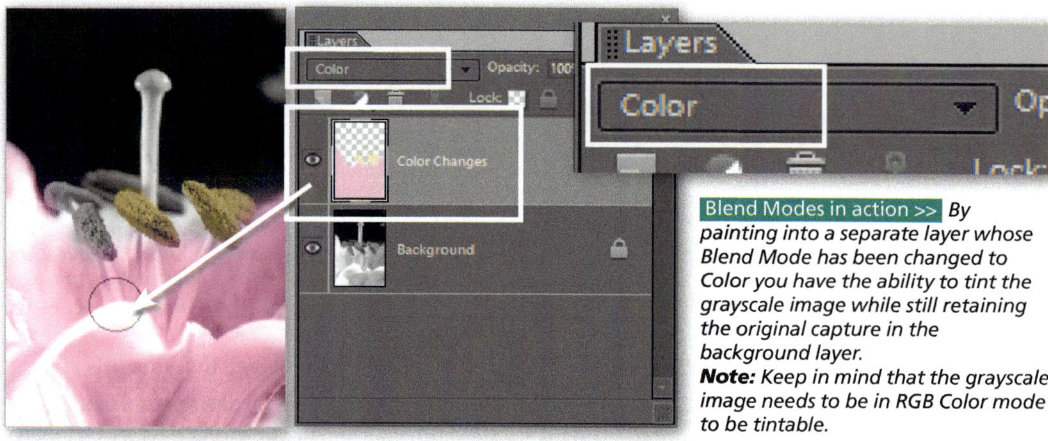

Blend Modes in action >> *By painting into a separate layer whose Blend Mode has been changed to Color you have the ability to tint the grayscale image while still retaining the original capture in the background layer.*
Note: *Keep in mind that the grayscale image needs to be in RGB Color mode to be tintable.*

That said, in applying the coloring directly to the background layer we are destructively altering the primary pixels. So let's rework the technique so that it still uses the Blend Mode but protects the original image. Start by creating a new layer to house the color changes. Next change the Blend Mode of the layer to Color. Select the foreground color and then the Brush tool. Make sure that the Blend Mode of the Brush is back to the default setting (Normal). With the new color changes layer selected, paint over the image. Notice that the same coloring effect is produced but this time the Blend Mode change is applied to the layer not the Brush.

5.16 Layer Masking

Suitable for Elements – 7.0, 6.0, 5.0, 4.0, 3.0, 2.0, 1.0 | Difficulty level – Basic

As we have already seen each time you add a fill or adjustment layer to an image two thumbnails are created in the Layers palette. The one on the left controls the settings for the adjustment layer. The thumbnail on the right represents the layer's mask that controls how the adjustment is applied to the picture.

The mask is a grayscale image. When it's colored white no part of the adjustment layer's effects are masked or held back from the picture below. The full changes are applied to the image. Conversely if the mask thumbnail is totally black then none of the layer's effects are applied to the picture. Shades of gray equate to various levels of transparency. In this way, the enhancement changes produced via an adjustment, or fill layer, can be selectively applied, or merged, with the layers beneath by painting (in black and white and gray) onto the layer mask.

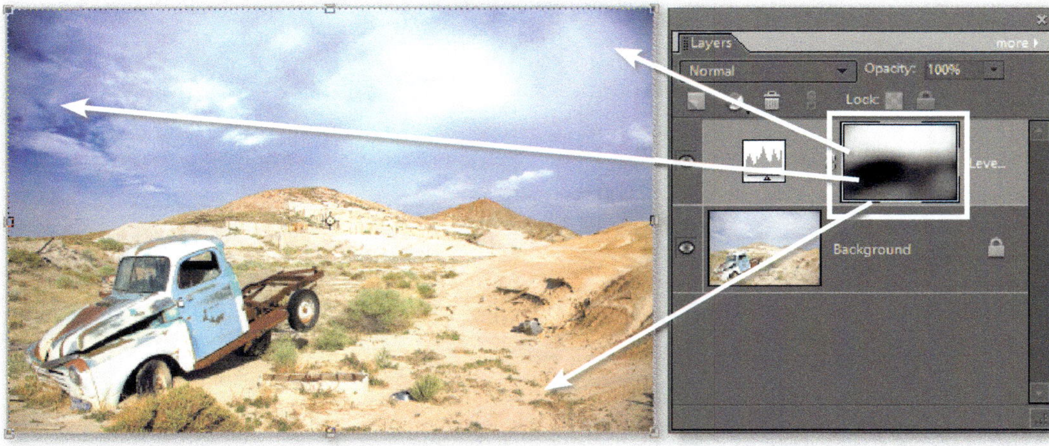

Masking >> *Modifying the mask associated with adjustment layers provides the option to customize where the effects of the layer are applied to the image layer. Using varying levels of gray will also change the strength of the enhancement effect. A darker gray will produce less noticeable changes whereas a light gray will allow more of the adjustment layer's effects to be seen.*

By default the layer mask is set to white so that the adjustment effect is fully applied. To customize the application of the effect, click onto the Layer Mask thumbnail (so that there is a second line border surround in the thumbnail), select the Brush tool and choose black, white or gray as the foreground color. Now paint over the surface of the image. Notice that the adjustment layer effect is reduced or eliminated in the areas where you paint with gray or black. Also notice that the mask thumbnail now displays the painted strokes. It is also worth noting that preselecting an area before creating the adjustment layer will result in a Mask the shape and size of the selection.

Many professionals use masks on a regular basis to help customize the application of adjustment layer changes and also for governing how the picture parts in separate image layers interact. Though Photoshop Elements doesn't contain all the masking power that its bigger brother Photoshop does, customizing adjustment layers is no problem and, with a simple 'work around' (see Technique 5.14), it is also possible to provide more masking functionality than is generally available to the Elements user.

5.17 Duplicate layers

Suitable for Elements – 7.0, 6.0, 5.0, 4.0, 3.0, 2.0, 1.0 | Difficulty level – Basic

In situations where none of the above techniques can be used to edit non-destructively it will be necessary to use other means to preserve the integrity of the original file. A clear example of this is when it comes time to add some sharpening to your photos. Now by design, applying a sharpening filter will pretty much change all the pixels in your photo in order to increase the clarity of the picture, which makes the action very destructive and one that should be avoided. So what other route can we take to provide the same results?

Well the simplest way is to duplicate the image layer, and then apply the sharpening filter to the copy, rather than the original layer. This way the primary pixels (in the original image layer) are

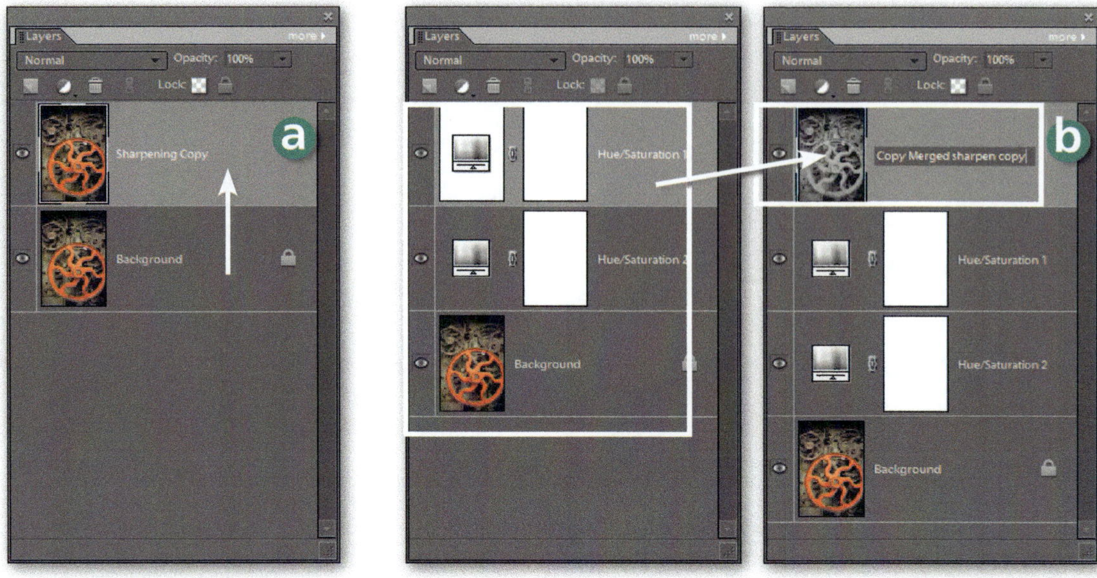

Editing layer copies >> *When there is no other option than apply editing changes directly to the image layer then the best way to ensure that your original pixels are protected is to duplicate the image layer and execute the changes on the copy (a). With multi-layer documents use the Copy Merge command to duplicate the contents of all layers first before applying the editing changes to the merge layer (b).*

protected and displaying the sharpened result is a simple matter of ensuring that it resides at the top of the layer stack. Alternatively the original can be hidden from view (click the 'eye' icon on the left of the layer entry).

In the case of a document that contains multiple image layers or a combination of image and adjustment layers some photographers would merge all the image layers before copying the resultant layer and applying the sharpen filter. The act of merging means that you will lose the ability to change the settings in the adjustment layers or edit any of the image layers independently. So forget the Layer > Merge Layers command, instead select the whole document using the Select > Select All command and then copy the contents of all the layers to memory by choosing the Copy Merged option from the Edit menu. Next select the uppermost layer in the layer stack and select Edit > Paste. This action inserts a new layer at the top of the stack that is the combination of all the layers in the document. This layer can then be filtered without fear of damaging the original photo.

Pro's Tip

Secret Pro's Tip: Instead of doing the select all, copy merged, paste to top of stack steps, pros simply add a new empty layer at the top of the stack and then do Shift-Alt-Control + E which is a undocumented Stamp Visible command that unfortunately has no menu equivalent.

Giving Elements a helping hand

It is true that Photoshop Elements contains a dazzling array of editing and enhancement tools. In fact, many would say that if you can't find a tool to perform the changes you desire, then you are not really trying. But as we have seen, just having the right tool to hand is not the whole story, it is also important to ensure that you are able to use the tools in a way that preserves the pixels first captured, and produces the best quality enhancements possible. This often means using the tools we have in ways that perhaps were not envisaged when the features were first designed. The next few techniques extend the editing abilities of Photoshop Elements beyond the standard workflow approaches advocated in most texts. These options may not need to be used with every photo, but they will certainly come in handy with specific enhancement tasks and will become an important technique in your editing kit bag.

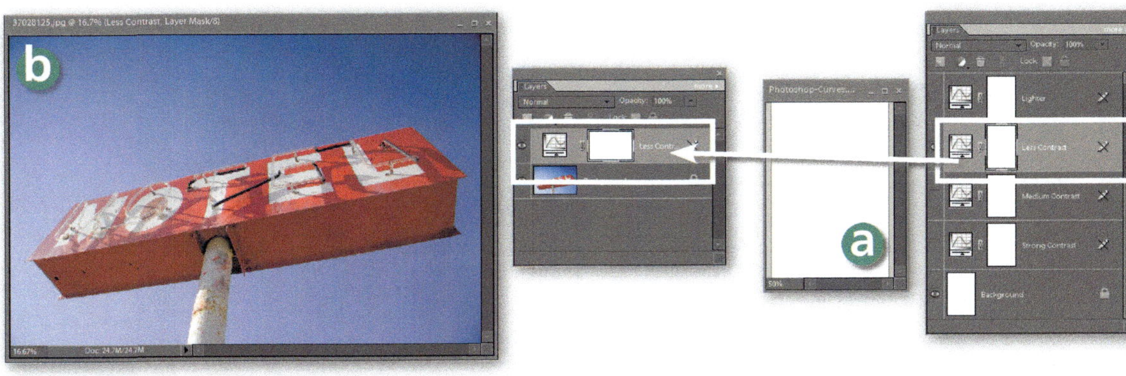

Photoshop features in Elements >> *Users can add to the functionality of Elements by opening Photoshop documents (a) containing Photoshop only adjustment layers (e.g. Curves, Selective Color, Black and White and Color Balance) and then dragging these layers to their Element documents (b). The adjustment layer's enhancements will be applied to the document, but the settings for these layers can not be altered in Elements.*

5.18 Borrowing Photoshop features

Suitable for Elements – 7.0, 6.0, 5.0, 4.0, 3.0, 2.0, 1.0 | Difficulty level – Basic

Because of the professional nature of Photoshop, it contains a range of high level features and tools that are not available in Elements. This said, both Photoshop and Elements contain a range of tools and features and technology in common and much of the nuts and bolts that sit behind the scenes are shared by both programs. This cross over leads to an interesting situation where some features that are Photoshop only can be borrow to be used, in a limited way, in Elements.

We have been talking about the importance of Adjustment Layers as a way of non-destructive enhancing and, as you would expect, Photoshop contains more adjustment layer options than Elements. Of interest to us particularly are the Curves, Color Balance, Selective Color and the new Black and White adjustment layers. Though these features can't be invoked or Adjusted in Elements, a Photoshop document containing the layers can be opened in the program. The Adjustment layers can be seen as separate entries in the layers palette, but for the most part, the settings can't be adjusted, Black and White is an exception, but more on this later. When this scenario is coupled with the fact that Photoshop adjustment layers can be dragged from one document to another, users end up with the ability to apply non Elements based adjustment layers to Elements documents. Cool!

In practice, I created several documents in Photoshop containing Adjustment Layers with a variety of settings, but no image data. I then open these files in Elements and drag the required adjustment layer from the Photoshop document to the Elements file and hey presto, the enhancement is applied. Now that is fine for me, as I have both Photoshop and Elements on my machine, but I know that most readers do not have this luxury, so for this reason I have created several different Photoshop documents that are available from the book's website that you can use for your own projects.

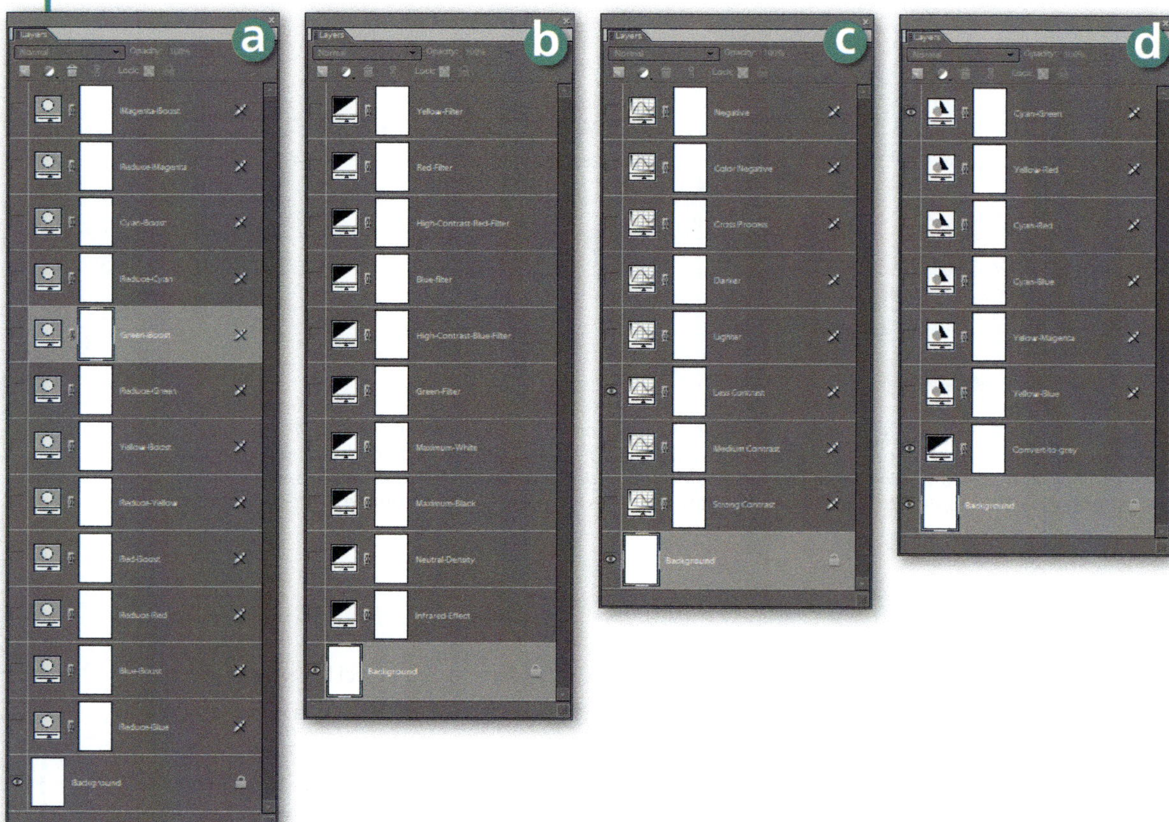

Photoshop donor documents >> *The book's website contains several documents created in Photoshop that can be used to donate Photoshop only adjustment layers to your Elements document.*
(a) Photoshop-Selective-Color.psd
(b) Photoshop-Convert-to-gray.psd
(c) Photoshop-Curves.psd
(d) Photoshop-Split-Tones.psd

Photoshop donor documents

The book's website contains four key Photoshop donor documents (the files containing adjustment layers which can be dragged to Elements documents) designed to be used for specific enhancement activities. Each document includes multiple layers for a single adjustment feature. The settings for each layer differ providing a bunch of preset enhancement options that can be applied to Elements documents by simply dragging and dropping the layer to the Elements files. The donor documents include:

Photoshop-Selective-Color.psd – For boosting or reducing specific colors using the Selective Color Adjustment layer.

Photoshop-Convert-to-Gray.psd – Monochrome conversions using the Black and White feature.

Photoshop-Curves.psd – Curves based adjustment of the tones in your photos.

Photoshop-Split-Tones.psd – Sophisticated split toning effects using Photoshop's Color Balance adjustment layer to separately tone highlights and shadows.

5.19 Advanced layer masks

Suitable for Elements – 7.0, 6.0, 5.0, 4.0, 3.0, 2.0, 1.0 | Difficulty level – Basic

Along with extra adjustment layers Photoshop also contains advanced masking options that are not available in Elements. We have already see how it is possible to use the masks associated with Adjustment Layers to customize where the layer's effects are applied, well, Photoshop allows users to

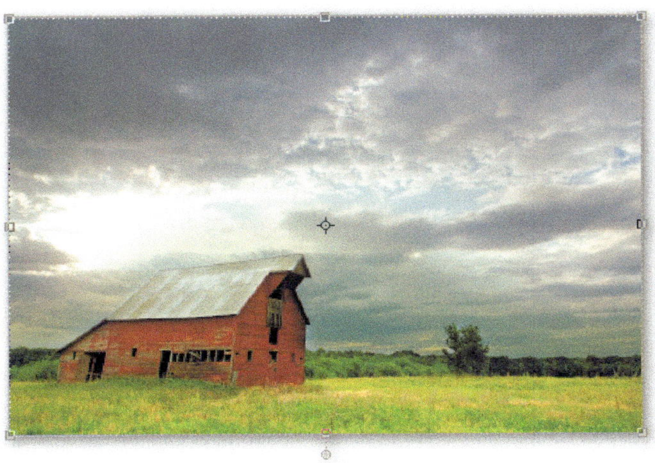

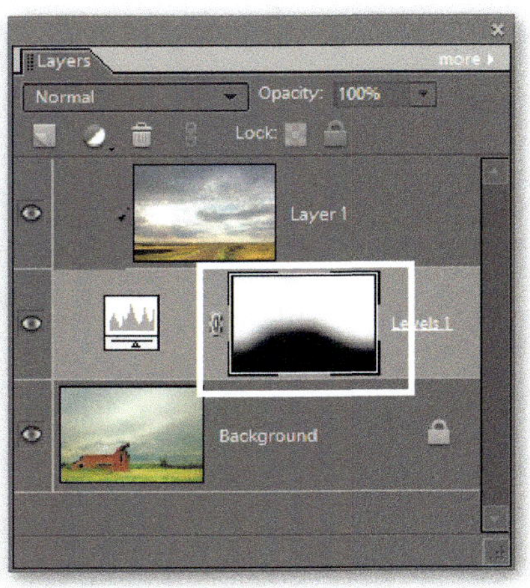

Image layer masks >> *Though not designed for this purpose it is possible to use the Layer Masks associated with adjustment layers to mask image layers. In the example above the sky from the upper image layer is HomeSite with the foreground detail from the layer below using the layer mask in the Levels adjustment layer. For this to occur the adjustment layer needs to be created with no settings and then the upper image layer is Grouped with the adjustment layer.*

use masks with image layers to provide the same level of customization when montaging. When a mask is attached to an image layer, it can be used to adjust which parts of the upper layer are visible, and which parts are hidden from view allowing the contents of the layer beneath to show through. This is a very handy function as it is provides non-destructive montage abilities. Elements users can access such masking abilities by highjacking the mask associated with an adjustment layer and use it with an image layer.

The process involves adding an adjustment layer, with no settings applied, to the layers stack in between the two image layers to be montaged. Next the upper image layer is grouped with the no-settings adjustment layer. This action essentially links the image layer with the mask of the adjustment layer. As the mask by default is white, the upper image layer is displayed in full, but paint onto the layer mask with a black (or gray) brush and details of the lower layer will be revealed. By using black, white and gray paint strokes on the mask it is possible to non-destructively mix the contents of the two image layers. Look for examples of this technique throughout the next chapters.

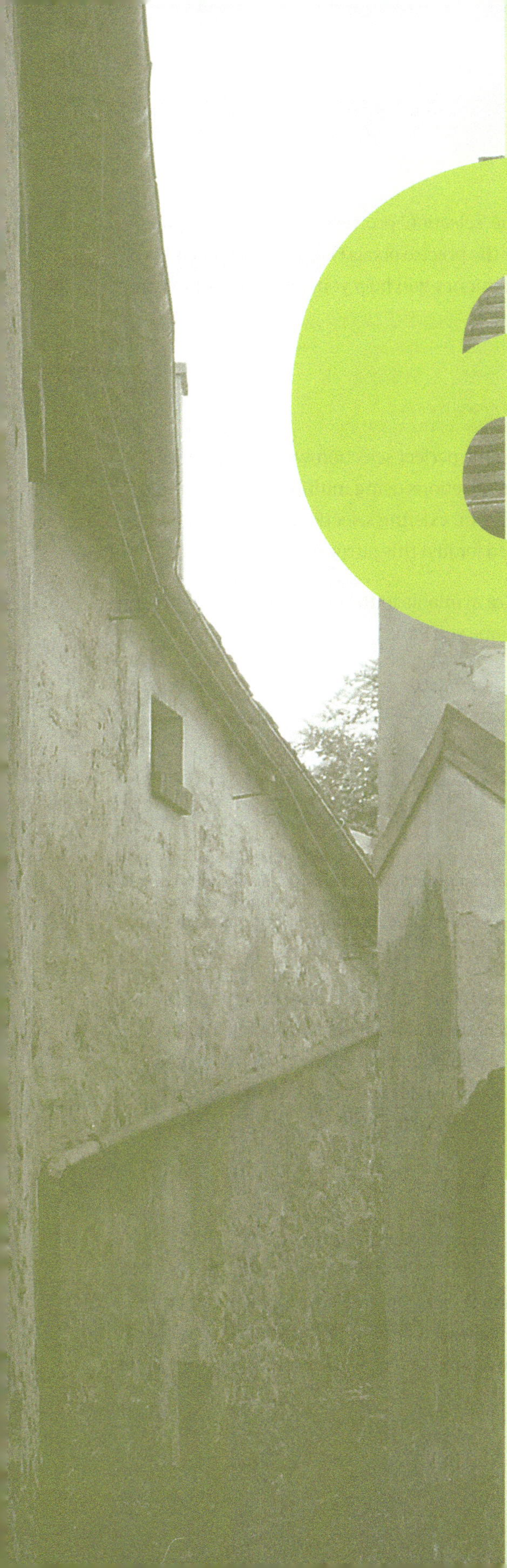

6

Image Changes – Beyond the Basics

Advanced selection techniques

Many great image editing techniques are based on the 'selection' prowess of the photographer. Being able to manipulate the selection tools to isolate the precise pixels that you wish to edit is a key skill that we all should possess. The following techniques will help you build on your existing selection skills.

6.01 Adding to and subtracting from selections

Suitable for Elements – 7.0, 6.0, 5.0, 4.0, 3.0, 2.0, 1.0 | Difficulty level – Basic
Related techniques – 6.02, 6.03, 6.04, 6.05 | Tools used – Magic Wand, Lasso, Marquee

Only on a very rare occasion will you be able to create the perfect selection with a single tool applied once. Most editing jobs require the building of selections using multiple tools, creating new selections that are either added to, or subtracted from, existing selections. Photoshop Elements provides a range of features that are designed for just this purpose.

When a selection tool is in use four selection modes are available in the options bar. By switching between these modes while making additional selections you can:

- Create a **new** selection each time the tool is applied,
- **Add** to an existing selection,
- **Subtract** from an existing selection, or
- Make a selection from the **intersection** of the new and old selections.

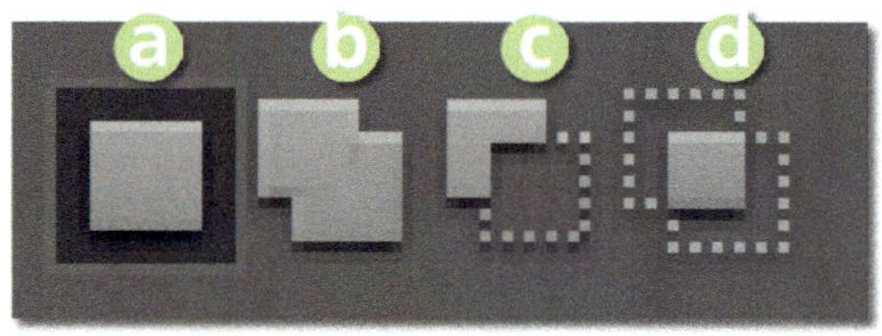

Adding to selections >> *Modify your selections by switching selection modes using the buttons found in the Options menu. (a) New selection. (b) Add to selection. (c) Subtract from selection. (d) Make new selection from the intersection.*

The modes are available for all selection tools the exception being that the Intersect mode can not be used with the Quick Selection Tool or the Selection Brush tools. The New Selection option is the default. Complex areas of a picture can be isolated by making a series of selections choosing the necessary tool (Lasso, Marquee, Magic Wand, Selection Brush or Quick Selection Tool) and mode (new, add to, subtract from, intersection of) as you go. The mode of the current tool can also be changed using a keyboard shortcut whilst selecting. Hold down the Shift key to add to a selection or the Alt key to take away or subtract from a selection.

6.02 Using the Selection Brush

Suitable for Elements – 7.0, 6.0, 5.0, 4.0, 3.0, 2.0 | Difficulty level – Intermediate | Resources – Web image 602
Related techniques – 6.01, 6.03, 6.04, 6.05 | Tools used – Selection tools | Menus used – Select

Responding to photographers' demands for even more options for making selections, Adobe included the Selection Brush for the first time in version 2.0 of Elements. The tool lets you paint a selection onto your image. The size, shape and edge softness of the selection are based on the brush properties you currently have set. These can be altered in the Brush Presets pop-up palette located in the options bar.

The tool can be used in two modes – Selection and Mask:

- The **Selection mode** is used to paint over the area you wish to select.
- The **Mask mode** is particularly well suited for showing the soft or feathered edge selections made when painting with a soft-edged brush or when making detailed edits to the selection. The Mask mode works by reverse painting in the areas you want to 'mask from the selection'.

Holding down the Alt (Windows) or Option (Mac) keys whilst dragging the brush switches the tool from adding to the selection to taking away from the area.

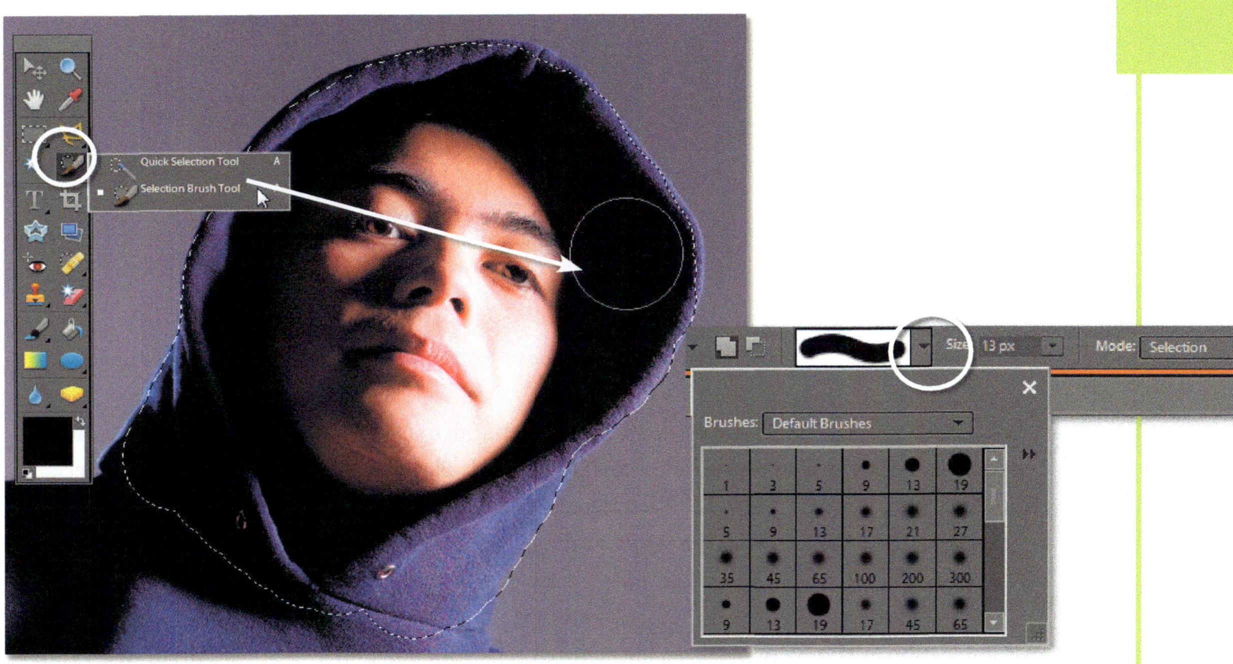

Painting selections >> *The Selection Brush tool allows the user to create selections by painting directly onto the picture surface.*

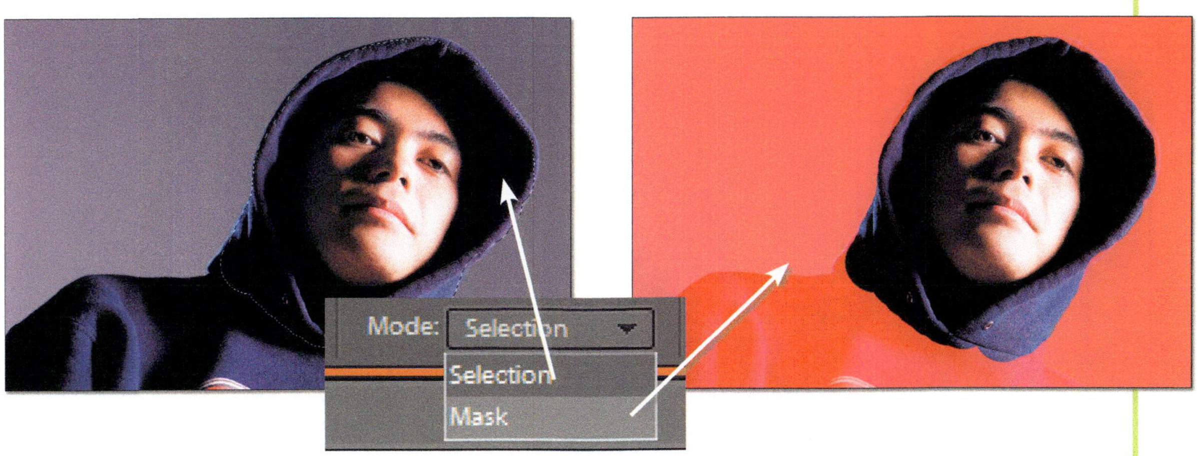

Selection Brush modes >> *The Selection Brush can work in either selection or mask modes.*

6.03 The Quick Selection Tool

Suitable for Elements – 7.0, 6.0 , 5.0, 4.0, 3.0, 2.0 | Difficulty level – Intermediate | Resources – Web image 6.02 Related techniques – 6.01, 6.03, 6.04, 6.05 | Tools used – Selection tools | Menus used – Select

Along with the Selection Brush tool, the new Quick Selection tool (previously the Magic Selection Brush) provides Elements users with a unique approach to creating and modifying selections. As we have seen, when using the Selection Brush the user must paint over the area to be encompassed by the selection. The accuracy of this painting step determines the accuracy of the final selection. For example, accidentally painting over an edge will result in the creation of a selection that goes beyond this picture part.

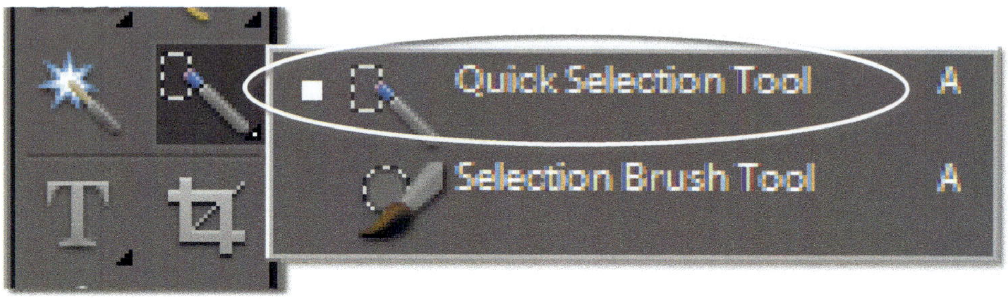

Quick 'magical' selections >> *The Quick Selection tool is coupled with the Selection Brush in the tool bar.*

The Quick Selection tool provides a quicker, easier and, in most cases, more accurate way to make selections by combining both the drawing and color selection approaches of the other tools we have covered. To make a selection choose the tool from the tool bar. If it is hidden from view click the small arrow at the bottom right of the Selection Brush button to reveal the tool. The Quick Selection tool doesn't require you to scribble or place some dots on the picture parts that you want to select as was the case with the Magic Selection Brush. Instead Elements creates the selection as you paint over specific picture areas. You don't have to be too careful with your initial painting as the program registers the color, tone and texture of the picture parts and then intelligently searches for other similar pixels to include in the selection.

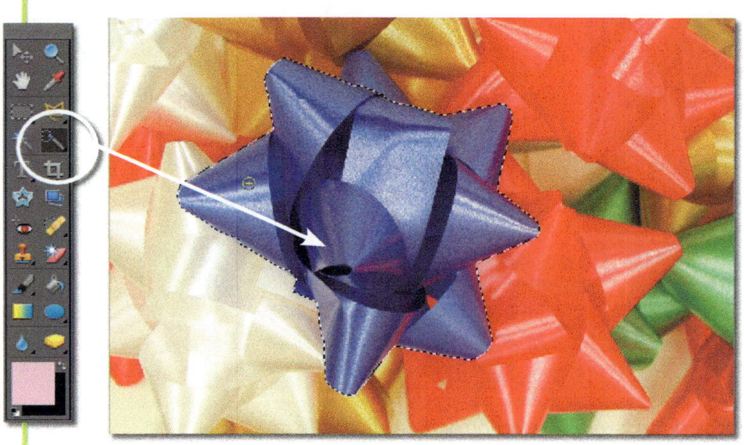

Elements does the selection work >> *As you are drawing with the Quick Selection tool Elements automatically generates a selection of all the adjacent areas in the picture that have similar color, texture or tone.*

Fine-tuning the areas selected with Quick Selection tool

Although this tool does a pretty good job of selecting alike areas, there will always be occasions when either too much or too little of the picture has been included. Just like the other tools we have looked at, the Quick Selection tool allows you to easily modify the selections it makes.

To include other areas in the selection, click the Add to Selection button in the tool's options bar (the cursor will change to include a small +) and paint over a new picture part. This step will cause Elements to regenerate the selection to include your changes. To remove an area from the selection, click on the Subtract from Selection button (cursor changes to the brush tip and a small - sign), and paint over the part to eliminate. Again, Elements will regenerate the selection to account for the changes. The Shift and Alt keys can be used whilst drawing to change modes on the fly and add to or subtract from the selection.

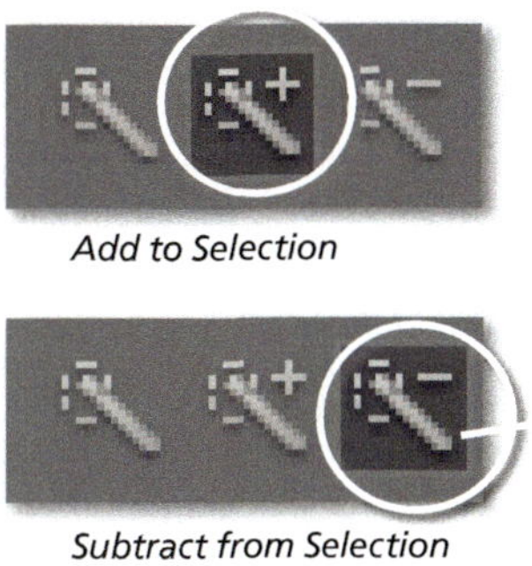

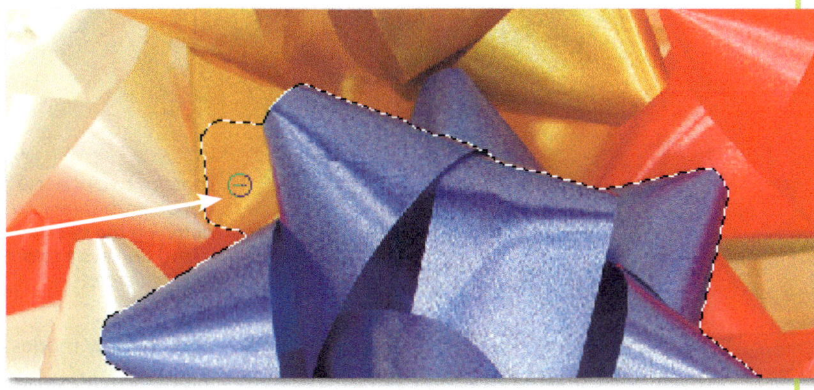

Adding to or subtracting from quick selections >> *The options bar of the Quick Selection tool contains several modes that can be used for altering or refining the selection created by the tool. You can add other picture parts to a selection by clicking on the Add to Selection button and then painting over the new area. Parts already selected can be removed by changing to the Subtract from Selection mode and painting on these areas.*

6.04 Advanced refining of selection edges

Suitable for Elements – 7.0, 6.0, 5.0, 4.0, 3.0, 2.0 | Difficulty level – Intermediate | Resources – Web image 602
Related techniques – 6.01, 6.03, 6.04, 6.05 | Tools used – Selection tools | Menus used – Select

Photoshop Elements also contains a way to modify the edges of the selections you create. Called the Refine Edge feature it is accessed either via the button now present in all the selection tools' options bars, or via the Select > Refine Edge menu entry. The feature brings together three different controls for adjusting the edges of the selection with two selection edge preview options. The edge controls previously existed as separate entries in either the Select or Select > Modify menu. Bringing them together in the one dialog, and then providing live preview options as well, means that the refining activity will be a lot more accurate, as you will be able to see the results of the changes made to any of the controls reflected in the image itself.

The feature's dialog contains a Preview toggle, and Zoom and Move tools which can be used for navigating around enlarged images to check the properties of the selection edge. The edge controls themselves come in the form of the following three sliders:

Smooth – This option removes stepped or jagged selection edges.

Feather – Softens the edge of the selection by a given pixel value. You can use this setting to provide a gradual transition between selected and non-selected areas.

Contract/Expand – Increase or decrease the size of the area outlined by the selection by the percentage value selected.

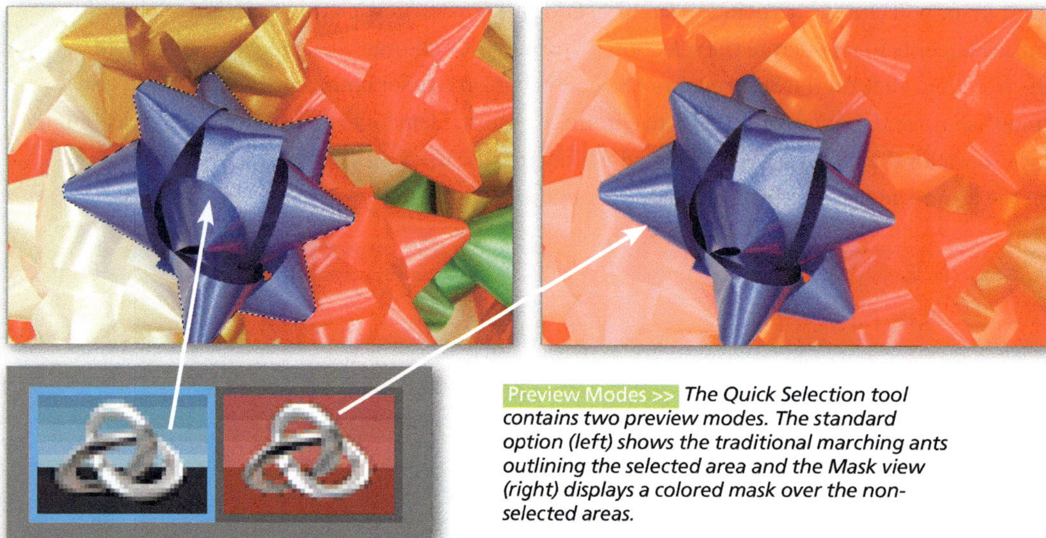

Preview Modes >> *The Quick Selection tool contains two preview modes. The standard option (left) shows the traditional marching ants outlining the selected area and the Mask view (right) displays a colored mask over the non-selected areas.*

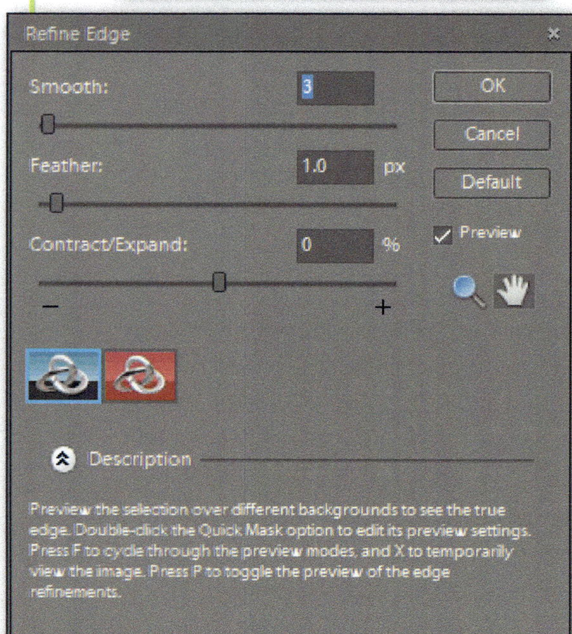

Refine Edges dialog >> *The Refine Edge dialog brings together all the controls used for altering the characteristics of the selection's edge into a single dialog. The feature also includes two edge preview options.*

The Preview modes buttons at the bottom of the dialog provide a range of different ways to view the selection on your picture. The left button displays a standard selection edge superimposed on the photo. The edge is outlined using the familiar 'marching ants' line.

The other button previews the selection as a mask, with the selected area displayed clear of color and the non-selected area colored with a specific color overlay. The color and transparency of the mask overlay can be altered by double-clicking the preview button.

Selecting the Mask option provides a much better way of viewing the quality of the selection edge as it is possible to preview the sharpness of the edge as well as how transparent the overlap is between selected and non-selected areas (feathering). For best results, use the Mask option in conjunction with the Zoom and Move tools to inspect an enlarged preview

IMAGE CHANGES – BEYOND THE BASICS

of the selection edge, as you make changes to the dialog's slider controls.

Press the 'P' key to turn off the preview of the current Refine Edge settings and the 'X' key to temporarily display the Full Image view.

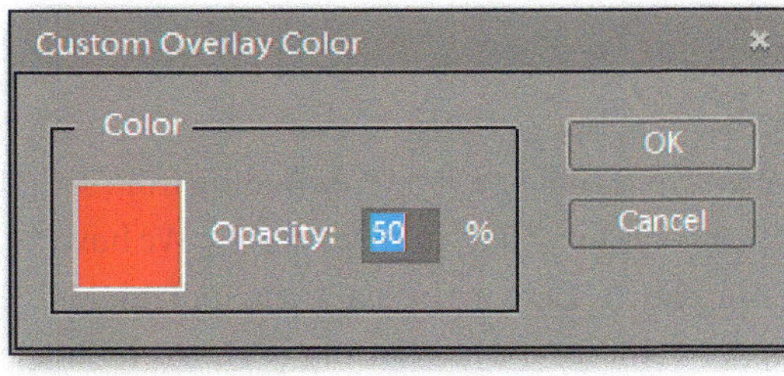

Overlay options >> *By double-clicking the Mask Preview option you can alter the color and opacity of the mask.*

6.05 Saving and loading selections

Suitable for Elements – 7.0, 6.0, 5.0, 4.0, 3.0, 2.0, 1.0 | Difficulty level – Intermediate | Resources – Web image 6.04
Related techniques – 6.01, 6.03, 6.04, 6.05 | Tools used – Selection tools | Menus used – Select

Photoshop Elements thankfully gives you the option to save all your hard selecting work so that it can be used again later. With your selection active choose the Save Selection option from the Select menu. Your selection will now be saved as part of the file when you save in PSD, TIFF, PDF or JPEG 2000 formats. When you open the file later you can retrieve the selection by choosing Load Selection from the same menu. This feature is particularly useful when making sophisticated multi-step selections, as you can make sequential saves, marking your progress and ensuring that you never lose your work. The Save Selection dialog also provides you with another way to modify your selections. Here you will find the option to save a newly created selection in any of the four selection modes we looked at earlier. This provides you with an alternative method for building complex selections which is based on making a selection and then saving it as an addition. In this way you can create a sophisticated selection one step at a time.

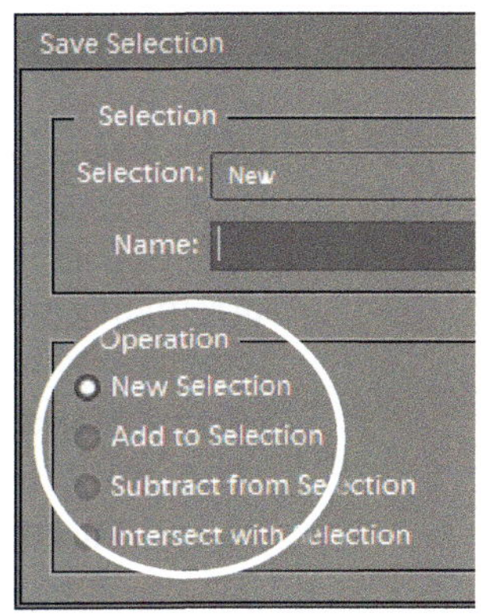

Save Selection dialog >> *You can also choose to modify your selection via the modes in the Save Selection dialog.*

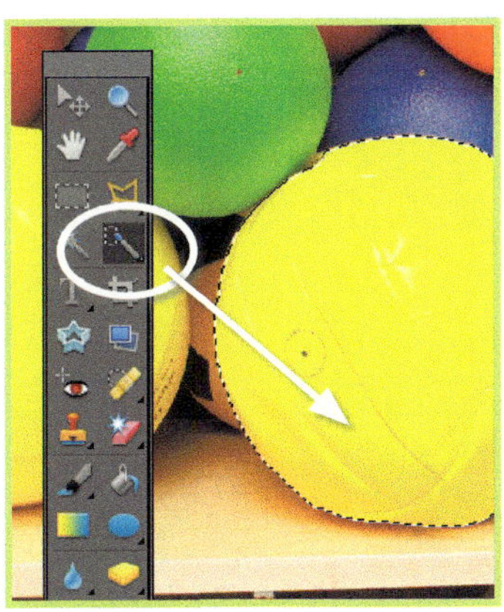

Step 1 >> *Use your favorite tool to make your first selection.*

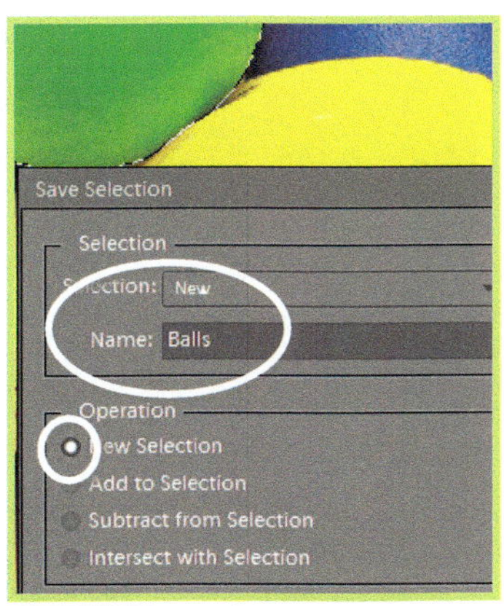

Step 2 >> *Save this as a new selection using the Select > Save Selection feature. Deselect (Ctrl + D).*

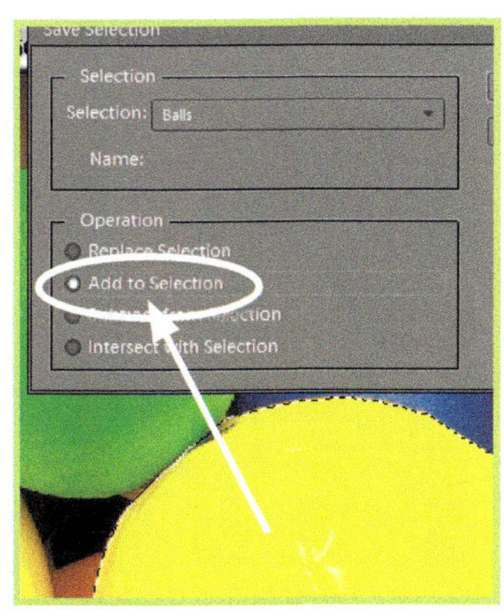

Step 3 >> *Make a new selection and then save it using the Add to Selection mode in the Save dialog.*

6.06 Modifying selections

Suitable for Elements – 7.0, 6.0, 5.0, 4.0, 3.0, 2.0, 1.0 | Difficulty level – Intermediate | Resources – Web image 6.04
Related techniques – 6.01, 6.02, 6.04 | Tools used – Selection tools | Menus used – Select

Apart from adding to and subtracting from selections, Photoshop Elements also offers several other ways to modify your selections. We have already seen some of these options in the Refine Edge feature. Here we look at them individually. Nested under the Select menu, most of these options change the positioning or character of the selection's edge. They can provide quick ways to adjust your selections. Use Refine Edge if you want to preview the changes to the selection before application.

- **Select > Feather** adjusts the smoothness of the transition between selected and non-selected areas. Low values are used for sharp-edged selections and higher values for softer ones.
- **Select > Modify > Border** creates a border of a specific pixel width at the selection's edge. Add color to this border using the Edit>Fill command. This option only creates soft edge borders. Use Edit>Stroke to create hard-edged lines around a selection.
- **Select > Modify > Smooth** searches for unselected pixels within the nominated radius. If these areas are surrounded by selected pixels then they will be included in the selection; if the surrounding areas are not selected then they will be removed from the selection.
- **Select > Modify > Expand** increases the size of the selection evenly by the pixel amount selected.
- **Select > Modify > Contract** decreases the selection size by the pixel amount selected.
- **Select > Grow** selects pixels adjacent to the selection that are within the tolerance range of the Magic Wand settings.
- **Select > Similar** chooses all pixels throughout the picture that fall within the Magic Wand tolerance settings.

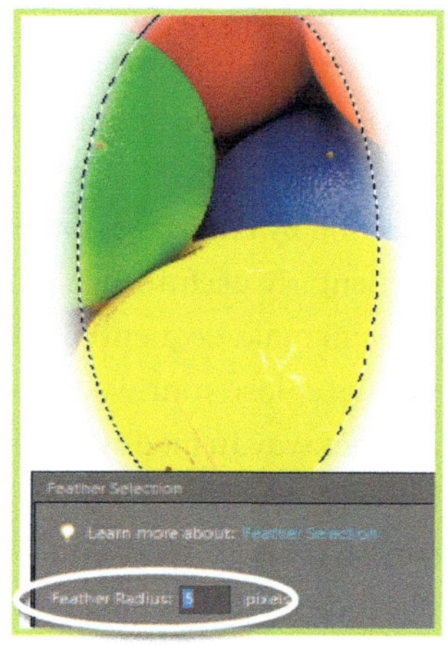

Feather >> *Use this option to create graduated edges to your selections.*

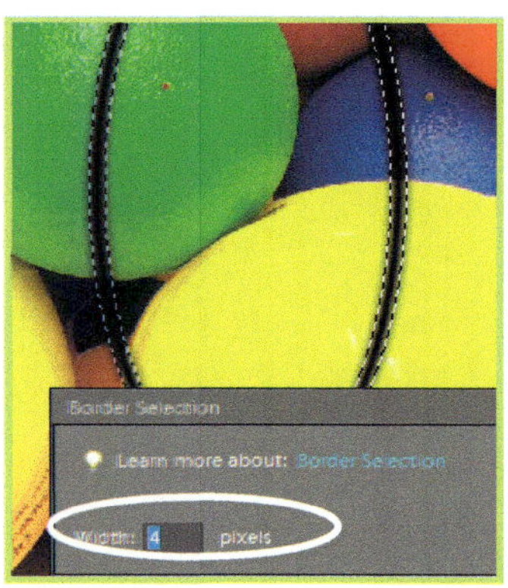

Border >> *This option creates a soft-edged border, a specific number of pixels wide.*

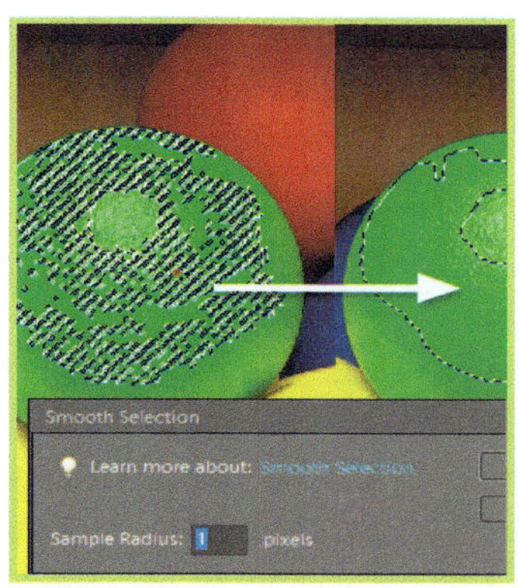

Smooth >> *Use this option to include random unselected pixels in an otherwise selected area.*

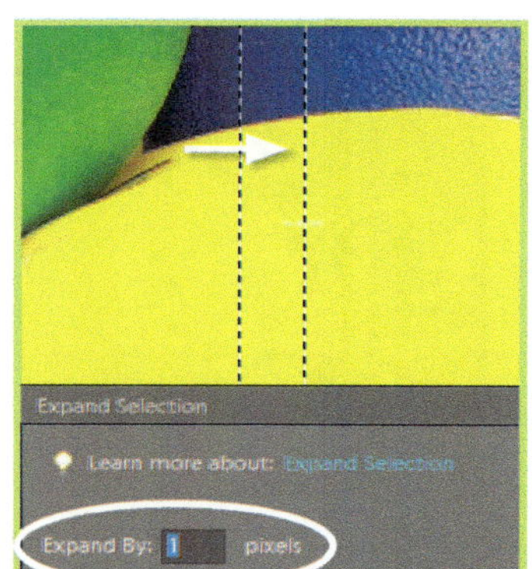

Expand >> *Increase a selection's size by a given number of pixels with this command.*

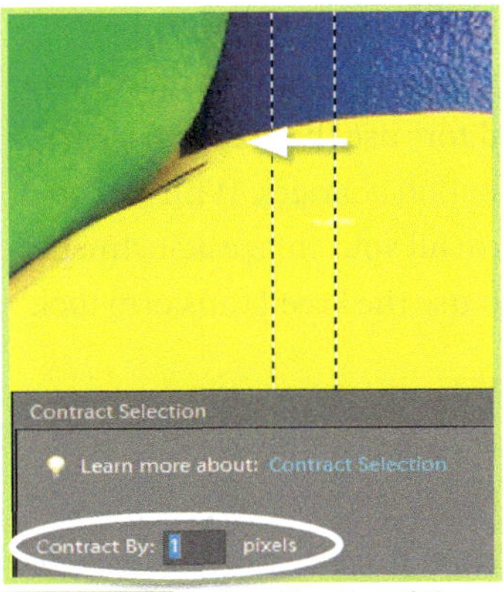

Contract >> *Reduce the size of the selection by a given number of pixels with this setting.*

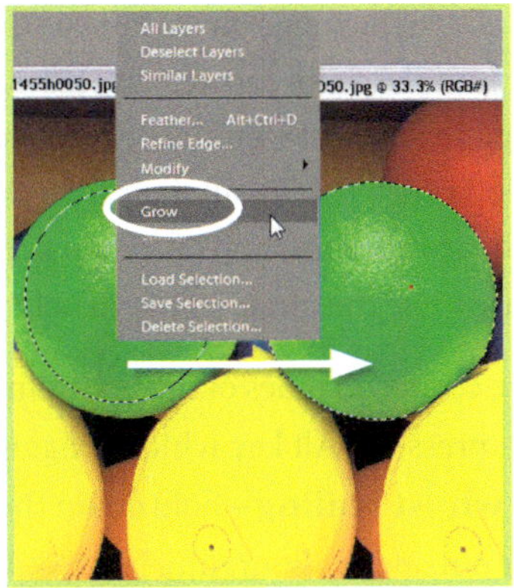

Grow >> *Use this option to select all adjacent pixels that fall within the current Magic Wand settings.*

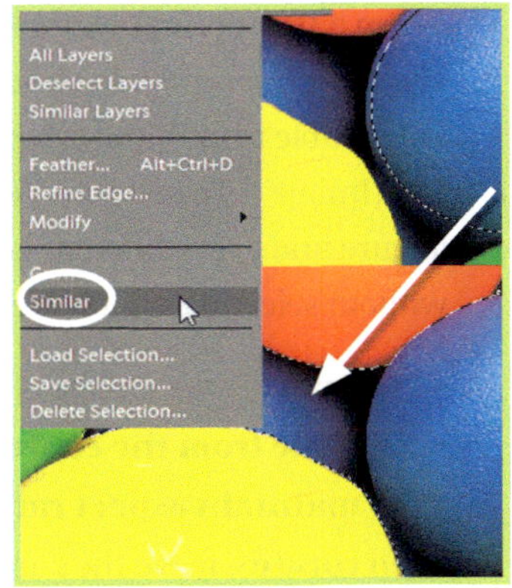

Similar >> *This command selects all other pixels in the whole image that fall within the Magic Wand settings.*

6.07 Transforming a selection

Suitable for Elements – 7.0, 6.0, 5.0, 4.0, 3.0, 2.0, 1.0 | Difficulty level – Intermediate | Resources – Web image 606
Related techniques – 6.01, 6.02, 6.03, 6.05 | Tools used – Selection tools | Menus used – Image

By combining the abilities of the transformation tools that Photoshop Elements provides with several selection techniques you have the power to seamlessly change the way that your pictures look. The features grouped under the Transform heading include tools that can alter the scale and rotation of your picture as well as those that can be used to skew, distort or apply perspective to the image. These changes can be made to the photograph as a whole, to the contents of a layer, to a selection or to a shape that you have drawn. Not all transformation options are available in all situations. For example, the Distort & Perspective options cannot be applied to the contents of a text layer.

Select, copy and paste >> *By manipulating selected parts of your picture you can change a straight image into something that on the one hand is obviously not real, but because it has been so seamlessly altered, it has an aspect of believability. Here the eyes and mouth of the subject have been selected, copied and enlarged before being blended back into the original picture.*

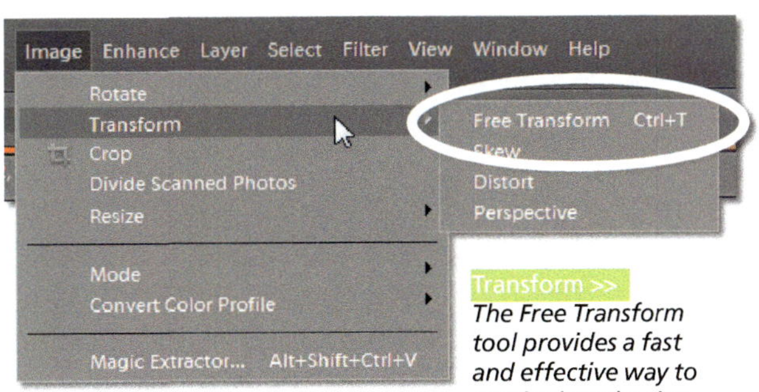

Transform >> *The Free Transform tool provides a fast and effective way to manipulate the size and shape of your pictures.*

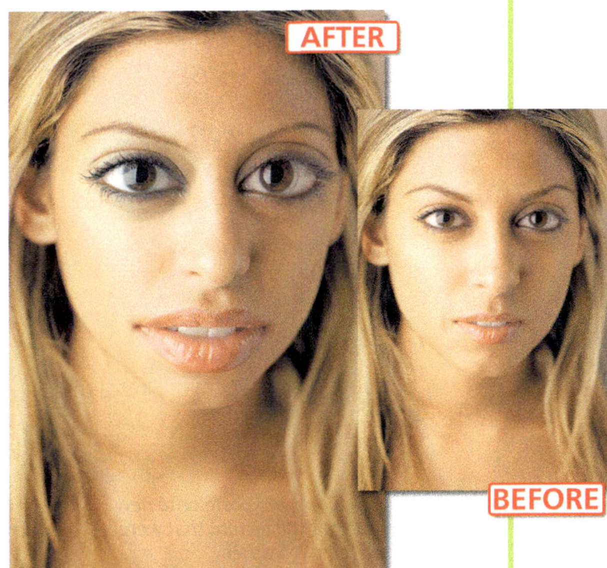

When a transformation tool is active the image area will be surrounded by a 'bounding box' containing several adjustment handles at its corners and sides. By dragging these handles you will be able to manipulate the picture. Most experienced image editors use the Free Transform tool (Image > Transform > Free Transform) for all their transformation changes. With this one feature and a few different keyboard combinations you can perform all your image adjustments without selecting another feature. Use the guide below to help you use the Free Transform tool:

- **To scale** – drag on one of the corner handles of the bounding box.
- **To scale from the center** – press the Alt key whilst dragging a corner handle.
- **To maintain aspect ratio whilst scaling** – hold down the Shift key whilst dragging.
- **To rotate** – move the cursor outside the bounding box until it changes to a curved two-ended arrow, then click and drag to rotate the picture or drag the Rotate handle at the bottom of the bounding box.
- **To distort** – hold down the Ctrl key whilst dragging any handle.
- **To skew** – hold down the Ctrl + Shift keys whilst dragging a side handle.
- **To apply a perspective change** – hold down Ctrl + Alt + Shift whilst dragging a corner handle.
- **To commit changes** – double-click inside the bounding box or hit Enter, or click the Commit icon (green tick) at the bottom of the marquee.

In the example the exaggerated eyes and mouth were created by firstly selecting the face parts, feathering the edge of the selection (Select > Feather) and then copying (Edit > Copy) and pasting (Edit > Paste) each part onto a new layer. With the appropriate layer selected the parts were then enlarged using the Free Transform feature (Image > Transform > Free Transform) and distorted a little (Image > Transform > Distort) to suit the rest of the face. As a final step a soft-edged eraser was used to remove sections of the face parts that didn't match the picture below. This step helped to blend changes into the original image.

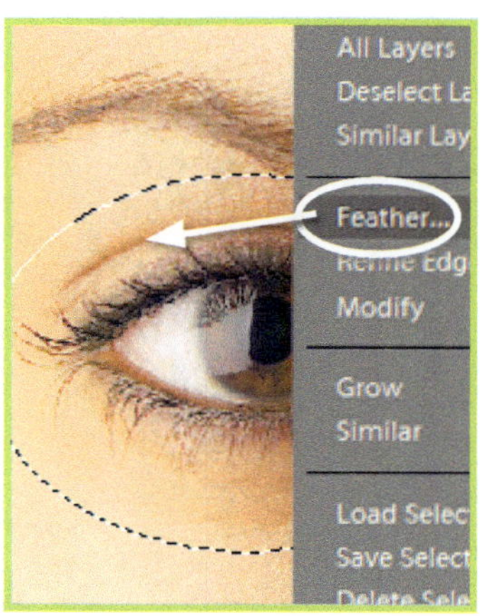

Step 1 >> Copy and paste onto new layers parts of the picture that were selected using a feather.

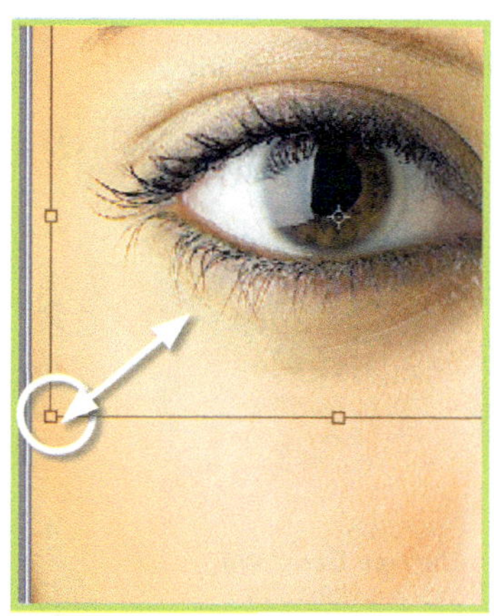

Step 2 >> Change the size of the face parts and apply some distortion using the Free Transform tool. Double-click inside the bounding box to commit your changes.

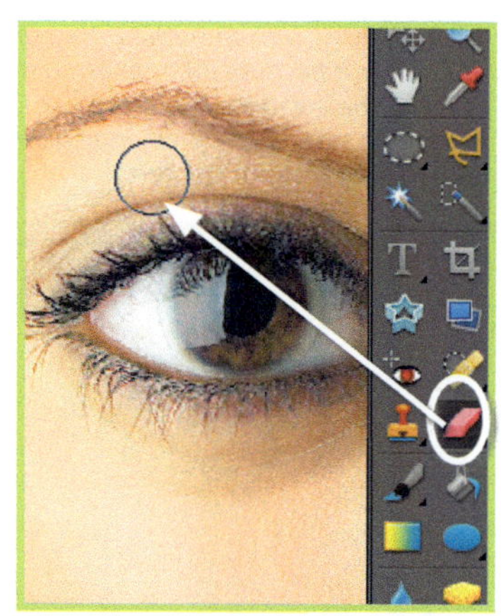

Step 3 >> Carefully erase the edge of the transformed face parts to blend them with the rest of the original image below.

6.08 Precise control of selection size

Suitable for Elements – 7.0, 6.0, 5.0, 4.0, 3.0, 2.0, 1.0 | Difficulty level – Intermediate | Related techniques – 6.01, 6.02, 6.03, 6.04
Tools used – Marquee | Menus used – Window, Edit, View

There will be times when you will need to know the precise size of the selections you make. You can get this information from the Info palette (Window > Info) where Elements reports the width and height of your selection in the units selected in the Units preferences (Edit > Preferences > Units and Rulers). This dialog also shows the exact position of the cursor. This can be helpful when you need to start and end a selection at a set screen reference.

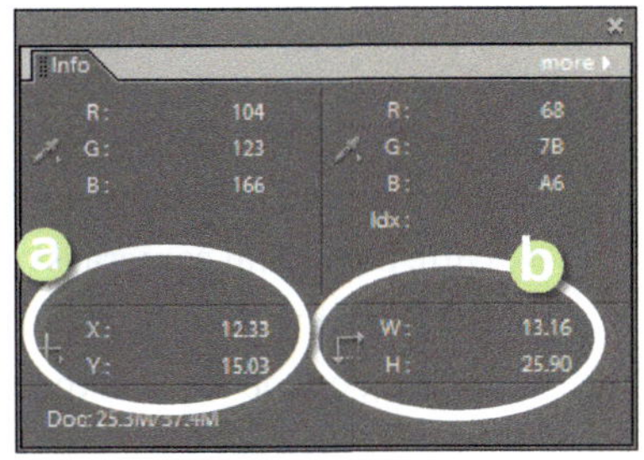

Info >> *The Info palette shows the position of the cursor (a) as well as the size of the selection (b).*

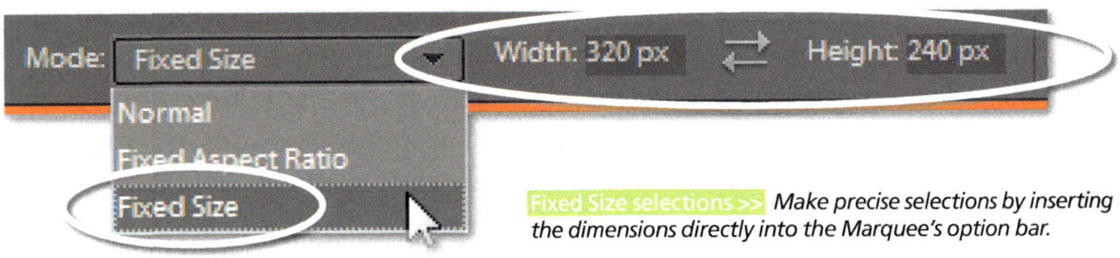

Fixed Size selections >> *Make precise selections by inserting the dimensions directly into the Marquee's option bar.*

If instead of just viewing the dimensions of the selection you actually want to specify the size, you can input these values into the options bar of the Marquee tool. After selecting the tool, choose Fixed Size from the Style drop-down menu in the Options bar. You can then enter the value for width and height into the fields in the bar. Now when you click on the canvas with the Marquee tool, a selection of the precise dimensions you input will appear on the picture. As with the Info dialog the measurement units used here are controlled by the settings in the Units and Rulers preferences.

Another way to precisely control the size of your selections is to use the Elements Grid system as a guide. Simply display the Grid over your picture (View >Snap To > Grid) and switch on the Snap to Grid option (View > Snap to Grid). Now as you are drawing a selection the cursor will align itself with the grid lines or intersections. The interval of the grid lines and spacings can be altered via the Grid preferences (Edit > Preferences > Grid).

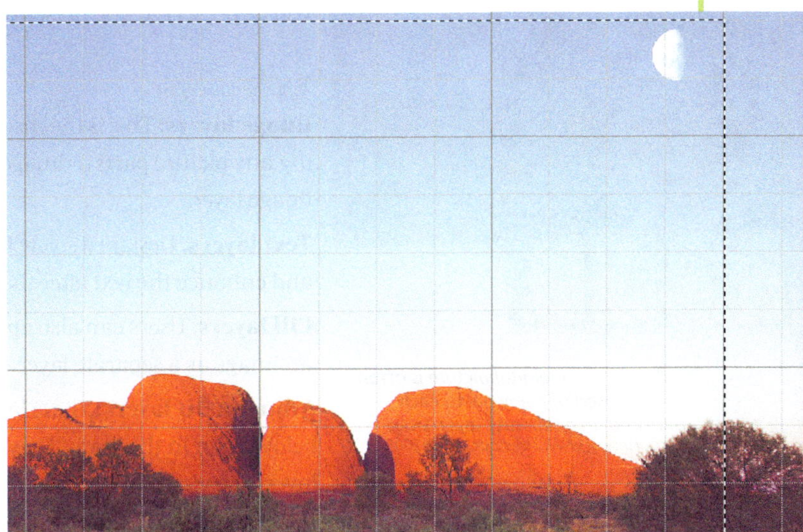

Grid as guide >> *Use the Elements Grid option to help make precise selection. Image courtesy of www.darranleal.com.au.*

Understanding layers

In a lot of ways traditional film-based shooting is very similar to digital photography. After all, apart from a few useful additions such as a preview screen on the back and a slot for my memory card, my digital camera is not unlike my film camera (in fact they even share the same lenses). But thinking that these similarities extend to the pictures themselves can mean that you are missing out on some of the more powerful capabilities of your digital pictures.

Digital pictures are not always flat

The traditional photograph contains all the picture elements in a single plane. Digital images captured by a camera or sourced from a scanner are also flat files. And for a lot of new digital photographers this is how their files remain – flat. All editing and enhancing work is conducted on the original picture, but things can be different.

Most image editing packages contain the ability to use layers with your pictures. This feature releases your images from having to keep all their information in a flat file. Different image parts, added text and certain enhancement tasks can all be kept on separate layers. The layers are kept in a stack and the image you see on screen in the work area is a composite of all the layers.

Sound confusing? Well try imagining for example that each of the image parts of a simple portrait photograph are stored on separate plastic sheets. These are your layers. The background sits at the bottom. The portrait is laid on top of the background and the text is placed on top. When viewed from above the solid part of each layer obscures the picture beneath. Whilst the picture parts are based on separate layers they can be moved, edited or enhanced independently of each other. If they are saved using a file format like Photoshop's PSD file (which is layer friendly) all the layers will be preserved and present next time the file is opened.

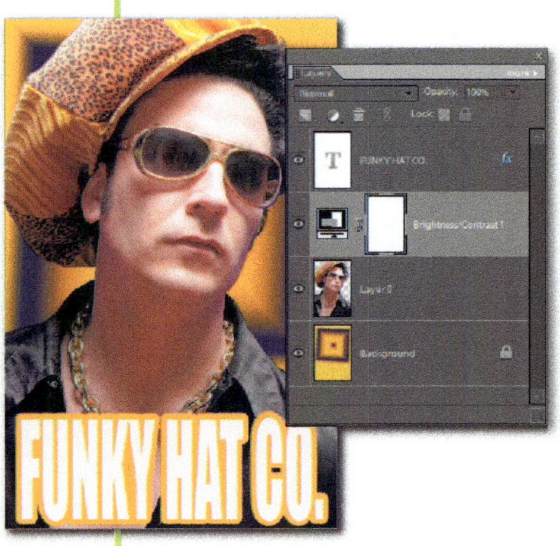

Layers >> *A digital picture is often composed of many parts, each stored on a separate layer. Image courtesy of www.ablestock.com © 2005.*

Types of layers

Image layers: This is the most basic and common layer type, containing any picture parts or image details. Background is a special type of image layer.

Text layers: Designed solely for text, these layers allow the user to edit and enhance the text after the layer has been made.

Fill layers: Users can also apply a Solid Color, Gradient or Pattern to an image as a separate layer.

Adjustment layers: These layers alter the layers that are arranged below them in the stack. They act as a filter through which the lower layers are viewed. You can use adjustment layers to perform many of the enhancement tasks that you would normally apply directly to an image layer without changing the image itself. Adjustment layers are added automatically when using the Smart Brush Tool.

Shape layers: Drawing with any of the shape tools creates a new vector-based Shape layer. The layer contains a thumbnail for the shape as well as the color of the layer.

Frame layers: From Elements 5.0 Adobe has included a new layer type to coincide with its Photo Layout and Photo Book projects. Called the Frame layer, its role is to store both the frame and the picture that sits within it. Both the component parts remain as separate individual images despite being stored as one layer. What does this mean in day-to-day editing? Well it means that you can do things like change the size, shape and orientation of either the frame and picture combination, or the picture, independently of each other.

Background layers: An image can only have one background layer. It is the bottom-most layer in the stack. No other layers can be moved beneath this layer. You cannot adjust this layer's opacity or its blending mode. You can convert background layers to standard image layer's by double-clicking the layer in the Layers palette, setting your desired layer options in the dialog provided and then clicking OK.

The magic of Frame layers

Adobe introduced Frame layers as part of its revamp of Photo Project creation in version 5.0. For most Elements users, frame layers are seen as a way to add decorative edges to their photos when creating albums or scrapbooking pages, but their quiet power goes beyond mere framing. Frame layers are built on a Photoshop Technology called Smart Objects.

Professionals in the know use Smart Objects as a way of protecting their photos from the damage associated with resizing, rotating and distorting image layers. A smart object keeps the pixels safe by applying the changes made to the layer to a copy of the pixels rather than the original photo.

It may not be immediately apparent when you are first playing with your images in this way, but each time you make a change to the size or orientation of your photo the pixels are resampled. This means that the original pixels are being changed with each adjustment, and you know how I feel about that! Perform enough of these changes and gradually the image becomes less and less defined. See the example images on the right. How can

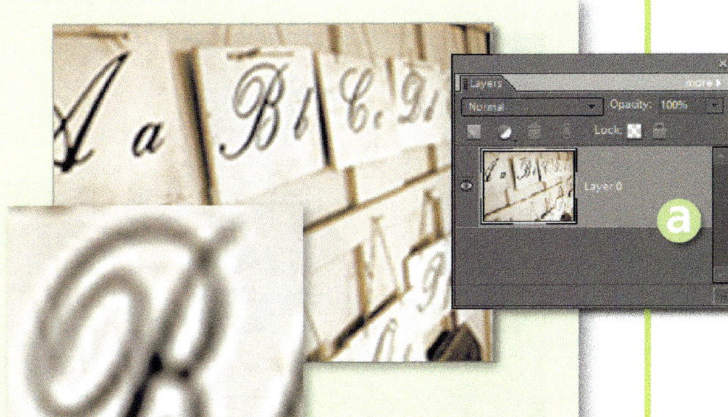

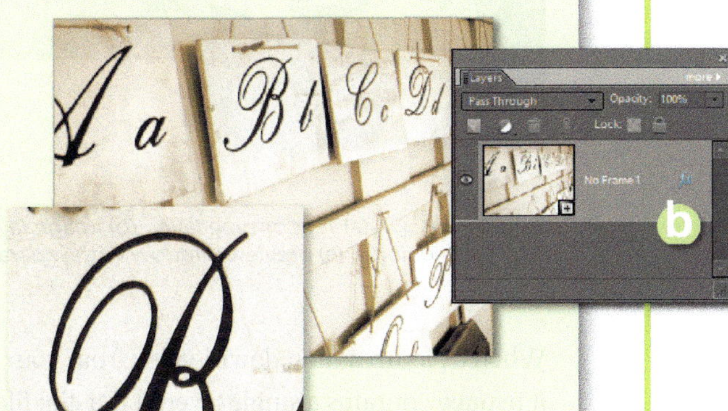

Non-destructive resizing with Frame layers >> *To give you an example of how destructive seemingly small changes to our image layers are I resized a standard image layer up and down three times. It is easy to see how blurry the photo has become (a). Next I added the same picture to a frame layer and performed exactly the same resizing activity. The result is an image as sharp as the original (b).*

we avoid this degradation? Well, one way to ensure that your files remain as crisp as the day that they were taken is to add the image to a frame layer before messing around with size and rotation. Don't want a frame around the photo? No problem just add the 'No Frame' frame layer to your document and then drag the picture from the project bin to the No Frame area in the composition. You can also simply drag a photo from the project bin onto an open document; it is added automatically as a Frame layer. Alternatively, you can right-click on a framed photo and choose Clear Frame from the context menu.

Now you can free transform to your heart's content without the fear of resampling, and therefore damaging, the pixels.

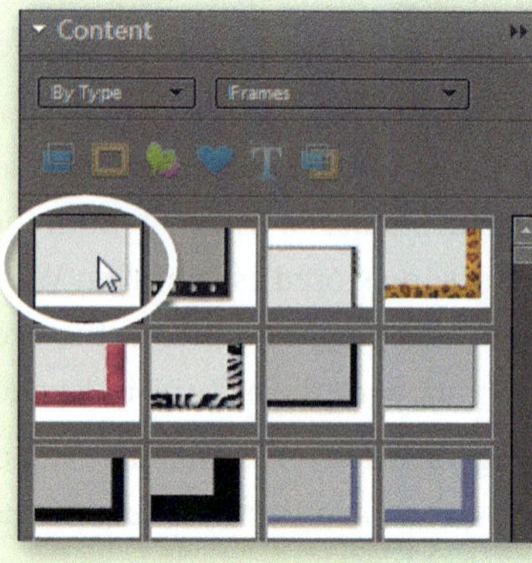

No Frame frame layer >> To gain the abilities of a frame layer without the frame, select the No Frame option from the Frames section of the Content palette.

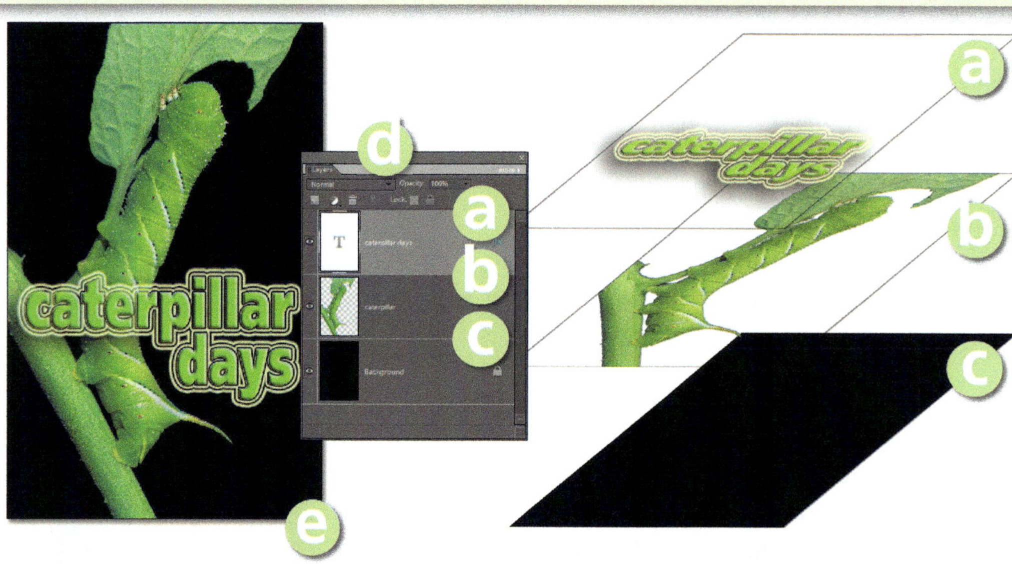

Layer types >> (a) Text or type layer, (b) image layer with chequered transparent area, (c) background layer, (d) Layers palette, (e) preview window with separate layers viewed as a composite image.

Adding layers

When a picture is first downloaded from your digital camera or imported into Photoshop Elements it usually contains a single layer. It is a 'flat file'. By default the program classifies the picture as a background layer. You can add extra 'empty' layers to your picture by clicking the New Layer button at the bottom of the Layers palette or choosing the Layer option from the New sub-menu in the Layer menu (Layer > New > Layer). The new layer is positioned above your currently selected layer. Some actions, such as adding text with the Type tool, automatically create a new layer for the content. This is true when adding adjustment and fill layers to your image. When selecting, copying and pasting image parts, Photoshop also creates a new layer for the copied portion of the picture. Also when you use the Background eraser or the Magic Eraser, a new layer will automatically be created.

Viewing layers

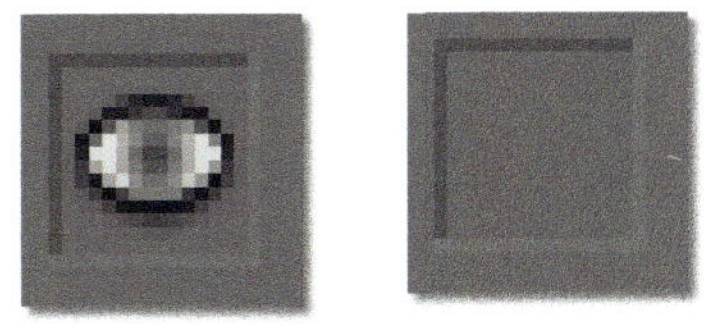

Visible layers >> *When the Eye icon is present the layer is visible. Clicking on the eye turns the icon off, removing the layer from the preview window.*

Photoshop Elements's Layers palette displays all your layers and their settings in the one palette. If the palette isn't already on screen when opening the program, it may be hidden in the Palette Bin or you may have to choose the option from the Window menu (Window > Layers). The individual layers are displayed, one on top of the other, in a 'layer stack'. The image is viewed from the top down through the layers. When looking at the picture on screen we see a preview of how the image looks when all the layers are combined. Each layer is represented by a thumbnail on the left and a name on the right. The size of the thumbnail can be changed, as can the name of the layer. By default each new layer is named sequentially (layer 1, layer 2, layer 3). This is fine when your image contains a few different picture parts, but for more complex illustrations it is helpful to rename the layers with titles that help to remind you of their content (portrait, sky, tree).

You can edit or enhance only one layer at a time. To select the layer that you want to change you need to click on the layer. At this point the layer will change to a different color from the rest in the stack. This layer is now the selected layer and can be edited in isolation from the others that make up the picture. Layers can be turned off by clicking the eye symbol on the far left of the layer so that it is no longer showing. This action removes the layer from view but not from the stack. You can turn the layer back on again by clicking the space where the eye symbol was. Holding down the Alt key whilst clicking on a layer's eye symbol will turn off or hide all layers other than the one that you are clicking.

Manipulating layers

Layers can be moved up and down the layer stack by click-dragging. Moving a layer upwards will mean that its picture content may obscure more of the details in the layers below. Moving downwards progressively positions the layer's details further behind the picture parts of the layers above.

You can reposition the content of any layers (except background layers) using the Move tool. Two or more layers can be linked together so that when the content of one layer is moved the other details follow precisely. Simply multi-select the layers in the Layers palette and then click on the Chain icon (Link Layers button) at the top of the palette. The chain will be added to all the linked layers on the right of the thumbnail. Unwanted layers can be deleted by click-dragging them to the Dustbin icon at the top of the Layers palette.

Layer styles

In early image editing programs creating a drop shadow edge to a picture was a process that involved many steps. Thankfully Elements includes this as one of the many built-in styles that can be quickly and easily applied to your layers. Users can add effects by clicking on the Effects palette tab in the Palettes pane and selecting a layer style from those listed in the Layer Styles section. You can edit the style settings by double-clicking on the small 'fx' icon on the right of the thumbnail in the Layers palette.

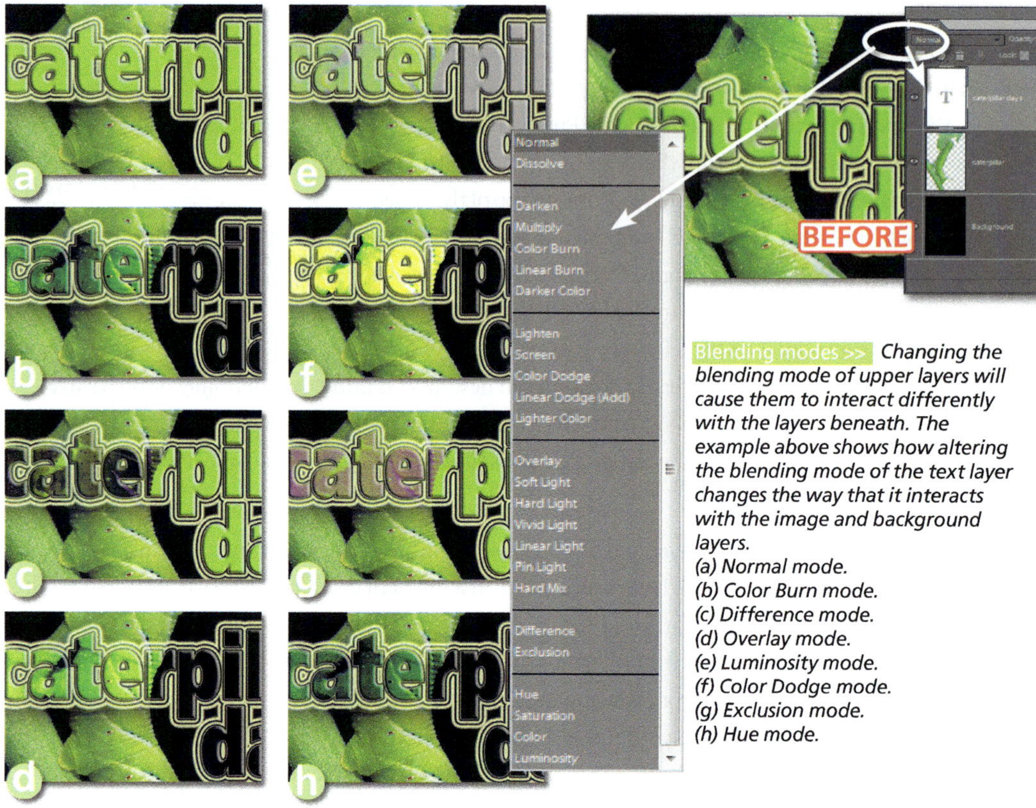

Blending modes >> *Changing the blending mode of upper layers will cause them to interact differently with the layers beneath. The example above shows how altering the blending mode of the text layer changes the way that it interacts with the image and background layers.*
(a) Normal mode.
(b) Color Burn mode.
(c) Difference mode.
(d) Overlay mode.
(e) Luminosity mode.
(f) Color Dodge mode.
(g) Exclusion mode.
(h) Hue mode.

Blending modes and opacity

As well as layer styles, or effects, the opacity (how transparent a layer is) of each layer can be altered by dragging the Opacity slider down from 100% to the desired level of translucency. The lower the number the more detail will show through from the layers below. The Opacity slider is located at the top of the Layers palette and changes the selected layer only. On the left of the Opacity control is a drop-down menu containing a range of blending modes. The default selection is 'normal', which means that the detail in upper layers obscures the layers beneath. Switching to a different blending mode will alter the way in which the layers interact. For more details see the full blending mode example in the Appendix.

Layer shortcuts

- **To display Layers palette** – Choose Window>Layers
- **To access Layers options** – Click the More button in the upper right-hand corner of the Layers palette
- **To change the size of layer thumbnails** – Choose Palette options from the Layers Palette menu and select a thumbnail size
- **To make a new layer** – Choose Layer>New>Layer or click the New Layer button in the Layers palette
- **To create a new adjustment layer** – Choose Layer>New Adjustment Layer and select the layer type or click the New Adjustment Layer in the layers palette
- **To add a style or effect to a layer** – Select the layer and choose a style from those listed in the Layer Styles section of the Artwork and Effects palette.

Masking techniques

Masking in traditional photography is used to physically protect part of the picture from development or exposure. In black and white darkrooms this process often involved the positioning of specially cut 'ruby' red sheets over the photographic paper, which shielded this part of the picture from being exposed during the enlargement process.

The digital version of masking is also designed to restrict effects to only certain portions of an image. Photoshop Elements provides a variety of ways to employ a masking system when editing your pictures.

6.09 Painting masks with the Selection Brush

Suitable for Elements – 7.0, 6.0, 5.0, 4.0, 3.0, 2.0 | Difficulty level – Intermediate | Resources – Web image 609
Related techniques – 6.02, 6.03 | Tools used – Selection Brush

The Selection Brush was a welcome addition to the Photoshop Elements tools line up when it was added in revision 2.0 of the program and, although its primary purpose is to aid the creation of complex selections, it can also be used in a 'Rubylith' Mask mode. Activate the mode by selecting the Mask option from the mode drop-down menu in the Tools options bar. Now when the brush is dragged across the surface of a picture it will leave a red, semi-transparent mask behind it. The mask will protect these parts of the picture from the effects of filters, color changes and tonal correction.

The size and edge softness of the Selection Brush as well as the mask opacity (overlay opacity) and mask color can be altered in the options bar. Switching back to the Selection mode will turn off the mask and make a selection from the parts of the picture that weren't painted. Whilst in Mask mode painting with the brush will add to the mask. Applying the brush in the Selection mode will add to the selection, which effectively is removing masked areas. You can also save carefully painted masks using the Save Selection option in the Select menu and pre-saved selections can be converted into a mask by loading the selection and then switching back to Mask mode. A quick tip for powers users – Alt-clicking the Layer Mask thumbnail displays shows the rubylith mask, which is handy when making lots of adjustments to the selected area.

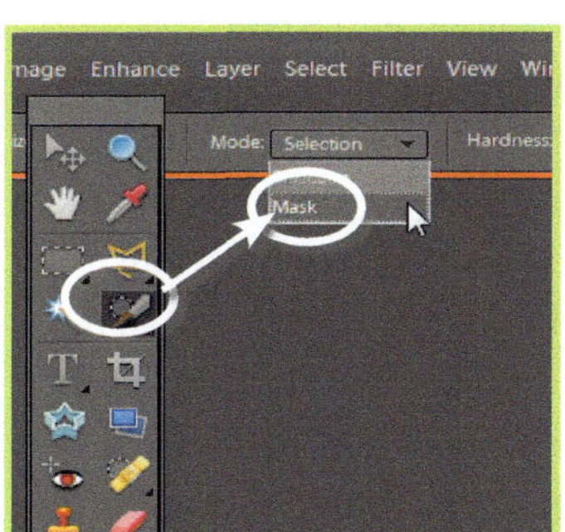

Step 1 >> *Choose the Selection Brush (under the Magic Selection Brush) from the tool box and switch the brush to Mask mode.*

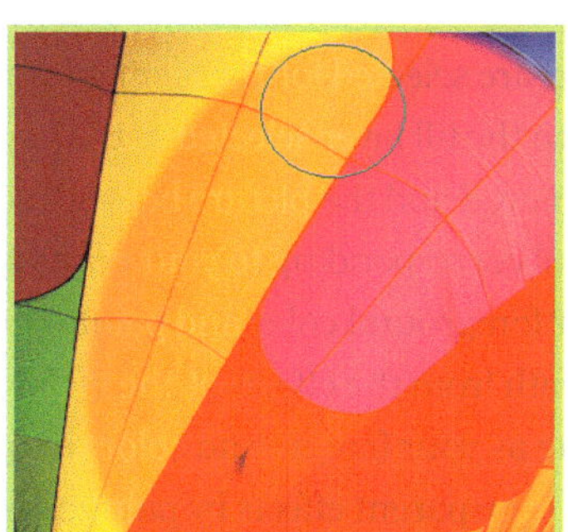

Step 2 >> *Paint on the parts of the picture that you want to shield from the editing process.*

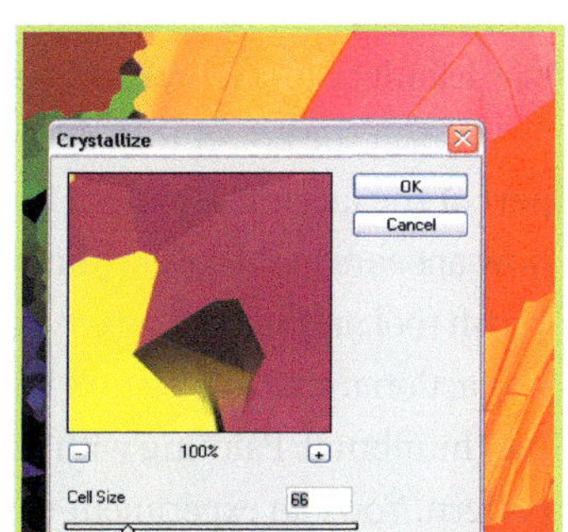

Step 3 >> *Apply the editing changes to the non-masked areas. Here we applied the Crystallize filter.*

6.10 Fill and adjustment layer masks

Suitable for Elements – 7.0, 6.0, 5.0, 4.0, 3.0, 2.0, 1.0 | Difficulty level – Intermediate | Resources – Web image 6.09
Related techniques – 6.07, 6.11, 6.12 | Menus used – Layer

Another form of masking is available to Elements users via the Fill and Adjustment Layers features. Each time you add one of these layers to an image, two thumbnails are created in the Layers palette. The one on the left controls the settings for the adjustment layer. Double-clicking this thumbnail brings up the dialog box and the settings used for the fill or adjustment layer. The thumbnail on the right represents the layer's mask which governs how and where the settings are applied to the image.

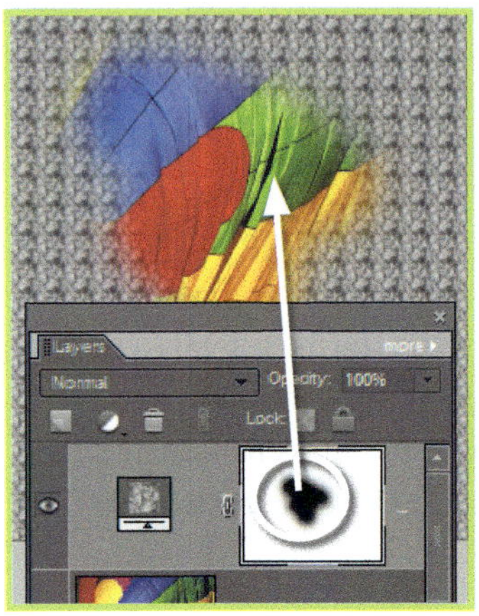

Eraser >> *Erasing parts of the fill layer reveals the picture beneath.*

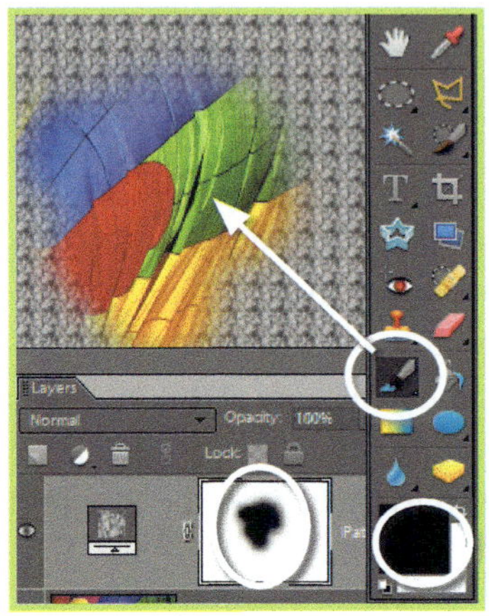

Black paint >> *Painting the mask with black paint has the same effect as erasing.*

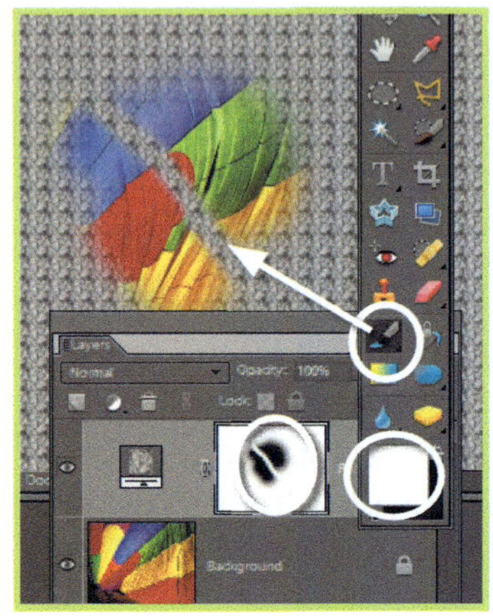

White paint >> *Painting with white paint restores the mask and the pattern.*

The mask is a grayscale image. In its default state it is colored white, meaning that no part of the layer's effects are being masked or held back from the picture below. Conversely, if the thumbnail is totally black then none of the layer's effects is applied to the picture. In this monochrome world shades of gray equate to various levels of transparency. With this in mind we can control which parts of the picture are altered by the fill or adjustment layer and which parts remain unchanged by painting (in black and white and gray) and erasing directly on the layer mask.

To start editing a layer mask, firstly apply a fill layer such as Pattern to the image. Check to see that the default colors (white and black) are selected for the Elements foreground and background colors. Next select the Eraser tool, and with the fill layer selected in the Layers palette, proceed to remove part of the layer. The pattern is removed and the picture beneath shows through and a black mark now appears in the layer thumbnail corresponding to your erasing actions. Switch to the Paint Brush tool and select black as your foreground color and paint onto the patterned surface. Again this action masks the picture beneath from the effects of the fill layer and adds more black areas to the thumbnail. Painting with white as your foreground color restores the mask and paints back the pattern. You can experiment with transparent effects by painting on the mask with gray. The lighter the gray the more the pattern will dominate, the darker the gray the less the pattern will be seen. A similar semi-transparent effect can be achieved if the opacity of the eraser or brush is reduced.

6.11 Using selections with layer masks

Suitable for Elements – 7.0, 6.0, 5.0, 4.0, 3.0, 2.0, 1.0 | Difficulty level – Intermediate | Resources – Web image 6.08 | Related techniques – 6.09, 6.10, 6.12 | Tools used – Select

In addition to employing painting and erasing tools to work directly on the layer mask you can also use a selection in conjunction with an adjustment or fill layer to restrict the area of your image that is altered. Make a selection in the normal way and then, with the selection still active, create a new adjustment or fill layer. The selection confines the changes made by the new adjustment/fill layer. You will notice the selected area is colored white in the Layer Mask thumbnail. A layer mask made in this way can be edited using the same painting techniques as discussed above.

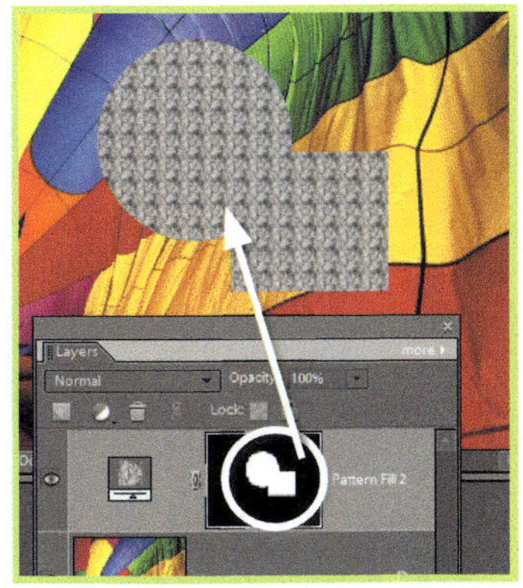

Selection >> *By having a selection active when you make a new adjustment or fill layer you immediately restrict the effects of this layer to just the confines of the selection.*

6.12 'Group with Previous' masks

Suitable for Elements – 7.0, 6.0, 5.0, 4.0, 3.0, 2.0, 1.0 | Difficulty level – Intermediate | Resources – Web image 609 | Related techniques – 6.09, 6.10, 6.110 | Menus used – Layer

The final masking technique that Photoshop Elements employs uses the special Group with Previous command found in the Layer menu. This command uses the transparency surrounding objects on a layer as a mask for the content of any layers that are above it in the stack. In the example the balloon image was placed above the test text layer. With the balloon layer active the Group with Previous command (Layer > Group with Previous) was selected. The example image now fills the text shape but is masked from showing through the rest of the layer by the transparency surrounding the type. This technique also works with shapes and filled selections drawn on a separate layer surrounded by transparency.

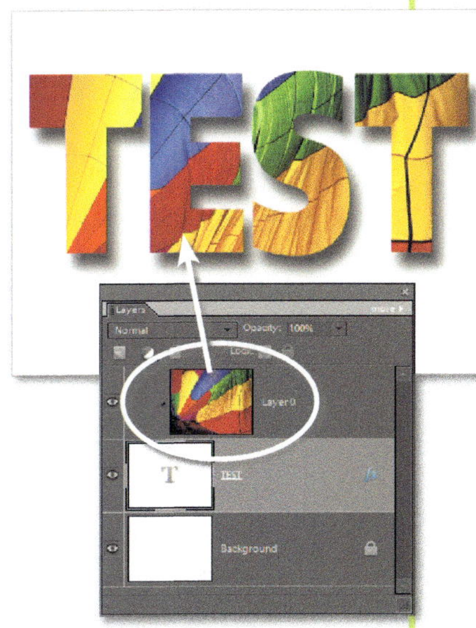

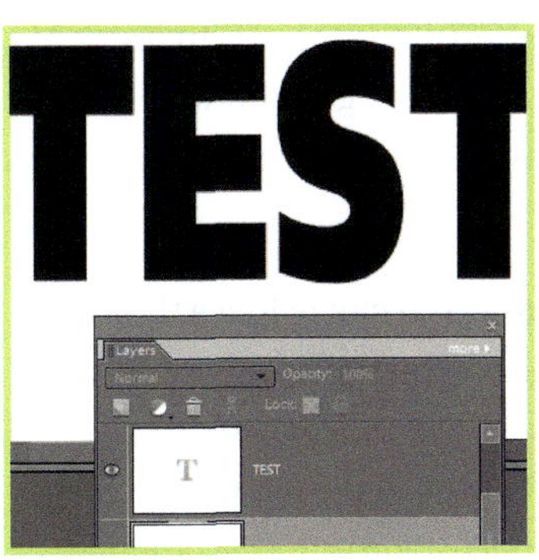

Step 1 >> *Create some bold text in a new document with a white background layer.*

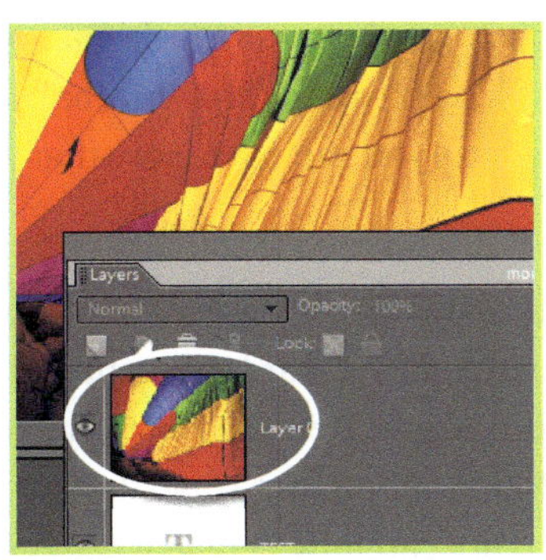

Step 2 >> *Copy and paste a color image in a layer above the text.*

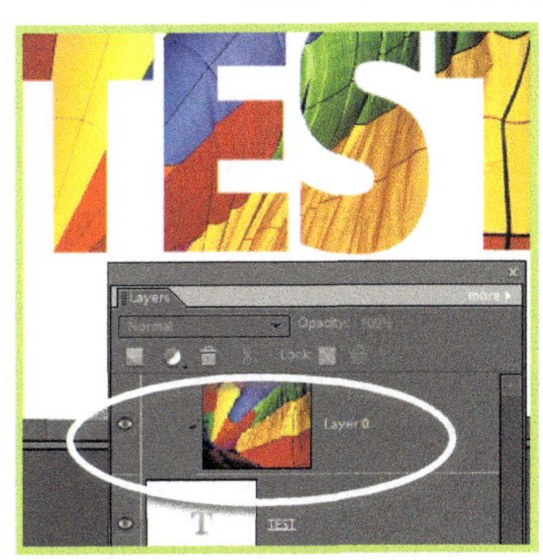

Step 3 >> *Select the color layer and choose the Group with Previous command from the Layers menu.*

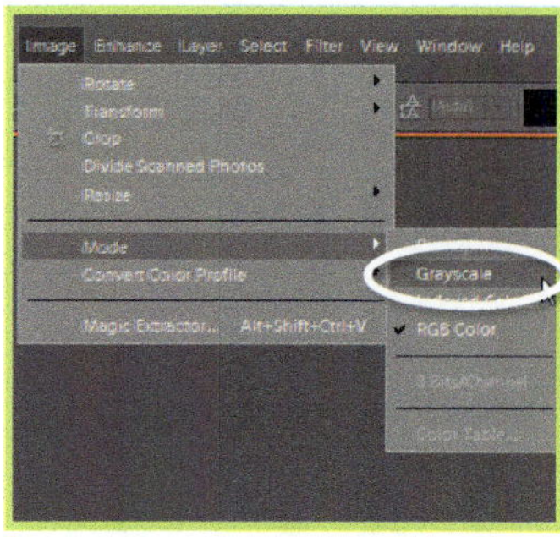

Step 1 >> Select Image > Mode > Grayscale and then click on the OK button in the Discard Color warning box.

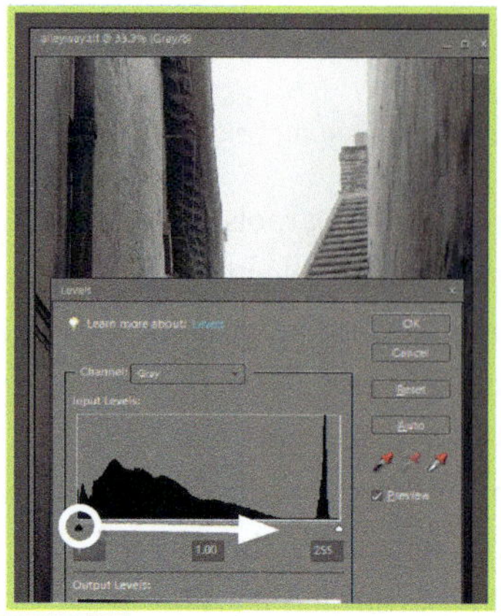

Step 2 >> Using the Levels control, map the dark pixels to black by dragging the black point slider to the right.

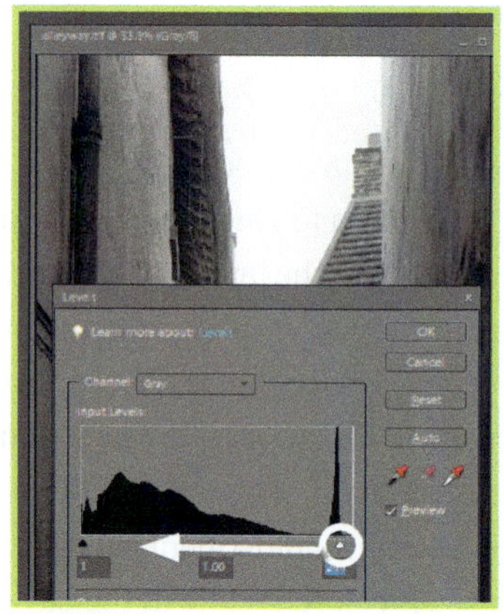

Step 3 >> Correct the highlights by dragging the white point slider to the left.

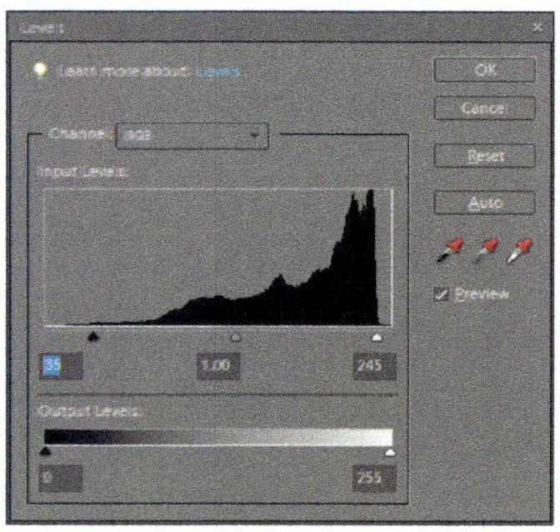

Increase contrast >> By moving the black and white input sliders towards the center of the dialog you can increase the contrast of your picture.

Converting color to black and white

One of the real advantages of shooting digital is the ease with which you can convert color images to black and white. Gone are the days of having to carry two camera bodies, one loaded with color film the other with black and white. Now you simply shoot color all the time and then convert selected images to black and white using a few simple steps.

6.13 Changing the mode to grayscale

Suitable for Elements – 7.0, 6.0, 5.0, 4.0, 3.0, 2.0, 1.0 | Difficulty level – Basic | Resources – Web image 610 | Related techniques – 6.14, 6.15 | Menus used – Image, Enhance

The simplest way to lose the colors in your picture is to convert the image to a grayscale. This process changes the photograph from having three color channels (red, green and blue) to being constructed of a single channel that contains the picture's detail only. Often this conversion produces a flat and lacklustre photograph and so a little manipulation of the tones is in order. My first point of call to help solve this problem would always be the Levels dialog (Enhance > Adjust Lighting > Levels). Using this control you can make sure that your image tones are spread across the grayscale spectrum.

Most grayscale conversion pictures need a general contrast increase. You can achieve this by moving the black and white input sliders towards the center of the dialog. Holding the Alt key down whilst you are moving the slider will enable you to preview the pixels that are being converted to pure black or pure white. Your aim is to map the darkest pixels in the picture to black and the lightest ones to white. Work carefully here as a heavy handed approach will produce pictures where delicate shadow and highlight details are lost forever.

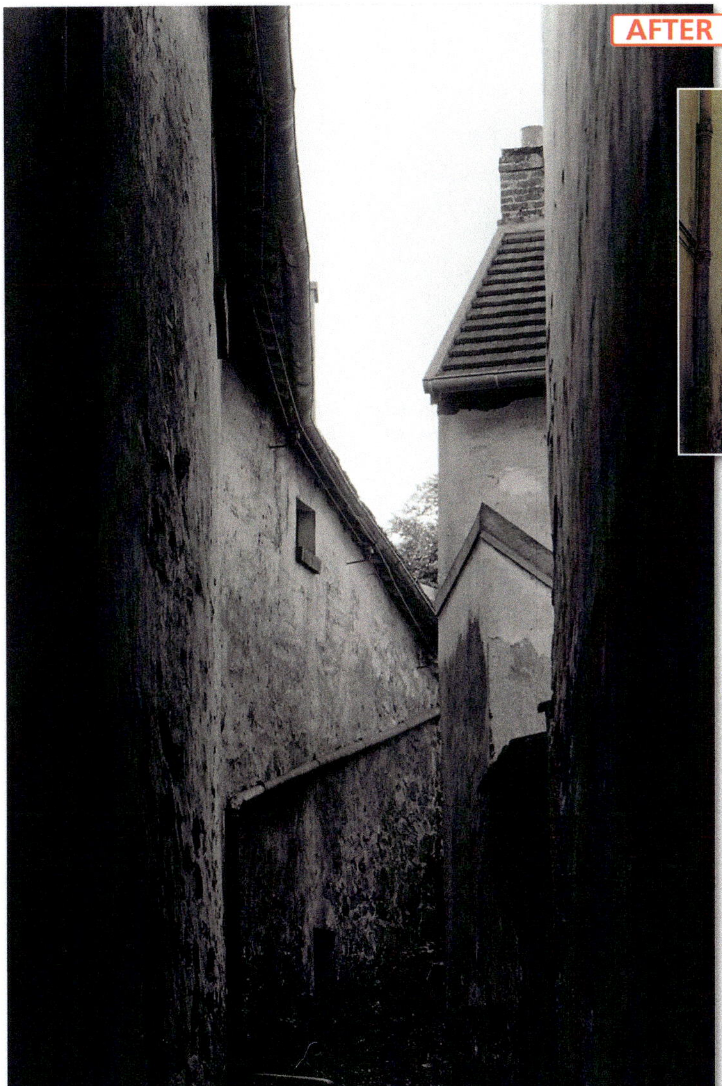

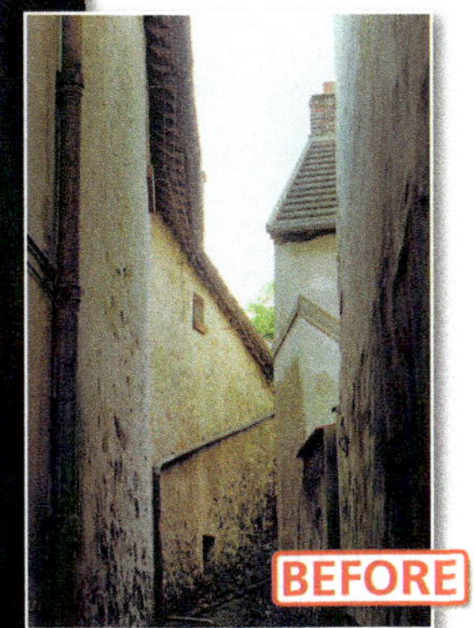

Grayscale >> You can convert your color digital photographs to grayscale using two different methods in Adobe Photoshop Elements.

The simplest is to change color modes from RGB to Grayscale. The alternative is to desaturate the photograph. This process has the added advantage of leaving the black and white picture in RGB mode so that color can be added to the monochrome later.

Images created with either process do benefit from some adjustment of tones after conversion.

6.14 Desaturate the color file

Suitable for Elements – 7.0, 6.0, 5.0, 4.0, 3.0, 2.0, 1.0 | Difficulty level – Basic | Resources – Web image 611 Related techniques – 6.13, 6.15, 6.16 | Tools used – Dodge and Burn-in | Menus used – Image

Photoshop Elements uses the term 'saturation' to refer to the strength of the colors in a picture. Increasing saturation makes the colors in a picture more vivid, decreasing saturation makes the hues weaker. The program employs the Hue/Saturation (Enhance > Adjust Color > Hue Saturation) control to adjust the color's strength. If the Saturation slider is moved all the way to the left of the dialog (to a setting of –100) then all color is removed from the picture. You are effectively left with a grayscale or black and white photograph that is very similar to the 'convert to grayscale' version above but with one important difference – the picture is still an RGB file. This means that even though the photograph no longer contains any color, the color mode it is stored in is capable of supporting

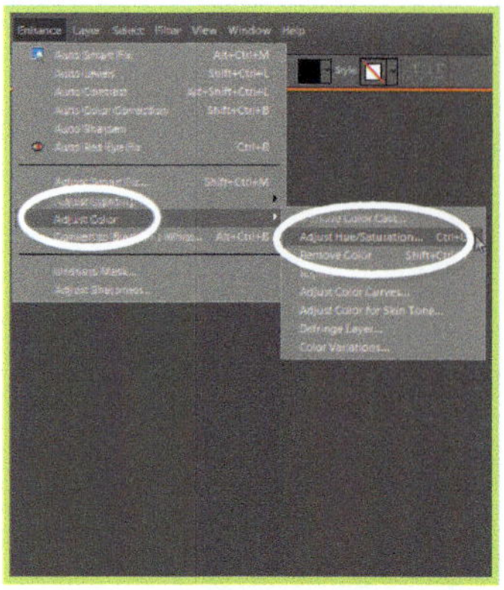

Step 1 >> Select the Hue/Saturation control from the Adjust Color heading in the Enhance menu.

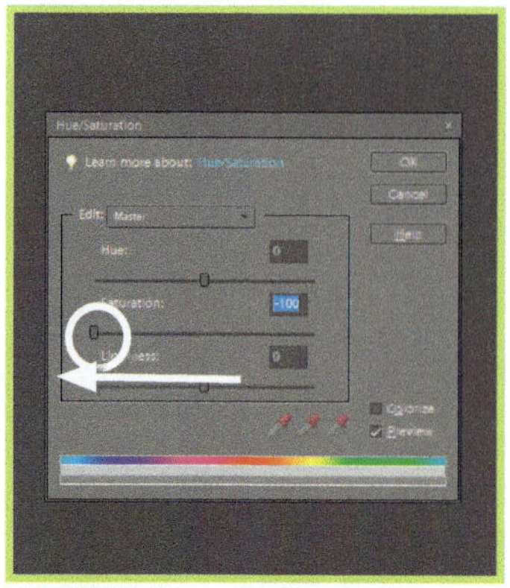

Step 2 >> Move the Saturation slider completely to the left, removing all color from the picture.

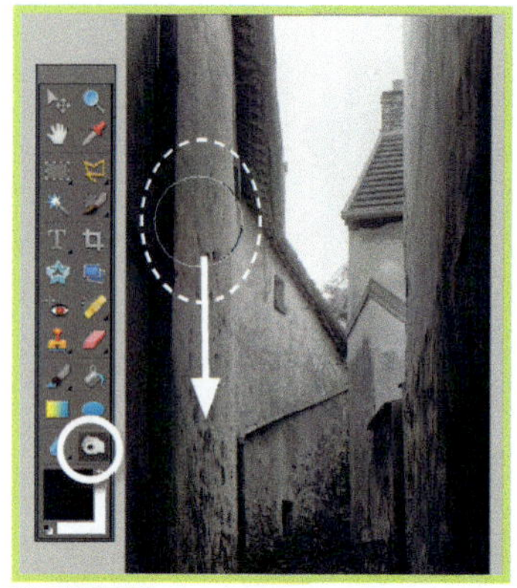

Step 3 >> Use the Dodging and Burning-in tools to lighten and darken selected areas of the picture.

color. So if you are wanting to try a little digital hand coloring, or experiment with pictures that contain monochrome as well as color components, then this is the technique for you. More details on these techniques can be found later in this book. Be warned though, once your picture is desaturated the color is lost for ever and so it is always a good idea to save a copy of the color version of the image before proceeding.

Pro's Tip: You can shortcut the desaturation process by selecting Enhance > Adjust Color > Remove Color, which provides the same results as using the Hue/Saturation control but in a single step.

Once the picture has been desaturated you may need to tweak the shadow, highlight and midtones using the Levels feature. Finally, add some drama to the picture by selectively lightening and darkening parts of the image using the Dodging and Burning-in tools. Used judiciously these devices can change the whole atmosphere of a photograph. In the example, I darkened the walls closest to the viewer and lightened those parts of the French alleyway that were in the background. These changes increased the sense of distance in the picture as well as helping to draw the viewer's eyes into the picture.

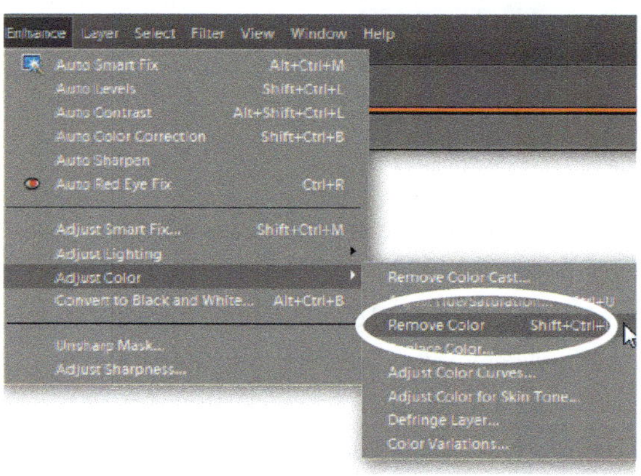

Desaturation shortcut >> The Enhance > Adjust Color > Remove Color option is a shortcut that produces the same results as moving the Saturation slider to -100 in the Hue/ Saturation feature.

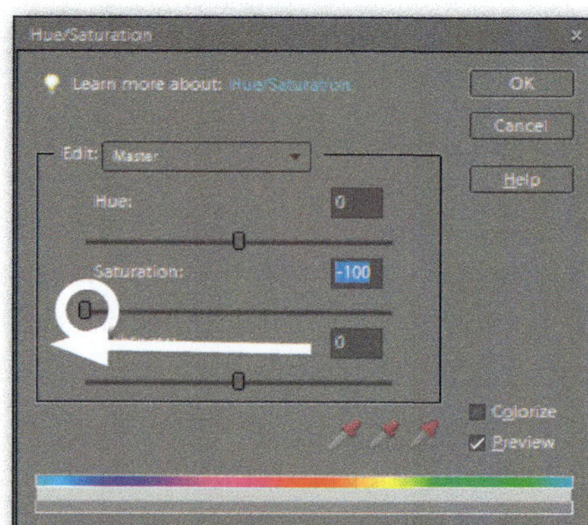

Saturation control >> By decreasing the saturation of the colors in a picture completely you convert the image to just black and white.

6.15 A more sophisticated approach

Suitable for Elements – 7.0, 6.0, 5.0, 4.0, 3.0, 2.0, 1.0 | Difficulty level – Basic | Resources – Web image 612
Related techniques – 6.13, 6.14, 6.16 | Menus used – Layer

Despite the straightforward nature of the two conversion approaches detailed above, transforming a color photo to grayscale is not as simple as it first seems. Many converted images seem a little flat and lack the separation of tones that existed in the original photo. The trick with good conversions from color to grayscale is ensuring that the hues in the original picture are translated into distinct and different tones. For this reason no one conversion process will be suitable for all pictures.

Take for instance the example of a red flower photographed against the background of rich green foliage. When converted to grayscale by switching modes or desaturating there is a tendency for both the red of the flower and the green of the leaves to be converted to the same gray tone, making the monochrome picture much less vibrant and dynamic than the original. In order to restore some visual separation between flower and background it is necessary to convert these hues to different grays.

Just such a technique was developed by the Adobe evangelist, Russell Brown (www.russellbrown.com). The original method was designed for Photoshop but works just as well with Elements. It uses the Adjustment Layers technology in Photoshop Elements as a way to both convert the color image to black and white and also to control how the colors are represented in the grayscale. Like a lot of Russell's techniques it leaves the original image unchanged in the background. Hence this style of image enhancing is called non-destructive editing.

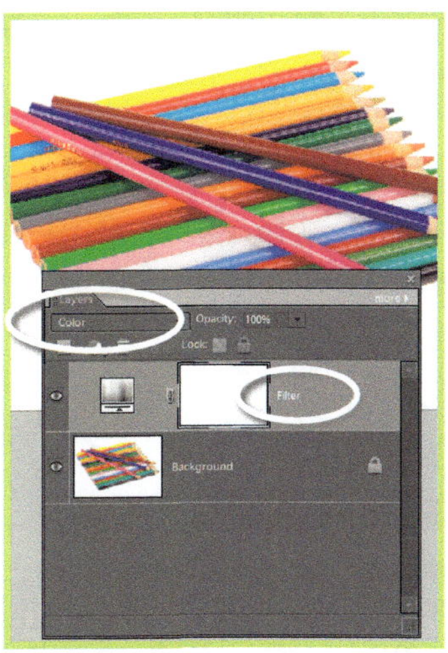

Step 1 >> *Make a new Hue/Saturation layer above your background. Don't make any changes to the default settings for this layer.*

Set the mode of the adjustment layer to Color. Label this layer 'Filter'.

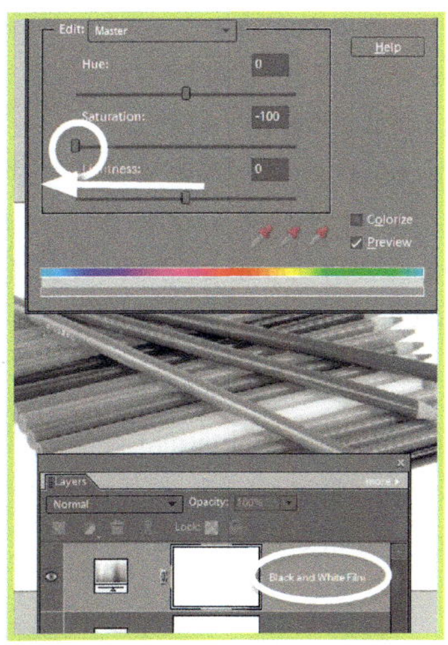

Step 2 >> *Make a second Hue/Saturation adjustment layer above the Filter layer and alter the settings so Saturation is -100. Call this layer Black and White Film. The monochrome image now on screen is the standard result we would expect if we just desaturated the colored original.*

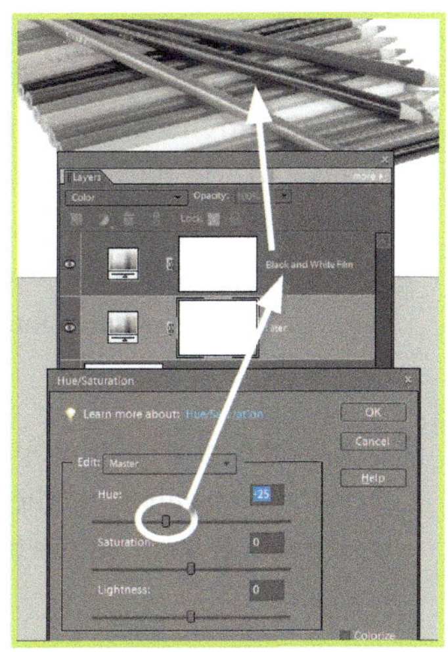

Step 3 >> *Next double-click on the layer thumbnail in the Filter layer and move the Hue slider. This changes the way that the color values are translated to black and white. Similarly, if you move the Saturation slider you can emphasize particular parts of the image.*

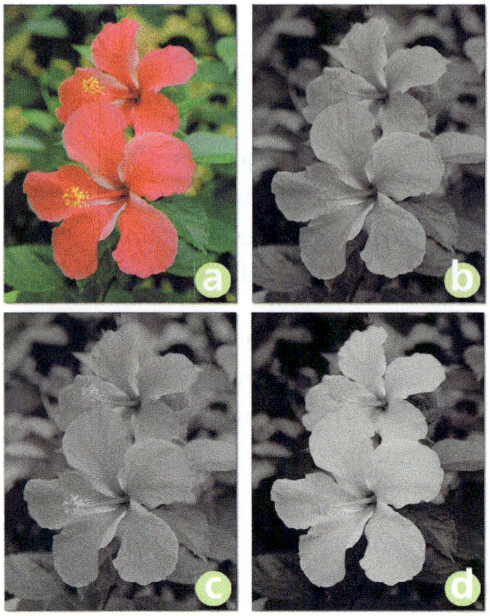

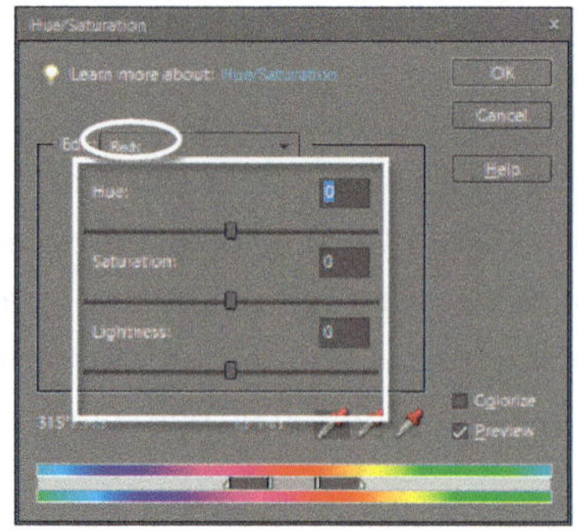

More control >> *For more precise control of the separation of tones you can restrict your changes to a single color group (red, blue, green, cyan, magenta) by selecting it from the drop-down menu before manipulating the Hue and Saturation controls.*

Gray conversion options >> *Photoshop Elements provides a variety of options when you are wanting to convert color pictures to a grayscale or black and white photo.*
(a) Original color photo.
(b) Change to grayscale mode.
(c) Desaturate the photo.
(d) The Russell Brown technique.

6.16 The Convert to Black and White feature

Suitable for Elements – 7.0, 6.0, 5.0 | Difficulty level – Basic Resources – Web image 613 | Related techniques – 6.13, 6.14, 6.15 | Menus used – Enhance

Taking this idea further in Elements 5 Adobe introduced a new Convert to Black and White feature (Editor: Enhance > Convert to Black and White). It provides the ability to customize the way that color areas are mapped to gray during the conversion process. The dialog consists of large before and after previews, a series of six conversion styles that are based on popular subject types or conversions and four slider control buttons for fine-tuning the results.

This feature provides the options for more sophisticated conversions by allowing the user to adjust which colors (red, green or blue) feature more prominently in the final result.

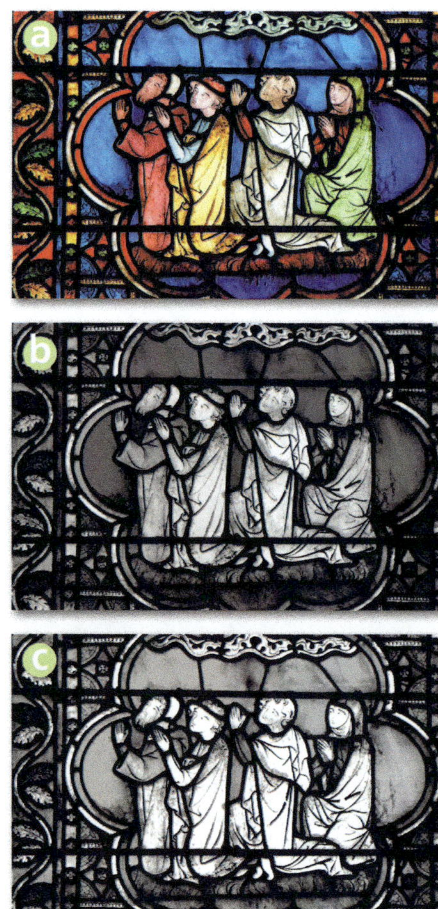

Convert to Black and White >> *From version 5.0 Photoshop Elements has contained a custom control for transforming color photos to grayscale. The Convert to Black and White feature allows you to control how the colors are mapped to gray.*
(a) Original color photo.
(b) Desaturate or Remove Color conversion.
(c) Convert to Black and White conversion emphasizing the blue areas in the original color photo.

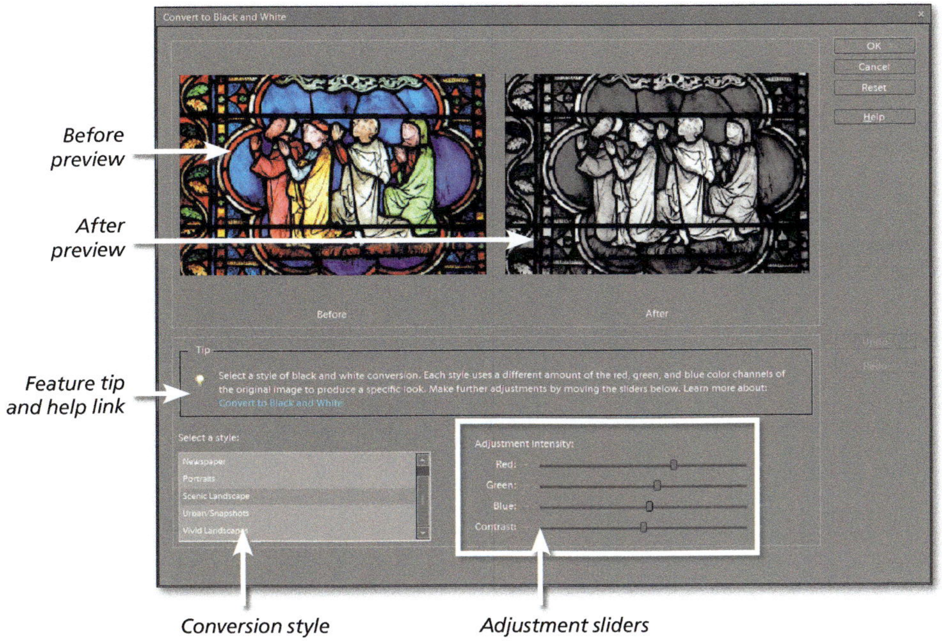

Convert to Black and White >> The Convert to Black and White dialog contains a before and after preview, six different conversion styles or flavor presets as well as a set of adjustment buttons that can be used for customizing the way that particular colors are mapped to gray.

This feature is great for situations where the color contrast of a scene isn't reflected in the monochrome conversion. Imagine the color contrast of a red rose against green foliage. Using a simple conversion feature such as Remove Color would result in both the rose and foliage being the same tone of gray. With Convert to Black and White the contrast of the original can be retained in the result by boosting or reducing the prominence of green or red parts of the picture.

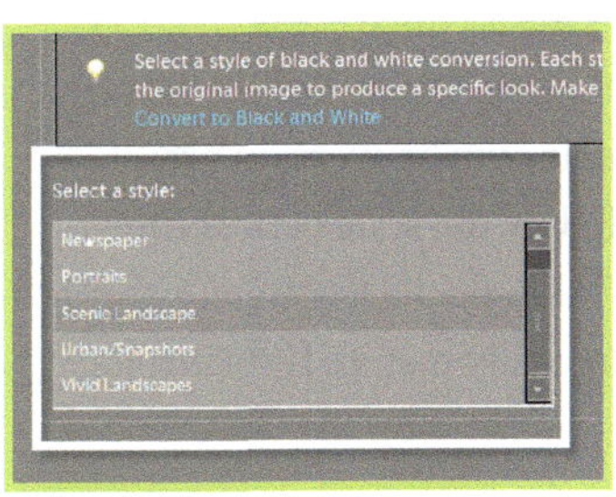

Step 1 >> With a suitable color image open in the Full Edit workspace select the Convert to Black and White feature from the Enhance menu. Click through the different conversion styles menu checking the After preview for a suitable result. Click OK to apply the conversion, Reset to remove current settings or Cancel to quit the feature.

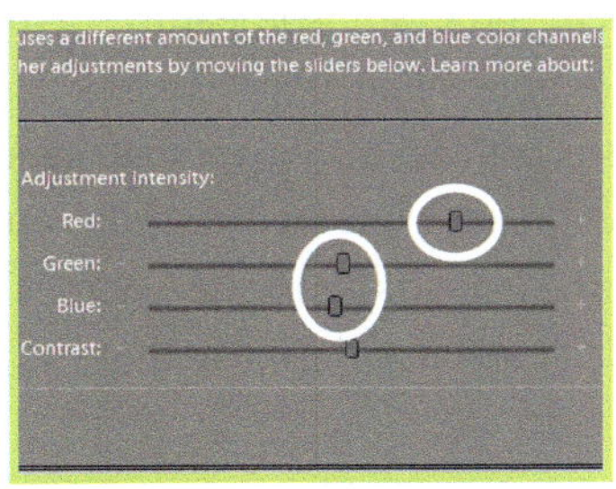

Step 2 >> For a more customized conversion start by selecting a conversion style that is closest to your desired result and then fine-tune the results with one of the Adjustment Intensity sliders. The effects can be more dramatic by also applying the opposite adjustment in the other two color channels.

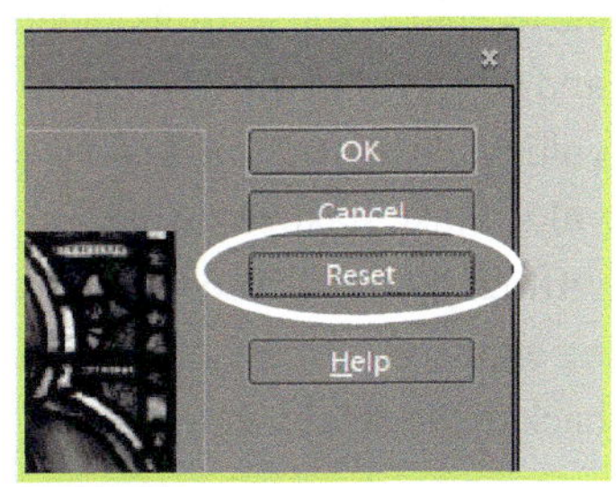

Step 3 >> In situations where the changes you make produce results that are undesirable you can return the after image back to its default state by clicking the Reset button in the top right of the dialog.

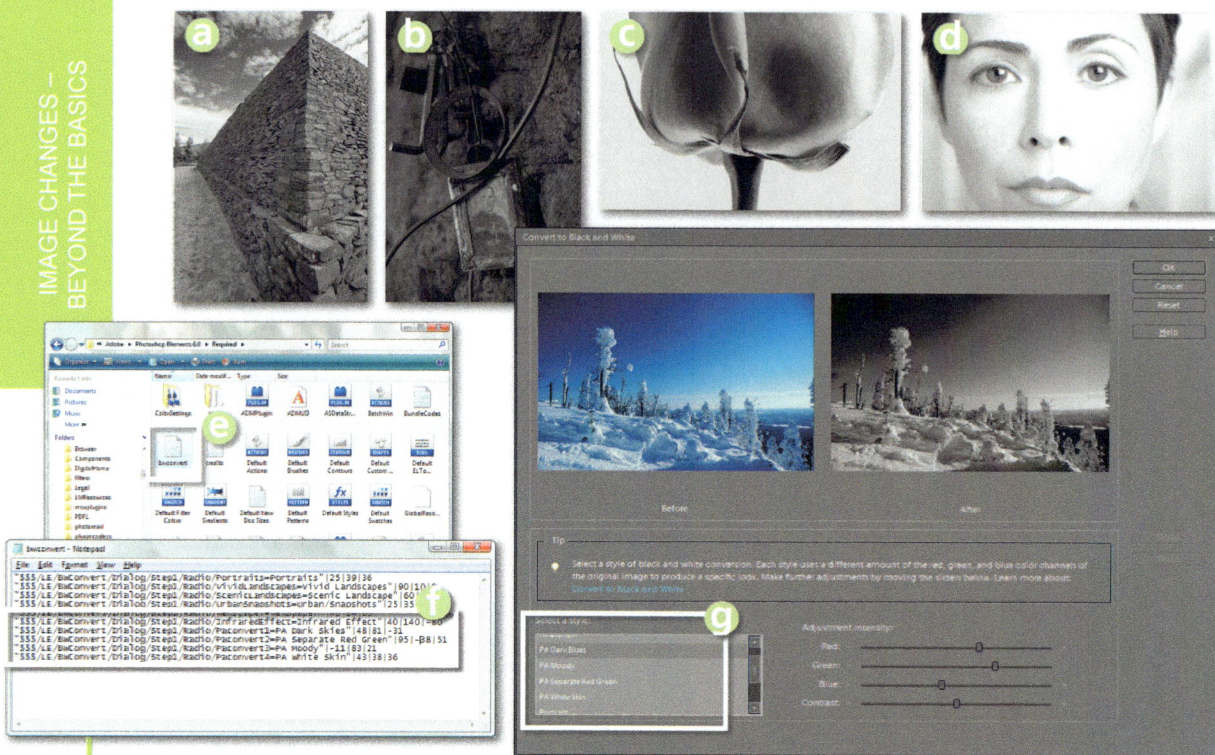

Custom Black and White >> *You can create your own custom black and white style presets by editing the bwconvert.txt file (f) located in the \Program Files\Adobe\Photoshop Elements 7.0\Required folder (e). Alternatively, you can download and copy my own version of this file to the directory. It contains four custom conversion options Dark Skies (a), Moody (b), Separate Red Green (c) and White Skin (d). After restarting Elements the new options will appear in the Styles menu of the feature (g).*

6.17 Custom entries in Convert to Black and White

Suitable for Elements – 7.0, 6.0, 5.0 | Difficulty level – Basic | Resources – Web image 614 | Related techniques – 6.14, 6.15, 6.16 | Menus used – Enhance

The preset style entries in the Convert to Black and White feature are controlled by a simple text file located in the settings folders of the program. The features settings file is called 'bwconvert.txt' and is located in the *C:\Program Files\Adobe\Photoshop Elements 7.0\Required* folder. The file sets the values for the styles and can be easily edited if a user wants to have their own conversion preset values. Just make sure that you create a new line for each entry and follow the style of the other settings. You will also need to restart Elements for the new entries to take effect. Of course, I highly recommend backing up the installed version of the file so that you can easily restore the settings back to the default values.

If all this sounds too difficult then just download my customized version of the 'bwconvert.txt' file and copy it to the *C:\Program Files\Adobe\Photoshop Elements 7.0\Required* folder. My version contains four extra presets (Dark Skies, Moody, Separate Red Green and White Skin) designed to extend the styles in the feature further and provide some example conversions that you might find useful. As with all styles, to fully suit your images, apply the style first and then tweak the results with the sliders.

6.18 The Gradient Map conversions

Suitable for Elements – 7.0, 6.0, 5.0 | Difficulty level – Basic | Resources – Web image 615
Related techniques – 6.13, 6.14, 6.15 | Menus used – Enhance

Yet another way to convert a color image to grayscale is to employ the abilities of a Gradient Map Adjustment Layer. When set to a black to white gradient, this feature maps the tones and colors in an image so that they are evenly distributed along the gradient's tonal range. This creates a conversion with good overall contrast, as the darkest point of the photo is mapped to black and the lightest to white, but by playing with the gradient itself, you can also tweak the brightness of other tonal areas in the image as well. So with this technique you get to make the conversion, and adjust how shadows, midtones and highlights are mapped to gray. Cool!

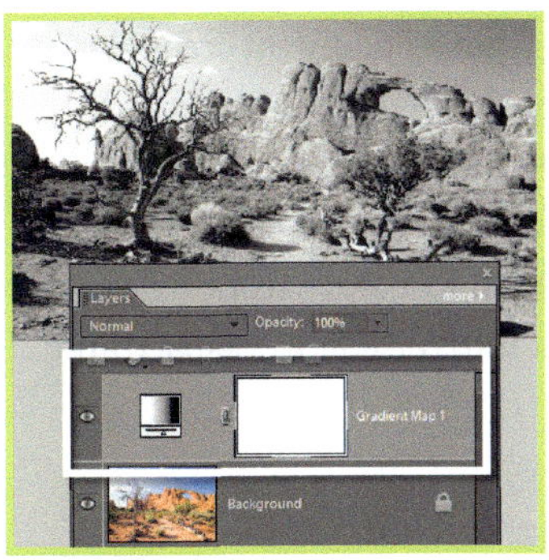

Step 1 >> To start let's make a simple Gradient Map grayscale conversion. Do this by adding a Gradient Map adjustment layer to the layers stack (Layer > New Adjustment Layer > Gradient Map). Next select a Black to White gradient from the drop-down menu. Click OK and the conversion is complete.

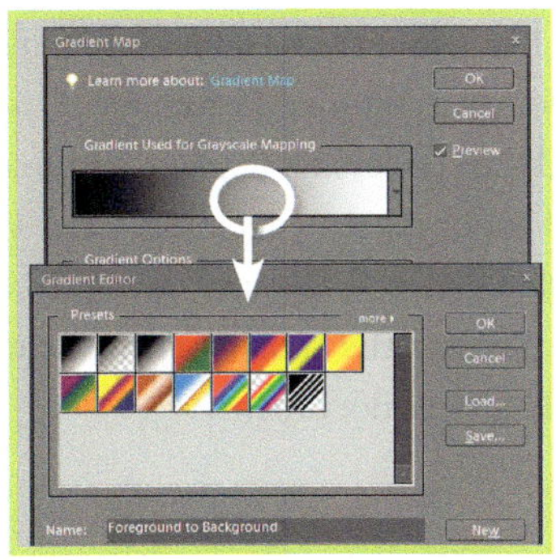

Step 2 >> To start to control how shadows midtones and highlights are mapped to gray we need to create a custom gradient In the Gradient Editor. Double-click on the Gradient Map thumbnail to open the feature's dialog. Next click onto the displayed gradient to open the Gradient Editor.

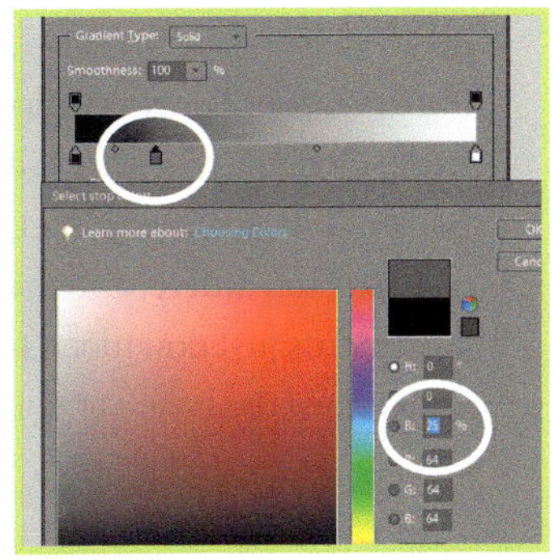

Step 3 >> At the moment the gradient has a color control (called Stops) at either end of the gradient – black and white. We want to add extra Stops for 25%, 50% and 75% brightness values. Do this by clicking just below the gradient. This adds a new Stop. Double-click the stop to open the Select Stop Color dialog. Type the gray value in the 'B' section for the HSB values. Click OK.

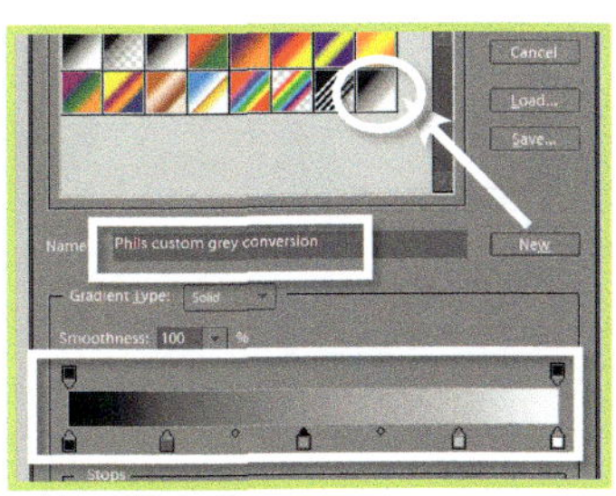

Step 4 >> Repeat the process adding in the other gray stops. Don't worry too much about their position along the gradient as we can alter this, just try to ensure that the 25% brightness value is left of center, 50% about center and 75% brightness is right of center. Once all the stops have been created add a name for the gradient in the Name area and click the New button to add the gradient to those listed in the palette. Don't click OK.

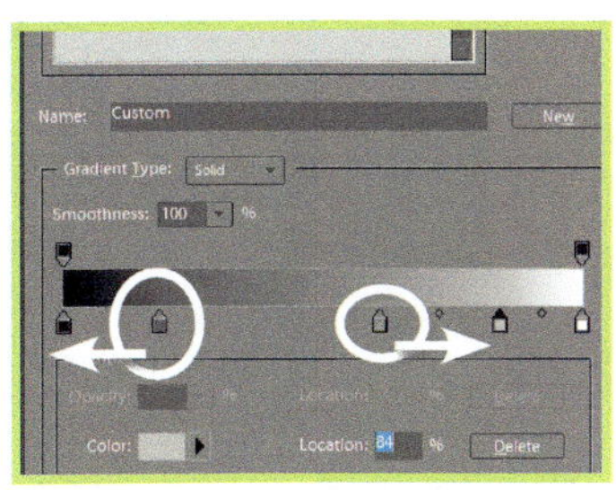

Step 5 >> To manipulate how the tones are mapped to gray click on a stop and drag it along the gradient in the Gradient Editor. In this example the shadows were lightened by dragging the 25% brightness stop to the left and midtones were darkened by dragging the 50% darkness to the right. The changes will be previewed in your image as long as the Preview option is ticked in the Gradient Map dialog.

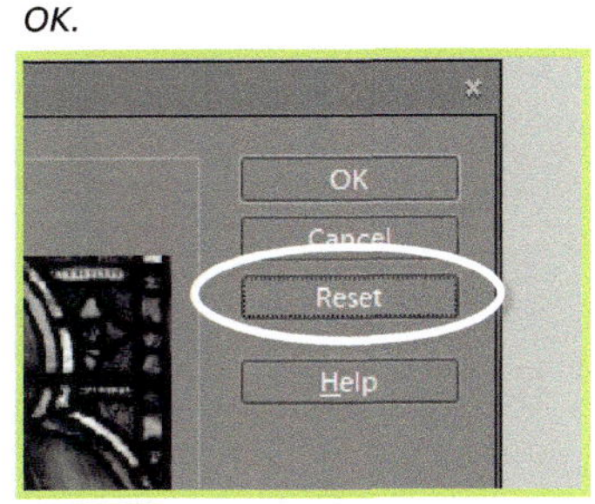

Step 6 >> Finally to apply the conversion click the OK buttons in the Gradient Editor and the Gradient Map dialogs. The tones can be adjusted at a later date by double-clicking on the adjustment layer thumbnail and then clicking the gradient. This will display the Gradient Editor complete with your custom gradient containing the three additional brightness stops.

6.19 Borrowing Photoshop's Black and White

Suitable for Elements – 7.0, 6.0, 5.0 | Difficulty level – Basic | Resources – Web image 6.16 | Related techniques – 6.13, 6.14, 6.15 | Menus used – Enhance

At the same time that Elements users were enjoying the monochrome mapping power of the Convert to Black and White feature, Photoshop CS3 users were also given a specialized conversion feature called, Black and White. The new feature is available for use directly on an image or via an Adjustment Layer. It contains six slider controls that adjust how specific color ranges are mapped to gray. In addition, there is a toning option at the bottom of the dialog which provides the ability to tint the converted monochrome.

Even though this is a Photoshop-only feature, we can make use of its color to gray mapping abilities. Just drag an existing Black and White adjustment layer from a document created in Photoshop, but opened into Elements, onto an Elements file. Just like magic the layer is added to the Elements document and the conversion applied. Just in case you don't have Photoshop handy I have created a special donor document called, *Photoshop-Convert-to-Gray.psd*, which contains ten different conversion layers. For you to have the Photoshop feature working on your documents just download the file from the book's website, open it into the edit workspace and drag one of the layers to your Elements document.

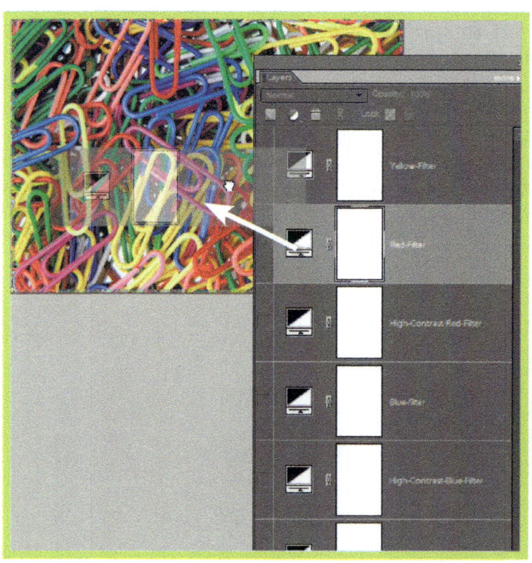

Step 1 >> *Start by opening both the Photoshop donor document (Photoshop-Convert-to-gray.psd) and the Elements file that you want to enhance. Click onto the Photoshop document and scroll through the list of adjustment layers available in the document. Select a layer and click-drag it onto the Elements document. The enhancement change will be immediately previewed in the workspace.*

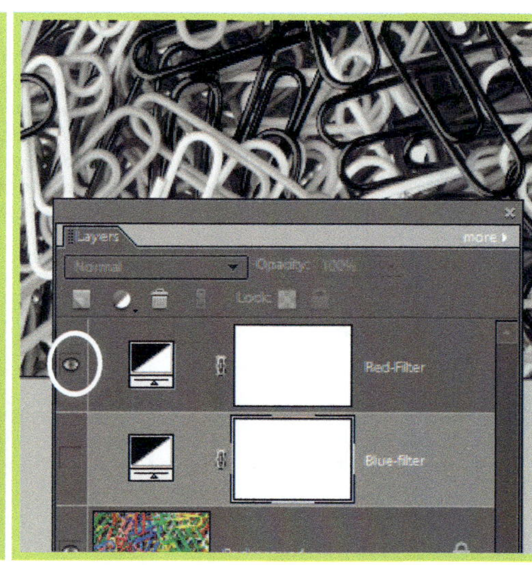

Step 2 >> *Multiple Photoshop layers can be dragged onto the Elements document and their effects hidden or applied by clicking the 'eye' icon on the left of the layer entry.*

Advanced dodging and burning-in

After years of my 'hit and miss' approach to dodging and burning in the darkroom I can still remember my reaction to seeing Photoshop Elements performing real-time lightening and darkening – 'You are kidding!'. Not only could I paint in light and dark areas on my picture using a soft-edged brush, I could also vary the strength of the effect and the size of the brush used for application. In addition, I could choose to alter shadow, midtones or highlights separately and 'undo' my actions with a single keystroke. All this flexibility and with the lights on as well!

I would think that most new users to Photoshop Elements would experience much of the same excitement as I did when they first discover the Dodge and Burn-in tools. For the majority of simple enhancement tasks a few quick strokes of these tools will provide plenty of control over your picture's tones, but there are occasions when you need a little more flexibility. I use the following techniques to provide a little more customization to my dodging and burning-in in my work.

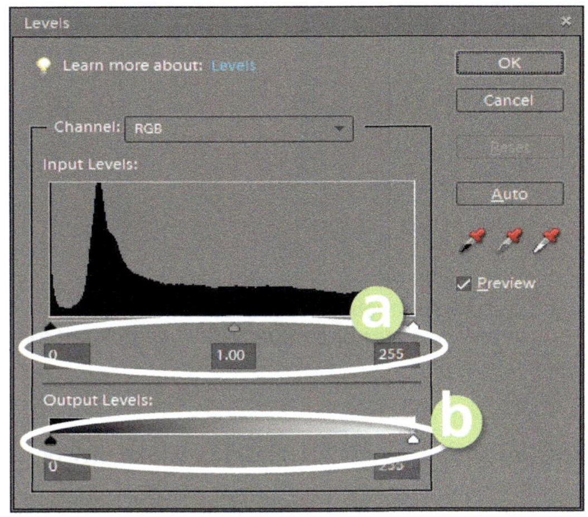

Input and output sliders >>
(a) Black, midtone and white Input sliders.
(b) Black and white Output sliders.

6.20 Using selections to change tone

Suitable for Elements – 7.0, 6.0, 5.0, 4.0, 3.0, 2.0, 1.0 | Difficulty level – Intermediate | Resources – Web Image 617
Related Techniques – 6.18 | Tools used – Selection tools| Menus used – Select

You can evenly alter the tone of a large area of your picture quickly by making a feathered selection of the area first and then using the Levels control to darken or lighten the pixels. The amount you feather the selection will determine how soft the transition will be between dodged or burnt areas and the original picture. Using the Levels feature gives you great control over the brightness of shadow, mid- tone and highlight areas.

By manipulating the Input and Output sliders you can selectively alter specific tones in your image. You can also decrease or increase the contrast of the selection as well.

Use this table to help get you started.

Required image change	Action to take
To lighten the midtones of a selected area	Move the midpoint input triangle to the left
To darken the midtones of a selected area	Move the midpoint input triangle to the right
To lighten the midtones and highlights	Move the white point input triangle to the left
To darken the midtones and shadows	Move the black point input triangle to the right
To lighten the shadow tones	Move the black point output triangle to the right
To darken the highlight tones	Move the white point output triangle to the left
To decrease contrast	Move the white and black point Output sliders closer together
To increase contrast	Move the white and black point Input sliders closer together

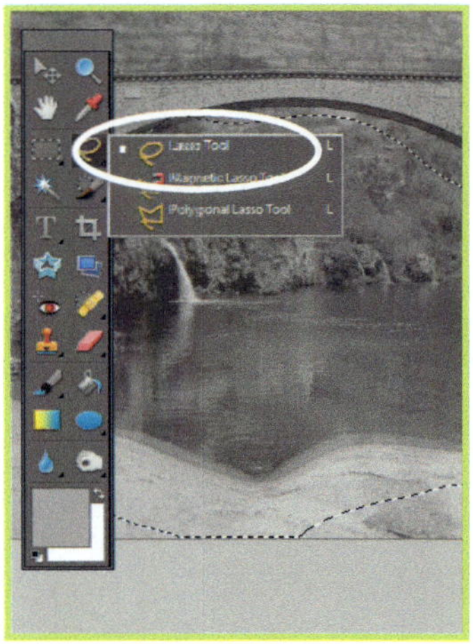

Step 1 >> *Using one of the selection tools draw a rough selection around the area to dodge or burn-in.*

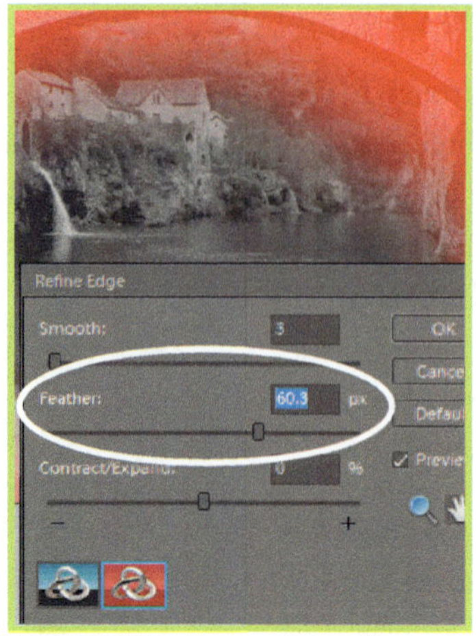

Step 2 >> *Feather and then inverse the selection. Use a large pixel amount for high-resolution pictures.*

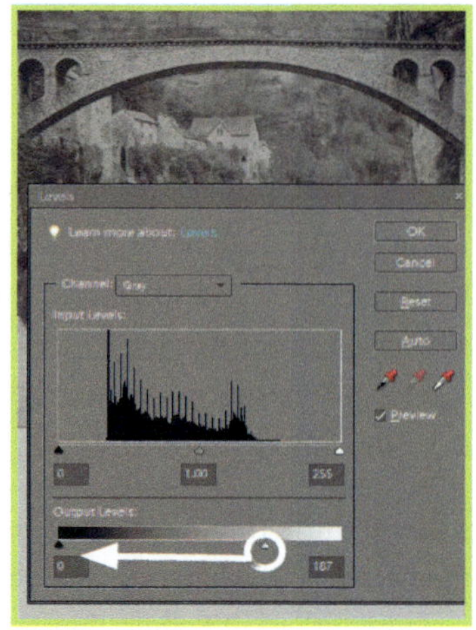

Step 3 >> *With the selection still active manipulate the Levels Input and Output sliders to darken/lighten tones.*

Pro's Tip: Non-destructive dodging and burning-in

If you want to dodge and burn but not make any permanent changes to the picture you can use the same feathered selection technique, but apply the changes through an adjustment layer. Make the selection as before, feathering (Select > Feather or Refine Edge) the edge and inversing (Select > Inverse) the selection. With the selection still active, click onto the Create New Adjustment Layer button on the top of the Layers palette and choose Levels. If the Layers palette is not visible then you can perform the same action via the Layer menu (Layer > New Adjustment Layer). The Levels dialog appears and any changes made with the sliders alter the tones in the selected area of the picture just as before. The difference with this approach is that the dodging and burning-in takes place via an adjustment layer, leaving the original picture unchanged in the layer beneath. The selection is used as a basis to form a mask in the adjustment layer. We view the levels changes through the clear areas of this mask only. A second advantage to this approach is that the levels settings can be changed at a later date. Simply double-click the thumbnail on the left-hand side of the layer and alter the Levels settings.

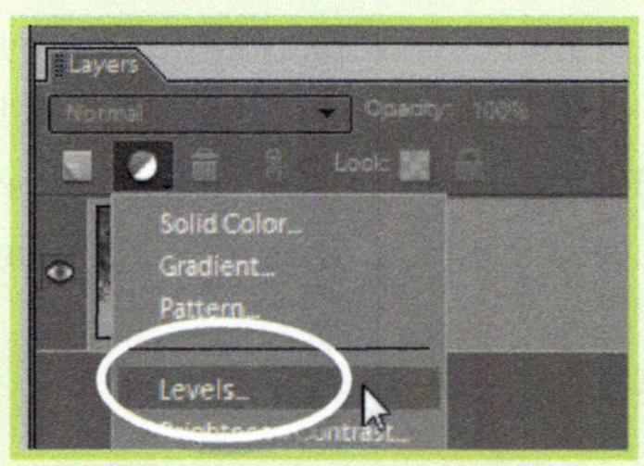

Step 1 >> *With your feathered selection active click the New Adjustment Layer button.*

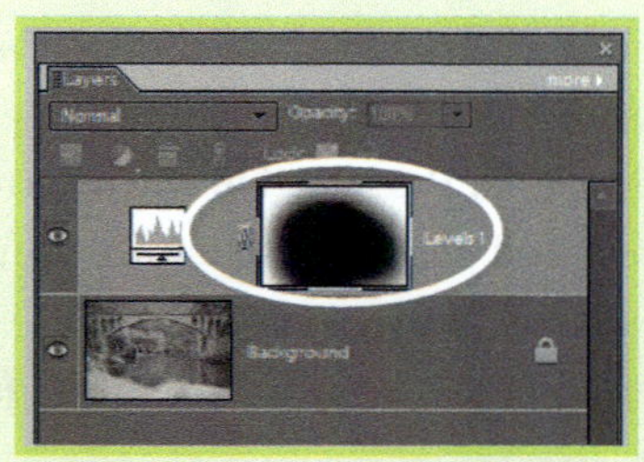

Step 2 >> *Select the Levels adjustment layer and adjust the dialog's settings to Dodge and Burn-in.*

A second non-destructive approach that was pioneered by Julianne Kost starts with you creating two empty layers above the background or image layer. Name them Dodge and Burn and set the blending mode for both of them to Soft Light. Using a Black brush at a low opacity (10–15%) paint on the burn layer to darken areas. Use a White brush at the same opacity on the dodge layer to lighten. This provides a non-destructive, subtle and artistic method for dodging and burning-in.

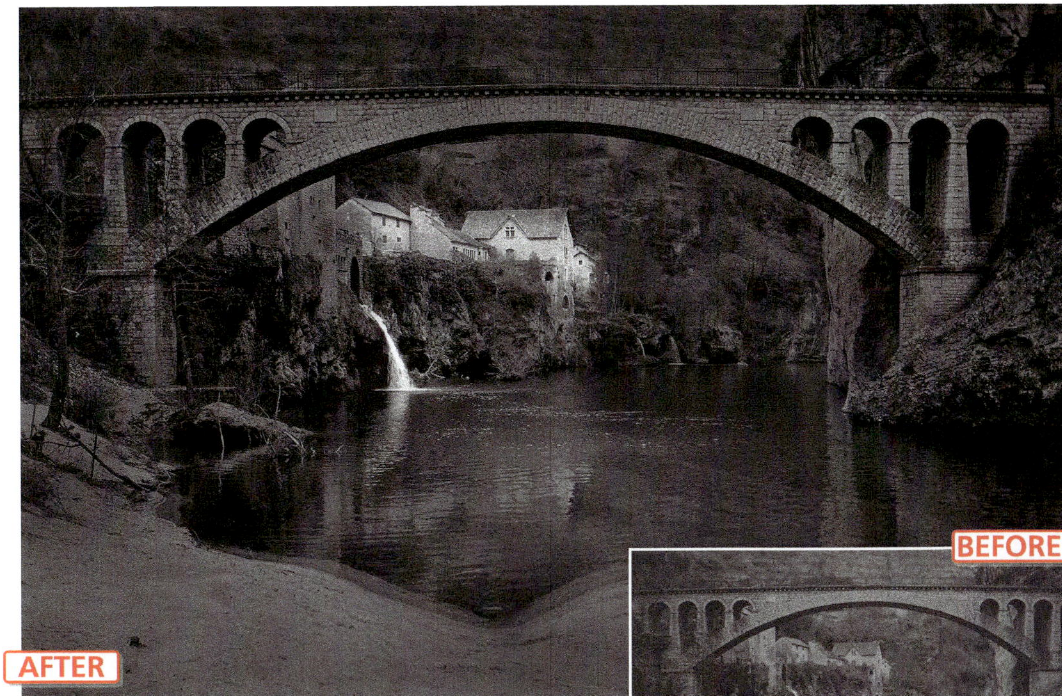

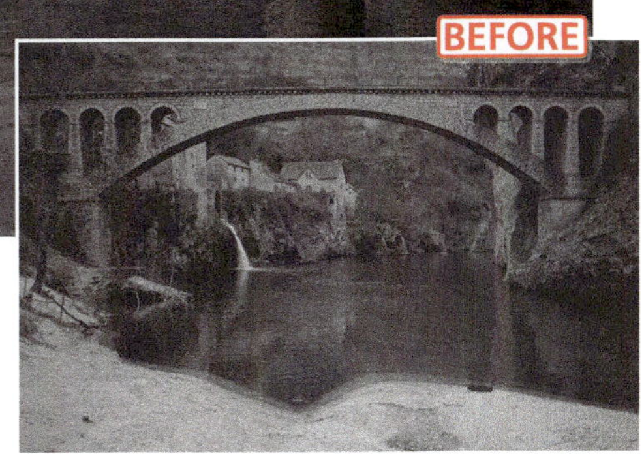

Dodging and burning-in >> *Dodging and burning-in has always been used to add a little visual drama into photographs. The careful lightening and darkening of areas of the print can create a sense of depth and also help to direct the viewer's eye to specific focal points in the image.* *Image courtesy of www.ablestock.com Copyright 2005.*

6.21 Erase back through tonal layers

Suitable for Elements – 7.0, 6.0, 5.0, 4.0, 3.0, 2.0, 1.0 | Difficulty level – Intermediate | Resources – Web image 617 | Related Techniques – 6.16 | Tools used – Eraser Menus used – Enhance, Layer

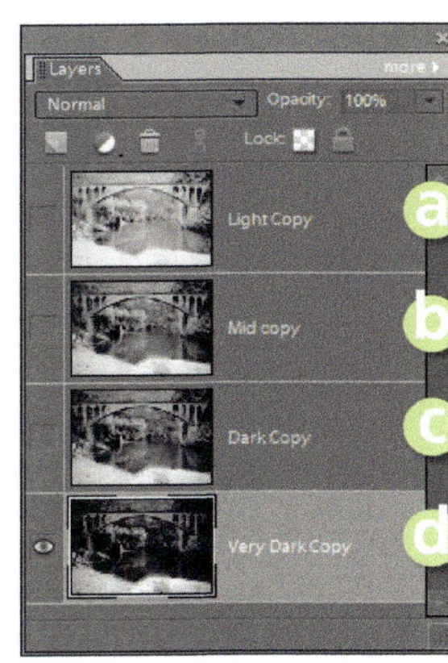

Dodge and burn via erase >> *Make creative tonal changes using the Eraser tool and several adjusted layer copies. (a) Light copy. (b) Midtone/normal copy. (c) Dark copy. (d) Very dark copy.*

A more artistic approach to dodging and burning-in can be found in a technique that involves making several different copies of the base picture. The background layer can be copied by either choosing Layer > Duplicate Layer or by dragging the layer to the Create New Layer button at the bottom of the Layers palette.

Each copy is stored on a separate layer and the overall tone of the duplicate image is changed using the Layers control. In the example I have created four layers, labelled them *light*, *midtone*, *dark* and *very dark*, and changed their tones accordingly. Next I selected the Eraser tool, set the mode to brush, the edge option to soft and the opacity to 20%. I then clicked on the Eye icon in both the light and midtone layers and selected the dark layer. Using the Eraser in overlapping strokes, I gradually removed sections of the dark layer to reveal the very dark layer beneath. I then selected the midtone layer and performed the same action and finally I selected the light layer and erased sections to reveal the darker layers below. If this all sounds a little confusing, try thinking of the erasing action as actually painting the image darker, or burning the picture area in, and take my advice – make sure that you name your layers as you create them. This technique works particularly well if used with a graphics tablet as the opacity of the erasing stroke can be linked to the pressure on the stylus. Pressing harder with the stylus erases more of the layer and creates a greater change. Lighter strokes can be used to produce more subtle adjustments.

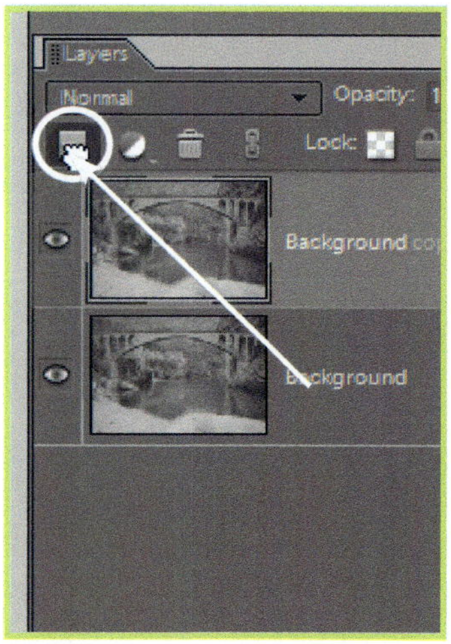

Step 1 >> *Make several copies of the basic image layer by dragging the layer to the Create New Layer button.*

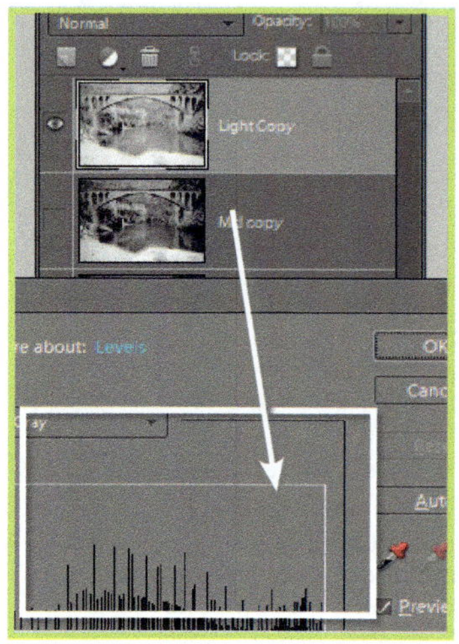

Step 2 >> *Select each layer in turn and alter the overall brightness using the Levels dialog.*

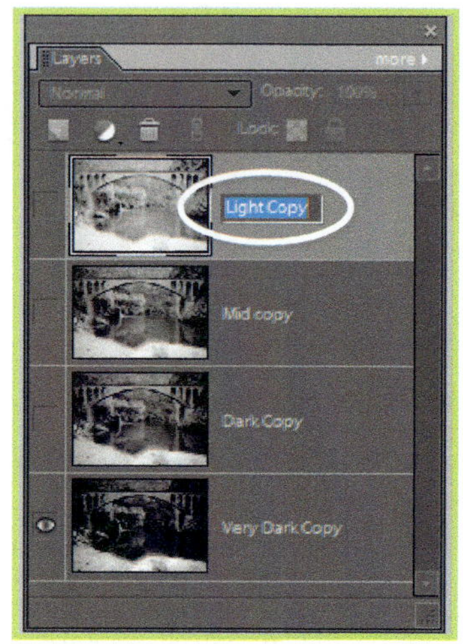

Step 3 >> *Rename the layers by double-clicking the names in the Layers palette.*

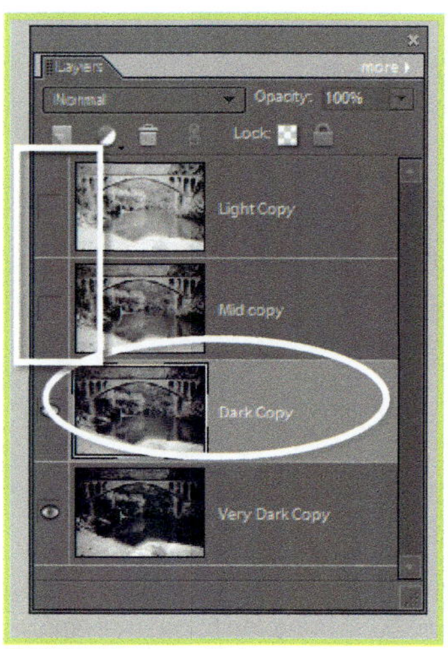

Step 4 >> *Turn off the Eye icon for the light and midtone layers and select the dark layer.*

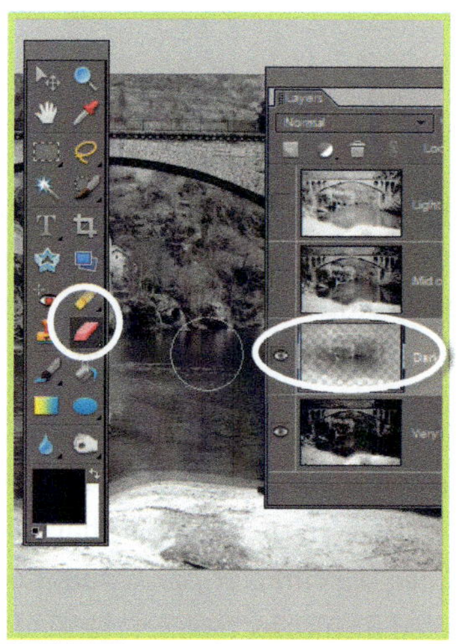

Step 5 >> *Using the Eraser tool remove parts of the dark layer to reveal the very dark picture below.*

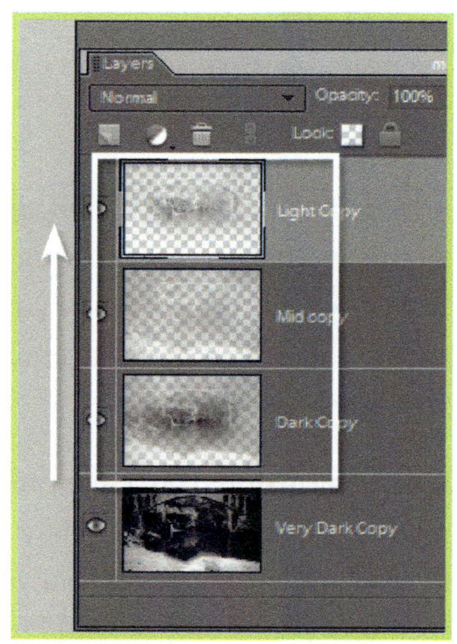

Step 6 >> *Work your way through the other layers gradually removing unwanted areas to build up the picture.*

Masked based layers

To ensure the maximum ability to customize how the layers are applied you can make use of the mask in a No Settings adjustment layer to hide or reveal the detail for any particular layer. To work this way add No Settings adjustment layers below each of the top three image layers. Then use the Group with Previous command to link the image and adjustment layers.

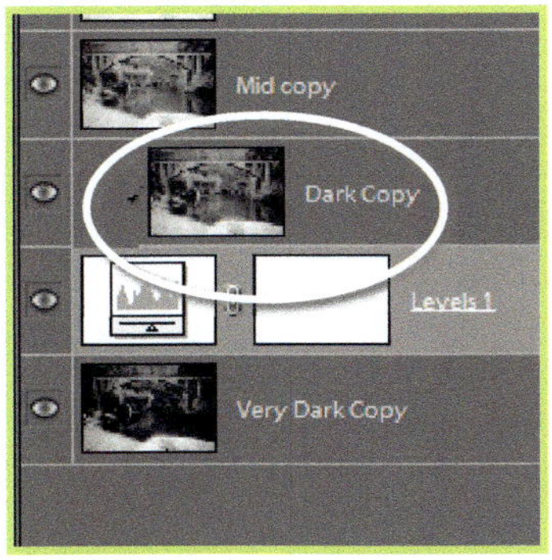

Step 1 >> *Start by adding a No Settings adjustment layer below each of the image layers. Next Select the image layer and then Choose Layer > Group With Previous to view the layer detail through the adjustment layer mask.*

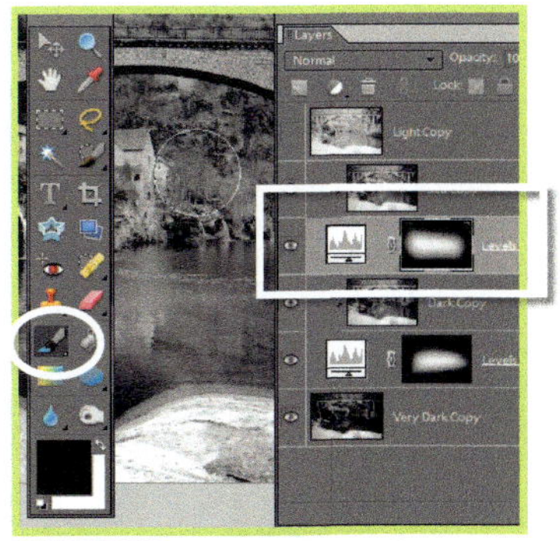

Step 2 >> *After selecting the Adjustment Layer Mask use a black Brush to paint in the areas of the layer that will be hidden from view (that will allow the detail from beneath to show through).*

6.22 Paint on dodging and burning-in

Suitable for Elements – 7.0, 6.0, 5.0, 4.0, 3.0, 2.0, 1.0
Difficulty level – Intermediate | Resources – Web image 618
Related Techniques – 6.20, 6.21 | Tools used – Brush Menus used – Layer

What if you want the flexibility of painting in your density changes (dodging and burning) but wanted to apply these changes non-destructively to your photo? Well, a solution can be found by combining aspects of the last technique with our understanding of adjustment layers and their associated layer masks.

Start by adding a Levels adjustment layer (Editor: Layer > New Adjustment Layer > Levels) to your photo. In the Levels dialog drag the Input midpoint slider to the right and the Output white point slider to the left. This will create an adjustment layer effect that darkens the whole image. Think of this change as how the image would look if you applied the Burn tool to the whole picture. Click OK to apply the change. Nothing new here you say. True, but what if we could selectively paint in this effect rather than apply it to the whole image? Well here is the trick. Click on the mask of the adjustment layer and fill it with black (Editor: Edit > Fill Layer). Remember black hides the adjustment layer effect so you should see the original tones of your photo restored in the preview window. With the mask still selected choose a soft-edged brush, lower the opacity slightly and make sure the paint colour is white.

Now paint onto the surface of the photo. The painted areas will darken. In reality you are not painting the photo but rather painting the mask and in so doing adding the adjustment layer effect in these areas.

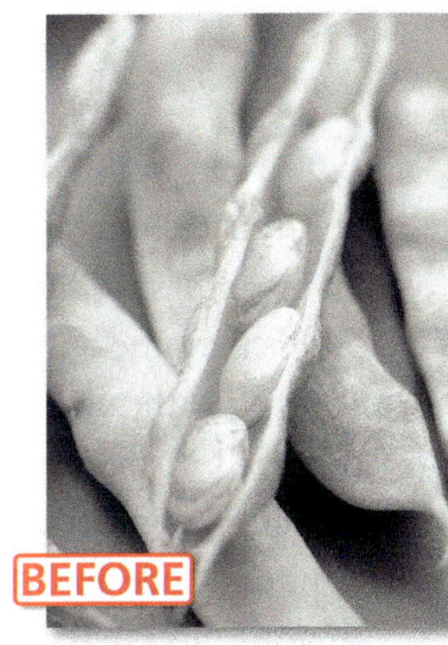

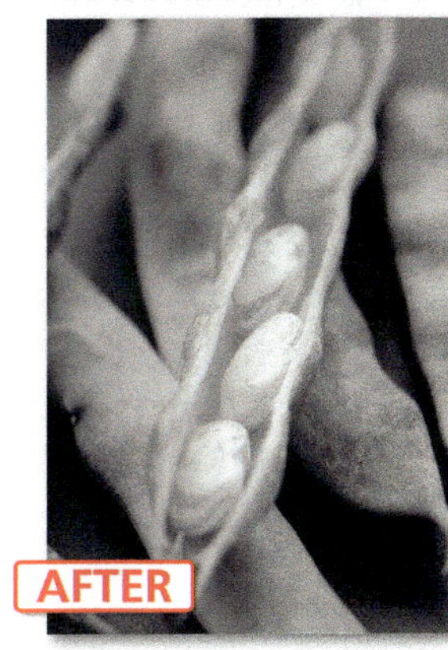

'Paint on' image changes >> *Use the mask of the Levels adjustment layer to paint burn and dodge effects non-destructively onto your photos.*

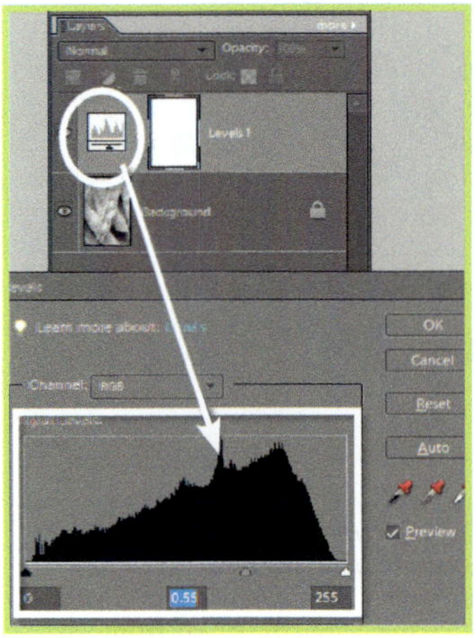

Step 1 >> *Create a new Levels adjustment layer that darkens the photo.*

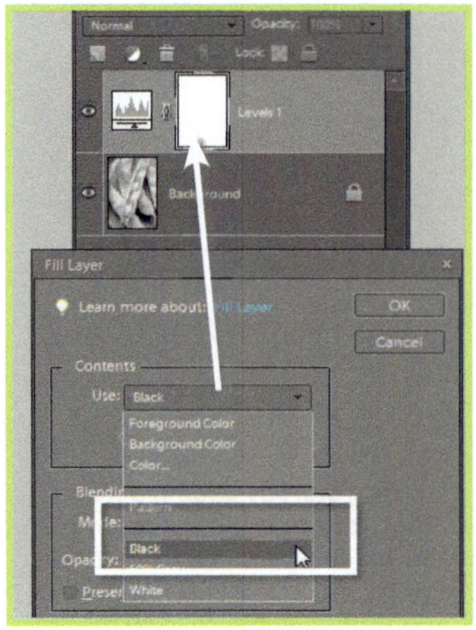

Step 2 >> *Select the layer mask of the adjustment layer in the Layers palette and fill with black.*

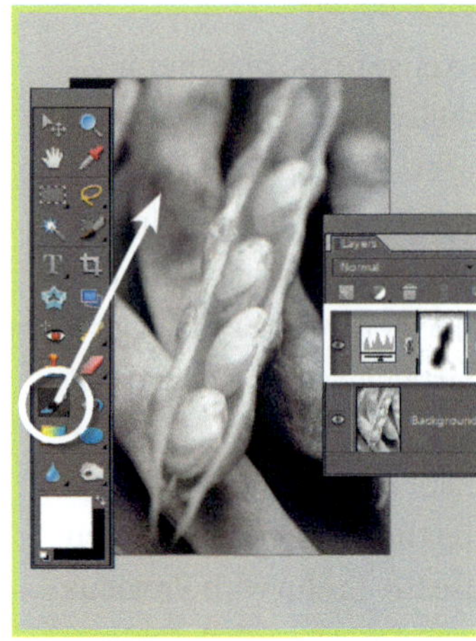

Step 3 >> *To burn non-destructively brush onto the photo with white whilst the layer mask is still selected.*

6.23 Blend mode Dodge and Burn

Suitable for Elements – 7.0, 6.0, 5.0, 4.0, 3.0, 2.0, 1.0 | Difficulty level – Intermediate | Resources – Web image 619 | Related Techniques – 6.20, 6.21 | Tools used – Brush | Menus used – Layer

One final technique for dodging and burning makes use of the Soft Light Blend Mode to change the brightness of different picture parts non-destructively. Start by adding a new layer above the background or main image layer. Next change the layer's Blend Mode setting to Soft Light. Now target the new layer and with a black soft-edged brush paint over the picture areas to be darkened. To lighten a portion of the image, switch to a white foreground color (click 'x' for a quick change between foreground and background colors) and paint over these areas. The Blending Mode applies the changes in brightness and the fact that the painting is stored in a separate layer makes the technique non-destructive.

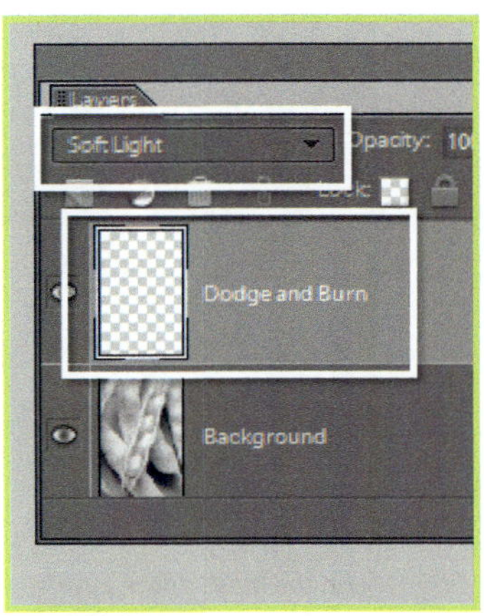

Step 1 >> *Create a new layer and then change the Layer Blend Mode to Soft Light.*

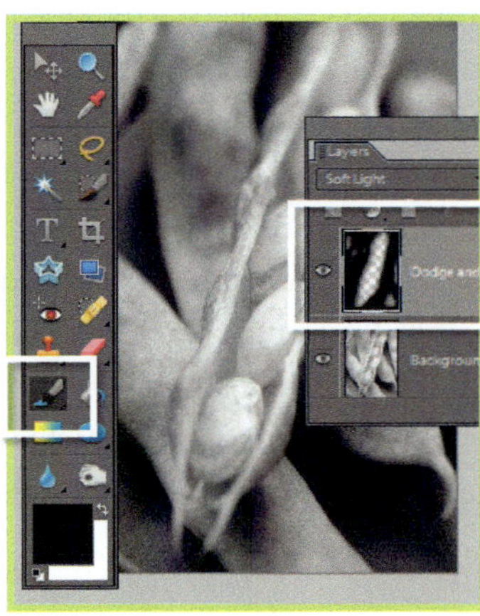

Step 2 >> *Target the new layer and paint over the areas to be burned in with a black soft-edged brush.*

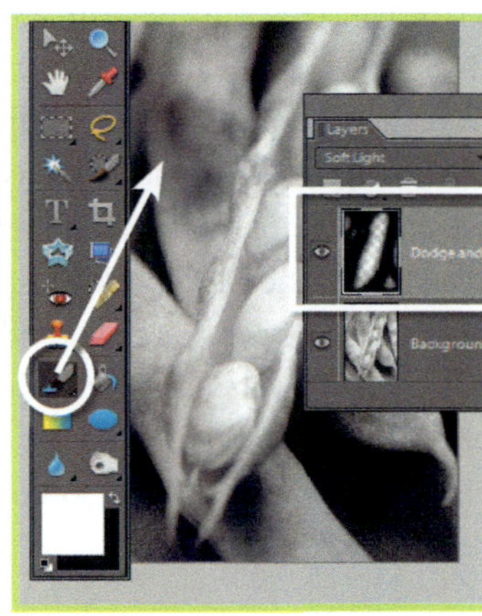

Step 3 >> *To lighten a picture part, switch the foreground color to white and paint again. Adjust the brushes opacity to fine tune the changes.*

Enhance your poorly exposed pictures

Good exposure is the cornerstone of great images. No matter how good your subject is, how well you have composed the image or how brilliantly you captured the scene, if your exposure is a little astray then you will be left with a less than perfect result. This is just as true for digital images as it was for traditional photographs. Overexposure leads to delicate highlight detail being recorded as pure white; underexposure on the other hand produces a picture with little detail in the shadow areas.

The best way to solve these problems is to re-shoot your picture using an aperture and shutter combination that will produce a well-exposed image but, as we all know, sometimes a 're-shoot' is just not possible. So how can Photoshop Elements help us enhance our poorly exposed pictures? I have found the following techniques particularly helpful when trying to enhance, or should that be disguise, images that are suffering from bad exposure.

6.24 Screening image layers to enhance tones

Suitable for Elements – 7.0, 6.0, 5.0, 5.0, 4.0, 3.0, 2.0, 1.0 | Difficulty level – Intermediate
Resources – Web image 620 | Related Techniques – 6.20 | Menus used – Layer, Enhance

The shadow and midtones of a picture are areas that suffer greatly when a photograph is underexposed. Valuable details are lost, the individual tones are too dark and the whole area is lacking in contrast. One way to help rectify this problem is to make an exact copy of the pictures and then combine the two images together in order to multiply the apparent detail and tone in the shadow areas. Photoshop Elements, via layers and blending modes, provides us with the tools necessary to perform these actions.

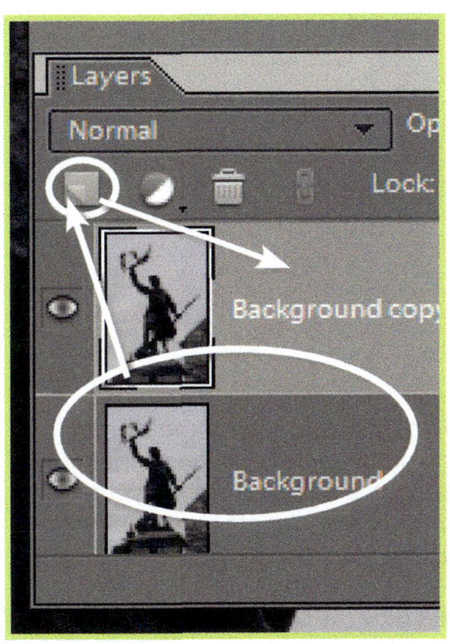

Step 1 >> *Copy the background layer by dragging it to the New Layer button in the Layers dialog.*

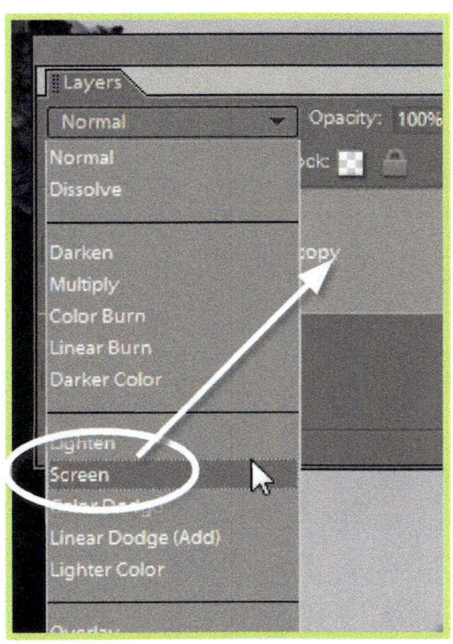

Step 2 >> *Select the copied layer and then change the blending mode to Screen.*

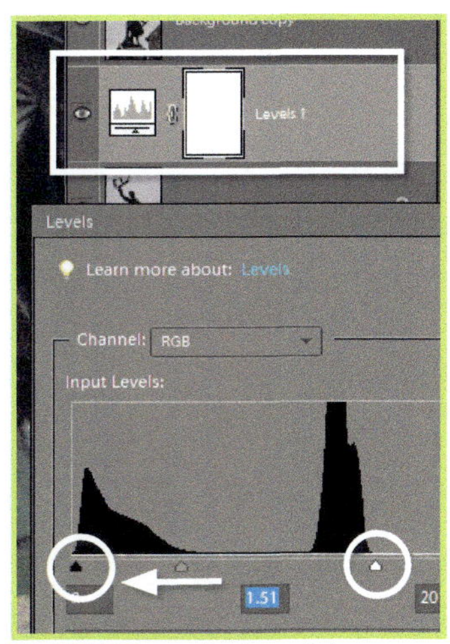

Step 3 >> *As a final touch insert a Levels Adjustment layer between the two layers. Peg the black and white points and lighten the midtones by dragging the midpoint to the left.*

Firstly, duplicate the background (image layer) by dragging it to the New Layer button at the bottom of the Layers dialog. Now, with the copy layer selected, change the layer blending mode to Screen. You should see an immediate brightening of the picture and the appearance of more detail in the shadow areas.

As a final tweaking of the image insert a Levels adjustment layer between the two layers. Do this by clicking on the bottom layer first and then selecting Levels from the drop-down list found when clicking the Create New Adjustment Layer button at the bottom of the Layers palette. Peg the highlights and shadows of the picture by moving the black and white points towards the center until they meet the first pixels in the histogram. Next, move the midtone to the left to increase the overall brightness of the image.

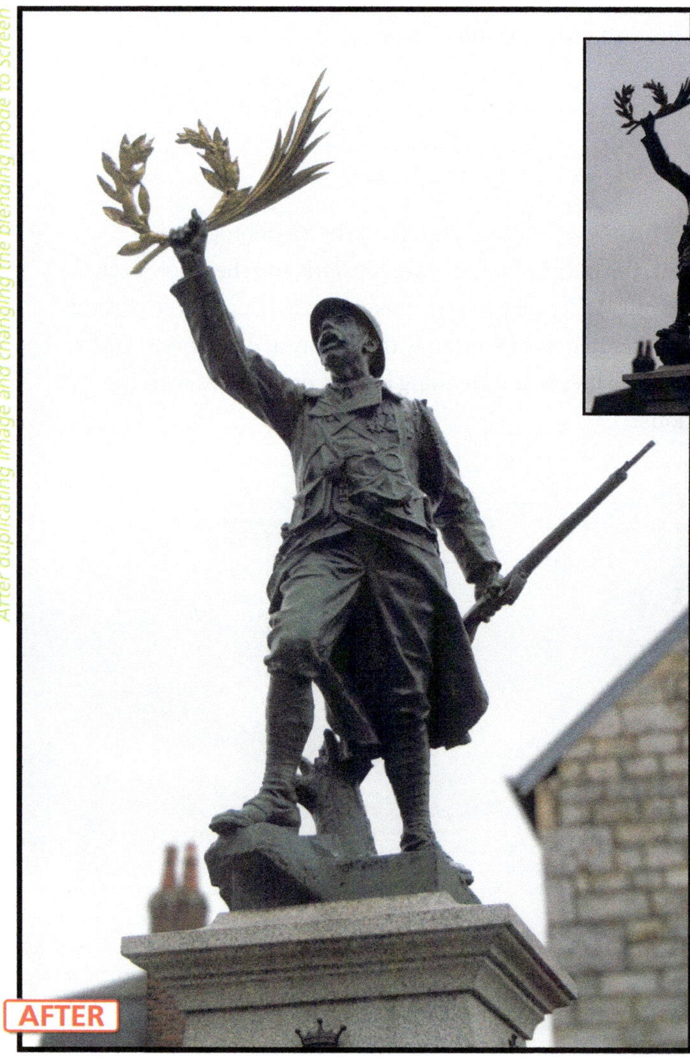

After duplicating image and changing the blending mode to Screen

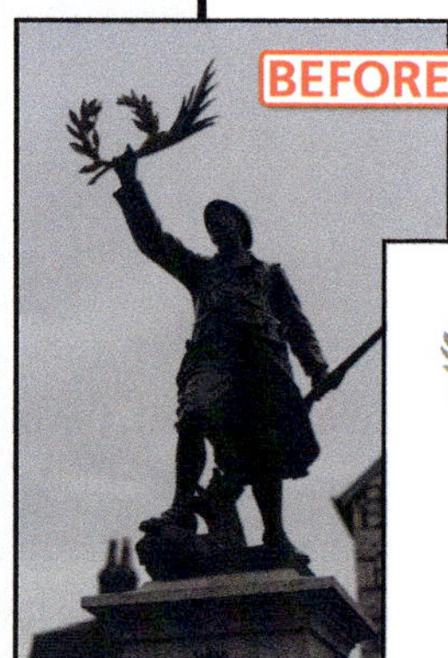

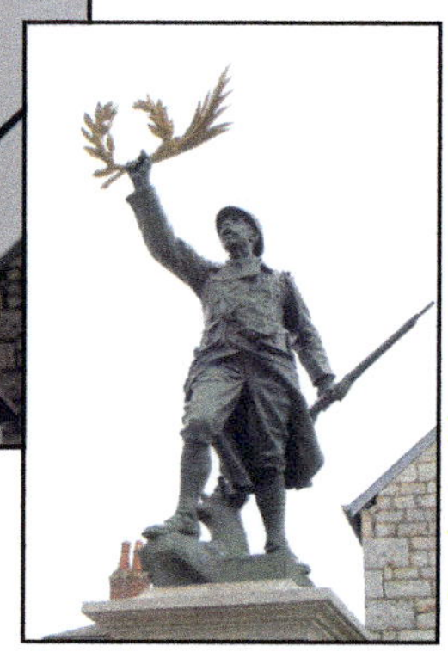

Re-shot with exposure compensation

Correcting underexposure >>

The best way to guarantee a great looking image where the tones are well distributed is to ensure that your exposure settings are correct before pushing the button. If, as is the case in this example, your camera meter is fooled by the scene then you can rescue an underexposed picture using a technique that involves duplicating the base image and then selecting the Screen option as the blending mode.

Those of you who are intimate with Elements will no doubt be asking 'Why not just use the Fill Flash or Shadows/Highlights feature to fix this underexposure problem?' and you are right to ask that question. The Fill Flash option is a great tool for lightening mid to dark tones that have plenty of details, but I have found that this 'duplication layers' technique provides a more pleasing result for underexposed images with little shadow information.

Solving exposure problems when shooting

The statue picture not only provides a great example for this technique but also demonstrates how such underexposure can occur. Set against a white overcast sky this dark statue was underexposed because the camera's meter was fooled by the bright sky behind the subject and therefore provided a shutter/aperture combination which was too dark. The thinking photographer would have predicted this problem and used the Exposure Compensation system on the camera to increase exposure by one to one-and-one-half stops to adjust for the back lighting. Most mid range digital cameras and above incorporate an Exposure Override system like this.

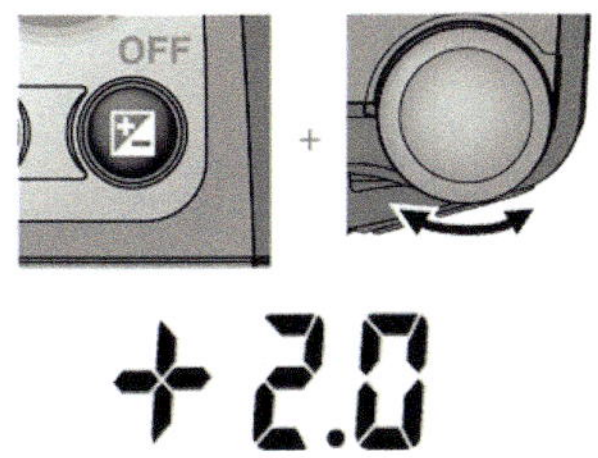

Exposure compensation >> *Use the camera's Exposure Compensation system to override your camera's settings.*

To try this for yourself, the next time you encounter a back lit scene shoot two pictures – one with the camera set to auto and the other where you have added to the exposure. Compare the results later on the desktop, or better still, check your exposure in the field by examining the histogram graph of your image on you camera's monitor. This graph works exactly the same way as the graph in the Levels feature in Photoshop Elements. It displays the spread of tones of your image across a grayscale from black to white. Underexposure will result in a graph that bunches towards the black end of the spectrum whereas overexposure moves the pixels towards the white point. A simple check of this graph when shooting can indicate whether you need to adjust your camera and re-shoot to compensate for an exposure problem.

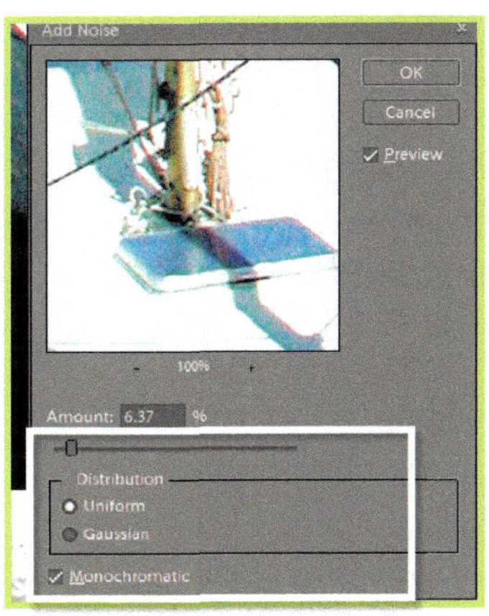

Step 1 >> *With the image at 100% magnification apply the Add Noise filter with Uniform/Monochrome settings.*

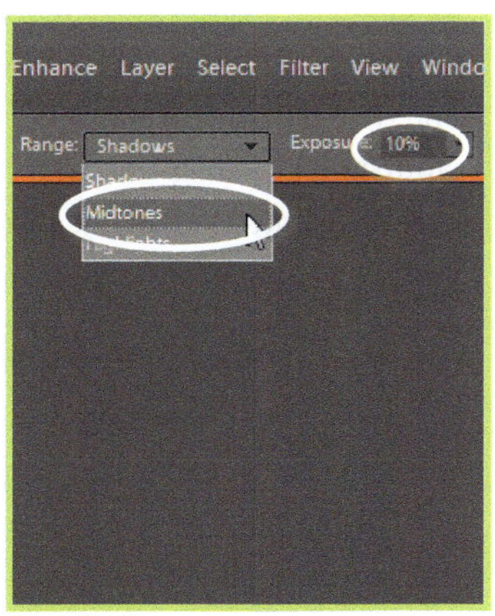

Step 2 >> *Select Burn-in tool, reduce exposure to 10% and choose mid-tone range. Set brush size and edge softness.*

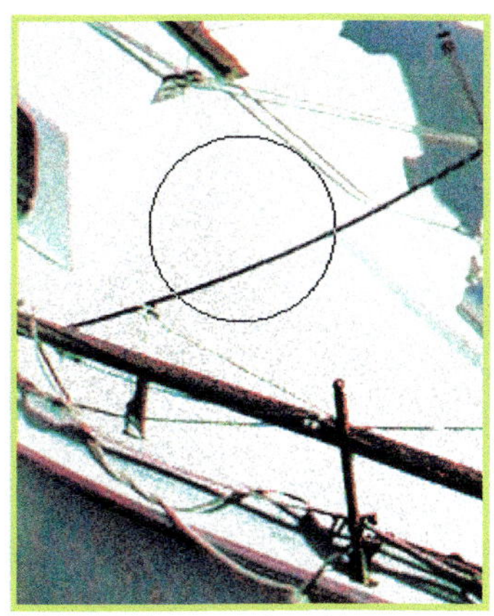

Step 3 >> *Burn-in the white area using several overlapping strokes to build up the effect. Change to Shadow range and repeat if necessary.*

6.25 Adding detail to highlights and shadows

Suitable for Elements – 7.0, 6.0, 5.0, 4.0, 3.0, 2.0, 1.0 | Difficulty level – Intermediate | Tools used – Dodging and Burning-in | Menus used – Filter

Sometimes, despite the utmost care on behalf of the photographer, digital images are captured with little or no shadow or highlight details. This scenario should ring true for any reader who has had the pleasure of photographing in very sunny countries. Along with the warmth, strong sun can provide a problem with contrast for the photographer. The deepest shadows and the brightest highlights are so far apart that even the best digital cameras have difficulty in recording all the tones. The result is a picture where either shadow or highlight detail (or in some extreme cases both) is not recorded. These parts of the picture are converted to pure black and white pixels in a process referred to as 'clipping'.

The same scenario can occur when using a scanner to convert slide or film originals into digital files. Incorrect scanner settings coupled with slides that are very dark or negatives that have been overdeveloped are the circumstances that most often produce 'clipped' files.

When presented with such pictures the experienced Elements user will attempt to restore detail in the highlight and shadow areas using the program's Dodging and Burning-in tools. But often such action only results in murky gray highlights and washed out shadow areas. The problem is that the program has no detail in these parts to actually lighten or darken. A solution to this scenario is to add a little (very little) texture to the image and then dodge and burn-in. The texture breaks up the pure white and pure black areas by filling these picture parts with random multi-tone (black, gray and white) pixels. This gives the tools some detail, albeit artificially created, to work on.

I use the Add Noise filter (Filter > Noise > Add Noise) to provide the texture and then select the Dodging tool set to midtones to work on the dark tones, or you could use the Burning-in tool also set to midtones to work on the highlights. A low exposure value of around 10% is coupled with repeated strokes over the offending area. To restrict the noise to just the highlight areas you could select these first using the Magic Wand and then apply the Noise filter.

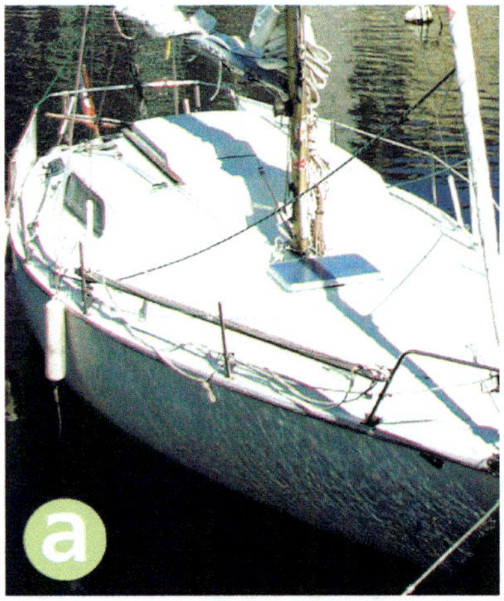

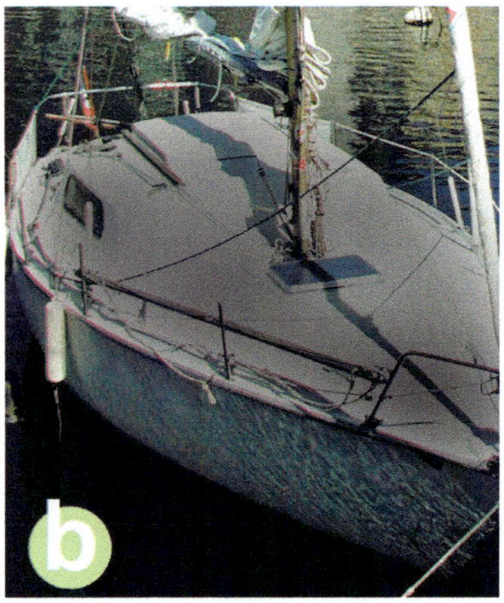

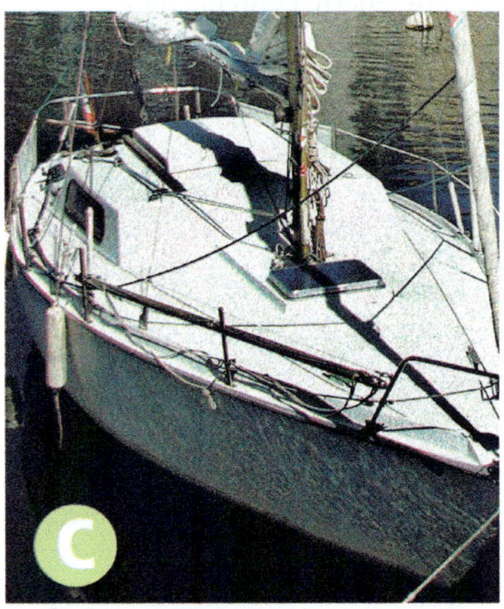

Texture burn-in >>
(a) Original image with blown highlights.
(b) Highlights burnt in using Burn-in tool.
(c) Highlights burnt in after adding a little texture.

This technique does have its down side. It doesn't recreate lost details and you will need to degrade your image by making it more noisy before you can dodge and burn. So it can't be considered a magic 'cure all' for problem pictures but it can help you get a little detail into that annoyingly white highlight or that equally frustrating blocked shadow area.

Tinted monochromes

One of the most enduring techniques utilized by photographers the world over is the practice of toning or changing the color of their black and white prints. The Sepia tone (brown) look has come to be linked with quality image production partly because it was a process that increased the longevity of black and white pictures and partly because only committed photographers would take their work through this extra processing step. Digital photographers have the tools at hand to not only 'tone' their black and white images but also to apply this same technique to their color ones.

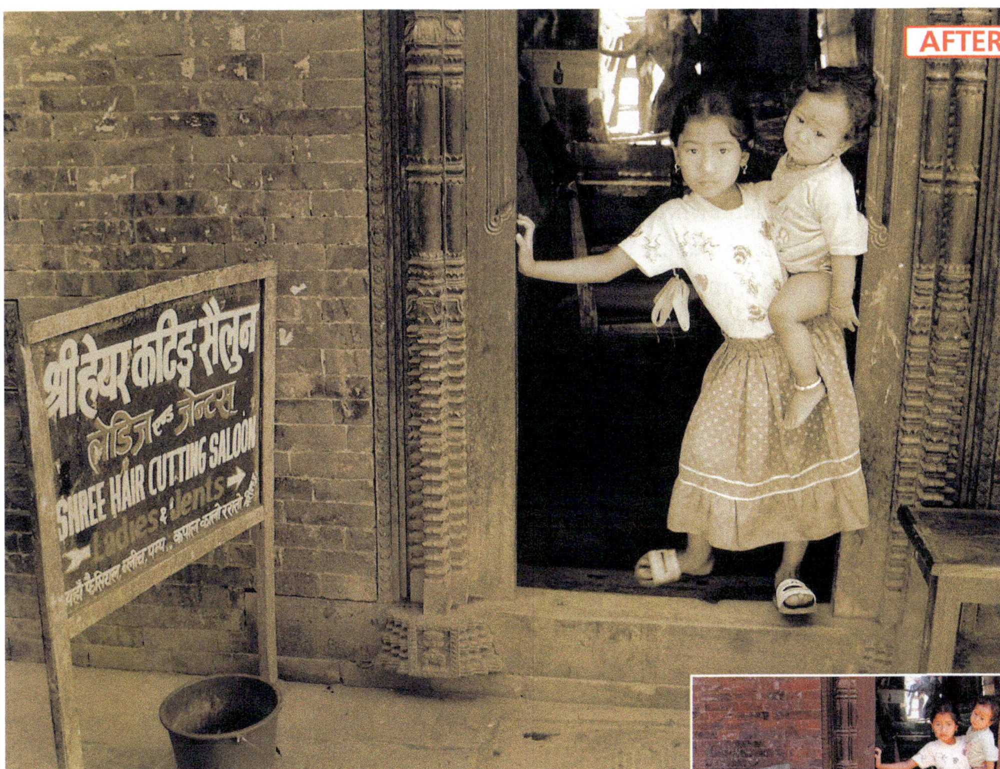

Toning >> *Use the Hue/Saturation control (Enhance > Adjust Color > Hue/ Saturation) to quickly and effectively add a tint to your color images.*

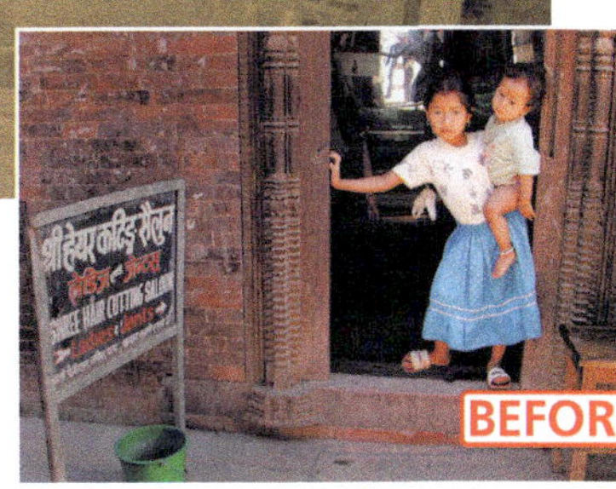

6.26 Using Hue and Saturation to tone your pictures

Suitable for Elements – 6, 5.0, 4.0, 3.0, 2.0, 1.0 | Difficulty level – Intermediate | Resources – Web image 621
Related techniques – 6.27 | Menus used – Enhance

The simplest and fastest way to add color is to use the Hue/Saturation control (Enhance > Adjust > Color > Hue/Saturation). This can be applied directly to the whole image or as an adjustment layer (Layer > New Adjustment Layer > Hue Saturation). To change the feature into a toning tool click the Colorize option in the bottom right of the box. The picture will switch to a single color monochrome (one color plus white and black). The Hue slider now controls the color of your tone.

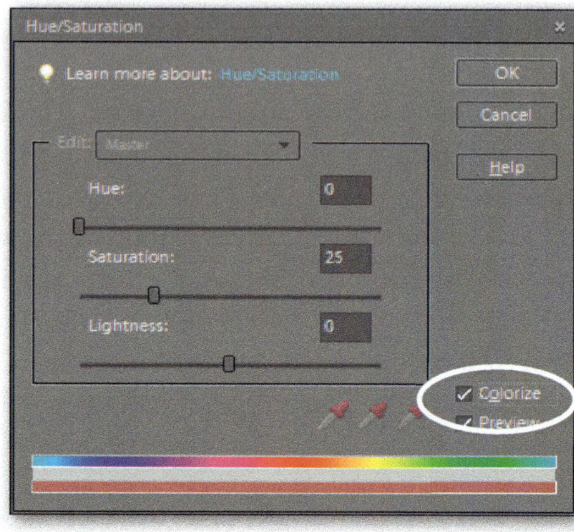

Hue/Saturation toning >> *Check the Colorize option to convert the dialog to Toning mode.*

The sepia look in the example is a value of 30 on the Hue slider. The Saturation slider varies the strength of the color. The Saturation value used in the example was 25. The Lightness slider adjusts the brightness of the image but changes of this nature should be left for the Levels feature.

The predictability of this digital toning system means that you can achieve the same tint in each image for a whole series of pictures. The recipes for regularly used tones, or favorite colors, can easily be noted down for later use or if toning using an adjustment layer then the layer can be dragged from one image to another. You can even create a Toning palette like the example on the next page, which provides a range of tint options as well as hue strengths.

IMAGE CHANGES – BEYOND THE BASICS

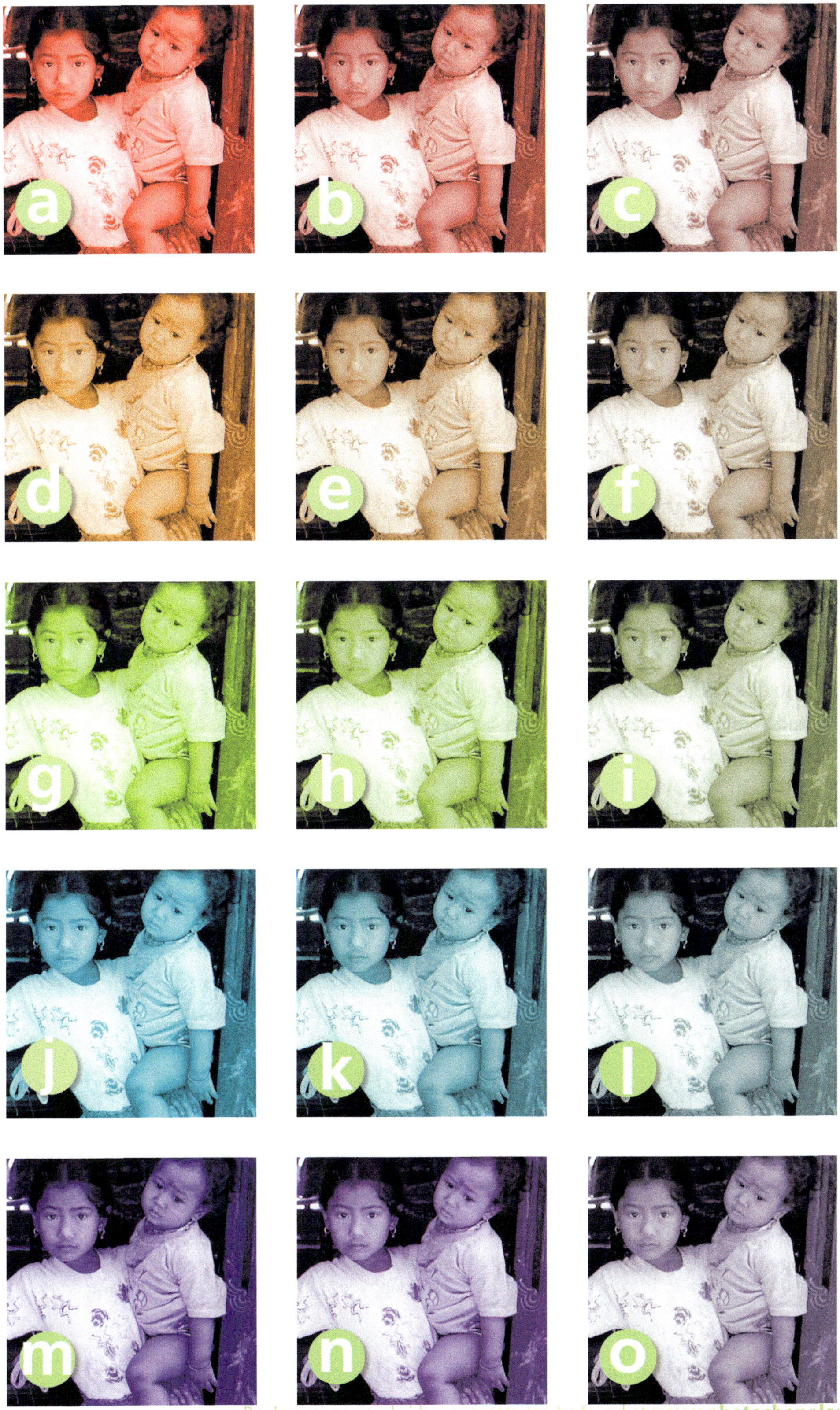

Toner recipes>>

Use the recipes for the tints below to help guide you when toning using the Hue/ Saturation control. Simply plug in the following numbers for the Hue, Saturation and Lightness sliders.

(a) 0, 75, 0
(b) 0, 50, 0
(c) 0, 25, 0

(d) 30, 75, 0
(e) 30, 50, 0
(f) 30, 25, 0

(g) 80, 75, 0
(h) 80, 50, 0
(i) 80, 25, 0

(j) 190, 75, 0
(k) 190, 50, 0
(l) 190, 25, 0

(m) 250, 75, 0
(n) 250, 50, 0
(o) 250, 25, 0

6.27 Tinting borrowed from Photoshop

Suitable for Elements – 7.0, 6.0, 5.0, 4.0, 3.0, 2.0, 1.0
Difficulty level – Intermediate | Resources – Web image 621 | Related Techniques – 6.26, 6.28
Tools used – Brush | Menus used – Layer

We have already seen how we can borrow adjustment layers from Photoshop documents to handle our conversions to grayscale, but there is also the opportunity to tint your photos with the same Black and White feature. Nestled at the bottom of the dialog is a tint control that contains the same Hue and Saturation sliders that feature in the Hue Saturation adjustment layer.

After setting the conversion sliders, ticking the Tint options changes the image from a grayscale to a toned monochrome. The Hue slider determines the color of the tint and the Saturation slider the strength of the tint color.

To gain access to this Photoshop feature simply drag a Black and White adjustment layer from the donor document ('Photoshop-Convert-to-gray-tinting.psd') which is available from the book's website, to an open Elements file. There are several different tinting adjustment layers to choose from.

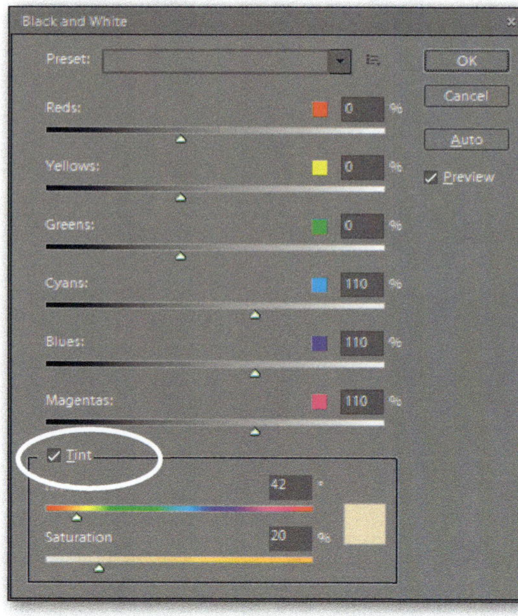

Photoshop's Black and White feature >> *After borrowing the Black and White adjustment layer, Elements users can open the feature's dialog by double-clicking the layer's thumbnail. At the base of the dialog is a Tint option that provides the opportunity for you to tone the images you convert to grayscale with the feature.*

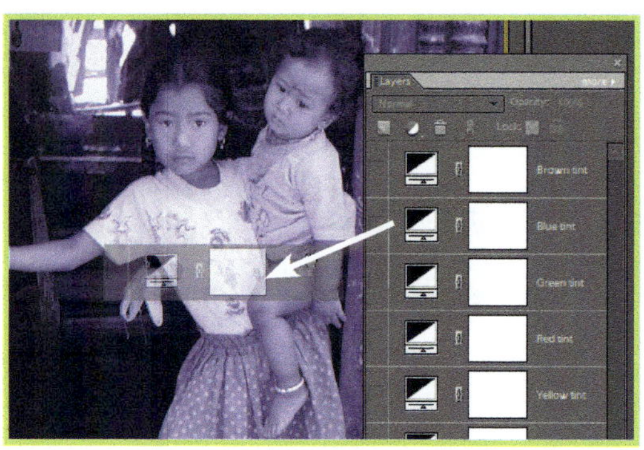

Step 1 >> *Start by opening both the Photoshop donor document (Photoshop-Convert-to-gray-tinting.psd) and the Elements file that you want to enhance. Click onto the Photoshop document and scroll through the list of adjustment layers available in the document. Select a layer and click-drag it onto the Elements document. The enhancement change will be immediately previewed in the workspace.*

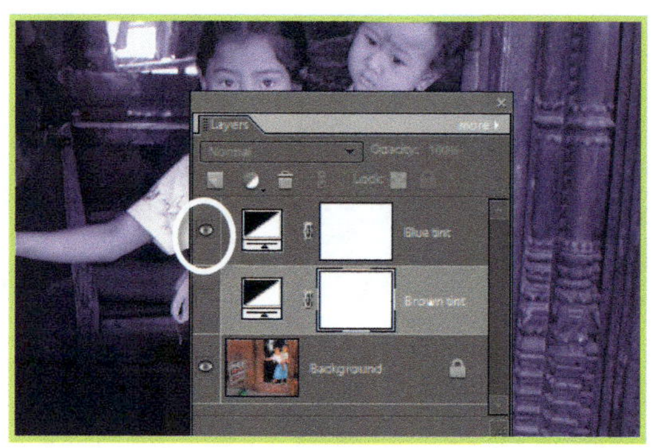

Step 2 >> *Multiple Photoshop layers can be dragged onto the Elements document and their effects hidden or applied by clicking the 'eye' icon on the left of the layer entry.*

Split toning

Once you have mastered the art of toning your pictures it is time to spread your 'tinting' wings a little. One of my favorite after-printing effects back in my darkroom days was split toning. This process involved passing a completed black and white print through two differently colored and separate toning baths. This resulted in the print containing a mixture of two different tints.

For example, when an image is split toned with sepia first and then blue toner the resultant picture has warm (brown) highlights and midtones, and cool (blue) shadows. Getting the right toning balance between the two solutions was difficult and then trying to repeat the process uniformly over a series of images was even harder. Thankfully I can replicate the results of split toning in my digital picture with a lot less trouble and a lot more predictability.

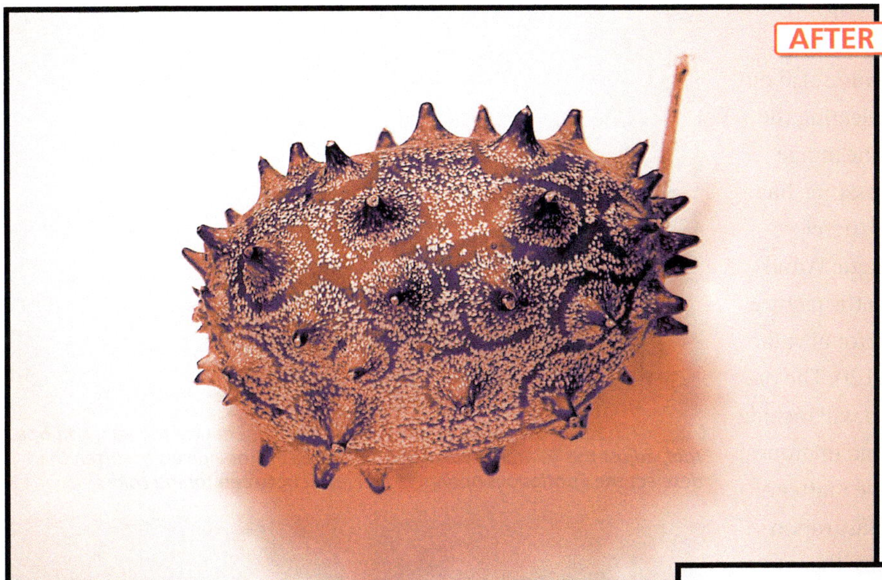

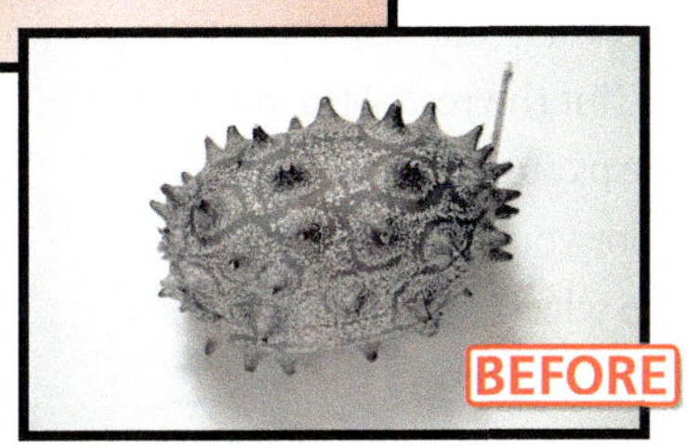

Split tone >> *With the aid of some tricky selection techniques it is possible to tint different tonal ranges of an image with alternative colors. This style of tinting is called split toning and traditionally is created by passing a photographic print through multiple toning baths.*

6.28 Select and tone

Suitable for Elements – 7.0, 6.0, 5.0, 4.0, 3.0, 2.0, 1.0 | Difficulty level – Intermediate| Resources – Web image 622 | Related techniques – 6.26 | Tools used – Magic Wand | Menus used – Select, Enhance

In order to tint a select range of tones such as midtones and shadows I must first select these areas of the image. The Magic Wand tool makes selections based on color and tone and so is perfectly suited for this type of selection. Normally we would use this tool with the Contiguous option turned on so that the selection comprises pixels that sit next to each other, but for this

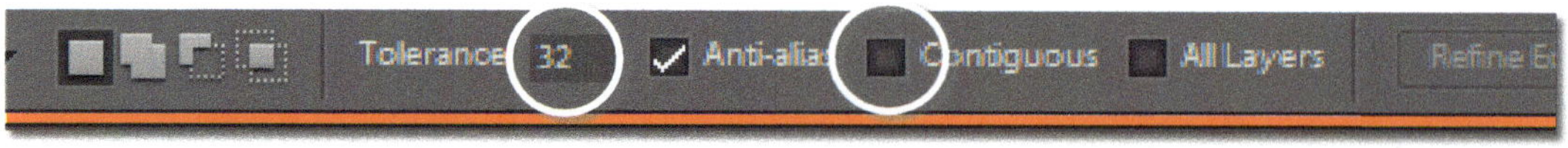

task turn this option off. The Tolerance value for the tool can range from 0 to 255. This setting determines how close to the selected pixel's tone the other pixels need to be before they too are included in the selection. The 0 setting is used to select other pixels in the image with exactly the same color and tone, whereas a setting of 20 will select other pixels that vary by as much as 20 tonal/color steps from the original.

Magic Wand settings >> When using the Magic Wand to select a range of tones in an image be sure to turn off the Contiguous setting, increase the Tolerance value and then select your reference pixel.

With this in mind we can easily employ this tool to select just the shadow and midtones of an image by setting the tolerance to a value of about 120 and then selecting the darkest part of the image (which we will assume has a value of 0 and therefore is black). The Magic Wand will then search the picture for pixels with a tonal value between 0 and 120. The resultant selection will include both shadows and midtones. It is then a simple matter of using the Hue/Saturation control to colorize these tones. To tint the rest of the pixels in the picture in an alternative color you must first invert the selection (Select>Inverse) and then repeat the Hue/Saturation toning procedure.

To soften the transition at the split of the two colors apply a feather of 1 or 2 pixels (Select > Feather) after your initial selection.

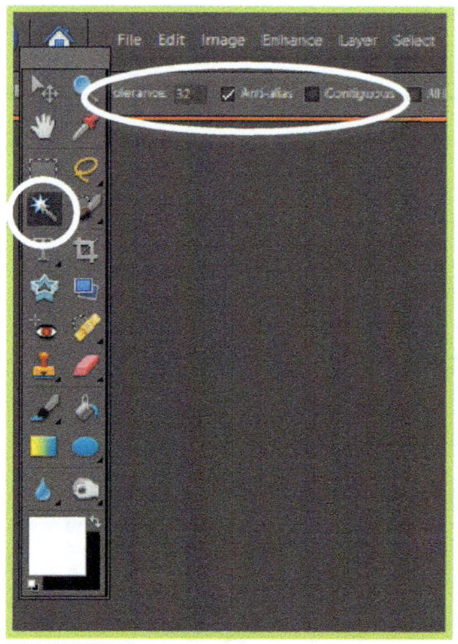

Step 1 >> Select the Magic Wand tool, adjust the Tolerance value and deselect the Contiguous option.

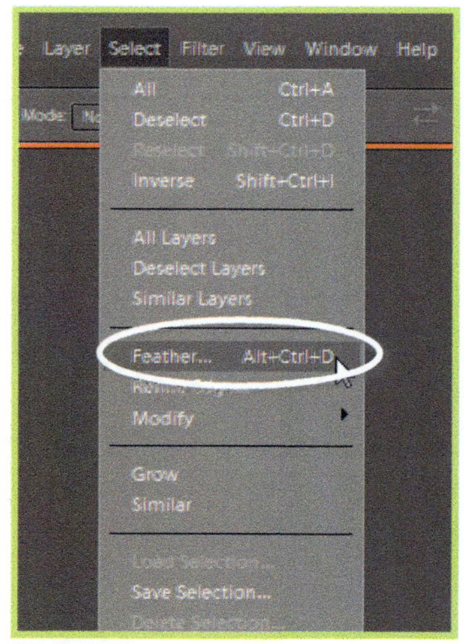

Step 2 >> Feather the selection by a value of 1 or 2 pixels to soften the split between toning colors.

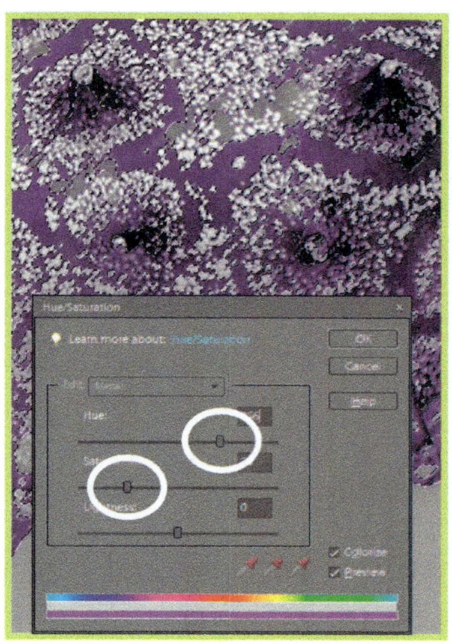

Step 3 >> Tone the selected areas using the Hue/Saturation control.

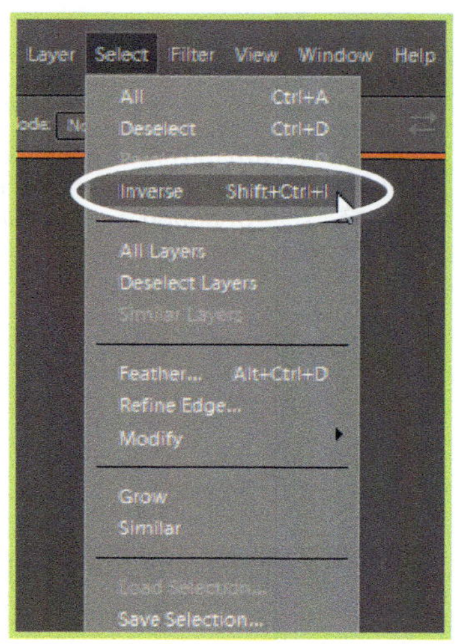

Step 4 >> Inverse the selection and tone the remaining pixels using an alternative color.

6.29 Two-layer erase

Suitable for Elements – 7.0, 6.0, 5.0, 4.0, 3.0, 2.0, 1.0 | Difficulty level – Intermediate | Resources – Web image 623
Related Techniques – 6.28 | Tools used – Eraser | Menus used – Layer, Enhance

You can extend the split toning idea beyond its darkroom origins by using this technique to create an image where one part of the picture is toned one color whilst the rest is colored in an alternative hue. To achieve this effect duplicate the image layer and then select and tone each layer in turn. Then use the mask from a No Settings adjustment layer to remove parts of the upper layer to reveal the color of the layer beneath.

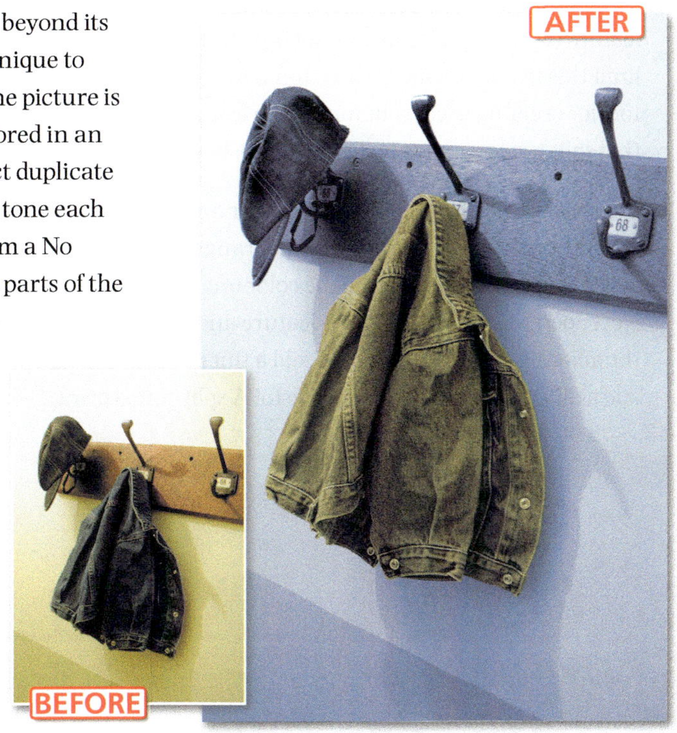

Erasing toned layers>> *By duplicating the image layer and then toning the two layers it is possible to use a No Settings adjustment layer mask to erase the upper layer to reveal the alternate colored layer below.*

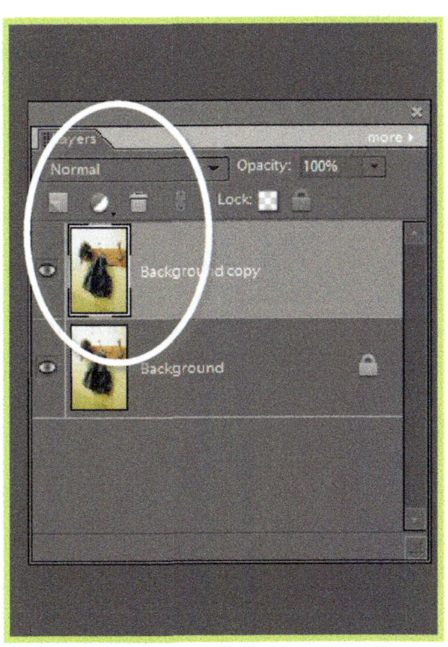

Step 1 >> *Duplicate the base image layer by dragging it to the New Layer button at the bottom of the Layers dialog.*

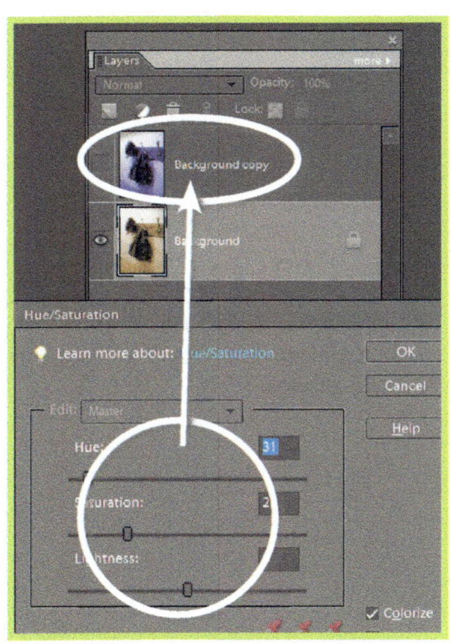

Step 2 >> *Select each layer in turn and tone using the Hue/Saturation control set to Colorize. Select the lower layer and add a new Levels Adjustment Layer with no settings applied between the layers.*

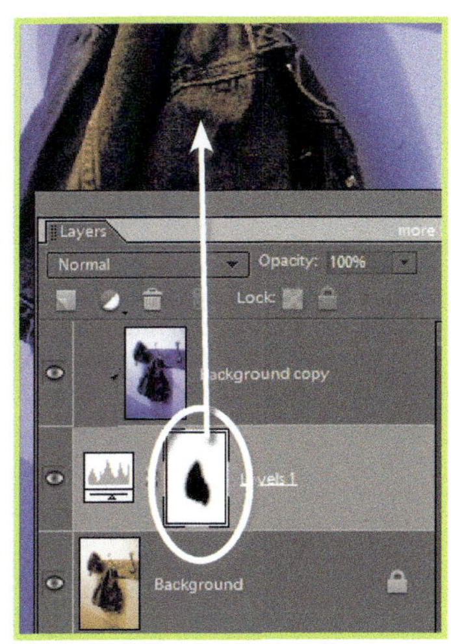

Step 3 >> *Select the uppermost layer and select Layer > Group with Previous. Now select the layer mask and a black soft brush and paint the details from the layer beneath.*

6.30 Color Variations based split toning

Suitable for Elements – 7.0, 6.0, 5.0, 4.0, 3.0, 2.0, 1.0 | Difficulty level – Intermediate | Resources – Web image 624 | Related Techniques – 6.28, 6.29 | Tools used – Brush | Menus used – Layer

The Color Balance feature in Photoshop provides a unique way of creating split tones. As the feature contains the ability to not only tint a grayscale image (that is in RGB Color mode), but also limit this tinting to one of three tonal ranges, shadows, midtones or highlights, it is the perfect tool for creating great split tones. The feature is also available as an Adjustment Layer meaning that split tones can be applied in Photoshop non-destructively.

Thankfully the Enhance > Adjust Color > Color Variations feature offers the same tinting abilities that are customized for specific tonal ranges. To start the toning process use the Convert to Black and White feature to change the color image to grayscale but still retain the RGB Color mode. Next open the Color Variations feature and target the Shadows, click onto one of the colored thumbnails a couple of times to add a tint to the shadows. Next choose the highlight setting and add a different color here. Hey presto! A split-toned print.

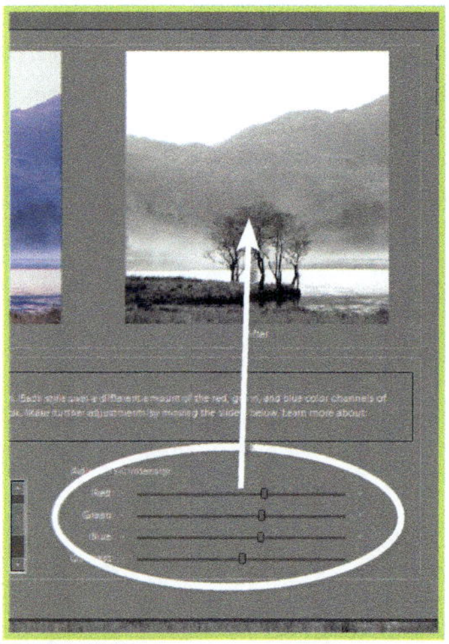

Step 1 >> *Start by converting the color original to gray using the Convert to Black and White feature. This removes the color but maintains the RGB Color mode of the file allowing for the split toning later.*

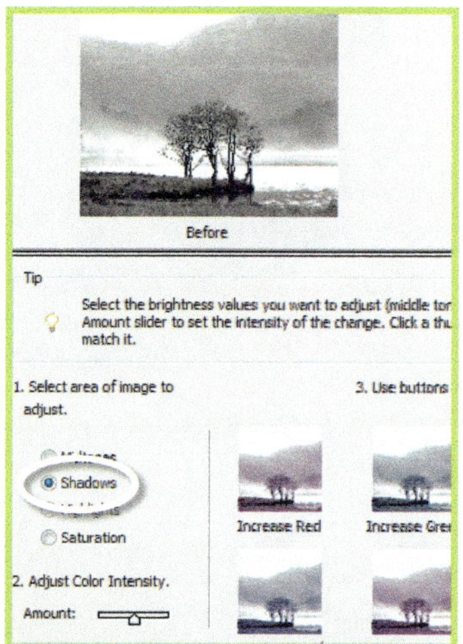

Step 2 >> *Next open the Color Variations feature and target the Shadow areas. Click onto one of the color thumbnails a couple of times to tint the shadows.*

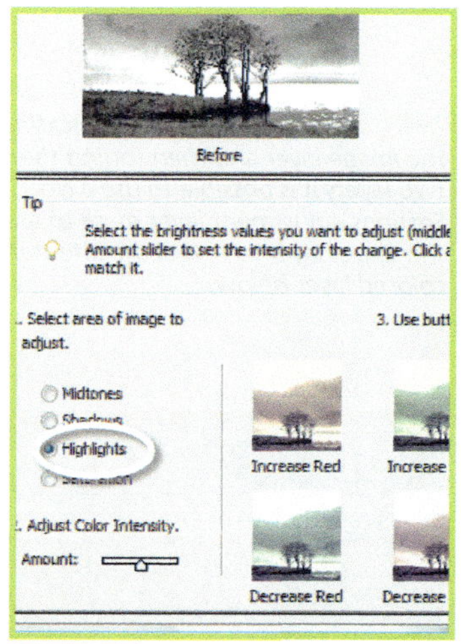

Step 3 >> *While the Color Variations dialog is still open, switch to the Highlight tonal range and tint these values a different color.*

6.31 Photoshop's Color Balance split toning in Elements

Suitable for Elements – 7.0, 6.0, 5.0, 4.0, 3.0, 2.0, 1.0 | Difficulty level – Intermediate | Resources – Web image 625 | Related Techniques – 6.16, 6.17 | Tools used – Brush | Menus used – Layer

For elements users who want to employ a non-destructive workflow, the Color Balance adjustment layer from Photoshop can be dragged and dropped from a Photoshop document onto an Elements file. To keep the whole technique non-destructive a Photoshop Black and White adjustment layer should be used first to convert the image to grayscale. To help with this process I have created a

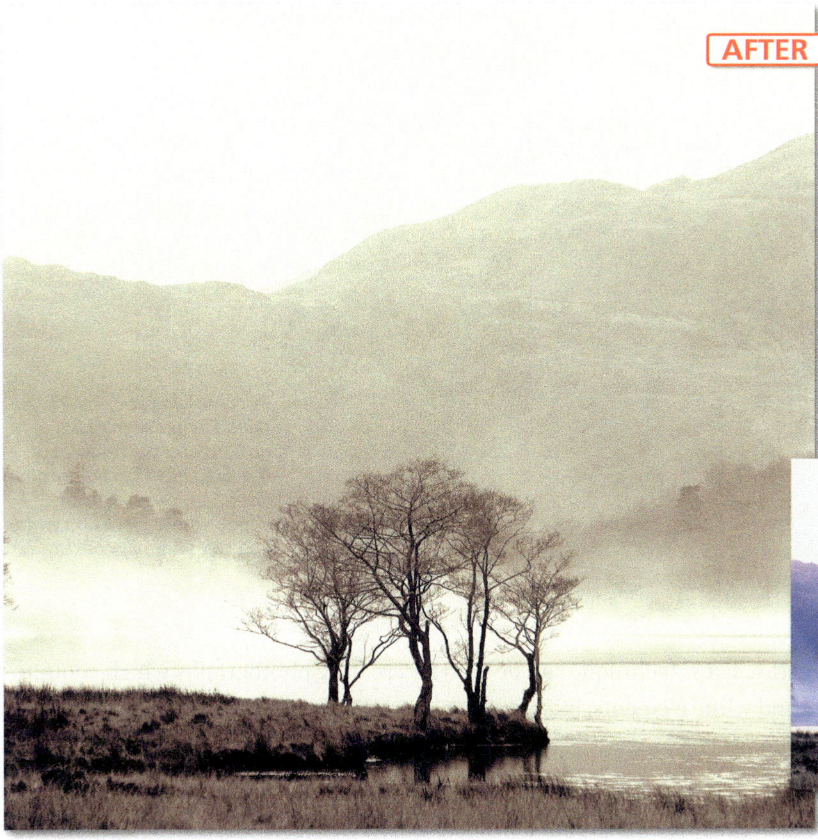

Split toning >> *Borrowing Color Balance and Black and White adjustment layers from Photoshop documents provides a way for Elements users to split tone non-destructively.*

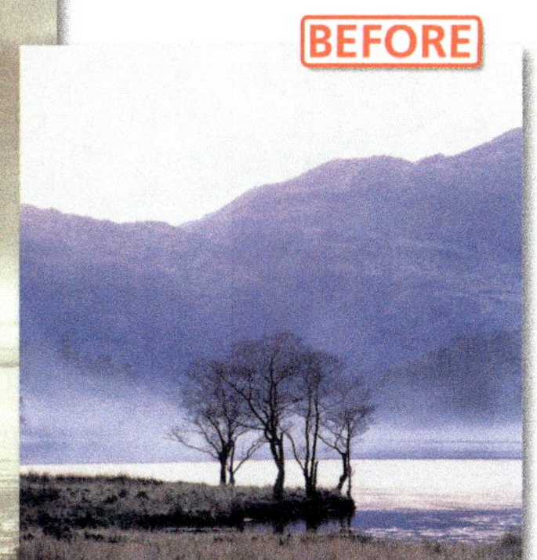

Photoshop file containing a convert to gray layer and a range of split-tone options. To use, download the Photoshop-Split-Tones.psd file from the book's website and open the document into Elements. Drag the Convert-to-Gray layer to the Elements file first and then add a split tone layer. Adjust the opacity of the split tone layer to control the strength of the split-tone colors.

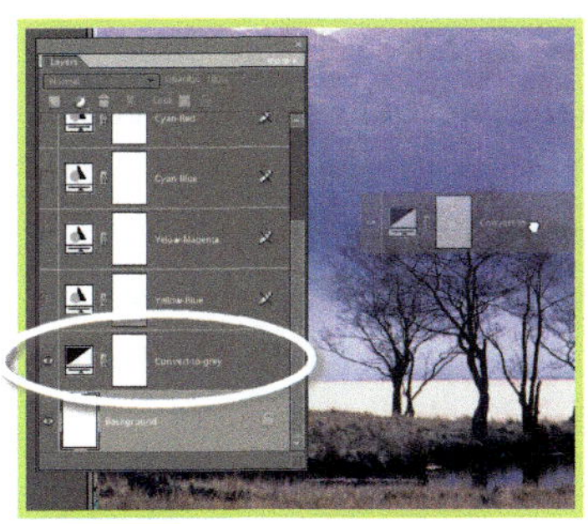

Step 1 >> *Start by opening the Photoshop-Split-tone.psd file into the Elements editing workspace. Drag the Convert-to-Gray layer from the Photoshop document to an open Elements file.*

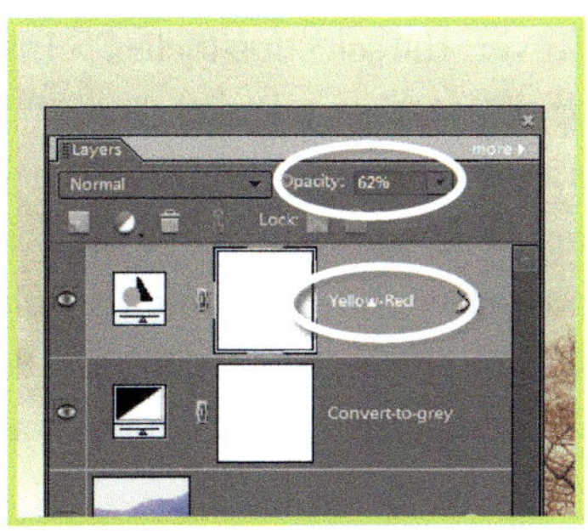

Step 2 >> *Now drag a split tone layer to the Elements document. If need be adjust the opacity of the layer to reduce the strength of the tinting colors.*

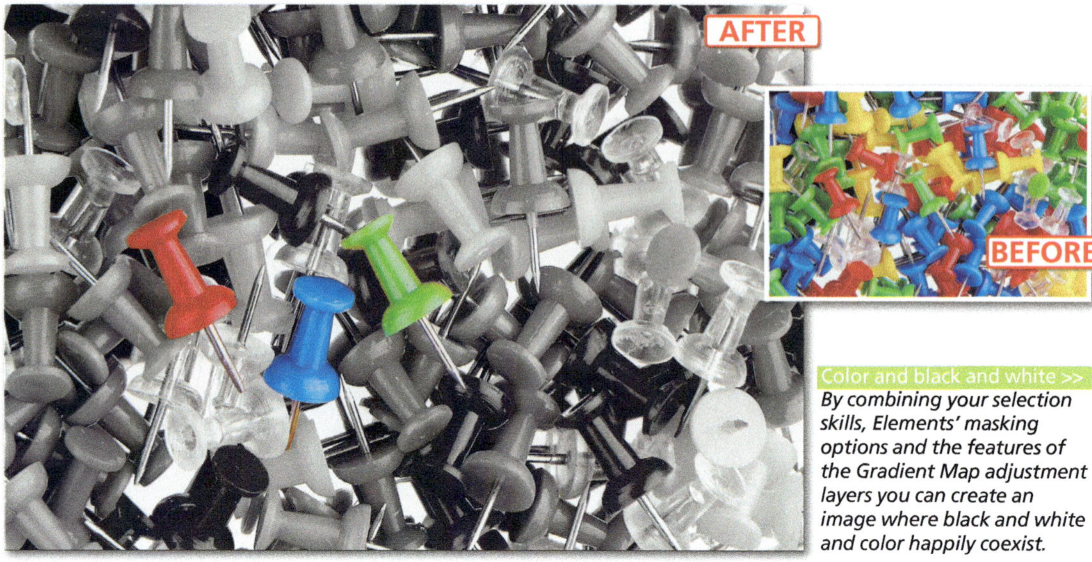

Color and black and white >> *By combining your selection skills, Elements' masking options and the features of the Gradient Map adjustment layers you can create an image where black and white and color happily coexist.*

Black and white and color

The same 'two-layer erase back' technique can be used for creating photographs which contain both color and black and white elements, but I prefer to use a different method based around Elements' masking options.

6.32 Layer mask and gradient map

Suitable for Elements – 7.0, 6.0, 5.0, 4.0, 3.0, 2.0, 1.0 | Difficulty level – Intermediate | Resources – Web image 626 | Related Techniques – 6.18 | Tools used – Selection tools | Menus used – Select, Layer

With the color image open make a selection of the objects that will not be converted to black and white. In the example I used a combination of the Magnetic Lasso and the standard Lasso tools to select the three map pins, but you could also use the Magic Selection Brush to achieve the same results. Next, feather the selection (Select > Feather) slightly with a setting of 1 pixel to soften the edge of the effect. Invert the selection (Select > Inverse) so that the background (everything other than the map pins) is now selected. Then, with the selection still active, create a new Gradient Map adjustment layer (Layer > New Adjustment Layer > Gradient Map). When the Gradient Map dialog appears select the map with a smooth transition from black to white and click OK. Elements uses your selection to mask out the adjustment layer effects and restrict them from being applied to the originally selected map pins. You can create a multitude of other effects using the same process but different gradient maps or adjustment layers.

More effects >> *You can create other effects using the same masking technique with the Threshold (a), Posterize (b) and Invert (c) Adjustment Layers options.*

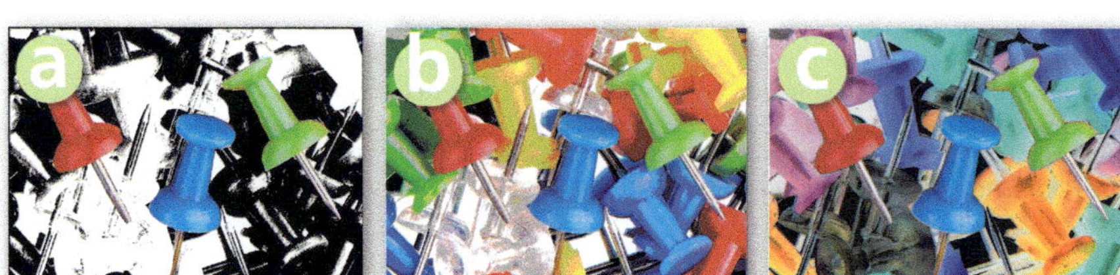

Pro's Tip: Make sure that you save your selections (Select > Save Selection) as you make them. This way you can always reload them later if you need to.

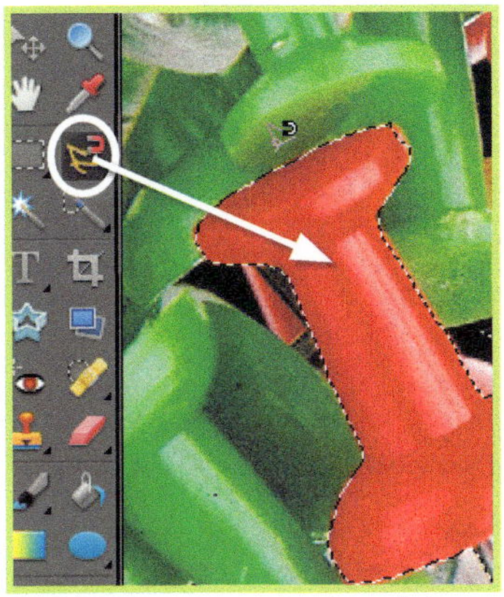

Step 1 >> Make a selection of the parts of the image that you want to remain in color.

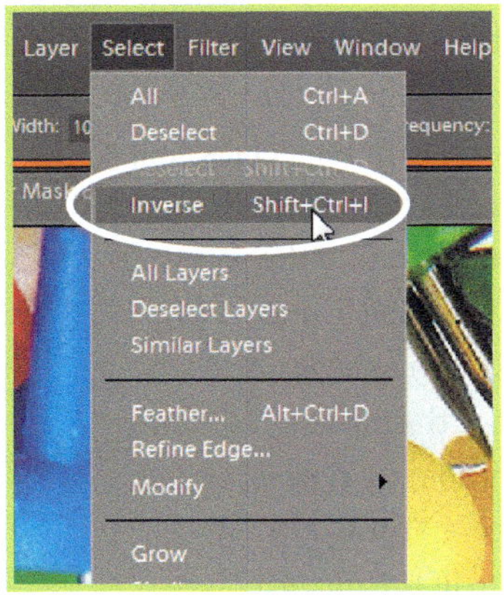

Step 2 >> Feather the selection by 1 pixel and then Inverse the selection.

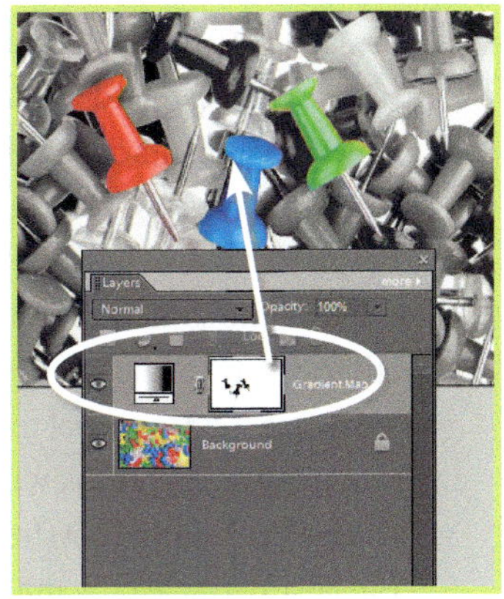

Step 3 >> With the selection still active create a new Gradient Map adjustment layer.

Border techniques

Creating a great border is one of those finishing touches that can really make your images stand apart from the crowd. Using Photoshop Elements you can easily create and apply a variety of different border styles to your photographs.

6.33 Simple borders

Suitable for Elements – 7.0, 6.0, 5.0, 4.0, 3.0, 2.0, 1.0 | Difficulty level – Intermediate | Resources – Web image 627 | Related Techniques – 6.34 | Tools used – Marquee | Menus used – Select, Window, Edit

A basic line border can be created by selecting the whole image (Select > Select All) and then stroking (Edit > Stroke) the selection on the inside with the foreground color. For fancier styles Elements provides a range of Frame and Edge treatments in its Artwork palette (Window > Effects). Some frames require you to make a selection first; others can be applied directly to the picture with no preliminary actions.

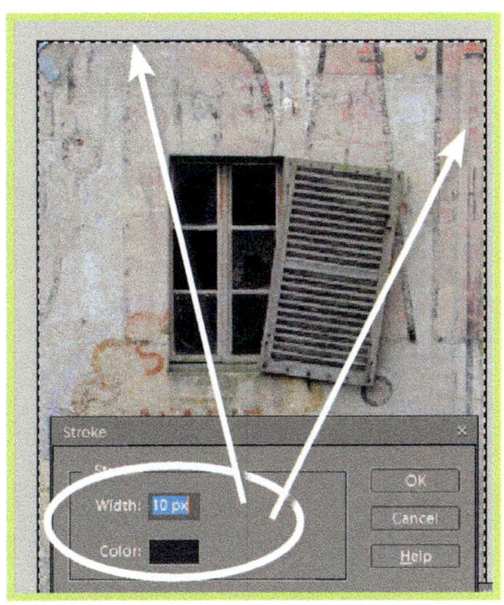

Stroked frame >> Use the Eyedropper tool to select a suitable border color from the image. Select all the picture (Select > Select All). Stroke the selection (Edit > Stroke Selection) on the inside with the foreground color and a width of 10 pixels.

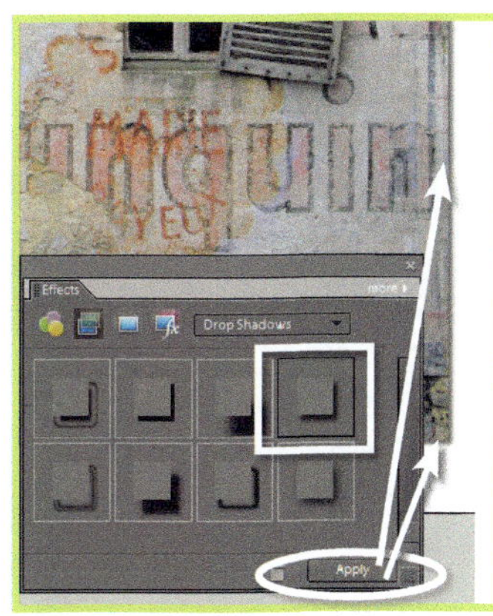

Layer Effects >> Display the Effects palette (Window > Effects) and then select the Special Effects > Photo Effects section. Choose frames from the drop-down list and then Drop Shadow from the thumb-nails. Press the Apply button.

6.34 Sophisticated edges using grayscale masks

Suitable for Elements – 7.0, 6.0, 5.0, 4.0, 3.0, 2.0, 1.0 | Difficulty level – Intermediate | Resources – Web image 628 | Related techniques – 6.33 | Tools used – Paint Brush | Menus used – layer

You can create truly imaginative edges by using a grayscale mask to hide the edges of the picture. Start by using the Elements drawing tools to paint a black shape with rough edges on a white background. This is our grayscale mask. Ideally the dimensions of the painting should be the same as the picture to be framed. With both the picture and the mask open as separate documents, use the Move tool to drag the mask image on top of the picture. The mask will become a new layer. Use the Free Transform tool (Image > Transform > Free Transform) to scale the mask to fit the image precisely.

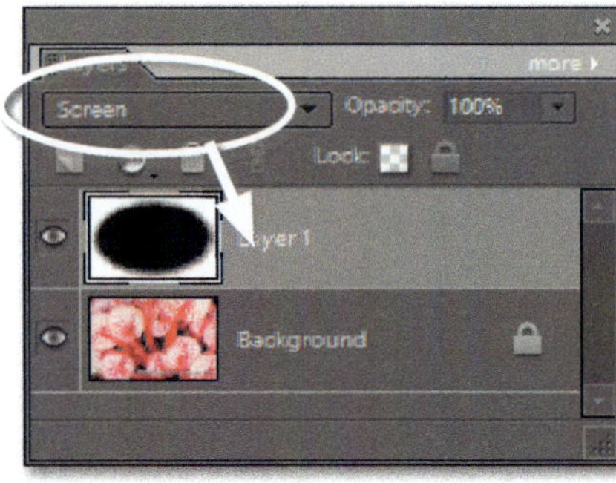

Grayscale mask borders >> *You can use a grayscale mask to produce a creative border effect by stacking the mask on top and then changing the layer mode to Screen.*

With the mask layer still active change the layer mode to Screen. This will cause the image from beneath to show through the black parts of the mask whilst the white areas of the mask hide the rest of the picture below.

This technique can also be used to create an image-filled border by inverting the mask before changing modes. This way the center of the picture is hidden by the white portion of the mask and the edges are filled with the image from below.

Pro's Tip

Search the web for pre-made grayscale masks that can be downloaded and used directly in Elements.

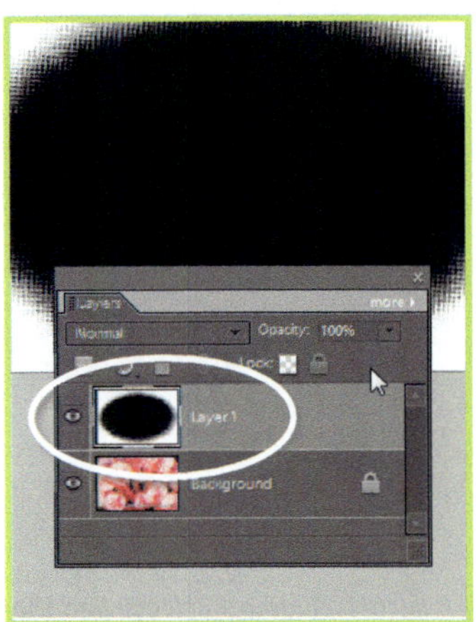

Step 1 >> *Create or download a grayscale mask. Open image and mask. Drag mask onto image as a new layer.*

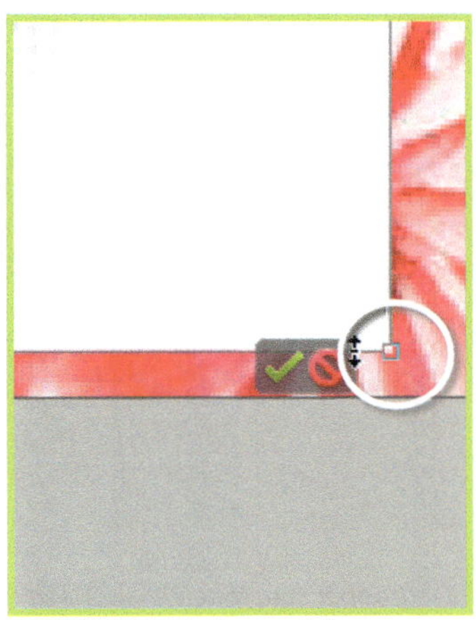

Step 2 >> *With the mask layer selected use the Transformation tool (Image>Transform>Free Transform) to scale the mask to fit the image.*

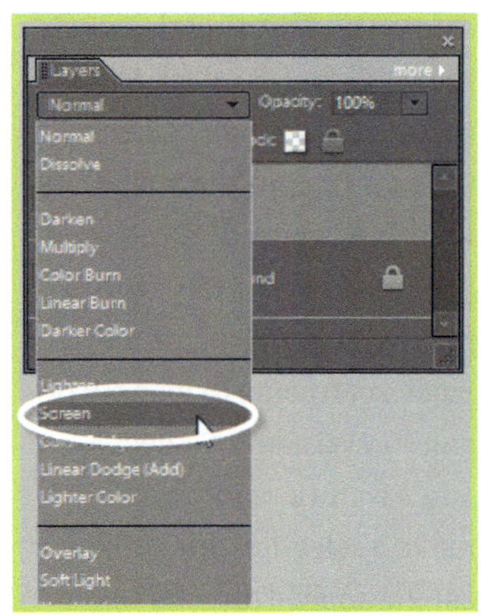

Step 3 >> *Switch the mask layer's mode to Screen to create the edge effect. To invert the effect select Image > Adjustments > Invert before changing the mode.*

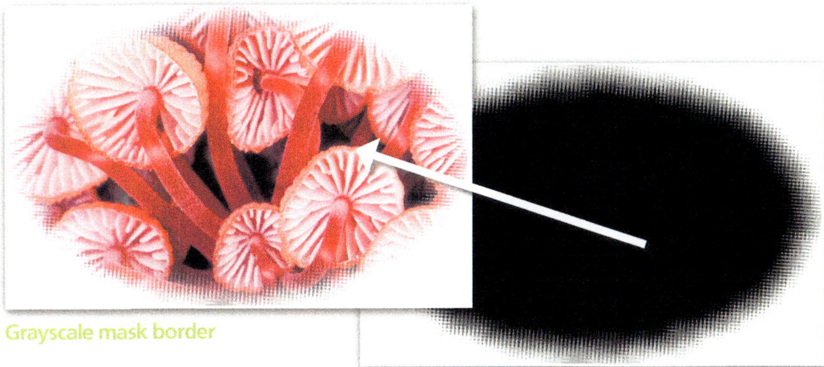

Grayscale mask border

Picture edges >> *More sophisticated masks of all manner of shapes, sizes and styles can be created using grayscale masks. By inverting the mask (Image > Adjustment > Invert) you can also create an edge filled with a picture rather than a picture surrounded by an edge.*

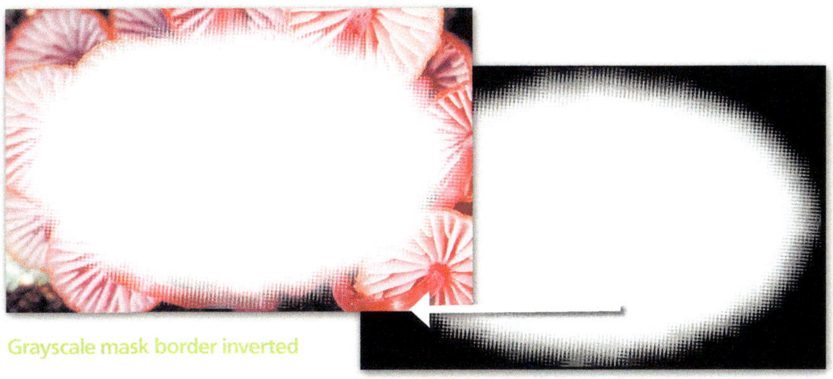

Grayscale mask border inverted

6.35 Creating frames with Frame layers

Suitable for Elements – 7.0, 6.0, 5.0 | Difficulty level – Intermediate Resources – Web image 629 | Related techniques – 6.34 Tools used – Paint Brush Menus used – layer

Frame layers are brand new to Elements and have been introduced as part of the new system of creating multi-page themed documents (Photo or .PSE documents). Here, we will just take a quick look at the framing abilities of the new technology, but for a fuller description of how to create and edit PSE files go to Chapter 12.

Frame layers combine both the picture and the frame in a single layer. This a really cool aspect of this technology as it means that not only can the frame and layer combination be sized and rotated as a single composition, but the picture can also be manipulated independent of the frame. Photoshop Elements ships with a huge collection of frames that can be quickly and easily added to your pictures.

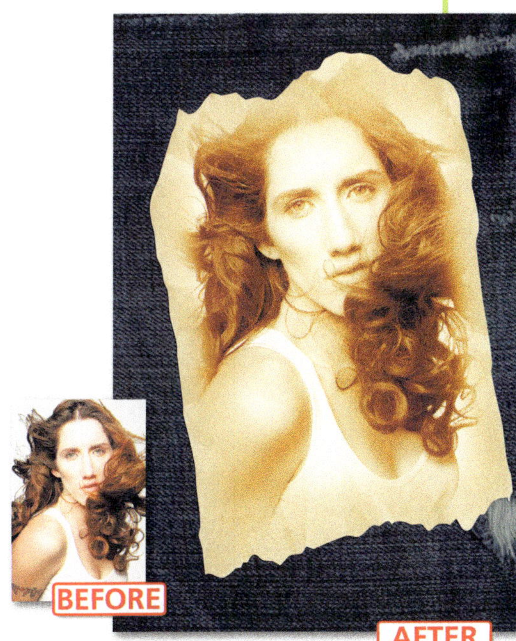

Frame layers >> *Frame layers are a new way to dynamically add fancy borders to your photos.*

The various designs are collated in the Content palette (under the Frames option in the By Type section of the palette). To add a frame to a picture that is already open in the Full Edit workspace display the palette first (Window > Content) and then click on the left-side drop-down menu and select By Type. Next choose the Frames option from the right-hand drop-down menu. After locating the frame type you want to add to your photo click on its thumbnail and then press the Apply button at the bottom of the palette.

Elements automatically creates a new Frame layer, adds your photo to it and then provides a small adjustment palette at the top of the framed image containing controls for sizing, rotating and replacing your photo. Alternatively, extra positioning and sizing options are available from the right-click menu. Click on the photo and then click-drag the corner handles to resize the frame and image together or the rotate handle to pivot the combination. Double-click the Move tool on the photo to select just the picture and use the handles to alter the photo independently of the frame.

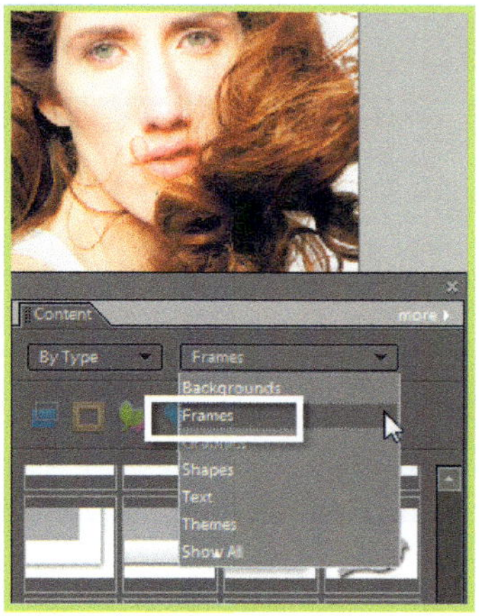

Step 1 >> *With a photo open in the editing space display the Frames section of the Content palette. Select the Frame Style thumbnail and click the Apply button.*

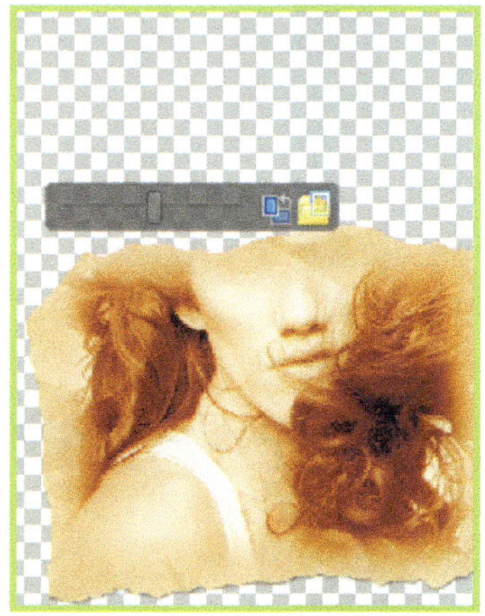

Step 2 >> *Elements automatically creates a new Frame layer and places your photo in the frame design. Adjust the size and orientation of the picture using the pop-up adjustment palette.*

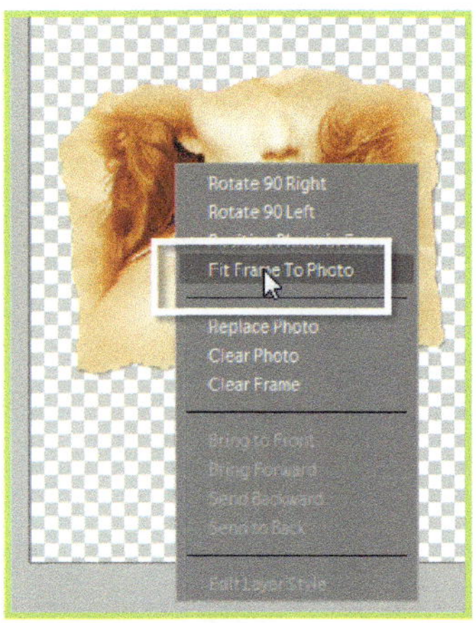

Step 3 >> *More picture controls are available from the right-click menu. In most cases the Fit Frame To Photo option should be selected first and then any fine-tuning added later.*

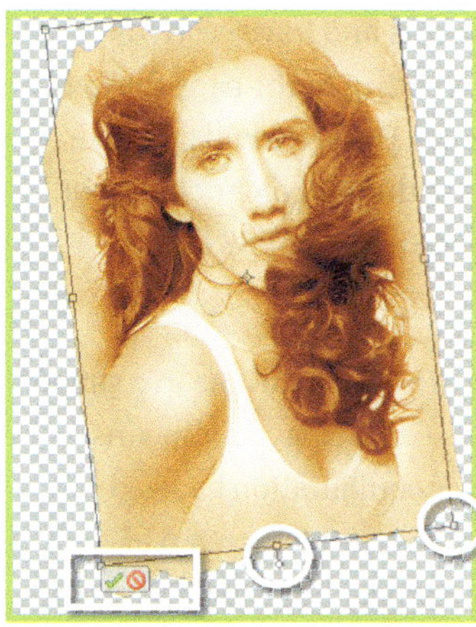

Step 4 >> *Single-click the photo to select both frame and photo. Double-click to pick the photo only. Use the corner and rotate handles to fine-tune the size of picture and frame.*

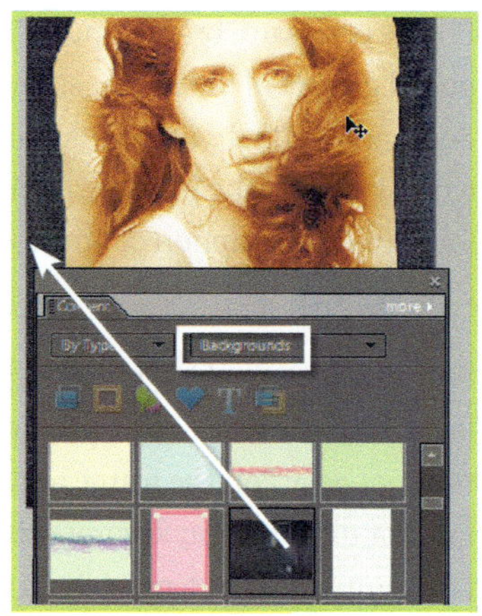

Step 5 >> *To finish add a background to the composition by selecting the Background option from the right-hand menu. Next Choose the background and then click Apply.*

Adding texture

Texture is a traditional photographic visual element that is often overlooked when working digitally. All but the highest quality professional films have visible grain when they are printed. This is especially true when the print size goes beyond the standard 6 x 4 inches. In fact we are so familiar with the idea that grain is part of the photographic process that putting a little texture into an otherwise grainless digital picture can lend a traditional 'look and feel' to the image.

Many photographers add a little texture to their pictures as part of their regular image editing process. Some go beyond this and produce photographs with huge clumps of grain that resemble the results often seen with prints made from old style high ISO films.

6.36 Add Noise filter

Suitable for Elements – 7.0, 6.0, 5.0, 4.0, 3.0, 2.0, 1.0 | Difficulty level – Intermediate | Resources – Web image 6.30 | Related techniques – 6.37, 6.38 | Menus used – Filter

The simplest method for adding texture to your picture is to use the Add Noise filter (Filter > Noise > Add Noise). The feature is provided with a preview dialog which allows you to alter the 'Amount' of noise that is added to the photograph, the style of noise – Gaussian or Uniform – and whether the noise is random colored pixels or just monochrome. As with most filters it is important to use this feature carefully as once the filter is applied and the file saved you will not be able to undo its effects. For this reason, it pays to make a duplicate file of your picture which you can texturize without risk of destroying the original image.

Pro's Tip

Be sure to preview the image at least 100% when adding noise to ensure that the effect is not too strong. If in doubt, make a test print of sections of the picture with different Add Noise settings to preview the hard copy results.

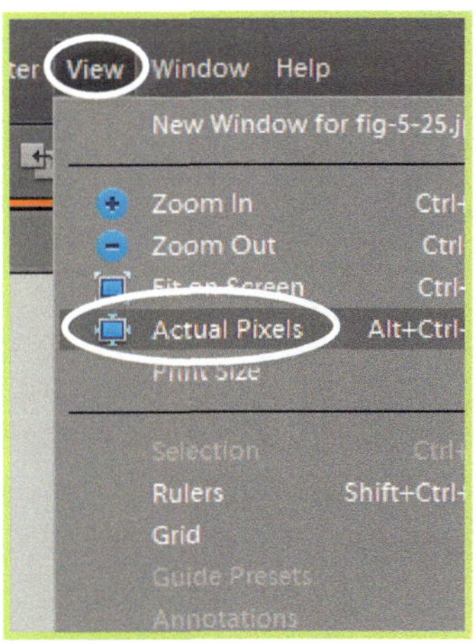

Step 1 >> *Zoom in so that the picture is at least at 100% view or the Actual Pixels entry.*

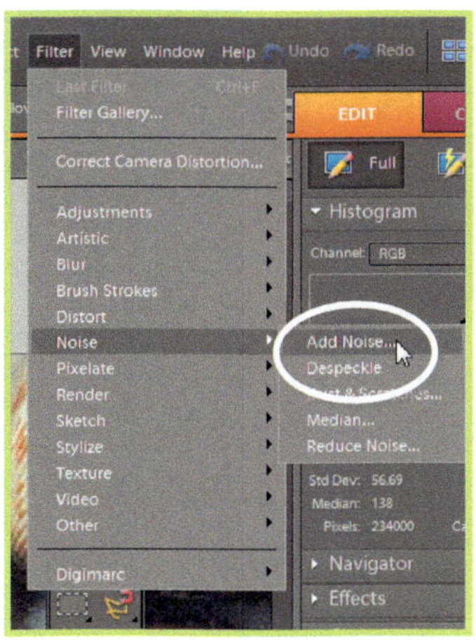

Step 2 >> *Select the Add Noise filter from the Filter menu.*

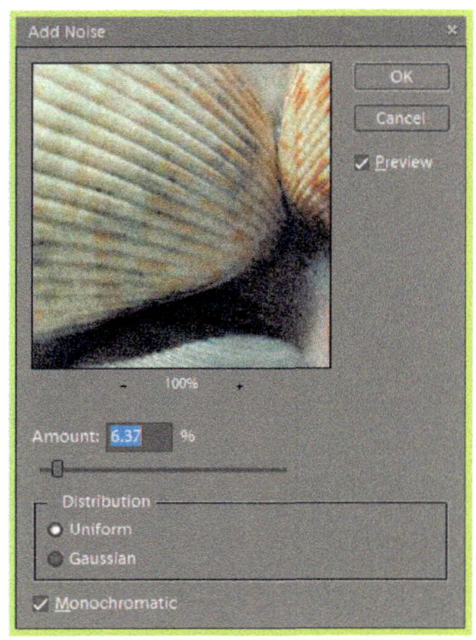

Step 3 >> *Adjust the Amount slider to change the strength of the effect and pick the noise type and color.*

6.37 Grain filter

Suitable for Elements – 7.0, 6.0,5.0, 4.0, 3.0, 2.0, 1.0
Difficulty level – Intermediate | Resources – Web image 630 | Related techniques – 6.36, 6.38
Menus used – Filter

As an alternative that provides a few more options than the technique above you can use the Grain filter (Filter > Texture > Grain) to add your choice of 10 different grain textures to your picture. Ranging from 'regular' through 'horizontal' to 'speckle' this filter produces a spectacular variety of texture effects. The feature's dialog also provides an Intensity slider to govern the strength of the texture and a Contrast control.

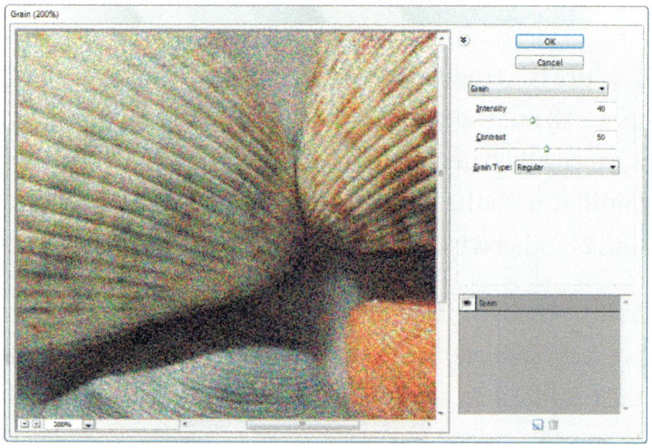

Adding grain >> *The Grain dialog provides a preview thumbnail, Intensity and Contrast sliders and a selection of 10 different grain types.*

The trick to creating good texture using this feature is the balancng of Intensity and Contrast settings. If the texture is too strong the shape and color of the original subject matter can be lost. If the contrast is too high then shadow and highlight details can be lost.

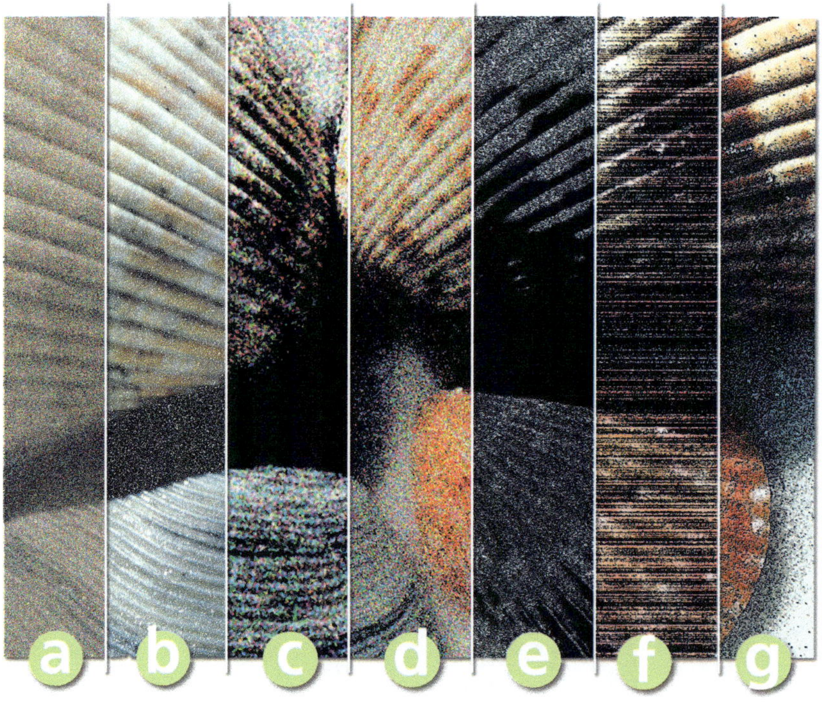

Texture options for the Grain filter >> *The Grain filter provides a range of unique texture options that can be applied to your picture. (a) Regular. (b) Sprinkles. (c) Clumped. (d) Enlarged. (e) Stippled. (f) Horizontal. (g) Speckle.*

6.38 Non-destructive textures

Suitable for Elements – 7.0, 6.0, 5.0, 4.0, 3.0, 2.0, 1.0 | Difficulty level – Intermediate | Resources – Web image 631 | Related techniques – 6.36, 6.37 | Menus used – Layer, Filter

As we have already seen adjustment layers are a great way to manipulate your pictures without actually altering the original image. This approach to image editing is referred to as 'non-destructive' as the integrity of the starting picture is always maintained. Mistakes or radical manipulations can always be reversed by switching off the adjustment layer leaving the untouched original below. Although there are no such things as Filter adjustment layers it would be handy to be able to use this same approach when making whole non-reversible image changes such as adding texture or noise to your pictures.

Such a technique was used in the following example. Despite the appearance of texture throughout the whole photograph the starting picture is still preserved at the bottom of the layer stack. To get the same results with your own pictures start by making a new layer (Layer > New > Layer) above the image. Next, fill this layer with 50% gray (Edit > Fill Layer) and Add Noise (Filter > Noise > Add Noise) to the layer. Change the mode of the gray textured layer to either Soft Light, Hard Light, Linear Light or Vivid Light. Notice how the texture is now applied to the picture. To soften the effect reduce the opacity of the texture layer.

Using this technique you not only preserve the integrity of the original picture but you can also alter the strength of the effect at any time. In addition, it is also a great way to apply the same amount and style of grain to several layers in a stack without having to individually select and filter each layer.

Pro's Tip

To apply the same texture settings to a series of images of the same size simply drag and drop the gray texture layer into each of the open documents.

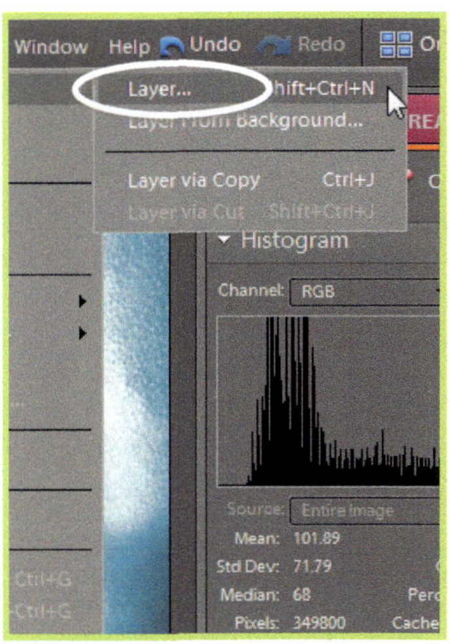

Step 1 >> *Create a new layer above the image layer or background.*

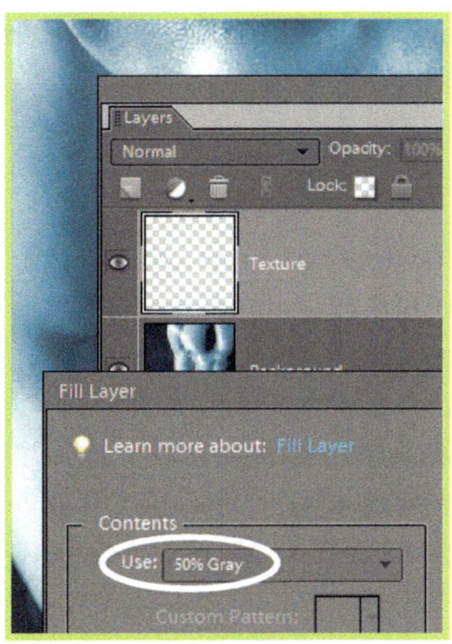

Step 2 >> *Fill the layer with 50% gray using the Edit > Fill layer command.*

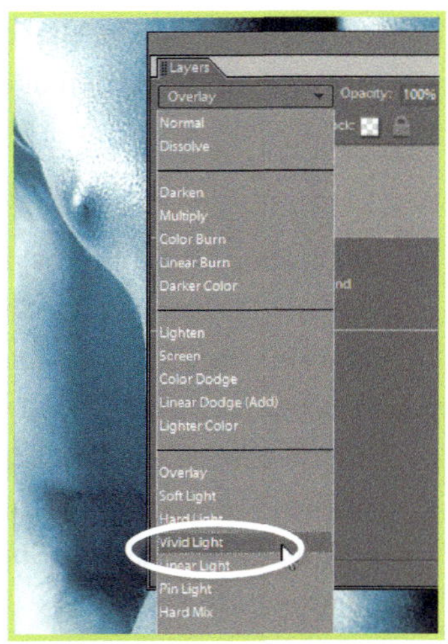

Step 3 >> *Texture the layer with Add Noise and switch the layer mode to Vivid Light.*

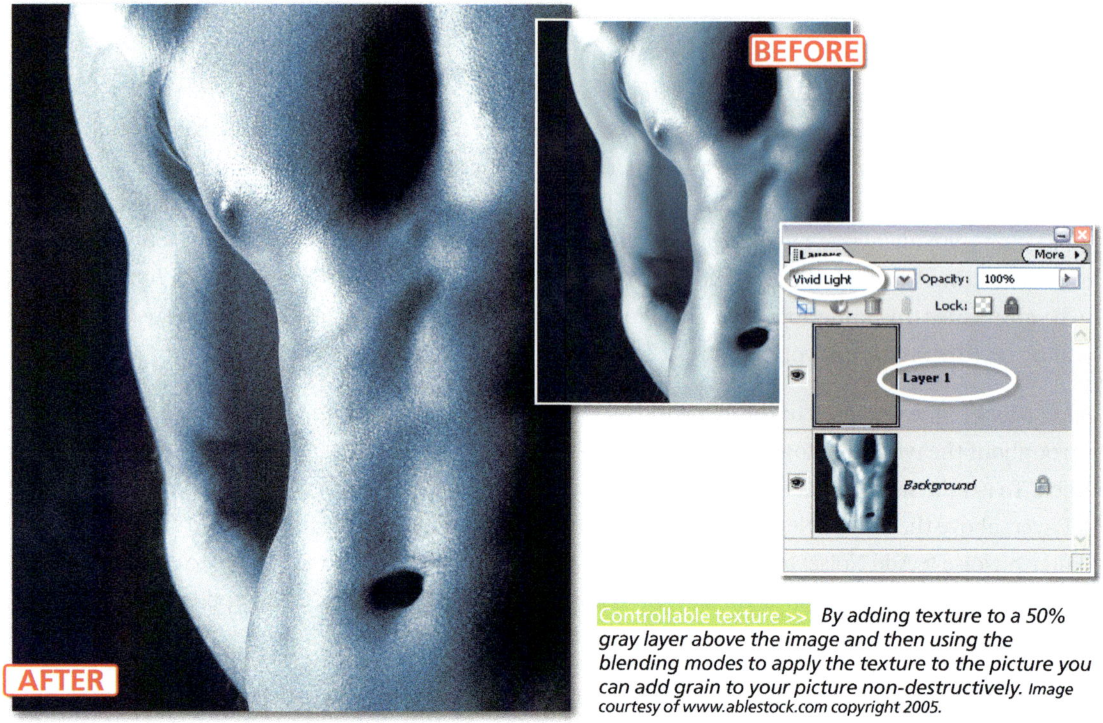

Controllable texture >> *By adding texture to a 50% gray layer above the image and then using the blending modes to apply the texture to the picture you can add grain to your picture non-destructively. Image courtesy of www.ablestock.com copyright 2005.*

Advanced sharpening secrets

To most of us sharpening is a way of improving the clarity of photos using a single-click option such as Enhance > Auto Sharpen in Elements, but why should we relinquish control when it comes to this final step in the editing process? Here we look a little deeper at some of the more customizable options that allow the user to more easily match the sharpening effect with the subject matter and output destination of their photos.

Sharpening – What are the options?

Photoshop Elements provides a variety of sharpening options designed to increase the clarity of digital photographs. In previous versions these options were listed in the Filter > Sharpen menu and include the Sharpen, Sharpen Edges, Sharpen More and Unsharp Mask filters. In version 5.0 the options were moved and are now grouped under the Enhance menu and include Auto Sharpen, Unsharp Mask and Adjust Sharpness filters.

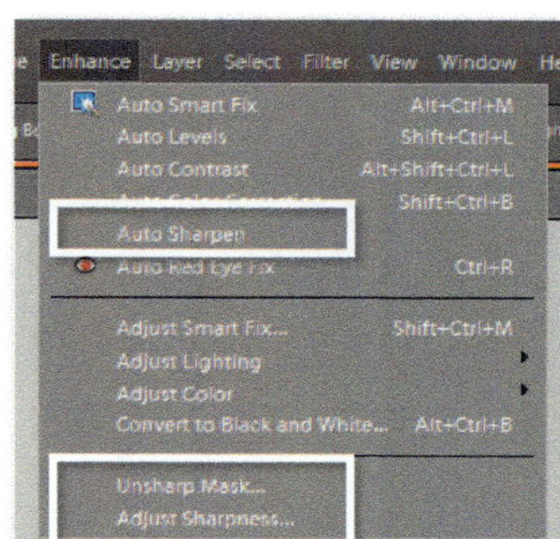

Sharpen options >> *Elements 5.0, 6.0 and 7 group the sharpening options under the Enhance menu. Unsharp Mask remains but the other filters have been replaced with the one-step Auto Sharpen and the sophisticated Adjust Sharpness options.*

Digital sharpening techniques are based on increasing the contrast between adjacent pixels in the image. When viewed from a distance, this change makes the picture appear sharper or more defined. So applying a sharpening filter does not, and will never, make a poorly focused picture suddenly appear as if it has been focused correctly. Instead these filters are designed to make your photos appear more sharply defined.

For many users selecting an option such as the Auto Sharpen is about as far as they go when it comes to thinking about how to sharpen their pictures, but this 'one-click' filter fail to take into account the content of the photo and the intended use for the image – two factors that should determine the amount of sharpening you apply. So for the ultimate control of your sharpening use the advanced features in the new Adjust Sharpness filter, or the tried and tested Unsharp Mask filter. Both these options contain controls that allow the user to manipulate the strength of the sharpening effect and adjust which parts of the picture the filters are applied. Let's look at each in turn.

6.39 Unsharp Masking to the rescue

Suitable for Elements – 7.0, 6.0, 5.0, 4.0, 3.0, 2.0, 1.0 | Difficulty level – Intermediate | Resources – Web image 632 | Related techniques – 6.40, 6.41 | Menus used – Enhance

Of the various sharpen filters that Photoshop Elements contains the Unsharp Mask provides some of the greatest control over the sharpening process by giving the user a range of sliders which, when adjusted, alter the way the effect is applied to pictures. Though a little confusing to start with, the Unsharp Mask filter is one of the best ways to make your scans or digital photographs clearer. However, to get the most out of the feature you must understand and control carefully each of the three sliders. So how does the feature work?

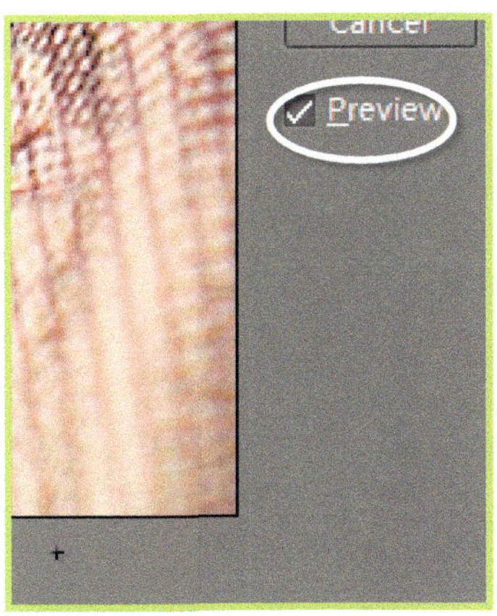

Step 1 >> *Make sure that your picture is zoomed in or magnified to at least 100% before selecting the Unsharp Mask option from the Enhance menu. Select the Preview option in the dialog to ensure that the sharpening effects are shown on the full image.*

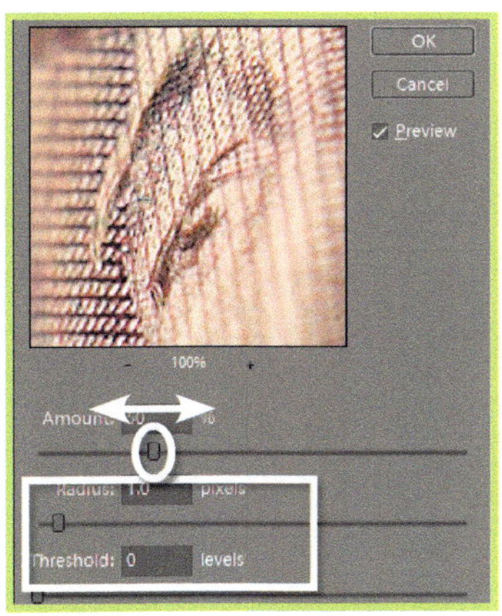

Step 2 >> *Start with the radius set to 1 and the Threshold value adjusted to 0. Gradually move the Amount slider upwards watching the sharpening effect as you go. Stop when you find a setting where the picture appears clearer but contains no sharpening 'halos'.*

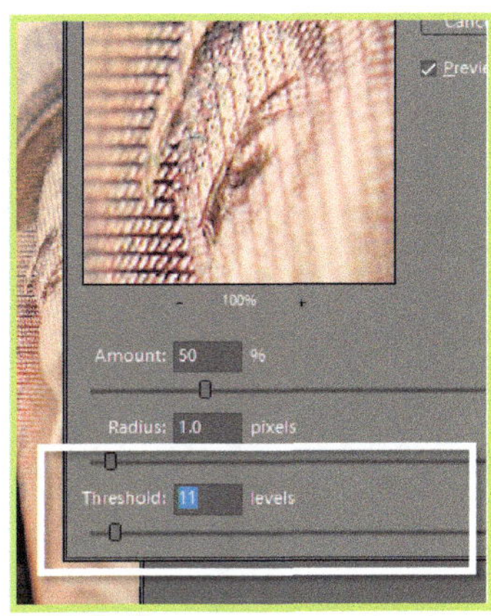

Step 3 >> *To restrict the effect from being applied to skin tones, blue skies or other areas of smooth tone gradually increase the Threshold slider until the sharpening is just being applied to the picture's edges.*

The **Amount** slider controls the strength of the sharpening effect. Larger numbers will produce more pronounced results whereas smaller values will create more subtle effects. Values of 50% to 100% are suitable for low-resolution pictures whereas settings between 150% and 200% can be used on images with a higher resolution.

The **Radius** slider value determines the number of pixels around the edge that are affected by the sharpening. A low value only sharpens edge pixels. High settings can produce noticeable halo effects around your picture so start with a low value first. Typically values between 1 and 2 are used for high-resolution images, settings of 1 or less for screen images.

The **Threshold** slider is used to determine how different the pixels must be before they are considered an edge and therefore sharpened. A value of 0 will sharpen all the pixels in an image whereas a setting of 10 will only apply the effect to those areas that are different by at least 10 levels or more from their surrounding pixels. To ensure that no sharpening occurs in sky or skin tone areas set this value to 8 or more.

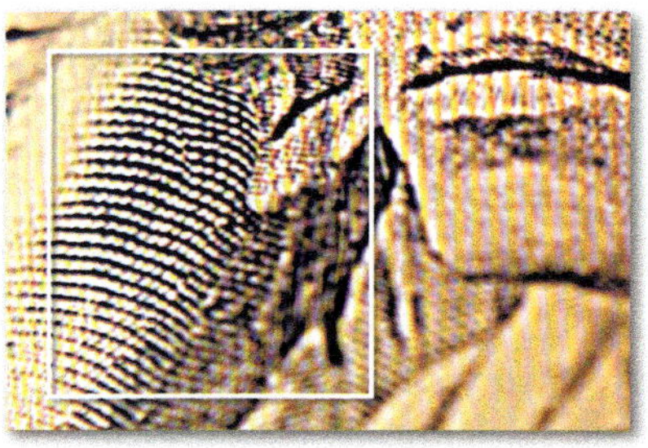

Unsharp Mask Top Tip:

Be careful when you are using the Unsharp Mask filter with your pictures. A little sharpening will improve the look of your photographs but too much sharpening is really noticeable and almost impossible to repair once applied to your picture. If you are unsure of your settings, apply the effect to a copy of the image first.

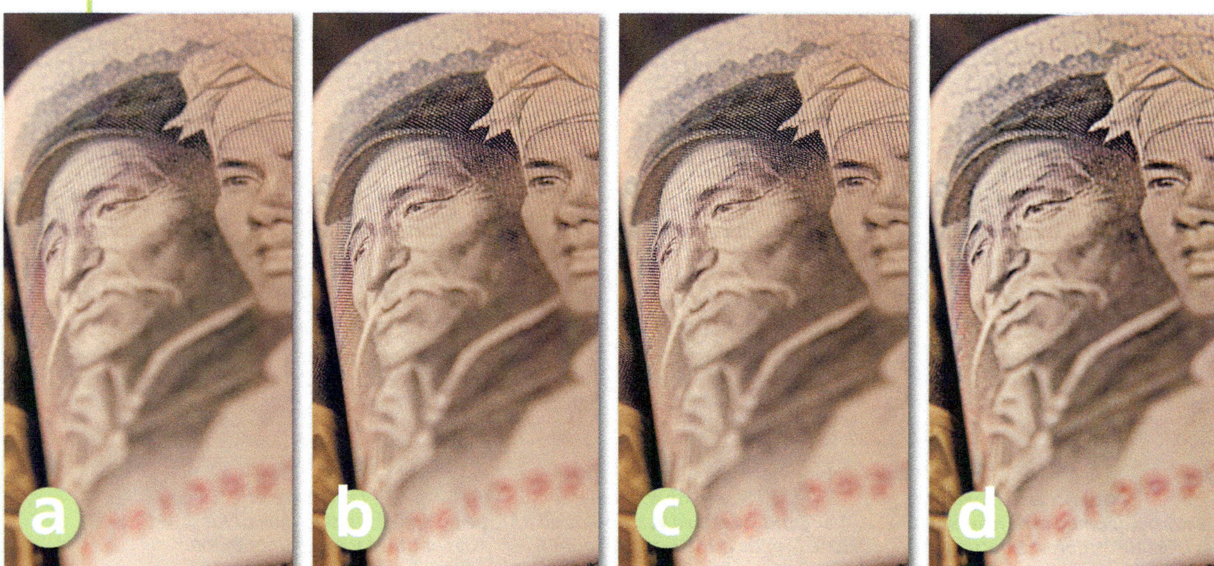

Adding clarity >> *Careful sharpening can really add to the clarity of a digital photo, but like most enhancement techniques it is best to make such changes subtly. (a) No-sharpening. (b) After Unsharp Mask. (c) After Adjust Sharpness. (d) High Pass/Blend Light mode approach.*

6.40 Adjust Sharpness for the ultimate control

Suitable for Elements – 7.0, 6.0, 5.0 | Difficulty level – Intermediate | Resources – Web image 632
Related techniques – 6.39, 6.41 | Menus used – Enhance

Until the release of Photoshop Elements 5.0 the best way to take control of the sharpening in your photographs was to use the Unsharp Mask filter. But the most recent release has included a brand new sharpening tool that will easily steal this crown. The Adjust Sharpness filter (Enhance > Adjust Sharpness) provides all the control that we are familiar with in the Unsharp Mask dialog plus better edge detection abilities, which leads to less apparent sharpening halos. The Filter dialog contains a zoomable preview, sliders to control the sharpening plus a drop-down menu where you can choose the type of sharpening to apply. You can control the sharpening effect with the following settings:

Amount – Strength of sharpening effect.

Radius – Determines the extent of sharpening. Higher values equal more obvious edge effects.

Remove – Determines sharpening algorithm used. Gaussian Blur uses the same approach as the Unsharp Mask filter. Lens Blur concentrates on sharpening details and produces results with fewer halos. Motion Blur reduces the effects of blur caused by camera shake or subject movement.

Angle – Sets Motion Blur direction.

More Refined – Longer processing for better results.

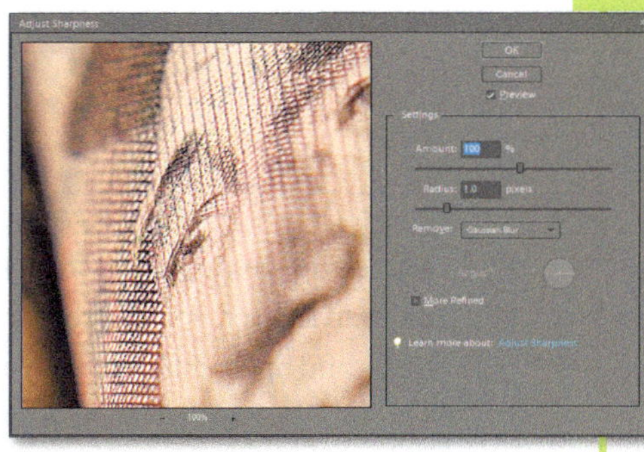

Adjust Sharpness >> *The Adjust Sharpness feature introduced in Elements 5.0 extends the customized sharpening ability first started with the Unsharp Mask filter.*

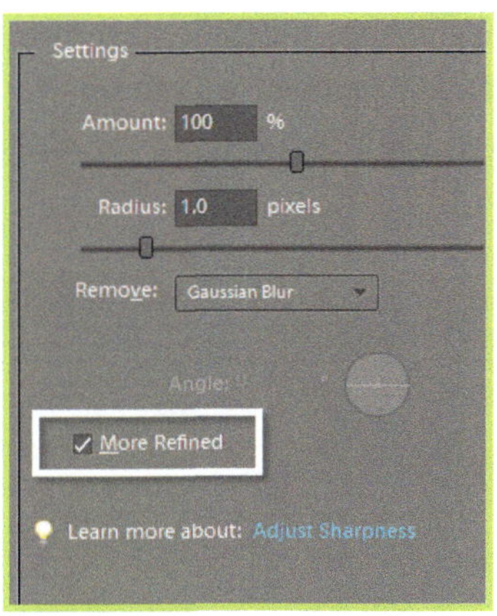

Step 1 >> *Make sure that your picture is zoomed in or magnified to at least 100% and then select the Enhance > Adjust Sharpness filter. Select the Preview option in the dialogue to ensure that the sharpening effects are shown on the full image and also tick the More Refined option unless you are working with a large file or a slow computer.*

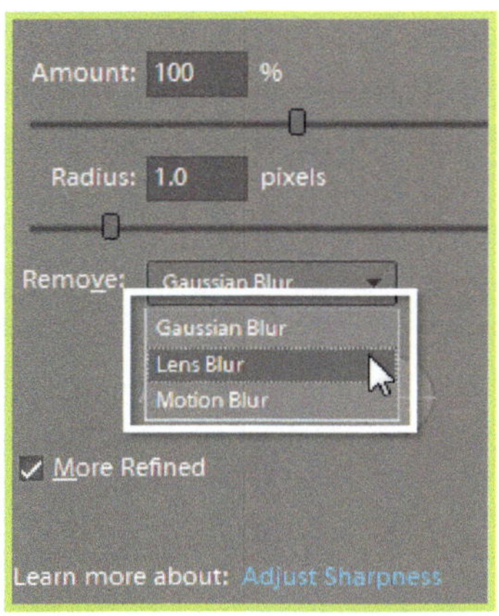

Step 2 >> *Choose the Lens Blur entry from the Remove menu. This option provides the best sharpening with least halo artifacts. Choose Gaussian Blur if you want to simulate Unsharp Mask results or Motion Blur if you are trying to get rid of the effects of camera shake.*

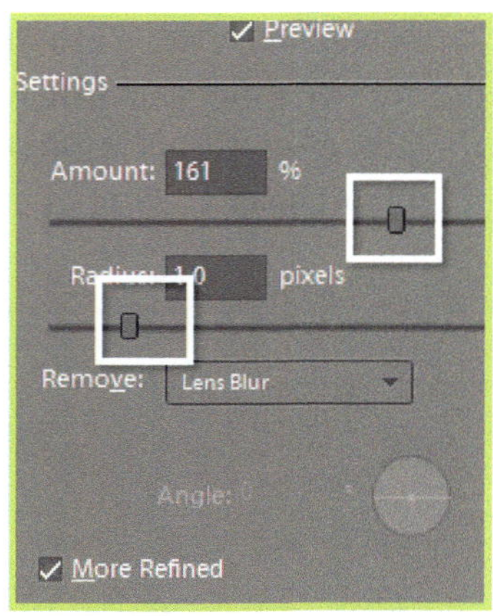

Step 3 >> *Start with the radius set to 1 and gradually move the Amount slider upwards watching the sharpening effect as you go. Stop when you find a setting where the picture appears clearer but contains no sharpening 'halos'.*

Adjust Sharpness Top Tip

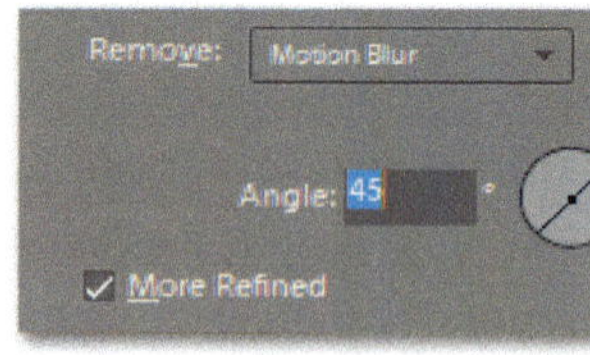

One of the options for the new Adjust Sharpness filter is the Motion Blur entry in the Remove menu. The options listed in this menu determine the way in which sharpening is applied to the picture or more specifically, the algorithm used when filtering. The Motion Blur option is different to the other choices as it provides a method of reducing the effects of blur in a photo due to the camera or subject moving during the exposure. When Motion Blur is selected you have the added option of inputting an angle for the blur reducing action. This can be achieved with the dial control by click-dragging the mouse or by inputting a specific angle.

6.41 Another approach

Suitable for Elements – 7.0, 6.0, 5.0, 4.0, 3.0, 2.0, 1.0 | Difficulty level – Intermediate | Resources – Web image 632 | Related techniques – 6.39, 6.40 | Menus used – Layer, Filter

There is no getting away from the fact that sharpening photos with filters alters them irreversibly and forever. For this reason many photographers duplicate their precious pictures multiple times and apply different sharpening options to the copies depending on their intended use. This is not a bad approach, especially if you have plenty of storage space to hand, but what if you could sharpen your photos without altering the original pixels? Well surprisingly the Blending Modes feature located in Photoshop Elements provides the key to just such a technique. In particular, we will use the Hard Light Blend Mode in conjunction with the High Pass filter to create a non-destructive sharpening effect. The High Pass filter provides the mechanism for controlling where the sharpening occurs by isolating the edges in a picture and then converting the rest of the image to mid gray. This is perfect for use with Hard Light blend mode as the mid gray areas will not be affected at all and the sharpening changes will only be applied to the edges of the photo.

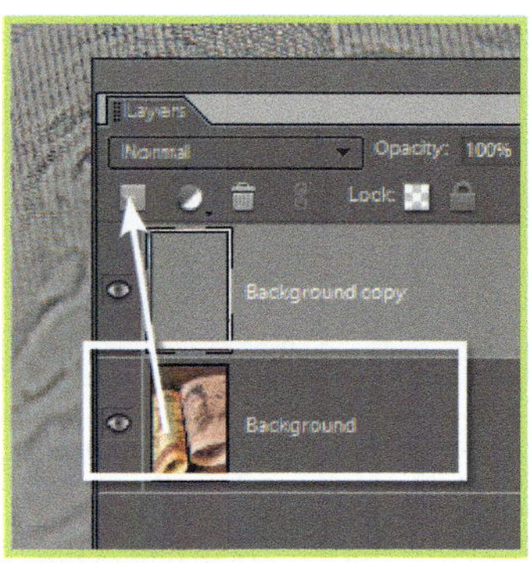

Step 1 >> Make a copy (Layer > Duplicate Layer) of the picture layer that you want to sharpen. Filter the copied layer with the High Pass filter (Filter > Other > High Pass) and press OK.

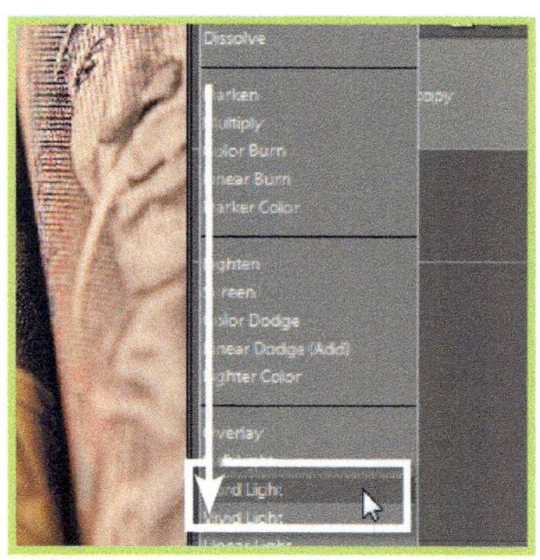

Step 2 >> With the filtered layer still selected switch the blend mode to Hard Light. This mode blends both the dark and light parts of the filtered layer with the picture layer, causing an increase in contrast.

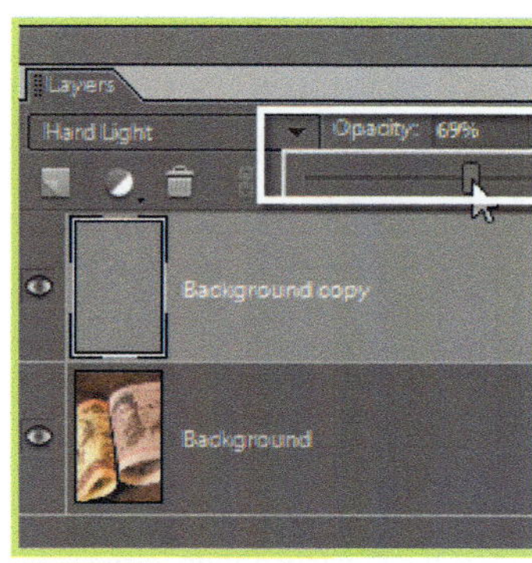

Step 3 >> Adjust the opacity of this layer to govern the level of sharpening. Sharpening using this technique means that you can remove or adjust the strength of the effect later by manipulating the filtered layer.

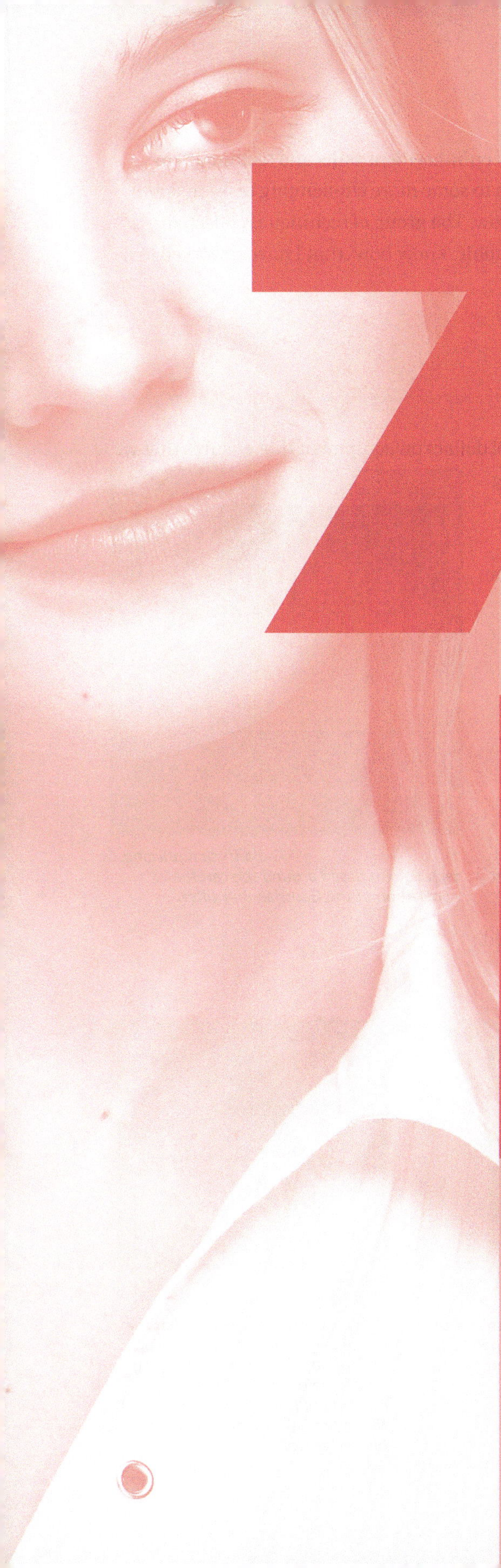

7

Darkroom Techniques on the Desktop

Once you have mastered the basic editing and enhancement skills and techniques in Elements you will no doubt want to move on to some more challenging tasks that will extend and build upon what you already know. The group of techniques collected together here is loosely based on traditional photographic 'know how' that I have reworked in a digital fashion.

7.01 Diffusion printing

Suitable for Elements – 7.0, 6.0, 5.0, 4.0, 3.0, 2.0, 1.0 | Difficulty level – Intermediate | Resources – Web image 701 | Tools used – Eraser | Menus used – Filter, Layer

Even though as image-makers we spend thousands of dollars on equipment that ensures that we make sharp photographs, there is something enticing about a delicately softened picture. Especially when this lack of sharpness is contrasted against a well-focused section of the picture. Diffusion printing is one traditional printing technique that played with this idea. Parts of the image were purposely blurred whilst other areas remained sharp.

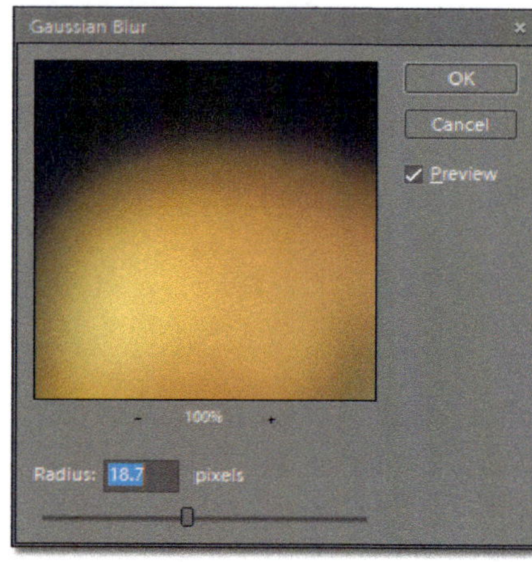

Gaussian Blur filter >> *The diffusion printing technique is based around the careful application of the Gaussian Blur filter.*

With non-digital photography, adding such an effect meant placing a 'mist' or 'fog' filter in front of the camera lens at the time of shooting. More recently, in an attempt to gain a little more control over the process, photographers have been placing diffusion filters below their enlarging lenses for part of the print's exposure time. This process gave a combination effect where sharpness and controlled blur happily coexisted in the final print.

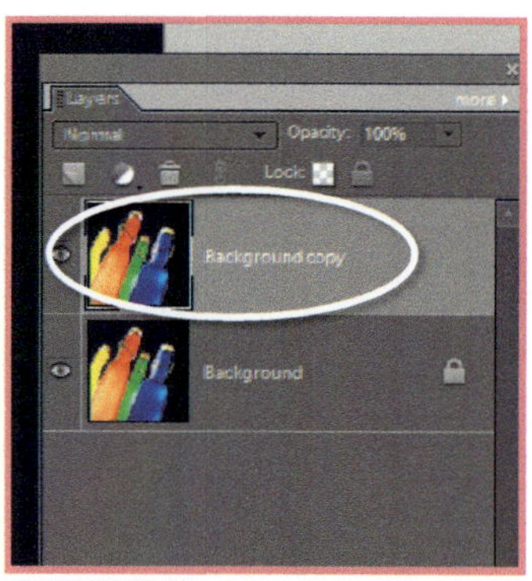

Step 1 >> *Duplicate the original picture by dragging it to the New Layer button or choosing the Layer>Duplicate Layer option.*

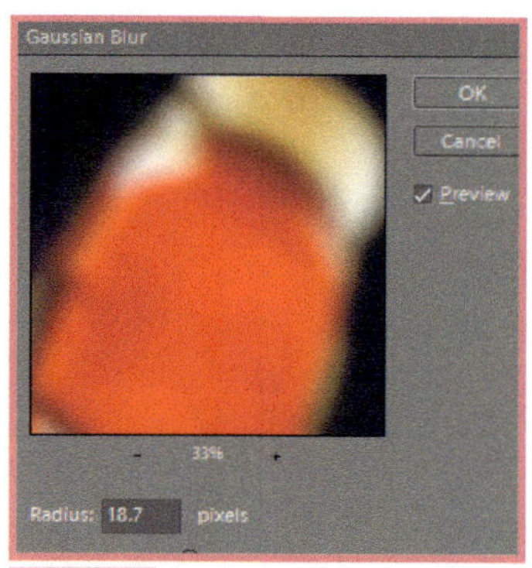

Step 2 >> *Apply the Gaussian Blur filter (Filter>Blur>Gaussian Blur) to the upper, duplicated, layer.*

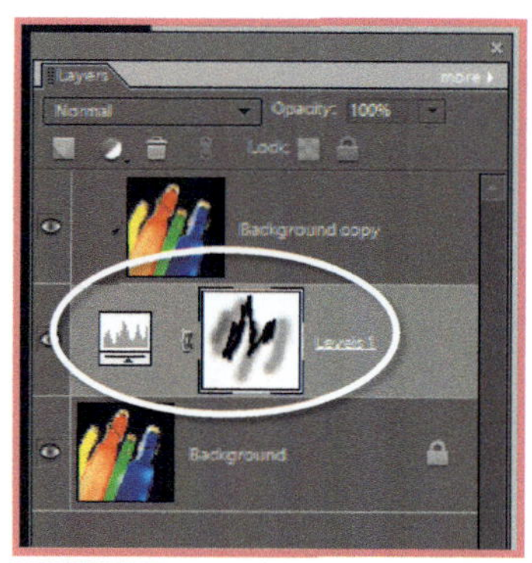

Step 3 >> *Control the way that the blurred layer interacts with the one beneath by adjusting the blending mode and/or using a No Settings adjustment layer mask grouped with the upper layer to remove unwanted blurred areas.*

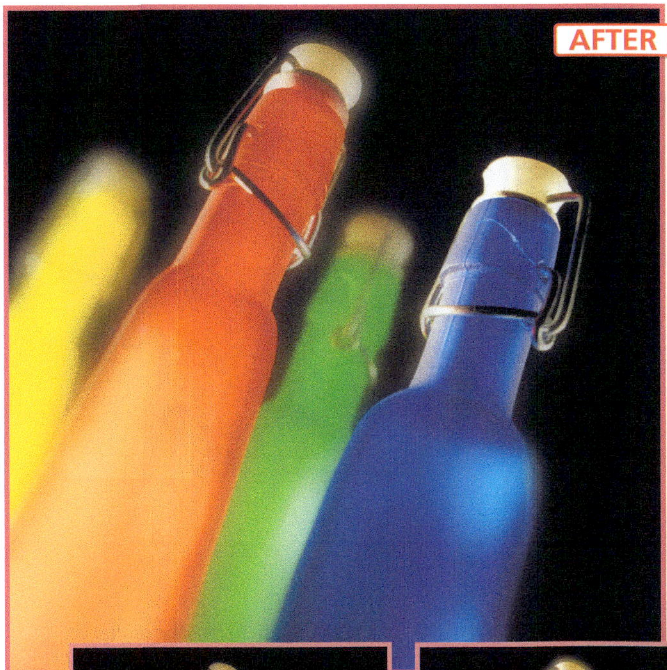

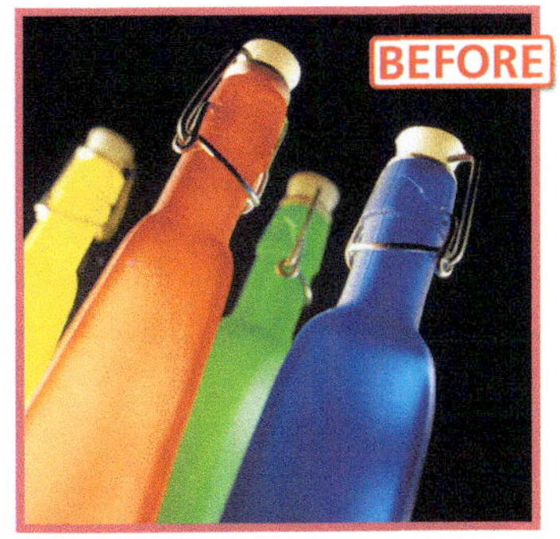

Diffusion printing >> *To control the style and position of the effect change the blending mode of the blurred layer and use the eraser to remove blurred areas to reveal the sharp original beneath. (a) Darken blending mode. (b) Lighten blending mode. (c) Normal blending mode.*

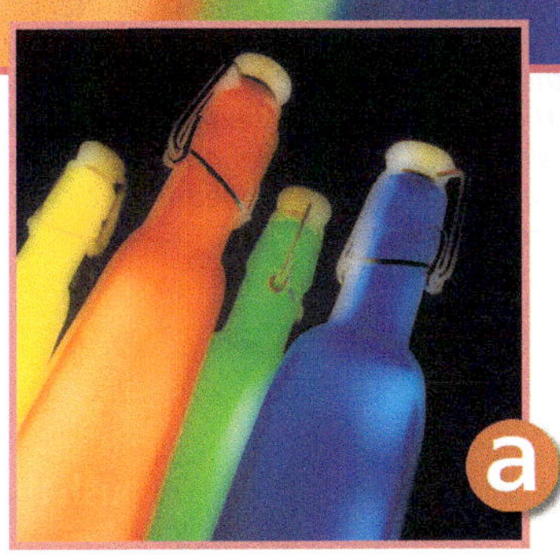

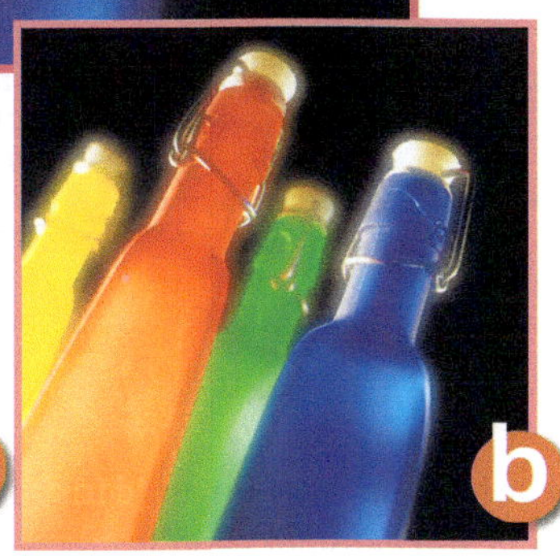

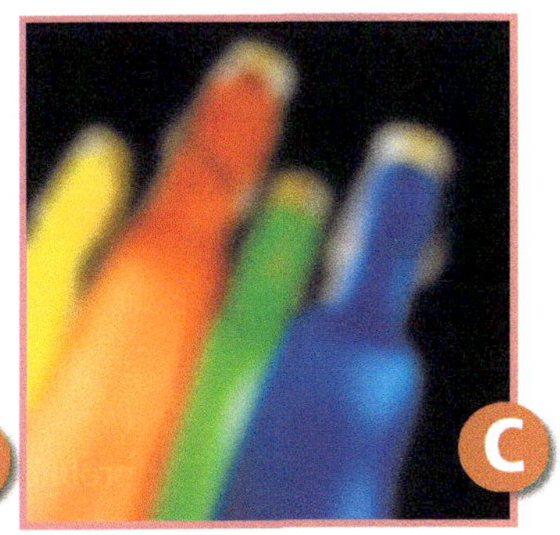

Creating this style of picture using digital processes offers the image-maker a lot more choice and control over the end results. The technique is based around the Gaussian Blur filter, which can be used to soften the sharp details of your photograph. A simple application of the filter to a base image produces a less than attractive result and one that doesn't combine the sharp and blurred imagery. Instead more control is possible if the filter is applied to a copy of the picture stored as a layer above the original image. This blurred layer is then combined with the original by either reducing the opacity of the blurred layer to allow the sharp original to show through, or by changing the blurred layer to a different blending mode such as Darken or Lighten.

Extending the technique

Blending mode or opacity changes provide control over the overall effect of the diffusion, but to fine-tune the results select the blur layer, add a No Settings adjustment layer below the blurred layer. Group the upper image layer with the adjustment layer and then use the mask of the adjustment layer to to gently remove parts of the top layer to reveal the sharpness beneath.

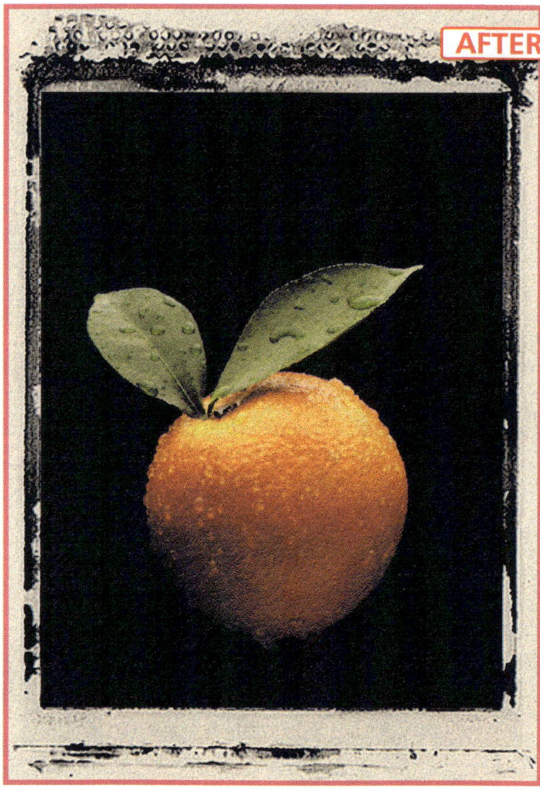

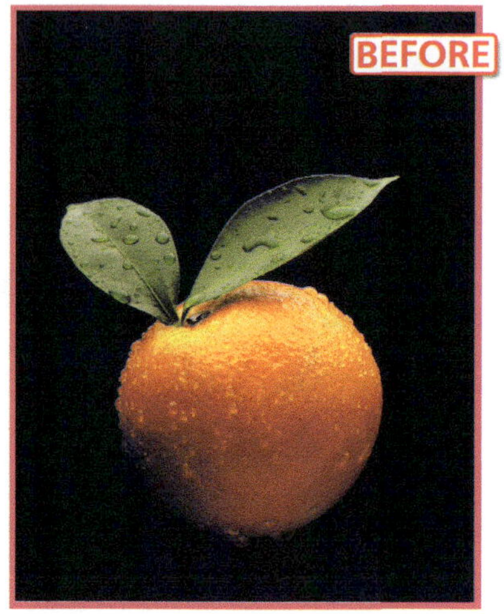

Polaroid transfer effect >> *The digital version of this traditional printing technique makes use of the two separate filters to construct the mottled image and the texturizer to create the paper effect before surrounding the whole picture with a frame scanned from a real Polaroid photograph.*

7.02 Instant film transfer effect

Suitable for Elements – 7.0, 6.0, 5.0 | Difficulty level – Advanced | Resources – Web images 702-1, 702-2, 702-3, Menus used – Filter, Layer, Enhance, Image

Most readers will probably be familiar with Polaroid instant picture products – you push the button and the print is ejected and develops right before your eyes. For many years professional image-makers have been using the unique features of this technology to create wonderfully textured images. The process involved substituting watercolor paper for the printing surface supplied by Polaroid. As a result the image is transferred onto the roughly surfaced paper and takes on a distinctly different look and feel to a standard Polaroid print.

Much acclaimed for its artistic appeal, the technique was not always predictable and, much to the frustration of photographers, it was often difficult to repeat the success of previous results. There were three main problems – dark areas of an image often didn't transfer to the new surface, colors and image detail would bleed unpredictably, and it was difficult to control how dark or light the final print would be. I know these problems intimately as it once took me 16 sheets of expensive instant film to produce a couple of acceptable prints.

A digital solution

This success ratio is not one that my budget or my temperament can afford. So I started to play with a digital version of the popular technique. I wanted to find a process that was more predictable, controllable and repeatable. My first step was to list the characteristics of the Polaroid transfer print so that I could simulate them digitally.

To me it seemed that there were four main elements: desaturated colors, mottled ink, distinct paper texture and color, and the Polaroid film frame.

If I could duplicate these on my desktop then I would be able to make an image that captured the essence of the Polaroid transfer process.

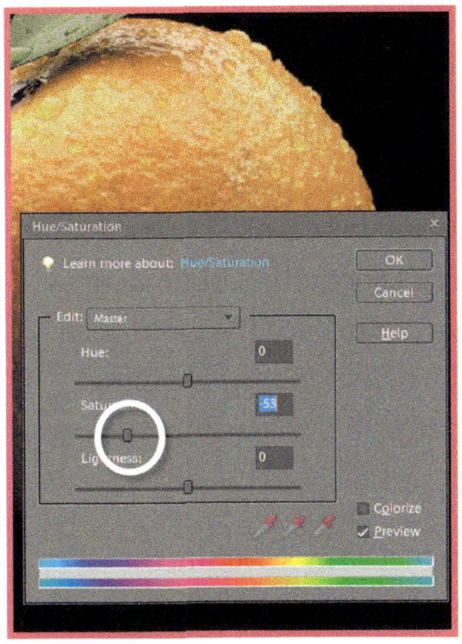

Step 1 >> *Desaturate the image tones slightly using the Hue/ Saturation feature.*

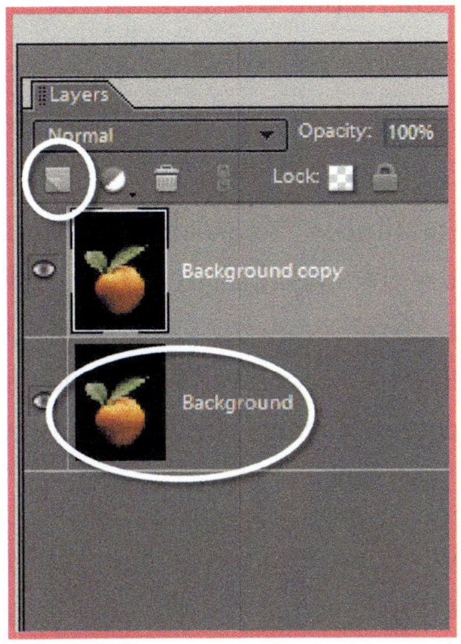

Step 2 >> *Duplicate the background layer by dragging it to the New Layers button at the top of the dialog.*

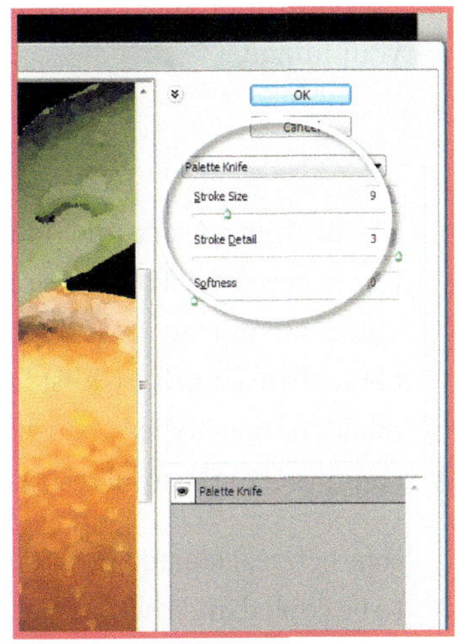

Step 3 >> *Apply both the Paint Daubs and Palette Knife filters to the upper layer (duplicate).*

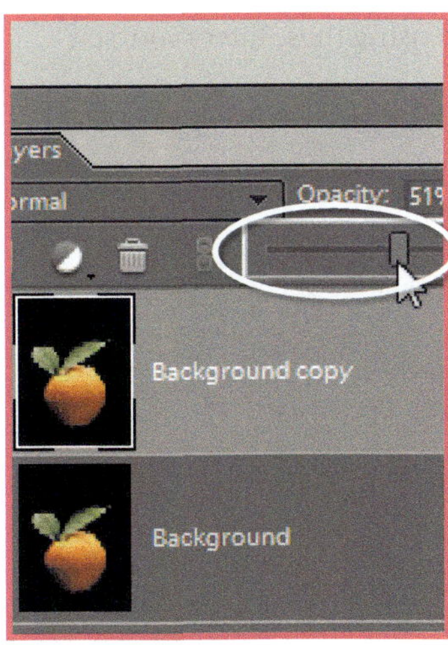

Step 4 >> *Reduce the opacity of the filtered upper layer to allow some of the sharp details of the original image to show through.*

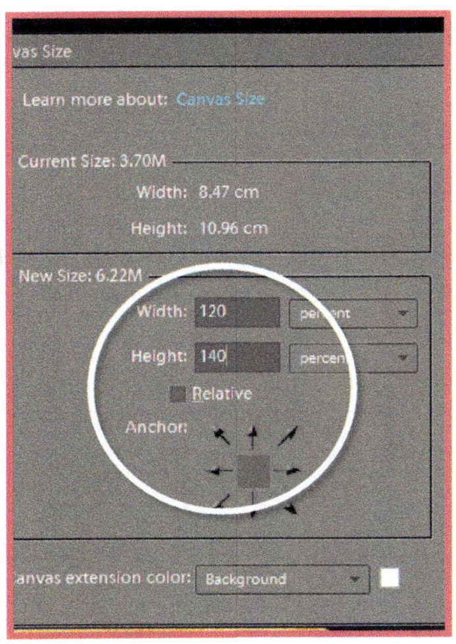

Step 5 >> *Check to see that the background color is set to white. Increase the size of the canvas to accommodate the Polaroid edge surround using the Canvas Size command with a setting of 120% for width and 140% for height. Copy Merge and paste the new layer.*

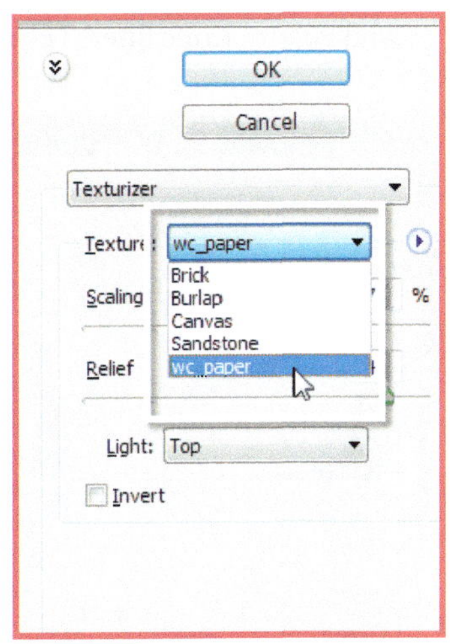

Step 6 >> *Either use one of the pre-installed textures available in the Texturizer filter or download and install the watercolor paper.psd file (web image 702-2) from this book's website. Use the filter to add the texture to the surround.*

Desaturate the image tones

The Polaroid technique requires the watercolor paper to be slightly wet at the time of transfer. The moisture, whilst helping the image movement from paper to paper, tends to desaturate the colors and cause fine detail to be lost. These characteristics are also the result of the coarse surface of the donor paper. So the first step of the digital version of the process is to desaturate the color of our example image. In Elements this can be achieved by using the Hue/Saturation control from the Adjust Color section of the Enhance menu. With the dialog open carefully move the Saturation slider to the left. This action will decrease the intensity of the colors in your image.

Mottle the ink

The distinct surface and image qualities of Polaroid transfer prints combine both sharpness and image break-up in the one picture. To reproduce this effect digitally, I copied the original image onto a second layer. My idea was to manipulate one version so that it displayed the mottled effect of the transfer print whilst leaving the second version untouched. Then, using the blending modes or opacity features of Elements' layers I could adjust how much sharpness or mottle was contained in the final result.

In practice, I started by duplicating the image layer. This can be achieved by selecting the layer to be copied and then using the Duplicate Layer command located under the Layer menu. Alternatively you drag the layer to the Create New Layer button at the top of the Layers palette. With the upper layer selected, I then needed to find a method to simulate the mottle of the transfer print. Though not exactly right, I found that by combining the effects of the Paint Daubs and Palette Knife filters I could produce reasonable results. When using these filters yourself

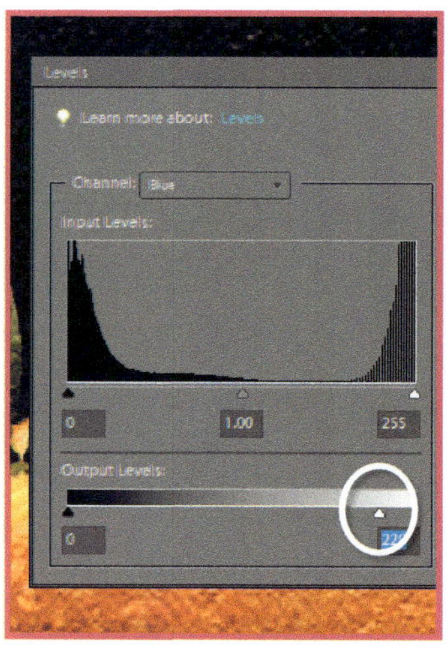

Step 7 >> *In the Levels feature select the blue and red channels separately, dragging in the white Output slider towards the center.*

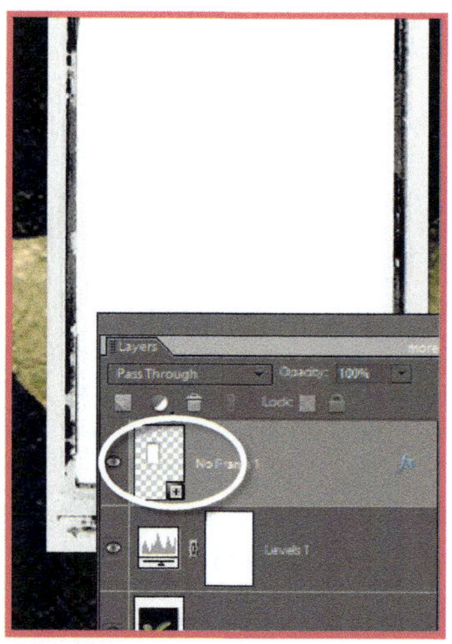

Step 8 >> *Open the edge file as a separate document, apply a 'No Frame' frame to the photo and drag it onto the original picture.*

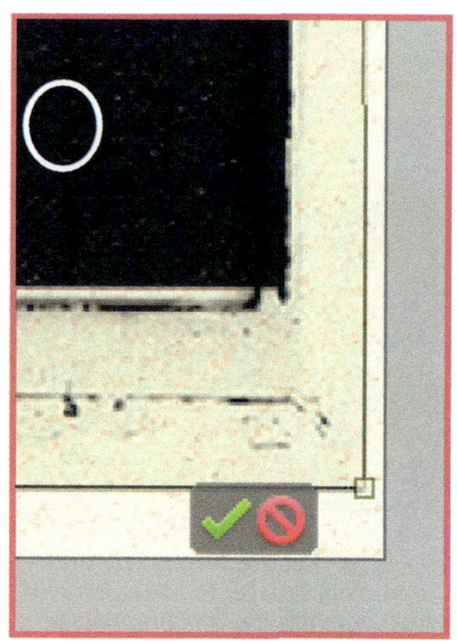

Step 9 >> *Switch the mode of the edge layer to Multiply and use the Scale command to adjust its frame or the edge to fit the picture below.*

keep in mind that the settings used will vary with the style and size of your image. This part of the process is not an exact science. Play and experimentation is the name of the game. You might also want to try other options in the Artistic, Sketch or Texture selections of the Filter menu. The last step in this stage is to combine the characteristics of the two layers. This can be achieved by either changing the Blending mode of the uppermost layer or by adjusting its opacity, or both. For the example image a simple opacity change was all that was needed, but don't be afraid to try a few different blend/opacity combinations with your own work.

Apply a paper texture and color

The paper color and texture is a critical part of the appeal of the transfer print. These two characteristics extend throughout the image itself and into the area that surrounds the picture. For this to occur in a digital facsimile it is necessary to provide some space around the image using Elements' Canvas Size feature. Unlike the Image Size command, this option allows the user to increase the size of the canvas without changing the image size (and all its associated layers). In the example the canvas width was increased by 120% and the height by 140%. To add the texture to both image and surround I copied and merged all of the document and then pasted the combined image to a new layer. Next, I photographed a section of watercolor paper to use as a customized texture with the Texturizer filter. You can download and use this very file from the book's website (*www.photoshopelements.net*). With the texture complete, I played with the overall color of the image using the Levels feature. I adjusted the blue and red channels independently and concentrated on the lighter tones of the image so that rather than the paper being a stark white it took on a creamy appearance.

Add the Polaroid frame

The last part of the process involves combining the final image with a photograph of a Polaroid film edge. The edge picture is nothing more complex than a scanned Polaroid print with the image removed. But rather than go to the trouble of making your own, you can download the edge I used for the example directly from the website (web image 702-3). Next, open the file as a separate Photoshop Elements document. Drag the No Frame frame from the Contents palette onto the Edge picture. Use the Fit Frame to Photo option from the right-click menu to adjust the frame to the edge. Click onto the edge frame layer and drag it onto your picture. The edge will automatically become a new layer on top of the existing image layer.

With the edge layer selected change the layer's mode to Multiply. Notice that the white areas of the layer are now transparent, allowing the picture beneath to show through. Finally, use the Scale or Free Transform command to adjust the size of the edge to fit the image. Remember that because the edge is sitting in a frame layer you click the picture once to adjust the frame and photo together and twice to change just the photo inside the frame. Though not an exact copy of the Polaroid transfer print, the digital version displays much of the character of the original and can be achieved for less cost and with more control.

7.03 Using the Unsharp Mask filter to add contrast

Suitable for Elements – 7.0, 6.0, 5.0, 4.0, 3.0, 2.0, 1.0 | Difficulty level – Basic | Resources – Web image 703
Tools used – Burning-in | Menus used – Enhance

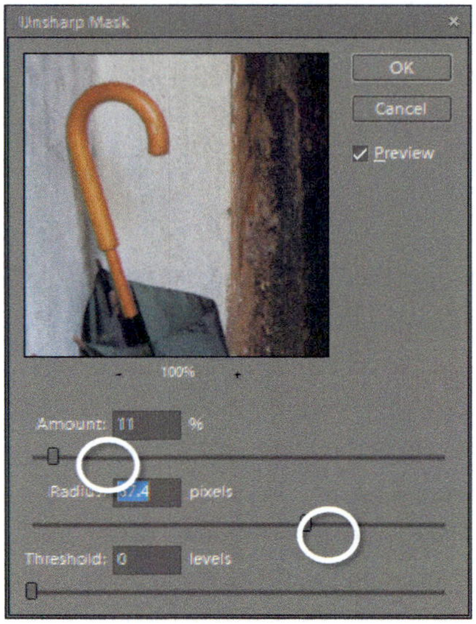

USM local contrast settings >> *Instead of using the modest radius settings that we normally associate with the Unsharp Mask filter this technique requires the radius to be set to a high value.*

Most digital photographers have used the Unsharp Mask filter as a way to add some crispness to pictures that are a little soft. In another application this feature can be used to add some local contrast to flat images in much the same way that multi-contrast printing provides a boost to black and white prints.

The trick with this technique is to forget the way that you have been using the feature. Instead of selecting a high amount and low radius setting you do the opposite. You drag the amount downwards and the radius upwards. This produces a change in local contrast rather than a sharpening of individual pixels. To use the technique as part of your standard enhancement process you would adjust highlight and shadow points to set the contrast of the whole picture first, then employ the Unsharp Mask filter to increase the local contrast and then use the filter a second time, with different settings, to increase the photograph's sharpness.

The new Adjust Sharpness filter also contains Amount and Radius sliders which can be employed to produce similar contrast changing effects.

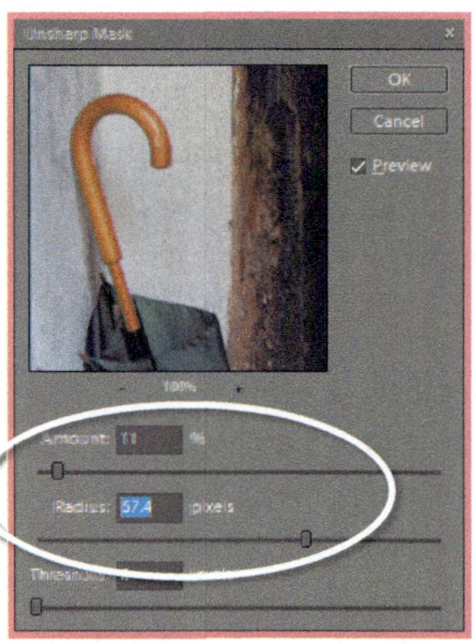

Step 1 >> *To change local contrast open the Unsharp Mask filter and select a low Amount value and a high Radius value.*

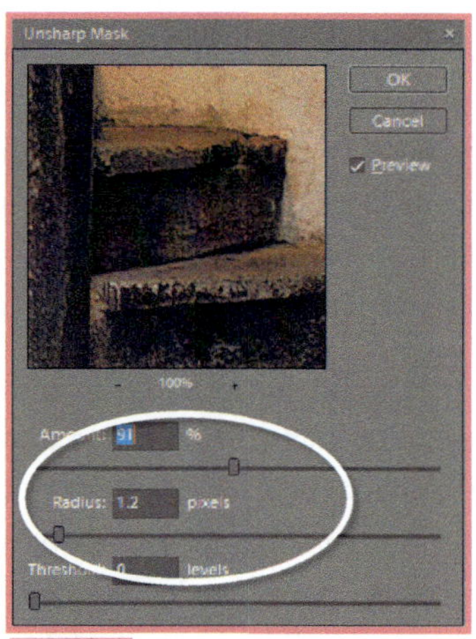

Step 2 >> *After adjusting the contrast sharpen the image using the Unsharp Mask filter in the normal fashion.*

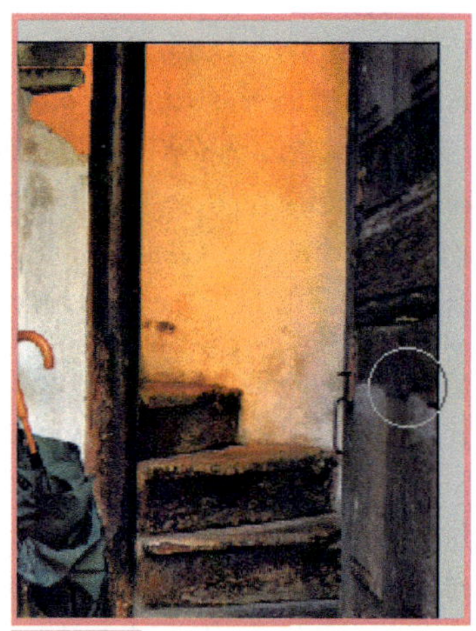

Step 3 >> *The final step in the example image was to darken some of the tones around the door opening with the Burn tool.*

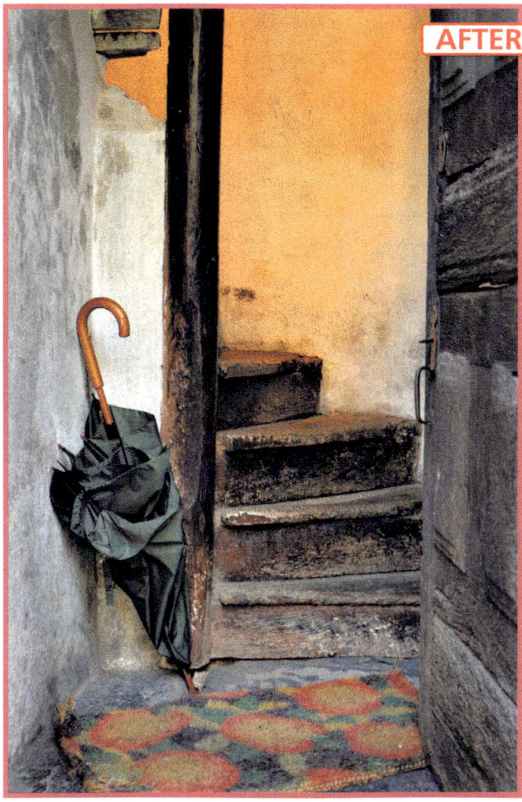

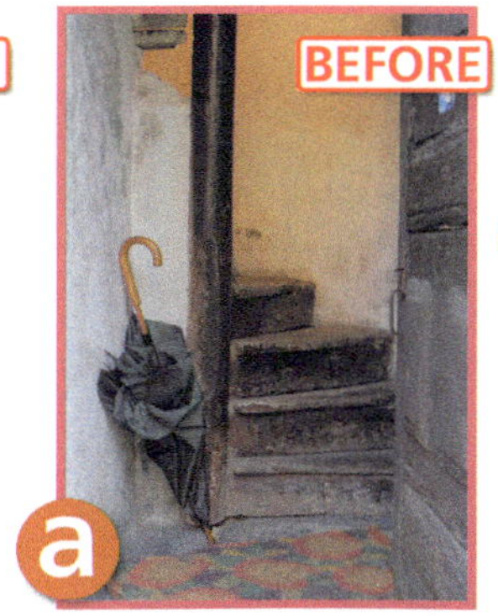

USM contrast change >> *Until now most of us have used the Unsharp Mask filter for the sharpening of pictures, but with this technique you can use the feature to increase the local contrast of an image as well.*

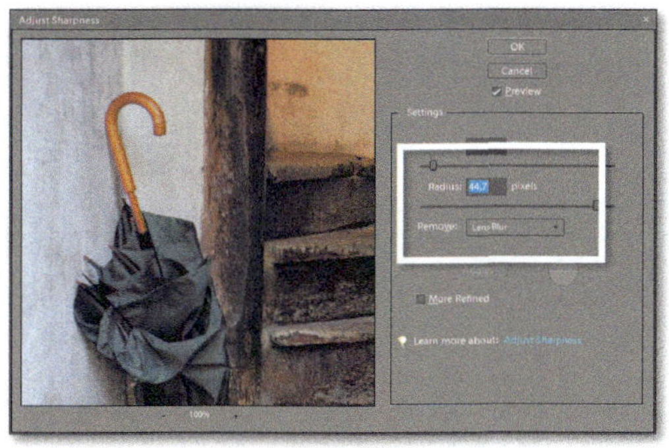

The Adjust Sharpness alternative >> *The Adjust Sharpness filter can also be used to provide similar local contrast changes.*

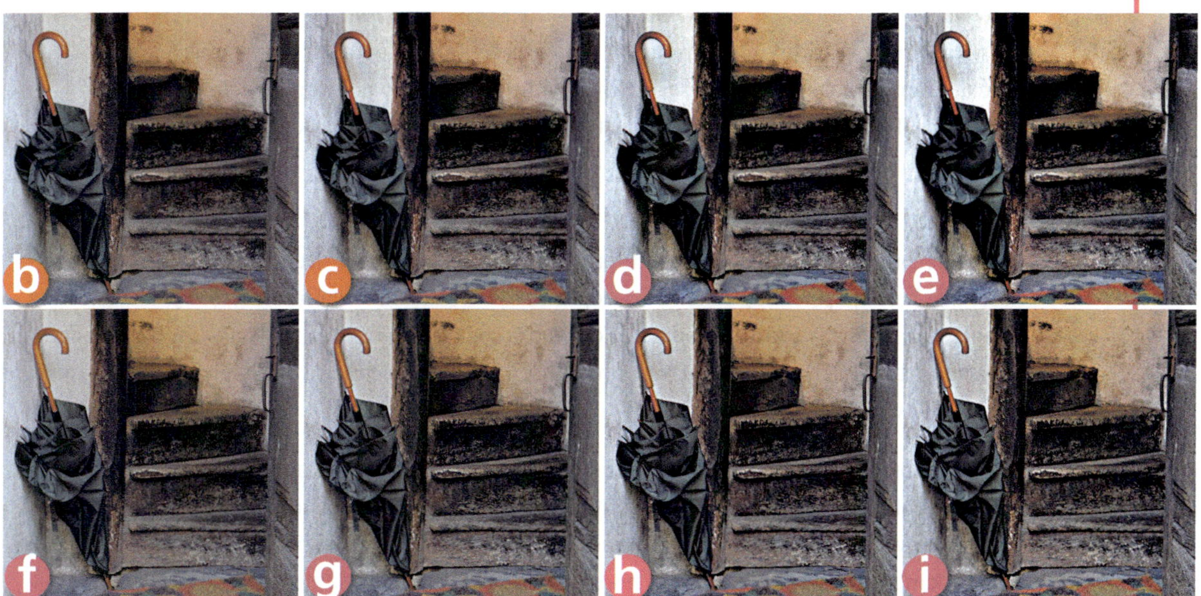

Recipes for USM contrast changes >> *(a) Original image, no contrast change.(b) Amount 30, Radius 80, Threshold 0. (c) Amount 60, Radius 80, Threshold 0. (d) Amount 90, Radius 80, Threshold 0. (e) Amount 120, Radius 80, Threshold 0. (f) Amount 30, Radius 20, Threshold 0. (g) Amount 60, Radius 20, Threshold 0. (h) Amount 90, Radius 20, Threshold 0. (i) Amount 120, Radius 20, Threshold 0.*

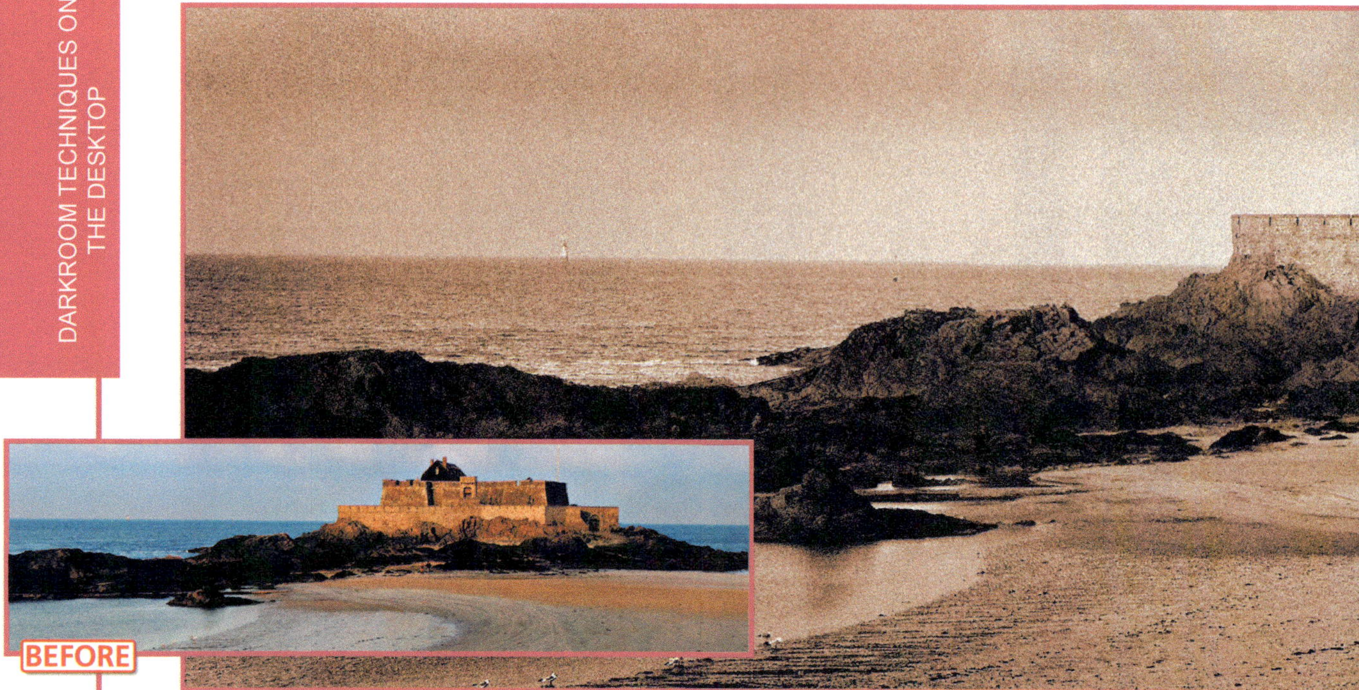

BEFORE

7.04 Lith printing technique

Suitable for Elements – 7.0, 6.0, 5.0, 4.0, 3.0, 2.0, 1.0 | Difficulty level – Basic | Resources – Web image 704
Tools used – Dodging, Burning-in | Menus used – Enhance, Image, Filter

Just a few short years prior to the massive uptake of digital photography many professional and amateur image-makers alike were discovering the beauty of a whole range of craft printing processes. There was a resurgence in the techniques involved in the production of high quality black and white pictures and a growing interest in 'alternative' processes that could create stunningly different monochromes.

One such process was lith printing. The process involves the massive overexposure of chloro-bromide-based papers coupled with development in a weak solution of lith chemistry. The resultant images are distinctly textured and richly colored and their origins are unmistakable. But rather than head back to the darkroom in pursuit of your first lith print you can use the following steps to recreate the results digitally.

Most lith prints have strong, distinctive and quite atmospheric grain that is coupled with colors that are seldom seen in a black and white print. They range from a deep chocolate, through warm browns, to oranges and sometimes even pink tones. If our digital version is to seem convincing then the final print will need to contain all of these elements.

Select a picture where the composition is strong. It should contain a full range of tones, especially in the highlights and shadows and good contrast will help make a more striking print. The first task is to lose the color. We want to achieve this change whilst still keeping the

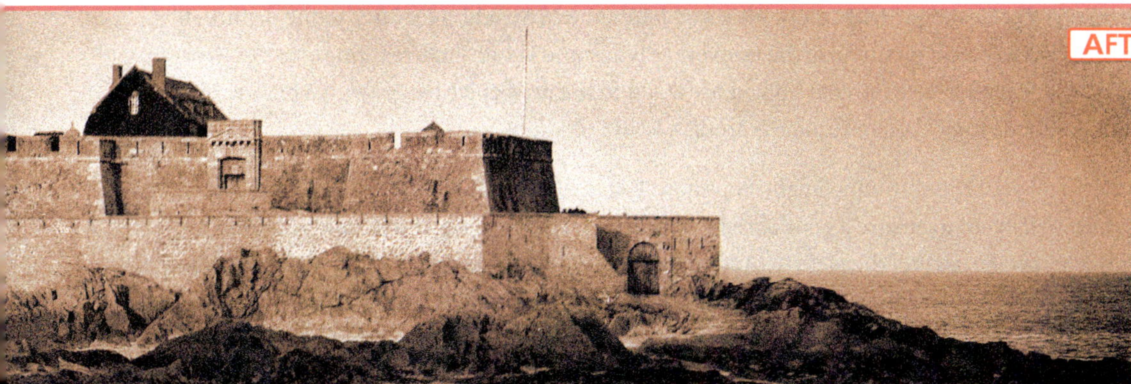

Lith printing >> *Recreating the highly textured, colored prints that result from the lith printing process involves the following steps:*
– losing the color from the image,
– adding some texture and then
– reapplying color to the picture.

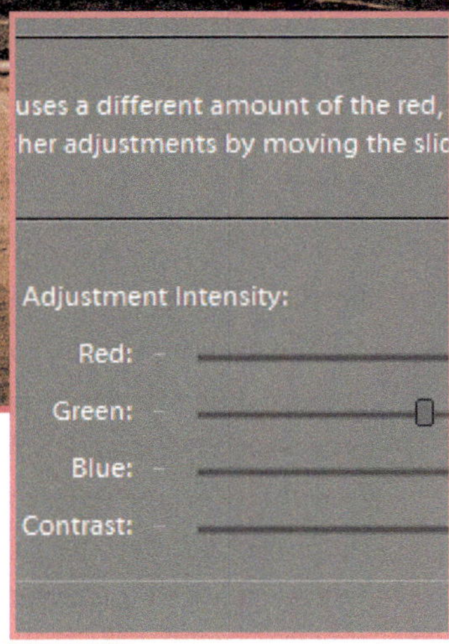

Step 1 >> *Convert your color picture to black and white with the Convert to Black and White feature.*

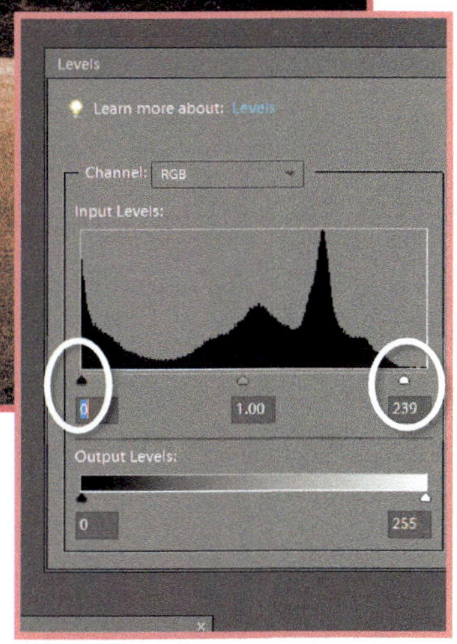

Step 2 >> *Adjust your picture's black and white points and check the spread of tones using the Levels feature.*

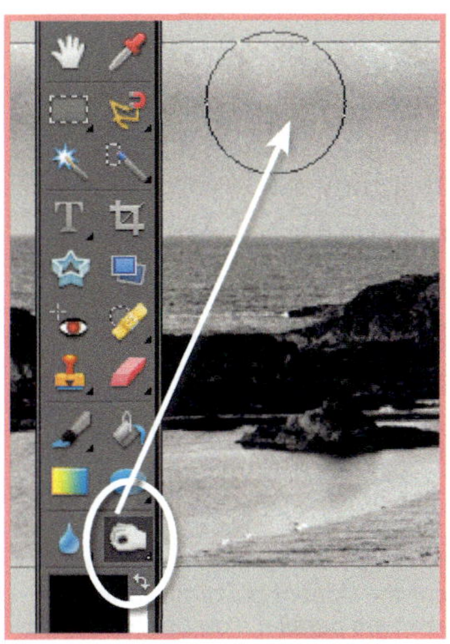

Step 3 >> *Use the Dodging and Burning-in tools to add drama to specific areas of the picture.*

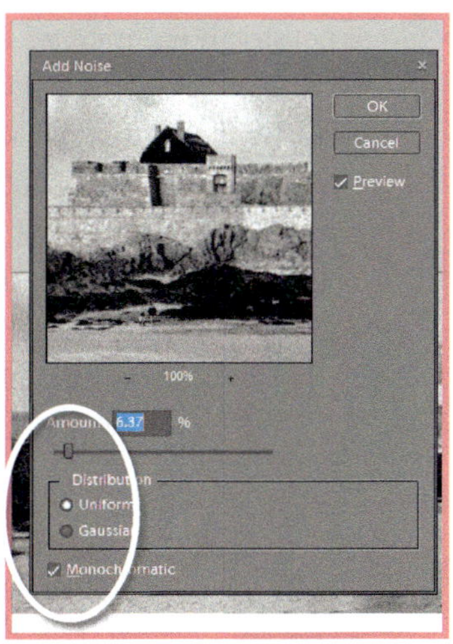

Step 4 >> *Add some texture to the image using the Add Noise filter set to Gaussian and Monochrome.*

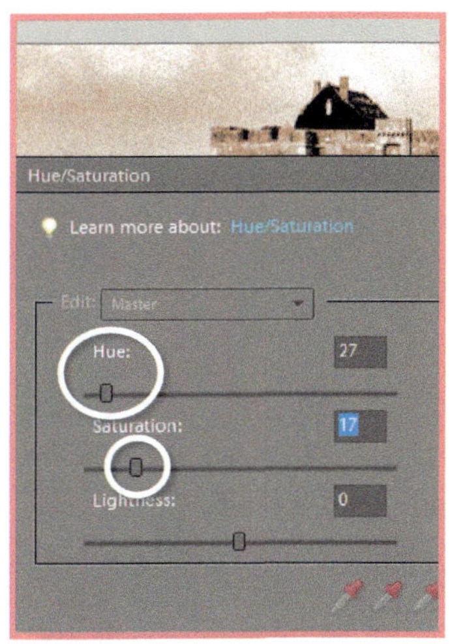

Step 5 >> *Apply some color using the Hue slider and Colorize option in the Hue/Saturation feature .*

picture in a color mode (RGB Color). This way later on we can add color back to the picture. If the original is a color picture use the Convert to Black and White feature (Enhance > Convert to Black and White) to lose the color. If you are starting the project with a grayscale picture change the color mode to RGB Color (Image > Mode > RGB Color).

Perform all your tonal enhancement steps now. Use the Levels feature (Enhance > Adjust Lighting > Levels) to ensure a good spread of tones and the Burning and Dodging-in tools to enhance specific parts of the picture. Add some texture to the image using the Add Noise filter (Filter > Noise > Add Noise) with the Gaussian and Monochrome options set. The final step is to add some color back to the picture. We can achieve this effect by selecting the Colorize option in the Hue/Saturation feature and then adjusting the Hue slider to select the color of the tint and the Saturation slider to alter the strength.

7.05 Correcting perspective problems

Suitable for Elements – 7.0, 6.0, 5.0 | Difficulty level – Basic
Resources – Web image 705 | Menus used – Filter

You know the story: you're visiting a wonderful city on holiday wanting to capture as much of the local scenes and architecture as possible. You enter the local square and point you camera towards an impressive three-spired building on the other side of the road only to find that you must tilt your camera upwards to get the peaks into the picture. At the time you think nothing of it and you move on to the next location. It is only when you are back at home about to print your photograph that you realize that the innocent 'tilt' has caused the edges of the building to lean inwards.

Now, to a certain extent this isn't a problem; even though it is not strictly accurate, we all know that most buildings have parallel walls and the majority of people who look at you picture will take this into account – won't they? Apart from a return trip and a re-shoot is there any way to correct these converging verticals? Well, I'm glad you asked. Armed with nothing except Elements 5.0, 6.0 or 7.0, the Correct Camera Distortion filter and the steps detailed here, you can now straighten all those leaning architectural shots without the cost of the return journey.

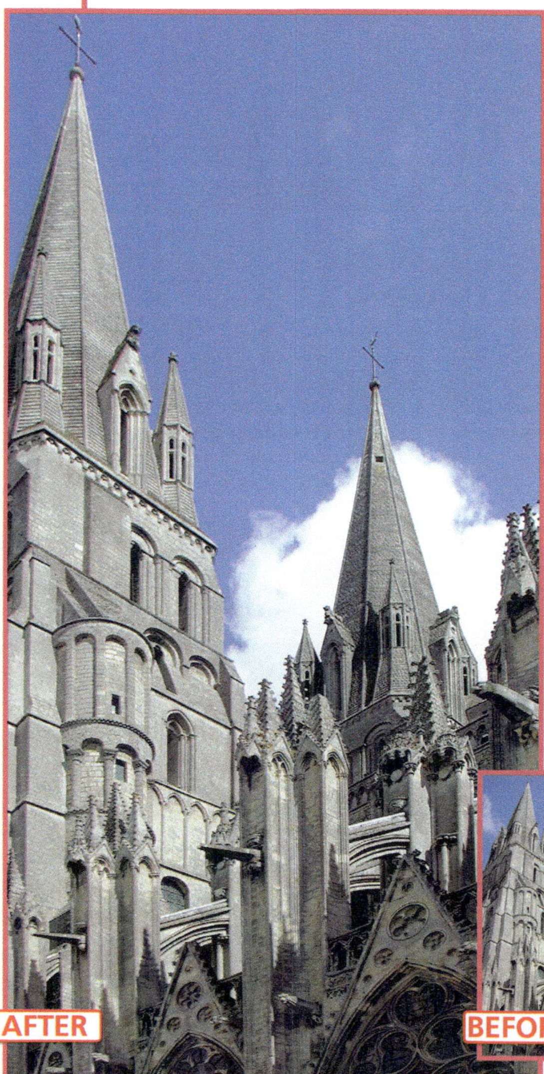

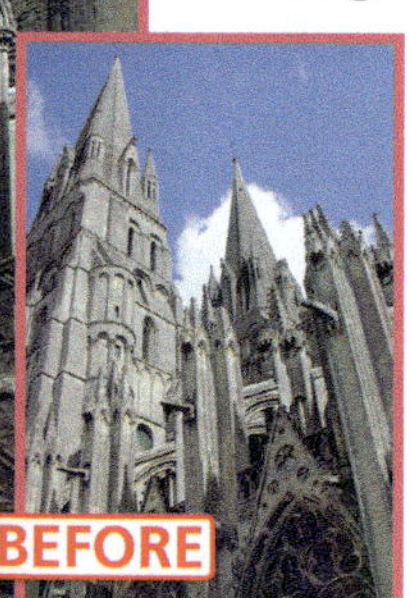

Correcting perspective >> *When shooting upwards with a wide angle lens the sides of buildings converge inwards rather than remain parallel. You can correct this problem using the new Correct Camera Distortion filter from Elements 5.0.*

DARKROOM TECHNIQUES ON THE DESKTOP

With the offending image open in the Full Edit workspace select Filter > Correct Camera Distortion. Ensure that the Grid option is switched on via the checkbox at the bottom of the dialog before starting to correct the photo. The dialog contains a variety of controls designed for correcting barrel and pincushion distortion, vertical and horizontal perspective, crooked horizons and the vignetting or the darkening of the corners of the picture frame. The key to using the feature is being able to identify the type of distortion that is present in the photo and then choosing the control to deal with the problem. The presence of a preview window means that you can see the results of the corrections as you apply them. Use the grid to guide your changes.

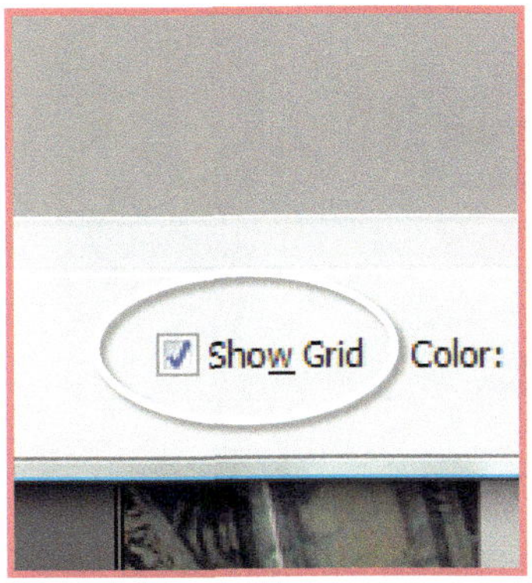

Step 1 >> *With the example image open in the Full Edit space of Elements select Filter > Correct Camera Distortion. Ensure that the Show Grid option at the bottom of the dialog is checked.*

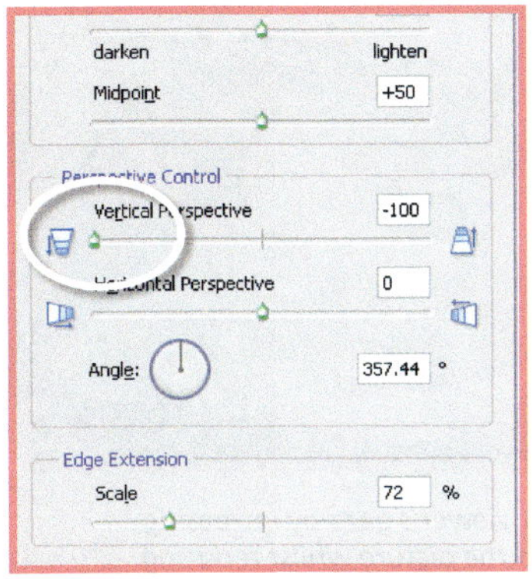

Step 2 >> *The main problem with the example image is converging verticals which can be corrected by moving the Vertical Perspective control to the left. Unlike the correction techniques in earlier versions of Elements this slider also adjusts the height of the building as well.*

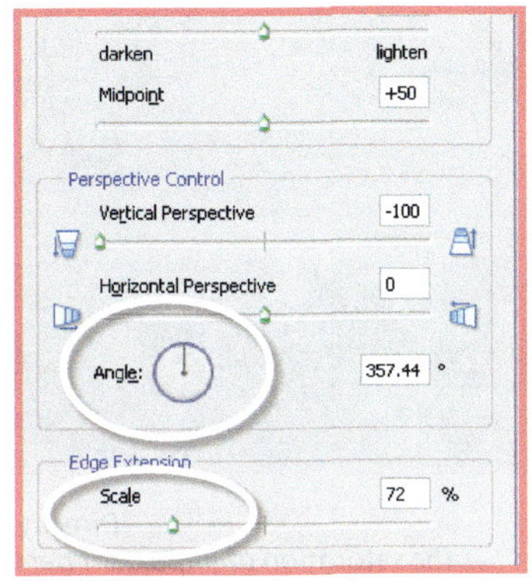

Step 3 >> *To complete the corrections straighten the photo with the Angle control and scale the results so that they fit within the original canvas area. Click OK to apply the changes and close the dialog – then use the Crop tool to remove unwanted areas of the photo.*

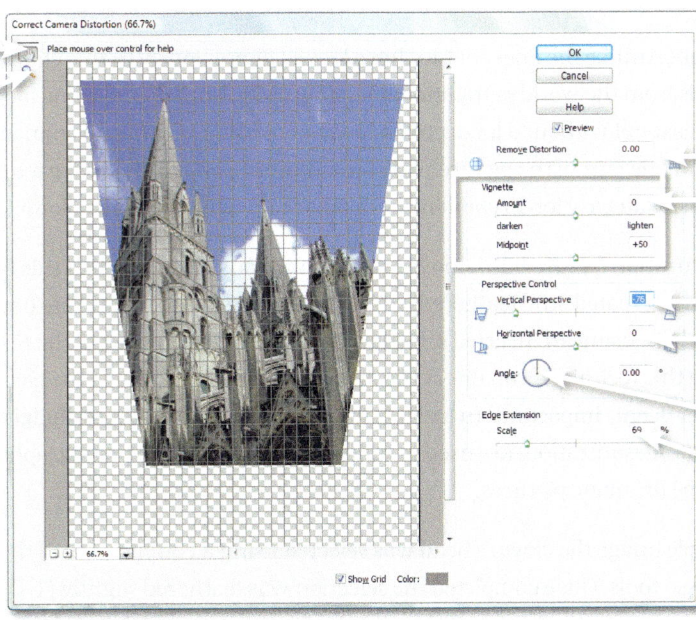

Lens correction >> *The new Correct Camera Distortion filter provides a variety of controls for correcting the distortion that results from tilting the camera or using a wide angle lens.*

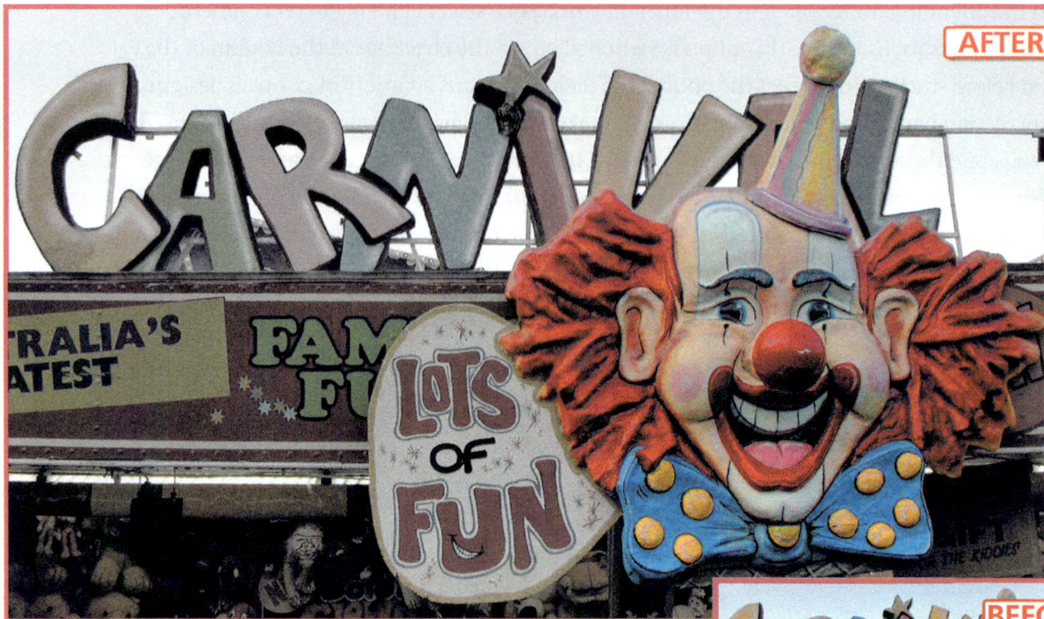

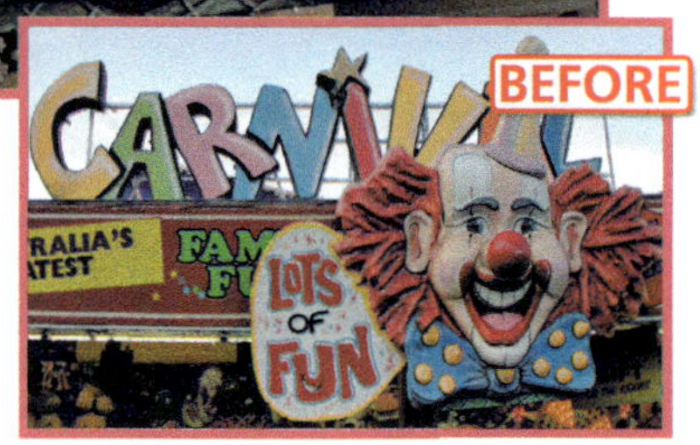

Desaturate/saturate >> *Direct your viewer's gaze by increasing the saturation of important parts of the picture whilst reducing the color vibrancy of the rest of the image.*

7.06 Add emphasis with saturation

Suitable for Elements – 7.0, 6.0, 5.0, 4.0, 3.0, 2.0, 1.0 | Difficulty level – Basic | Resources – Web image 706
Tools used – Selection tools | Menus used – Enhance, Select

This technique, unlike the ones that we have looked at previously in this chapter, does not draw easy parallels from the world of traditional photography. Until digital came along it was not possible, at least not without a lot of professional smoke and mirrors, to change the vibrancy of the color in one part of the picture whilst maintaining or even boosting it in another part. It certainly wasn't an easy job to combine both black and white and full color in a single picture.

The Hue/Saturation feature has removed such limitations forever. When this tool is combined with a carefully created (and feathered) selection it is possible to desaturate one part of the picture and then, using an inverted selection, increase the saturation of the rest. Like dodging and burning this technique can direct the viewer's interest to a part of the picture that the photographer deems important. In fact it is when these two techniques, dodging and burning and saturation/desaturation, are used in tandem that the desktop photographer can really start to create some dramatic pictures.

In the example image the clown's head was selected using a combination of the Magnetic and standard Lasso tools. Once completed the selection was feathered slightly (1–2 pixels) (Select > Feather) to soften the transition of the effect and saved (Select > Save Selection). With the selection still active the Hue/Saturation feature was opened and the color vibrancy of the clown increased by moving the Saturation slider to the right. To add more contrast, the selection was then inverted (Select > Inverse) and the saturation of the background was decreased almost to the point of just being black and white. An alternative way of working this technique is to create masked Hue/Saturation adjustment layers using the saved selection. This would allow you to readjust the amount of saturation and desaturation at any point later in time and would keep the original picture intact.

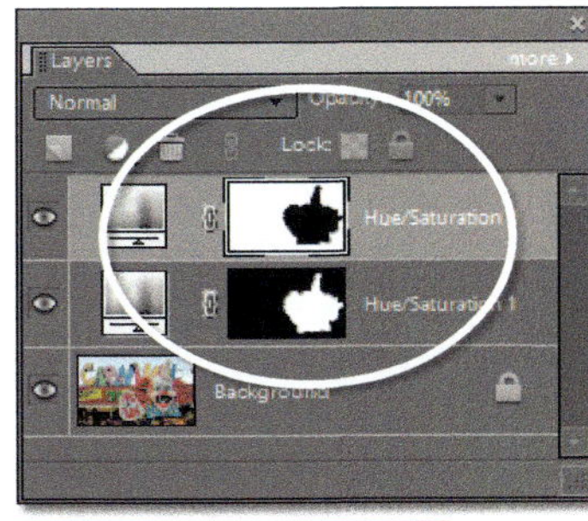

Non-destructive version >> *Use masked Hue/Saturation layers to produce the same results with fine-tuning options.*

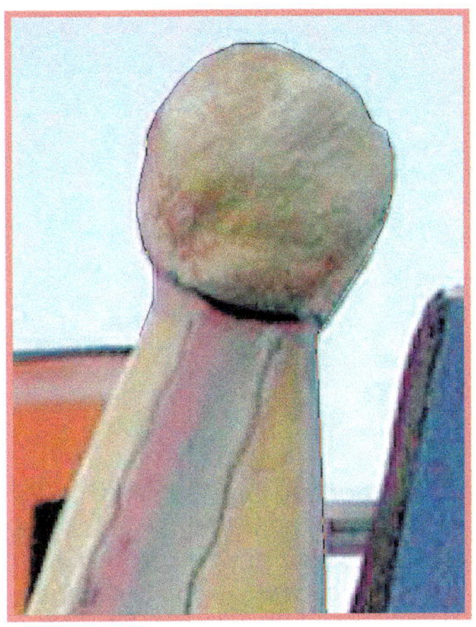

Step 1 >> *Carefully select the area to saturate/desaturate using your favorite selection tools.*

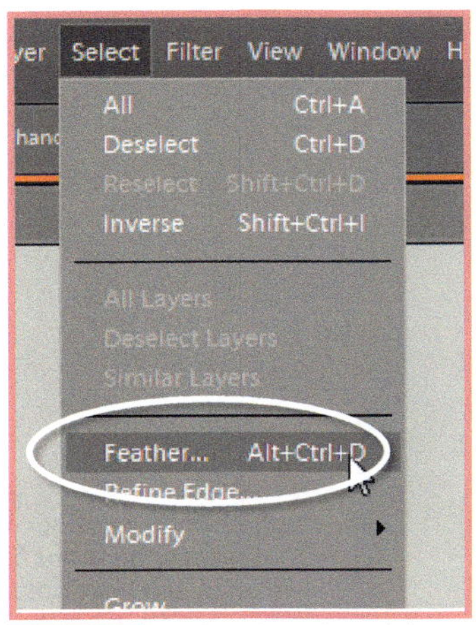

Step 2 >> *Feather the edge of the selection slightly so that the transition will be smoother.*

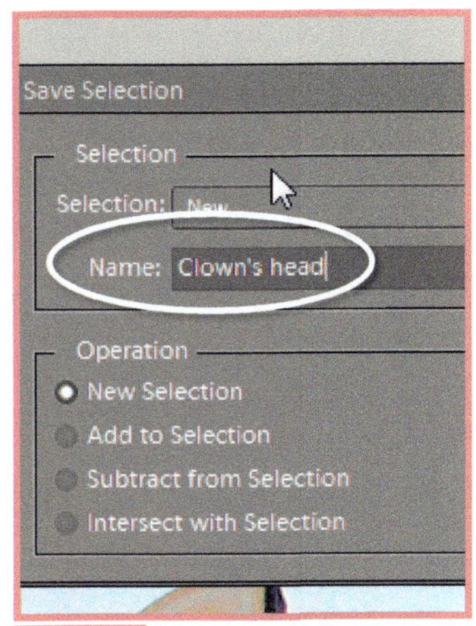

Step 3 >> *Save the selection so that you can use it or edit it later.*

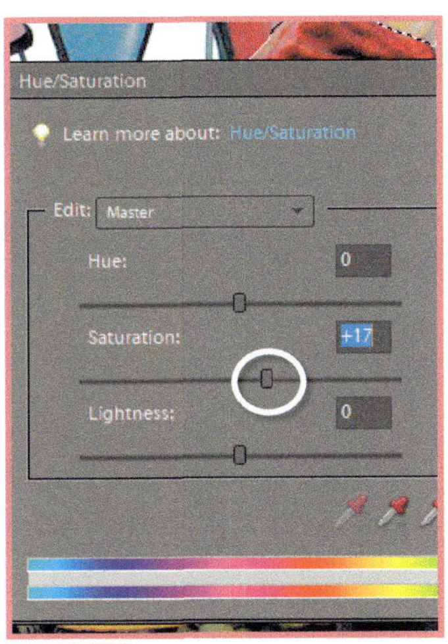

Step 4 >> *With the selection still active use the Hue/Saturation feature to increase the saturation of the clown's face.*

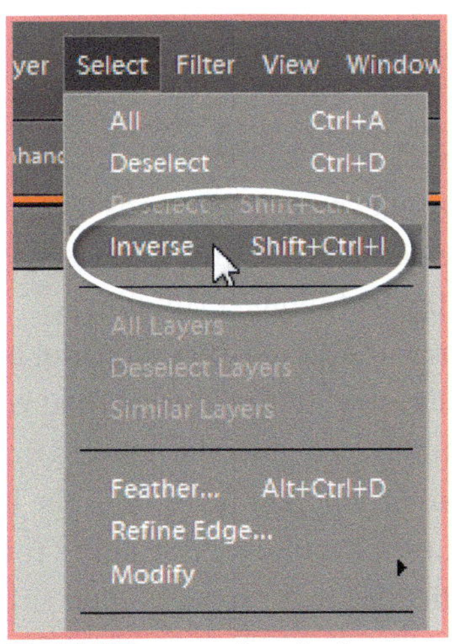

Step 5 >> *Inverse the selection so that the rest of the picture is now selected.*

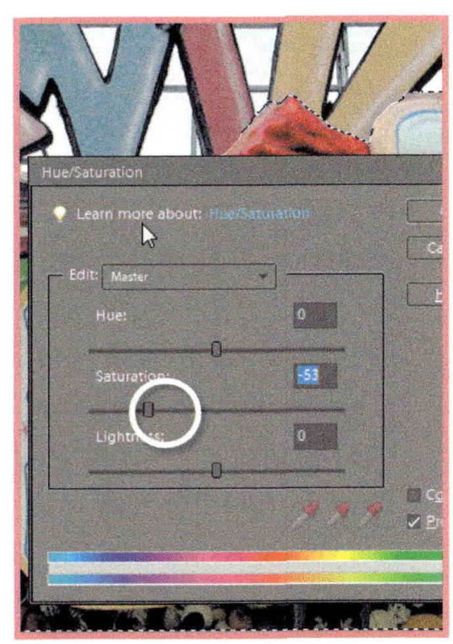

Step 6 >> *Use the Hue/Saturation slider to decrease the saturation and provide color contrast between the two picture parts.*

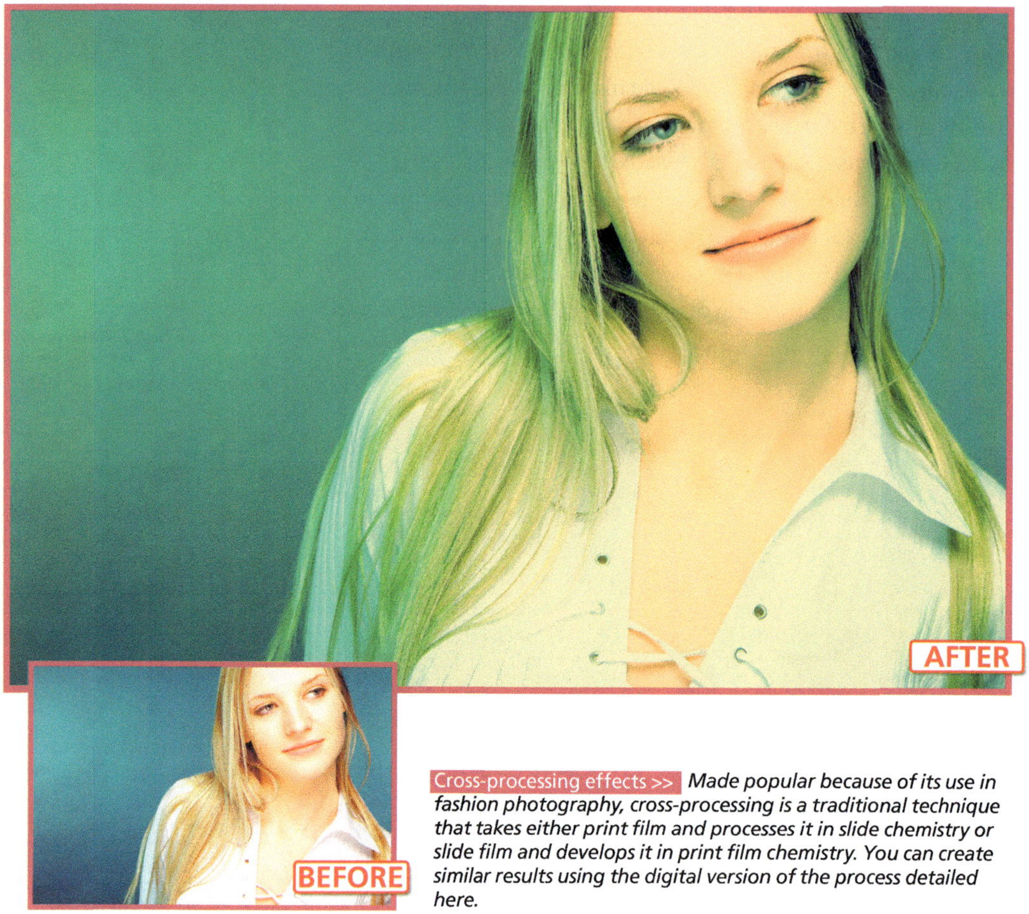

Cross-processing effects >> *Made popular because of its use in fashion photography, cross-processing is a traditional technique that takes either print film and processes it in slide chemistry or slide film and develops it in print film chemistry. You can create similar results using the digital version of the process detailed here.*

7.08 Cross-processing effects

Suitable for Elements – 7.0, 6.0, 5.0, 4.0, 3.0, 2.0, 1.0 | Difficulty level – Intermediate | Resources – Web image 708 | Menus used – Enhance

Processing your film in the wrong chemistry sounds like an action that will guarantee disaster, but this is precisely the basis of the cross-processing technique. Print film is developed using slide chemistry or alternatively slide film is processed using print film chemistry. Whichever method you use the process results in distinctly recognizable images that have found their way into many fashion magazines in the last few years. As with many of these alternative techniques the process can be a little unpredictable, with strange color shifts and massive under- and overexposure problems, reducing the number of usable pictures resulting from any shooting session.

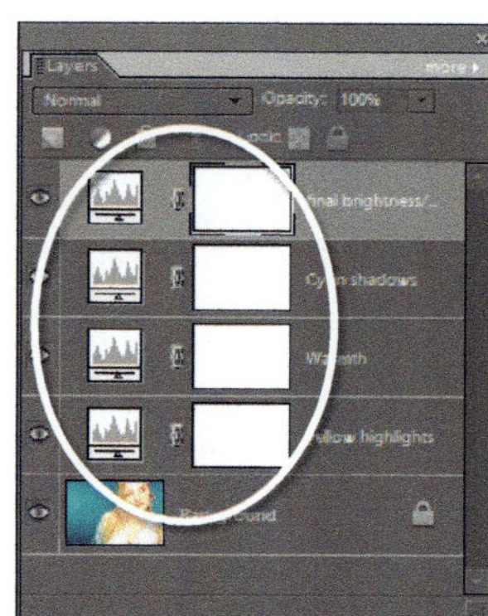

Four adjustment layers >> *This technique relies on the application of four different adjustment layers being stacked upon the original image.*

Martin Evening of 'Adobe Photoshop for Photographers' Focal Press fame created a digital version of this process that uses a series of curve changes to create images that have a similar look and feel to those produced with the chemical cross-processing effect. Here I present an Elements-friendly version of the technique that provides equally impressive results without using the Photoshop curves feature. In addition, as the technique uses a series of adjustment layers to create the effect, the original picture remains unaltered throughout and the settings for each of the layers can be altered at any time to tweak the final result.

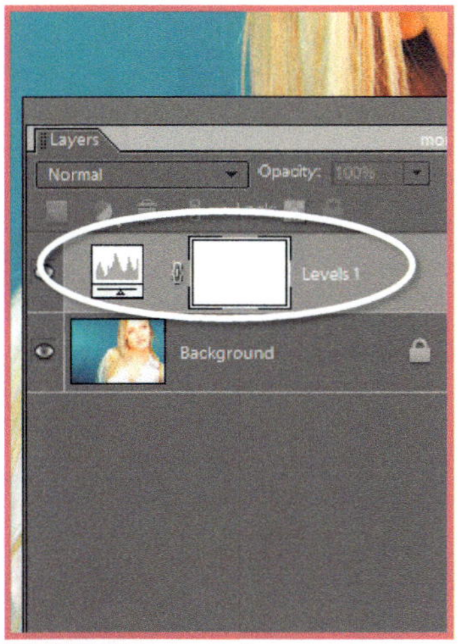

Step 1 >> *To start the process open a color image and create a Levels adjustment layer.*

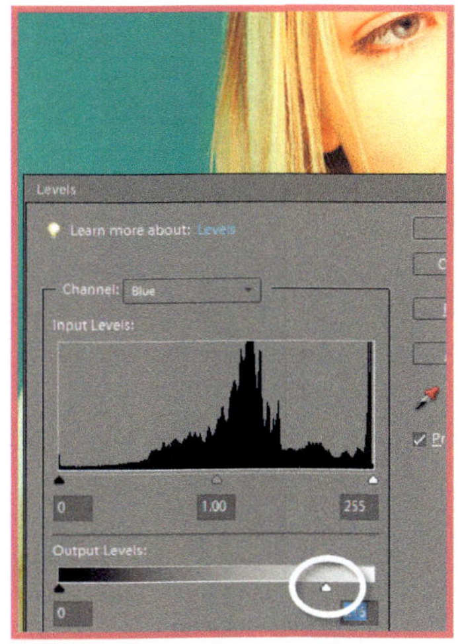

Step 2 >> *To make the yellow highlights select the blue channel in the Levels feature and drag down the white Output slider. This adds some yellow to the highlights.*

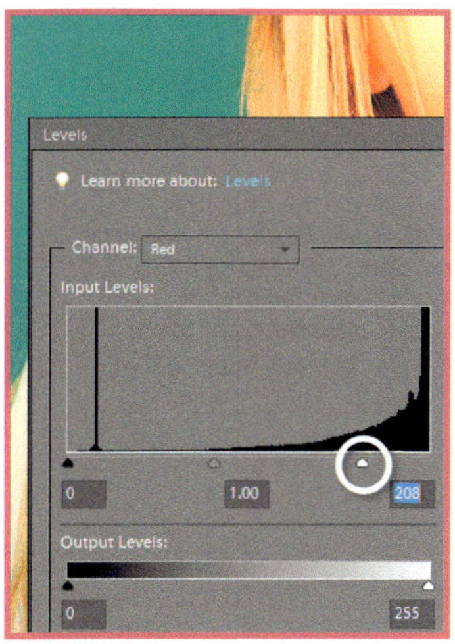

Step 3 >> *Create another Levels adjustment layer, select the red channel and drag down the white input layer. This adds some warmth to the highlights.*

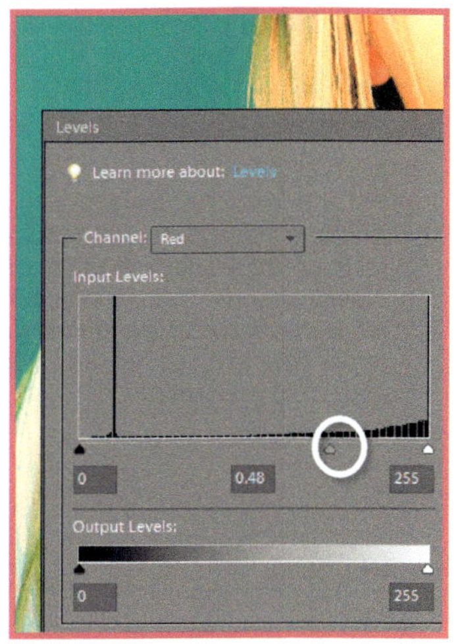

Step 4 >> *To add cyan to the shadow areas create another Levels adjustment layer, select the red channel and move the midtone Input slider to the right.*

To recreate the look of cross-processing (print film developed in slide chemistry) we must change the image so that it contains creamy highlights, cyan shadows and is generally reduced in contrast. Start with a standard color image. Create a Levels adjustment layer and select the blue channel. Move the white Output slider to the left to flatten the highlights and color them yellow. Create a second Levels adjustment layer and with the red channel selected move the white Output slider to the left as well. This adds some warmth. Next create another Levels adjustment layer and select the red channel again. This time you need to move the mid point Input slider to the right to make the shadows and midtones cyan. With the Levels feature still open, and the red channel still selected, move the white and black Input sliders until they meet the first group of pixels in the histogram. To fine-tune the overall tones you can add yet another Levels adjustment layer and with the composite of all channels selected (RGB), alter contrast and brightness of the whole picture.

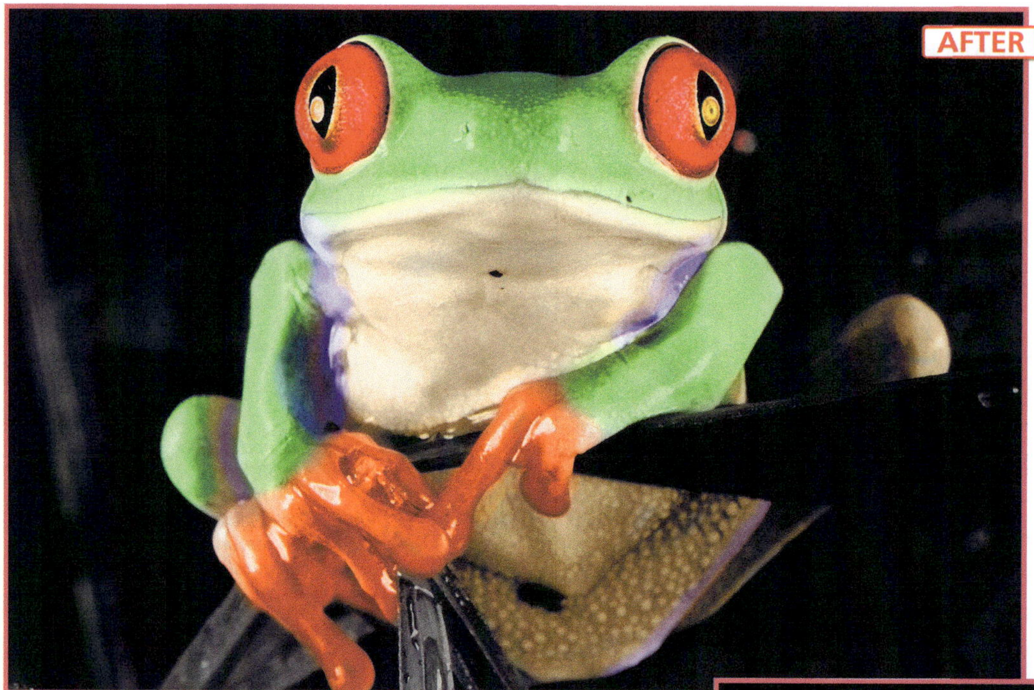

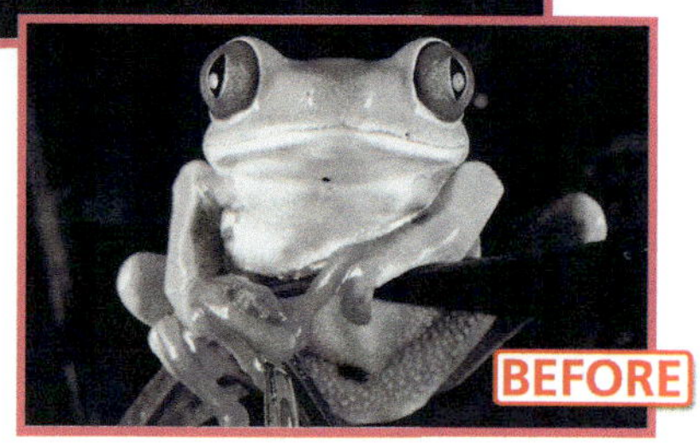

Hand coloring >> *Digital hand coloring works by applying painted sections of the image to the black and white original using the Color blending mode. This technique preserves the detail of the monochrome picture and tints the surface with the color of the upper layer in much the same way as oil paint was used to tint black and white prints of old.*

7.09 Digital hand coloring

Suitable for Elements – 7.0, 6.0, 5.0, 4.0, 3.0, 2.0, 1.0 | Difficulty level – Basic | Resources – Web image 709
Tools used – Brush | Menus used – Layer

Before the advent of color film the only way to add a hue to a picture was to apply water- or oil-based paints over the top of a black and white print. Most of us will have old photographs of family weddings that are delicately colored in this way. There is a simplicity and subtlety about this approach that is worth recapturing in the digital age.

If you look at the old images you will notice that the detail of the black and white picture shows through the colored paint. The combination of these details and the applied color creates the hand colored effect. To simulate this technique digitally we can use the Color blending mode in Elements. The color is applied to a separate layer using the paint brush and then the mode of the layer is changed to Color. This allows the details of the image beneath to show through the color above. Using the paint brush in the Normal mode will create large flat areas of color that hide the detail beneath.

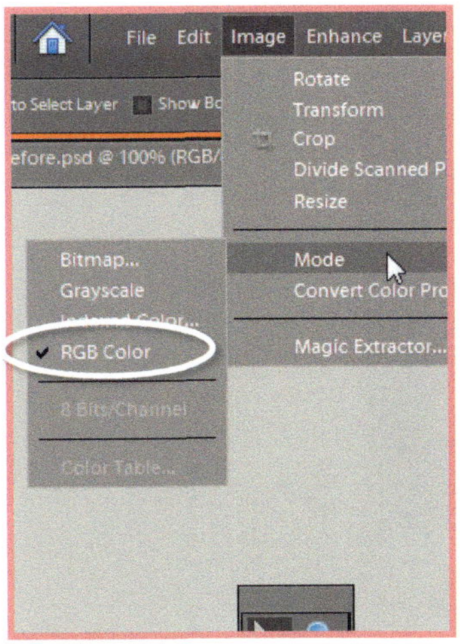

Step 1 >> *Open a black and white picture and make sure that it is in RGB color mode. Make a new layer in the document.*

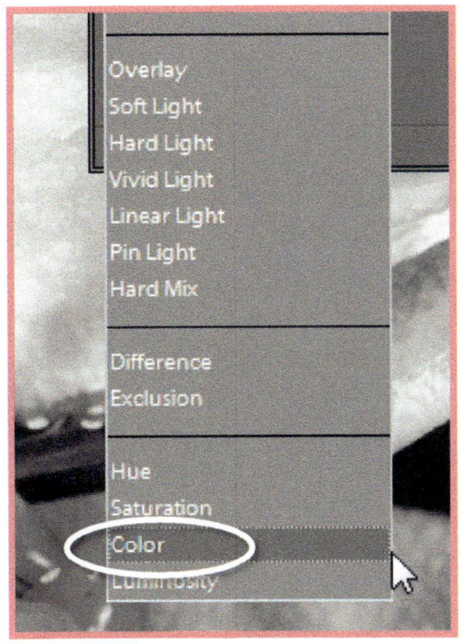

Step 2 >> *Select the layer and change its Blending mode to Color.*

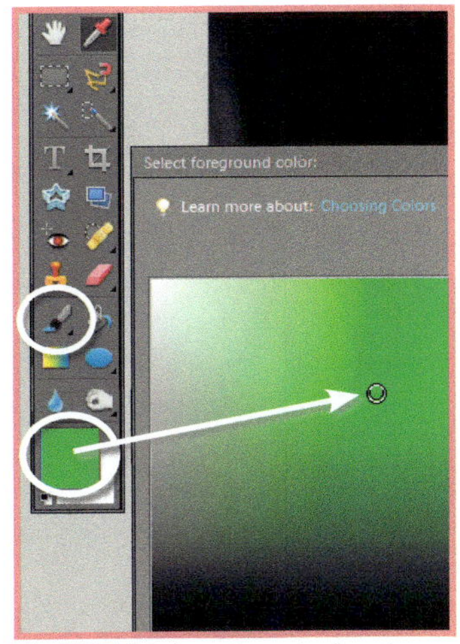

Step 3 >> *Select the paint brush from the tool box and then select a foreground color to paint with from the Swatches palette.*

The color can be removed from any part of the picture with the eraser tool and the vibrancy of the hues can be altered by changing the opacity of the color layer.

For the ultimate control each individual color can be added via a new layer. This approach means that the various colors that make up the picture can be edited individually.

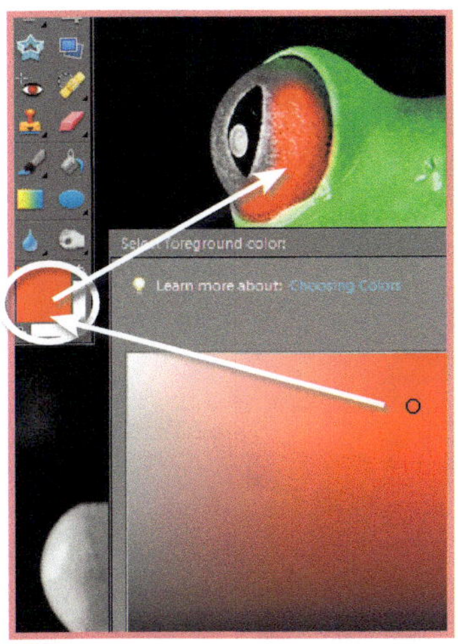

Step 4 >> *Paint over the area of the image that you want to hand color. Switch foreground colors and continue to paint.*

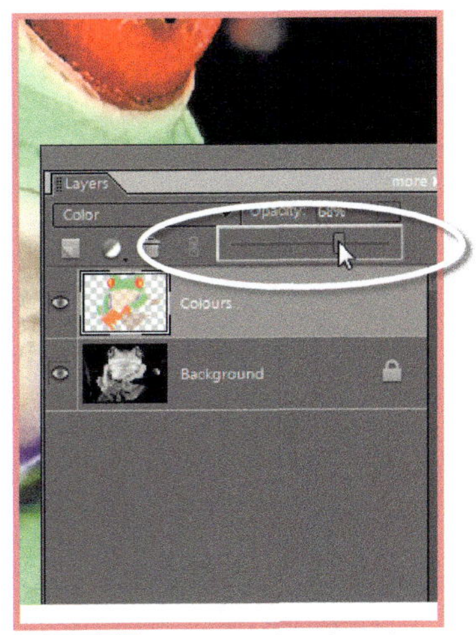

Step 5 >> *Make sure that the colors are being applied to the newly created layer. The strength of the coloring can be altered by adjusting the opacity of the layer.*

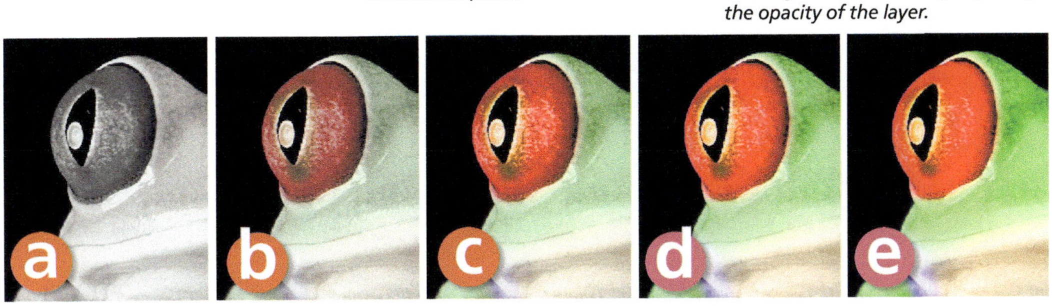

Hand coloring >> *Changing the opacity of the color layer will alter the strength of the hand coloring effect. (a) 0% opacity. (b) 25% opacity. (c) 50% opacity. (d) 75% opacity. (e) 100% opacity.*

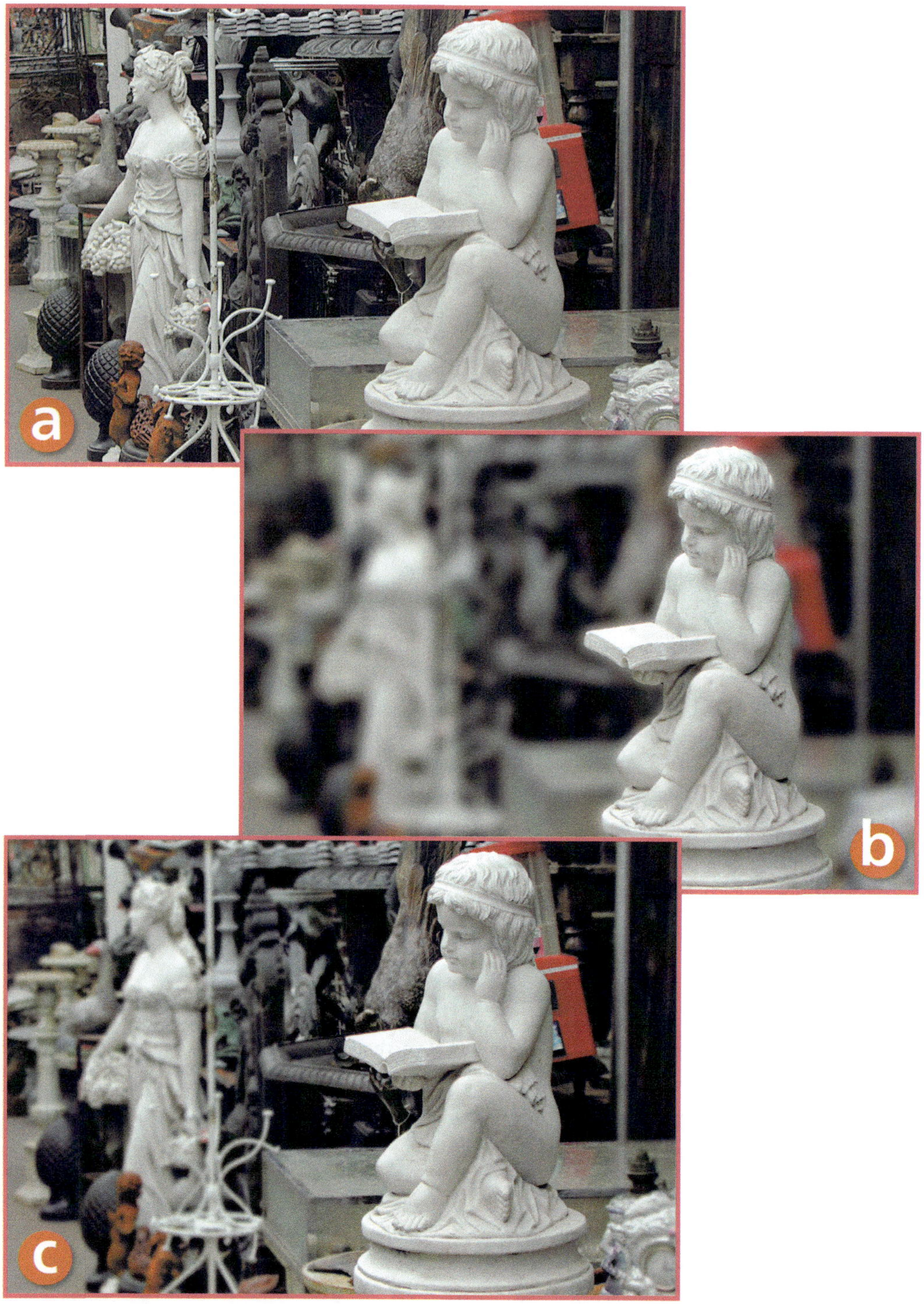

Artificial depth of field effects >>

It is possible to create realistic depth of field effects by making and blurring a series of selections that gradually increase in size. (a) Straight print. (b) Simple selection with Gaussian Blur. (c) Multiple selections with increasing Gaussian Blur values.

7.10 Realistic depth of field effects

Suitable for Elements – 7.0, 6.0, 5.0, 4.0, 3.0, 2.0, 1.0 | Difficulty level – Advanced
Resources – Web image 710 | Tools used – Selection tools | Menus used – Filter, Select

The shallow depth of field effect that is created when you select a small F-stop number (use a long lens or get in very close to your subject) controls the way that a viewer sees your picture. The eye is naturally drawn to the sharpest part of the image and shallow depth of field restricts the sharpness in a photograph to often only a single subject. The Gaussian Blur filter can be used in a similar way to produce results that help to direct the viewer's gaze. Areas of an image can be selected and blurred so that our eyes will be redirected to the sharp part of the print. In a way, by blurring parts of an otherwise sharp picture, this process is creating artificial depth of field.

When the potential of the Blur filter is first discovered many enthusiastic digital photographers take to the task of creating shallow DOF pictures from their sharp originals with gusto. The process they use is simple – select and blur. The results certainly provide a contrast in sharpness, but the pictures lack the sense of realism that is needed for the effect to be truly convincing.

To recreate shallow depth of field more effectively there needs to be a gradual decrease in sharpness as you move in front of, or behind, the main point of focus. Making a single selection doesn't provide the gradual change that is needed. In its place we need to use a series of overlapping selections that gradually move further away from the point of focus. Each selection is feathered to smooth the transition of the effect and then the selected area is blurred using the Gaussian Blur filter. The amount of blur is increased as the selection gets more distant from the point of focus.

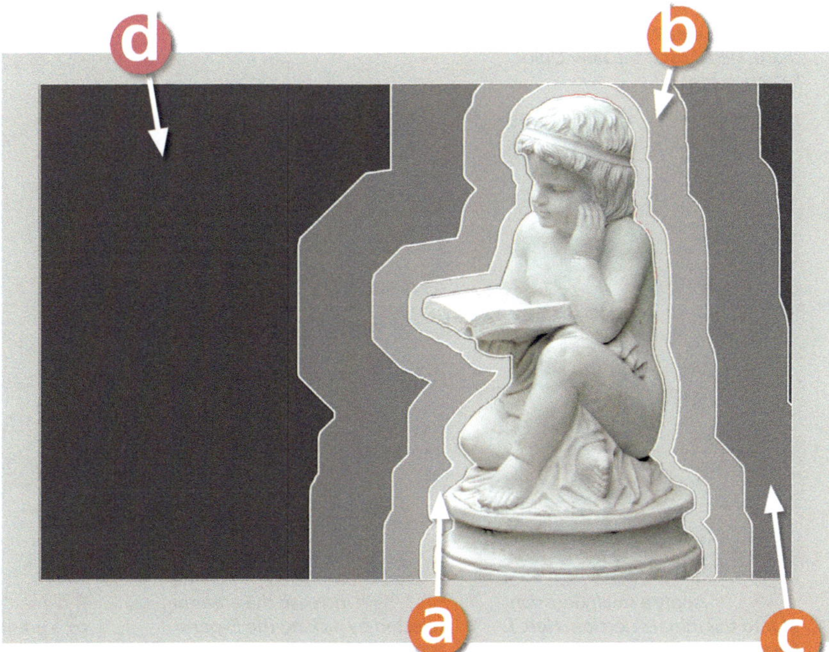

Multiple selections >>
Convincing depth of field effects are based on the sequential blurring of multiple overlapping selections.

(a) First selection.
(b) Second selection.
(c) Third selection.
(d) Fourth selection.

This simulates lens-based depth of field by surrounding the point of focus with the area of least blur and then gradually increasing the out of focus effect as the eye moves further from this part of the picture.

Start the process by creating a selection of the subject area that you want to remain sharp. Feather (Select > Feather) the edge slightly to ensure that the transition between blurred and sharp picture parts is less obvious. Inverse (Select > Inverse) the selection so that the rest of the picture is selected. Apply the Gaussian Blur filter (Filter > Blur > Gaussian Blur) to the selection

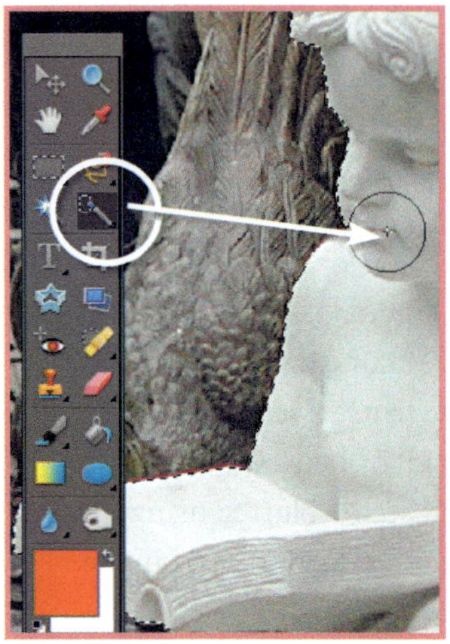

Step 1 >> *Carefully select the part of the picture that is to be your point of focus – the area that will remain sharp. Here I used the new Quick Selection tool.*

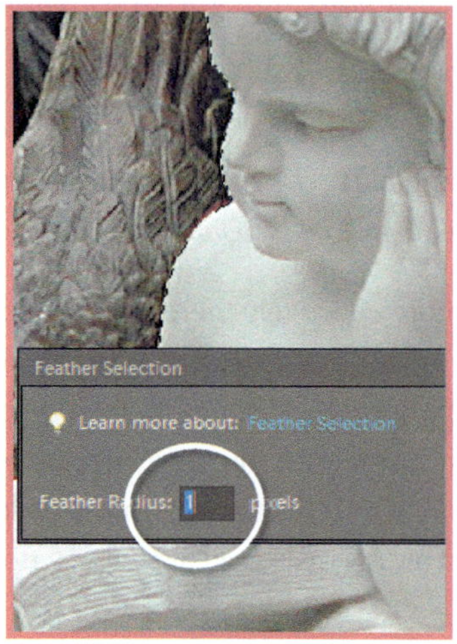

Step 2 >> *Feather (1 or 2 pixels) and then save the selection.*

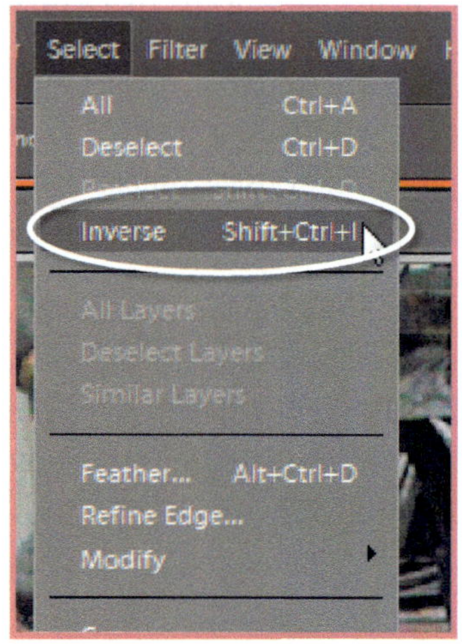

Step 3 >> *Use the Inverse command to select the rest of the picture.*

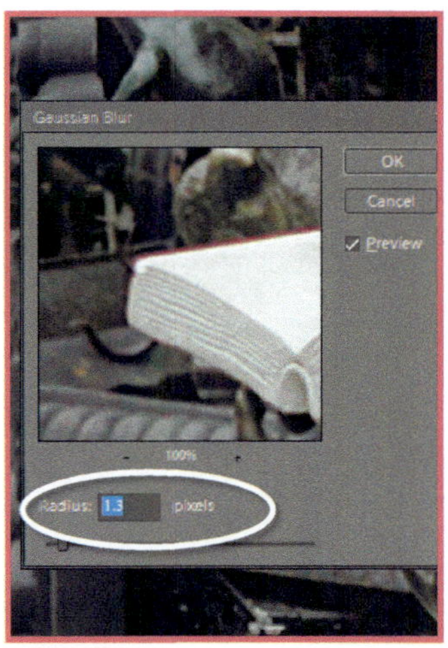

Step 4 >> *Apply a small Gaussian Blur to this initial selection. Here I have used a radius of 1.0 pixels. Inverse the selection again.*

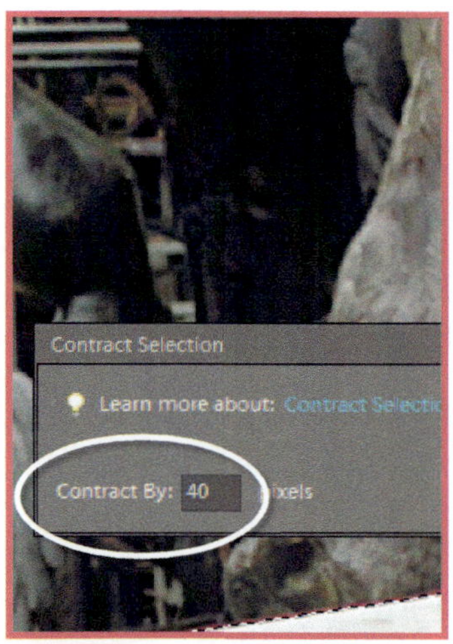

Step 5 >> *Increase the area that is selected by picking the Expand command from the Select > Modify menu. Inverse the selection again.*

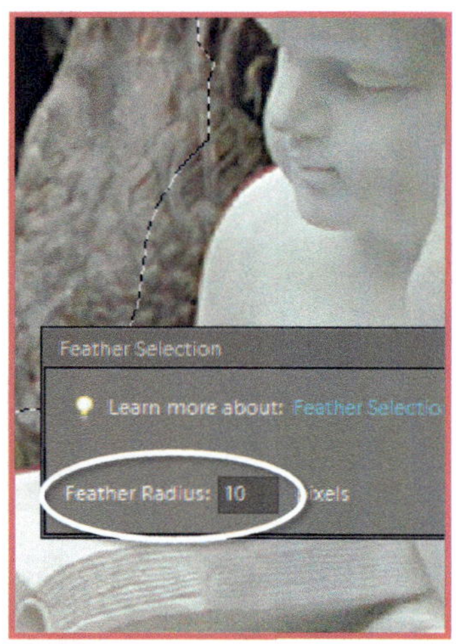

Step 6 >> *Feather the new selection by a greater amount. Here I have used 10 pixels. Save the selection.*

using a low Radius value of 1 pixel. Now to recede the selection away from the point of focus. Here I have used the Contract command (Select > Modify > Contract) but you could just as easily draw another selection that is further away from the statue. The edge is feathered again, this time by a larger amount, and the whole thing blurred with a larger radius.

This process – contract, feather blur – is repeated as many times as is needed to ensure that the picture's background details are suitably unsharp. In the example image I used four selections to get the shallow depth of field effect.

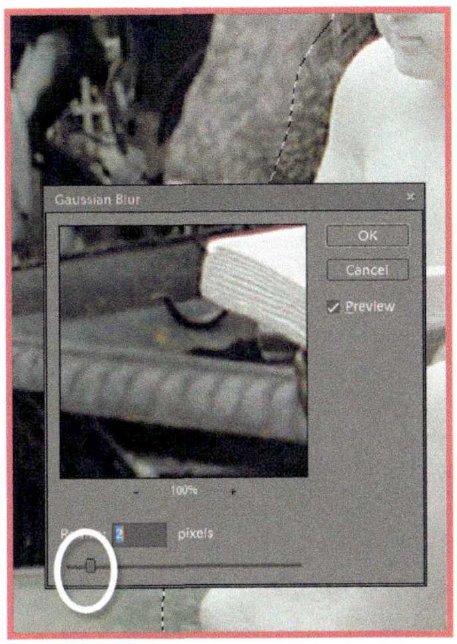

Step 7 >> *Apply a larger Gaussian Blur (2 pixels) to this new section of the picture. Inverse the selection.*

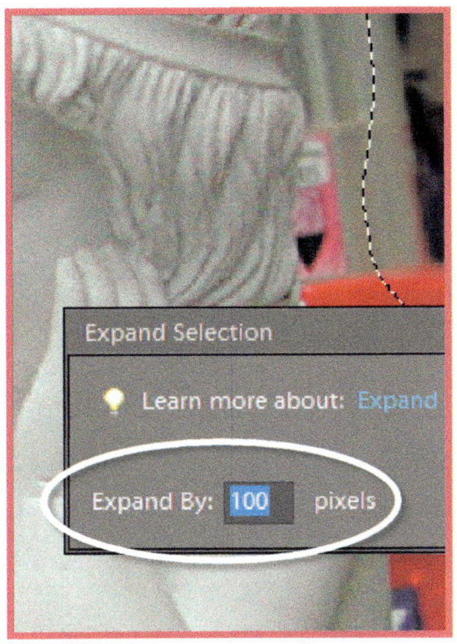

Step 8 >> *Create a new larger selection around the statue using the Expand command set to 100 pixels. Inverse the selection.*

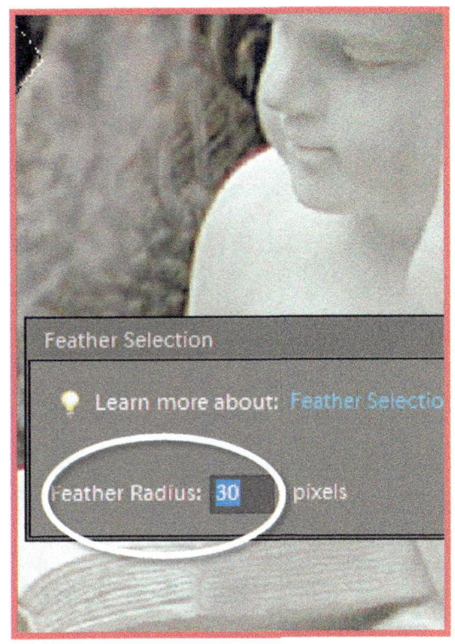

Step 9 >> *Feather and save the new selection. Here I have used a radius of 30 pixels.*

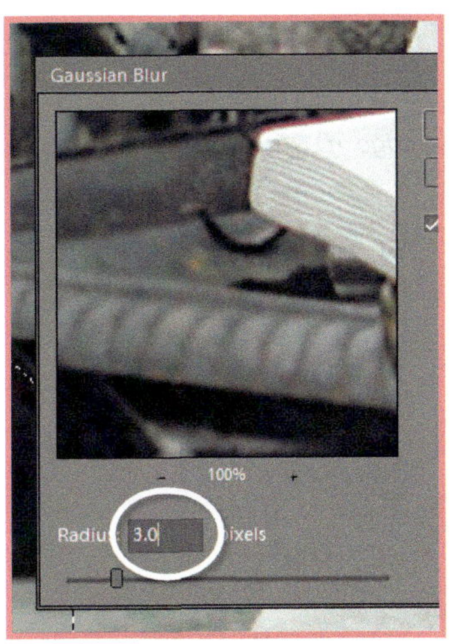

Step 10 >> *Blur the new selection with a higher Gaussian Blur setting. Inverse the selection again.*

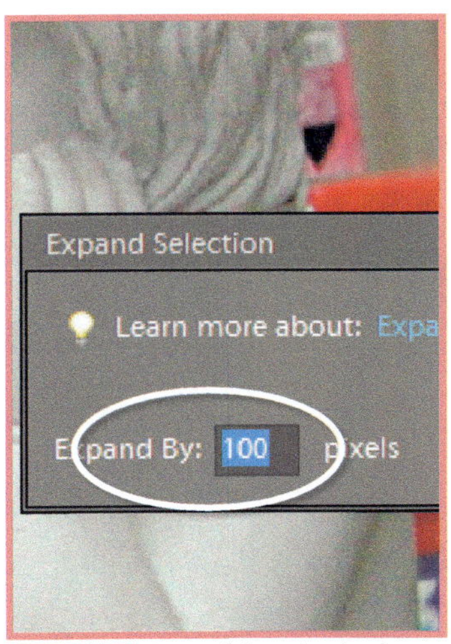

Step 11 >> *Expand the selection by 100 pixels and then again by another 100 pixels before feathering the edge by 60 pixels and saving the selection.*

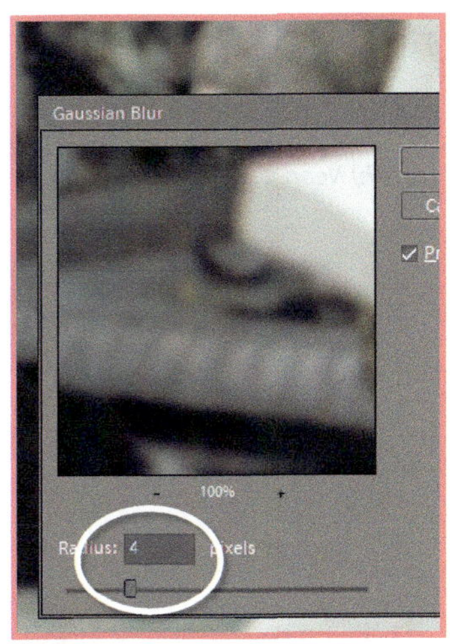

Step 12 >> *Inverse the selection and then apply the final Gaussian Blur to the selection using a radius of 4 pixels.*

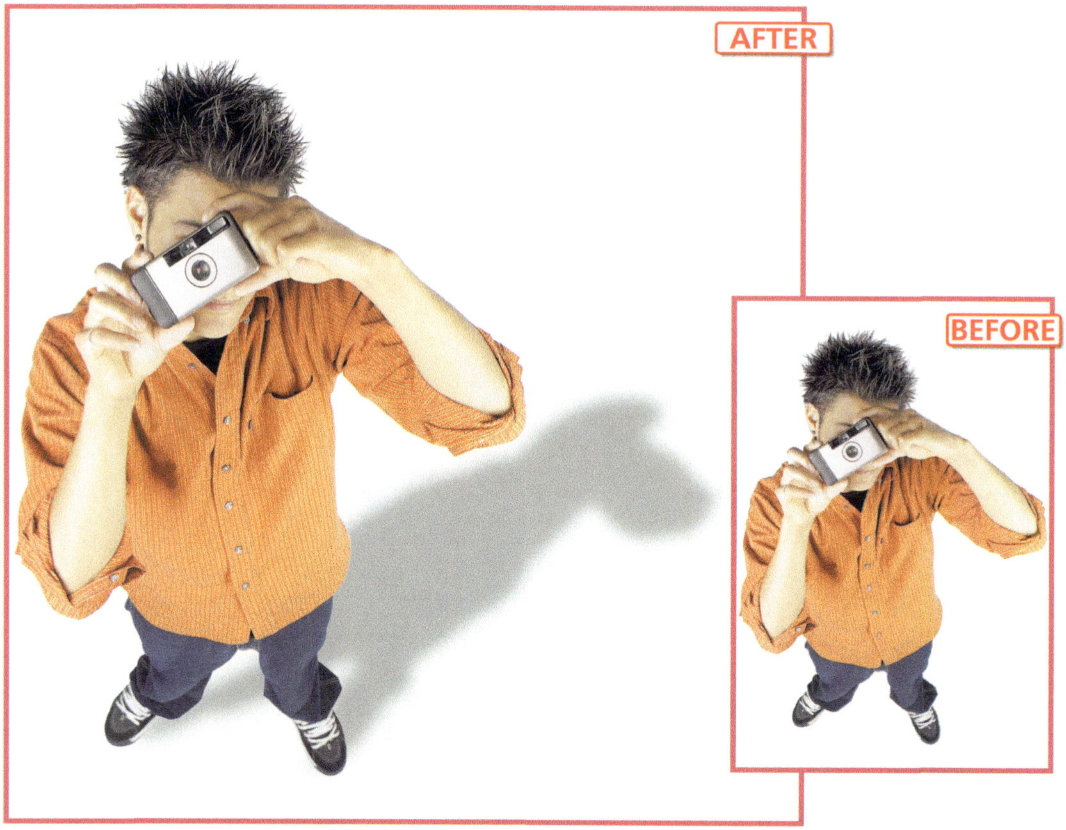

Creating realistic shadows >> *Simple shadows can be applied to any layer using the Drop Shadow options in the Elements Styles palette. More complex shadows, like the one in the example that looks like it is falling on the ground, can be created by making a shadow layer beneath the image.* *Image courtesy of www.ablestock.com. Copyright © 2003 Hamera and its licensors. All rights reserved.*

Elements' drop shadow styles >> *Elements provides a range of ready-made drop shadow styles that can be applied directly to any layer. (a) High. (b) Low. (c) Noisy. (d) Hard edge. (e) Soft edge. (f) Outline. (g) Fill/outline. (h) Neon.*

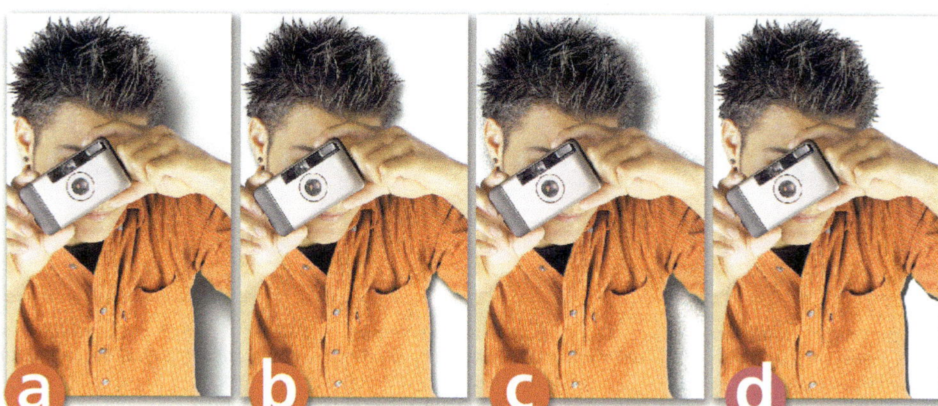

7.11 Beyond the humble drop shadow

Suitable for Elements – 7.0, 6.0, 5.0, 4.0, 3.0, 2.0, 1.0 | Difficulty level – Advanced | Resources – Web image 711
Tools used – Selection tools | Menus used – Edit, Filter, Image

The drop shadow effect has become very popular in the last few years as a way of making an image or some text stand out from the background. To coincide with this popularity Adobe created a series of drop shadow styles that can be applied directly to any layer. These options are suitable for many applications and Elements users can even customize the look of the effect by altering variables like the direction of the light and the shadow distance using the Style Settings dialog (Layer > Layer Style > Style Settings).

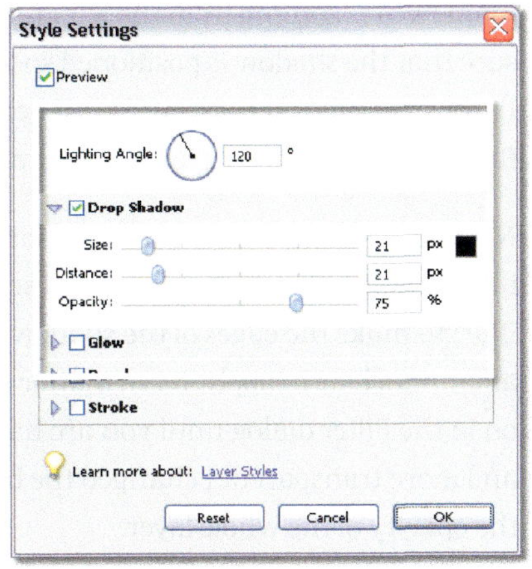

Drop shadow style settings >> *Alter the look of your drop shadows by changing the value of the options in the Style Settings dialog.*

But what if you want a more sophisticated shadow than these preset choices allow? Well then you will need to create your own shadows. Using the example image let's make a shadow that lies upon the ground that the model is standing on. To do so, we will need to revisit the steps that I used to use to create even the simplest drop shadow before the days of layer styles.

First select the subject with one of your favorite selection tools and copy it to memory (Edit > Copy). Next paste the picture (Edit > Paste) twice to form two new layers. Fill the background layer with white. Next fill the second image layer with black making sure that the Preserve Transparency option is turned on. This creates a silhouette exactly the same size and shape as the main picture. To allow for the shadow we will need to create some more space on the right-hand side of the picture. Use the Canvas Size feature for this (Image > Resize > Canvas Size). Here I have anchored the canvas on the left side and set the option to percent and then increased the width to 150%.

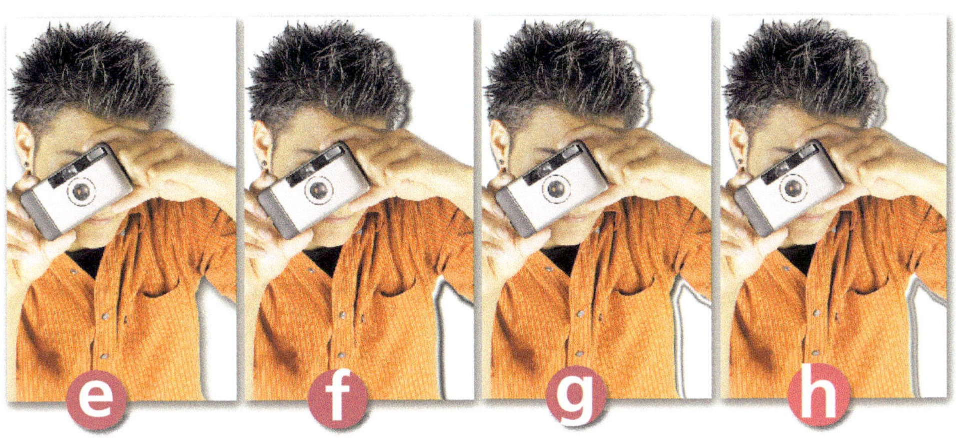

With the shadow layer still selected I used the Distort feature (Image > Transform > Distort) to push the shadow downwards and to the right. Keep in mind that for this type of shadow to be convincing it must be consistent with the lighting in the image generally. In the example the main light is coming from the left and so the shadow should be projected to the right. Also make sure that the shadow is positioned so that it grows from where the subject touches the ground. In the example it is the feet. If need be, use the Move tool and even the Rotate feature (Image > Rotate > Free Rotate Layer) to orientate the shadow so that it meets the shoes.

Next we need to blur the edges of the shadow and adjust its transparency to complete the illusion. With the shadow layer still selected use the Gaussian Blur filter (Filter > Blur > Gaussian Blur) to make the edges of the shadow less sharp. There are no hard and fast rules about the amount of blur to apply. It is a matter of trying a few settings with the Preview option switched on in the Filter dialog until you are happy with the results. To make the shadow a little brighter and more transparent I changed the blending mode from Normal to Multiply and dragged down the opacity of the whole layer.

Although not immediately obvious here, changing the blending mode to Multiply will give a more realistic shadow effect when laid over other picture areas. When used in conjunction with the layer's Opacity slider the density of the shadow can be adjusted to allow the detail from the picture beneath to show through.

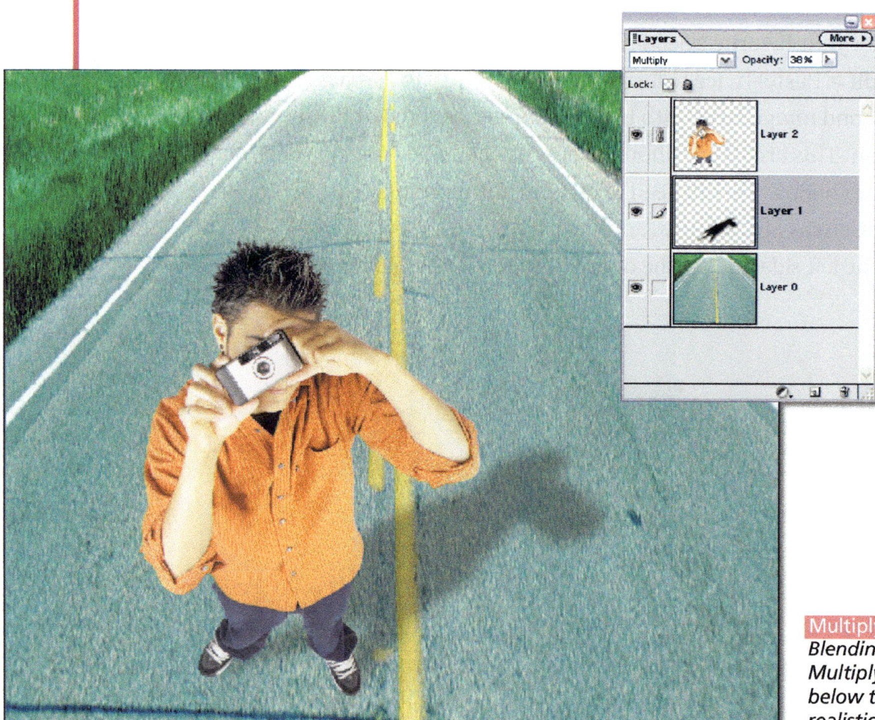

Multiply shadows >> *Switching the Blending mode of the shadow layer to Multiply will allow the detail of the layer below to show through, producing a more realistic effect.*

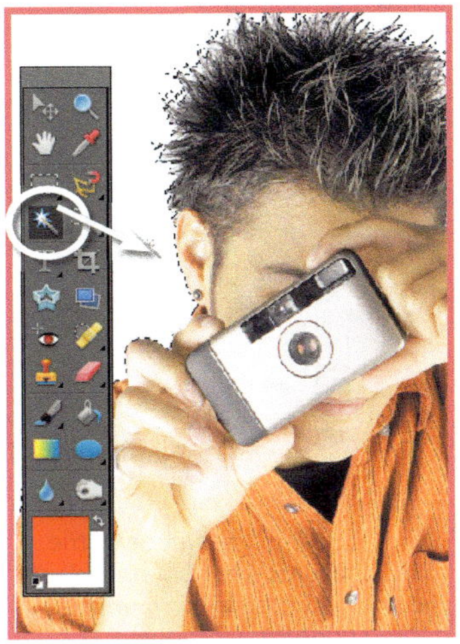

Step 1 >> *Carefully select the main subject using your favorite selection tools. Here it was easier to select the uniform background and adjust the selection around the hair region rather than selecting the model.*

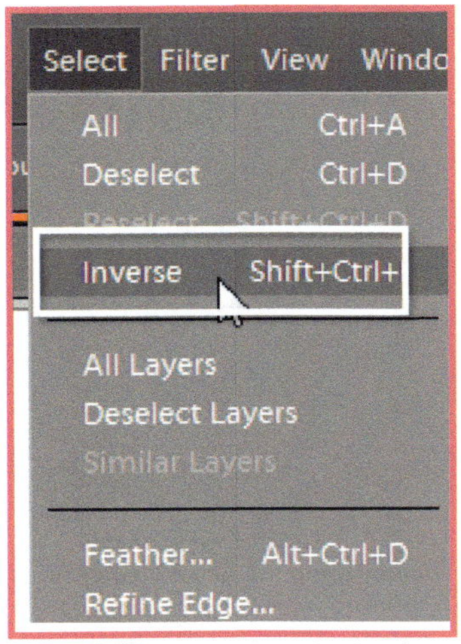

Step 2 >> *Change the selection from the background to the model by inversing the selection.*

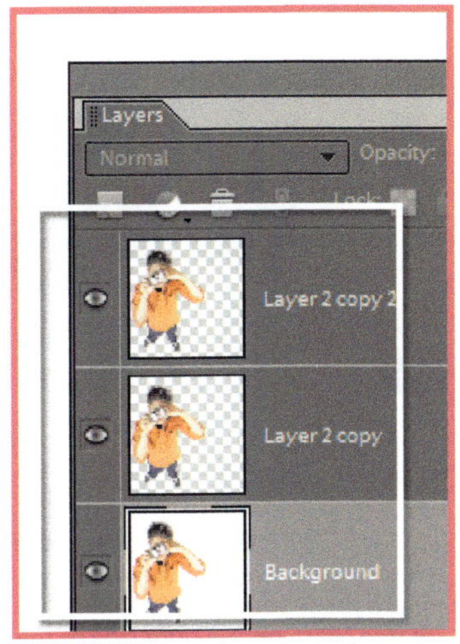

Step 3 >> *Copy the selected area to the computer memory and then paste the contents twice to form two new image layers containing the copied model picture.*

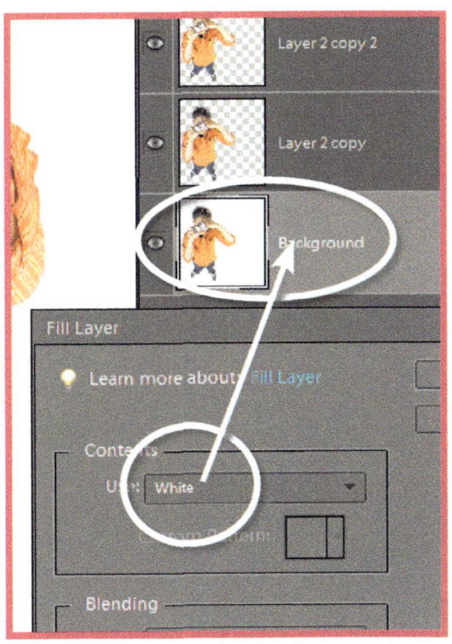

Step 4 >> *Select the background layer and fill it with white.*

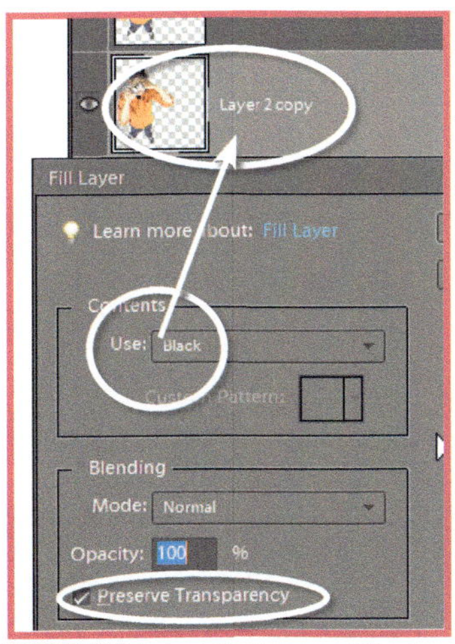

Step 5 >> *Select the lower of the two new layers and fill this layer with black, this time making sure that the Preserve Transparency option is turned on.*

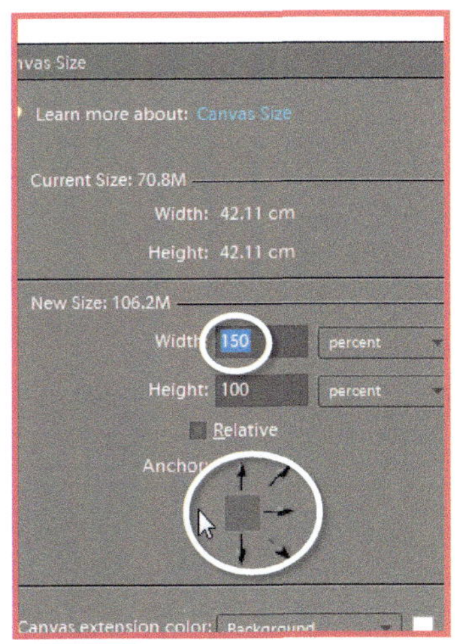

Step 6 >> *Increase the size of the canvas to accommodate the shadow by anchoring the image on the left side and increasing the width by 150%.*

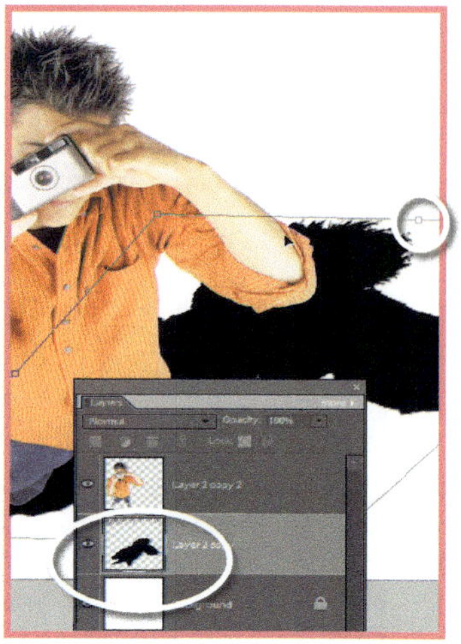

Step 7 >> *With the shadow layer still selected use the Distort tool to squash the shadow into the newly created space on the right side of the model.*

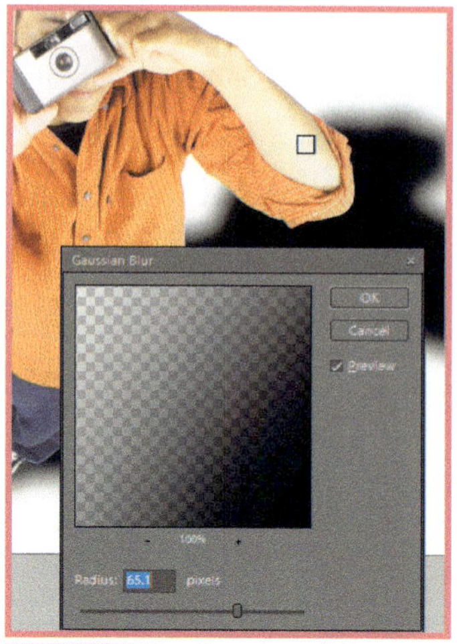

Step 8 >> *Blur the edge of the shadow using the Gaussian Blur filter.*

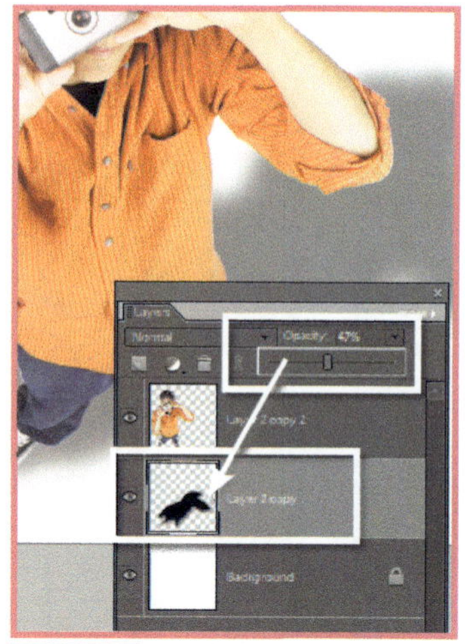

Step 9 >> *Switch the mode of the shadow layer to Multiply and adjust the opacity of the shadow until the desired brightness is shown.*

AFTER

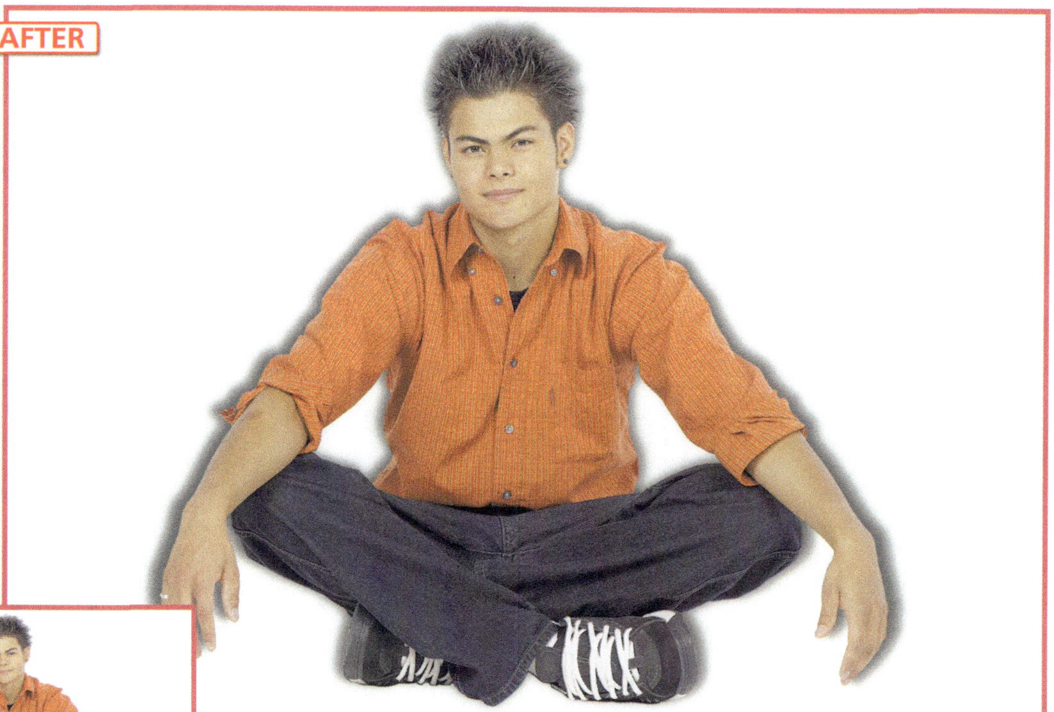

BEFORE

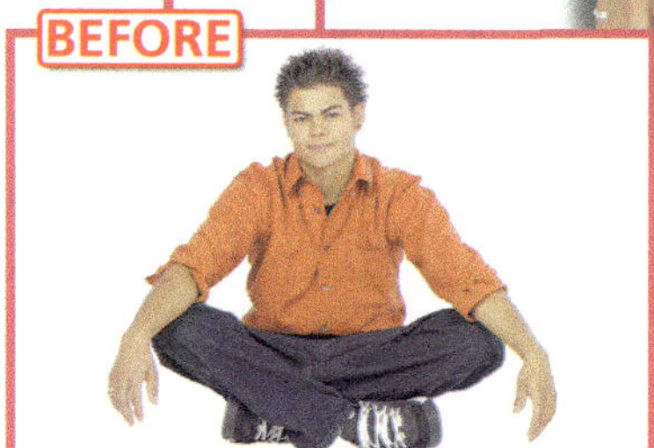

Ring flash shadow >> *You can extend the technique detailed above to allow you to create shadows similar to those created when using a ring flash that surrounds the camera's lens.* *Image courtesy of www.ablestock.com.*

7.12 Ring flash shadow

Suitable for Elements – 7.0, 6.0, 5.0, 4.0, 3.0, 2.0, 1.0 | Difficulty level – Advanced | Resources – Web image 712
Tools used – Selection tools | Menus used – Edit, Filter, Image

You can extend the technique detailed above to create a shadow that is similar to those found in pictures created with a ring flash attached to the camera lens. These pictures are characterized by the model having a shadow projected onto the wall behind. As the light is coming from the same position as the camera the shadow is larger but directly behind the subject.

The first few steps are the same as those found in the previous technique. Start by selecting the main subject and copy and pasting it twice to form two new layers. Next fill the background with white. Select the lower image layer and fill it with black, making sure that the Preserve Transparency option is selected. Blur the shadow using the Gaussian Blur filter (Filter > Blur > Gaussian Blur). With the Preview option selected in the Filter dialog, adjust the Blur Radius so that the edge of the shadow is visible as a halo around the top image layer.

With the shadow layer still selected use the Move tool to shift its location upwards by a few pixels. For accuracy you can use the arrow keys instead of the mouse. Each arrow key press moves the shadow one pixel. To finalize the technique change the blending mode of the shadow to Multiply and reduce its opacity.

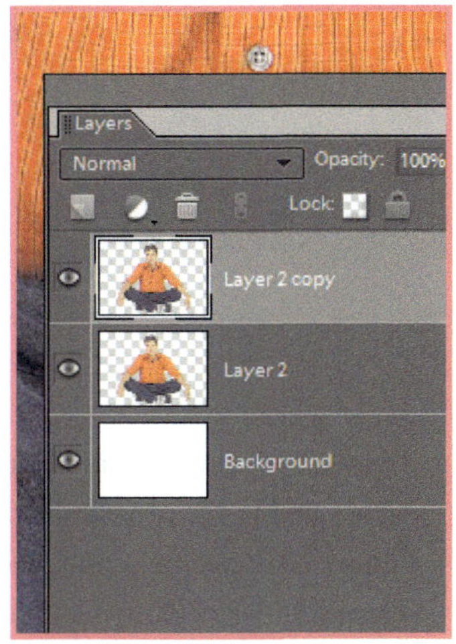

Step 1 >> *Select, copy and paste the model twice to create two image layers. Fill the background with white.*

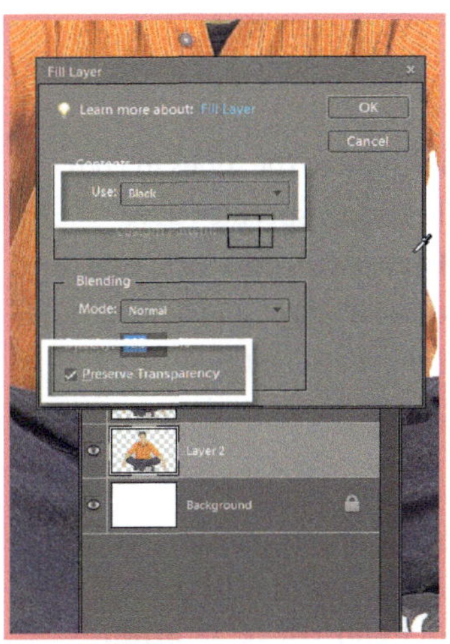

Step 2 >> *Select the lower image layer and fill the image area with black. Make sure that the Preserve Transparency option is selected.*

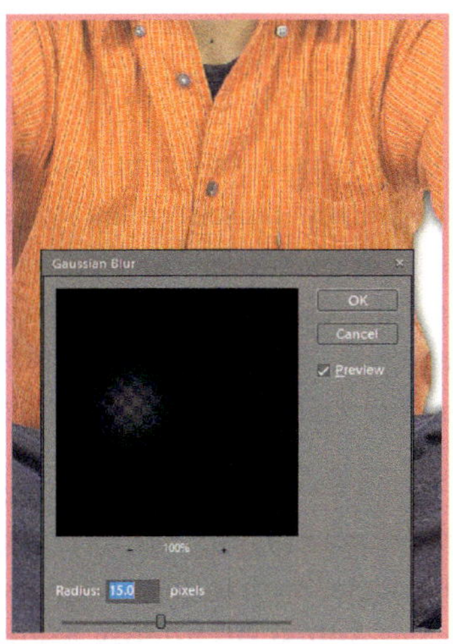

Step 3 >> *Use the Gaussian Blur filter to blur the shadow so that it shows as a halo around the top image layer.*

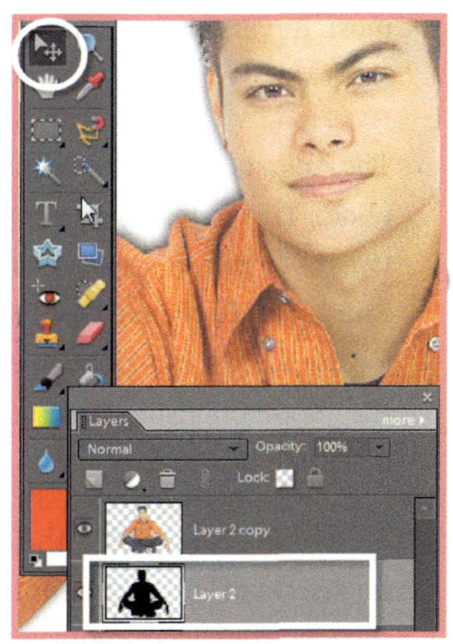

Step 4 >> *Use the arrow keys to move the shadow gradually upwards so that it shows to the left, right and above but not below the model. Change the Blending mode to Multiply and adjust the opacity.*

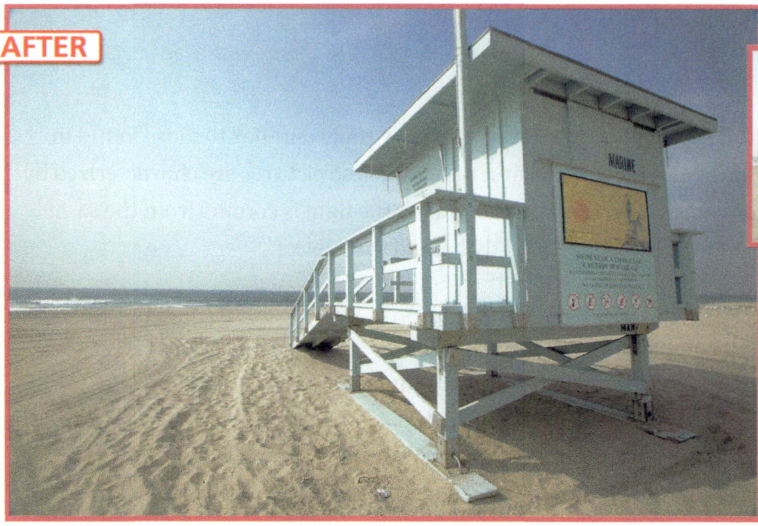

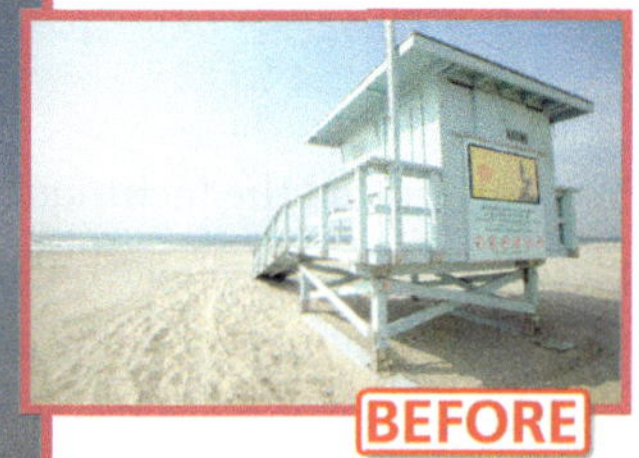

Altering specific tones >>
Images with bright highlights often need a little curve tweak to darken these tones without changing the white and black points of the picture.

7.13 Elements' Curves features

Suitable for Elements – 5.0 | Difficulty level – Intermediate | Resources – Web image 713 | Menu used – Enhance

One of the regular complaints from Photoshop enthusiasts trying to put Elements users in their place is that the program 'doesn't contain curves' and so can't really be considered as a serious photo enhancement package. For the first four versions of the program this was indeed true, but in 5.0 Adobe included an easy-to-use version of Photoshop's famous Curves feature. This is great news as the Curves feature in Photoshop does offer a great deal of flexibility and creativity over manipulating the tones in your image. In particular, curves provide a great way to lighten shadow areas and darken highlights and it is precisely these two tasks that I use Curves for most. In version 6.0 curves was revamped and now has a simpler interface.

Adjust Color Curves feature

The Adjust Color Curves feature contains two different ways to manipulate the tones in your photo. The first is a series of enhancement presets, called Styles, that apply specific curve tweaks to your photos. These adjustments include the options to **Increase Midtones**, **Lighten Shadows**, **Increase Contrast**, **Darken Highlights**, create a **Solarize** effect and compensate for **Backlight** in a photo. Selecting one of these options adds the selected adjustment to the photo. Choosing a second option replaces the first tonal tweak with the second curves adjustment.

The second way to alter the tones in your photo when using the new Adjust Color Curves feature is via a set of four slider controls coupled with a graphical curves display located in the Adjust section. The sliders controls include **Adjust Highlights**, **Midtone Brightness**, **Midtone Contrast** and **Adjust Shadows** options. Moving any of the sliders directly alters the way that the tones are distributed in your photo and changes the shape of the curve. Using these controls you can fine-tune specific areas of your photo.

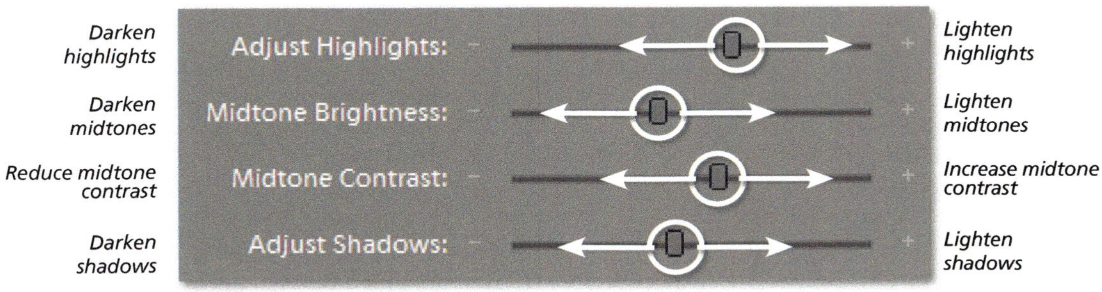

Advanced Options slider controls >> *Moving the position of the sliders in the Advanced Options section of the Adjust Color Curves dialog produces the changes listed above to specific tonal ranges in a photo.*

The Reset button removes all curves changes, both thumbnail selections and slider movements, and restores the feature back to the default setting, which does not apply any changes to image. Note that in the version 5.0 the Reset button switches the control to the Increase Midtones sample.

The easiest and most effective way to use this new Elements' Curves control is to use the Styles menu to select the general correction to apply to the photo first and then use the sliders to fine-tune the results.

Adjust Color Curves >> *The new Adjust Color Curves feature provides two different ways to tweak the tones in your photo. You can use each set of controls independently but the best results are obtained when the global changes are set by clicking a Styles entry and small fine-tuning to specific tonal ranges added next via the Slider controls.*

(a) Adjust Sliders section containing Slider controls for specific tonal ranges.

(b) The Styles presets which apply a set adjustment to the picture when clicked.

(c) Changes in the shape of the curve based on clicking the Sample thumbnails. Left to right: Increase Midtones, Lighten Shadows, Backlight, Increase Contrast, Darken Highlights and Solarize.

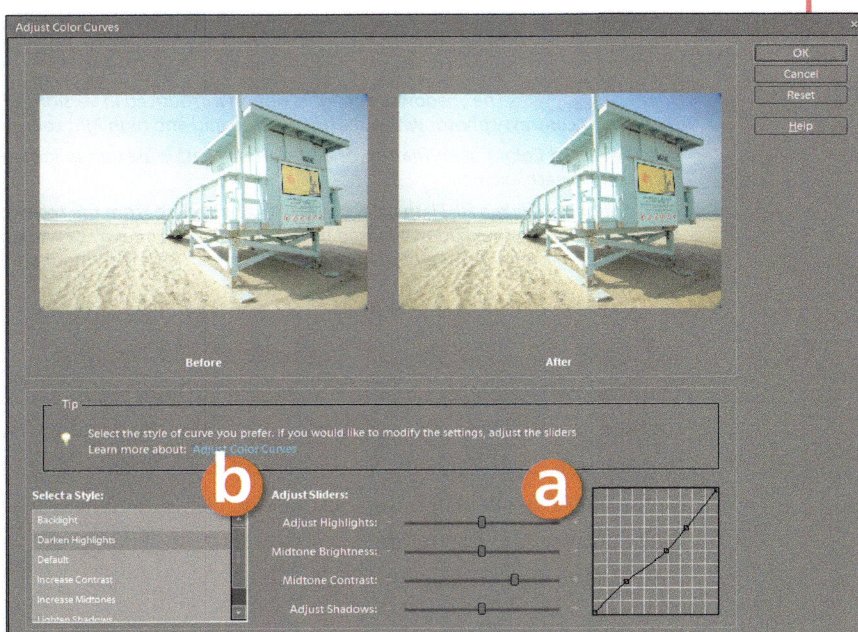

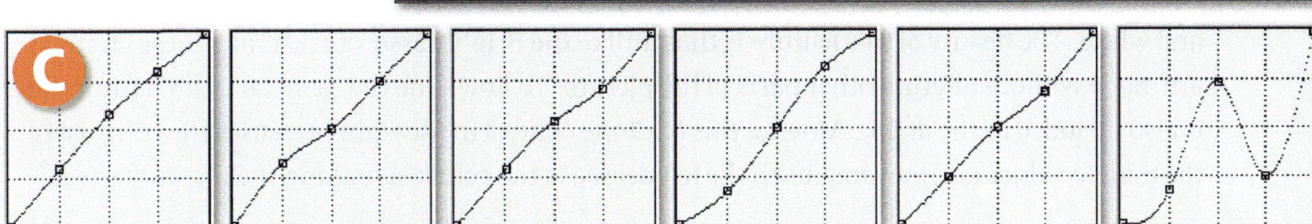

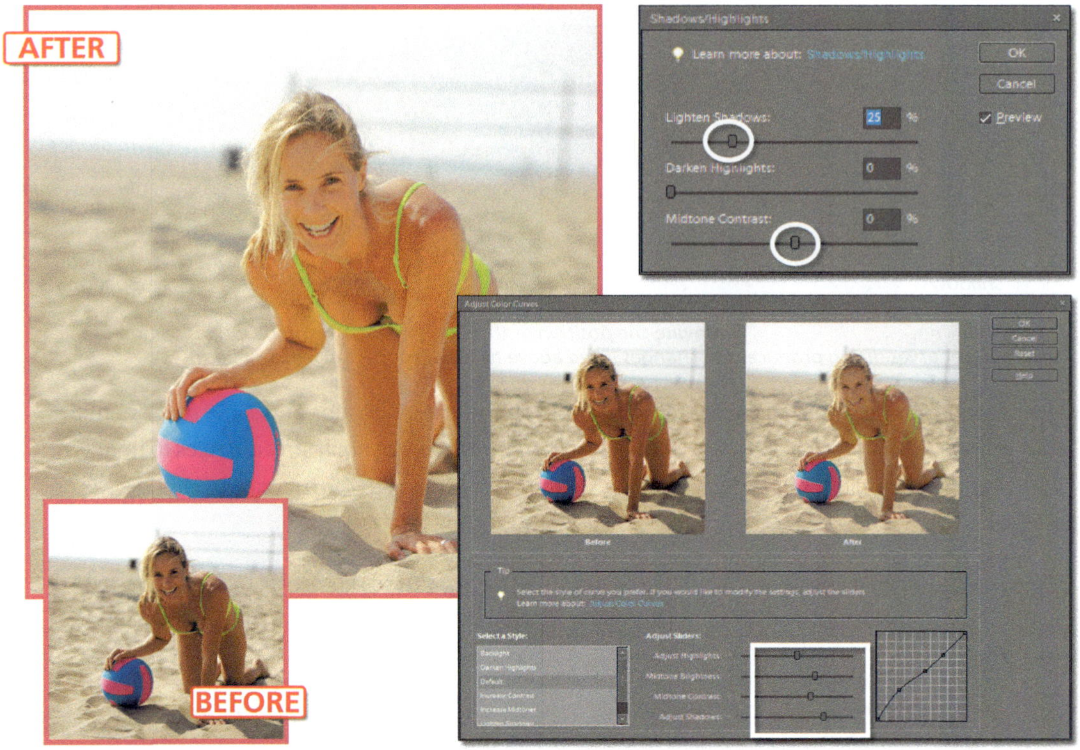

Fill Flash effects >> *The Shadows/Highlights option introduced in version 3.0 of Elements also easily lightens the shadows of contrasty photos without affecting the mid and highlight tones in the picture.*

Like the Adjust Color Curves feature, Shadows/Highlights is useful for lightening the shadows in backlit images such as this beach example.

Both options provide a Fill Flash effect which takes its name from the technique of using an on-camera flash in daylight to lighten the shadows caused by direct sunlight. This way of working is popular with photojournalists who in their haste to capture hard news images have little time to modify the lighting on their subjects.

Curves like control via the Shadows/Highlights feature

The Shadow/Highlights tool can also be used to alter specific tonal ranges in your photos. It contains three sliders – the upper one is for lightening shadows, which replaces the old Fill Flash tool (included up to version 2.0), the control in the middle darkens highlights and is a substitute for the old Adjust Backlighting tool (included up to version 2.0) and the final slider adjusts mid-tone Contrast. Moving the Shadows control to the right lightens all the tones that are spread between the middle values and black.

Sliding the Darken Highlights control to the right darkens those tones between middle values and white. The beauty of this feature is that unlike the Brightness/Contrast tool, these changes are made without altering other parts of the picture. To fine-tune the tonal changes a third slider is also included in the dialog. Moving this Midtone control to the right increases the contrast of the middle values and movements to the left decrease the contrast making the image 'flatter'.

7.14 Using Photoshop's Curves in Elements

Suitable for Elements – 7.0, 6.0, 5.0 | Difficulty level – Intermediate | Resources – Web image 713 | Menu used – Enhance

Though Photoshop's curves feature is not supported in Elements it is possible to make use of Curves Adjustment Layers in Elements documents. Like other Photoshop Adjustment Layer features, it is possible to create a series of Curves layers in Photoshop and save them to a donor PSD document. When this document is opened into Elements the adjustment layers are present and they still enhance the layers below them in the stack. It is not possible to change the settings of each layer but they can be dragged to an Elements document and be used to change the tones in that image.

As most Elements users will not have access to Photoshop, I have created a document with multiple Curves adjustment layers (Photoshop-Curves.psd). To use simply download the file from the website, open in Elements and drag the appropriate layer to your Elements file.

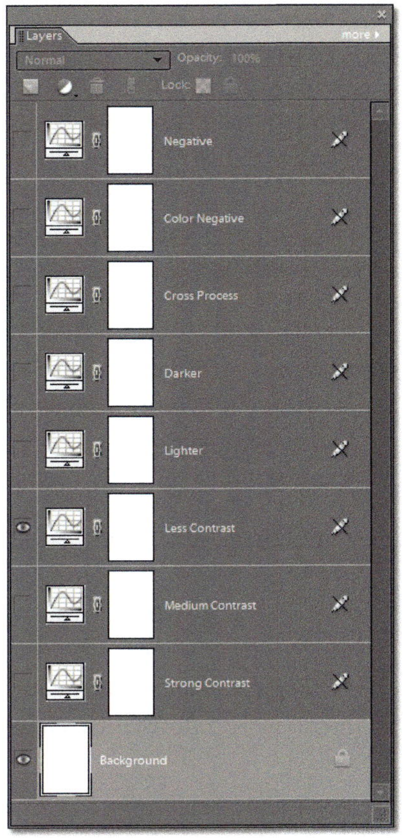

Photoshop Curves layers >> *The Photoshop-Curves.psd document available from the book's website contains a variety of Curves Adjustment layers that you can use with your Elements files.*

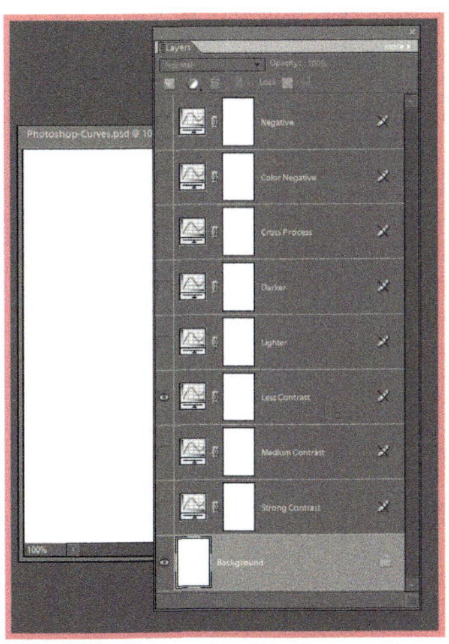

Step 1 >> *Download and open the Photoshop-Curves.psd from the website. Make sure that the layers palette is also visible.*

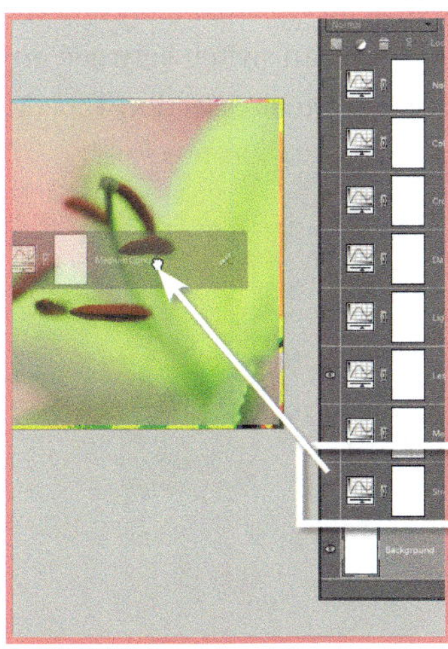

Step 2 >> *Open your Elements file and drag a suitable Curves layer from the layers palette onto the photo.*

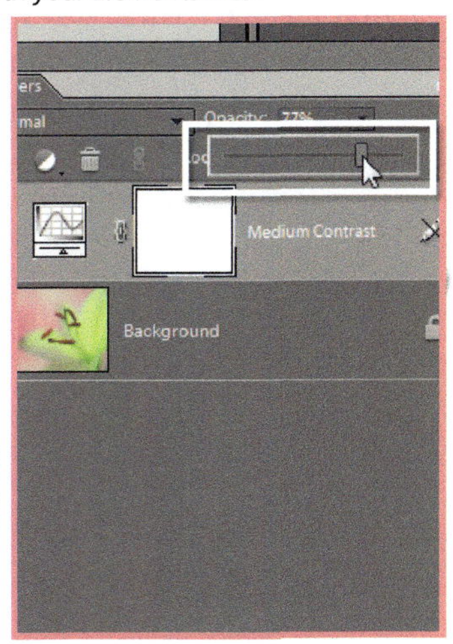

Step 3 >> *Fine tune the effects of the curve by adjusting the opacity of the adjustment layer.*

7.15 Combining images seamlessly

Suitable for Elements – 7.0, 6.0, 5.0, 4.0, 3.0, 2.0, 1.0 | Difficulty level – Intermediate
Resources – Web images 715-1, 715-2 | Tools used – Selection tools | Menus used – Select, Layer

One of the most basic yet critical skills for any digital photographer to learn is the art of careful selection of image parts. Whether you need to isolate a portion of a picture so that it is not affected by a filter, or use a selection as a prelude to copying an image section from one photograph to another, being able to manipulate your program's selection tools is a very important skill.

The success of a simple task such as creating a montage from two separate pictures is largely dependent on how well the image parts are isolated and copied. As an example I will add an extra ornament from a separate picture to an existing shadow box image and in the process demonstrate some basic selection and montaging steps that will help you to increase your image editing skills.

With both images open in Elements check to see that they are similar in size (and resolution) by viewing both the images at the same magnification. Make image size adjustments using the Scale feature. This step can also be performed after copying and pasting have occurred. Using the Lasso tool carefully work your way around the edge of the subject to be copied, in this example it is an angel, being sure to pick out as much edge detail as possible. In scenarios where there is more contrast between the edge and the background the Magnetic Lasso could be used instead.

Most selections are not perfect first time round, but rather than scrapping the initial selection try using the modifying keys to adjust your results. To take away part of the selection hold down the Alt key and draw around the area. Increase the image magnification to ensure accuracy around areas or detail. To add to the selection hold down the Shift key and draw around the image part to be included. These keys work with all selection tools and can be used repeatedly to build up a perfect result. Keep in mind that you can switch between any of the selection tools during the modification process; this includes the Quick Selection Tool (Magic Selection Brush in PSE6).

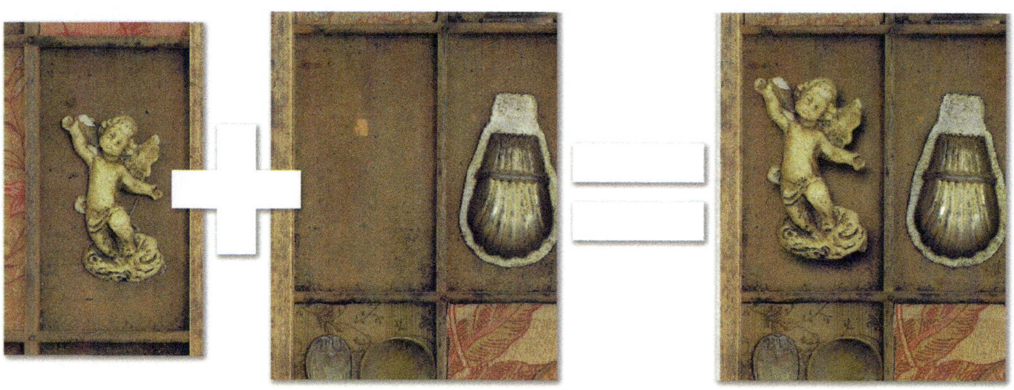

Montaging picture parts >> *Selecting, copying and pasting picture parts from one image to another is a basic skill that most digital photographers should learn. Seamless integration is based on careful selection techniques so it is on developing these skills that you should spend your time.*

At this point a lot of digital photographers would copy the angel and paste it onto the shadow box image, but such an action can produce a very sharp edge to the selection, which is a dead give-away in the final montage. The best approach is to apply a little feathering (Select > Feather) to the edge of the selection before copying. In most cases a value of between 1 and 3 pixels will give a realistic result.

With the feather applied copy (Edit > Copy) the selected portion of the image. This action stores the copy in the computer's memory ready for the Paste command. Switch to the shadow box image and paste the copied angel onto the picture. At this point you should see the object sitting on top of the shadow box picture. Any problems with the relative sizes of the two images will now become obvious. To make small changes in size you can use the Image > Transform > Free Transform tool. When the angel picture was pasted onto the shadow box image a new layer was created. Keeping these two image parts on separate layers means that they can be altered, edited and moved independently of each other; just keep in mind that the changes will only be made to the layer that is selected. Using the Move tool the angel picture is placed in the spare box space in the shadow box. As a final touch of realism a small drop shadow is applied to the angel using the Layer Styles > Drop Shadow options (via the Layer Style menu in the Special Effects section of the Artwork and Effects palette). The direction and size (shadow distance) of the shadow can be altered via the Layer > Layer Styles > Style Settings dialog box. The shadow helps integrate the new picture element with the other ornaments already in the box.

Typically, as your skills increase you will attempt more and more complex selection tasks, some of which may take many minutes to complete. For this reason Adobe has included in version 2.0 of Elements a Save Selection (Select > Save Selection) feature that will allow you to store a copy of your carefully created selection with your image file, ready for later use. Input a name for the selection in the Save Selection dialog. It is good practice to save progress on complex selections as you go. This way if at any point you lose the work you have done you can simply reload the lost selection. Reinstating a saved selection is as simple as selecting the Load Selection option from the Select menu (Select > Load Selection) and choosing the particular selection name from the drop-down menu.

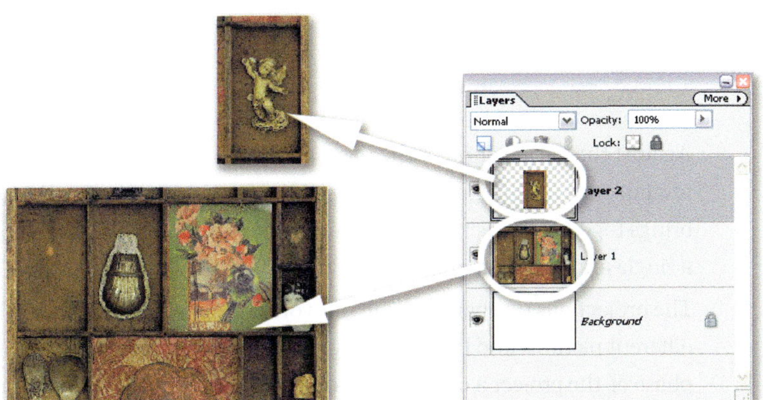

Edit>Paste >> *When part of a picture is selected, copied and pasted into a different document, Elements automatically creates a new layer to hold the pasted part. Having the element stored separately means that you can easily move, scale, change brightness or even add texture without altering the background image. In the example I added a drop shadow to the separate layer to help unify the new subject with the background.*

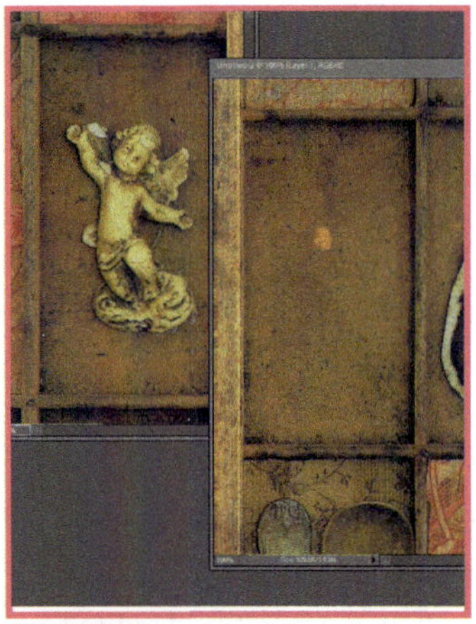

Step 1 >> *Open both images into the Elements workspace. Check their relative sizes by displaying them at the same magnification rate.*

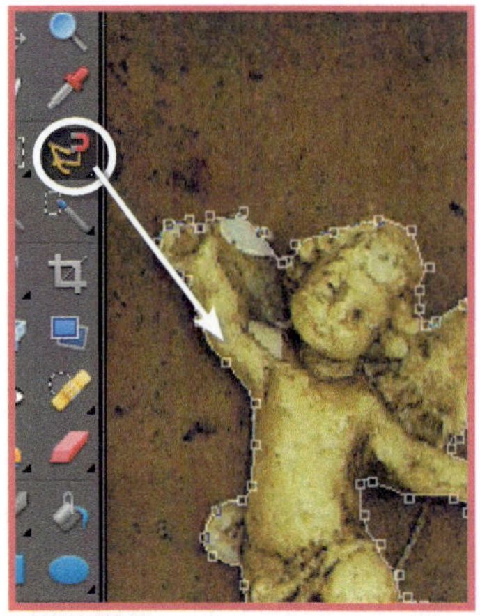

Step 2 >> *Carefully select the subject to be copied using your favorite selection tool. Zoom in closer to ensure accuracy.*

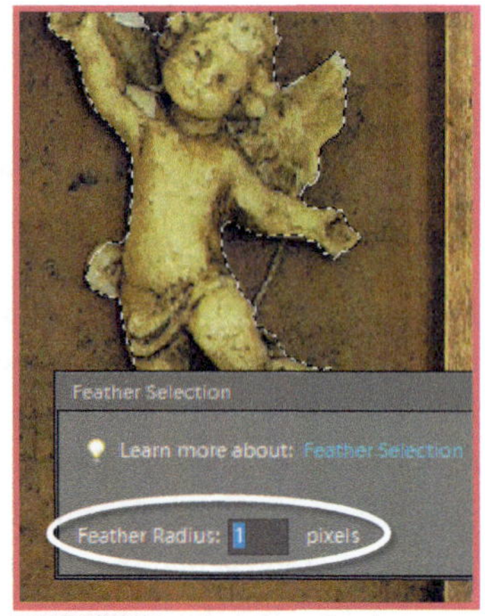

Step 3 >> *Feather the selection slightly (1–2 pixels) to ensure that the edge of the copied part is not too crisp to appear real.*

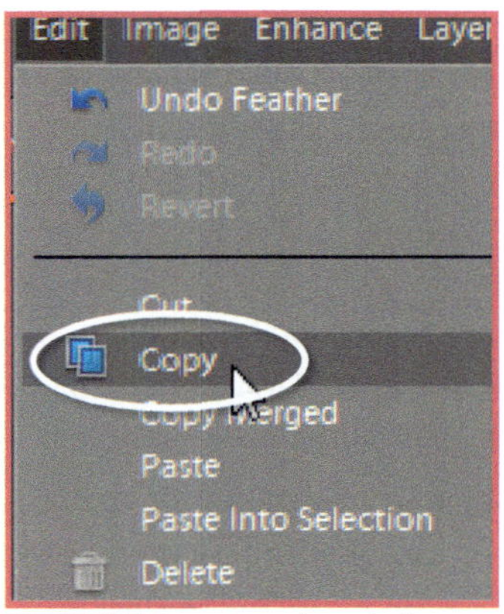

Step 4 >> *Copy the selected picture part. This places the part into the computer's memory.*

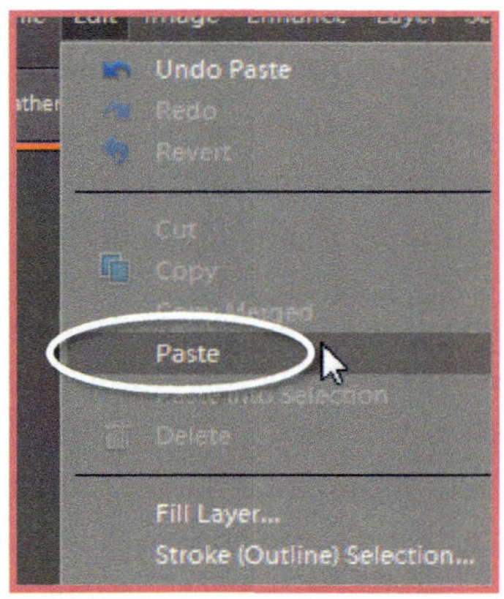

Step 5 >> *Click onto the background document to make it active and paste the copied part. Use the Move tool to position it and, if need be, use the Free Transform tool to adjust its size to suit.*

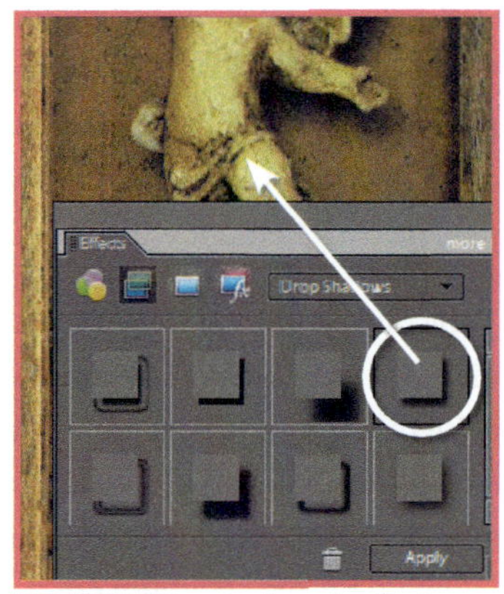

Step 6 >> *To complete the illusion add a drop shadow to the object. Make sure that the size and direction of the shadow are consistent with the others in the background.*

7.16 Believable montages – a step further

Suitable for Elements – 7.0, 6.0, 5.0, 4.0, 3.0, 2.0, 1.0 | Difficulty level – Intermediate
Resources – Web images 716-1 to 716-5 | Tools used – Selection tools, Eraser, Clone Stamp
Menus used – Select, Layer, Filter, Enhance

Against the background of the basic montaging skills developed in the last technique let's really test out your abilities to combine disparate images by stepping through the following project that brings together five very different source pictures and with the aid of Photoshop Elements creates a single and hopefully convincing final illustration.

The project has two parts. The first involves creating a background street scene from three different pictures and then unifying the composition by applying a lighting effect. In the second phase of the project a car and bus are added, the street lights are turned on and a little blur is mixed in to create a sense of speed and motion.

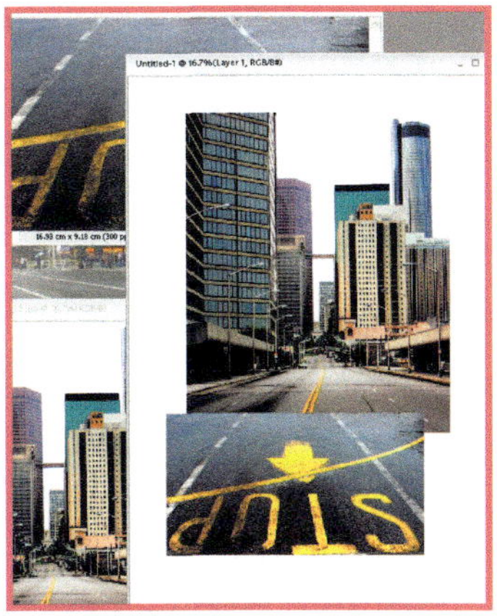

Step 1 >> *Open the background images. Be careful to choose pictures with similar pixel dimensions and try to pick photographs with a consistent perspective. Create a new document (File > New) large enough to encompass all three photos and then click-drag the open pictures onto the canvas of the new document.*

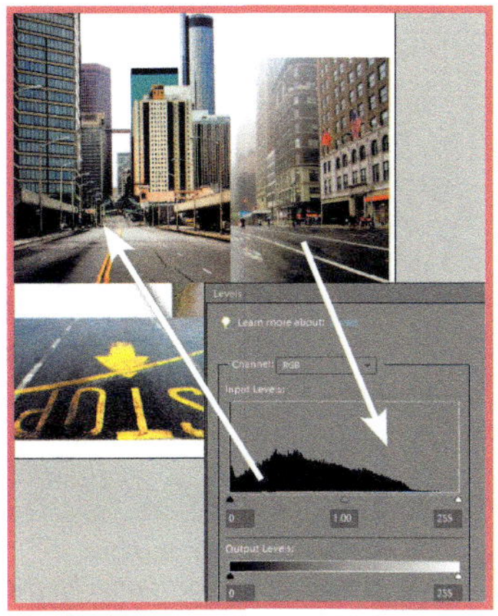

Step 2 >> *To match the picture parts select the most different photo and adjust the brightness using the Levels feature. Next alter the color using the Color Variations feature. Finally, make a copy of the right background layer (Layer > Duplicate Layer). This will be used later in the process.*

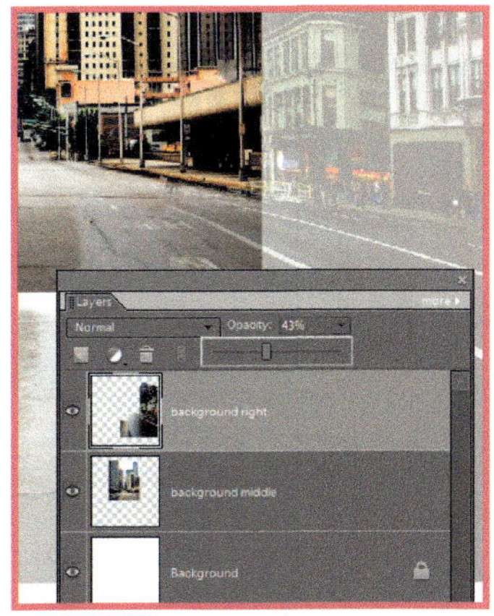

Step 3 >> *Using the background as the base match the perspective, size and shape of the other background pieces to fit. Do this by reducing the opacity of the layer to be changed and then using the Free Transform feature to resize, rotate and change layer position. To alter perspective hold down the Ctrl key whilst dragging a corner or side handle.*

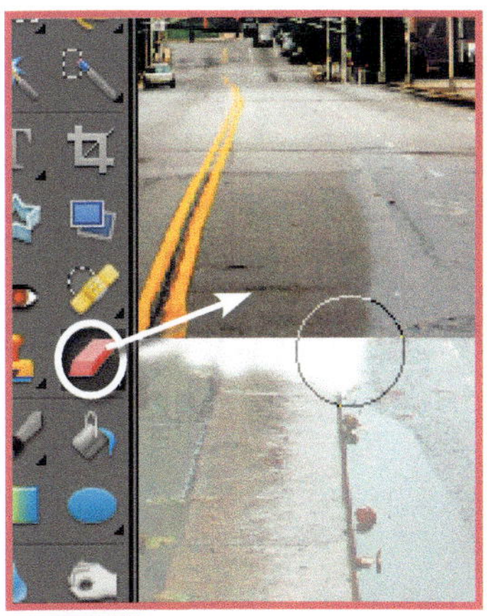

Step 4 >> *Use the Eraser tool set to Brush mode, low opacity and soft edge to carefully remove the sharp edges of the upper layers to allow them to blend with the lower ones. Alternatively, you can use a mask from a No Settings Adjustment Layer to hide parts of each layer.*

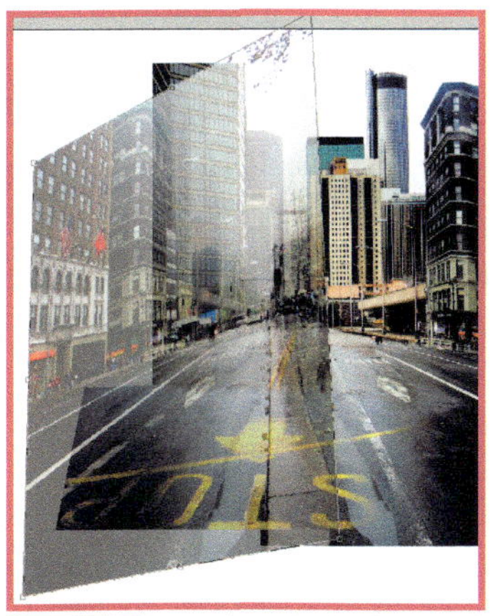

Step 5 >> *Complete the background by selecting the duplicate layer (Step 2) and flipping it horizontally (Image > Rotate > Flip Horizontal). Use this copy to form the left side of the composition. Size, shape and rotate the layer before blending it into the existing background.*

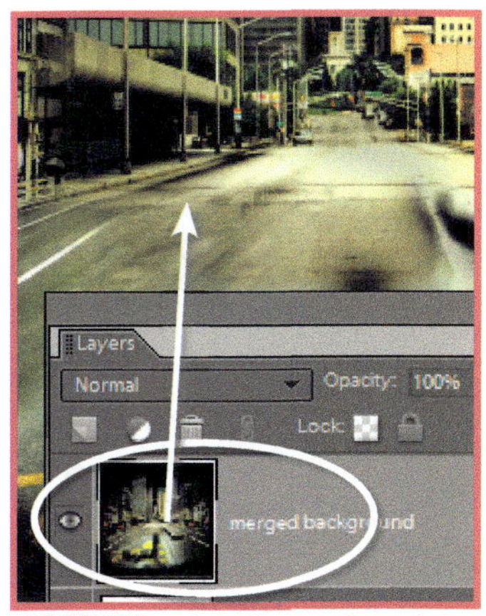

Step 6 >> *Make a flat version of the background by selecting all of the document (Select > All) and then choosing the Copy Merged command (Edit > Copy Merged). The merged copy is then pasted (Edit > Paste) as a new layer.*

Creating convincing montages:

1. When using a selection tool to cut out an object that will be pasted onto another background always apply a 1-pixel feather to the selection before cutting.

2. Try to ensure that all source images have similar lighting direction and quality.

3. Match the color, contrast and brightness of all picture parts before starting to merge them together.

4. Make sure that all source images are the same (or very similar) size and resolution.

5. Label all layers as you create them as this will help you keep track of the many layers that often make up a complex montage.

7. Don't flatten all the layers and masks that you have used for editing – instead Select > All, then Edit > Copy Merged and finally Edit > Paste a composite of all the detail as a new layer.

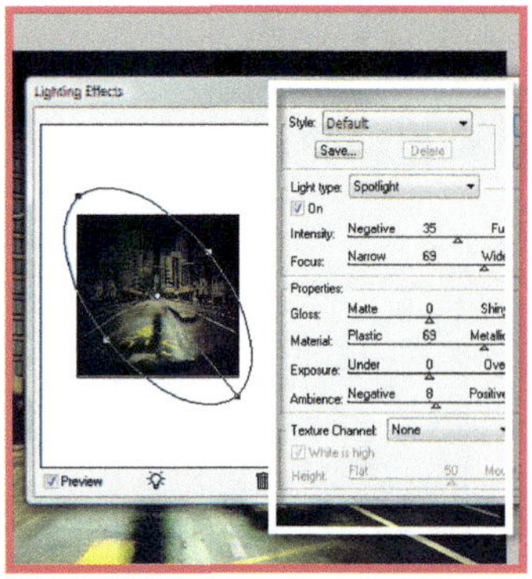

Step 7 >> *Use the Clone Stamp to even out the textures and tones and the Burn and Dodge tools to darken or lighten areas. Next select white sky area with the Magic Wand tool and fill (Edit > Fill) with black. Use the Lighting Effects filter (Filter > Render > Lighting Effects) to add a yellow hotspot in the center of the picture, fading the edges of the buildings into the newly created black sky.*

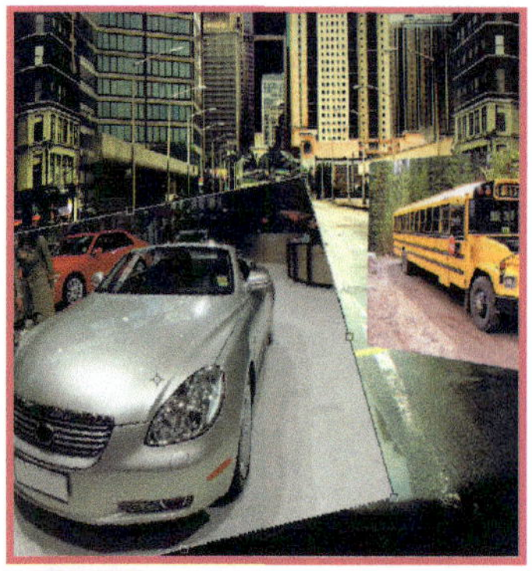

Step 8 >> *Drag the car and bus images onto the background. Flip the bus horizontally (Image > Rotate > Flip Horizontal) and select the bus destination display and flip it back. Using the Free Transform tool (Image > Transform > Free Transform) both the car and bus images are resized and their perspective adjusted to suit the scene.*

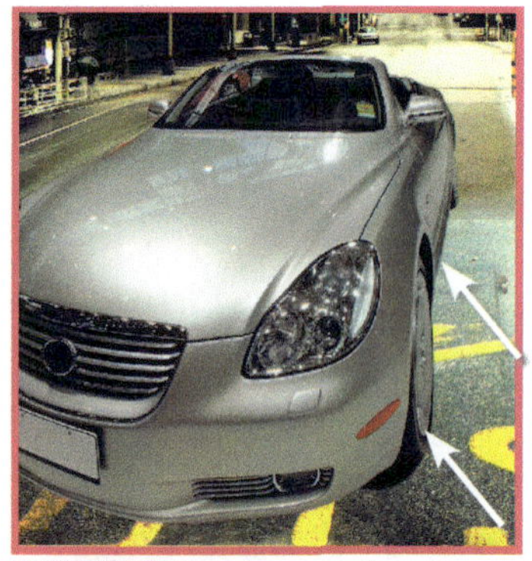

Step 9 >> *Use a low opacity soft-edged eraser to remove the unwanted areas around the car and bus. Next darken the side of the bus and add a shadow underneath using the Burn-in tool. Apply similar burning-in changes to the car including shadows and darkening the front and windscreen areas. Use the Sponge tool to desaturate vivid color areas that can appear after burning-in.*

AFTER

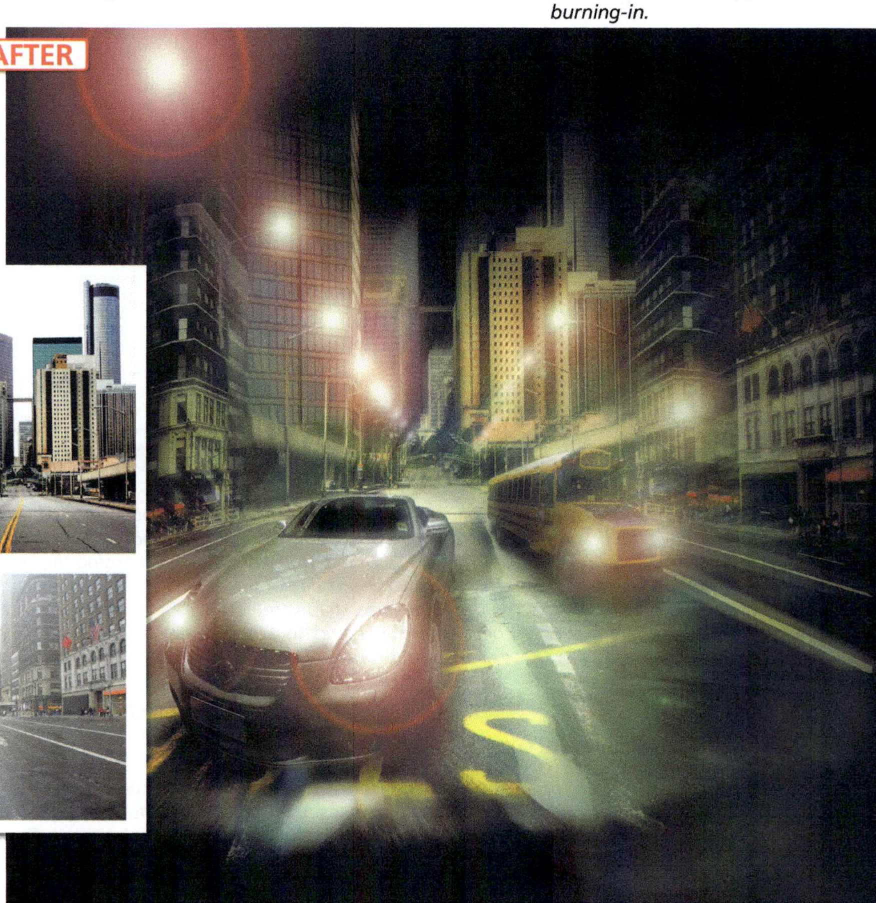

BEFORE

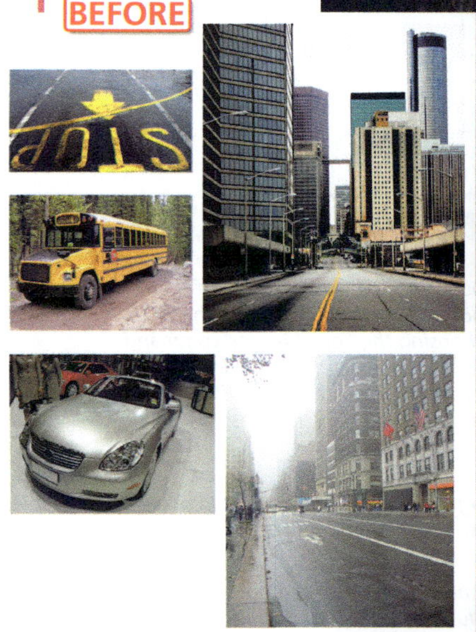

All images courtesy of www.istockphoto.com © 2005.

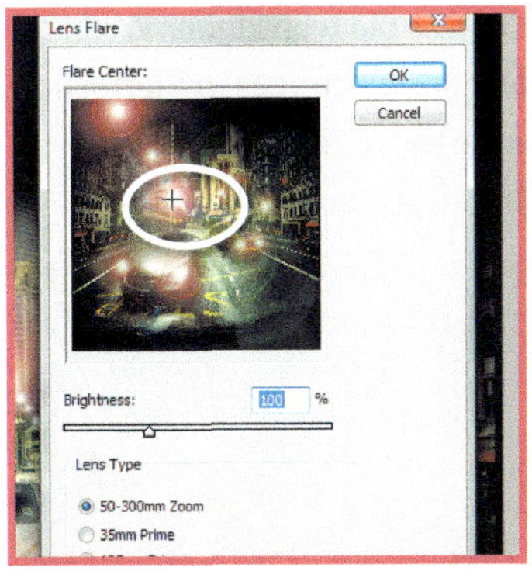

Step 10 >> *Next select the Lens Flare filter (Filter > Render > Lens Flare) and add glows to the headlights of the car and bus and to most of the bigger street lamps using the filter. Because the filter preview window is so small, it is more difficult to apply the changes to the more distant lamp posts. Instead add these with a soft-edged, slightly transparent brush that is colored white.*

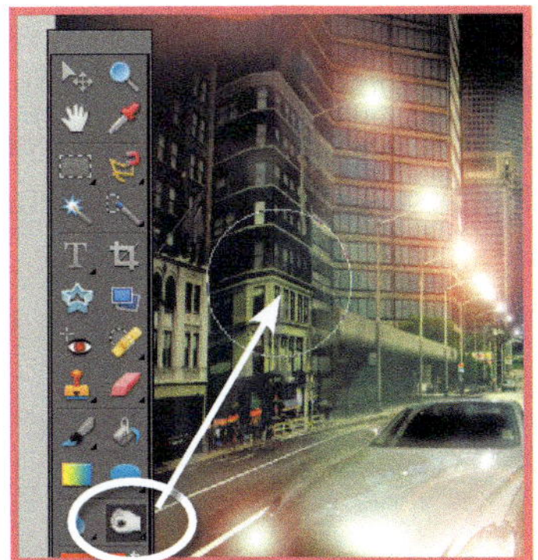

Step 11 >> *One of the side effects of the Lens Flare filter is a general lightening of shadow areas in the picture. For this reason use the Burn tool to restore some of the depth of tone to the shadow areas. Selecting Midtone or Shadows as the target range ensures that the highlights remain bright during the changes.*

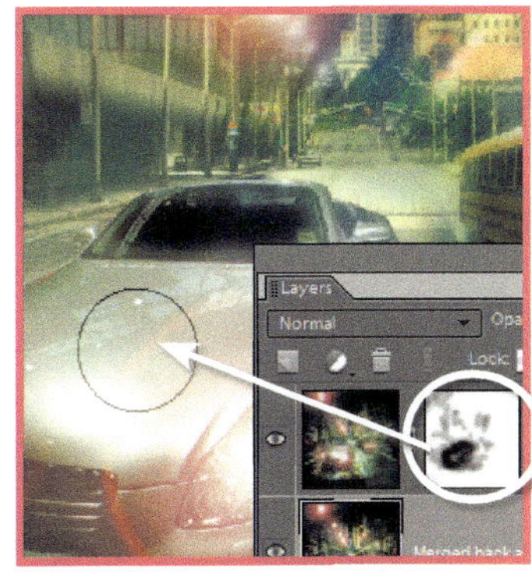

Step 12 >> *Make a copy of the merged layer of the work to date using the technique outlined in Step 6 and then apply the Radial Blur filter (Filter > Blur > Radial Blur), set to zoom and with the center positioned over the car, to the copy. Reduce the opacity of the blurred layer to restore a little detail and then use a soft-edged eraser or No Settings mask to remove layer parts to reveal the detail beneath.*

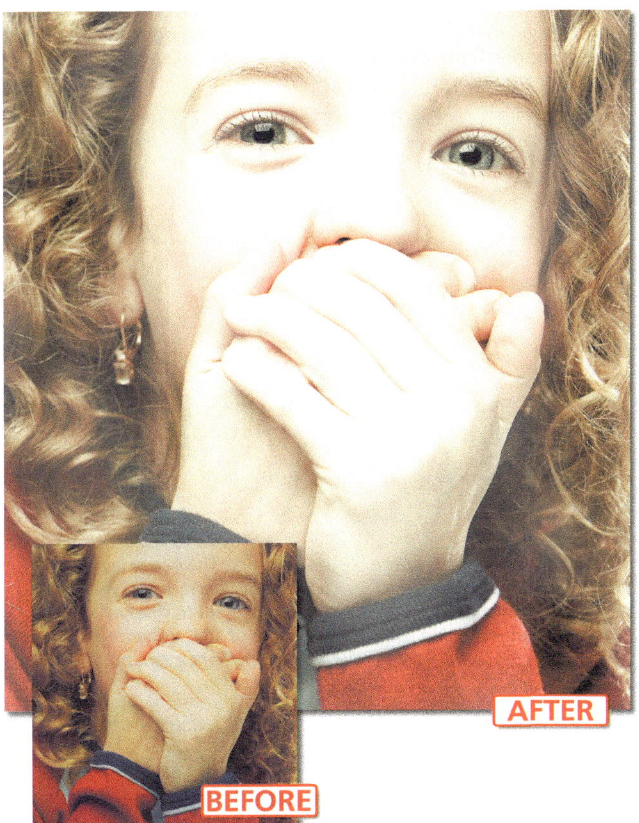

7.17 Producing high-key pictures

Suitable for Elements – 7.0, 6.0, 5.0, 4.0, 3.0, 2.0, 1.0 | Difficulty level – Intermediate
Resources – Web image 717
Tools used – Selection tools
Menus used – Select, Layer

When, as a student, I was asked to produce a high-key portrait I can remember the extreme lengths that I went to making sure that my lighting was just right, my exposure perfect and my printing spot on. So finicky was the process that many photographers veer away from making many of these stylized portraits. There is no doubting the beauty of a well-produced high-key portrait. The skin tones become almost white, but still manage to retain just a hint of detail, whilst the shadows keep their depth and the detail throughout remains crisp.

With digital now dominant, what new spin can this technology offer to this old technique? Well I'm glad you asked. This technique takes a standard portrait and with a few basic changes in Photoshop Elements creates a new high-key version. Just like the original technique the digital approach concentrates on lightening the subject's skin tones whilst still retaining depth in the shadows.

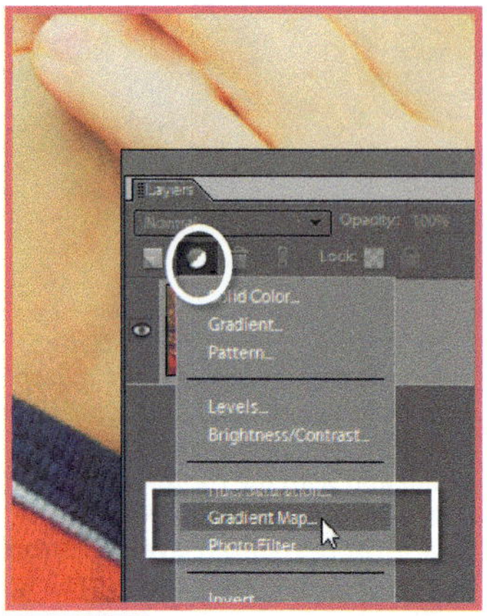

Step 1 >> With the image open in Photoshop Elements, the first task is to create a Gradient Map adjustment layer. Do this by selecting the option from the Adjustment Layer button at the top of the Layers palette.

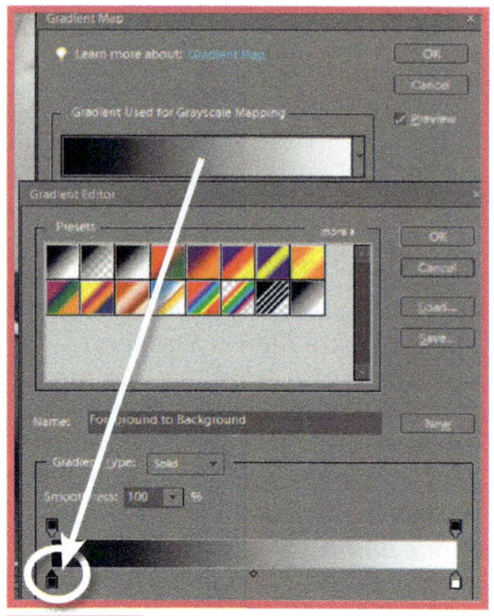

Step 2 >> Double-click in the gradient area in the dialog to display the Gradient editor. Now to change the tones that make up the start and end points of the gradient. Start with the left end of the gradient – double-click on the Color Stop box.

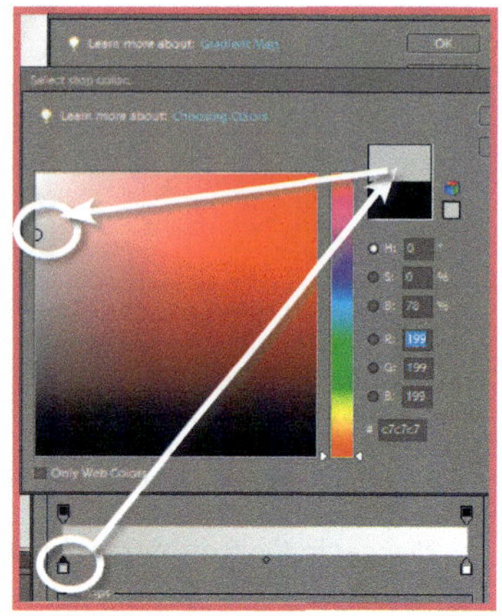

Step 3 >> The Color Picker dialog will open. Select a light gray and click OK. This sets this color as the left end of the gradient. Now double-click the color stop on the right end and select white as the gradient end point.

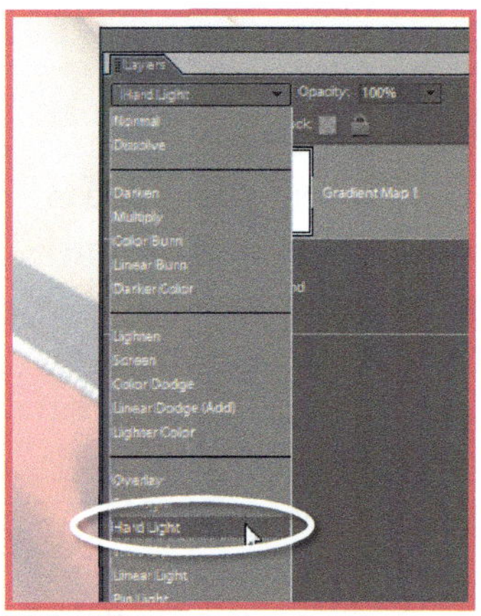

Step 4 >> Select the adjustment layer and change the blending mode to Hard Light. This will produce a much lighter color image but still hold most of your highlight details.

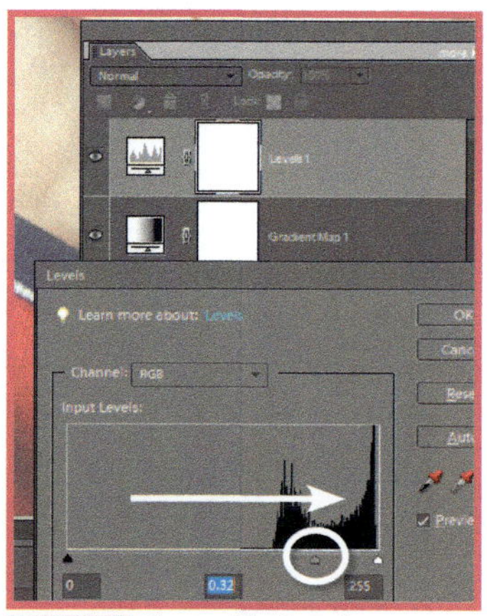

Step 5 >> Now add a Levels adjustment layer so that it sits at the top of the Layer Stack. Adjust the Midtone slider to control the brightness of the subject's skin tones.

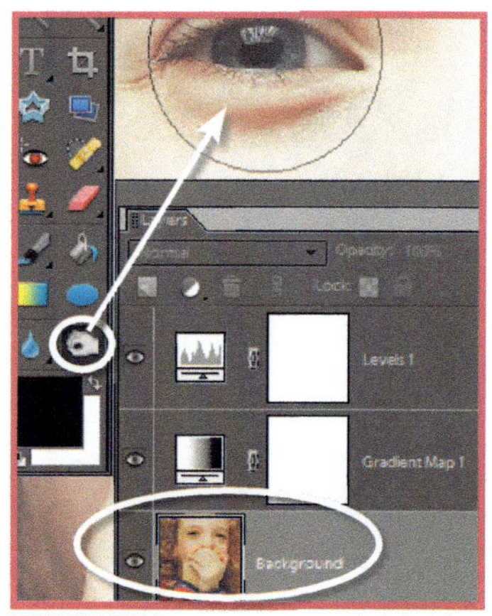

Step 6 >> Now to restore the shadow detail. Select the image layer at the bottom of the stack and with the Burn-in tool set to shadow and an exposure of 10% enhance the shadow areas using light overlapping strokes.

Gradient map?

This feature switches the colors in your picture with tones from a gradient. This option is often used to convert color images to black and white by using a black-to-white gradient map. The colors in your picture are mapped to the grays in the gradient. The feature works just as easily with colors and complex rainbow gradients as well. Try it yourself.

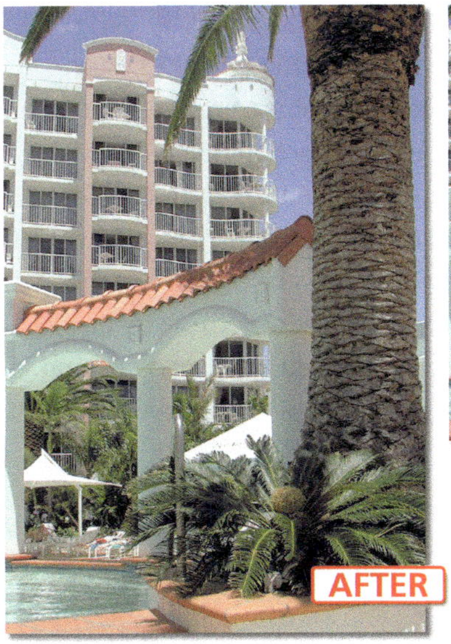

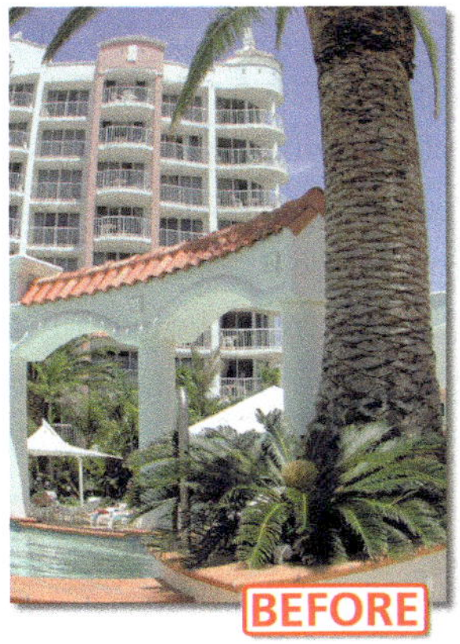

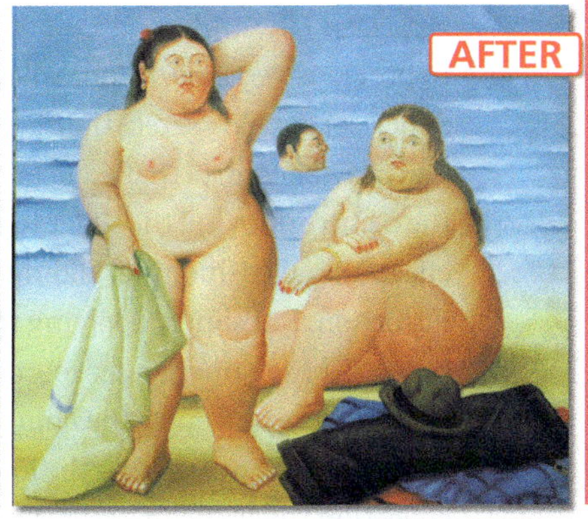

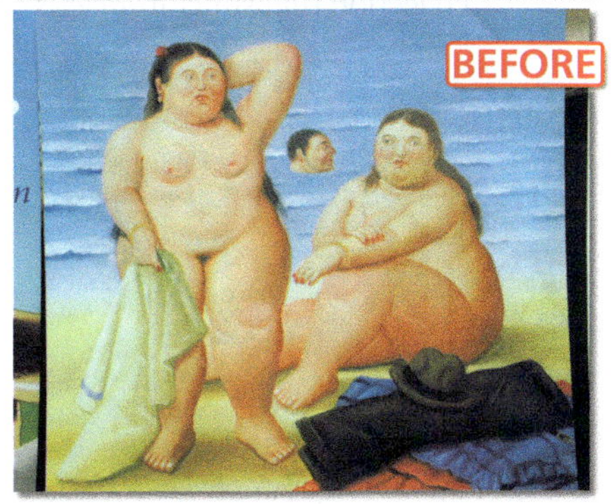

7.18 Correcting lens problems

Suitable for Elements – 7.0, 6.0, 5.0, 4.0, 3.0, 2.0, 1.0 | Difficulty level – Intermediate | Resources – Web images 718-1, 718-2 | Menus used – Filter, Image

The following techniques are designed to correct two of the most common lens problems:

- **Barrel distortion** and
- **Pincushion distortion**.

As we have already seen in technique 7.05 the new Correct Camera Distortion filter that ships with Photoshop Elements 6.0 and 7.0 can quickly and easily correct perspective problems in your photos, but this isn't the end of the feature's abilities. The Remove Distortion slider is designed specifically for removing the barrel distortion or pin cushioning effects common with some lenses. For best results this slider can be used in conjunction with the Rotate, Perspective and Vignetting controls to fine-tune the look of your photo. This feature can also be used to intentionally add the effects of each of these lens problems in order to produced bloated or pinched photos.

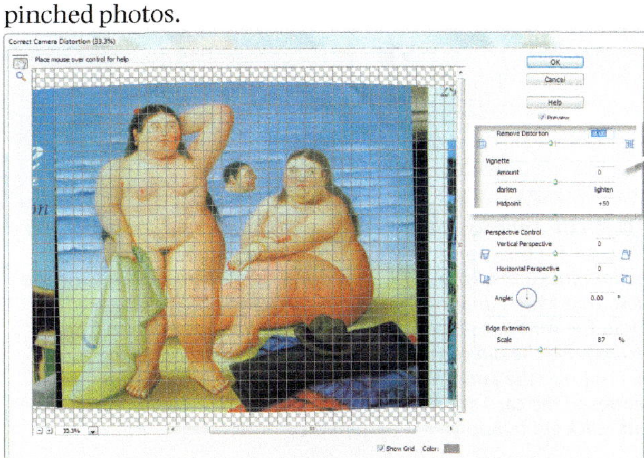

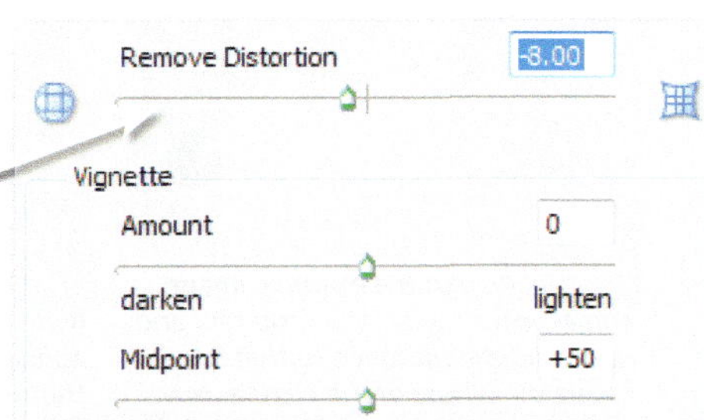

The Remove Distortion control >>
Moving the slider to the right removes the effect of pin cushioning by causing the picture to bulge. Sliding the control to the right pinches the picture inwards correcting barrel distortion.

Before Correct Camera Distortion filter (for previous Elements versions)

In previous versions of Photoshop Elements you could use the Spherize filter (Filter > Distort > Spherize) to help correct the distortion problems in your photos. It contains a preview thumbnail and a slider control that adjusts the degree of barrel or pin cushion correction that is applied to the picture. Moving the slider to the right balloons the picture and therefore counteracts the effects of pin cushioning. Sliding the control to the left contracts the image and reduces barrel distortion. But simply applying this filter to the problem picture will cause some parts of the photo to be left unchanged (corners) whilst the rest of the image is 'spherized'. To overcome this problem and apply the changes to all the picture, you will need to add some space around the image before applying the filter. Use the steps below to correct the photos you have in your collection that suffer from lens distortion.

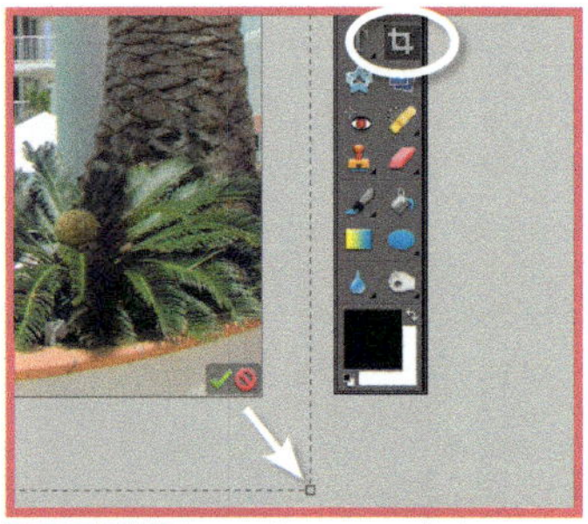

Step 1 >> *Open the example image. Next select the Crop tool and click-drag the marquee so that it covers the whole of the picture. Now click on the marquee corner handles in the top left and bottom right and drag these outwards beyond the edge of the picture. Double-click in the center of the marquee to add the new canvas space.*

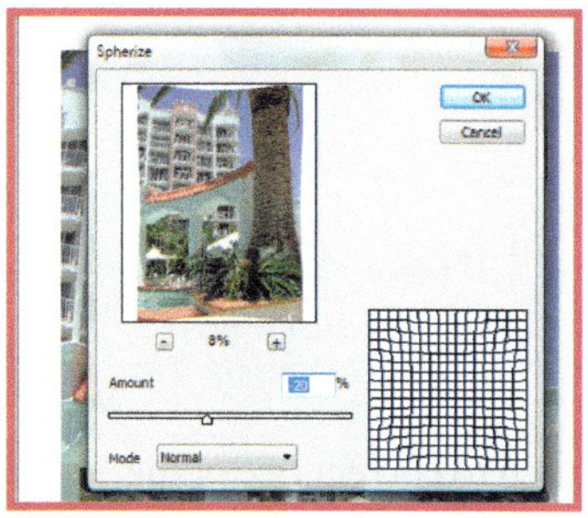

Step 2 >> *Open the Spherize filter (Filter > Distort > Spherize) and adjust the magnification of the thumbnail so that all the image can be seen. Drag the Amount slider to the left to remove the barrel distortion. Continue the adjustment until the ballooning effect is no longer evident. Click OK to apply.*

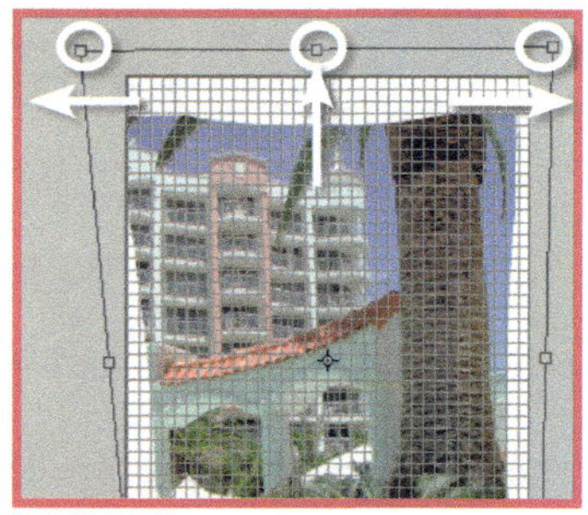

Step 3 >> *Next choose View > Grid and then select Image > Transform > Free Transform. Click-drag the top corner handles outwards until the building parts that should be vertical are aligned to a grid line. Drag the top handle upwards to counteract the squashing action and then double-click to transform. Use the Crop tool to remove edges.*

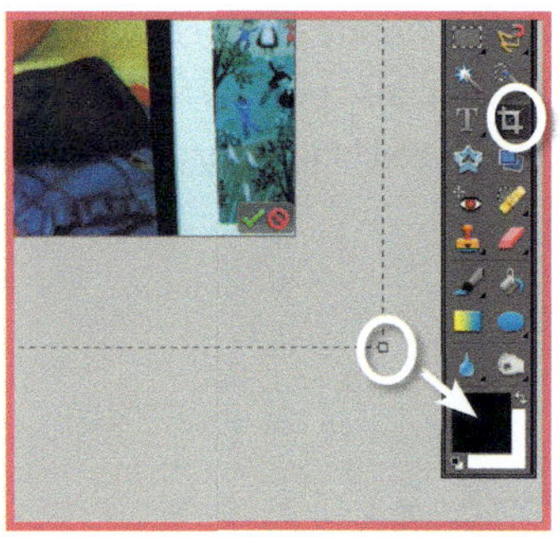

Step 1 >> *Open the example image and as before select the Crop tool and click-drag the marquee so that it covers the whole of the picture. Now click on the marquee corner handles in the top left and bottom right and drag these outwards beyond the edge of the picture. Double-click in the center of the marquee to add the new canvas space.*

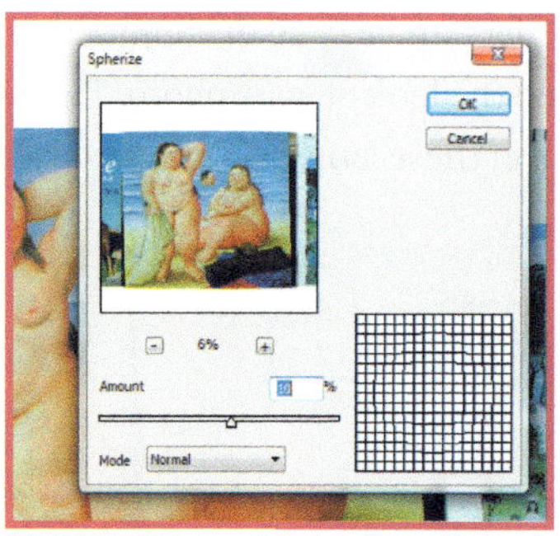

Step 2 >> *Open the Spherize filter (Filter > Distort > Spherize) and adjust the magnification of the thumbnail so that all the image can be seen. Drag the Amount slider to the right to remove the pin cushion distortion. Continue the adjustment until the edges of the card are no longer bent. Click OK to apply.*

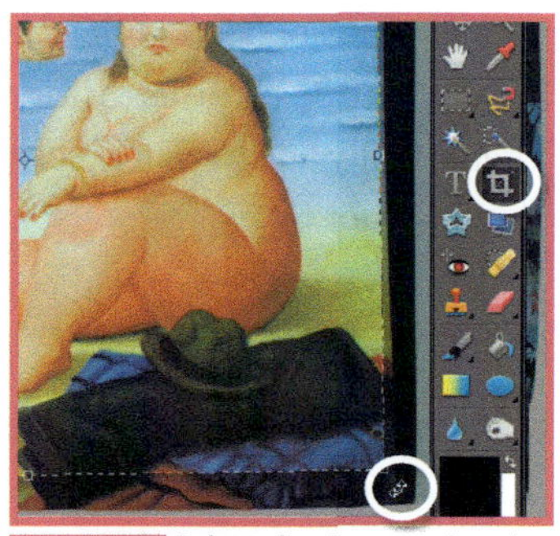

Step 3 >> *Select the Crop tool and after drawing the crop marquee around the picture click outside the marquee and drag to rotate the marquee until the edges of the marquee are parallel to the card's sides. Double-click in the centre of the marquee to crop and rotate the photo.*

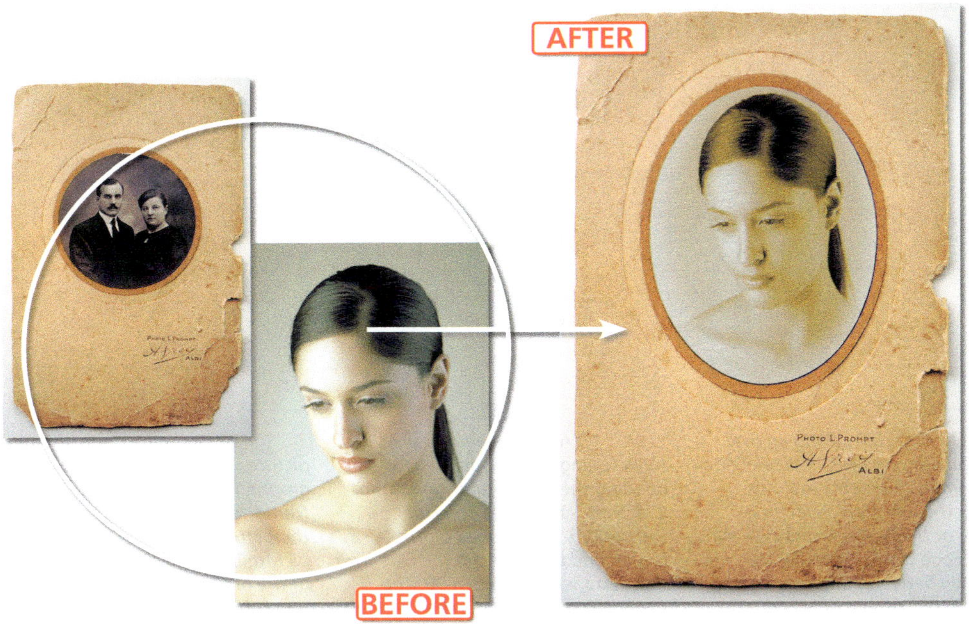

7.19 Change to old

Suitable for Elements – 7.0, 6.0, 5.0, 4.0, 3.0, 2.0, 1.0 | Difficulty level – Intermediate | Resources – Web images 719-1, 719-2 | Tools used – Selection tools, Free Transform | Menus used – Select, Layer, Enhance, Filter, Edit

Most people would say that old photographs have a certain look and feel about them that can almost be described as magical. It is hard to pin down exactly why we can be so fascinated by these aged images; it may be nostalgia pure and simple, or the knowledge that you are holding a piece of captured history in your hands or it may even be the fact that they look so different from their modern, dare I say it, digital, counterparts. But such is the fascination with old images that many contemporary shooters use a range of digital techniques to recapture this 'look and feel' in their pixel-based photographs. In this section we will gracefully add years of age to a straight portrait with the help of some of the features in Photoshop Elements.

Sepia toned vignettes with old background

In this technique we will take a modern portrait that uses a classic pose, give it an old time treatment and then add it to an original antique background. Such picture surrounds can be easily located at car boot sales or, as with my example, a French brocante shop. The state of the photograph itself is not all that important; it is the surround that we are interested in. The circular cutout won't suit the oval vignette of the example picture so some quick copy, paste and transform steps modify the original to fit our modern portrait. The last part of the process adds some texture and a little unsharpness to the original to ensure that it matches its new (or is that old?) surround.

Pro's Tip

To see how to create similar results using the new Frame layer technology included in Photoshop Elements go to Chapter 12.

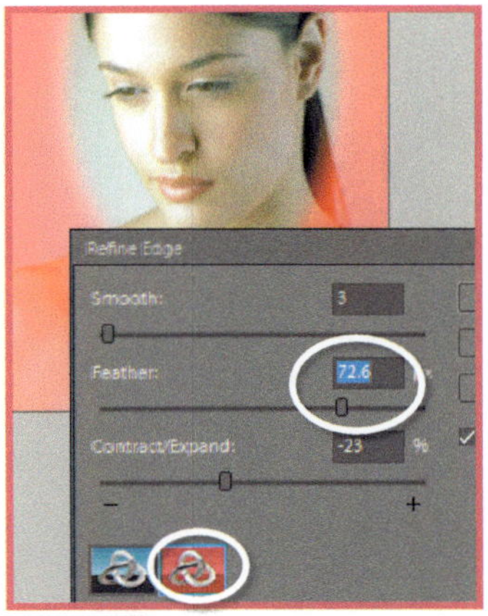

Step 1 >> *Start by making an oval selection using the Elliptical selection tool from the Elements tool box. Feather the selection (Select > Feather or the Feather option in the Refine Edge dialog) to make the transition between the selected and non-selected areas more gradual. Inverse the selection (Select > Inverse) and then press the Delete key to remove the background of the portrait.*

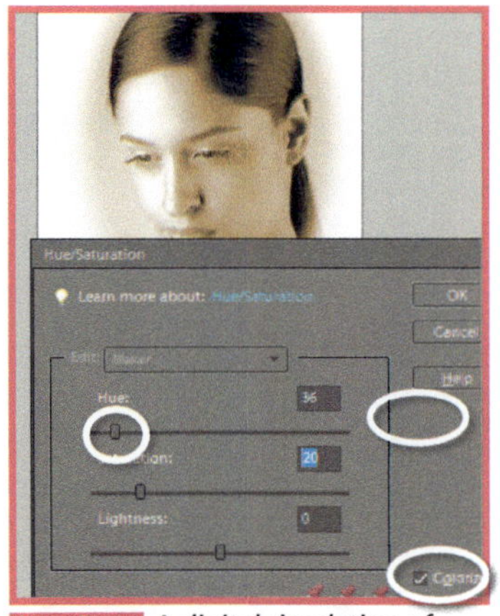

Step 2 >> *A digital simulation of sepia toning can be obtained by opening the Hue/Saturation feature (Enhance > Adjust Color > Hue/ Saturation), ticking the Colorize option and then moving the Hue slider to a value of about 30. The strength of the color can be changed by sliding the Saturation slider.*

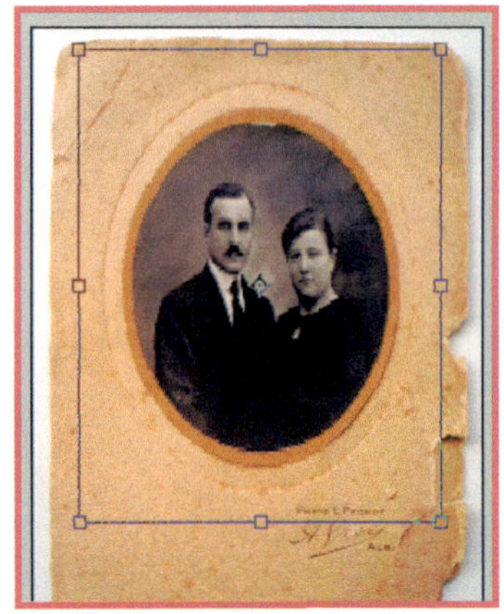

Step 3 >> *Open the photo-frame picture. This example was photographed using window light directed from the top of the picture. Change the circular cutout to suit the oval picture by making a feather selection of the oval and Edit > Copy and Edit > Paste the selection. Next use the Free Transform tool to make the circle taller. Double-click to apply the transformation.*

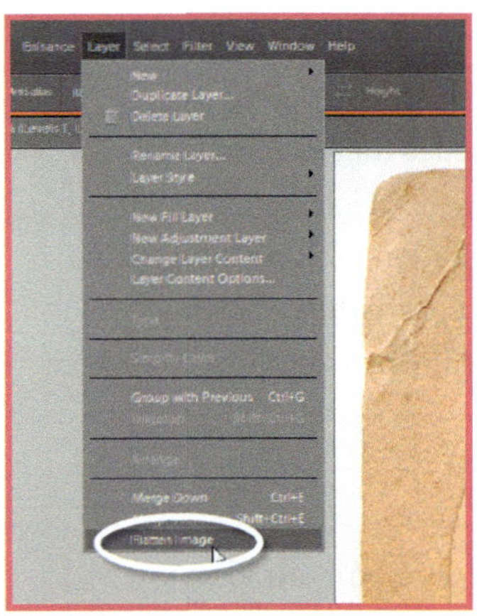

Step 4 >> *Flatten the picture (Layer > Flatten Image) and carefully select the inside of the cutout using one of the Lasso tools. Feather the selection by 1 pixel. Save the selection (Select > Save Selection) just in case you lose it during the next couple of steps. Switch back to the sepia-toned portrait and select (Select > All) and copy (Edit > Copy) the whole picture to memory. Click onto the background document and make sure that the cutout selection is still active. Now select the Paste Into Selection option from the Edit menu (not the Paste option).*

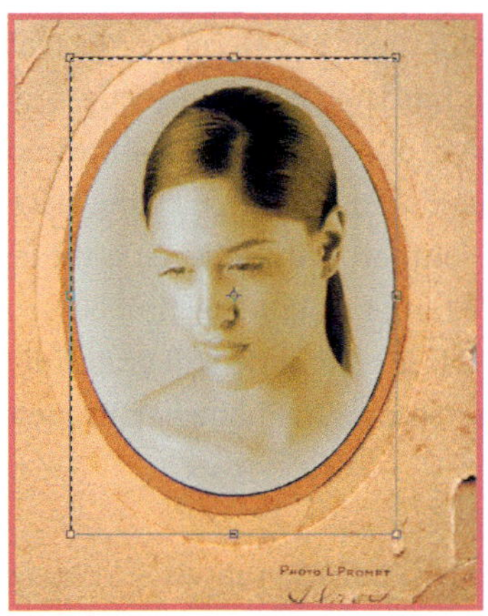

Step 5 >> *Straight after you paste the portrait into the surround select the Free Transform feature using the shortcut key – Ctrl T. This will place the familiar transformation handles around the pasted picture allowing you to manipulate the size of the portrait to suit the cutout. Check that the Constrain Proportions option is checked in the Options bar. This will help guarantee that the portrait remains in proportion when resizing. Double-click to apply the transformation.*

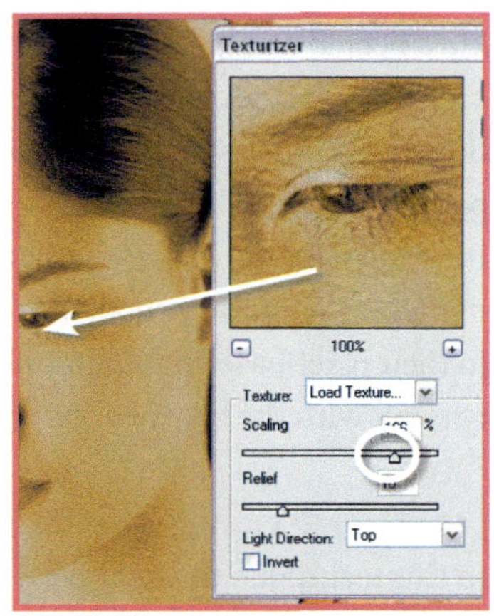

Step 6 >> *Although the picture now fits the surround well there is an obvious difference between the texture of the two parts. To help match these areas, select a portion of the picture surround and then copy and paste this into a new Elements document. Save the texture as a PSD file. Reload the original selection made for the cutout (Select > Load Selection). Now apply the saved copied texture to the portrait area using the Load Texture option in the Texturizer filter (Filter > Texture > Texturizer).*

7.20 Painterly photos

Suitable for Elements – 7.0, 6.0, 5.0, 4.0, 3.0, 2.0, 1.0
Difficulty level – Intermediate | Resources – Web image 720
Menus used – Filter

Before photography was even invented or digital became the way to take and make pictures, artists had been creating great pictures for centuries using such diverse materials as chalk, pastel, pen and ink, and, of course, paint. Now you can emulate the look of these old masterpieces by using your very own photographs as the starting point and adding the artistic 'look and feel' with a few well-chosen, but simple, digital embellishments. Here we will recreate four distinct artistic illustrations from a single humble photographic beginning using several enhancement steps and the filters contained in Elements.

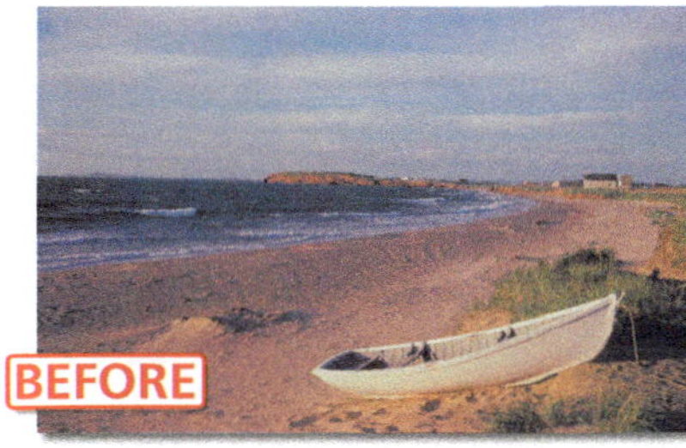

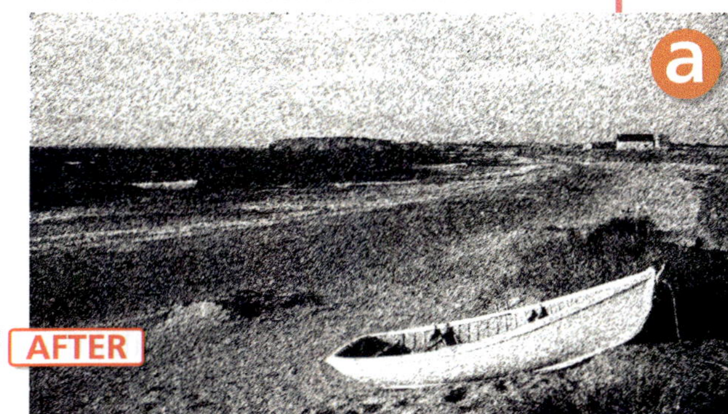

Changing to a pen and ink drawing (See a)

Using the Graphic Pen filter it is possible to simulate the effect of making a drawing of a photograph with a thin graphic arts pen. Close overlapping strokes are used for the shadow areas; midtones are represented by balancing strokes with the paper color showing through; and highlight details are drawn with a few sparse strokes.

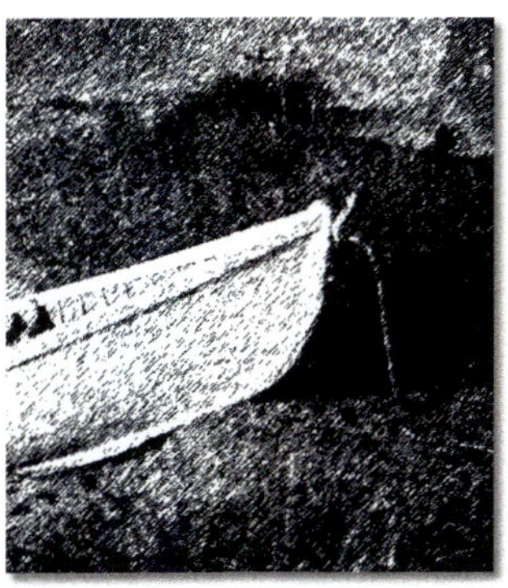

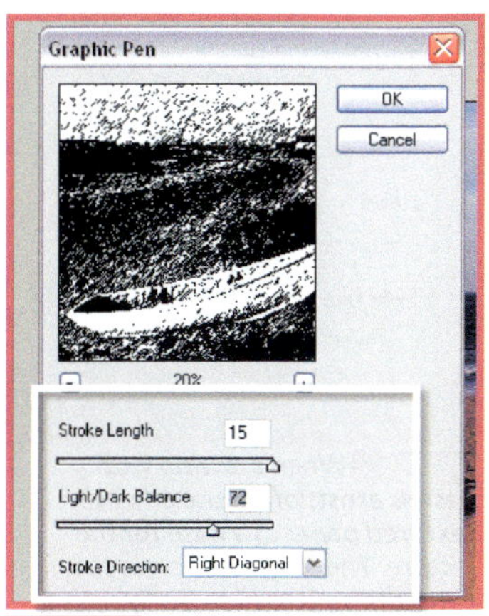

Step 1 >> *Set the foreground colors to default by clicking the small black and white squares in the bottom left of the toolbar. The Graphic Pen filter uses the foreground color as the 'ink' color and the background color as the 'paper' color. Select the filter from the Sketch menu. Using the preview as a guide adjust the Stroke Length, Light/Dark Balance and Stroke Direction controls. Click OK.*

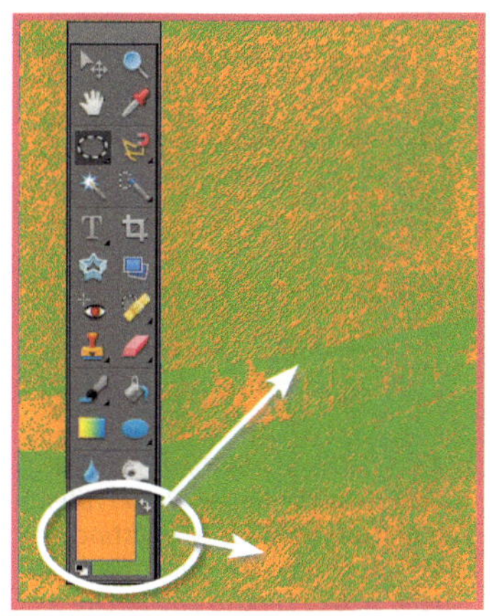

Step 2 >> *To add a little more color to your Graphic Pen 'drawings' select colors other than black and white for the foreground and background values. Double-click each swatch to open the Color Swatch palette where you can select the new color. Here I changed the pen color to brown and the paper color to light cream.*

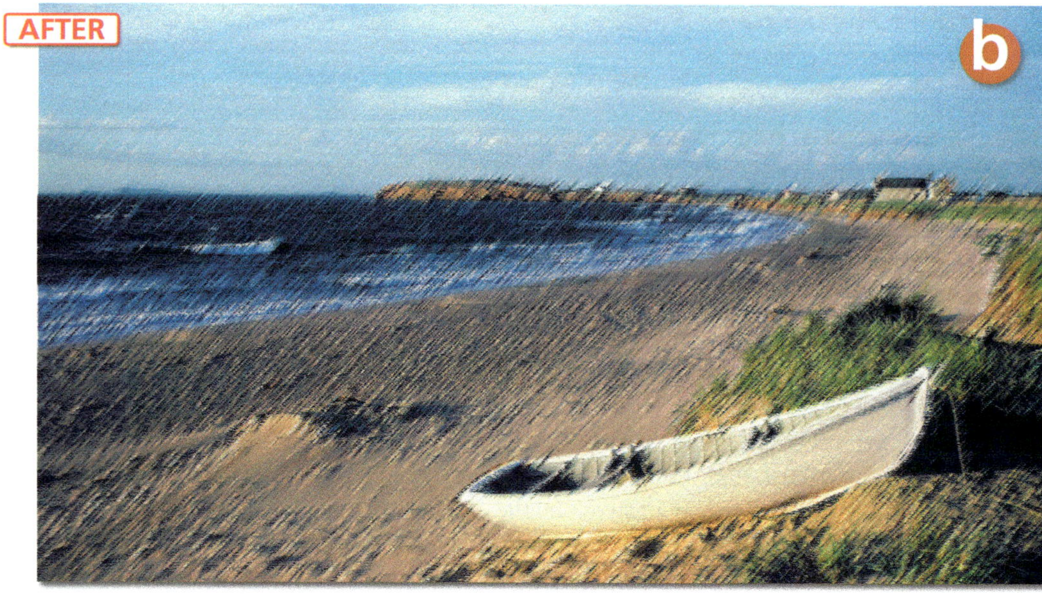

Switching photographic tones with pastel strokes (See b)

As well as the pen and ink approach used above, another favorite with artists is the use of pastels or chalks on a roughly textured paper surface. The tones of the picture are layered upon the paper's texture so that the image detail gradually emerges from the background as a combination of stroke, color and texture.

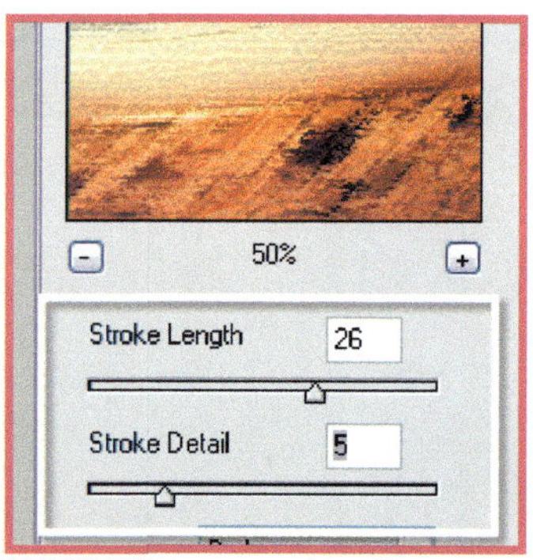

Step 1 >> *To create this effect we make use of the Rough Pastel filter. The feature contains two distinct control sections. The upper two sliders, Stroke Length and Stroke Detail, are used to adjust the way that the photographic tone is converted to pastel strokes. With the preview window zoomed in to 100% move both sliders until you are happy with the mix of detail and tone.*

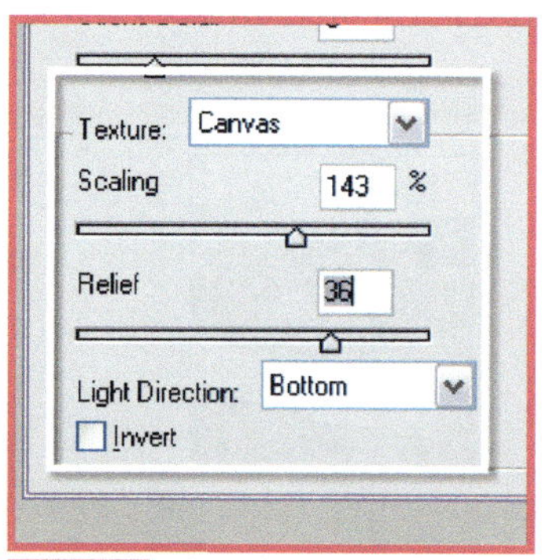

Step 2 >> *When drawing with pastels artists often use a heavily textured paper as a base for the picture. The lower section in the Filter dialog is used to apply such a surface texture to your pastel image. Here you can select the texture type (canvas, burlap, sandstone), the size of the texture (scaling), the strength of the texture effect (relief) and the direction of the light that provides shadow for the surface. After making your texture selections, check the preview and readjust the stroke length and detail if necessary before clicking OK to complete.*

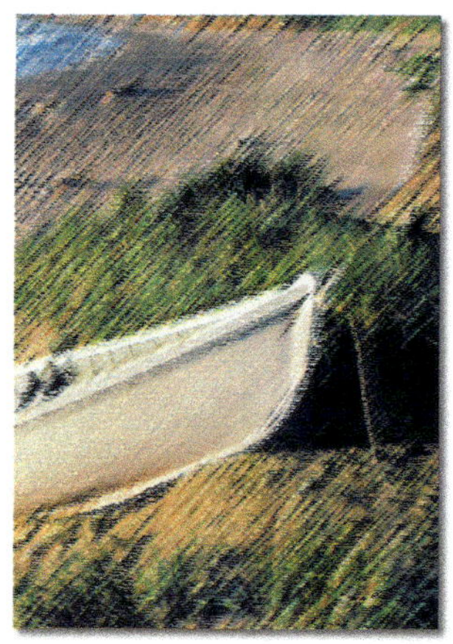

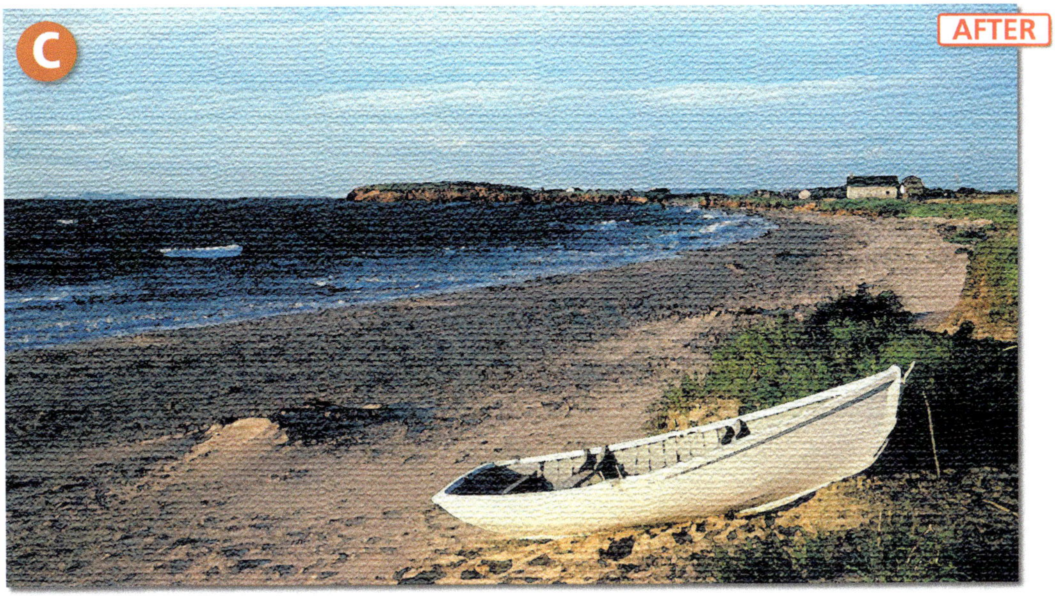

Creating a watercolor painting (See c)

If you want to create the feeling of a painted surface rather than a drawn one then the Watercolor filter in Photoshop Elements is a good place to start. With this feature the tone and hue of the original photograph is converted to daubs of semi-transparent color with the larger areas surrounded by a darker border edge. To make the effect even more convincing I have applied a texture to the picture after the watercolor conversion.

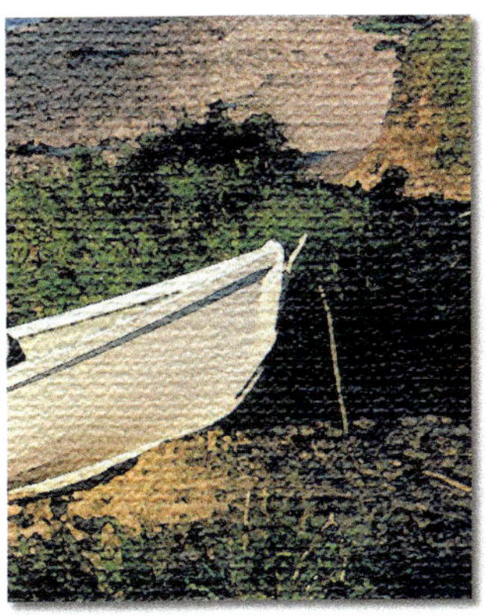

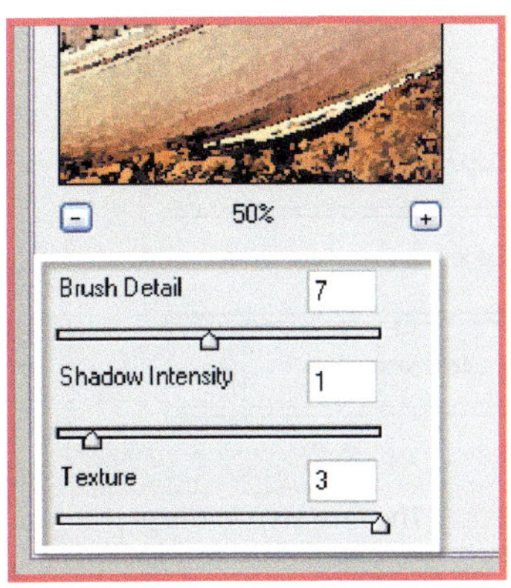

Step 1 >> *Start by opening the Watercolor filter from the Artistic option of the Filter menu. Next, with the preview set to 100%, adjust the Brush Detail and Shadow Intensity sliders to suit the picture. The third slider, Texture, is used to control the break-up of the painted areas rather than any simulated paper texture. This comes in the next step. Click OK to filter.*

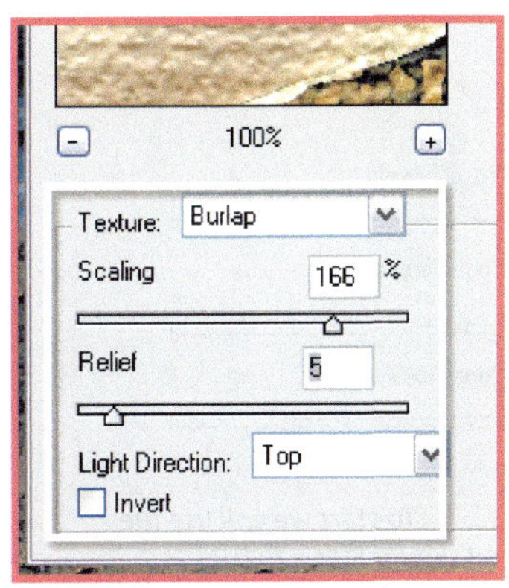

Step 2 >> *Now to add a surface treatment to the picture that will really make the conversion to a watercolor painting complete. For this task we will use the Texturizer (Filter > Texture > Texturizer) filter which has the same controls and options that we looked at in the Rough Pastel filter. We can choose the type, scale, relief and light direction that will be used for the texture. Be sure to preview the effect of the settings at 100% before clicking OK to apply.*

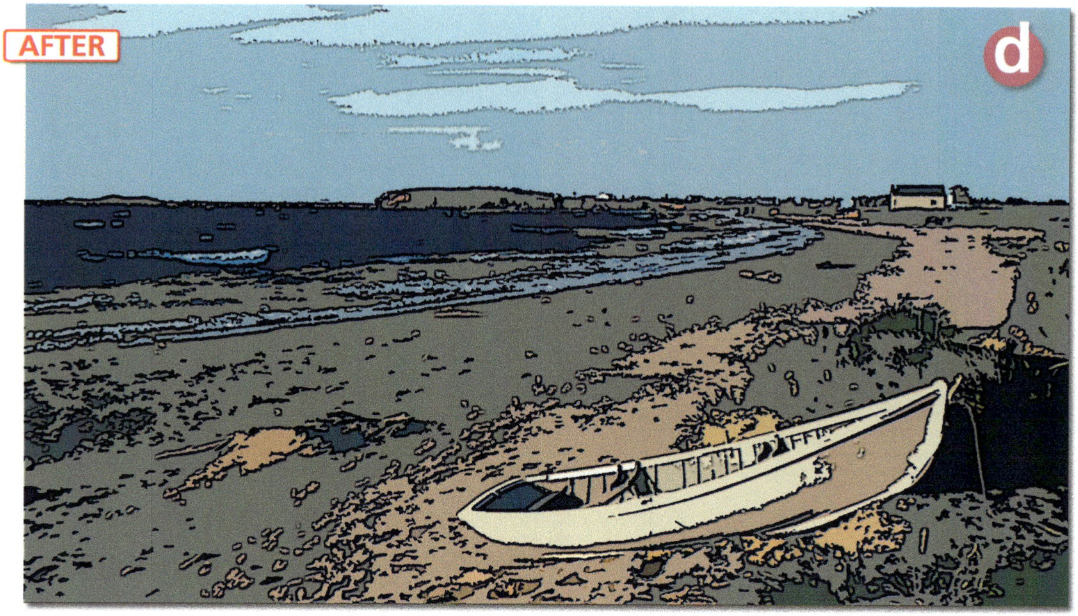

Pop art posters (See d)

Andy Warhol made the technique famous in the sixties and now you can recreate his posterized effect using your own pictures. Warhol's images were extremely graphic and constructed of very few colors, which were then applied in broad flat areas of the picture. Others like Roy Lichtenstein added a cartoon-like feeling to the pop art pictures by including a black line around colored areas. Here we will use the Cutout and Poster Edges filters to recreate this image style.

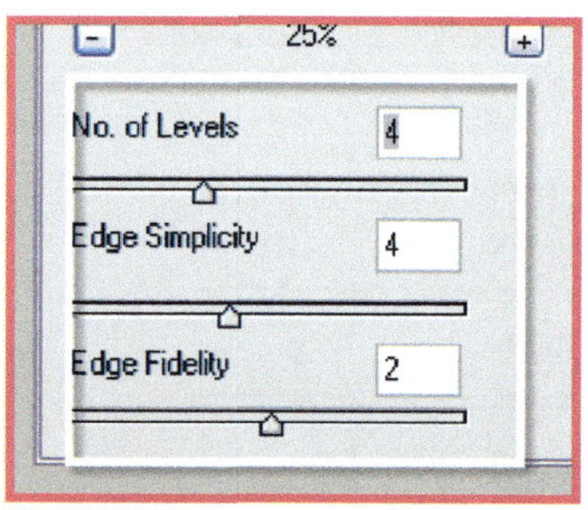

Step 1 >> *To start we will use the Cutout filter (Filter > Artistic > Cutout) to reduce the colors in the picture and to simplify the photographs detail. The feature contains three sliders. The first , No. of Levels, determines the number of colors that will be present in the final picture. Smaller values mean less colors. The Edge Simplicity and Fidelity sliders are used to determine the amount of detail that is retained in the picture. Try several settings to ensure that you have a good balance of detail and flat tone. Click OK to filter.*

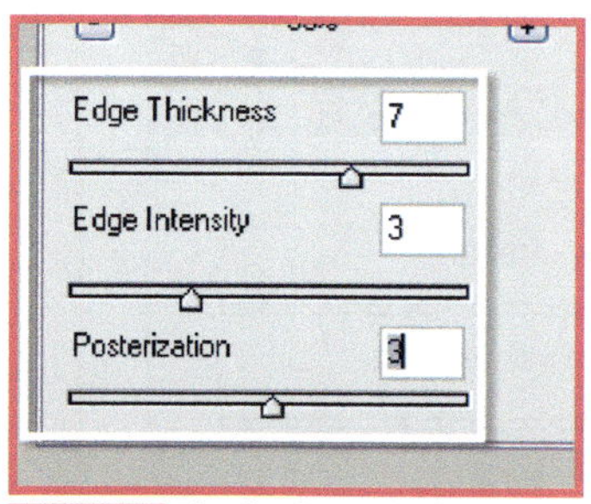

Step 2 >> *The final step in the pop art transformation is to add a black surround to the flat areas of color. For this job we will use the Poster Edges filter (Filter > Artistic > Poster Edges). The Edge Thickness slider adjusts the width of the line drawn around the picture parts, the Edge Intensity slider controls the darkness of the line and the Posterization setting is a further color reduction control. Check how the results of your settings appear when previewed at 100% and then click OK to complete.*

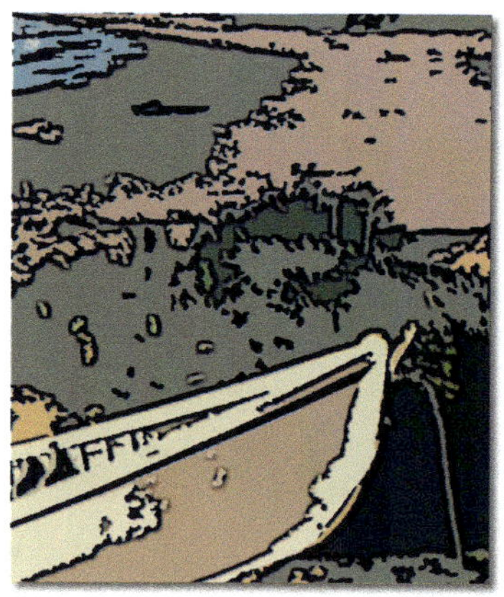

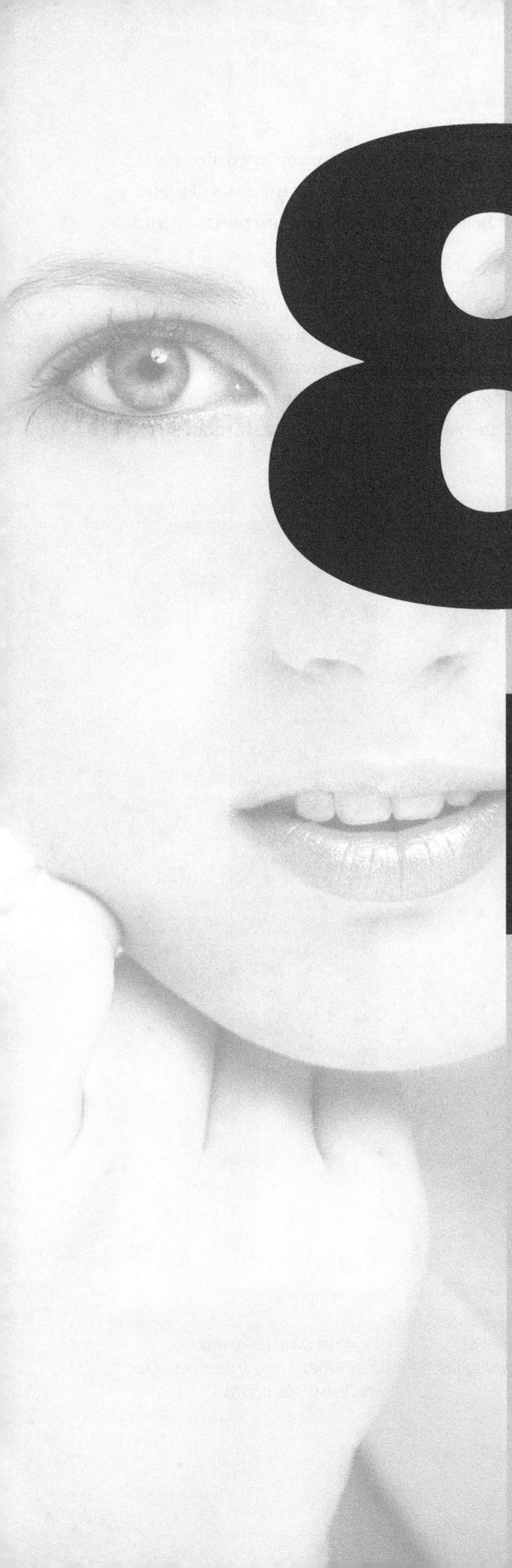

8

Professional Retouching

When it comes to retouching, Photoshop Elements and Photoshop are definitely the royalty amongst image-editors. The programs jointly contain hosts of tools, filters and adjustment options that can help turn ordinary looking portraits into something that is truly dazzling.

The shear power and dominance of the programs in this area is not difficult to see as most glossy magazine covers, family scrapbooks and wedding albums contain a plethora of photos that have been 'shopped' in one way or another. The results, in most cases, are amazing and in a few instances, even a little scary. But for the average photographer (judging by the requests from readers) the interest is not about wanting to recreate the plastic look of celebrity stardom but

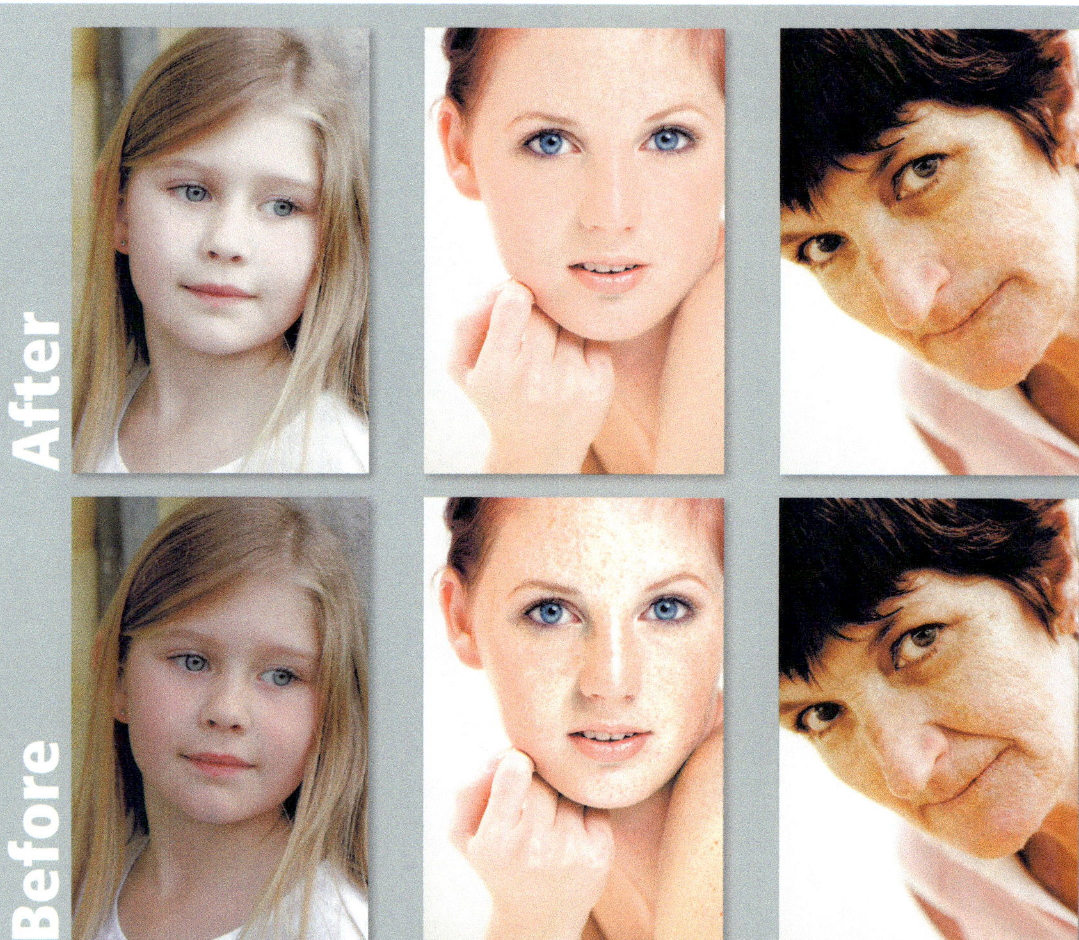

Technique 8.01>>
Add a dreamlike glow to your portraits using the Diffuse Glow filter.

Technique 8.02>>
Decrease the appearance of freckles whilst still retaining the texture of the skin.

Technique 8.03>>
Remove wrinkles and skin blemishes without destroying the realism of the photo.

rather it centers around the gentle art of photo enhancement. And in truth, I feel that this is the best use of the retouching power of programs like Elements.

Visual surgery without a hint of anything plastic

So with this in mind, I present here a few of the basic techniques that are used by portrait photographers on a daily basis. Most work with, rather than paint over, the basic structure and texture of the model's face and in so doing they carefully enhance what already exists rather than replace it with something that is manufactured.

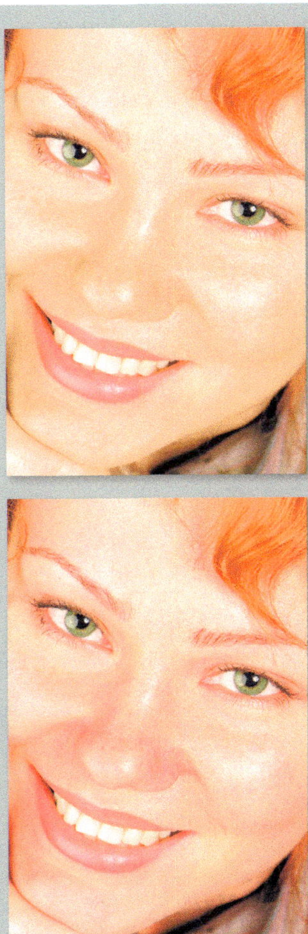

Technique 8.04>>
Correct the red skin tones that sometimes appear around noses, cheeks and ears.

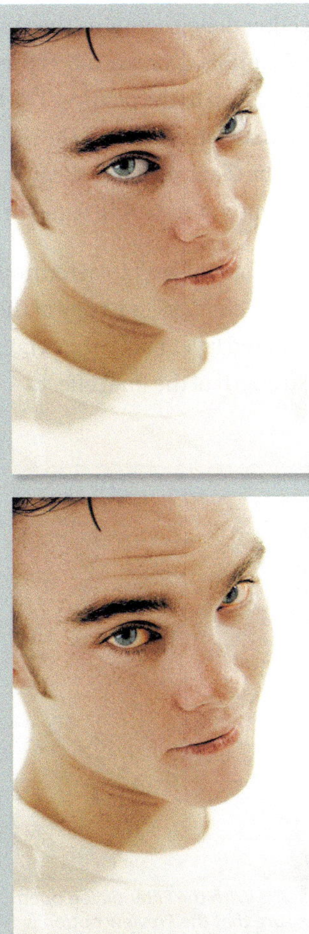

Technique 8.05>>
Clean up tired looking eyes with two simple adjustment layers.

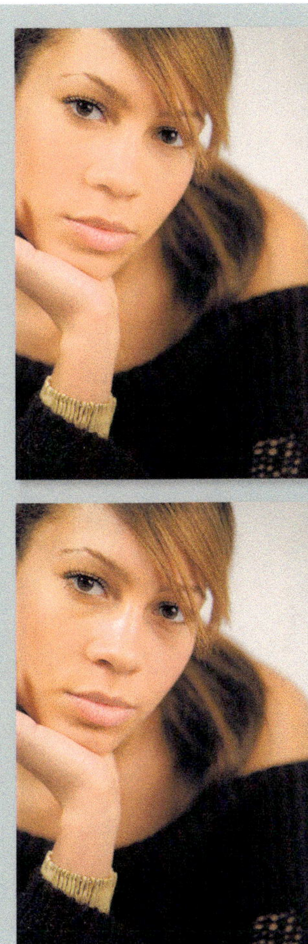

Technique 8.06>>
Remove shiny areas of skin and the dark tones beneath the eyes.

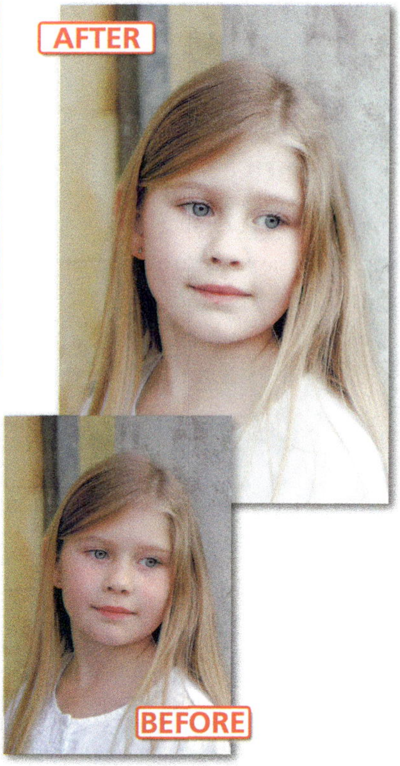

The Diffuse Glow filter adds a glamorous touch to standard portrait images.

8.01 Adding a dreamy effect

Suitable for Elements – 7.0, 6.0, 5.0, 4.0, 3.0, 2.0, 1.0 | Difficulty level – Basic
Menus used – Filter | Resources – Web image 801

The Diffuse Glow filter is one of the Distort group of filters that can be found in Photoshop Elements. The feature creates a high-key (very light), glamorous and slightly grainy glowing version of your picture. The filter is great for smoothing out surface marks on the skin of your subject and is often used to add a Hollywood feel to portraits. Try low settings to start with, keeping an eye on the changes in the filter's preview window to ensure that you are not losing important picture detail in the surface glow.

The Filter dialog contains three sliders and a preview window. The Graininess control alters the dominance of the noise that will be added to the picture. The Glow Amount slider changes the strength of white glow in the picture (and how much detail is lost to it). The Clear Amount slider acts as a counter balance to the Glow Amount restoring detail in the glowing areas of the picture.

As it is often difficult to determine how well the filter will work, apply the changes to a copy of the image layer first and then, with this filtered layer above the original, change its opacity to vary the strength of the final effect.

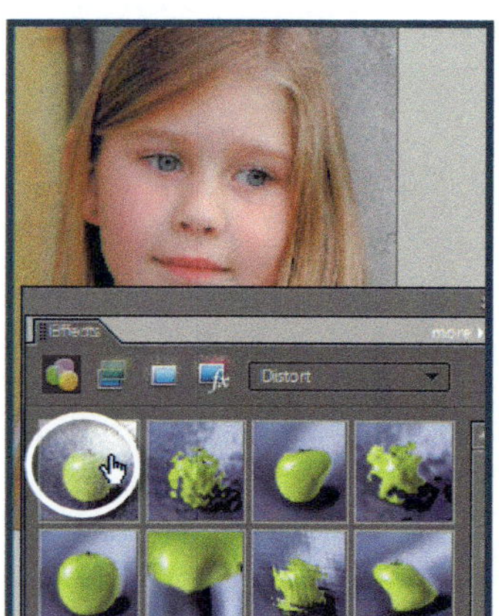

Step 1 >> *Make sure that the default foreground and background colors are selected and then with your picture open select the Diffuse Glow filter from the Distort group in the Filter menu. Alternatively you can also choose the feature from the Effects palette (Filters > Distort).*

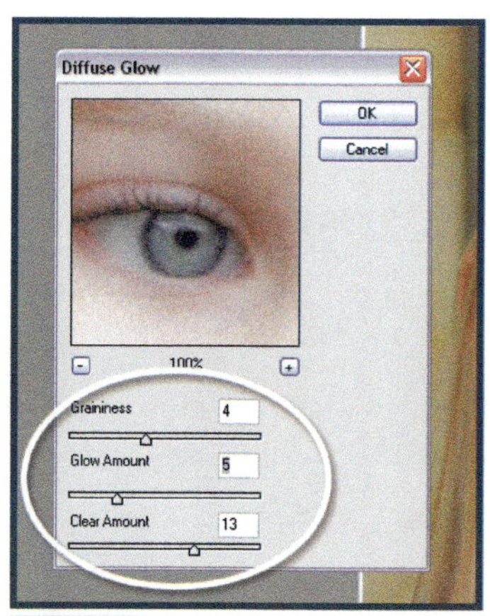

Step 2 >> *With the Filter dialog open make sure that the Preview option is clicked and that the preview window is set to 100%. Adjust the three sliders in turn carefully previewing the results. If necessary, drag the visible area in the preview window to examine more closely the changes in other areas of the picture. Click OK.*

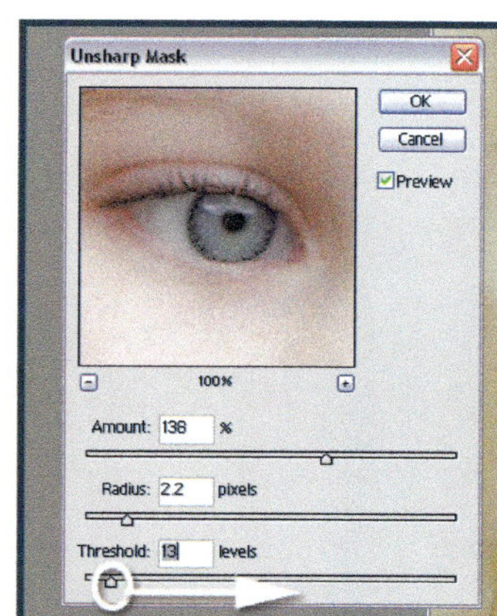

Step 3 >> *As a finishing touch for this example I decided to apply a little sharpening to the eyes to ensure that they stood out from the rest of the scene. Using the Filter > Sharpen > Unsharp Mask feature increase the Levels value to restrict the changes to the areas of the picture with the greatest contrast. Click OK to complete.*

8.02 Softening freckles

Suitable for Elements – 7.0, 6.0, 5.0, 4.0, 3.0, 2.0, 1.0 | Difficulty level – Intermediate Tools – Brush | Resources – Web image 802

So many good retouching techniques are not about totally removing or changing the basic structure or make-up of the model's face. Instead, the aim should be to gently enhance the existing skin tones and textures. There is nothing worse, nor more obvious, than an overworked portrait where the skin's original texture and tone are replaced with a flat (or sometimes even shiny) surface that has more in common with plastic appliances than anyone I know.

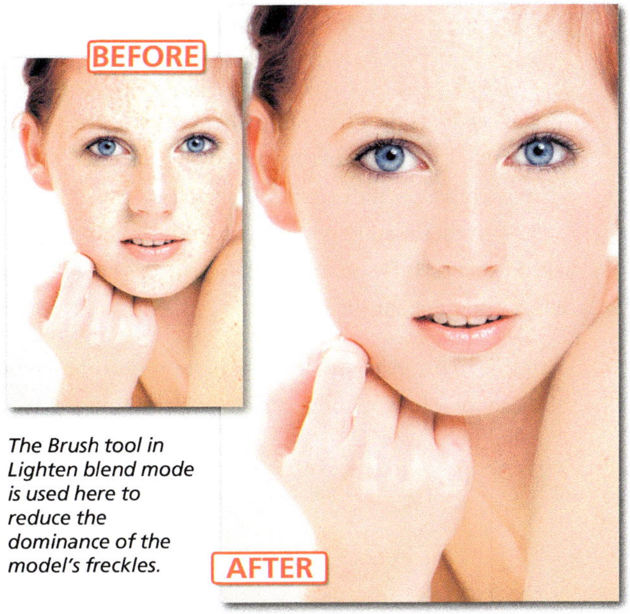

The Brush tool in Lighten blend mode is used here to reduce the dominance of the model's freckles.

The example image is typical of the sort of photograph that is normally overworked. In an attempt to smooth out the appearance of the model's freckly skin most photographer's completely remove this skin characteristic with the result that the final portrait resembles a computer-generated model rather than an actual living and breathing person. This technique aims to reduce the dominance of the freckles rather than removing them totally. In this way the underlying structure of the face shines through and is complemented with, rather than over-ridden by, just a hint of the freckles.

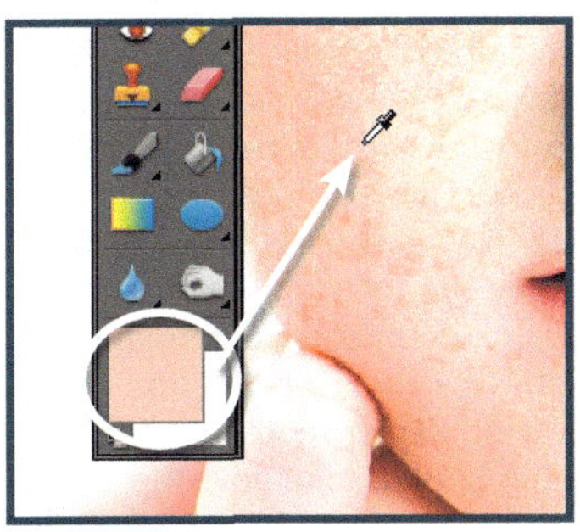

Step 1 >> *Select the Eyedropper tool and then check to see that the Sample Size (in the options bar) is set to average 3 × 3 or 5 × 5 pixels. Next select a flesh color from the portrait that represents a midtone of the range available across the face surface.*

Pro's Tip: *The tone you select at this point in the process will determine which freckles are lightened. Choosing a darker skin tone will change only a few of the darkest freckles whereas a lighter tone selection will alter both midtone and dark freckles.*

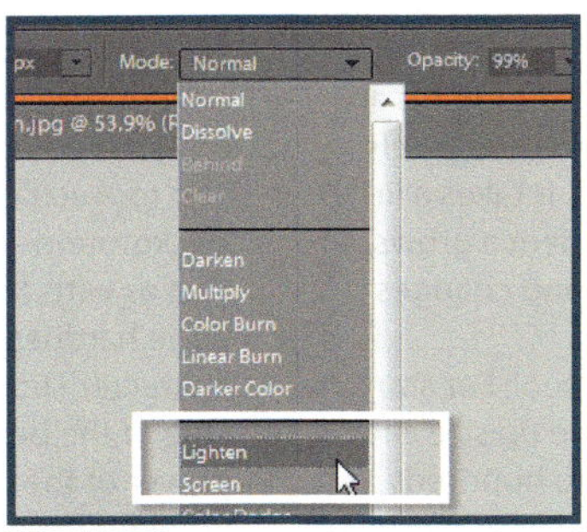

Step 2 >> *With the skin tone selected the next step is to select the Brush tool and then switch the tool's blend mode to Lighten. Do this by selecting the Lighten option from the drop-down mode list in the tool's option bar. When the brush is in the Lighten mode Elements compares the paint color with the pixels being painted over. If the pixels are darker then they are replaced with the paint color, effectively lightening the area.*

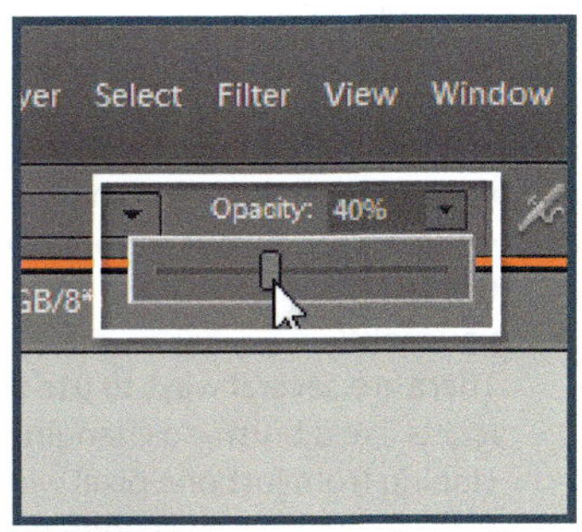

Step 3 >> *The next step is to adjust the opacity of the Brush. Turn again to the options bar and this time reduce the opacity to about 40%. An opacity setting of 100% would produce a result that was too smooth. Reducing the opacity has the effect of allowing a little of the old freckle texture to show through – maintaining the feeling of realism whilst reducing the freckle's dominance. Now paint away, being careful not to paint over details like eyelashes as you go.*

8.03 Eliminating blemishes

Suitable for Elements – 7.0, 6.0, 5.0, 4.0, 3.0, 2.0, 1.0 | Difficulty level – Intermediate
Tools – Spot Healing Brush, Healing Brush, Clone Stamp | Resources – Web image 803

Ethical issues aside, Photoshop Elements is a great tool for removing, or at least making less pronounced, a variety of unwanted photo elements. Despite the fact that skin blemishes and wrinkles are a normal everyday occurrence for most of us, photographers are constantly asked to retouch these sections of portrait photos. Like all other techniques discussed here, the secret behind successful retouching of these areas is not to remove them completely but rather to reduce their appearance.

With this in mind let's look at the three tools that Elements offers for blemish removal and then set these tools to work on a typical portrait image.

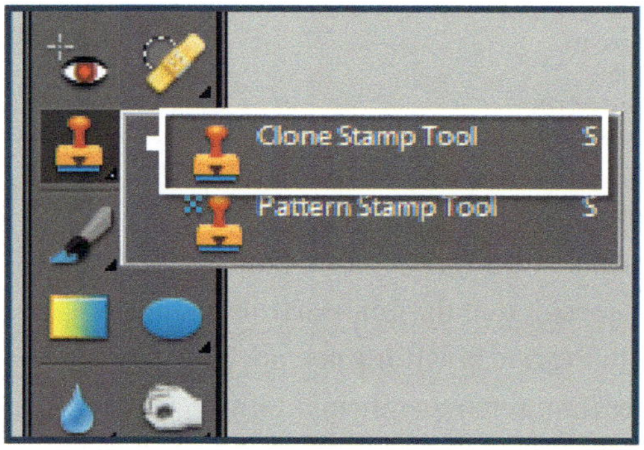

Clone Stamp tool

The most basic of all the retouching tools is called the Clone Stamp tool (or sometimes the Rubber Stamp tool). The feature selects and samples an area of your picture and then uses these pixels to paint over the offending marks. It takes a little getting used to, but as your confidence grows, so too will the quality of the repairs and changes you make.

There are several ways to use the tool. For starters, it acts like a brush, so changing the tip size allows cloning from just one pixel wide to hundreds across. You can also change the opacity in order to produce a range of subtle clone effects. It can be used in conjunction with any one of the options from the Blend menu and, most importantly, there's a choice between Cloning aligned or non-aligned with the sample area.

Select Aligned and the sample cursor will follow the destination cursor around keeping a constant distance between the two. When the Aligned option is unchecked the sample cursor starts where you left off with all ensuing paint strokes. Both choices have their advantages.

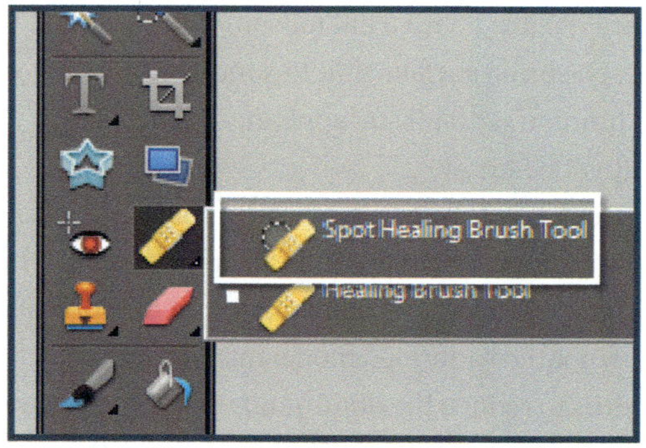

Healing Brush tool

The Healing Brush is designed to work in a similar way to the Clone Stamp tool; the user selects the area (Alt-click) to be sampled and then proceeds to drag the brush tip over the area to be repaired.

The tool achieves great results by merging background and source area details as you paint. Just as with the Clone Stamp tool, the size and edge hardness of the current brush determines the characteristics of the Healing Brush tool tip.

One of the best ways to demonstrate the sheer power of the Healing Brush is to remove the wrinkles from an aged face. In the step-by-step example image we used here, the deep crevices of the model's face have been easily removed with the tool.

The texture, color and tone of the face remain even after the 'healing' work is completed because the tool merges the new areas with the detail of the picture beneath.

Note: Sometimes the best source for sampling can be found in a different photo. With these both the Clone Stamp and Healing Brush tools, you can Alt-click in any open photo and sample from it.

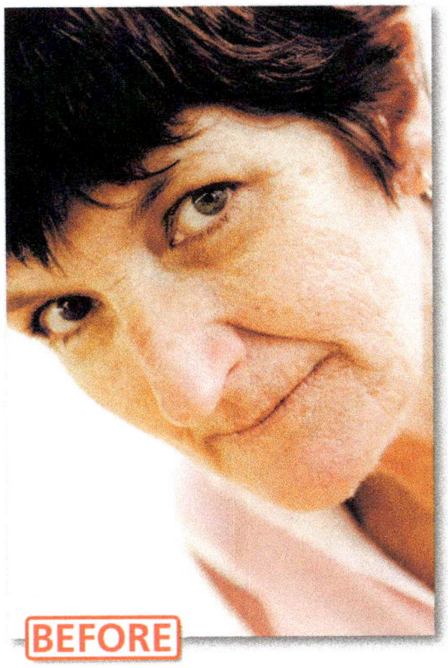

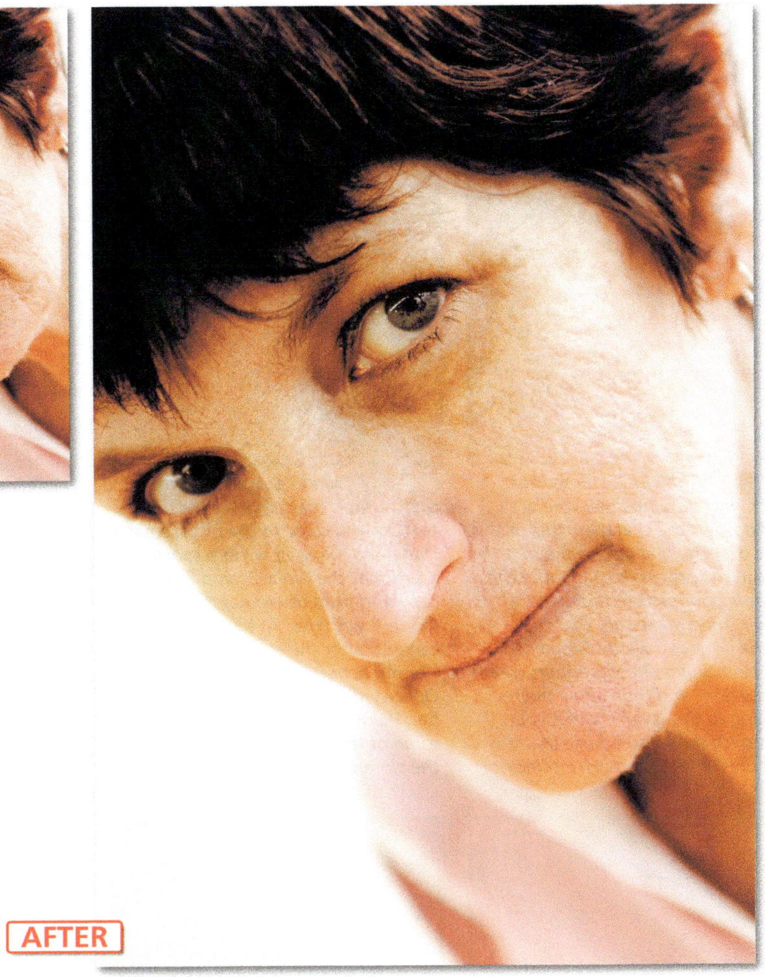

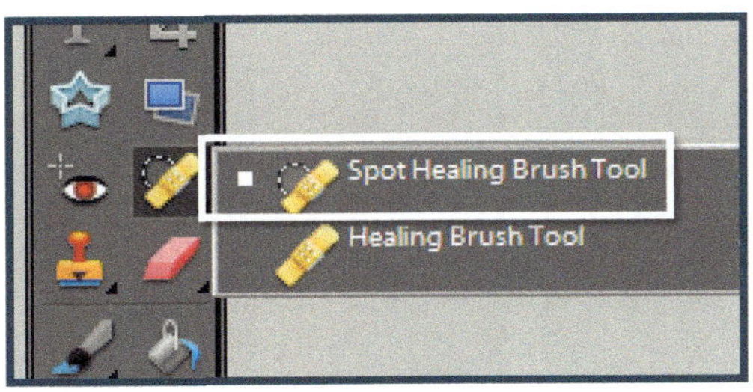

By carefully using any of the three retouching tools in Photoshop Elements it is possible to gently remove skin blemishes and signs of age like wrinkles and cracks.

Spot Healing Brush

In recognition of just how tricky it can be to get seamless dust removal with the Clone Stamp tool, Adobe decided to include the Spot Healing Brush in Photoshop Elements.

After selecting the new tool you adjust the size of the brush tip using the options in the tool's option bar and then click on the dust spots and small marks in your pictures.

The Spot Healing Brush uses the texture that surrounds the mark as a guide to how the program should 'paint over' the area. In this way, Elements tries to match color, texture and tone whilst eliminating the dust mark.

But don't just use this tool for spots, scratches too can get the treatment by click-dragging the tool's tip across the mark. The results are terrific and this tool should be the one that you reach for first when there is dust to remove from your photographs.

Clone Stamp tool step-by-step

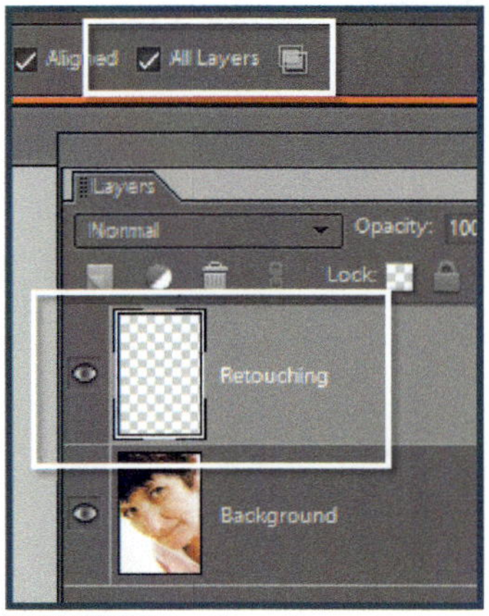

Step 1 >> *The Clone Stamp tool works by sampling a selected area and pasting the characteristics of this area over the blemish, so the first step in the process is to identify the areas in your picture that need repair. Then make sure that the image layer you want to repair is selected. Some photographers create a new layer and then apply their cloning to this layer. If this is your approach then also ensure that the Sample All Layers option is selected.*

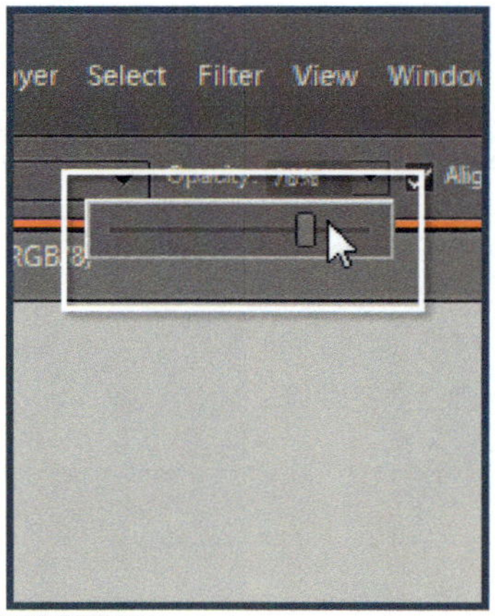

Step 2 >> *Next, locate areas in the photograph that are a similar tone, texture and color to the picture parts that need fixing. It is these sampled areas that the Clone Stamp tool will copy and then use to paint over the model's wrinkles. At this point you can also alter the transparency of the cloning action by adjusting the Opacity slider in the tool's options bar. Values less than 100% will let some of the original texture through the clones areas.*

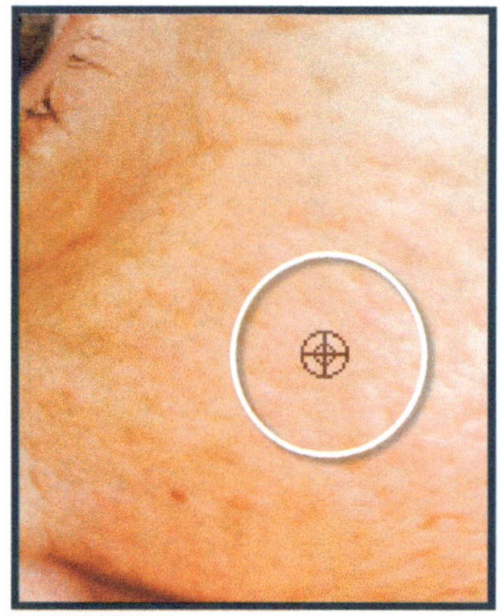

Step 3 >> *Now select the area to be sampled, or the 'Sample Point'. Do this by holding down the Alt key and clicking the left mouse button when the cursor (now changed to cross hairs) is over a part of the image that suits the area to be repaired.*

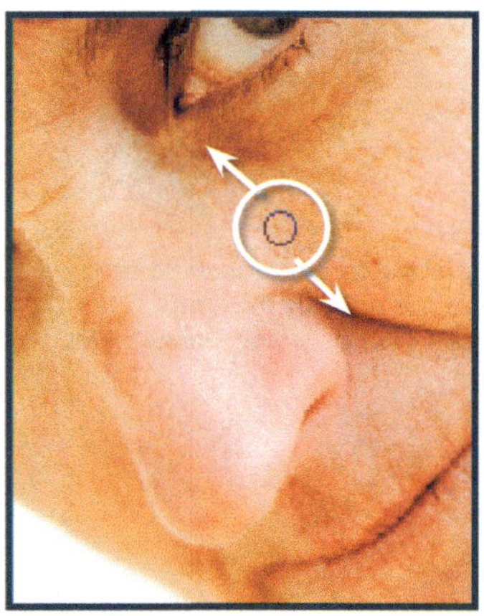

Step 4 >> *With the sample point selected you can now move the cursor to the area to be fixed. Click on the blemish and a copy of the sample point area is pasted over the mark. Depending on how well you chose the sample area, the blemish will now be blended into the background seamlessly. Continue to click and drag to repair more areas.*

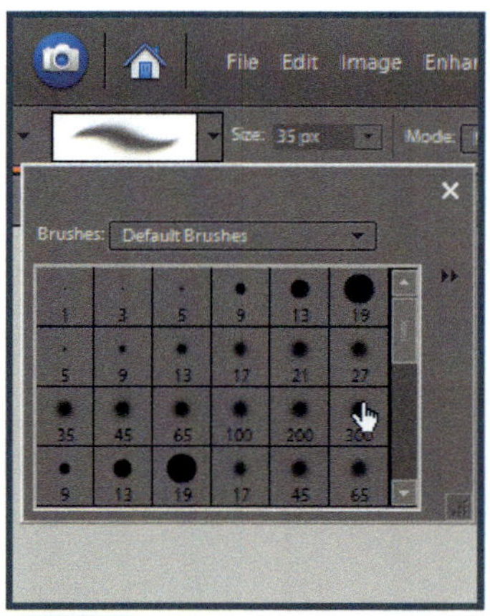

Step 5 >> *You may need to reselect your sample point if you find that the color, texture or tone doesn't match the surrounds of the blemish. You can also change the brush size and hardness to alter the characteristics of both the sample and stamp areas. A softer edge helps blend the edge areas of the newly painted parts of the picture with the original image. Simply select a different brush tip from the Brush Preset drop- down palette.*

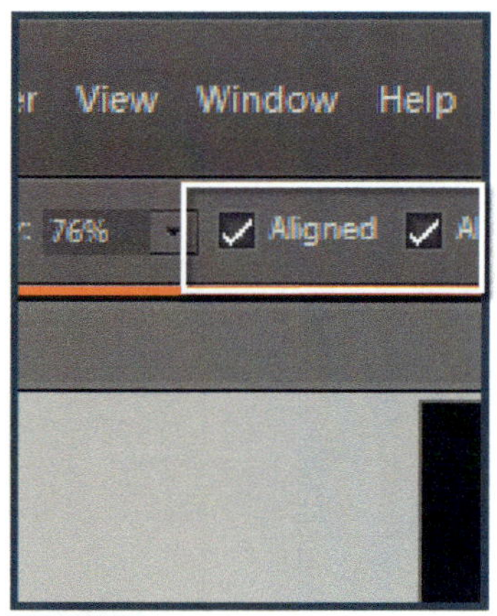

Step 6 >> *Switching between aligned and non-aligned (when the Aligned option is not selected) can really help when you are rebuilding missing parts of your restoration project. 'Aligned' sets the sample point so that it remains the same distance from the stamped area no matter where on the picture you start to click, and 'Non-aligned' repositions the sample point back to the original sample spot each time the mouse is moved and then clicked.*

Healing Brush tool step-by-step

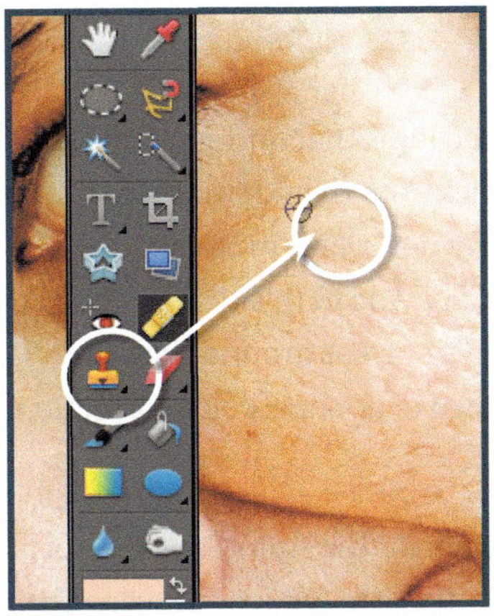

Step 1 >> *The Healing Brush is also a two-step process. After selecting the tool hold down the Alt/Option key and click a clear skin area to use as the sample for the healing. This action is the same as you would take when using the Clone Stamp tool to select a sample point.*

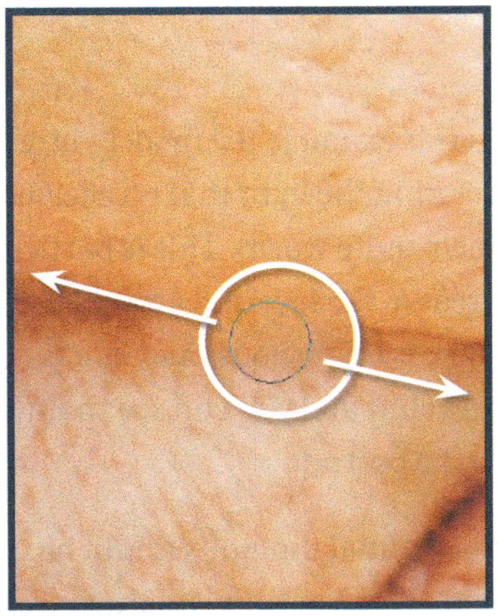

Step 2 >> *Now move to the area to be repaired and click-drag the cursor over the blemish. The Healing Brush will use the tones, textures and color of the sampled area to paint over the blemish but unlike the Clone Stamp tool, the Brush takes into account the general tone of the repair area and does a great job of seamlessly merging the new detail with the old.*

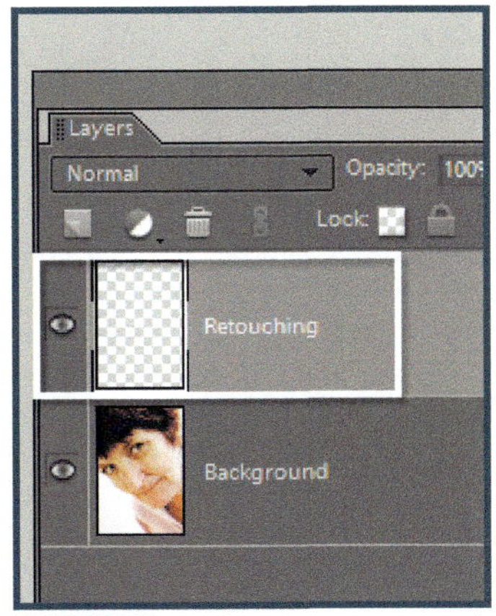

Step 3 >> *Like the Clone Stamp tool the Healing Brush contains a Sample All Layers option enabling photographers to perform non-destructive editing of their photos by painting the retouched areas onto a separate layer. Using a retouching layer also means that you can interactively adjust the strength of the changes via the layer's Opacity settings.*

Spot Healing Brush tool step-by-step

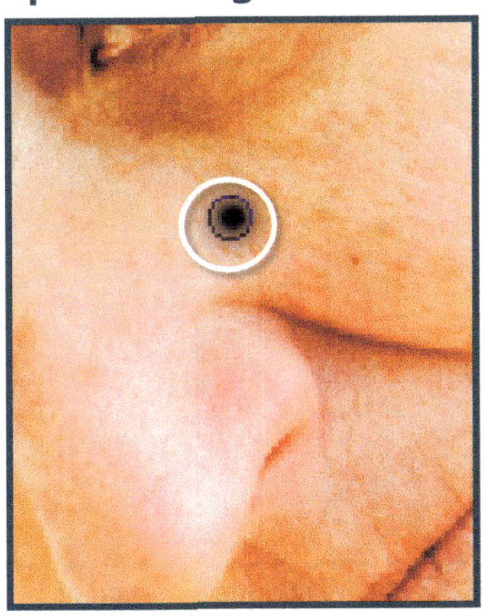

Step 1 >> *The Spot version of the Healing Brush removes the sampling step from the process. To use the brush you simply select the feature, adjust the brush tip size and harness and then click onto the blemish. Almost magically the Brush will analyse the surrounding texture, color and tones and use this as a basis for painting over the problem area.*

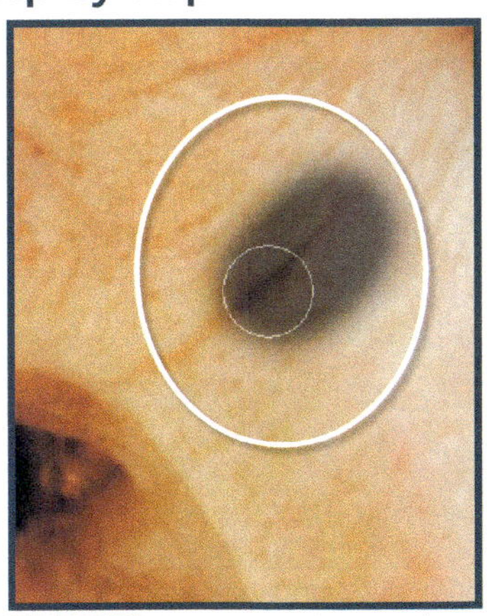

Step 2 >> *The Spot Healing Brush can also be used for removing marks, hairs, streaks or cracks by click-dragging the tool across the offending blemish.*
Pro's tip: *If unwanted detail is used to cover the repaired area undo the changes and then draw around the area to be healed with the Lasso tool and apply the brush again. This restricts the area around the blemish that the tool uses to heal.*

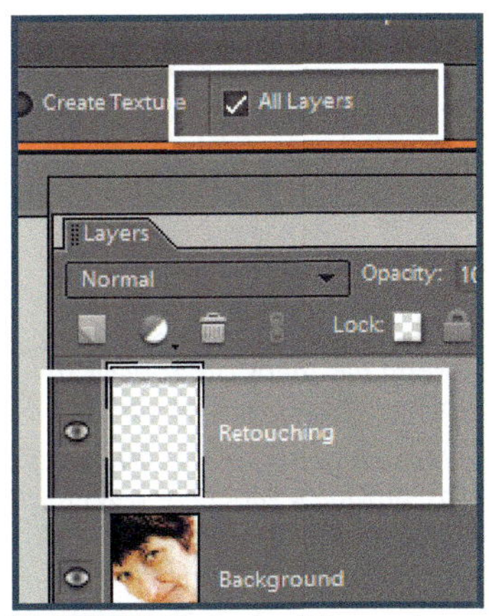

Step 3 >> *Like both of the previous tools the Spot Healing Brush also contains a Sample All Layers option enabling photographers to perform non-destructive editing of their photos by painting the retouched areas onto a separate layer. Using a retouching layer also means that you can interactively adjust the strength of the changes via the layer's Opacity settings.*

8.04 Removing the Red

Suitable for Elements – 7.0, 6.0, 5.0, 4.0, 3.0, 2.0, 1.0 | Difficulty level – Intermediate | Tools – Lasso | Resources – Web image 804

In this example the model's bright red (or is that orange?) hair is coloring the light that is reflected back onto the skin tones making them quite warm. This is particularly noticeable in the shadow areas of the face and around the hands. Add to this the fact that there is an obvious magenta tinge to the areas around the nose and chin and you can see that we need to do some color correction to the portrait.

Your initial thoughts might be to reach for the Auto Color Correct and Color Variations feature and use these to reduce the warmth in the photo but this action has the effect of reducing the vibrancy of the hair color at the same time as neutralizing the skin tones. This is not a desired scenario as the hair color is one of the strongest aspects of the image. So instead of making global (all over) changes to the picture this technique uses the Eyedropper tool to sample an area of neutral skin and then employs the Brush tool in Color mode to paint out the overly warm tones. This technique can be used to neutralize 'red ears' or the 'red nose' that is a sure sign of too much indulgence of the wine variety.

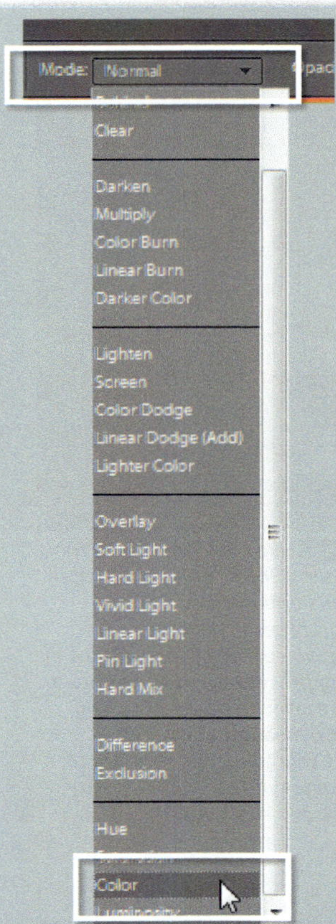

The way that color applied with the Brush tool interacts with the pixels being painted over is determined by the blend mode selected at the time of painting.

By default the Brush tool's mode is set to normal which causes the paint to obscure the pixels beneath, but Photoshop has many other ways to control how these pixels interact.

Called blend modes, these different options provide a variety of ways to control the mixing, blending and general interaction of the paint and the content beneath.

Blend modes can also be applied to the drawing tools via a drop-down menu in the tool's options bar as well as individual layers via the drop-down menu located at the top left of the Layers palette.

The retouching technique outlined here makes use of the Color blend mode to neutralize the red or magenta tinges that sometimes appear in portraits.

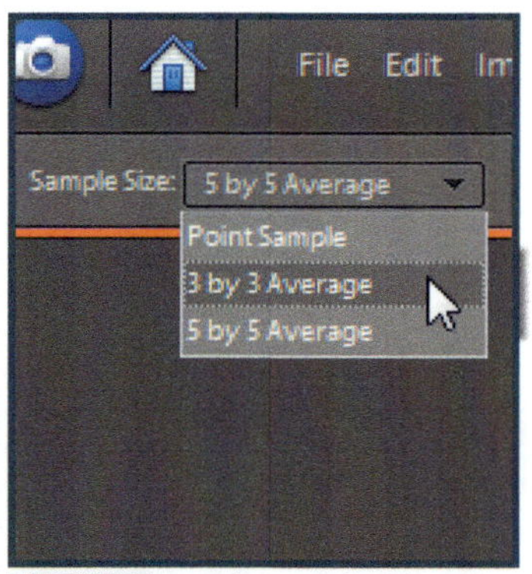

Step 1 >> *Start by ensuring that the Eyedropper tool's Sample Size is set to an average of either '3 × 3' or '5 × 5' pixels and not the Point Sample setting. To do this select the tool and then choose a different option from the drop-down list on the tool's options bar. This change will make sure that when you use the tool that you sample an average of the pixel tones and colors rather than just a single pixel's value.*

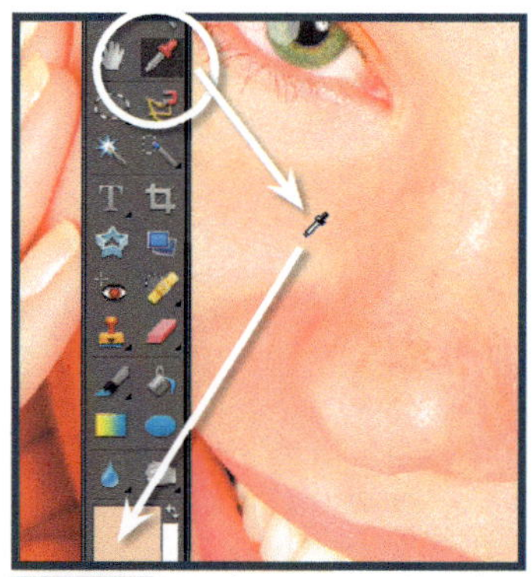

Step 2 >> *Next locate a portion of skin tone that is free from red or magenta casts and click on it with the Eyedropper tool. You will notice that the foreground color in the toolbox now contains the color you sampled. Check to see that the color is not too dark or light and that the hue is free from any strange casts. If this isn't the case, then resample a different areas of skin until you are happy with the color.*

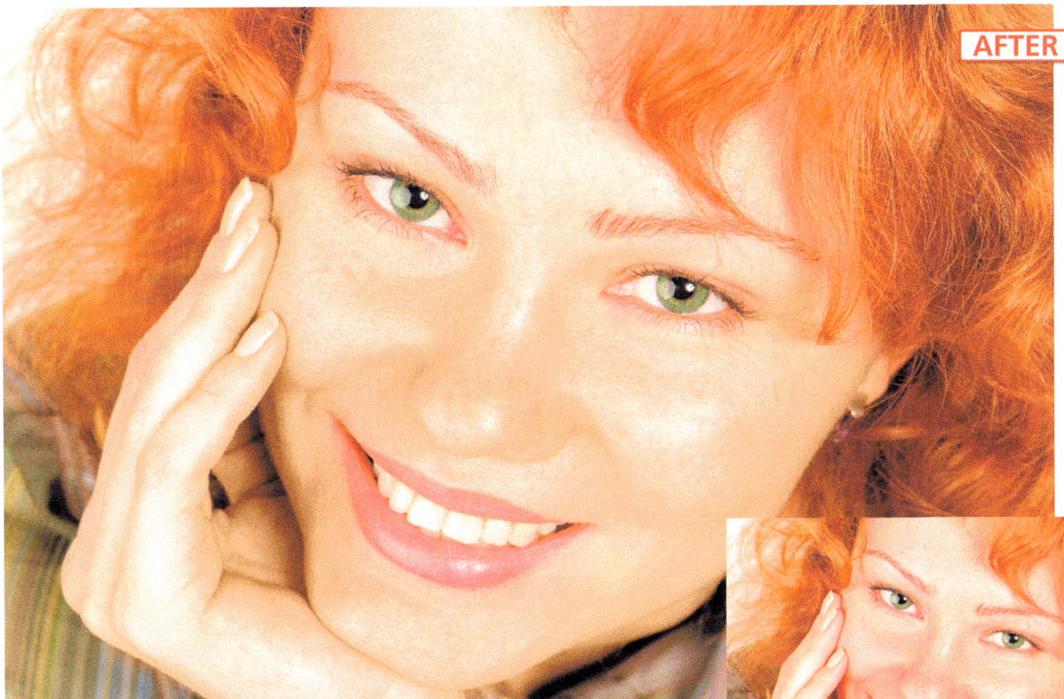

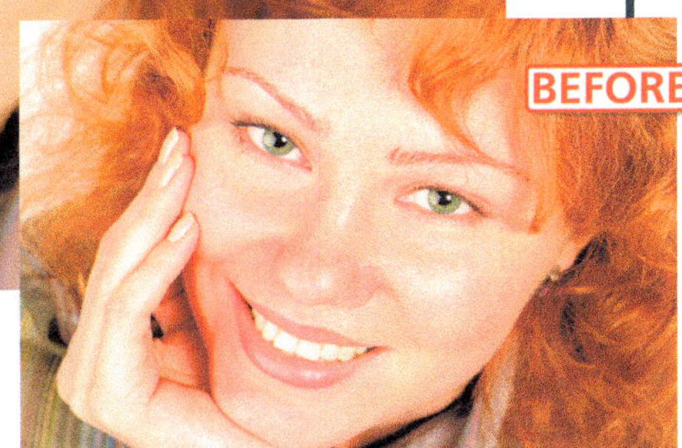

Even out skin tones by sampling and using the model's own skin color to remove unwanted areas of red and magenta.

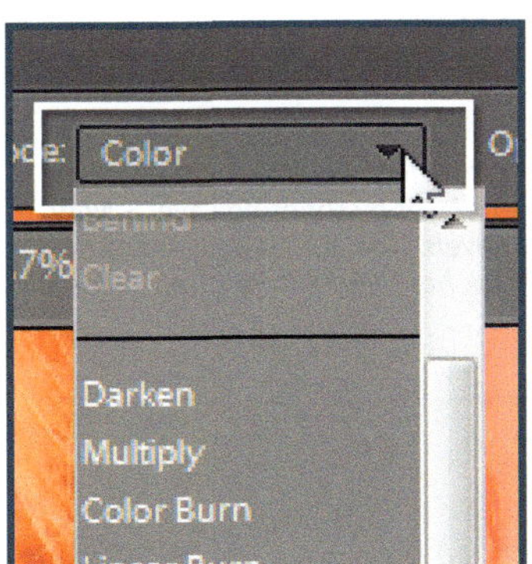

Step 3 >> *With the skin color set as the foreground color select the Brush tool and change the Blend mode from Normal to Color (towards the bottom of the drop-down list in the Brush tool's options bar).*

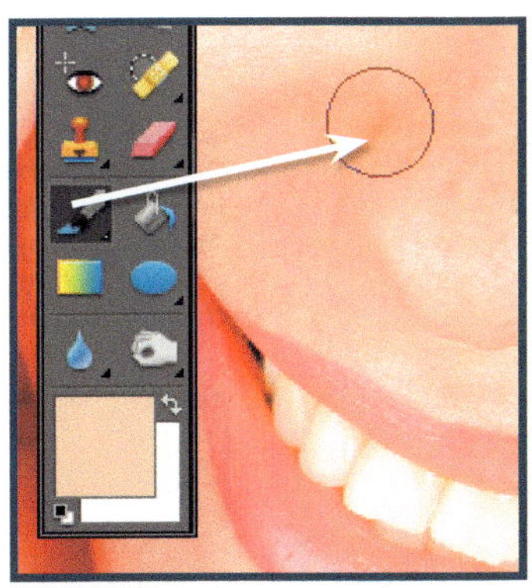

Step 4 >> *The last step in the process is to apply the skin colored paint over the red/magenta areas in the photo. Notice that because the brush is in the Color mode that the paint is laid down in such a way that the details of the photo beneath are retained and only the color is altered.*

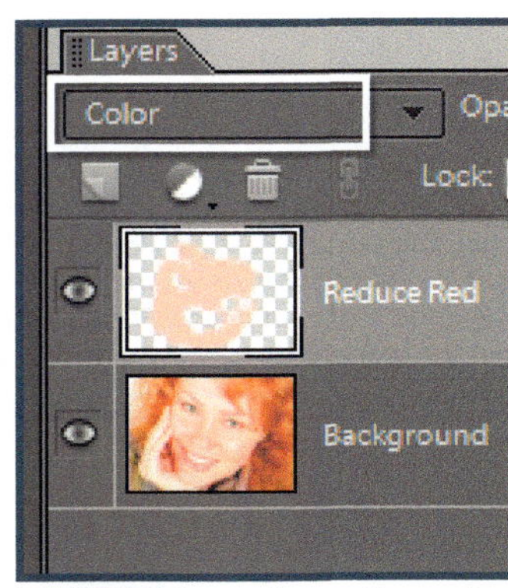

Step 5 >> *A non-destructive version of this technique starts with creating a new empty layer above the original photo. Next change the Blend mode of the new layer to Color using the drop-down list at the top of the Layers palette. Select the skin tone with the Eyedropper tool and then switch to the Brush tool. Make sure it is set to the Normal mode and then brush this color onto the new layer. With this approach the colorization of the skin is handled by the layer's blend mode.*

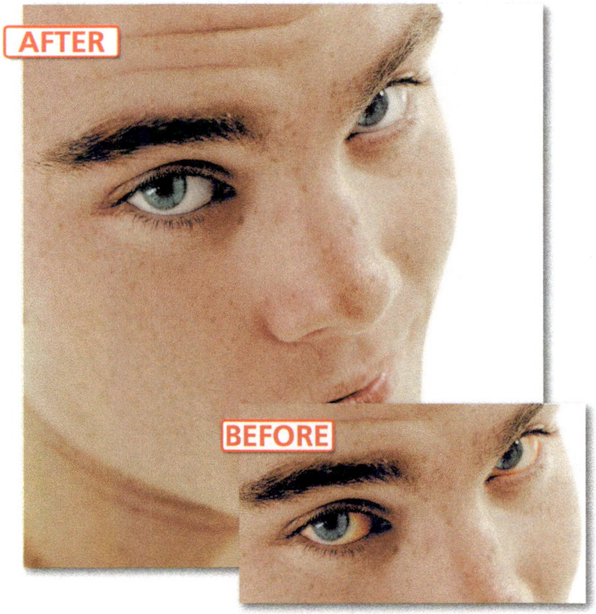

8.05 Brighten Eyes

Suitable for Elements – 7.0, 6.0, 5.0, 4.0, 3.0, 2.0, 1.0 Difficulty level – Intermediate
Tools – Lasso | | Resources – Web image 805

No amount of clever photography or tricky lighting can cover the traces of lack of sleep or overindulgence in the eyes of your model. A set of 'sore red eyes' staring back at you can easily ruin an otherwise well-produced photo. Elements certainly has the tools to add back the sparkle and life, but over enhancing can easily lead to sci-fi-like results. This technique uses a selection with a couple of adjustment layers for its effect, allowing changes and fine-tuning to the strength of the effect at a later date.

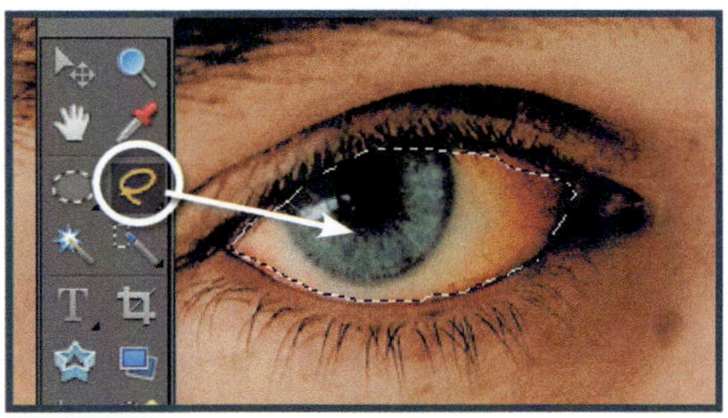

Step 1 >> *Use the Lasso tool to make a careful selection around the main part of the eye. Soften the edge by choosing Select > Feather. Here I used a value of 5 pixels but the setting you use will be determined by the pixel dimensions of your photo. Photos with more pixels will need a larger feather, those with less a smaller amount.*

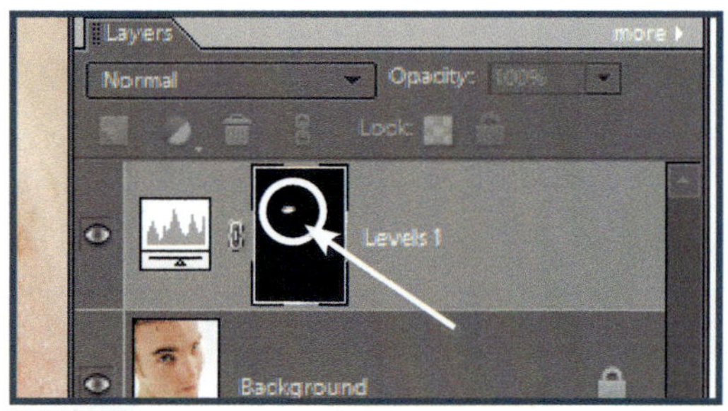

Step 2 >> *With the Eyes selections still active, create a new Levels adjustment layer by choosing Layer > New Adjustment Layer > Levels. Notice that because of the active selection, a mask has been automatically added to the adjustment layer.*

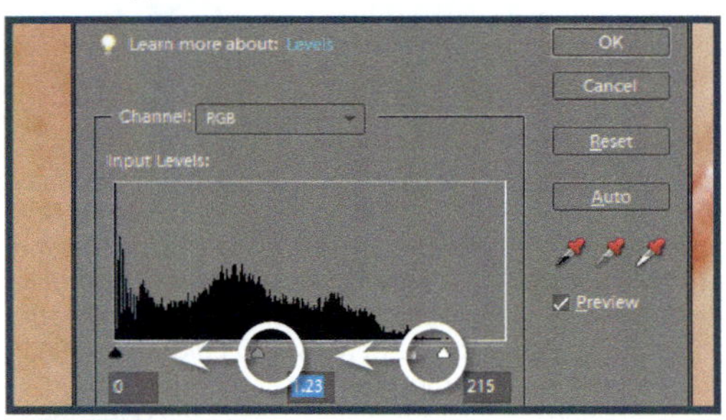

Step 3 >> *The addition of a mask means that the changes made in the Levels dialog will be restricted to the clear part of the mask (the eyes). Add a simple brightening and contrast adjustment by dragging the black and white. Click the OK button to apply the changes. Re-select the eye areas by Ctrl/Command clicking the mask section of the adjustment layer.*

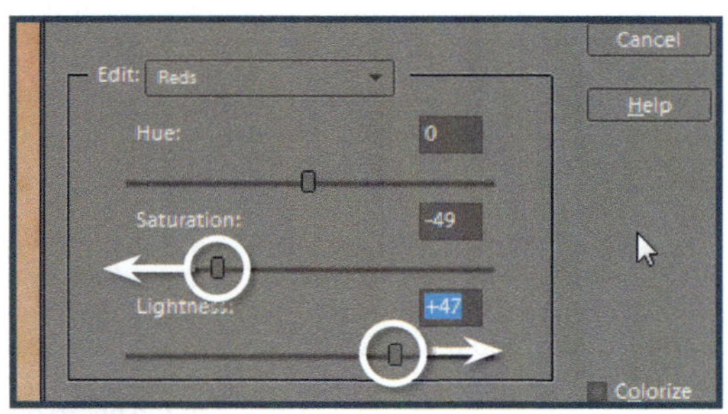

Step 4 >> *Now add a Hue/Saturation adjustment layer. Again the changes will be limited to the eyes via the mask. Select Red in the drop-down Edit menu at the top of the dialog and then pull down the Saturation slider and push up the Lighten setting. This will help to lessen the red veins in the eyes. Click OK to apply.*

PROFESSIONAL RETOUCHING

8.06 Tone down skin highlights and shadows

Suitable for Elements – 7.0, 6.0, 5.0, 4.0, 3.0, 2.0, 1.0 | Difficulty level – Intermediate Tools – Brush | Resources – Web image 806

The example image has all the attributes of a great portrait but as with a lot of photos of this type there are a couple of places where the model's skin is a little shiny and the area under her eyes is a little dark. Gentle lightening of the dark areas and darkening of the light area are two techniques that, when mastered, you will use often when enhancing your portrait images.

This technique makes use of the Brush tool in both Lighten and Darken blending modes, along with the model's own skin color, to reduce the appearance of these areas in the final image.

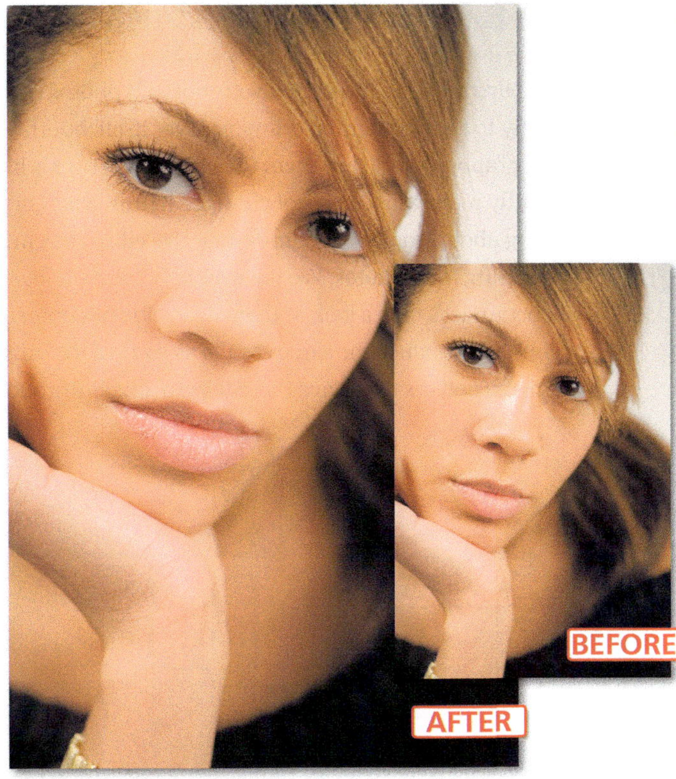

Remove shiny skin areas and bags under the eyes using the Brush in Lighten/Darken modes.

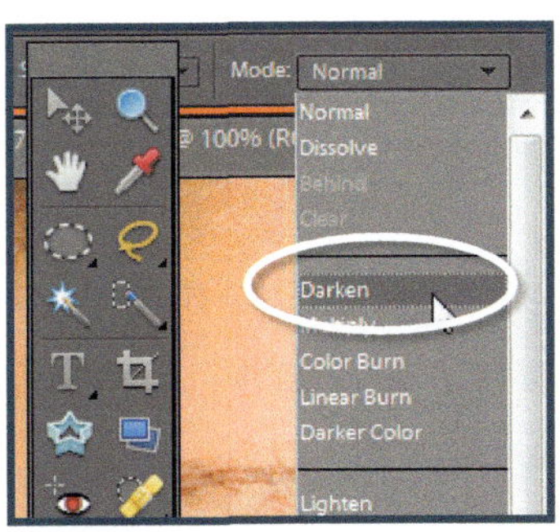

Step 1 >> *Start by selecting the Brush tool from the tool bar. Next go to the tool's options bar and select Darken as the Brush mode. At the same time I also adjust the opacity of the tool so that a little of the original texture remains after retouching. Then select a flesh tone that is slightly darker than the highlight areas whilst still using the brush by holding down the Alt key and clicking on the skin color.*

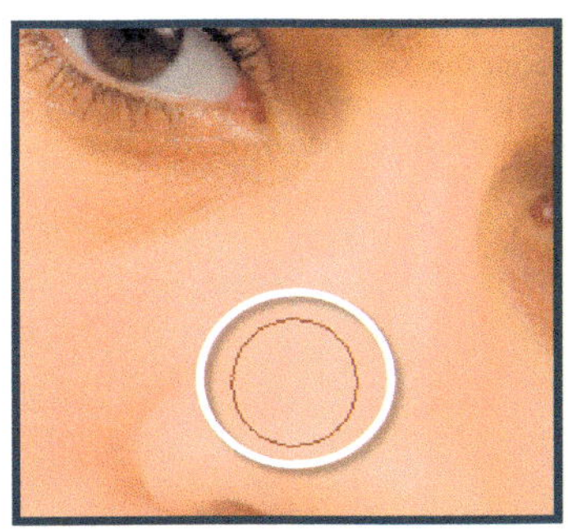

Step 2 >> *Next gently brush over the shiny areas on the model's nose, forehead and cheek regions. When brushing using the Darken mode, only the pixels that are lighter than the sampled color will be adjusted. For the best results keep selecting different sample colors as you brush.* ***Pro's tip:*** *For even more control apply the enhancement changes to a separate layer. The strength of the changes can then be adjusted via the layer's Opacity setting.*

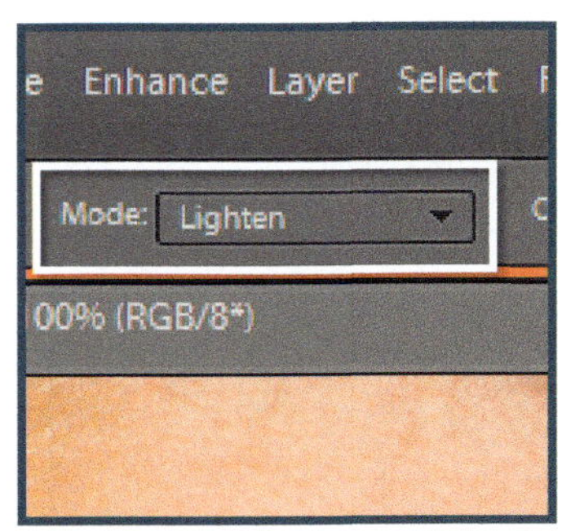

Step 3 >> *The same technique can also be used to lighten the dark areas under the model's eyes. This time select the Lighten mode before sampling a flesh tone that is slightly lighter than the dark areas you want to fix. Again make sure that you choose a range of sample tones whilst brushing to ensure that the results are not too uniform and plastic looking. If you applied the changes to a separate layer, adjust the opacity of the layer to bring back some of the underlying face structure.*

8.07 Retouching non-destructively

Suitable for Elements – 7.0, 6.0, 5.0, 4.0, 3.0 | Difficulty level – Intermediate

When first starting to retouch your portrait photos it seems logical to apply the changes directly to the photograph or image layer itself, but this is not the way that most professional photographers work. For them the original picture is like the negatives of old and should be carefully maintained and not changed in any way. For this reason you will often hear them talking about employing non-destructive editing techniques as an alternative method for retouching their photos. We have already touched on some of these techniques but they are so important let's take a look at them again in the context of enhancing portraits. Remember these techniques produce the same results as editing the original image but employ some advanced Elements options that leave these 'virgin' pixels untouched.

Sample all layers

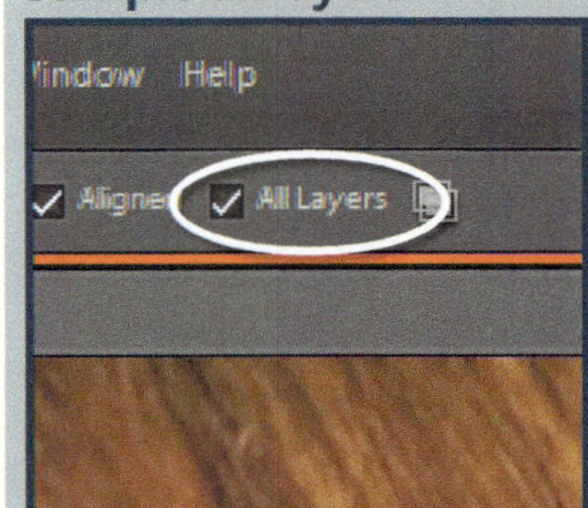

Step 1 >> *Retouching features such as the Clone Stamp, Spot Healing Brush and Healing Brush tools all contain an All Layers setting on their options bar. Designed to allow the tools to retouch the contents of several layers this option can also be used to protect your original photo pixels.*

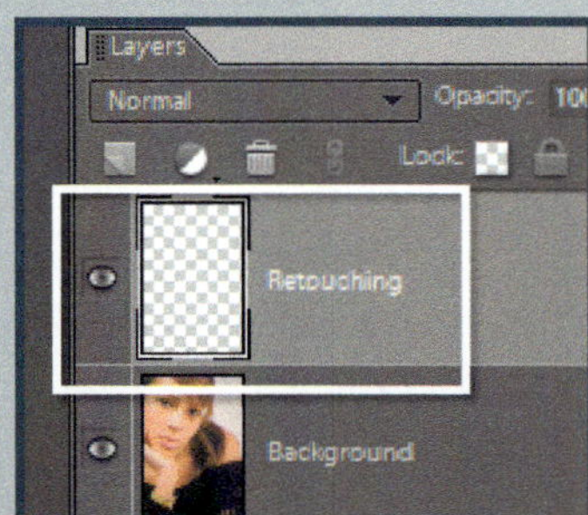

Step 2 >> *To make use of this option for non-destructive retouching firstly create a new blank layer above the image layer. Make this the active layer and then select the retouching tool and choose the Sample All Layers option. Now when you retouch the changes will be stored on the newly created layer.*

Use Adjustment layers

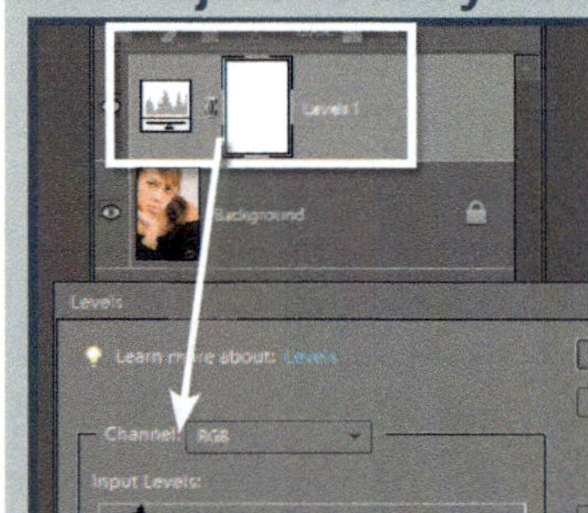

Step 1 >> *Many of the editing or enhancement changes that are possible via the options in the Enhance menu can also be applied via Adjustment Layers. Wherever possible use an Adjustment Layer to make a change rather than applying the alteration directly to the image.*

Retouch duplicate layer

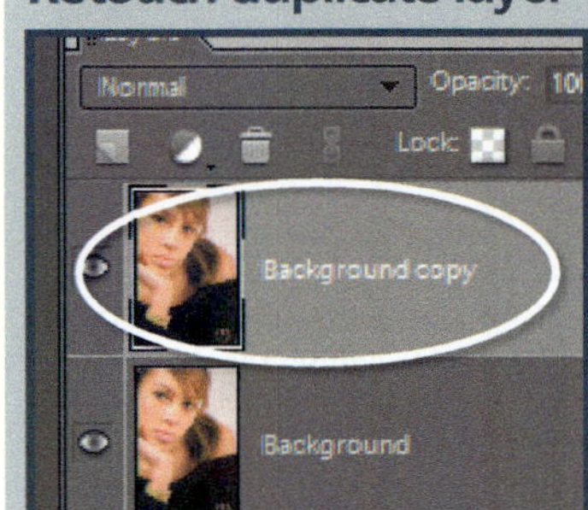

Step 1 >> *If the technique you are using can't be applied non-destructively then make a duplicate of the image layer and make the changes to the copied image instead of the original. This also gives you the chance to adjust the strength of the changes with the layer's Opacity slider.*

Mask editing adjustments

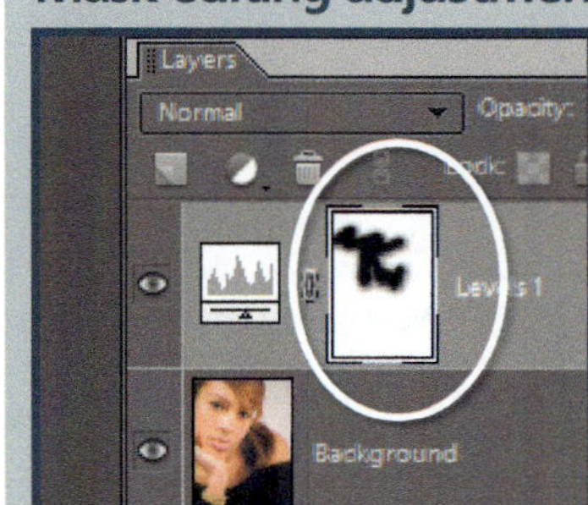

Step 1 >> *Keep in mind that you can mask the effects of adjustment layers by selecting the layer mask in the Layers palette and then painting onto the image with black to hide the effect and white to apply the change.*

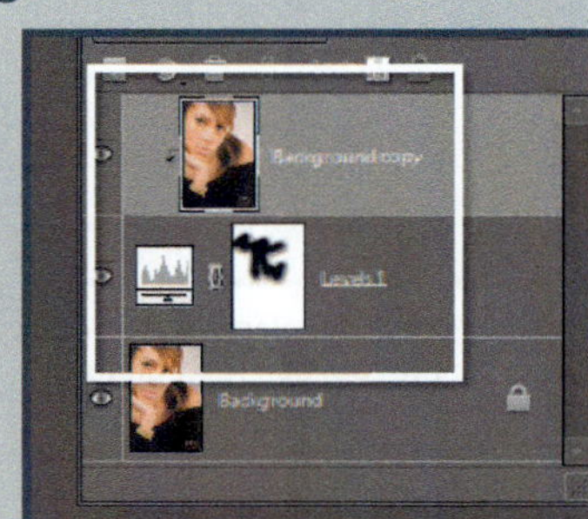

Step 2 >> *You can also selectively apply the effects of a duplicate image layer by grouping this layer with a blank (no settings applied) Levels adjustment layer. Once grouped painting onto the Levels layer mask will either hide or apply the changes made in the duplicate layer.*

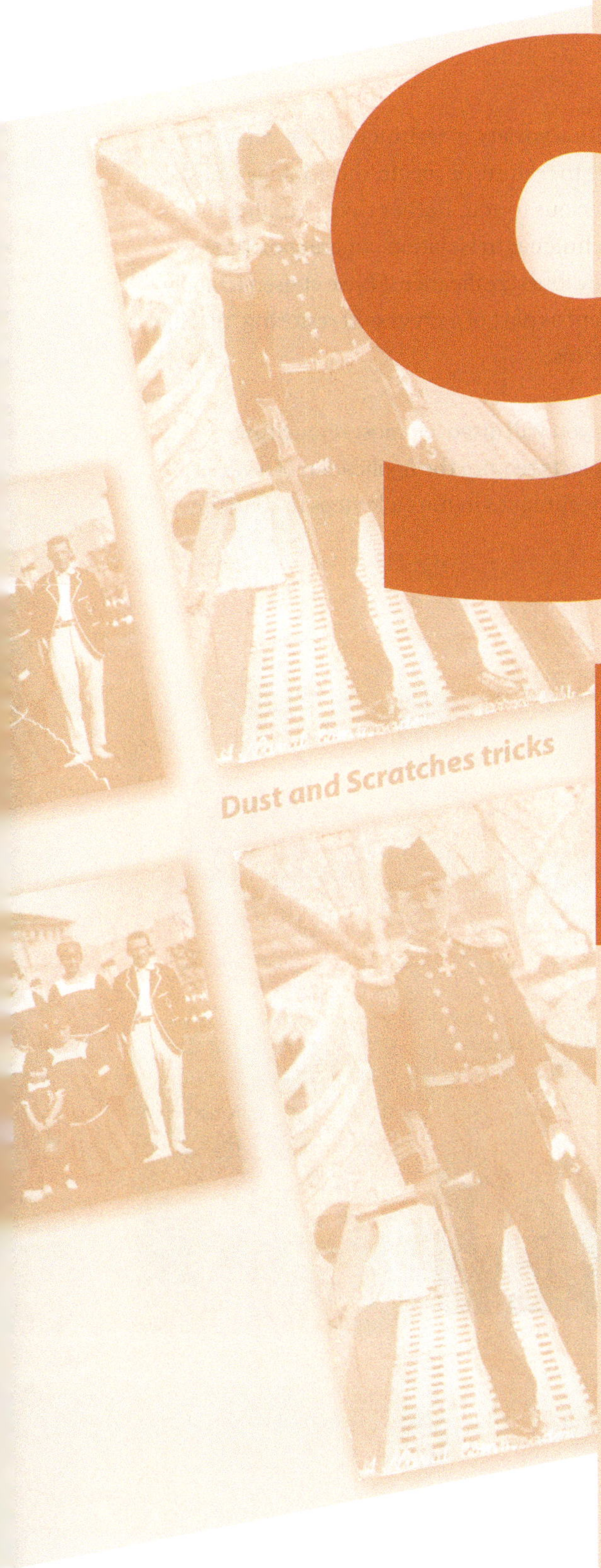

9

Photo Restoration

As a digital photography author one of the areas that I am often asked about is photo restoration. As photographers, it is an editing activity that most of us will attempt at least once during our life time. After all, many of the memories of important family events and history are associated with images of the time and, even with the right care and attention, lots of these photos end up a little worse for wear. In this chapter I thought that I would present you with a variety of techniques that you can use to restore, or repair, those images most precious to you. Rather than detailing the techniques in isolation, where sometimes they lose significance, I have chosen to apply them as part of a process of restoring 'real life' photos.

As you will discover, most retouching projects require the application of a variety of techniques in multiple steps to coax the

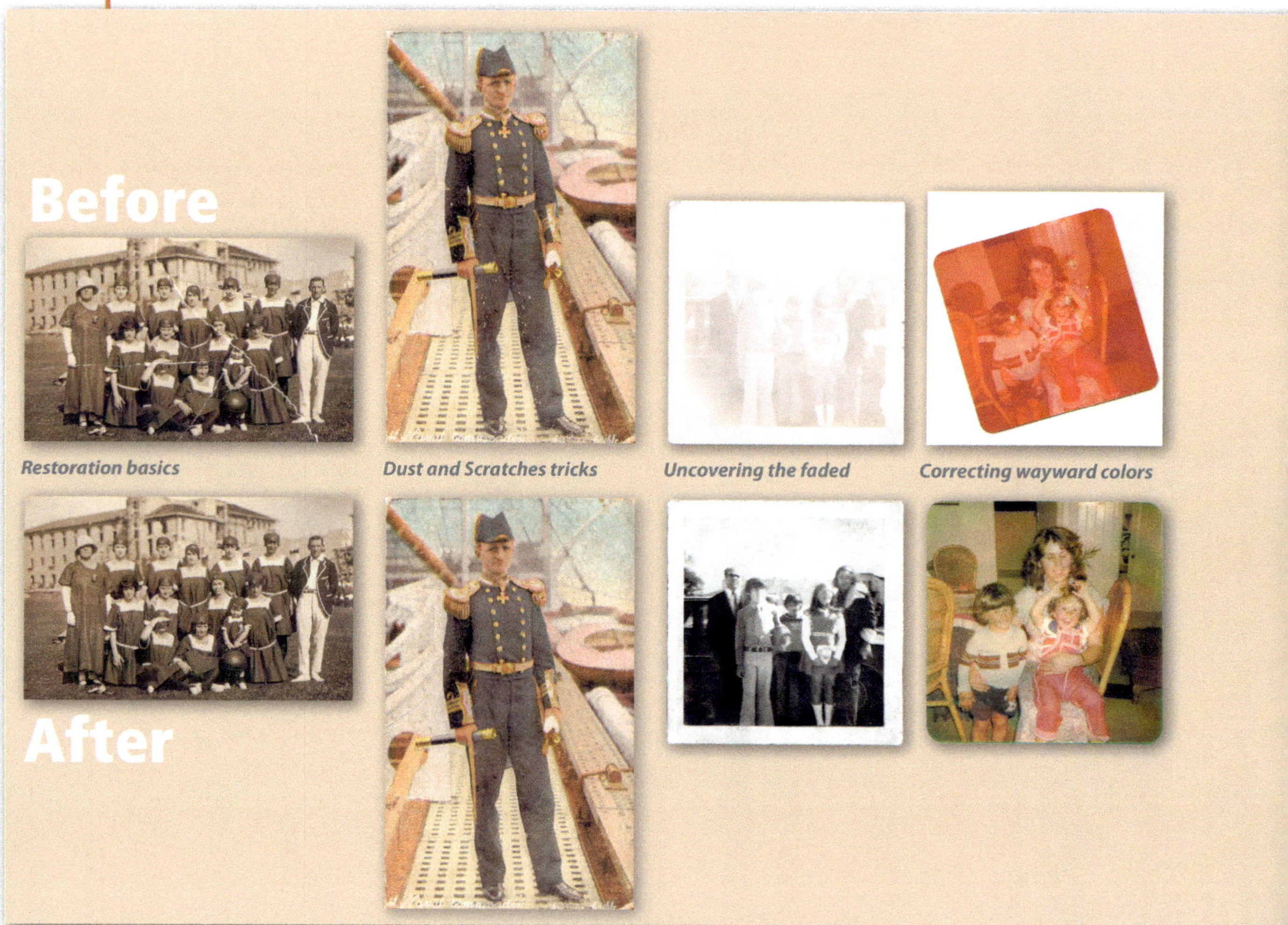

Restoration basics

Dust and Scratches tricks

Uncovering the faded

Correcting wayward colors

aged photo back to its best. So even though the example photos presented here have quite different problems (and associated solutions) they also contain some degree of overlap in areas such as removing of dust and scratches. These techniques are by no way an exhaustive list of all that are possible, but they will provide you with a good basis to start your restoration work.

Below and opposite >> *The example images here are shown with the before versions above and the after results below. The main restoration tasks involved with each photo are listed in the headings and all the techniques used to produce the results displayed here are contained on the following pages.*

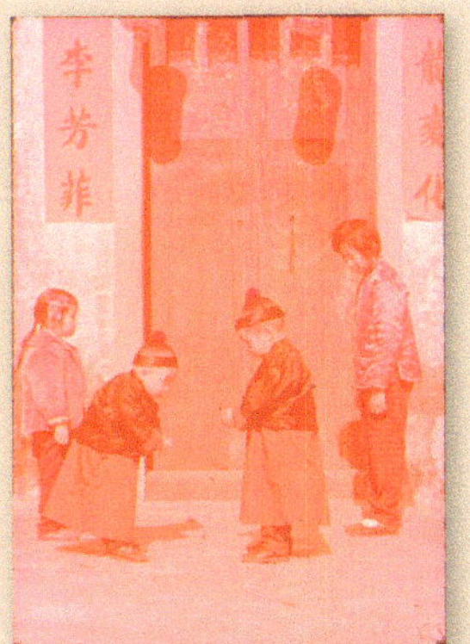

Restoring old slides

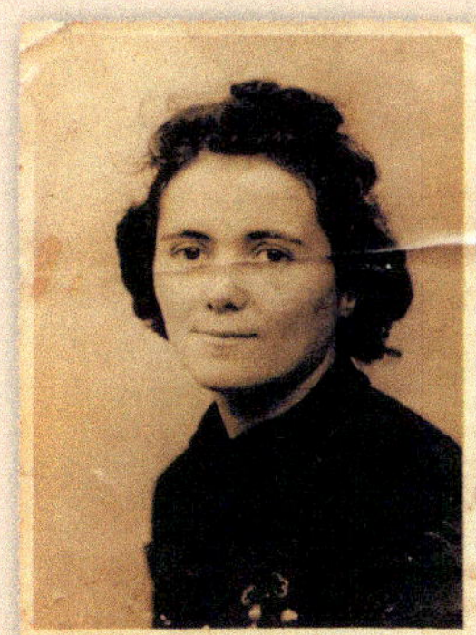

Adjusting shadow tones

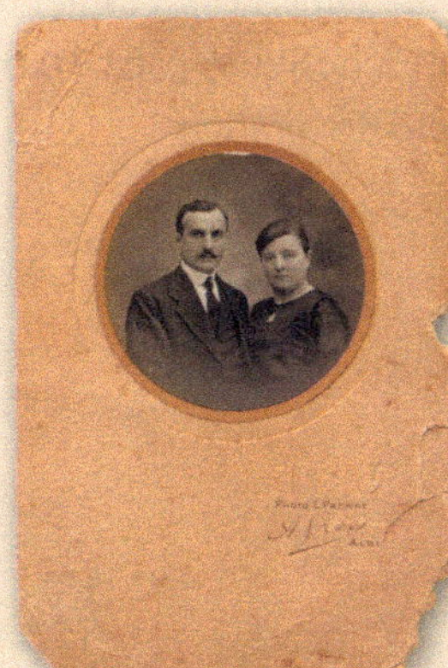

Recreating missing content

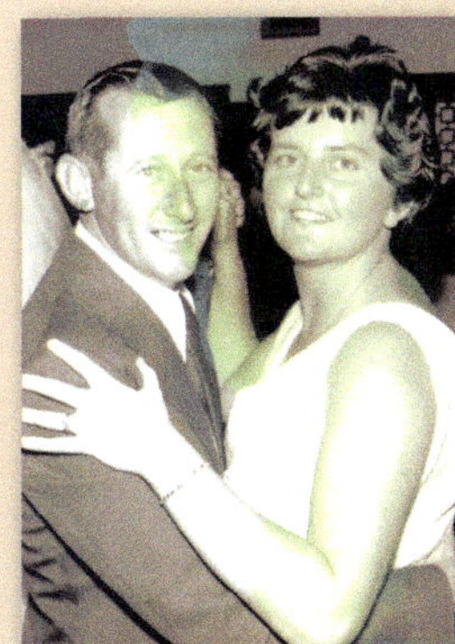

Removing stains

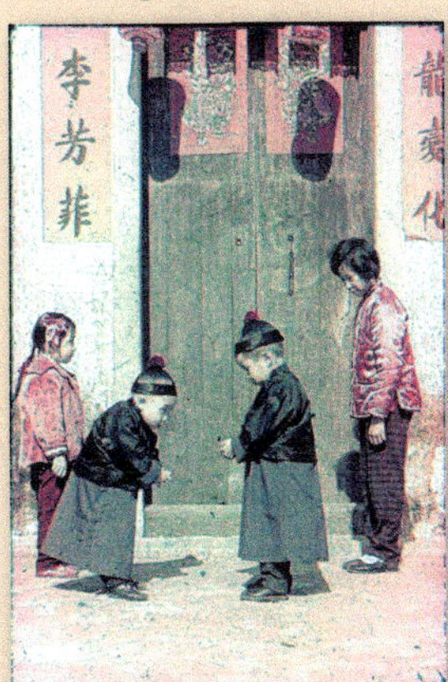

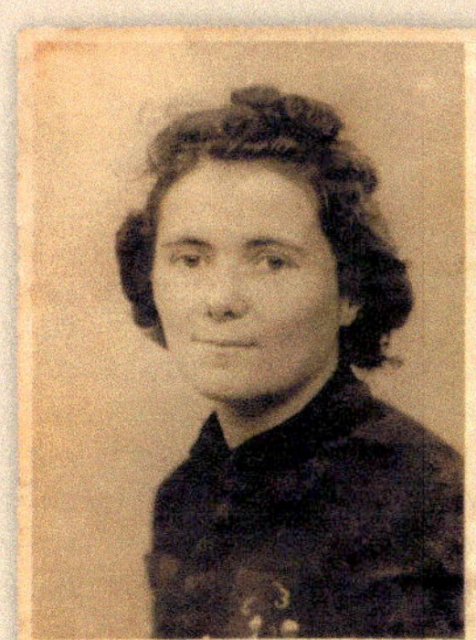

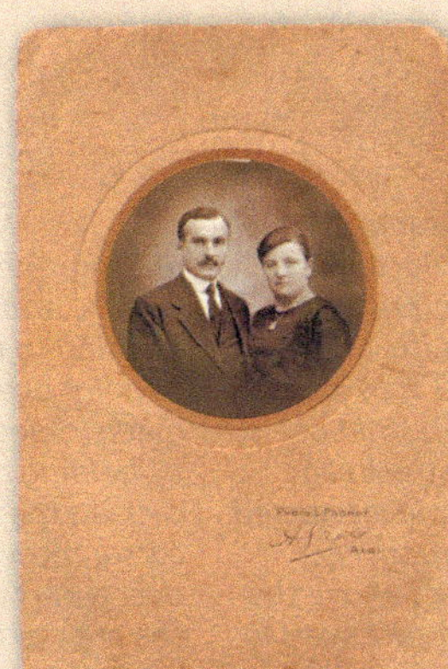

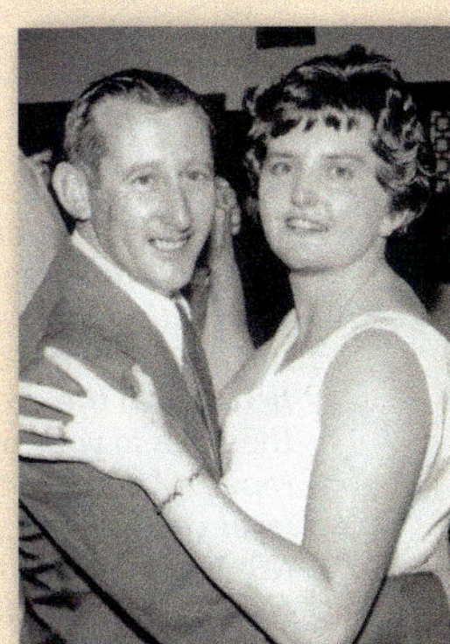

9.01 Restoration basics

Suitable for Elements – 7.0, 6.0, 5.0, 4.0, 3.0, 2.0, 1.0 | Difficulty level – Intermediate | Resources – Web image 901

In the last chapter we looked at how the retouching tools in Photoshop Elements can be used to remove unwanted marks and skin details in portraits. In this chapter the same tools are used for critical restoration and surgery work and with some photos, they are even called upon, to recreate detail that has been lost.

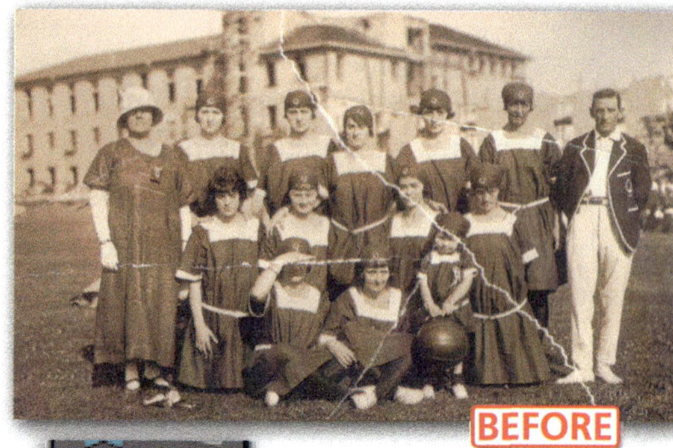

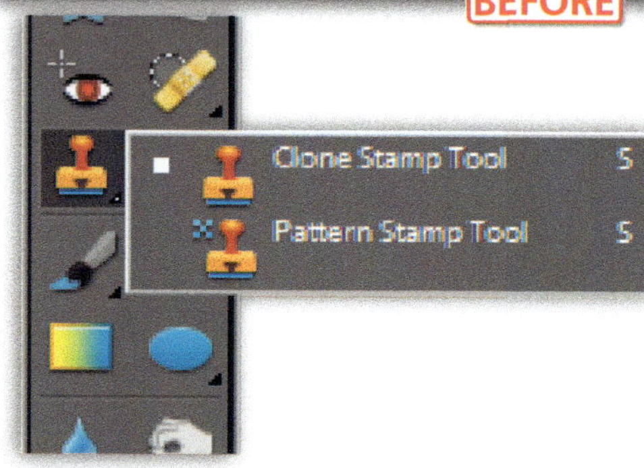

Though the application is different, the basic functionality of features such as the Clone Stamp Tool, Spot Healing Brush and Healing Brush, remains the same. Let's look at how a feature like the Clone Stamp can be used in the world of Photo Restoration.

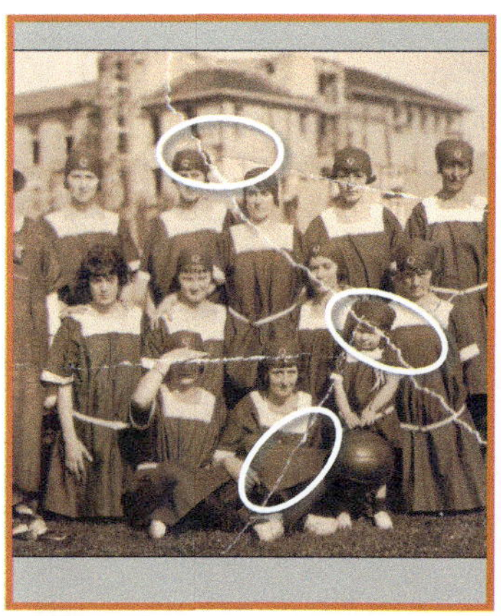

Step 1 >> *The Clone Stamp tool works by sampling a selected area and pasting the characteristics of this area over the blemish, so the first step in the process is to identify the areas in your picture that need repair. Make sure that the image layer you want to sample is selected. NB: To work non-destructively, create a new blank layer above the background and select All Layers in the options bar.*

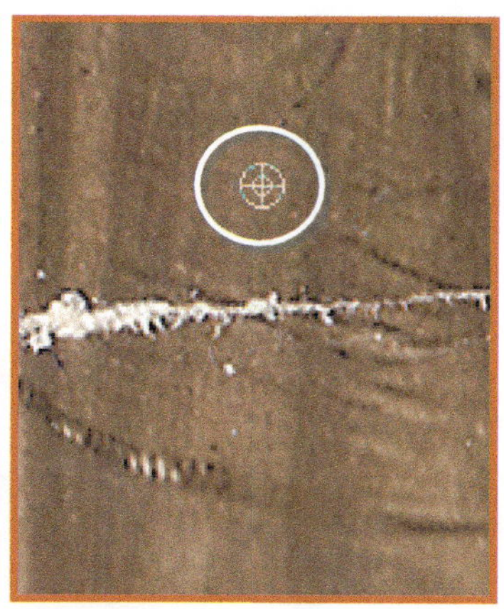

Step 2 >> *Next locate areas in the photograph that are a similar tone, texture and color as the areas needing to be fixed. Use these areas to paint over the dust and scratches marks. Select the area to be sampled by holding down the Alt key and clicking the mouse button when the cursor (now changed to cross hairs) is over a part of the image that suits the area to be repaired.*

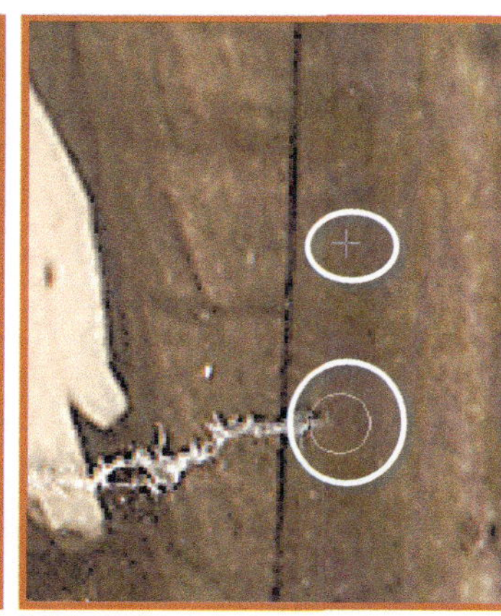

Step 3 >> *With the sample point selected you can now move the cursor to the area to be fixed. Click on the blemish and a copy of the sample point area is pasted over the mark. Depending on how well you chose the sample area, the blemish will now be blended into the background seamlessly. Continue to click repairing more blemishes as you go.*

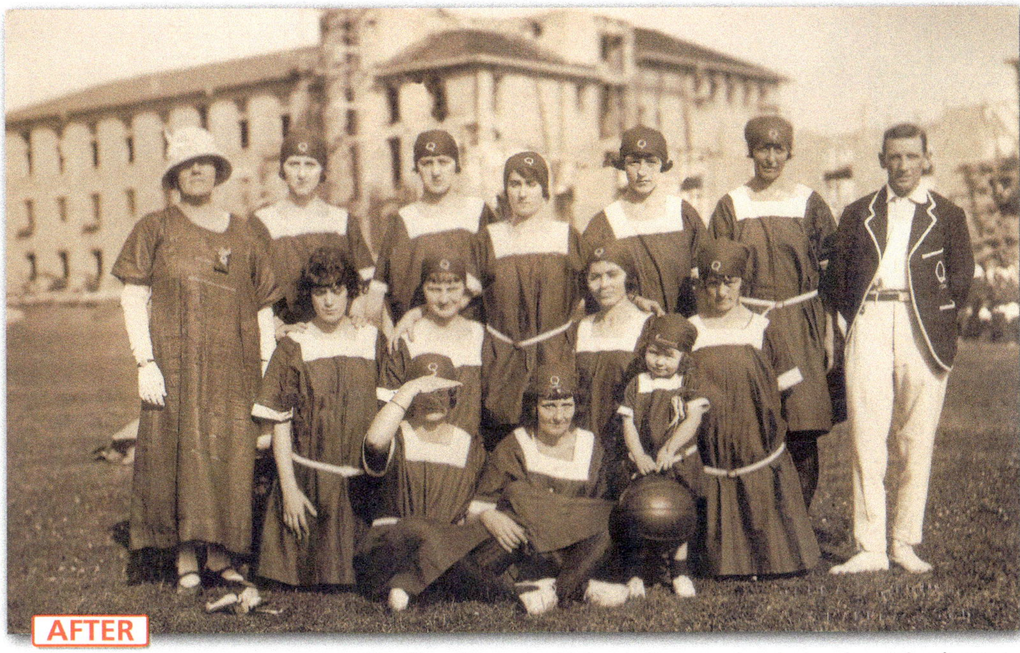

The Clone Stamp tool is handy for removing dust and scratches but can also be used for recreating the detail lost in areas such as cracks or tears.

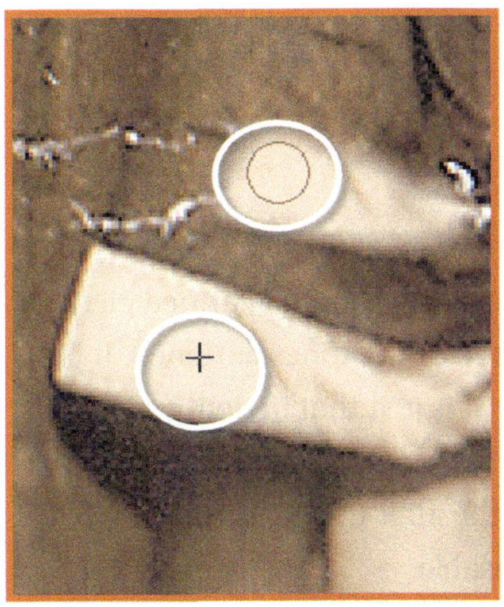

Step 4 >> *You may need to reselect your sample point if you find that the color, texture or tone doesn't match the surrounds of the blemish. It may also be necessary to change brush size to suit different repair tasks. Changing the brush size will alter the size of both the sample and stamp areas.*

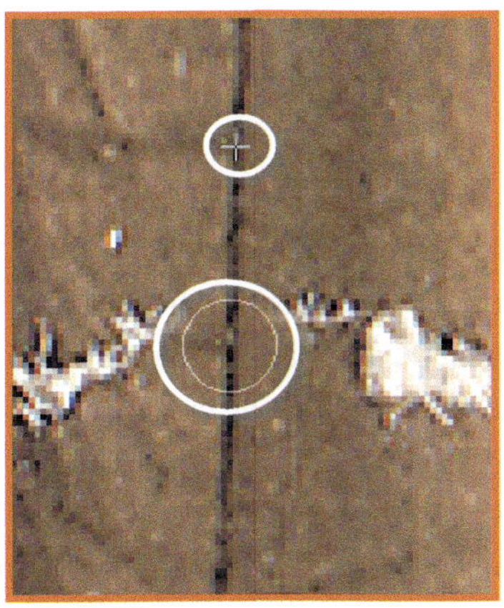

Step 5 >> *For difficult repair jobs where you need to recreate picture elements select a similar part from the photograph as your sample point. Here the seam in the dress above the scratch is sampled to repair the damaged area. The same process is used to recreate the folds in the fabric and the texture of the glove.*

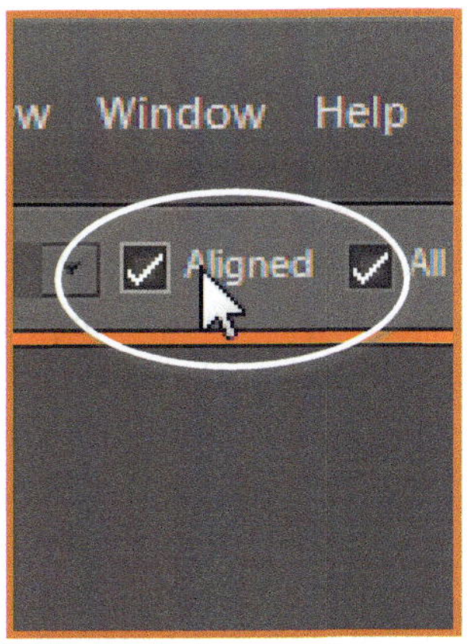

Step 6 >> *Switching between aligned and non-aligned options can really help you rebuild picture parts. Aligned – sets the sample point so that it remains the same distance from the stamped area no matter where on the picture you start to click, and Non-aligned – repositions the sample point back to the original sample spot each time the mouse is moved and then clicked.*

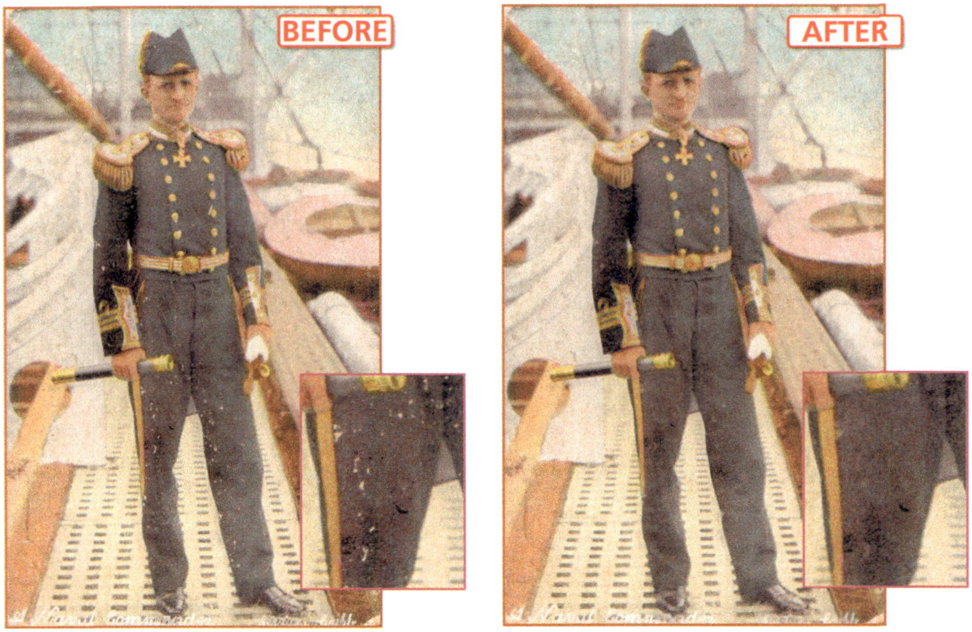

Removing dust automatically >> *One of the most tedious jobs for the digital photographer is the removal of dust and scratch marks from a badly damaged slide or print. Using the Clone Stamp tool to patch each individual mark can take considerable time and effort. A more automated approach that doesn't soften the detail in an image is detailed here. It uses the much besmirched Dust and Scratches filter in conjunction with the Layer blending modes to restrict changes to just the areas where it is needed.*

9.02 Dust and scratches be gone

Suitable for Elements – 7.0, 6.0, 5.0, 4.0, 3.0, 2.0, 1.0 | Difficulty level – Intermediate
Resources – Web image 902 | Menus used – Layer, Filter

The enticingly named Dust and Scratches filter (Filter > Noise > Dust and Scratches) teases us with the promise of a simple solution to repairing the dust and scratches in our scanned pictures. Nearly always the results of using the filter are disappointingly soft or the tones flattened. It is not that the filter doesn't obscure or disguise the problem marks, it is just that in doing so the rest of the image is also filtered. In areas where there is no dust this causes a deterioration of the picture. If only we could restrict the application of the filter to just the areas where the dust marks appear the results would be more usable.

Pro's Tips for using the Dust and Scratches filter:

1. Always start with both sliders set to 0.

2. Move the Radius slider first until the marks disappear.

3. Next move the Threshold slider until the texture of the image returns. Do not move this slider so far that the marks start to reappear.

The Lighten and Darken blending modes in Elements can be used for just this purpose. By applying the Dust and Scratches filter to a copy of the background and then blending this filtered layer using the Darken mode, the layer will only change the light dust marks of the original image and will leave the rest of the image unaffected. Similarly a second copy layer also filtered for dust and scratches could also be applied to the original image using the Lighten blending mode to remove the black marks from the picture. If we control where the effects are applied with a layer mask then it is possible to restrict the changes made by the Dust and Scratches filter to just the areas where it is needed most.

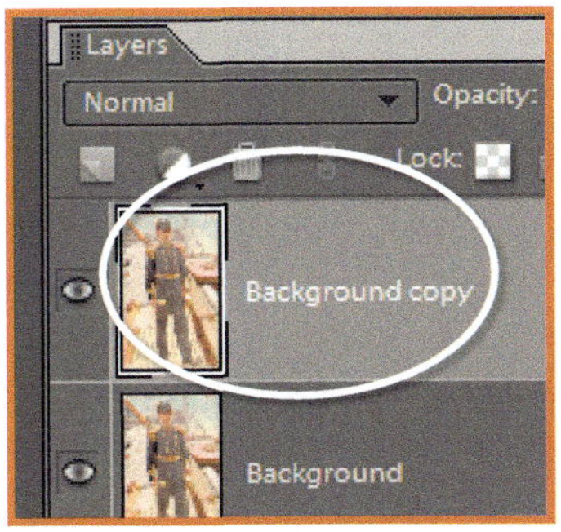

Step 1 >> *Start the technique by copying the base layer by dragging the background to the New Layer button at the bottom of the Layers palette. Label the new layer Darken Light Spots.*

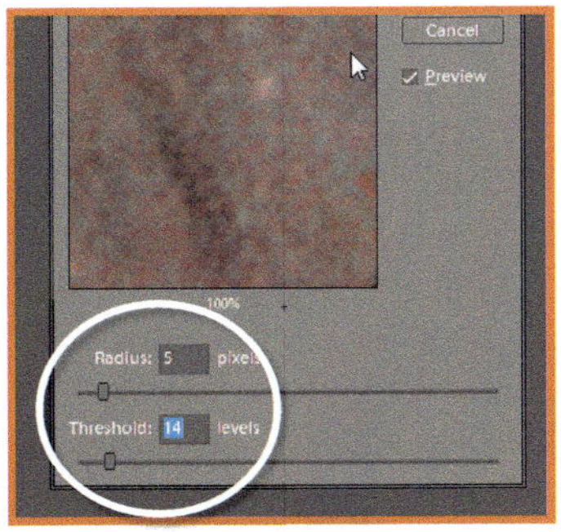

Step 2 >> *With the new layer selected apply the Dust and Scratches filter. Start with both sliders set on 0. Move the Radius slider first until you see the dust spots disappear. Next gradually move the Threshold slider to the right until the texture returns to the picture – not so far that you start to see the spots again.*

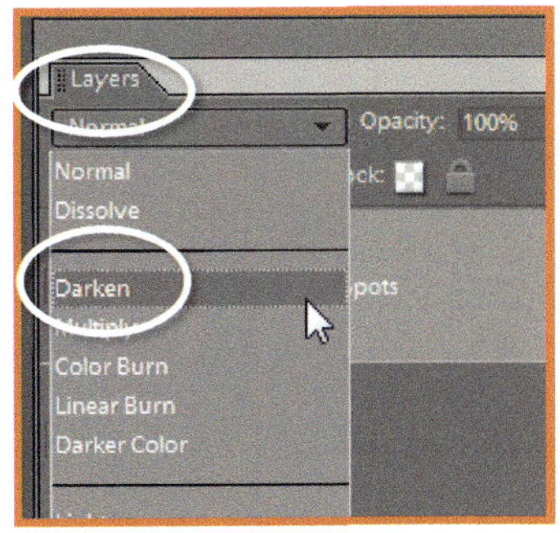

Step 3 >> *With the Darken Light Spots layer still selected change the mode of the layer to Darken. This will only apply the dust and scratches changes to the areas where this original layer is lighter – the white dust spots.*

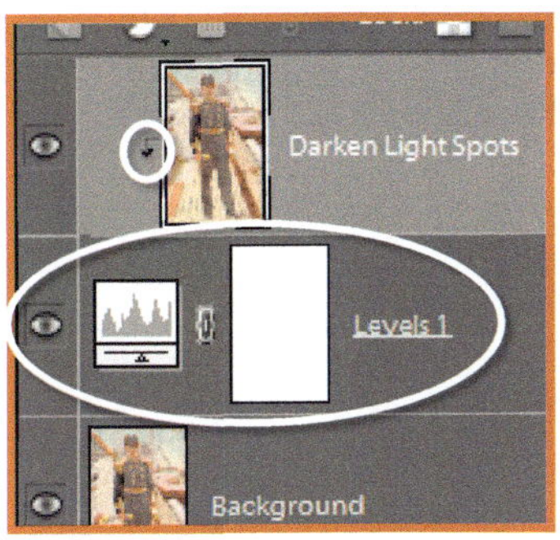

Step 4 >> *Add a Levels adjustment layer with no changes to the default settings above the background layer. Select the Darken White Spots layer and the choose Layers > Group with Previous.*

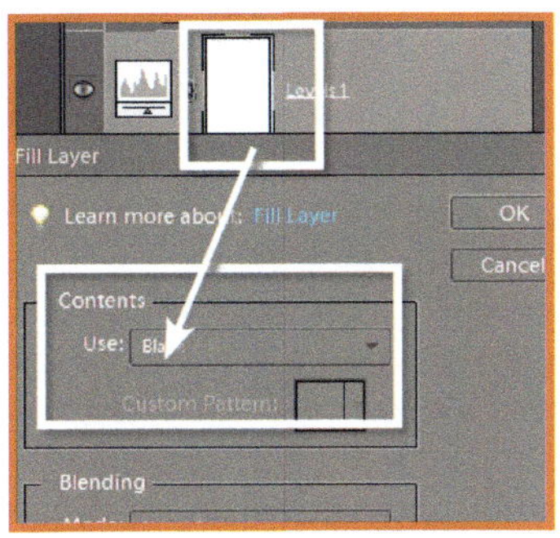

Step 5 >> *Select the layer mask of the Levels adjustment layer and then choose the Edit > Fill Layer option to fill the mask with black. This action hides the upper layer and reveals the unretouched layer beneath.*

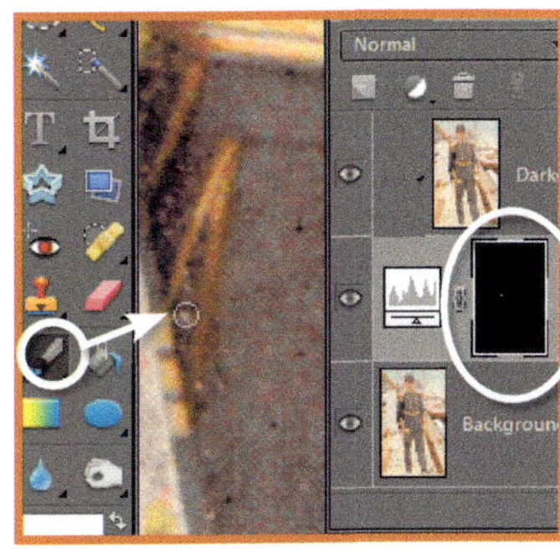

Step 6 >> *With the layer mask still selected choose white as the foreground color and proceed to paint onto the canvas over the white marks in the photo. The white strokes will reveal the results of the upper layer.*

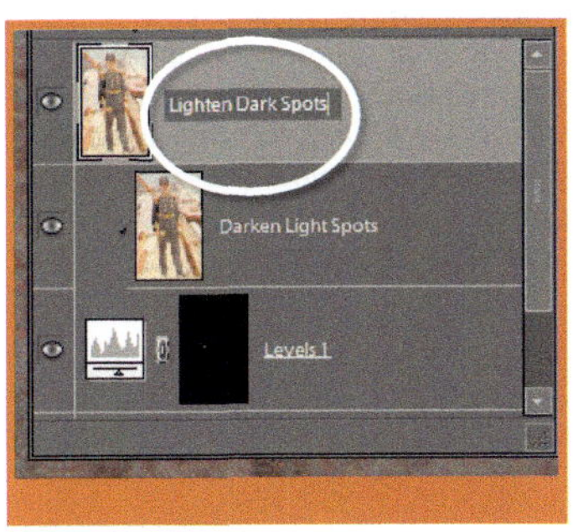

Step 7 >> *Create a copy of the background layer and label it Lighten Dark Spots. Apply the Dust and Scratches filter to remove the black marks and change the mode of this layer to Lighten.*

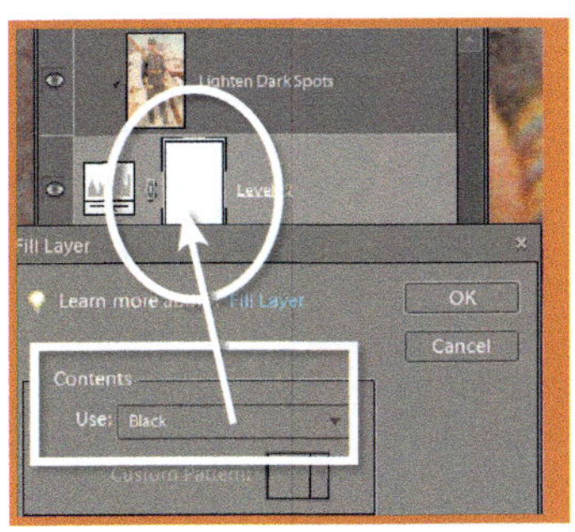

Step 8 >> *Create a blank Levels adjustment layer and then group it with the Lighten Dark Spots layer. Fill the Levels layer mask with black to hide the filtered results.*

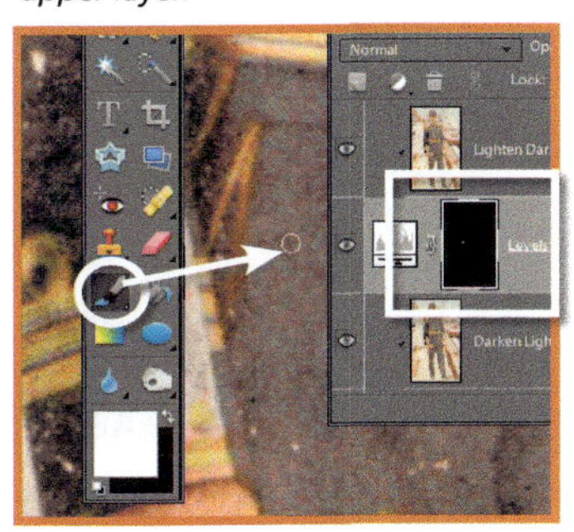

Step 9 >> *With white set as the foreground color and the mask still selected paint over the dark marks on the picture with the Brush tool.*

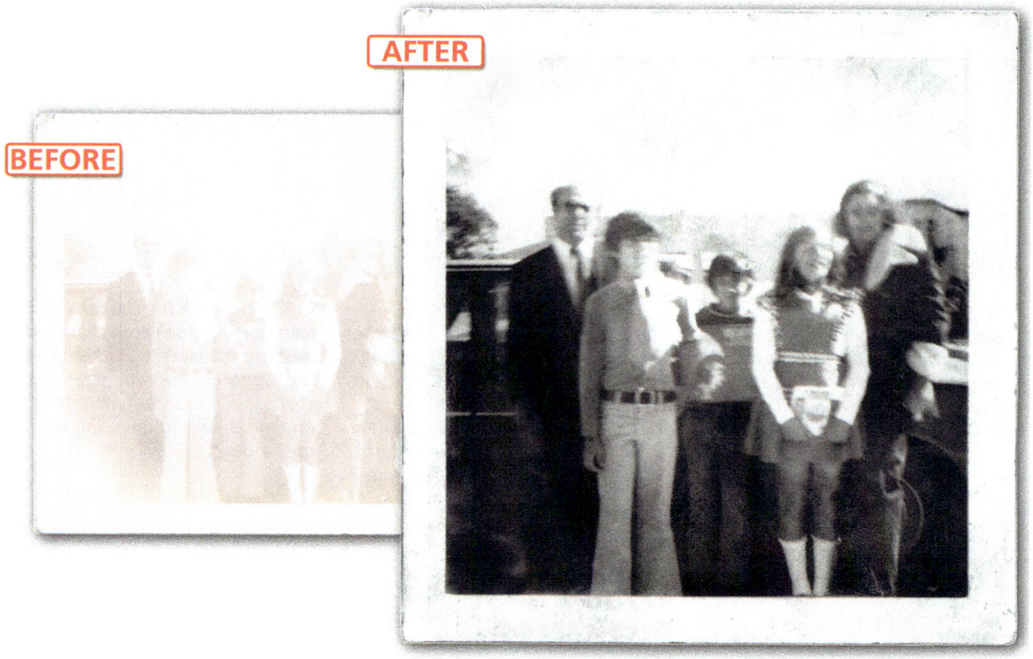

9.03 Uncovering the faded

Suitable for Elements – 7.0, 6.0, 5.0, 4.0, 3.0, 2.0, 1.0 | Difficulty level – Intermediate | Resources – Web image 903 | Menus used – Layer, Enhance

Unfortunately this treasured family photo is well and truly past its prime. Poor storage and exposure to bright light has caused the image to almost fade completely. Though complete restoration is almost impossible due to the extent of the fading it is worth noting the techniques that are used here to conjure hidden detail from the vintage photo.

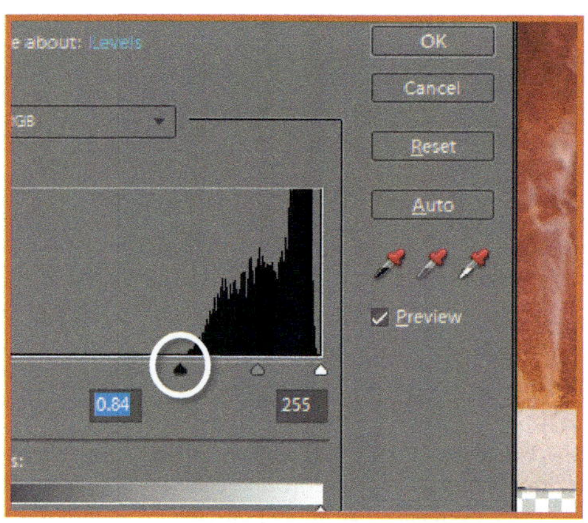

Step 1 >> *Using the Levels feature (Layer > New Adjustment Layer > Levels) in Photoshop Elements you can adjust black and white points of the photo. To set the shadow tones, hold down the Alt key and then drag the black point input slider to the right until the first pixels are revealed in the preview. Now move the slider slightly to the left until no clipped pixels are shown.*

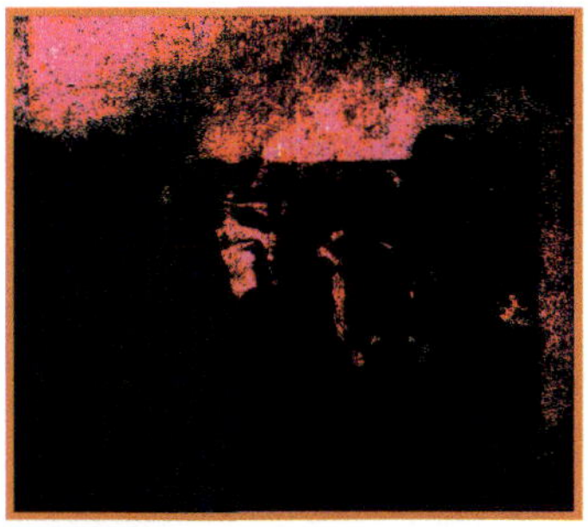

Step 2 >> *Next we will set the highlight tones. With the Alt key still pressed, drag the white point slider towards the left until you see the first clipped pixels displayed in the preview, then move the slider slightly to the right until no pixels are shown.*

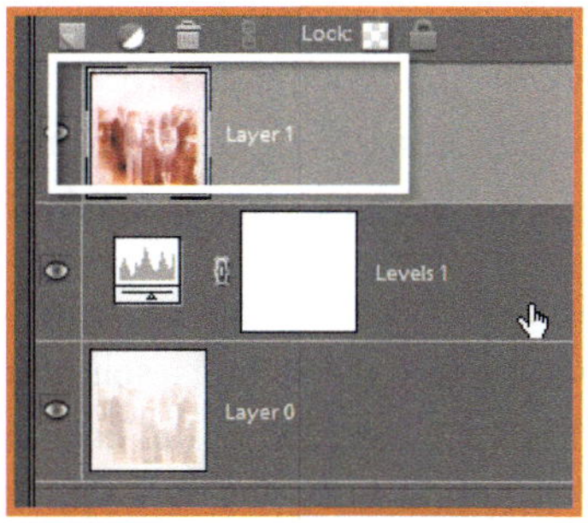

Step 3 >> *With the white and black points set, it is time to encourage hitherto hidden detail from the rest of the photo. We can do this with some careful adjustment with Adjust Color Curves control, but this feature can not be used as an Adjustment Layer so the first step is to Select > All the document and the Edit > Copy Merge to store a composite of all the visible layers in memory. Final Edit > Paste to create a new layer based on the merged details.*

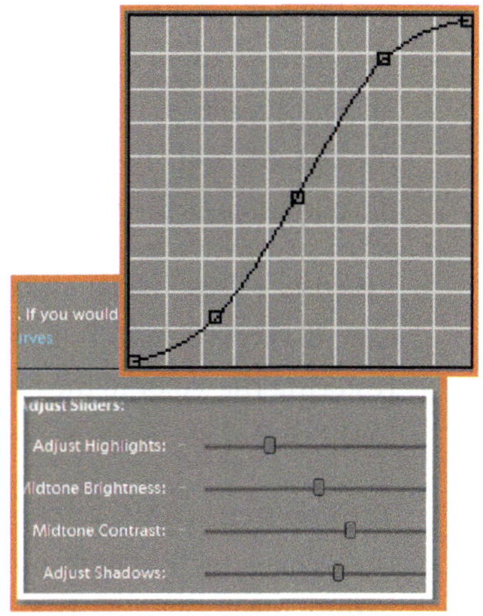

Step 4 >> *Now we can alter this layer with the Adjust Color Curves option. Here I selected the Increase Contrast Style first and then customized the enhancement by moving the Adjust Sliders until the Curve diagram resembled the classic steep 'S' shape. This adjustment spreads the tones and provides more contrast overall.*

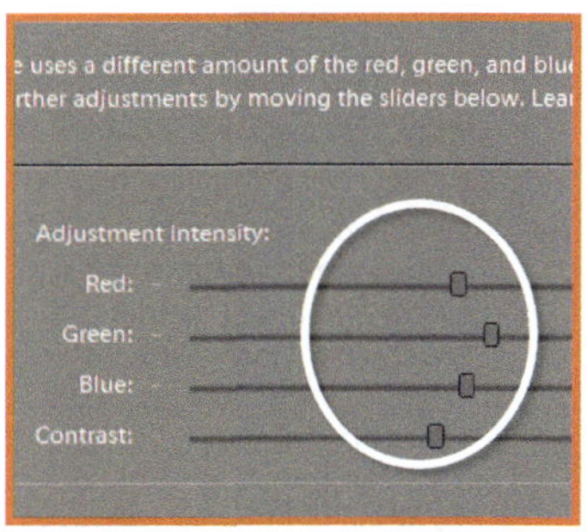

Step 5 >> *In the process of removing the red cast and converting the picture to grayscale it is also possible to emphasize other hidden detail using the Convert to Black and White feature (Enhance > Convert to Black and White). Adjusting the red and blue color range changes how these hues are mapped to gray provided more opportunity to reveal details hidden by the cast.*

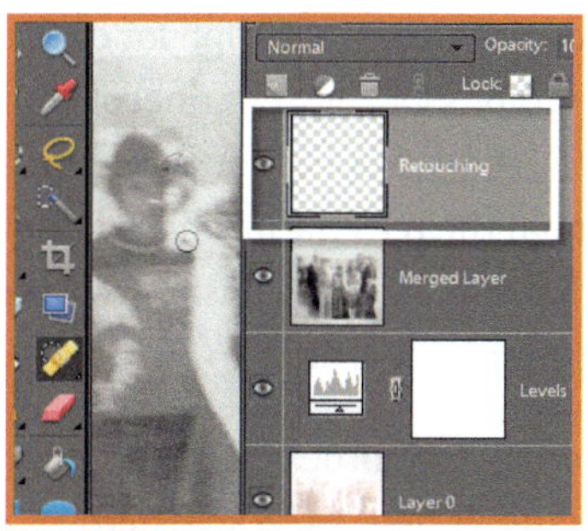

Step 6 >> *To remove marks, spots and scratches a new blank layer is added to the layers palette above the picture merged layer. Target the new layer and then use the Spot Healing Brush with the Sample All Layers option selected to repair the damaged areas.*

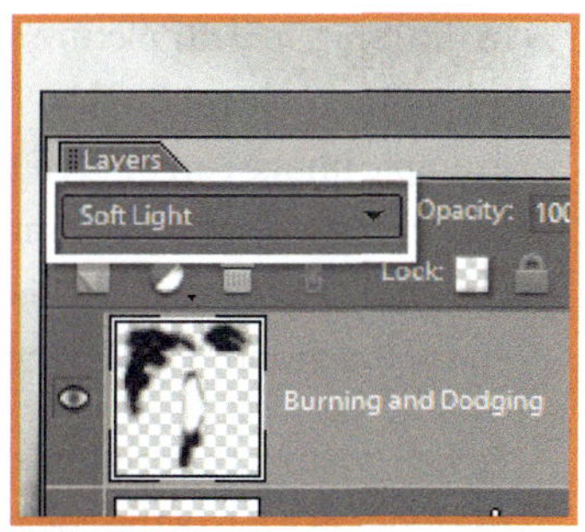

Step 7 >> *The final step is to add some definition to flat or faded sections of the photo. Do this by adding a new blank layer (Layer > New > Layer) at the very top of the layers stack. Change the Blend Mode to Soft Light and then use a black soft-edged brush to burn-in detail, or a soft-edged white brush to lighten sections.*

9.04 Levels based color restoration

Suitable for Elements – 7.0, 6.0, 5.0, 4.0, 3.0, 2.0, 1.0 | Difficulty level – Intermediate
Resources – Web image 904 | Menus used – Enhance

Old images, whether they be captured on color films, negatives or slides, are prone to fading and color changes as the dyes they are constructed of break down. It is a source of concern for all photographers who have big collections of images stored away in attics, cupboards or under the bed. After all, many of these photographs, though not valuable in the commercial sense, are irreplaceable as they hold glimpses of a family's history and echoes of days gone by.

Recently a loyal reader and avid Elements user emailed me with exactly this problem. Tom Edwards asked me if I had a solution for restoring the color to the hundreds of fading slides that he had taken in the Orient in the early 70s as they now all appear to be turning red.

The first step in any such restoration work is diagnosing the problem that is causing the color shift and fading. To get a good understanding of the cause I always turn to the Levels feature (Enhance > Adjust Lighting > Levels) for help. It contains a descriptive display of the spread pixels in the image and also includes the tools needed to coax the picture back to life.

When the Levels feature is first opened it displays a graph of the combined red, green and blue pixels. This is signified by the RGB label in the Channels drop-down menu. To really see what is happening to the tones in your picture select and view the graph for each of the individual color channels. The graphs for each channel of Tom's example image can be seen to the right. Notice how the green and blue channels are fairly similar but the red channel has all the signs of being overexposed, that is, all the tones being pushed to the right end of the graph. This is where our problem lies.

To help restore the original color and brightness of the photograph the tones of each of the color channels have to be adjusted individually. Starting with the red channel, drag the black input triangle towards the center of the graph until it meets the first major group of pixels. Do the same for the green and blue channels, but with these also adjust the white point Input slider in the same way.

This action will help to restore the color and contrast of the picture and will give good results for all but the most faded slides or prints. Final adjustments to tone and the removal of any slight color casts that remain can be achieved using levels on the combined RGB channel setting and the Color Variations features.

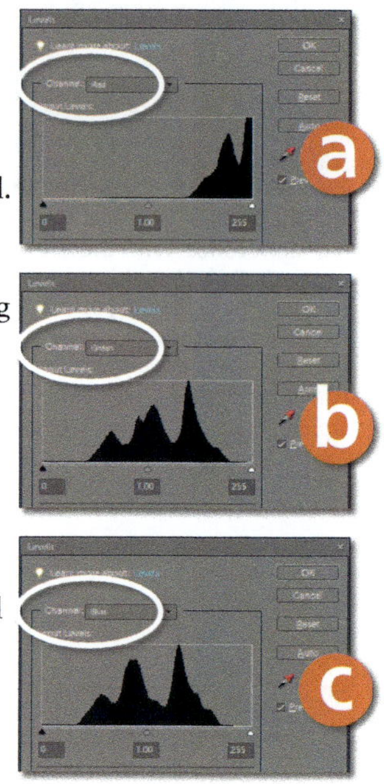

Restoring faded slides >>
When you look at the histogram for each of the red, green and blue channels separately it is easy to see why the faded slide appears so warm.

(a) Red channel.
(b) Green channel.
(c) Blue channel.

To restore the color in the image work on each channel separately, dragging the white and black points in to meet the first major group of pixels.

This will balance the distribution of the tones in each of the channels and restore the slide's color and contrast.

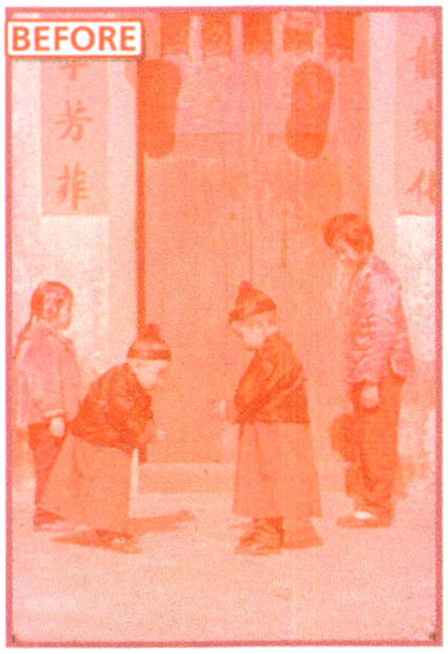

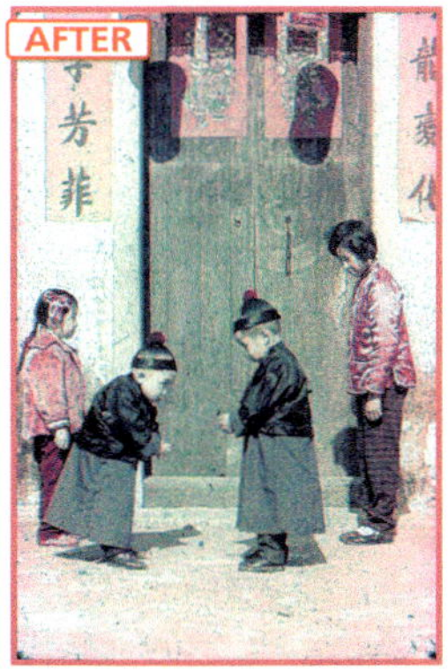

Fading slides >> *Over time traditional color photographs, slides and negatives can show signs of fading and take on a dominant color cast. Using the color correction and tonal change tools in Elements might not be aggressive, or selective enough, to correct these problems. Instead use the steps detailed here to rebalance the tones and colors in your picture.* *Image courtesy of Tom Edwards © 1972.*

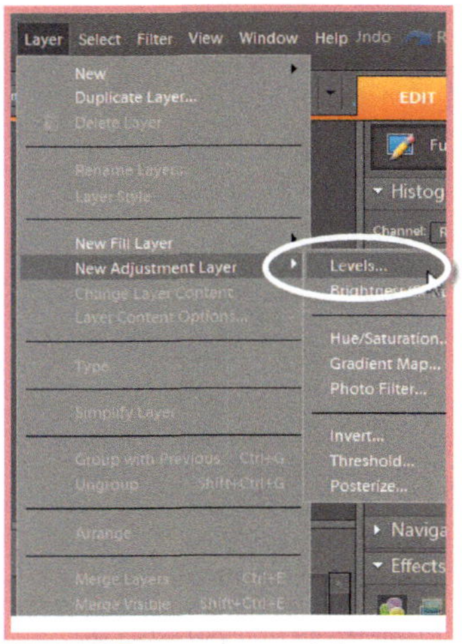

Step 1 >> *Open the Levels feature from the Enhance > Adjust Lighting or Layer > New Adjustment Layer menus.*

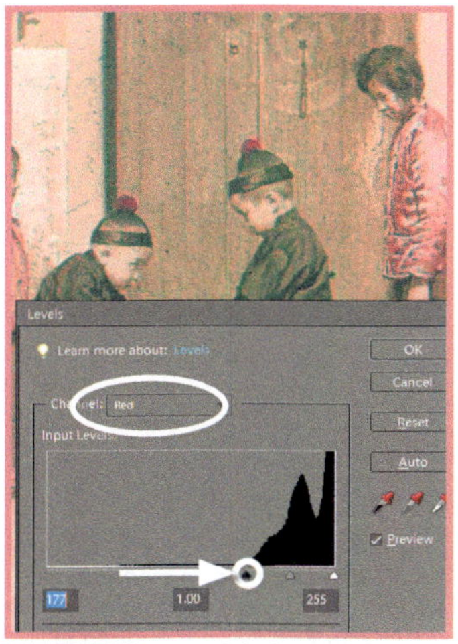

Step 2 >> *Start with the red channel and drag the black input triangle to meet the first group of pixels.*

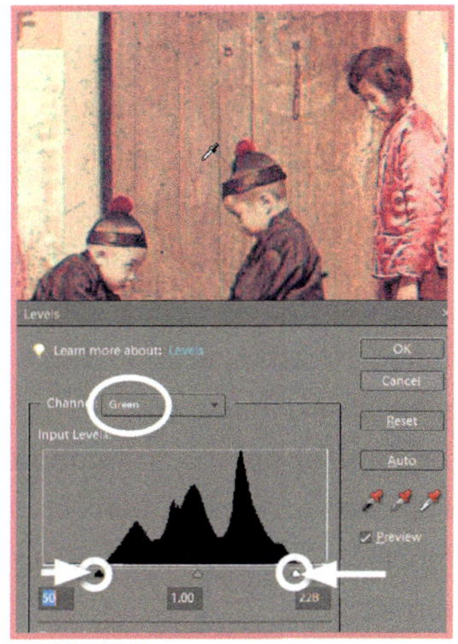

Step 3 >> *Next select the green channel and move both the white and black input sliders to the first group of pixels.*

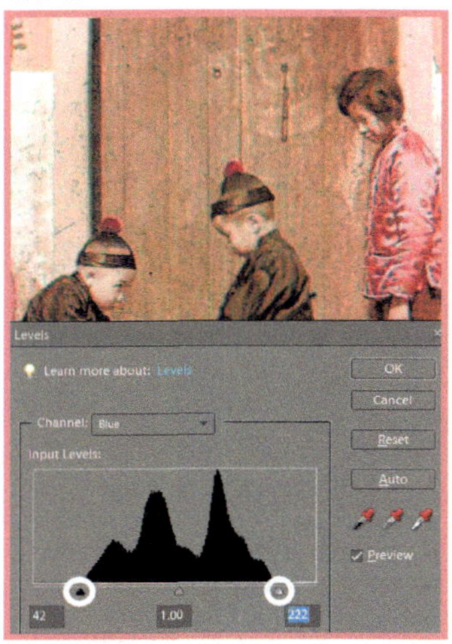

Step 4 >> *Make the same black and white point adjustments for the blue channel as well.Click OK and then Select All, Copy Merge and Paste.*

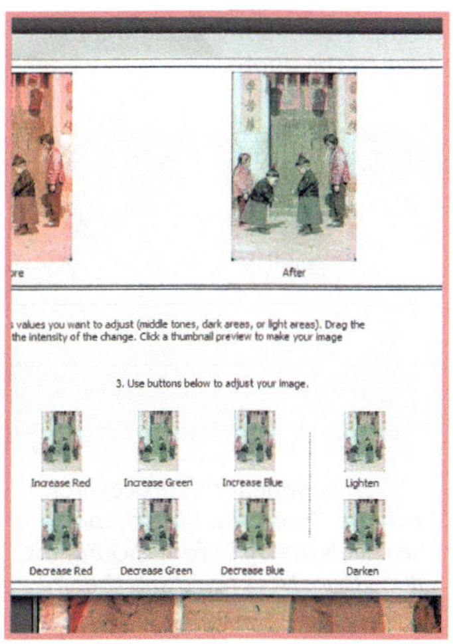

Step 5 >> *With the image now balanced, target the Copy Merged layer and use Color Variations to remove any color casts that remain.*

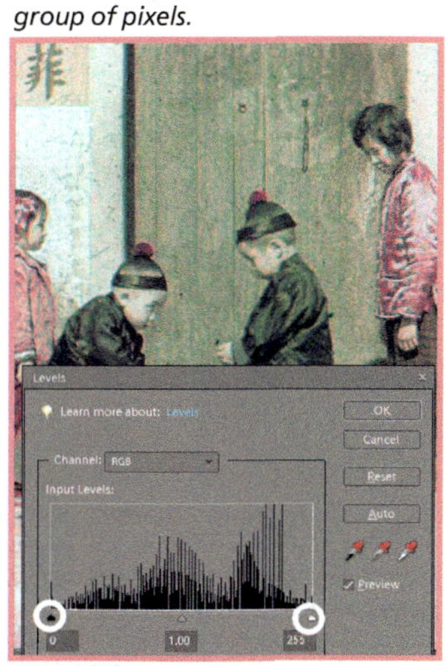

Step 6 >> *As a final check of the tones open the Levels feature again and adjust white, middle and black points for the composite channel (RGB).*

9.05 Working with a scanned print

Suitable for Elements – 7.0, 6.0, 5.0, 4.0, 3.0, 2.0, 1.0
Difficulty level – Intermediate
Resources – Web image 905
Menus used – Enhance

Okay with these basics under our belt let's look at how to restore a scanned print rather than a scanned slide. Unlike their traditional black and white counterparts, color photographic prints often suffer from dramatic fading, or color changes, after only a few years of viewing. In this example, as was the case with the previous slide, the image has become very red. Apart from the removal of dust marks and the lightening of the photo, restoration will involve the reorientation of the photo and the correction of the dominant color.

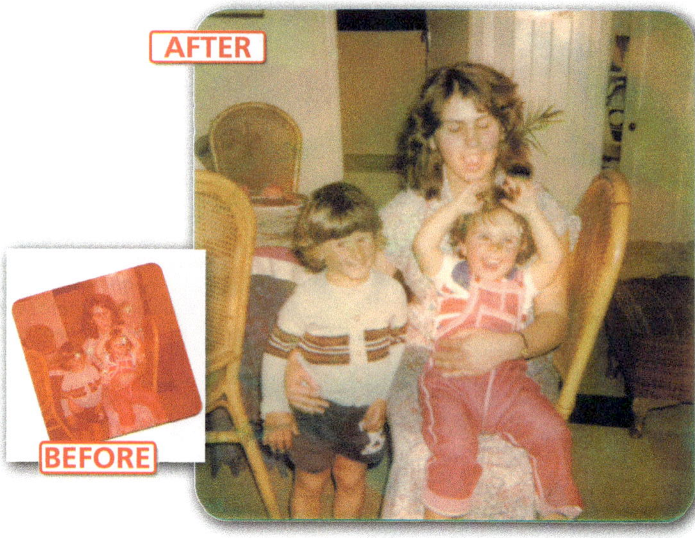

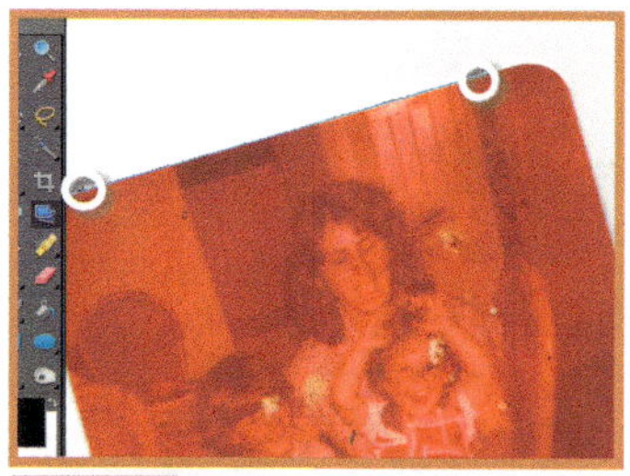

Step 1 >> Like many a scanned image, this photo ended up being a 'little' crooked when it opened in Elements. So the first step is to straighten the photo. To do this select the Straighten tool from the toolbar and click-drag a measurement line a along the top edge of the photo.

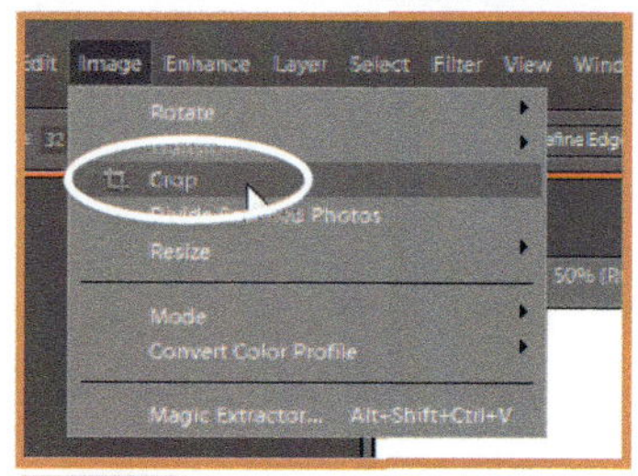

Step 2 >> To remove the excess background automatically, select the Magic Wand tool and select the background. Now Inverse the selection and choose the image > Crop command. Hit the Ctrl D keys to deselect.

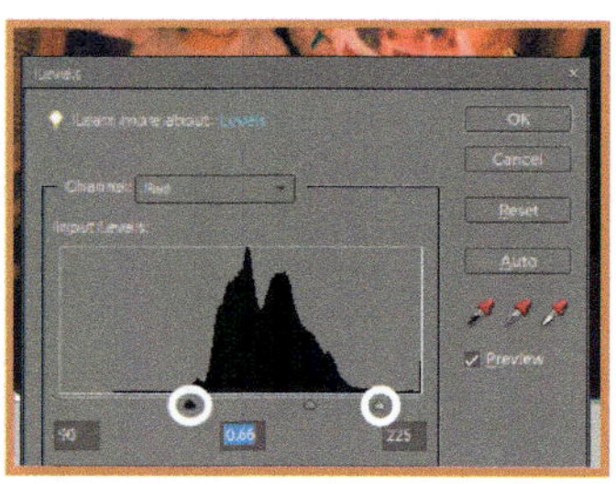

Step 3 >> To remove the dominant red cast, start by adding a new Levels adjustment layer. In the Levels dialog, select the Red channel from the drop-down menu and drag the black and white input sliders inwards. Hold down the Alt key while you do this to ensure that no pixels are clipped.

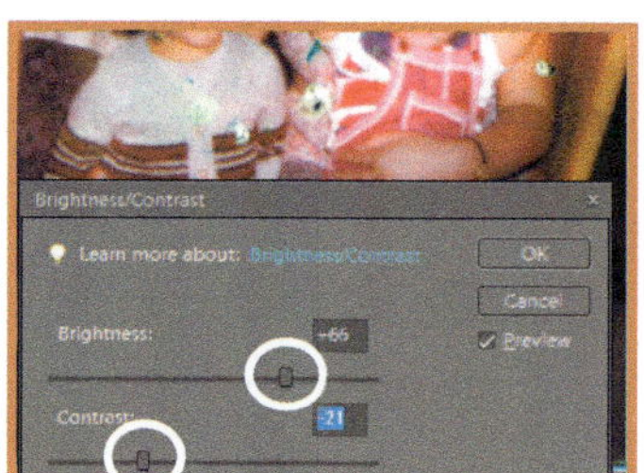

Step 4 >> Repeat this process for both the Green and Blue channels in the Levels dialog before clicking the OK button. Now fine-tune the brightness and contrast of the picture with the addition of a Brightness/Contrast adjustment layer. Make any final color changes with a Color Variations feature to a Copy Merged layer.

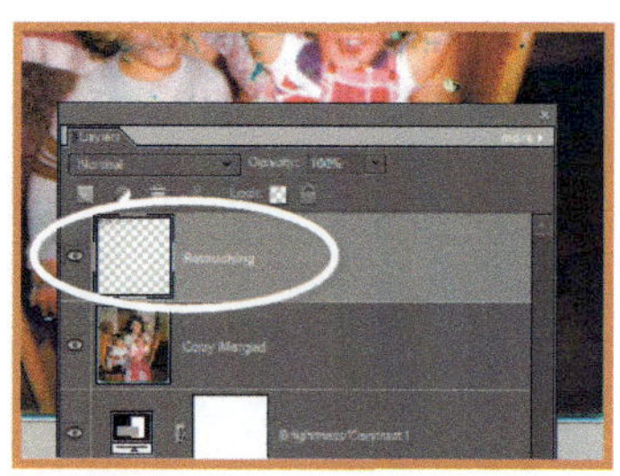

Step 5 >> Now let's turn our attention to the marks and scratches on the photo. A new layer is added above the copy merged layer. Using the Spot Healing Brush and with the new blank layer targeted in the Layers palette. The Sample All Layers setting is selected in the tool's options bar and the small marks removed.

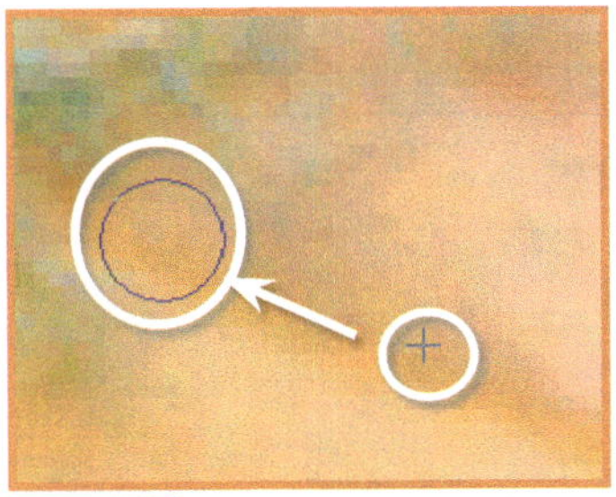

Step 6 >> *Targeting the same layer, the Spot Healing Brush is switched to the Clone Stamp tool. The Current and Below setting is selected in the Sample drop-down menu of the tool's options bar before cloning away marks and scratches not able to be corrected with the Spot Healing Brush.*

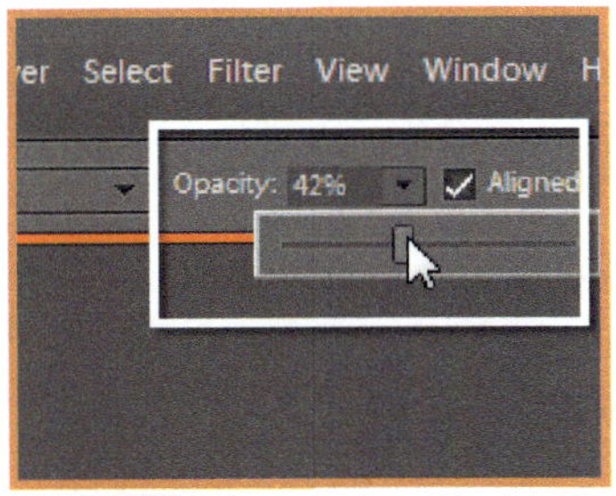

Step 7 >> *When cloning skin detail it is often a good idea to reduce the opacity of the tool and build up the repair areas slowly with repeated strokes. It also pays to move the sample point regularly to reduce the repetition of cloning content. Many photographers use a graphics tablet and stylus setup for this type of editing.*

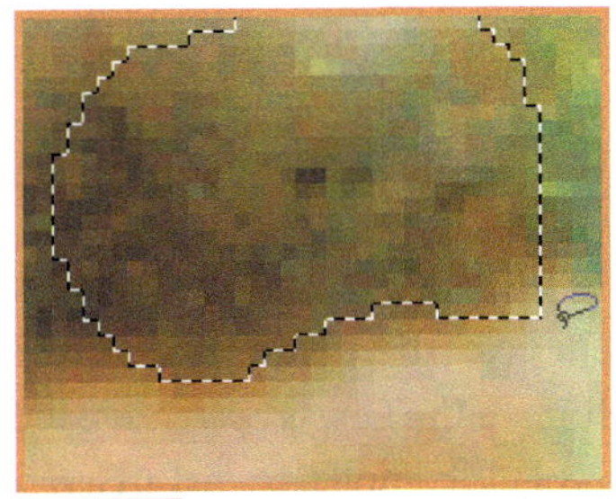

Step 8 >> *With the simple marks and scratches removed it is now time to tackle the larger damaged areas in the photo. Here the missing detail must be reconstructed from other areas in the photo. Here I created a soft-edged selection of the boy's hair and then copied and pasted the detail as a new layer.*

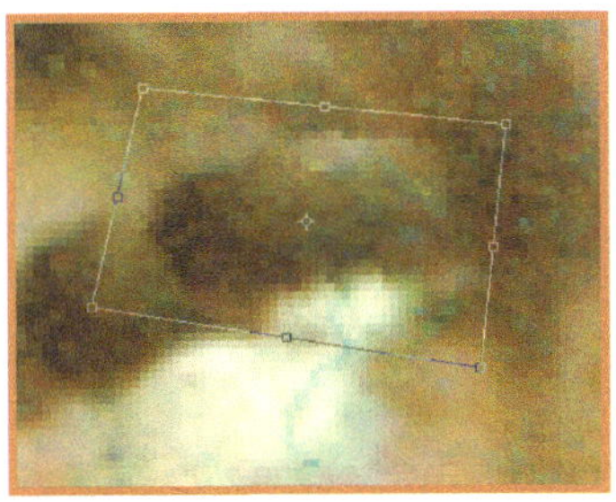

Step 9 >> *I then duplicated this new layer. To quickly create a copy of a layer hold down the Alt key and click-drag a new copy to a different position in the document. Next each of the new 'hair' layers was selected in turn and the Free Transform tool (Ctrl T) used to deform the content to cover the damaged area.*

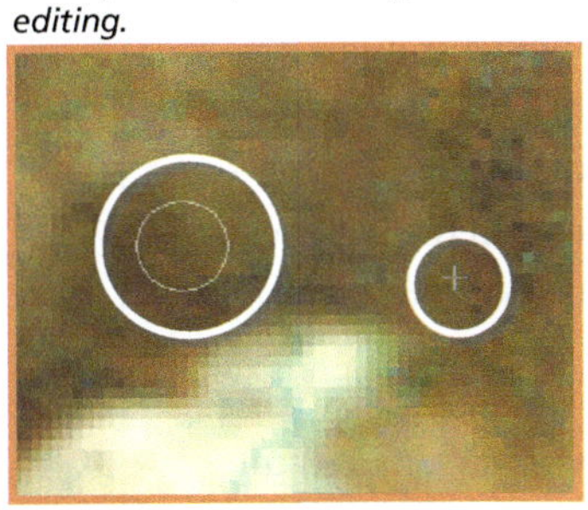

Step 10 >> *After creating, and targeting, a new blank layer above the copied hair layers, the Clone Stamp tool is then used to sample existing hair detail, color and tone and carefully blend the pasted detail with the background. Again the opacity of the tool was reduced and detail was built gradually with different sample points.*

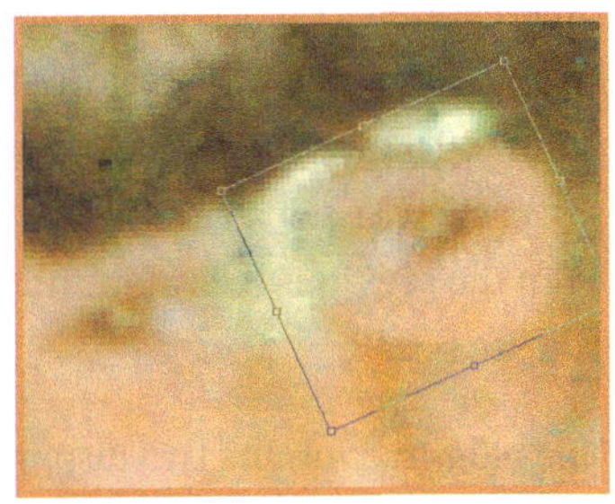

Step 11 >> *A similar approach was used when reconstructing the missing portions of the faces in the photo. This time a soft-edge selection of the cheek and eye was created, copied and pasted into position on the opposite side of the face. Next this layer was flipped (Image > Rotate > Flip Horizontal) and the content rotated to fit.*

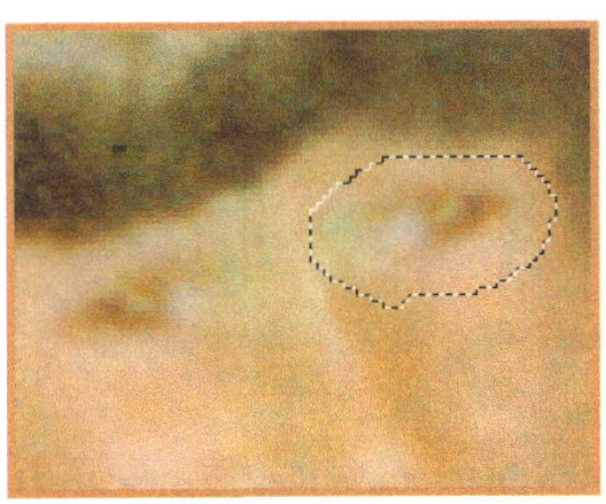

Step 12 >> *Flipping the copied face content meant that the cheek details were correctly position but left the eyes looking 'cross eyed'. To correct this problem a second feathered selection was created of just the eye area. The eye was then copied, pasted and flipped horizontally before the Move and Free Transform tools were used to massage the detail into place.*

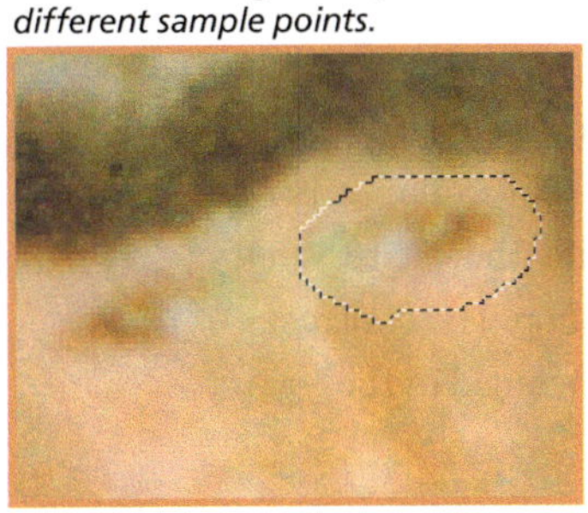

Step 13 >> *The Clone Stamp tool and Spot Healing brush were then used to help blend the edges of the newly pasted content with the background details. This same process was used to reconstruct the other damaged areas in the photo.*

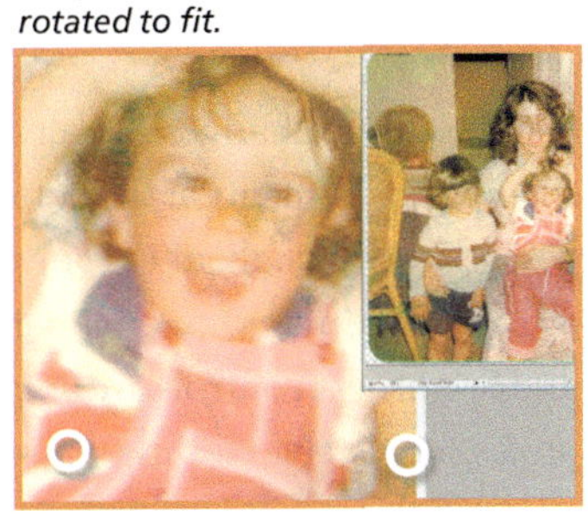

Step 14 >> *When making small adjustments or edits on highly magnified sections of the photo it is a good idea to use the View > New Window for... option to display a second 100% view of the document being corrected. This provides a great way to check your work up close and at a distance at the same time.*

9.06 Extra correction help

Suitable for Elements – 7.0, 6.0, 5.0, 4.0, 3.0, 2.0, 1.0 | Difficulty level – Intermediate | Resources – Web image 906 | Menus used – Enhance

In the previous techniques we looked at how to balance the color of a photo with a dominant cast. With some images the Levels correction method still doesn't provide completely cast-free results.

An alternative method for achieving good results is to employ a specialist plug-in for the task. ASF (Applied Science Fiction) now owned by Kodak produces some specialist plug-ins for Photoshop Elements that work well with restoration projects. The Digital ROC (Recreation Of Color) plug-in automatically analyzes corrects, balances and restores the color in problematic images. To give you an idea of how the plug-in performs we used it to correct the cast in the picture from the previous technique and it produced the results you see here.

The plug-in contains two display windows. By default the left window previews the file after changes and the one on the right as a navigator panel and displays a before version of the photo. When first opened the plug-in analyzes the color problems with the image and then automatically displays, what it considers, a 'best correction'. You can modify the results with the color and brightness sliders on the right of the dialog.

Some contrast changes can also be applied using the slipping adjustments at the bottom of the dialog. For best results, though, alter contrast with features such as Levels or Curves back in Photoshop. The contrast and brightness controls are only included in the professional version of the plug-in.

For more details about Digital ROC or any of the other ASF plug-ins or to download a trial version go to www.asf.com.

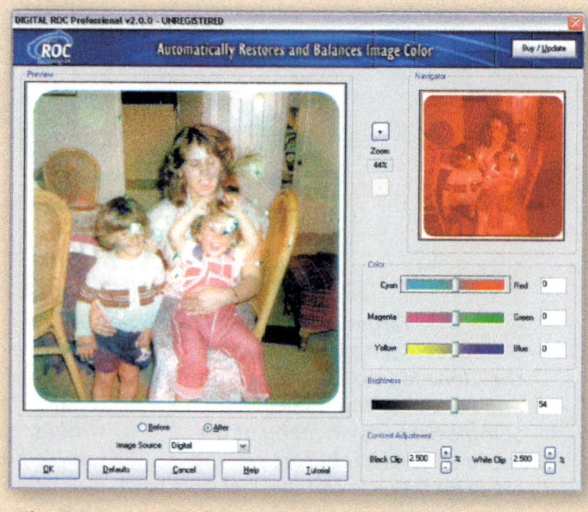

The Digital ROC plug-in quickly restores the color to a problematic image like this one.

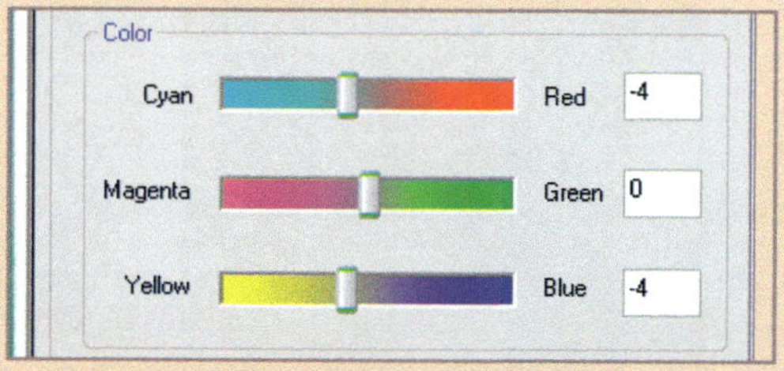

Step 1 >> *When first opened the plug-in automatically analyzes the color in the photo and then displays a corrected version of the picture. You can switch between before and after versions of the file with the settings under the main preview window. Use the three color slider controls to fine-tune the correction. Moving the slider towards a color will add the color to the photo and remove its opposite.*

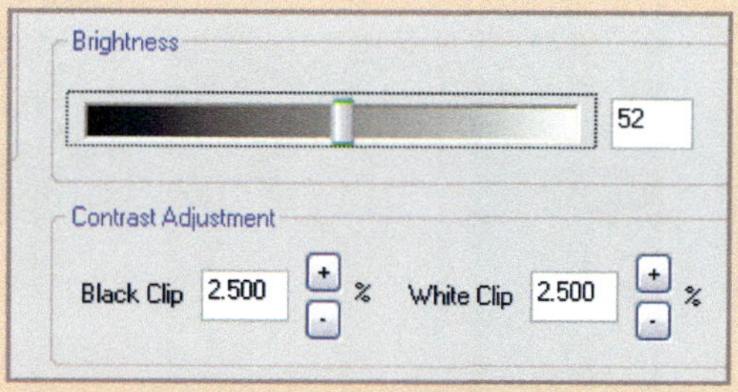

Step 2 >> *As a final step, in the Pro version of the plug-in, you can also adjust the brightness and contrast of the photo. If these options are not available then these changes can be made when the photo is back in Elements. Click the OK button to apply the changes, close the plug-in and return the corrected image to Elements. Complete the restoration by removing dust and scratches using the techniques described in the previous pages.*

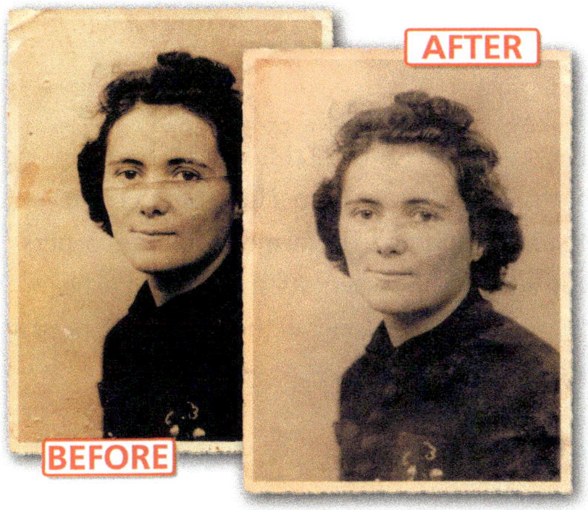

9.07 Adjusting shadow tones

Suitable for Elements – 7.0, 6.0, 5.0, 4.0, 3.0, 2.0, 1.0 | Difficulty level – Intermediate | Resources – Web image 907 | Menus used – Enhance

Some family heirloom images survive the ravages of time pretty much intact. This is the case with the example portrait we see here. Of course, there are a few marks, scratches, creases and a slight stain on the left to remove, but in addition to these enhancements, a good restoration job would also include the revealing of shadow details lost because of print over-exposure or incorrect scanner settings.

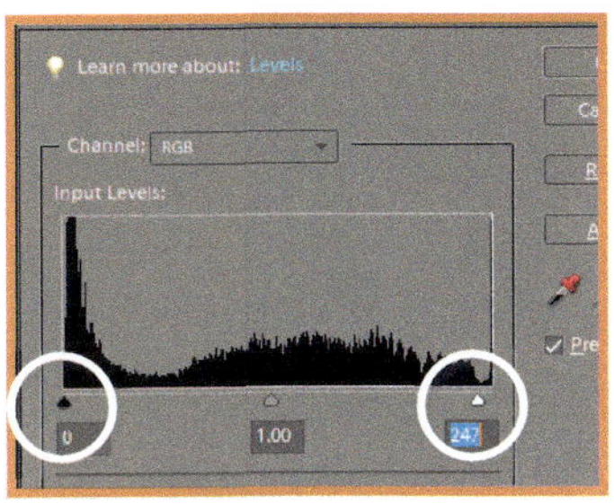

Step 1 >> *The first step is for us to 'peg' the white and black points. Using a Levels Adjustment layer, the black and white point input sliders are dragged in towards the middle of the histogram while holding down the Alt key. Move the sliders until the point just before you start to see clipped pixels in the preview.*

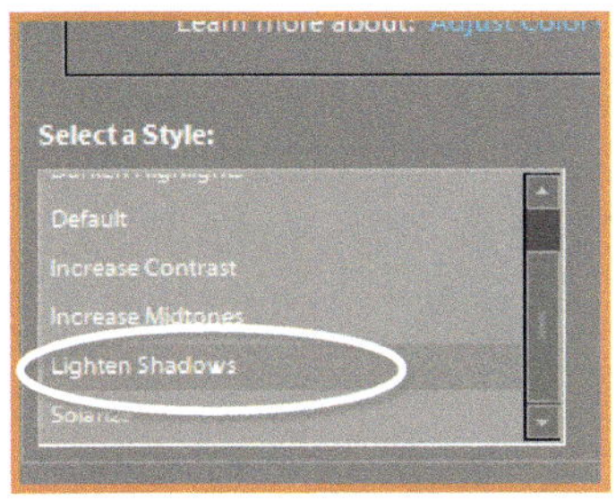

Step 2 >> *Now that the black and white points are set, let's reveal some of the hidden shadow details. Start by selecting all (Select > Select All), Edit > Cop Merged and then pasting (Edit > Paste) the content as a new layer. Then using the Adjust Color Curves feature select the Lighten Shadows Style from the menu.*

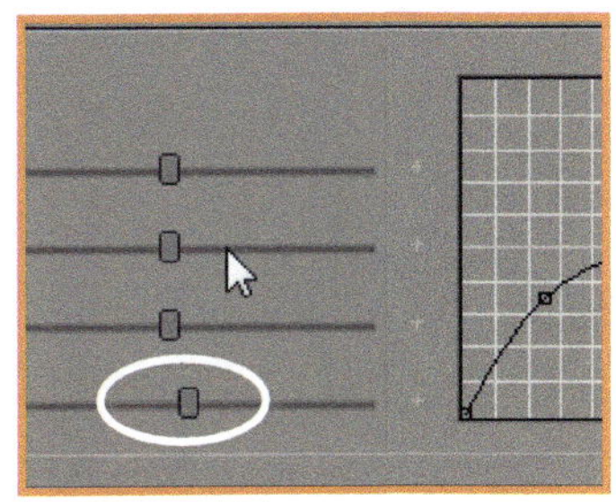

Step 3 >> *Now to fine-tune the preset enhancment. First we will concentrate on the shadow areas. Move the Adjust Shadows slider to the right of the dialog. This will lighten and add contrast and separation to the shadow areas.*

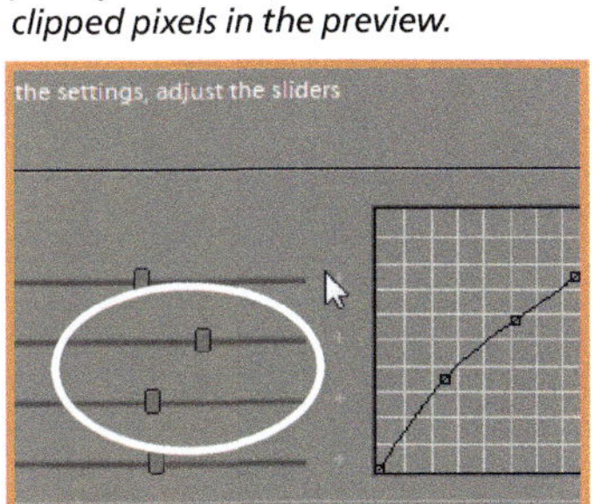

Step 4 >> *This change will also slightly affect the midtones and highlights in the photo. To control these tones separately use the Midtone Brightness and Midtone Contrast sliders. Here I pushed the brightness slider to the right to lighten the midtones and the contrast slider to the left to reduce the contrast slightly.*

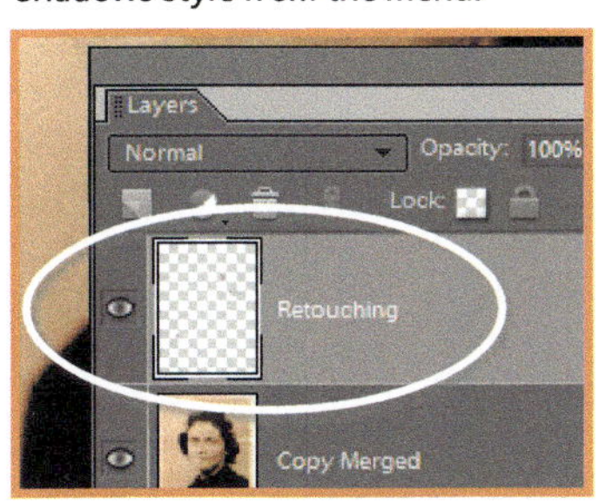

Step 5 >> *With the tones adjusted, the next task is to remove spots, creases and marks. A new layer is added (and targeted) above the copy merged layer. The Spot Healing Brush in the Sample All Layers mode is then used to non-destructively retouch these problem areas.*

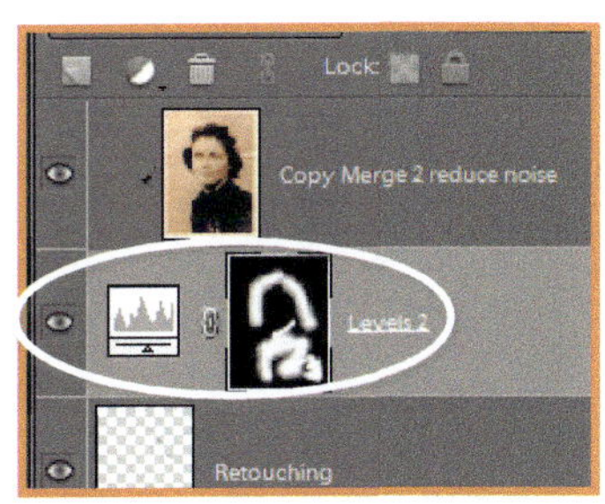

Step 6 >> *To remove the noise that pervades the shadow area, a new copy merge layer was created and pasted above the other layers. This later was filtered with the Reduce Noise filter targeting the shadow noise. A No Settings Levels adjustment layer was then grouped with the filtered layer, the mask filled with black and a white brush used to paint in the noise reduction to the areas that need it.*

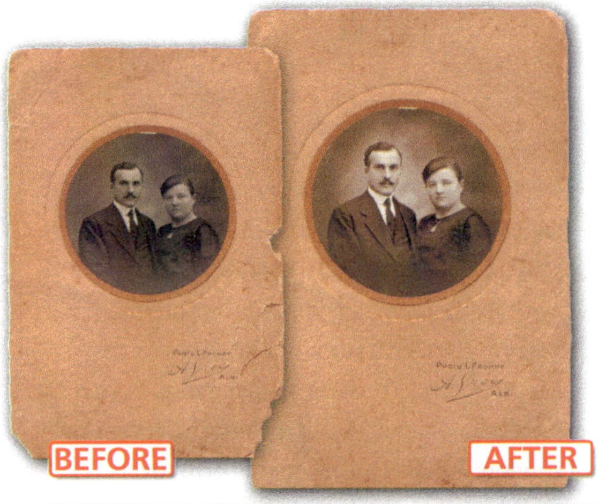

9.08 Recreating missing content

Suitable for Elements – 7.0, 6.0, 5.0, 4.0, 3.0, 2.0, 1.0 | Difficulty level – Intermediate | Resources – Web image 908 | Menus used – Enhance

The stylish surround of this vintage French portrait is suffering from a little neglect. To restore the photo to its former glory the corners and edge of the presentation card need to be recreated and the tones of the photo itself need a little tweaking.

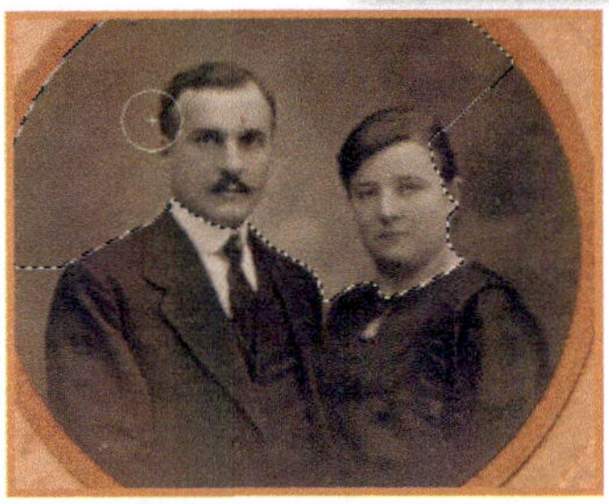

Step 1 >> Before commencing any corrective work we will adjust the tones in the picture section of the document. So that these changes are applied to the photo only and not the textured background use the new Quick Selection Tool to isolate the circular shaped image.

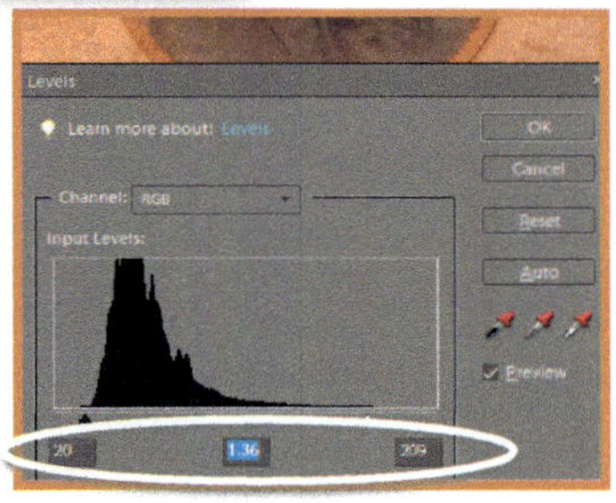

Step 2 >> Next with the selection still active, a Levels adjustment layer is added to the document. Automatically a mask, the shape and size of the selection, is attached to the layer so that the changes are only applied to the selected area. Set the black and white points first and then drag the middle input slider to the left to lighten.

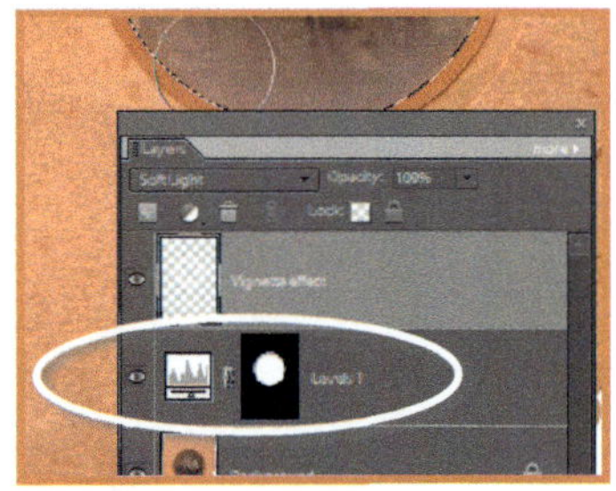

Step 3 >> In the process of lightening and adding contrast, the strength of the vignetting effect has been diminished. Add a new layer above the adjustment layer and change the Blend mode to Soft Light. To rectify this Ctrl click the Levels mask to load the original selection. Now select a soft-edged black brush and paint around the selection's edge to create a new vignette.

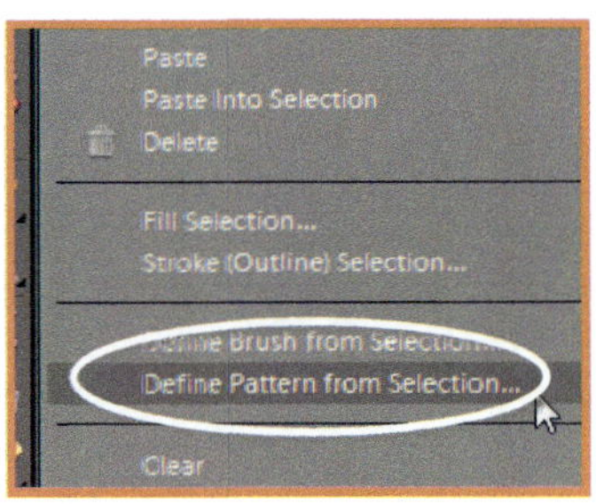

Step 4 >> Now to recreate the corner content. Start by targeting the background layer and then selecting an unblemished section of the card surround with the Rectangular Marquee tool. Now choose Edit > Define Pattern. Enter a name in the Define Pattern dialog that appears and click OK. This pattern will be used for the repair work in the next two steps.

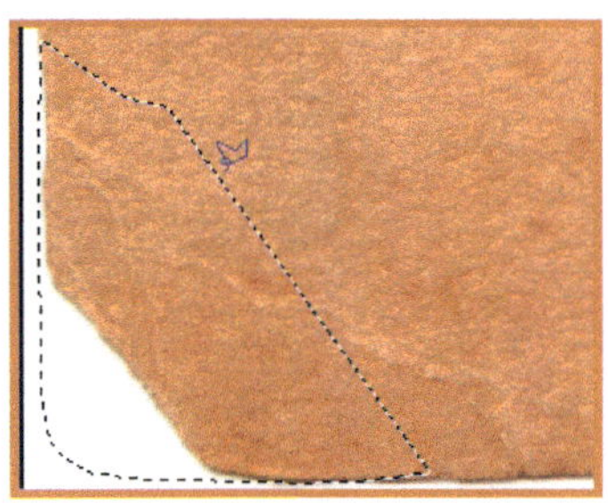

Step 5 >> To recreate the missing corners make a 1 pixel feathered selection in the same shape as the top left-hand corner but positioned at the bottom right of the card. This selection will confine our pattern filling activities and rebuild the corner of the photo frame.

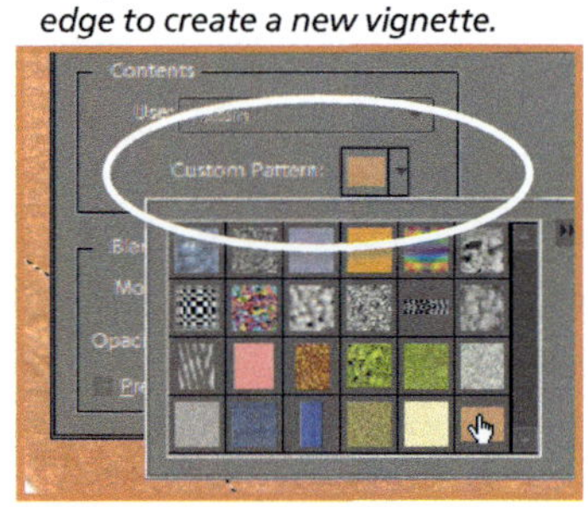

Step 6 >> Now fill the selection (Edit > Fill) with the newly created pattern (select Pattern in the Use menu). Create another selection in the opposite corner and fill it also. Now Lasso the torn side sections, add a 1 pixel feather and pattern fill this selection also. Next use the Healing Brush in Pattern mode with the new pattern selected as the source to disguise the new areas and repair the other wrinkles.

9.09 Removing stains

Suitable for Elements – 7.0, 6.0, 5.0, 4.0, 3.0, 2.0, 1.0
Difficulty level – Intermediate | Resources – Web image 909 | Menus used – Enhance

In this example, the repair work centered around the removal of a yellowish stain running through the middle of the photo. There was also the need to try to restore some details in the highlights sections of the photo.

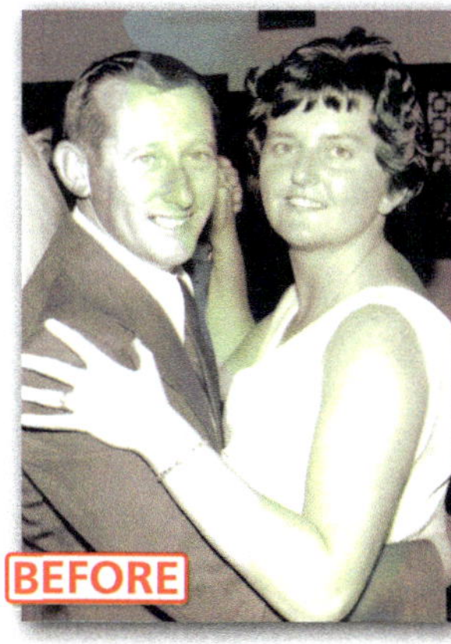

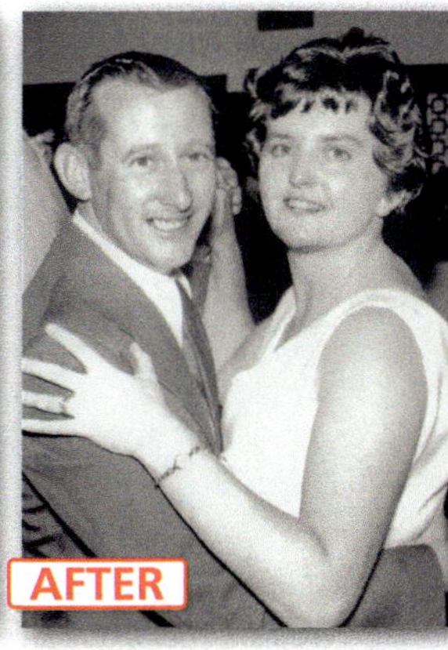

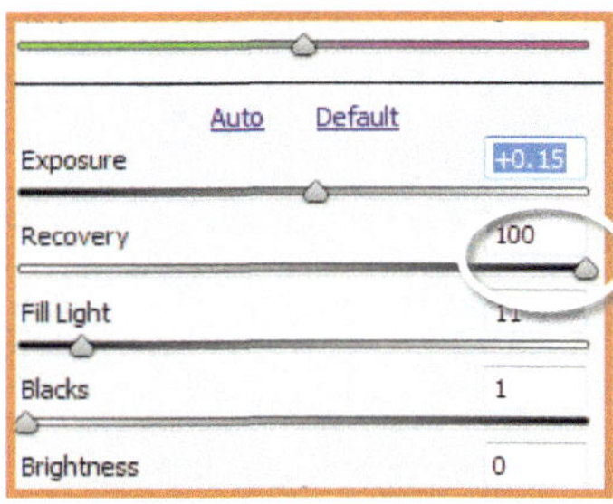

Step 1 >> *Some of the highlight areas in the example file are clipped. The Recovery slider in Adobe Camera Raw 4 is able to reconstruct details in some blown highlights by referencing the details in the other channels. So the first step is to rebuild as much lost detail as possible using this control. NB: ACR 4 also works with TIFF and JPEG files as well as RAW formats. See side panel.*

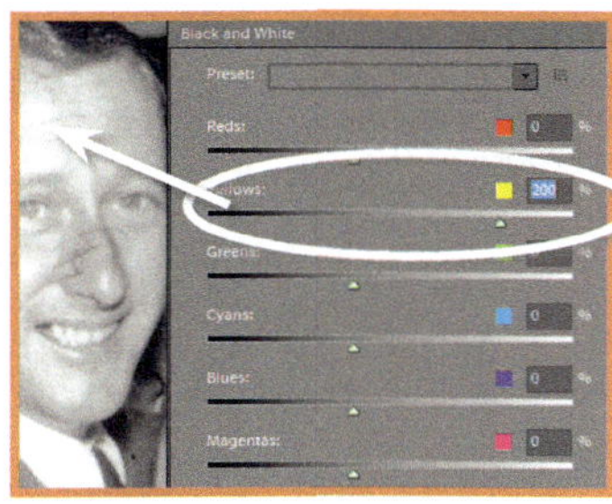

Step 2 >> *Next the file is opened into Elements from Adobe Camera Raw. To remove the yellow stain a Black and White Adjustment layer was dragged from a Photoshop donor document and added above the image layer. Double-click the layer thumbnail to open the feature. By adjusting the Yellow slider it is possible to hide the stain in the grayscale conversion process.*

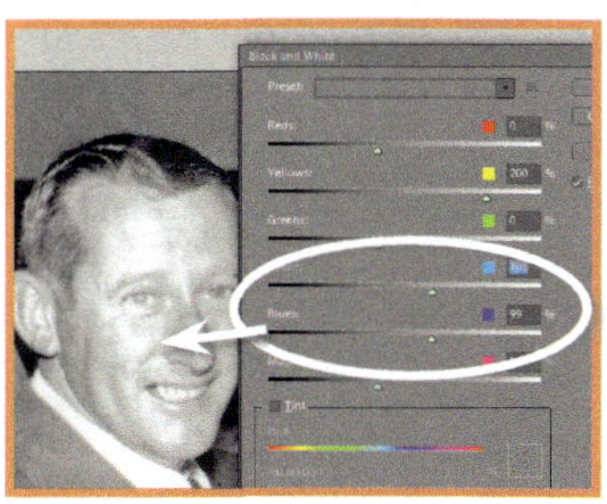

Step 3 >> *To minimize the blue pen scribble on the subject's nose, adjust the Blue and Cyan sliders. Variation in density of the stain or scribble may cause some or only part of the stain to disappear. This is the case here so we will have to resort to another process for the final touch up of these problems.*

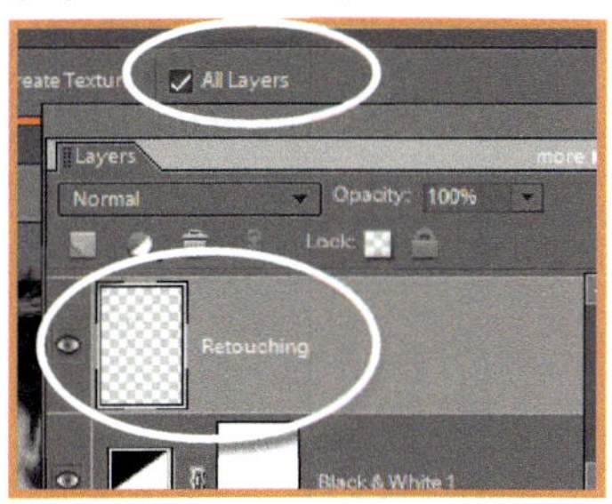

Step 4 >> *To retouch residual stains and other marks. Create a new layer above the background image layer but under the Black and White adjustment layer. Select the new layer and then choose the Spot Healing Brush. Change the brush settings to Sample All Layers in the options bar and proceed to retouch problem areas.*

ACR and JPEG/TIFF files

The version of Adobe Camera Raw that ships with Photoshop Elements 6.0 and 7.0 is also capable of enhancing JPEG and TIFF files. Use the steps below to open your non-raw files in ACR:

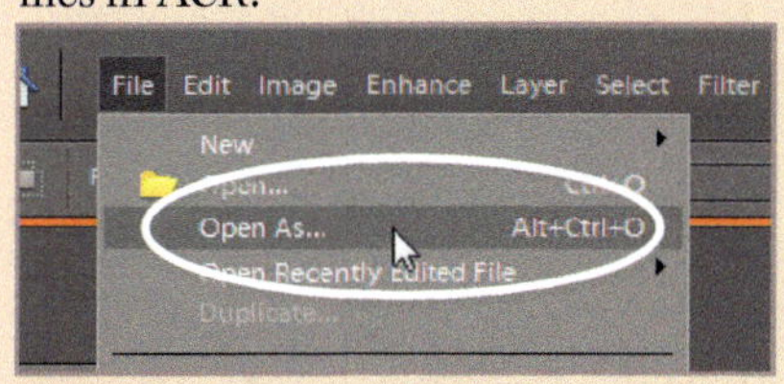

Step 1 >> *Display the Elements Full Edit workspace. Next Select the File > Open As option. This enables the user to open specific documents as if they were created in a different format. In this scenario, we will use the option to open a TIFF or JPEG file as if it were a Raw file.*

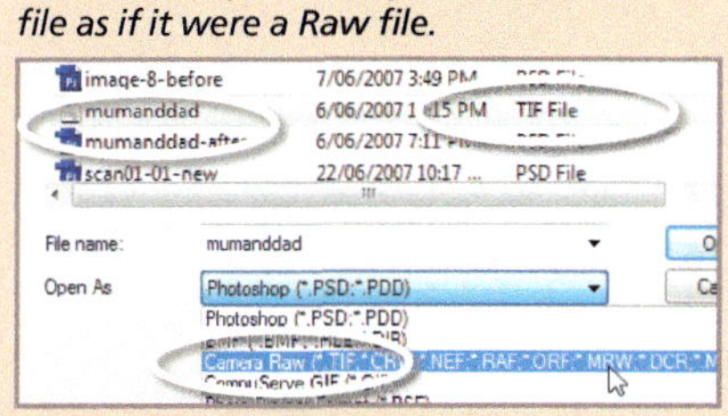

Step 2 >> *Next navigate to the file in the file browser window and single click the entry. Choose the Camera Raw option from the Open As menu at the bottom of the Dialog. Click OK and the file will appear in the Adobe Camera Raw dialog. Process as you would normally and then select Open to transfer the converted file in to the Full Edit workspace with the enhancements applied.*

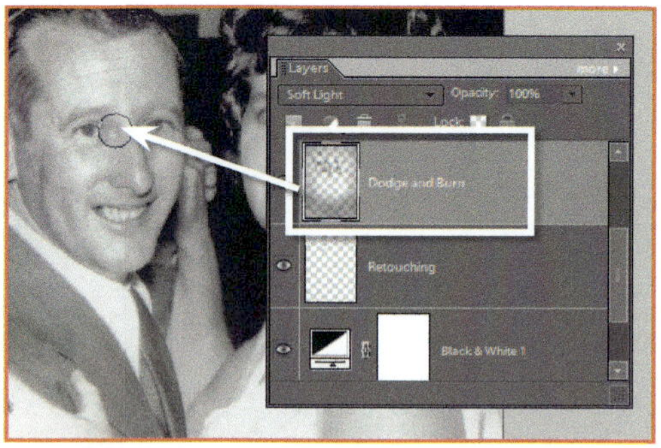

Step 5 >> *After removing dust marks and scratches add another blank layer at the top of the layers stack. Change the Blend Mode of the layer to Soft Light and choose a black soft-edged brush. This set up works like the Burn tool but the changes are made non-destructively. Carefully add some depth to the areas of the image that appear flat because of the harsh, direct, flash lighting.*

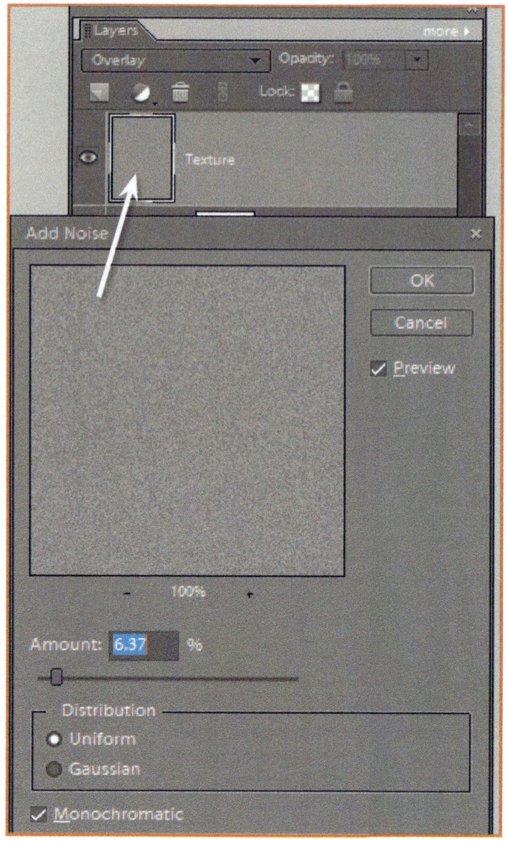

Step 6 >> *The last part of the restoration process is to add a very small amount of texture to the photo to provide detail in the blown-out areas. Add a new blank layer and change the mode to Overlay. Next fill the layer with 50% gray and filter the layer with the Add Noise filter. Make sure that you view the photo at 100% in order to properly gauge the appearance of the texture.*

9781138401167